PREFACE

Cricket's long history is littered with crises and controversy which, at the time, all seemed to be threatening the future of our great game. Now, we stand on the edge of another precipice as cricket's administrators – the men charged with safeguarding and nurturing the sport – dash frantically and, in some cases, thoughtlessly, after the riches that Twenty20 can deliver. Never before have politics and greed combined to form such a dangerous force.

The Stanford affair was an unmitigated disaster yet, maybe, something that was desperately needed to ram home to cricket's bosses – who are becoming increasingly entrepreneurial – that nothing should supersede the integrity of the game. Not even money. The whole tawdry business of the Texan landing at Lord's in his (rented) helicopter with a chest full of dollars (although nothing close to the million it was supposed to contain) looks even worse in retrospect. We now know that every aspect of his spectacular arrival as some sort of saviour of English cricket was a sham, and yet so desperate was the England and Wales Cricket Board to plough its own furrow, and keep one step ahead of the Indians, that he was welcomed with open arms.

The saddest aspect of this race for cash is that it has put the future of Test cricket in jeopardy. Of course the administrators all make the right reassuring noises when pressed about their views of the longer form of the game, but it is one-day cricket that pays the bills. As an indication of the current imbalance one need only to look at England's winter tour of West Indies. There, with the exception of only one game, they played back-to-back Tests with three days between them for rest and recovery. Yet the one-day series of just five games lasted three weeks!

The great challenge for the game's administrators now is to use Twenty20 cricket intelligently and sparingly: to protect it from the danger of over-exposure. If this is done prudently, Test cricket will be bankrolled for years to come. Sadly, there is the real danger of television coverage of Twenty20 competitions reaching saturation point, not merely for the television companies but also the viewers. They surely will tire of wall-to-wall coverage of games that actually mean something to only a very few and nothing to the vast majority. To this end, the move by the IPL to South Africa on security grounds will face a fascinating test: will South Africans be drawn to watch the most over-hyped cricket tournament in the world?

The television companies have, themselves, been drawn into this mad dash and have seriously overstretched themselves in promising the IPL, and others, ludicrously inflated fees. If broadcasting revenue dries up – and in these economic times that must be a serious likelihood – the result will be swift and disastrous. Cricket's exciting future will have been destroyed by short-term opportunism. We are well beyond the crossroads and urgently need a U-turn in order to return to a time when the administrators came from a firm cricketing background – not former professionals, necessarily, but men who held the interests of cricket close to their hearts.

JONATHAN AGNEW

ACKNOWLEDGEMENTS AND THANKS

HEADLINE
David Wilson (Editorial Director)
Rhea Halford (Assistant Editor)
Ian Marshall (Acting Editor)
John Skermer (proofs)

LETTERPART
Lorraine Byfield
Chris Leggett
Caroline Leggett

CAREER RECORDS
Philip Bailey
Cricket Archive
Robin Abrahams
Andrew Roberts

ECB
Alan Fordham

COUNTY SCORER/STATISTICIANS
John Brown (Derbyshire)
Brian Hunt (Durham)
Tony Choat (Essex)
Andrew Hignell (Glamorgan)
Keith Gerrish (Gloucestershire)
Tony Weld (Hampshire)
Jack Foley (Kent)
Alan West (Lancashire)
Graham York (Leicestershire)
Don Shelley (Middlesex)
Tony Kingston (Northamptonshire)
Brian Hewes (Nottinghamshire)
Gerry Stickley (Somerset)
Keith Booth (Surrey)
Mike Charman (Sussex)
David Wainwright (Warwickshire)
Neil Smith (Worcestershire)
John Potter (Yorkshire)

UNIVERSITIES
Ray Markham (Cambridge)
Graeme Fowler (Durham)
Margaret Folwell (Loughborough)
Neil Harris (Oxford)

TASTATS
Ric Finlay
David Fitzgerald

OVERSEAS
Rajesh Kumar (India)
Andrew Samson (South Africa)
Cheryl Styles (New Zealand)
Charlie Wat (Australia)

COUNTY ADMINISTRATIONS
Tom Holdcroft (Derbyshire)
Ellen Johnson (Durham)
Danny Macklin (Essex)
Caryl Watkin (Glamorgan)
Lizzie Allen (Gloucestershire)
Tim Tremlett (Hampshire)
Carolyn Dunne (Kent)
Diana Lloyd (Lancashire)
Elaine Pickering (Leicestershire)
Rebecca Hart (Middlesex)
David Capel (Northamptonshire)
Helen Palmer (Nottinghamshire)
Guy Wolfenden (Somerset)
Stephen Howes (Surrey)
Simon Dyke (Sussex)
Keith Cook (Warwickshire)
Joan Grundy (Worcestershire)
James Buttler (Yorkshire)

ENGLAND v WEST INDIES

SERIES RECORDS
1928 to 2008-09

HIGHEST INNINGS TOTALS

England	in England	619-6d	Nottingham	1957
	in West Indies	849	Kingston	1929-30
West Indies	in England	692-8d	The Oval	1995
	in West Indies	751-5d	St John's	2003-04

LOWEST INNINGS TOTALS

England	in England	71	Manchester	1976
	in West Indies	46	Port-of-Spain	1993-94
West Indies	in England	54	Lord's	2000
	in West Indies	47	Kingston	2003-04

HIGHEST MATCH AGGREGATE 1815 for 34 wickets Kingston 1929-30
LOWEST MATCH AGGREGATE 309 for 29 wickets Bridgetown 1934-35

HIGHEST INDIVIDUAL INNINGS

England	in England	285*	P.B.H.May	Birmingham	1957
	in West Indies	325	A.Sandham	Kingston	1929-30
West Indies	in England	291	I.V.A.Richards	The Oval	1976
	in West Indies	400*	B.C.Lara	St John's	2003-04

HIGHEST AGGREGATE OF RUNS IN A SERIES

England	in England	506	(av 42.16)	G.P.Thorpe (6 Tests)	1995
	in West Indies	693	(av 115.50)	E.H.Hendren	1929-30
West Indies	in England	829	(av 118.42)	I.V.A.Richards	1976
	in West Indies	798	(av 99.75)	B.C.Lara	1993-94

RECORD WICKET PARTNERSHIPS – ENGLAND

1st	229	A.J.Strauss (142)/A.N.Cook (94)	Bridgetown	2008-09
2nd	291	A.J.Strauss (137)/R.W.T.Key (221)	Lord's	2004
3rd	303	M.A.Atherton (135)/R.A.Smith (175)	St John's	1993-94
4th	411	P.B.H.May (285*)/M.C.Cowdrey (154)	Birmingham	1957
5th	218	P.D.Collingwood (161)/M.J.Prior (131*)	Port-of-Spain	2008-09
6th	205	M.R.Ramprakash (154)/G.P.Thorpe (103)	Bridgetown	1997-98
7th	197	M.J.K.Smith (96)/J.M.Parks (101*)	Port-of-Spain	1959-60
8th	217	T.W.Graveney (165)/J.T.Murray (112)	The Oval	1966
9th	109	G.A.R.Lock (89)/P.I.Pocock (13)	Georgetown	1967-68
10th	128	K.Higgs (63)/J.A.Snow (59*)	The Oval	1966

RECORD WICKET PARTNERSHIPS – WEST INDIES

1st	298	C.G.Greenidge (149)/D.L.Haynes (167)	St John's	1989-90
2nd	287*	C.G.Greenidge (214*)/H.A.Gomes (92*)	Lord's	1984
3rd	338	E.de C.Weekes (206)/F.M.M.Worrell (167)	Port-of-Spain	1953-54
4th	399	G.St A.Sobers (226)/F.M.M.Worrell (197*)	Bridgetown	1959-60
5th	265	S.M.Nurse (137)/G.St A.Sobers (174)	Leeds	1966
6th	282*	B.C.Lara (400*)/R.D.Jacobs (107*)	St John's	2003-04
7th	155*	G.St A.Sobers (150*)/B.D.Julien (121)	Lord's	1973
8th	99	C.A.McWatt (54)/J.K.Holt (48*)	Georgetown	1953-54
9th	150	E.A.E.Baptiste (87*)/M.A.Holding (69)	Birmingham	1984
10th	70	I.R.Bishop (44*)/D.Ramnarine (19)	Georgetown	1997-98

BEST INNINGS BOWLING ANALYSIS

England	in England	8-103	I.T.Botham	Lord's	1984
	in West Indies	8- 53	A.R.C.Fraser	Port-of-Spain	1997-98
West Indies	in England	8- 92	M.A.Holding	The Oval	1976
	in West Indies	8- 45	C.E.L.Ambrose	Bridgetown	1989-90

BEST MATCH BOWLING ANALYSIS

England	in England	12-119	F.S.Trueman	Birmingham	1963
	in West Indies	13-156	A.W.Greig	Port-of-Spain	1973-74
West Indies	in England	14-149	M.A.Holding	The Oval	1976
	in West Indies	11- 84	C.E.L.Ambrose	Port-of-Spain	1993-94

HIGHEST AGGREGATE OF WICKETS IN A SERIES

England	in England	34	(av 17.47)	F.S.Trueman	1963
	in West Indies	27	(av 18.66)	J.A.Snow	1967-68
		27	(av 18.22)	A.R.C.Fraser	1997-98
West Indies	in England	35	(av 12.65)	M.D.Marshall	1988
	in West Indies	30	(av 14.26)	C.E.L.Ambrose	1997-98

RESULTS SUMMARY

ENGLAND v WEST INDIES – IN ENGLAND

	Tests	Series			Lord's			Manchester			The Oval			Nottingham			Birmingham			Leeds			Chester-le-St		
		E	WI	D	E	WI	D	E	WI	D	E	WI	D	E	WI	D	E	WI	D	E	WI	D	E	WI	D
1928	3	3	–	–	1	–	–	1	–	–	1	–	–	–	–	–	–	–	–	–	–	–	–	–	–
1933	3	2	–	1	1	–	–	–	–	1	1	–	–	–	–	–	–	–	–	–	–	–	–	–	–
1939	3	1	–	2	1	–	–	–	–	1	–	–	1	–	–	–	–	–	–	–	–	–	–	–	–
1950	4	1	3	–	–	1	–	1	–	–	–	1	–	–	1	–	–	–	–	–	–	–	–	–	–
1957	5	3	–	2	1	–	–	–	–	–	1	–	–	–	–	1	–	–	1	1	–	–	–	–	–
1963	5	1	3	1	–	–	1	–	1	–	–	1	–	–	–	–	1	–	–	–	1	–	–	–	–
1966	5	1	3	1	–	–	1	–	1	–	1	–	–	–	1	–	–	–	–	–	1	–	–	–	–
1969	3	2	–	1	–	–	1	1	–	–	–	–	–	–	–	–	–	–	–	1	–	–	–	–	–
1973	3	–	2	1	–	1	–	–	–	–	–	1	–	–	–	–	–	–	1	–	–	–	–	–	–
1976	5	–	3	2	–	–	1	–	1	–	–	1	–	–	–	1	–	–	–	–	1	–	–	–	–
1980	5	–	1	4	–	–	1	–	–	1	–	–	1	–	1	–	–	–	–	–	–	1	–	–	–
1984	5	–	5	–	–	1	–	–	1	–	–	1	–	–	–	–	–	1	–	–	1	–	–	–	–
1988	5	–	4	1	–	1	–	–	1	–	–	1	–	–	–	1	–	–	–	–	1	–	–	–	–
1991	5	2	2	1	–	–	1	–	–	–	1	–	–	–	1	–	–	1	–	1	–	–	–	–	–
1995	6	2	2	2	1	–	–	1	–	–	–	–	1	–	–	1	–	1	–	–	1	–	–	–	–
2000	5	3	1	1	1	–	–	–	–	1	1	–	–	–	–	–	–	1	–	1	–	–	–	–	–
2004	4	4	–	–	1	–	–	1	–	–	1	–	–	–	–	–	1	–	–	–	–	–	–	–	–
2007	4	3	–	1	–	–	1	1	–	–	–	–	–	–	–	–	–	–	–	1	–	–	1	–	–
78		**28**	**29**	**21**	**7**	**4**	**7**	**6**	**5**	**4**	**7**	**6**	**3**	**–**	**4**	**4**	**2**	**4**	**2**	**5**	**6**	**1**	**1**	**–**	**–**

ENGLAND v WEST INDIES – IN WEST INDIES

	Tests	Series			Bridgetown			Port-of-Spain			Georgetown			Kingston			St John's			North Sound		
		E	WI	D	E	WI	D	E	WI	D	E	WI	D	E	WI	D	E	WI	D	E	WI	D
1929-30	4	1	1	2	–	–	1	1	–	–	–	1	–	–	–	1	–	–	–	–	–	–
1934-35	4	1	2	1	1	–	–	–	1	–	–	–	1	–	1	–	–	–	–	–	–	–
1947-48	4	–	2	2	–	–	1	–	–	1	–	1	–	–	1	–	–	–	–	–	–	–
1953-54	5	2	2	1	–	1	–	–	–	1	1	–	–	1	1	–	–	–	–	–	–	–
1959-60	5	1	–	4	–	–	1	1	–	1	–	–	1	–	–	1	–	–	–	–	–	–
1967-68	5	1	–	4	–	–	1	1	–	1	–	–	1	–	–	1	–	–	–	–	–	–
1973-74	5	1	1	3	–	–	1	1	1	–	–	–	1	–	–	1	–	–	–	–	–	–
1980-81	4	–	2	2	–	1	–	–	1	–	–	–	–	–	–	1	–	–	1	–	–	–
1985-86	5	–	5	–	–	1	–	–	2	–	–	–	–	–	1	–	–	1	–	–	–	–
1989-90	4	1	2	1	–	1	–	–	–	1	–	–	–	1	–	–	–	1	–	–	–	–
1993-94	5	1	3	1	1	–	–	–	1	–	–	1	–	–	1	–	–	–	1	–	–	–
1997-98	6	1	3	2	–	–	1	1	1	–	–	1	–	–	–	1	–	1	–	–	–	–
2003-04	4	3	–	1	1	–	–	1	–	–	–	–	–	1	–	–	–	–	1	–	–	–
2008-09	5	–	1	4	–	–	1	–	–	1	–	–	–	–	1	–	–	–	1	–	–	1
65		**13**	**24**	**28**	**3**	**4**	**7**	**6**	**7**	**6**	**1**	**4**	**4**	**3**	**6**	**6**	**–**	**3**	**4**	**–**	**–**	**1**

Totals	**143**	**41**	**53**	**49**																		

ENGLAND v AUSTRALIA

SERIES RECORDS

1876-77 to 2006-07

HIGHEST INNINGS TOTALS

England	in England	903-7d	The Oval	1938
	in Australia	636	Sydney	1928-29
Australia	in England	729-6d	Lord's	1930
	in Australia	659-8d	Sydney	. 1946 47

LOWEST INNINGS TOTALS

England	in England	52	The Oval	1948
	in Australia	45	Sydney	1886-87
Australia	in England	36	Birmingham	1902
	in Australia	42	Sydney	1887-88

HIGHEST MATCH AGGREGATE   1753 for 40 wickets   Adelaide   1920-21
LOWEST MATCH AGGREGATE   291 for 40 wickets   Lord's   1888

HIGHEST INDIVIDUAL INNINGS

England	in England	364	L.Hutton	The Oval	1938
	in Australia	287	R.E.Foster	Sydney	1903-04
Australia	in England	334	D.G.Bradman	Leeds	1930
	in Australia	307	R.M.Cowper	Melbourne	1965-66

HIGHEST AGGREGATE OF RUNS IN A SERIES

England	in England	732	(av 81.33)	D.I.Gower (6 Tests)	1985
	in Australia	905	(av 113.12)	W.R.Hammond	1928-29
Australia	in England	974	(av 139.14)	D.G.Bradman	1930
	in Australia	810	(av 90.00)	D.G.Bradman	1936-37

RECORD WICKET PARTNERSHIPS – ENGLAND

1st	323	J.B.Hobbs (178)/W.Rhodes (179)	Melbourne	1911-12
2nd	382	L.Hutton (364)/M.Leyland (187)	The Oval	1938
3rd	262	W.R.Hammond (177)/ D.R.Jardine (98)	Adelaide	1928-29
4th	310	P.D.Collingwood (206)/K.P.Pietersen (158)	Adelaide	2006-07
5th	206	E.Paynter (216*)/D.C.S.Compton (102)	Nottingham	1938
6th	215	L.Hutton (364)/J.Hardstaff jr (169*)	The Oval	1938
	215	G.Boycott (107)/A.P.E.Knott (135)	Nottingham	1977
7th	143	F.E.Woolley (133*)/J.Vine (36)	Sydney	1911-12
8th	124	E.H.Hendren (169)/H.Larwood (70)	Brisbane	1928-29
9th	151	W.H.Scotton (90)/W.W.Read (117)	The Oval	1884
10th	130	R.E.Foster (287)/W.Rhodes (40*)	Sydney	1903-04

RECORD WICKET PARTNERSHIPS – AUSTRALIA

1st	329	G.R.Marsh (138)/M.A.Taylor (219)	Nottingham	1989
2nd	451	W.H.Ponsford (266)/D.G.Bradman (244)	The Oval	1934
3rd	276	D.G.Bradman (187)/A.L.Hassett (128)	Brisbane	1946-47
4th	388	W.H.Ponsford (181)/D.G.Bradman (304)	Leeds	1934
5th	405	S.G.Barnes (234)/D.G.Bradman (234)	Sydney	1946-47
6th	346	J.H.W.Fingleton (136)/D.G.Bradman (270)	Melbourne	1936-37
7th	165	C.Hill (188)/H.Trumble (46)	Melbourne	1897-98
8th	243	R.J.Hartigan (116)/C.Hill (160)	Adelaide	1907-08
9th	154	S.E.Gregory (201)/J.M.Blackham (74)	Sydney	1894-95
10th	127	J.M.Taylor (108)/A.A.Mailey (46*)	Sydney	1924-25

BEST INNINGS BOWLING ANALYSIS

England	in England	10- 53	J.C.Laker	Manchester	1956
	in Australia	8- 35	G.A.Lohmann	Sydney	1886-87
Australia	in England	8- 31	F.Laver	Manchester	1909
	in Australia	9-121	A.A.Mailey	Melbourne	1920-21

BEST MATCH BOWLING ANALYSIS

England	in England	19- 90	J.C.Laker	Manchester	1956
	in Australia	15-124	W.Rhodes	Melbourne	1903-04
Australia	in England	16-137	R.A.L.Massie	Lord's	1972
	in Australia	13- 77	M.A.Noble	Melbourne	1901-02

HIGHEST AGGREGATE OF WICKETS IN A SERIES

England	in England	46	(av 9.60)	J.C.Laker	1956
	in Australia	38	(av 23.18)	M.W.Tate	1924-25
Australia	in England	42	(av 21.26)	T.M.Alderman (6 Tests)	1981
	in Australia	41	(av 12.85)	R.M.Hogg (6 Tests)	1978-79

RESULTS SUMMARY
ENGLAND v AUSTRALIA – IN ENGLAND

	Tests	Series			The Oval			Manchester			Lord's			Nottingham			Leeds			Birmingham			Sheffield		
		E	A	D	E	A	D	E	A	D	E	A	D	E	A	D	E	A	D	E	A	D	E	A	D
1880	1	1	–	–	1	–	–																		
1882	1	–	1	–	–	1	–																		
1884	3	1	–	2	–	–	1	–	–	1	1	–	–												
1886	3	3	–	–	1	–	–	1	–	–	1	–	–												
1888	3	2	1	–	1	–	–	1	–	–	–	1	–												
1890	2	2	–	–	1	–	–				1	–	–												
1893	3	1	–	2	1	–	–	–	–	1	–	–	1												
1896	3	2	1	–	1	–	–	–	1	–	1	–	–												
1899	5	–	1	4	–	–	1	–	–	1	–	1	–	–	–	1	–	–	1						
1902	5	1	2	2	1	–	–	–	1	–	–	–	1							–	–	1	–	1	–
1905	5	2	–	3	1	–	–	1	–	–	–	–	1	1	–	–	–	–	1						
1909	5	1	2	2	–	–	1	–	1	–	–	1	–				–	1	–	1	–	–			
1912	3	1	–	2	1	–	–	–	–	1	–	–	1												
1921	5	–	3	2	–	–	1	–	–	1	–	1	–	–	1	–	–	1	–						
1926	5	1	–	4	1	–	–	–	–	1	–	–	1	–	–	1	–	–	1						
1930	5	1	2	2	–	1	–	–	–	1	–	1	–	1	–	–	–	–	1						
1934	5	1	2	2	–	1	–	–	–	1	1	–	–	–	–	1	–	1	–						
1938	4	1	1	2	1	–	–				–	–	1	–	–	1	–	1	–						
1948	5	–	4	1	–	1	–	–	–	1	–	1	–	–	1	–	–	1	–						
1953	5	1	–	4	1	–	–	–	–	1	–	–	1	–	–	1	–	–	1						
1956	5	2	1	2	–	–	1	1	–	–	–	1	–	–	–	1	1	–	–						
1961	5	1	2	2	–	–	1	–	1	–	–	1	–	1	–	–				–	–	1			
1964	5	–	1	4	–	–	1	–	–	1	–	–	1	–	–	1	–	1	–						
1968	5	1	1	3	1	–	–	–	1	–	–	–	1	–	–	1	–	–	1						
1972	5	2	2	1	–	1	–	1	–	–	–	1	–	–	–	1	1	–	–						
1975	4	–	1	3	–	–	1	–	–	1	–	–	1				–	1	–						
1977	5	3	–	2	–	–	1	1	–	–	–	–	1	1	–	–	1	–	–						
1980	1	–	–	1							–	–	1												
1981	6	3	1	2	–	–	1	1	–	–	–	–	1	–	1	–	1	–	–	1	–	–			
1985	6	3	1	2	1	–	–	–	–	1	–	1	–	–	–	1	1	–	–	1	–	–			
1989	6	–	4	2	–	1	–	–	1	–	–	1	–	–	–	1	–	1	–	–	–	1			
1993	6	1	4	1	1	–	–	–	1	–	–	1	–	–	–	1	–	1	–	–	1	–			
1997	6	2	3	1	1	–	–	–	1	–	–	–	1	–	1	–	–	1	–	1	–	–			
2001	5	1	4	–	1	–	–	–	1	–	–	1	–	–	1	–	1	–	–	–	1	–			
2005	5	2	1	2	–	–	1	–	1	–	–	1	–	1	–	–	–	1	–						
	151	43	46	62	15	6	13	7	7	14	5	14	14	4	7	9	7	8	8	5	3	4	–	1	–

8

	Tests	Series			Melbourne			Sydney			Adelaide			Brisbane			Perth		
		E	A	D	E	A	D	E	A	D	E	A	D	E	A	D	E	A	D
1876-77	2	1	1	–	1	1	–	–	–	–	–	–	–	–	–	–	–	–	–
1878-79	1	–	1	–	–	1	–	–	–	–	–	–	–	–	–	–	–	–	–
1881-82	4	–	2	2	–	–	2	–	2	–	–	–	–	–	–	–	–	–	–
1882-83	4	2	2	–	1	1	–	1	1	–	–	–	–	–	–	–	–	–	–
1884-85	5	3	2	–	2	–	–	–	2	–	1	–	–	–	–	–	–	–	–
1886-87	2	2	–	–	–	–	–	2	–	–	–	–	–	–	–	–	–	–	–
1887-88	1	1	–	–	–	–	–	1	–	–	–	–	–	–	–	–	–	–	–
1891-92	3	1	2	–	–	1	–	–	1	–	1	–	–	–	–	–	–	–	–
1894-95	5	3	2	–	2	–	–	1	1	–	–	1	–	–	–	–	–	–	–
1897-98	5	1	4	–	–	2	–	1	1	–	–	1	–	–	–	–	–	–	–
1901-02	5	1	4	–	–	2	–	1	1	–	–	1	–	–	–	–	–	–	–
1903-04	5	3	2	–	1	1	–	2	–	–	–	1	–	–	–	–	–	–	–
1907-08	5	1	4	–	1	1	–	–	2	–	–	1	–	–	–	–	–	–	–
1911-12	5	4	1	–	2	–	–	1	1	–	1	–	–	–	–	–	–	–	–
1920-21	5	–	5	–	–	2	–	–	2	–	–	1	–	–	–	–	–	–	–
1924-25	5	1	4	–	1	1	–	–	2	–	–	1	–	–	–	–	–	–	–
1928-29	5	4	1	–	1	1	–	1	–	–	1	–	–	1	–	–	–	–	–
1932-33	5	4	1	–	–	1	–	2	–	–	1	–	–	1	–	–	–	–	–
1936-37	5	2	3	–	–	2	–	1	–	–	–	1	–	1	–	–	–	–	–
1946-47	5	–	3	2	–	–	1	–	2	–	–	–	1	–	1	–	–	–	–
1950-51	5	1	4	–	1	1	–	–	1	–	–	1	–	–	1	–	–	–	–
1954-55	5	3	1	1	1	–	–	1	–	1	1	–	–	–	1	–	–	–	–
1958-59	5	–	4	1	–	2	–	–	–	1	–	1	–	–	1	–	–	–	–
1962-63	5	1	1	3	1	–	–	–	1	1	–	–	1	–	–	1	–	–	–
1965-66	5	1	1	3	–	–	2	1	–	–	–	1	–	–	–	1	–	–	–
1970-71	6	2	–	4	–	–	1	2	–	–	–	–	1	–	–	1	–	–	1
1974-75	6	1	4	1	1	–	1	–	1	–	–	1	–	–	1	–	–	1	–
1976-77	1	–	1	–	–	1	–	–	–	–	–	–	–	–	–	–	–	–	–
1978-79	6	5	1	–	–	1	–	2	–	–	1	–	–	1	–	–	1	–	–
1979-80	3	–	3	–	–	1	–	–	1	–	–	–	–	–	–	–	–	1	–
1982-83	5	1	2	2	1	–	–	–	–	1	–	1	–	–	1	–	–	–	1
1986-87	5	2	1	2	1	–	–	–	1	–	–	–	1	1	–	–	–	–	1
1987-88	1	–	–	1	–	–	–	–	–	1	–	–	–	–	–	–	–	–	–
1990-91	5	–	3	2	–	1	–	–	–	1	–	–	1	–	1	–	–	1	–
1994-95	5	1	3	1	–	1	–	–	–	1	1	–	–	–	1	–	–	1	–
1998-99	5	1	3	1	1	–	–	–	1	–	–	1	–	–	–	1	–	1	–
2002-03	5	1	4	–	–	1	–	1	–	–	–	1	–	–	1	–	–	1	–
2006-07	5	–	5	–	–	1	–	–	1	–	–	1	–	–	1	–	–	1	–
	165	54	85	26	19	27	7	21	25	7	8	16	5	5	10	4	1	7	3
Totals	316	97	131	88															

Matches abandoned without a ball bowled (Manchester 1890 and 1938, Melbourne 1970-71) are excluded from these tables.

2000 RUNS

	Tests	I	NO	HS	Runs	Avge	100	50
D.G.Bradman (A)	37	63	7	334	5028	89.78	19	12
J.B.Hobbs (E)	41	71	4	187	3636	54.26	12	15
A.R.Border (A)	47	82	19	200*	3548	56.31	8	21
D.I.Gower (E)	42	77	4	215	3269	44.78	9	12
S.R.Waugh (A)	46	73	18	177*	3200	58.18	10	14
G.Boycott (E)	38	71	9	191	2945	47.50	7	14
W.R.Hammond (E)	33	58	3	251	2852	51.85	9	7
H.Sutcliffe (E)	27	46	5	194	2741	66.85	8	16
C.Hill (A)	41	76	1	188	2660	35.46	4	16
J.H.Edrich (E)	32	57	3	175	2644	48.96	7	13
G.A.Gooch (E)	42	79	0	196	2632	33.31	4	16
G.S.Chappell (A)	35	65	8	144	2619	45.94	9	12
M.A.Taylor (A)	33	61	2	219	2496	42.30	6	15
M.C.Cowdrey (E)	43	75	4	113	2433	34.26	5	11
L.Hutton (E)	27	49	6	364	2428	56.46	5	14
R.N.Harvey (A)	37	68	5	167	2416	38.34	6	12
V.T.Trumper (A)	40	74	5	185*	2263	32.79	6	9
D.C.Boon (A)	31	57	8	184*	2237	45.65	7	8
W.M.Lawry (A)	29	51	5	166	2233	48.54	7	13
M.E.Waugh (A)	29	51	7	140	2204	50.09	6	11
S.E.Gregory (A)	52	92	7	201	2193	25.80	4	8
W.W.Armstrong (A)	42	71	9	158	2172	35.03	4	6
I.M.Chappell (A)	30	56	4	192	2138	41.11	4	16
K.F.Barrington (E)	23	39	6	256	2111	63.96	5	13
A.R.Morris (A)	24	43	2	206	2080	50.73	8	8

D.G.Bradman holds the unique record of scoring 2000 runs in both countries in this series (2674 runs in England and 2354 in Australia); J.B.Hobbs is the only other batsman to score 2000 runs in either country (2493 runs in Australia). R.T.Ponting (A) had scored 1978 runs against England before the 2009 Ashes series.

100 WICKETS

	Tests	Balls	Runs	Wkts	Avge	Best	5wI	10wM
S.K.Warne (A)	36	10757	4535	195	23.25	8- 71	11	4
D.K.Lillee (A)	29	8516	3507	167	21.00	7- 89	11	4
G.D.McGrath (A)	30	7280	3286	157	20.92	8- 38	10	–
I.T.Botham (E)	36	8479	4093	148	27.65	6- 78	9	2
H.Trumble (A)	31	7895	2945	141	20.88	8- 65	9	3
R.G.D.Willis (E)	35	7294	3346	128	26.14	8- 43	7	–
M.A.Noble (A)	39	6845	2860	115	24.86	7- 17	9	2
R.R.Lindwall (A)	29	6728	2559	114	22.44	7- 63	6	–
W.Rhodes (E)	41	5791	2616	109	24.00	8- 68	6	1
S.F.Barnes (E)	20	5749	2288	106	21.58	7- 60	12	1
C.V.Grimmett (A)	22	9224	3439	106	32.44	6- 37	11	2
D.L.Underwood (E)	29	8000	2770	105	26.38	7- 50	4	2
A.V.Bedser (E)	21	7065	2859	104	27.49	7- 44	7	2
G.Giffen (A)	31	6457	2791	103	27.09	7-117	7	1
W.J.O'Reilly (A)	19	7864	2587	102	25.36	7- 54	8	3
R.Peel (E)	20	5216	1715	101	16.98	7- 31	5	1
C.T.B.Turner (A)	17	5195	1670	101	16.53	7- 43	11	2
T.M.Alderman (A)	17	4717	2117	100	21.17	6- 47	11	1
J.R.Thomson (A)	21	4951	2418	100	24.18	6- 46	5	–

100 WICKET-KEEPING DISMISSALS

	Tests	Ct	St	Total
R.W.Marsh (A)	42	141	7	148
I.A.Healy (A)	33	123	12	135
A.P.E.Knott (E)	34	97	8	105

R.W.Marsh (141 catches) and W.A.S.Oldfield (31 stumpings) hold the respective individual records in Anglo-Australian Tests.

TOURING TEAMS REGISTER 2009

Neither West Indies nor Australia had selected their 2009 touring teams at the time of going to press. The following players who had represented those teams in Test matches since 1 November 2007 were still available for selection:

WEST INDIES

Full Names	Birthdate	Birthplace	Team	Type	F-C Debut
BAKER, Lionel Sionne	06.09.84	Montserrat	Leeward Is	RHB/RMF	2002-03
BENN, Sulieman Jamaal	22.07.81	St James	Barbados	LHB/SLA	1999-00
BRAVO, Dwayne John	07.10.83	Santa Cruz	Trinidad	RHB/RFM	2001-02
CHANDERPAUL, Shivnarine	16.08.74	Unity Village	Guyana	LHB/LB	1991-92
CHATTERGOON, Sewnarine	03.04.81	Berbice	Guyana	LHB/LB	1999-00
EDWARDS, Fidel Henderson	06.02.82	St Peter	Barbados	RHB/RF	2001-02
GANGA, Daren	14.01.79	Barrackpore	Trinidad	RHB/OB	1996-97
GAYLE, Christopher Henry	21.09.79	Kingston	Jamaica	LHB/OB	1998-99
HINDS, Ryan O'Neal	17.02.81	St James	Barbados	LHB/SLA	1998-99
JAGGERNAUTH, Amit Sheldon	16.11.83	Trinidad	Trinidad	LHB/OB	2002-03
LEWIS, Rawl Nicholas	05.09.74	Union Village	Windward Is	RHB/LBG	1991-92
MARSHALL, Xavier Melbourne	27.03.86	Jamaica	Jamaica	RHB/OB	2003-04
MORTON, Runako Shakur	22.07.78	Rawlins, Nevis	Leeward Is	RHB/OB	1996-97
NASH, Brendan Paul	14.12.77	Attadale, W Aus	Jamaica	LHB/LM	2000-01
PARCHMENT, Brenton Anthony	24.06.82	St Elizabeth	Jamaica	RHB/OB	1999-00
POWELL, Daren Brentlyle L	15.04.78	Malvern	Jamaica	RHB/RFM	2000-01
RAMDIN, Denesh	13.03.85	Freeport, Couva	Trinidad	RHB/WK	2003-04
SAMMY, Darren Julius Garvey	20.12.83	Micoud, St Lucia	Windward Is	RHB/RM	2002-03
SARWAN, Ramnaresh Ronnie	23.06.80	Wakenaam Is	Guyana	RHB/LB	1995-96
SIMMONS, Lendl Mark Platter	25.01.85	Port-of-Spain	Trinidad	RHB/RMF	2001-02
SMITH, Devon Sheldon	21.10.81	Sauters, Grenada	Windward Is	LHB/OB	1998-99
TAYLOR, Jerome Everton	22.06.84	St Elizabeth	Jamaica	RHB/RF	2002-03

AUSTRALIA

Full Names	Birthdate	Birthplace	Team	Type	F-C Debut
BOLLINGER, Douglas Erwin	24.07.81	Sydney	NSW	LHB/LF	2002-03
CASSON, Beau	07.12.82	Perth	NSW	RHB/SLC	2002-03
CLARK, Stuart Rupert	28.09.75	Sydney	NSW	RHB/RFM	1997-98
CLARKE, Michael John	02.04.81	Liverpool	NSW	RHB/SLA	1999-00
HADDIN, Bradley James	23.10.77	Cowra	NSW	RHB/WK	1999-00
HAURITZ, Nathan Michael	18.10.81	Wondai	NSW	RHB/OB	2000-01
HILFENHAUS, Benjamin William	15.03.83	Ulverstone	Tasmania	RHB/RFM	2005-06
HODGE, Brad John	29.12.74	Sandringham	Victoria	RHB/OB	1993-94
HUGHES, Phillip Joel	30.11.88	Macksville	NSW	LHB	2007-08
HUSSEY, Michael Edward Killeen	27.05.75	Morley	W Australia	LHB/RM	1994-95
JAQUES, Philip Anthony	03.05.79	Wollongong	NSW	LHB/LM	2000-01
JOHNSON, Mitchell Guy	02.11.81	Townsville	Queensland	LHB/LF	2001-02
KATICH, Simon Mathew	21.08.75	Middle Swan	NSW	LHB/SLC	1996-97
KREJZA, Jason John	14.01.83	Sydney	Tasmania	RHB/OB	2004-05
LEE, Brett	08.11.76	Wollongong	NSW	RHB/RF	1994-95
McDONALD, Andrew Barry	15.06.81	Wodonga	Victoria	RHB/RFM	2001-02
McGAIN, Bryce Edward	25.03.72	Mornington	Victoria	RHB/LBG	2001-02
NORTH, Marcus James	28.07.79	Melbourne	W Australia	LHB/OB	1998-99
PONTING, Ricky Thomas	19.12.74	Launceston	Tasmania	RHB/RM	1992-93
ROGERS, Chris John Llewellyn	31.08.77	Sydney	Victoria	LHB/LBG	1998-99
SIDDLE, Peter Matthew	25.11.84	Traralgon	Victoria	RHB/RFM	2005-06
SYMONDS, Andrew	09.07.75	Birmingham, Eng	Queensland	RHB/RM/OB	1994-95
TAIT, Shaun William	22.02.83	Adelaide	S Australia	RHB/RF	2002-03
WATSON, Shane Robert	17.06.81	Ipswich	Queensland	RHB/RFM	2000-01
WHITE, Cameron Leon	18.08.83	Bairnsdale	Victoria	RHB/LBG	2000-01

THE FIRST-CLASS COUNTIES REGISTER, RECORDS AND 2008 AVERAGES

Career statistics are to the end of the 2008 season.
Test Match and LOI career bests have been updated to 22 March and 14 March respectively.
Where possible, other personal bests from the 2008-09 season have been included.

ABBREVIATIONS – General

*	not out/unbroken partnership	IT20	International Twenty20
b	born	l-o	limited-overs
BB	Best innings bowling analysis	LOI	Limited-Overs Internationals
Cap	Awarded 1st XI County Cap	Tests	Official Test Matches
f-c	first-class	F-c Tours	Overseas tours involving first-class
HS	Highest Score		appearances

Awards

PCA 2008 Professional Cricketer's Association Player of 2008
Wisden 2008 One of *Wisden Cricketers' Almanack's* Five Cricketers of 2008
YC 2008 Cricket Writers' Club Young Cricketer of 2008

ECB Competitions

BHC	Benson & Hedges Cup (1972-2002)
CC	LV County Championship
CGT	Cheltenham & Gloucester Trophy (2001-06)
FPT	Friends Provident Trophy
NL	National League (1999-2005)
NWT	NatWest Trophy (1981-2000)
P40	NatWest PRO 40 League
SL	Sunday League (1969-98)
T20	Twenty20 Competition

Education

ARU	Anglia Ruskin University
BHS	Boys' High School
C	College
CFE	College of Further Education
CHE	College of Higher Education
CS	Comprehensive School
GS	Grammar School
HS	High School
I	Institute
IHE	Institute of Higher Education
RGS	Royal Grammar School
S	School
SFC	Sixth Form College
SM	Secondary Modern School
SS	Secondary School
TC	Technical College
T(H)S	Technical (High) School
U	University
UMIST	University of Manchester Institute of Science and Technology
UWIC	University of Wales Institute, Cardiff

Playing Categories

LBG	Bowls right-arm leg-breaks and googlies
LF	Bowls left-arm fast
LFM	Bowls left-arm fast-medium
LHB	Bats left-handed
LM	Bowls left-arm medium pace
LMF	Bowls left-arm medium fast
OB	Bowls right-arm off-breaks
RF	Bowls right-arm fast
RFM	Bowls right-arm fast-medium
RHB	Bats right-handed
RM	Bowls right-arm medium pace
RMF	Bowls right-arm medium-fast
RSM	Bowls right-arm slow-medium
SLA	Bowls left-arm leg-breaks
SLC	Bowls left-arm 'Chinamen'
WK	Wicket-keeper

Teams (see also p 136)

ACT	Australian Capital Territory
ADBP	Agricultural Development Bank of P
B	Bangladesh
CD	Central Districts
EP	Eastern Province
FS	Free State
GW	Griqualand West
HK	Hong Kong
K	Kenya
KRL	Khan Research Laboratories
NBP	National Bank of Pakistan
ND	Northern Districts
NSW	New South Wales
NT	Northern Transvaal
NW	North West
(O)FS	(Orange) Free State
PIA	Pakistan International Airlines
PNSC	Pakistan National Shipping Corp
PTC	Pakistan Telecommunication Co
Q	Queensland
REDCO	Really Efficient Development Co
SAU	South African Universities
Tas	Tasmania
UP	Uttar Pradesh
Vic	Victoria
WA	Western Australia
WAPDA	Water & Power Development Auth.
WP	Western Province

DERBYSHIRE

Formation of Present Club: 4 November 1870
Inaugural First-Class Match: 1871
Colours: Chocolate, Amber and Pale Blue
Badge: Rose and Crown
County Champions: (1) 1936
Gillette/NatWest/C&G/FP Trophy Winners: (1) 1981
Benson and Hedges Cup Winners: (1) 1993
Pro 40/National League (Div 1) Winners: (0); best – 4th (Div 2) 2002
Sunday League Winners: (1) 1990
Twenty20 Cup Winners: (0) best – Quarter-Finalist 2005.

Chief Executive: Keith Loring, Derbyshire County Cricket Club, Grandstand Road, Derby DE21 6AF • Tel: 01332 388101 • Fax: 0844 500 8322 • Email: info@derbyshireccc.com • Web: www.derbyshireccc.com

Head of Cricket: J.E.Morris. **Captain:** C.J.L.Rogers. **Vice-Captain:** None. **Overseas Player:** C.J.L.Rogers. **2009 Beneficiary:** None. **Head Groundsman:** Neil Godrich. **Scorer:** John M.Brown. ‡ New registration. ^{NQ} Not qualified for England.

BIRCH, Daniel John (Kimberley CS, Nottingham), b Nottingham 21 Jan 1981. Son of J.D.Birch (Nottinghamshire 1973-88). 6'3". LHB, RM. Debut (Derbyshire) 2007, scoring 130 v CU (Cambridge), including 122* before lunch. HS 130 (*see above*). CC HS 95 v Glos (Derby) 2007 – on Championship debut. LO HS 76 v Northants (Northampton) 2008 (P40). T20 HS 25.

BORRINGTON, Paul Michael (Repton S; Chellarton S; Loughborough U), b Nottingham 24 May 1988. Son of A.J.Borrington (Derbyshire 1971-80). 5'10". RHB, OB. Debut (Derbyshire) 2005. Loughborough UCCE 2008. HS 102* Loughborough v Worcs (Kidderminster) 2008. De HS 85 v Worcs (Worcester) 2008. BB – .

CLARE, Jonathan Luke (St Theodore's HS), b Burnley, Lancs 14 Jun 1986. 6'4". RHB, RMF. Lancashire 2nd XI. Derbyshire 2nd XI 2006-07. Debut (Derbyshire) 2007, taking 5-90 v Notts (Chesterfield). HS 129* and BB 7-74 v Northants (Northampton) 2008. LO HS 18 v Kent (Canterbury) 2008 (P40). LO BB 3-39 v Scotland (Derby) 2008 (FPT). T20 HS 4*. T20 BB 2-20.

‡^{NQ}GROENEWALD, Timothy Duncan (Maritzburg C; South Africa U), b Pietermaritzburg, South Africa 10 Jan 1984. 6'0". RHB, RFM. Debut Cambridge UCCE 2006. Warwickshire 2006-08. HS 78 Wa v Bangladesh A (Birmingham) 2008. CC HS 76 Wa v Durham (Chester-le-St) 2006. BB 3-26 Wa v Hants (Birmingham) 2007. LO HS 36 Wa v Lancs (Manchester) 2007 (FPT). LO BB 3-25 Wa v Worcs (Birmingham) 2007 (P40). T20 HS 41. T20 BB 3-40.

NQHINDS, Wavell Wayne (Camperdown HS), b Kingston, Jamaica 7 Sep 1976. 6'0". LHB, RM. Jamaica 1995-96 to date. Derbyshire debut 2008 (Kolpak registration). **Tests** (WI): 45 (1999-00 to 2005-06); HS 213 v SA (Georgetown) 2004-05; BB 3-79 v SA (Johannesburg) 2003-04. **LOI** (WI): 114 (1999 to 2006-07); HS 127* v Z (Harare) 2003-04; BB 3-24 v E (Oval) 2004. F-c Tours (WI): E 2000; A 2000-01, 2005-06; SA 1997-98, 2003-04; NZ 1999-00; I 1998-99, 2002-03; P (Sharjah) 2001-02; Z 2001, 2003-04; B 1998-99, 2002-03. HS 213 (*see Tests*). De HS 76 v Northants (Northampton) 2008. BB 3-9 WI B v Jamaica (Montego Bay) 2000-01. De BB 3-22 v Middlesex (Derby) 2008. LO HS 127* (*see LOI*). LO BB 4-35 WI v Zim A (Kwekwe) 2003-04. IT20 HS 14. T20 HS 72*. T20 BB 2-14.

HUNTER, Ian David (Fyndoune Community C, Sacriston; New C, Durham), b Durham City 11 Sep 1979. 6'2". RHB, RMF. Durham 2000-03. Derbyshire debut 2004. HS 65 Du v Northants (Northampton) 2002. De HS 48 v Somerset (Taunton) 2006. BB 5-63 v Du (Chester-le-St) 2005. LO HS 39 Du v Leics (Leicester) 2002 (BHC). LO BB 4-29 Du v Essex (Ilford) 2000 (NL). T20 HS 25*. T20 BB 3-26.

JONES, Edward Peter (Trentham HS; Stoke-on-Trent SFC; Derby U), b Stoke-on-Trent, Staffs 23 Oct 1989. 6'4" RHB, RMF. Derbyshire 2nd XI 2007-08. Staffordshire 2008. Summer contract – awaiting 1st XI debut.

NQLANGEVELDT, Charl Kenneth (Luckhoff SS), b Stellenbosch, South Africa 17 Dec 1974. RHB, RFM.Boland 1997-98 to 2002-03. Border 2003-04. Lions 2004-05 to 2006-07. Somerset 2005; cap 2005. Leicestershire 2007. Cape Cobras 2007-08 to date. Derbyshire debut/cap 2008 (Kolpak registration). **Tests** (SA): 6 (2004-05 to 2005-06); HS 10 v WI (Georgetown) 2004-05; BB 5-46 v E (Cape Town 2004-05 – on debut. **LOI** (SA): 59 (2001-02 to 2007-08); HS 12 v P (Lahore (2007-08); BB 5-39 v SL (Providence, Guyana) 2006-07. F-c Tours (SA): A 2002-03 (SA A), 2005-06; WI 2000 (SA A), 2004-05; I 2007-08 (SA A); Z 1998 (SA Acad), 2004 (SA A), 2007-08 (SA A). HS 56 Boland v E Province (Port Elizabeth) 1999-00. UK/De HS 40 v Glamorgan (Cardiff) 2008. 50 wkts (1): 55 (2008). BB 6-48 Lions v Titans (Potchefstroom) 2006-07. UK/De BB 5-40 v Middlesex (Derby) 2008. LO HS 33* S Africa A v SL (Potchefstroom) 2002-03. LO BB 5-7 SA President's XI v B (Pietermaritzburg) 2000-01. IT20 HS 2. IT20 BB 2-14. T20 HS 9*. T20 BB 5-16; took 4-9 v Yorkshire (Leeds) 2008 – a De record.

LAWSON, Mark Anthony Kenneth (Castle Hall Language C, Mirfield), b Leeds, Yorkshire 24 Oct 1985. 5'8". RHB, LB. Yorkshire 2004-07. Middlesex (1 match) 2008. Derbyshire debut (1 match) 2008. HS 44 Y v Hants (Southampton) 2006. De HS 88 Y v Middlesex (Scarborough) 2006. De HS 5. LO HS 20 Y v Warwks (Birmingham) 2005 (NL). LO BB 2-50 Y v Hants (Leeds) 2006 (P40). T20 HS 4*. T20 BB 2-34.

LUNGLEY, Tom (St John Houghton SS; SE Derbyshire C), b Derby 25 Jul 1979. 6'1". LHB, RM. Debut (Derbyshire) 2000; cap 2007. HS 50 v Warwks (Derby) 2008. 50 wkts (1): 59 (2007). BB 5-20 v Leics (Derby) 2007. LO HS 45 v Essex (Chelmsford) 2001 (NL). LO BB 4-28 v Essex (Derby) 2001 (NL). T20 HS 25. T20 BB 4-11.

NEEDHAM, Jake (Nottingham Bluecoat S, Aspley), b Portsmouth, Hants 30 Sep 1986. 6'1". RHB, OB. Debut (Derbyshire) 2008. HS 48 v Notts (Chesterfield) 2007. BB 6-49 v Leics (Leicester) 2008. LO HS 42 and BB 2-36 v Somerset (Taunton) 2007 (P40). T20 HS 7*. T20 BB 1-4.

PARK, Garry Terence (Eshowe HS, Natal; Anglia Ruskin U), b Empangeni, Zululand, South Africa 19 Apr 1983. 5'7". RHB, WK, RM. Cambridge UCCE 2003-05. Durham 2006-08. Cambridgeshire 2005. HS 100* Du v Yorks (Leeds) 2006. LO HS 42* v Lancs (Chester-le-St) 2008 (FPT). T20 HS 25*.

14

PATEL Akhil (Kimberley CS, Nottingham), b Nottingham 18 Jun 1990. Younger brother of S.R.Patel (see *NOTTINGHAMSHIRE*). 5'10". LHB, SLC. Debut (Derbyshire) 2007 (summer contract). Awaiting CC debut. HS 31 v CU (Cambridge) 2007 – on debut.

PIPE, David **James** (Queensbury S, Bradford), b Bradford, Yorks 16 Dec 1977. 5'11". RHB, WK. Worcestershire 1998-2005. Derbyshire debut 2006; cap 2007. HS 133* v Essex (Chelmsford) 2007. LO HS 83 v Leics (Leicester) 2007 (FPT). Held 8 catches Wo v Herts (Hertford) 2001 (CGT) to equal 1-o record. T20 HS 45.

POYNTON, Thomas (John Taylor HS, Barton-under-Needwood; Repton S), b Burton upon Trent, Staffs 25 Nov 1989. 5'10". RHB, WK. Debut (Derbyshire) 2007 (summer contract). HS 14 v Bangladesh A (Derby) 2008. CC HS 2 v Glamorgan (Derby) 2007. LO HS – . T20 HS 3.

REDFERN, Daniel James (Adam's GS, Newport, Shropshire), b Shrewsbury, Shropshire 18 Apr 1990. 5'9". LHB, OB. Debut (Derbyshire) 2007 (summer contract). HS 69* v Glamorgan (Derby) 2008. BB 1-7. LO HS 57* v Yorkshire (Derby) 2007 (P40). T20 HS 9.

[NO]**ROGERS, Christopher** John Llewellyn (Wesley C, Perth; Curtin U, Perth), b St George, Sydney, Australia 31 Aug 1977. Son of W.J.Rogers (NSW 1968-69 to 1969-70). 5'10". LHB, LBG. W Australia 1998-99 to 2007-08. Derbyshire 2004, 2008, cap 2008; captain 2008 (part) to date. Leicestershire 2005. Northamptonshire 2006. Victoria 2008-09. Shropshire 2003. Wiltshire 2005. **Tests** (A): 1 (2007-08); HS 15 v I (Perth) 2007-08 – on debut. F-c Tour (Aus A): P 2007-08. 1000 runs (2+1); most – 1372 (2008). HS 319 Nh v Glos (Northampton) 2006. De HS 248* v Warwks (Birmingham) 2008. BB 1-16 Nh v Leics (Northampton) 2006. LO HS 117* WA v Q (Perth) 2003-04. BB 2-22 Nh v Durham (Northampton) 2006. T20 HS 35.

SADLER, John Leonard (St Thomas A'Becket S, Sandal), b Dewsbury, Yorks 19 Nov 1981. 5'11". LHB, LBG. Leicestershire 2003-07. Derbyshire debut 2008. 1000 runs (1): 1024 (2006). HS 145 Le v Surrey (Leicester) 2003 and 145 Le v Sussex (Hove) 2003. De HS 50 v Bangladesh A (Derby) 2008. BB 1-5 v Middlesex (Southgate) 2007. De BB 1-57 v Essex (Derby) 2008. LO HS 113* Le v Derbys (Leicester) 2007 (FPT). LO BB 1-33 Le v Yorks (Leeds) 2007 (FPT). T20 HS 73. T20 BB – .

SAFFELL, Oliver Henry James (De Lisle S, Loughborough; Derby U), b Derby 16 Jul 1986. 6'1". RHB, RMF. Debut (Derbyshire) 2007 (match contract). No f-c appearances in 2008. Awaiting CC debut. HS 35* and BB 3-37 v CU (Cambridge) 2007 – on debut.

[NO]**SMITH, Gregory** Marc (St Stithins C), b Johannesburg, South Africa 20 Apr 1983. 5'9". RHB, RM/OB. Griqualand West 2003-04. Derbyshire debut 2006 (Kolpak registration). HS 113 v Middlesex (Derby) 2008. BB 3-31 v Middlesex (Southgate) 2007. LO HS 88 v Kent (Derby) 2007 (P40). LO BB 3-19 v Scotland (Edinburgh) 2007 (FPT). T20 HS 100* v Yorks (Leeds) 2008 – county record.

STUBBINGS, Stephen David (Frankston HS, Aus; Swinburne U, Aus), b Huddersfield, Yorks 31 Mar 1978. 6'3". LHB, OB. Debut (Derbyshire) 1997; cap 2001; benefit 2008. 1000 runs (3); most – 1126 (2005). HS 151 v Somerset (Taunton) 2005. LO HS 110 v Northants (Northampton) 2006 (CGT). T20 HS 57.

NQTELO, Filipe Dominic (Wynberg BHS; Unitek C), b Cape Town, South Africa 4 Mar 1986. 5'6". RHB, OB. Western Province 2005-06 to 2007-08. Cape Cobras 2005-06 to 2007-08. SA Academy 2006 to 2006-07. Derbyshire debut 2008 (Kolpak registration). HS 134* WP v Boland (Paarl) 2007-08. De HS 6 v Essex (Chelmsford) 2008. BB 1-36 v Essex (Derby) 2008. LO HS 90 WP v Border (East London) 2005-06. T20 HS 48.

WAGG, Graham Grant (Ashlawn S, Rugby), b Rugby, 28 Apr 1983. 6'0". RHB, LM. Warwickshire 2002-04; contract terminated after ECB imposed a 15-month ban, expiring 1 Jan 2006, for taking cocaine. Derbyshire debut 2006; cap 2007. F-c Tour (Eng A): I 2003-04. HS 108 v Northants (Northampton) 2008. 50 wkts (2); most – 59 (2008). BB 6-38 v Somerset (Taunton) 2006. LO HS 45 Eng A v Karnataka (Bangalore) 2003-04 and 45 v Yorks (Derby) 2007. LO BB 4-35 v Durham (Derby) 2008 (FPT). T20 HS 27*. T20 BB 3-23.

WHITELEY, Ross Andrew (Repton S), b Sheffield, Yorks 13 Sep 1988. RHB, WK. Derbyshire 2nd XI 2006-08. Debut (Derbyshire) 2008. HS 27 v Leics (Leicester) 2008 – on debut. LO HS 24 v Glamorgan (Cardiff) 2008.

RELEASED/RETIRED
(Having made a County First-Class or List A appearance in 2008)

CLARKE, R. – see WARWICKSHIRE.

DEAN, Kevin James (Leek HS; Leek CFE), b Derby 16 Oct 1975. 6'5". LHB, LMF. Derbyshire 1996-2008; cap 1998; benefit 2006. MCC 2002. HS 54* v Worcs (Derby) 2002. 50 wkts (2): most – 83 (2002). BB 8-52 v Kent (Canterbury) 2000. 2 hat-tricks (1998, 2000). LO HS 16* v Glamorgan (Cardiff) 1998 (SL) and 16* v Middlesex (Derby) 2002 (NL). LO BB 5-32 v Glos (Derby) 1996 (SL). T20 HS 8*. T20 BB 2-14.

DOSHI, Nayan Dilip (King Alfred S, London), b Nottingham 6 Oct 1978. Son of D.R.Doshi (Bengal, Notts, Warwks, Saurashtra, and India 1968-69 to 1986). 6'4". RHB, SLA. Saurashtra 2001-02 to 2007-08. Surrey 2004-07; cap 2006. Derbyshire 2008. Buckinghamshire 2001. 50 wkts (1): 51 (2006). HS 37 Saurashtra v Vidarbha (Rajkot) 2005-06. UK HS 33 Sy v Notts (Oval) 2005. De HS 17* and BB 3-84 v Bangladesh A (Derby) 2008. BB 7-110 (10-183 match) Sy v Sussex (Hove) 2004. LO HS 38* Saurashtra v Baroda (Bombay) 2001-02. LO BB 5-30 Sy v Derbys (Chesterfield) 2006 (P40). T20 HS 5. T20 BB 4-22; took 3-1 inc hat-trick v Durham (Chester-le-Street) 2008.

KLOKKER, Frederik Andreas (Hindsholm S), b Odense, Denmark 13 Mar 1983. LHB, WK. Warwickshire (1 match) 2006. Derbyshire 2007-08 – scoring 100* v CU (Cambridge) on debut. Denmark (not f-c) 1999-00 to 2005. MCC YC 2002-05. HS 103* v Warwks (Derby) 2008. LO HS 138* Denmark v USA (Armagh) 2005.

NEW, T.J. – see LEICESTERSHIRE.

WHITE, Wayne Andrew (John Port S, Etwall; Nottingham Trent U), b Derby 22 Apr 1985. 6'2". RHB, RMF. Derbyshire 200-08. HS 19* Surrey (Derby) 2006. BB 5-87 v Northants (Northampton) 2007. LO HS 25 v Somerset (Taunton) 2007 (P40). LO BB 3-47 v Glamorgan (Cardiff) 2008 (P40).

C.D.Paget left the staff, without making a County First-Class or List A appearance for Derbyshire in 2008.

DERBYSHIRE 2008
RESULTS SUMMARY

	Place	Won	Lost	Tied	Drew	No Result
County Championship (2nd Division)	6th	4	3		9	
All First-Class Matches		4	4		10	
FP Trophy (North Division)	3rd	3	2			3
Pro40 League (2nd Division)	8th	1	6	1		
Twenty/20 Cup (North Division)	5th	3	7			

LV COUNTY CHAMPIONSHIP AVERAGES
BATTING AND FIELDING

Cap		M	I	NO	HS	Runs	Avge	100	50	Ct/St
2008	C.J.L.Rogers	14	24	2	248*	1232	56.00	3	8	13
	J.L.Clare	13	18	5	129*	555	42.69	1	5	5
2007	D.J.Pipe	8	14	3	133	453	41.18	1	2	21/1
2007	T.Lungley	4	4	1	50	108	36.00	–	1	2
	D.J.Birch	11	18	1	77	609	35.82	–	3	6
	G.M.Smith	11	18	1	113	575	33.82	1	5	1
2001	S.D.Stubbings	9	17	2	62*	499	33.26	–	2	5
	T.J.New	6	8	1	58	224	32.00	–	1	12/2
	D.J.Redfern	4	6	1	69*	159	31.80	–	1	1
	W.W.Hinds	9	13	–	76	407	31.30	–	3	1
	P.M.Borrington	8	13	1	85	324	27.00	–	3	7
2007	G.G.Wagg	15	22	3	108	498	26.21	1	2	6
	F.A.Klokker	4	8	1	103*	160	22.85	1	–	10
	R.Clarke	10	16	–	81	317	19.81	–	1	19
	J.Needham	7	15	2	36	135	19.28	–	–	4
	F.D.Telo	7	14	–	69	263	18.78	–	2	2
	J.L.Sadler	6	11	–	49	195	17.72	–	–	1
2008	C.K.Langeveldt	12	15	3	40	208	17.33	–	–	5
	W.A.White	3	5	1	18	38	9.50	–	–	1
	I.D.Hunter	4	5	1	17	28	7.00	–	–	1
	N.D.Doshi	7	7	2	2	6	1.20	–	–	3

Also batted: K.J.Dean (2 matches – cap 1998) 8, 3*, 25; M.A.K.Lawson (1) 5, 3*; R.A.Whiteley (1) 27, 18.

BOWLING

	O	M	R	W	Avge	Best	5wI	10wM
C.K.Langeveldt	418.1	105	1238	55	22.50	5-40	3	–
J.Needham	135.1	23	410	16	25.62	6-49	1	–
W.W.Hinds	88	13	261	10	26.10	3-22	–	–
G.G.Wagg	443	86	1549	57	27.17	6-56	2	1
J.L.Clare	257.4	47	871	31	28.09	7-74	1	–
R.Clarke	131.2	16	522	11	47.45	4-87	–	–
Also bowled:								
T.Lungley	85.1	13	326	9	36.22	4-70	–	–
I.D.Hunter	110.2	23	303	6	50.50	2-62	–	–
G.M.Smith	115.3	10	428	8	53.50	1- 7	–	–
W.A.White	68	8	296	5	59.20	2-66	–	–
N.D.Doshi	211.1	48	646	8	80.75	2-69	–	–

P.M.Borrington 1-0-5-0; K.J.Dean 42.3-8-154-4; F.A.Klokker 10-0-99-0; D.J.Redfern 18-3-54-1; C.J.L.Rogers 3.4-0-13-0; J.L.Sadler 10-0-57-1; S.D.Stubbings 6-0-42-0; F.D.Telo 5-0-36-1; R.A.Whiteley 11-1-38-0.

The First-Class Averages (pp 136–153) give the records of Derbyshire players in all first-class county matches (Derbyshire's other opponents being Bangladesh A and Durham UCCE), with the exception of M.A.K.Lawson and T.J.New, whose first-class figures for Derbyshire are as above, and:

P.M.Borrington 9-15-1-85-359-25.64-0-3-8ct. 1-0-5-0.
R.Clarke 11-17-0-81-396-23.29-0-2-20ct. 144.2-20-543-13-41.76-4/87-0-0.

DERBYSHIRE RECORDS

FIRST-CLASS CRICKET

Highest Total	For 801-8d		v	Somerset	Taunton	2007
	V 662		by	Yorkshire	Chesterfield	1898
Lowest Total	For 16		v	Notts	Nottingham	1879
	V 23		by	Hampshire	Burton upon T	1958
Highest Innings	For 274	G.A.Davidson	v	Lancashire	Manchester	1896
	V 343*	P.A.Perrin	for	Essex	Chesterfield	1904

Highest Partnership for each Wicket

1st	322	H.Storer/J.Bowden	v	Essex	Derby	1929
2nd	417	K.J.Barnett/T.A.Tweats	v	Yorkshire	Derby	1997
3rd	316*	A.S.Rollins/K.J.Barnett	v	Leics	Leicester	1997
4th	328	P.Vaulkhard/D.Smith	v	Notts	Nottingham	1946
5th	302*†	J.E.Morris/D.G.Cork	v	Glos	Cheltenham	1993
6th	212	G.M.Lee/T.S.Worthington	v	Essex	Chesterfield	1932
7th	258	M.P.Dowman/D.G.Cork	v	Durham	Derby	2000
8th	198	K.M.Krikken/D.G.Cork	v	Lancashire	Manchester	1996
9th	283	A.Warren/J.Chapman	v	Warwicks	Blackwell	1910
10th	132	A.Hill/M.Jean-Jacques	v	Yorkshire	Sheffield	1986

† 346 runs were added for this wicket in two separate partnerships

Best Bowling (Innings)	For 10- 40	W.Bestwick	v	Glamorgan	Cardiff	1921
	V 10- 45	R.L.Johnson	for	Middlesex	Derby	1994
Best Bowling (Match)	For 17-103	W.Mycroft	v	Hampshire	Southampton	1876
	V 16-101	G.Giffen	for	Australians	Derby	1886

Most Runs – Season	2165	D.B.Carr	(av 48.11)	1959
Most Runs – Career	23854	K.J.Barnett	(av 41.12)	1979-98
Most 100s – Season	8	P.N.Kirsten		1982
Most 100s – Career	53	K.J.Barnett		1979-98
Most Wkts – Season	168	T.B.Mitchell	(av 19.55)	1935
Most Wkts – Career	1670	H.L.Jackson	(av 17.11)	1947-63
Most Career W-K Dismissals	1304	R.W.Taylor	(1157 ct; 147 st)	1961-84
Most Career Catches in the Field	563	D.C.Morgan		1950-69

LIMITED-OVERS CRICKET

Highest Total	FPT	365-3		v	Cornwall	Derby	1986
	P40	304-3		v	Kent	Maidstone	2005
	T20	195-8		v	Yorkshire	Leeds	2005
Lowest Total	FPT	79		v	Surrey	The Oval	1967
	P40	60		v	Kent	Canterbury	2008
	T20	98		v	Lancashire	Manchester	2005
Highest Innings	FPT	173*	M.J.Di Venuto	v	Derbys CB	Derby	2000
	P40	141*	C.J.Adams	v	Kent	Chesterfield	1992
	T20	100*	G.M.Smith	v	Yorkshire	Leeds	2008
Best Bowling	FPT	8-21	M.A.Holding	v	Sussex	Hove	1988
	P40	6- 7	M.Hendrick	v	Notts	Nottingham	1972
	T20	4- 9	C.K.Langeveldt	v	Yorkshire	Leeds	2008

DURHAM

Formation of Present Club: 23 May 1882
Inaugural First-Class Match: 1992
Colours: Navy Blue, Yellow and Maroon
Badge: Coat of Arms of the County of Durham
County Champions: (1) 2008
Gillette/NatWest/C&G/FP Trophy Winners: (1) 2007
Benson and Hedges Cup Winners: (0); best –
Quarter-Finalist 1998, 2000, 2001
Pro 40/National League (Div 1) Winners: (0); best – 3rd
(Div 2) 2008
Sunday League Winners: (0); best – 7th 1993
Twenty20 Cup Winners: (0); best – Semi-Finalist 2008

Chief Executive: David Harker, County Ground, Riverside, Chester-le-Street, Co Durham
DH3 3QR • Tel: 0191 387 1717 • Fax: 0191 387 1616 • Email: marketing@durham-ccc.co.uk •
Web: www.durhamccc.co.uk

Director of Cricket: G.Cook. **Captain**: W.R.Smith. **Vice-Captain**: none. **Overseas Player**:
S.Chanderpaul. **2009 Beneficiary**: Brian Hunt. **Head Groundsman**: David Measor. **Scorer**:
Brian Hunt. ‡ New registration. ^{NQ} Not qualified for England.

*Durham initially awarded caps immediately after their players joined the staff but revised
this policy in 1998, again capping players on merit, past 'awards' having been nullified.
Durham abolished both their capping and 'awards' systems after the 2005 season.*

^{NQ}**BENKENSTEIN, Dale** Martin (Durban HS; Michaelhouse HS), b Salisbury, Rhodesia
9 Jun 1974. Son of M.M.Benkenstein (Rhodesia, Natal B 1970-71 to 1980-81); brother of
twins B.R. (Natal B 1993-94) and B.N. Benkenstein (Natal B, GW 1994-95 to 1996-97).
5'9". RHB, RM/OB. Natal/KwaZulu-Natal 1993-94 to 2003-04. Dolphins 2004-05 to
2007-08. MCC 2004. British passport. Durham debut/cap 2005; captain 2006-08. *Wisden*
2008. **LOI** (SA): 23 (1998-99 to 2002-03); HS 69 v WI (Cape Town) 1998-99; BB 3-5 v K
(Colombo) 2002-03. F-c Tours (SA A): WI 2000; NZ 1998-99 (SA); SL 1995 (SA U-24),
1998. 1000 (3); most – 1500 (2006). HS 259 KZ-Natal v Northerns (Durban) 2001-02. Du
HS 162* v Derby (Chester-le-St) 2005. BB 4-16 Dolphins v Warriors (Durban) 2005-06. Du
4-29 v Northants (Northampton) 2005. LO HS 107* Natal v North West (Fochville)
1997-98. LO BB 4-16 v Surrey (Chester-le-St) 2005. T20 HS 56*. T20 BB 3-10.

‡**BLACKWELL, Ian** David (Brookfield Community S), b Chesterfield, Derbys 10 Jun
1978. 6'2". LHB, SLA. Derbyshire 1997-99. Somerset 2000-08; cap 2001; captain 2006
(part). **Tests**: 1 (2005-06): HS 4 v I (Nagpur) 2005-06. **LOI**: 34 (2002-03 to 2005-06); HS
82 v I (Colombo) 2002-03; BB 3-26 v A (Adelaide) 2002-03. F-c Tour: I 2005-06. 1000 runs
(3); most – 1256 (2005). HS 247* Sm v Derbys (Taunton) 2003 – off 156 balls and
including 204 off 98 balls in reduced post-lunch session. Won Walter Lawrence Trophy
2005 for 67-ball hundred v Derbys (Taunton). HS 7-90 Sm v Glamorgan (Taunton) 2004
and 7-90 Sm v Notts (Nottingham) 2004. LO HS 134* v Sussex (Taunton) 2005 (NL). LO
BB 5-26 v Derbys (Taunton) 2005 (NL). T20 HS 82. T20 BB 4-26.

‡**BORTHWICK, Scott** George (Farringdon Community Sports C, Sunderland), b Sunderland 19 Apr 1990. 5'9". LHB, LBG. Durham 2nd XI 2006-08. Awaiting f-c debut. T20 HS – .
T20 BB 3-23.

19

BREESE, Gareth Rohan (Wolmer's BHS, Kingston; Kingston U of Technology, Jamaica), b Montego Bay, Jamaica 9 Jan 1976. 5'7". RHB, OB. Jamaica 1995-96 to 2005-06; captain/overseas player 2003-04 to 2005-06. British passport (Welsh father). Durham debut 2004; cap 2005. **Tests** (WI): 1 (2002-03); HS 5 and BB 2-108 v I (Madras) 2002-03. F-c Tours (WI): E 2002 (WI A); I 2002-03. HS 165* v Somerset (Taunton) 2004. BB 7-60 Jamaica v Barbados (Bridgetown) 2000-01. Du BB 5-41 (10-151 match) v Yorks (Scarborough) 2004 – scored 35 and 68 to complete match double. LO HS 68* v Notts (Chester-le-St) 2007 (FPT). LO BB 5-41 v Derbys (Chester-le-St) 2008 (FPT). T20 HS 24*. T20 BB 4-14.

NQ**CHANDERPAUL, Shivnarine** (Cove and John SS, Unity Village), b Unity Village, Demerara, Guyana 16 Aug 1974. 5'6". LHB, LB. Guyana 1991-92 to 2007-08. Durham debut 2007. **Tests** (WI): 119 (1993-94 to 2008-09, 14 as captain); HS 203* v SA (Georgetown) 2004-05; BB 1-2 v A (Adelaide) 1996-97. **LOI** (WI): 224 (1994-95 to 2008-09, 16 as captain); HS 150 v SA (E London) 1998-99; BB 3-18 v I (Sharjah) 1997-98. F-c Tours (WI) (C=Captain): E 1995, 2000, 2004, 2007; A 1995-96, 1996-97, 2000-01, 2005-06C; SA 1998-99, 2003-04, 2007-08; NZ 1994-95, 1999-00, 2005-06C, 2008-09; I 1994-95, 2002-03; P 1997-98, 2001-02 (Sharjah), 2006-07; SL 2005C; Z 2001, 2003-04; B 1999-00, 2002-03; K 2001. 1000 runs (1+1); most – 1107 (2004-05). HS 303* Guyana v Jamaica (Kingston) 1995-96. Du HS 138 v Sussex (Chester-le-St) 2008. BB 4-48 Guyana v Leeward Is (Basseterre) 1992-93. Du BB – . LO HS 150 (see LOI). LO BB 4-22 Guyana v Trinidad (Hampton Court) 1995-96. IT20 HS 41. T20 HS 48.

NQ**CLAYDON, Mitchell** Eric (Westfield Sports HS, Sydney), b Fairfield, NSW, Australia 25 Nov 1982. 6'4". LHB, RMF. Yorkshire 2005-06. Durham debut 2007. HS 40 v Lancs (Manchester) 2008. BB 3-26 v DU (Durham) 2006. CC BB 1-42 Y v Durham (Chester-le-St) 2007. LO HS 9 Y v Worcs (Worcester) 2006 (CGT). LO BB 3-31 v Bangladesh A (Chester-le-St) 2008. T20 HS 12*. T20 BB 2-6.

COETZER, Kyle James (Aberdeen GS), b Aberdeen, Scotland 14 Apr 1984. 5'11". RHB, RM. Debut (Durham) 2004. Scotland 2004. **LOI** (Scot): 1 (2008); HS 0 v E (Edinburgh) 2008. HS 153* v DU (Durham) 2007. CC HS 142 v Warwks (Chester-le-St) 2007. LO HS 76 v Surrey (Guildford) 2007 (P40). IT20 HS 48*. T20 HS 48*.

COLLINGWOOD, Paul David (Blackfyne CS; Derwentside C), b Shotley Bridge 26 May 1976. 5'11". RHB, RMF. Debut (Durham) 1996 v Northants (Chester-le-St) taking wicket of D.J.Capel with his first ball before scoring 91 and 16; cap 1998; benefit 2007. MBE 2005. Wisden 2007. **ECB central contract 2008-09. Tests**: 46 (2003-04 to 2008-09); HS 206 v A (Adelaide) 2006-07; BB 3-23 v NZ (Wellington) 2007-08. **LOI**: 154 (2001 to 2008-09, 24 as captain); HS 120* v A (Melbourne) 2006-07; BB 6-31 v B (Nottingham) 2005 – first to score a hundred (112*) and take six wickets in same LOI. F-c Tours: A 2006-07; WI 2003-04, 2008-09; NZ 2007-08; I 2005-06, 2008-09; P 2005-06; SL 2003-04, 2007-08. 1000 runs (2); most – 1120 (2005), inc six hundreds (Du record). HS 206 (see Tests). Du HS 190 v SL (Chester-le-St) 2002 and 190 v Derbys (Derby) 2005. BB 5-52 v Somerset (Stockton) 2005. LO HS 120* (see LOI). LO BB 6-31 (see LOI). IT20 HS 79. IT20 BB 4-22. T20 HS 79. T20 BB 5-14 v Derbys (Chester-le-St) 2008 – Du record.

DAVIES, Anthony Mark (Northfield CS, Billingham; Stockton SFC), b Stockton-on-Tees 4 Oct 1980. 6'3". RHB, RMF. Debut (Durham) 2002; cap 2005. Nottinghamshire 2007 (on loan). F-c Tour (Eng A): NZ 2008-09. HS 62 v Somerset (Stockton) 2005. 50 wkts (1): 50 (2004). BB 8-24 (11-75 match) v Hampshire (Basingstoke) 2008. LO HS 31* v Warwks (Chester-le-St) 2002 (NL). LO BB 4-13 v Sussex (Chester-le-St) 2001 (NL). T20 HS 6. T20 BB 2-14.

NQDi VENUTO, Michael James (St Virgil's C; Hobart), b Hobart, Australia 12 Dec 1973. 6'0". LHB, RM/LBG. Tasmania 1991-92 to 2007-08. Sussex 1999; cap 1999. Derbyshire 2000-06; cap 2000; appointed captain for 2004 but missed entire season – back surgery. Durham debut 2007, carrying his bat for 155* v Worcs (Worcester) on debut. Italian passport 2008. **LOI** (A): 9 (1996-97 to 1997-98); HS 89 v SA (Johannesburg) 1996-97. F-c Tours: Z 1995-96 (Tas); Scotland/Ireland 1998 (Aus A). 1000 runs (8); most – 1538 (2002). HS 230 De v Northants (Derby) 2002. Du HS 204* v Kent (Chester-le-St) 2007. BB 1-0 Tas v Q (Brisbane) 1999-00. UK BB 1-3 Sx v Somerset (Taunton) 1999. LO HS 173* v Derbys CB (Derby) 2000 (NWT). LO BB 1-10 Tas v Q (Hobart) 1995-96. T20 HS 95*. T20 BB 3-19.

EVANS, Luke (St Aidan's S, Sunderland), b Sunderland 26 Apr 1987. 6'7". RHB, RMF. Debut (Durham) 2007 – awaiting CC debut. No 1st XI appearances in 2008. HS 1 and BB 2-39 v SL A (Chester-le-St) 2007.

GIDMAN, William Robert Simon (Wycliffe C; Berkshire C of Agriculture), b High Wycombe, Bucks 14 Feb 1985. Younger brother of A.P.R.Gidman (*see GLOUCESTER-SHIRE*). 6'2". LHB, RM. Debut (Durham) 2007 (awaiting CC debut). No f-c appearances in 2008. MCC YC 2004-06. HS 8 and BB 3-37 v SL A (Chester-le-St) 2007. HS LO 12 Gs CB v Surrey CB (Bristol) 2002. BB 2-21 v Bangladesh A (Chester-le-St) 2008.

GODDARD, Lee James (Batley GS; Huddersfield TC; Loughborough U), b Dewsbury, Yorks 22 Oct 1982. 5'10". RHB, WK. Loughborough UCCE 2003. Derbyshire 2004, 2006. Durham debut 2007. No f-c appearances in 2008. HS 91 De v Surrey (Derby) 2006. Du HS 52 v SL A (Chester-le-St) 2007. LO HS 36 De v Kent (Canterbury) 2006 (P40). T20 HS – .

HARMISON, Ben William (Ashington HS), b Ashington, Northumb 9 Jan 1986. Younger brother of S.J.Harmison. 6'5". LHB, RMF. Debut (Durham) 2006, scoring 110 v Oxford UCCE (Oxford). Scored 105 in his second match (v West Indies A) to emulate A.Fairbairn (Middlesex 1947) in scoring hundreds in first two f-c matches, those matches being in England. HS 110 (*see above*). CC HS 101 v Warwks (Chester-le-St) 2007. BB 4-27 v Surrey (Guildford) 2008. LO HS 57 v Notts (Chester-le-St) 2006 (P40). LO BB 3-43 v Scotland (Chester-le-St) 2008 (FPT). T20 HS 21. T20 BB 1-21.

HARMISON, Stephen James (Ashington HS), b Ashington, Northumb 23 Oct 1978. Elder brother of B.W.Harmison. 6'4". RHB, RF. Debut (Durham) 1996; cap 1999. Lions 2007-08. MCC 2007. *Wisden* 2004. MBE 2005. **ECB central contract 2008-09. Tests**: 60 (2002 to 2008-09); HS 49* v SA (Oval) 2008; BB 7-12 (9-73 match) v WI (Kingston) 2003-04. **LOI**: 54 (2002-03 to 2008-09); HS 13* v NZ (Chester-le-St) 2003; BB 5-33 v A (Bristol) 2005; hat-trick v I (Nottingham) 2004. F-c Tours: A 2002-03, 2005-06 (RW), 2006-07; SA 1998-99 (Eng A), 2004-05; WI 2003-04, 2008-09; NZ 2007-08; I 2005-06, 2008-09; P 2005-06; SL 2007-08; Z 1998-99 (Eng A); B 2003-04. HS 49* (*see Tests*). Du HS 36* v Hampshire (Chester-le-St) 2008. 50 wkts (5); most – 65 (2008). BB 7-12 (*see Tests*). Du BB 6-52 (9-84 match) v Lancs (Manchester) 2005. Hat-tricks (2): v Worcs (Chester-le-St) 2005 and v Sussex (Hove) 2008. LO HS 25* v Somerset (Chester-le-St) 2008 (P40). LO BB 5-33 (*see LOI*). IT20 HS – . IT20 BB 1-13. T20 HS 5. T20 BB 4-38.

‡HINDMARCH, Paul Robert (Keswick S), b Carlisle, Cumbria 8 Feb 1988. 6'2". RHB, RMF. Durham 2nd XI 2006-08. Cumberland 2006. Development contract – awaiting 1st XI debut.

KILLEEN, Neil (Greencroft CS; Derwentside C; Teesside U), b Shotley Bridge 17 Oct 1975. 6'2". RHB, RMF. Debut (Durham) 1995; cap 1999; benefit 2006. MCC 1999-2000. Tour (MCC) B 1999-00. HS 48 v Somerset (Chester-le-St) 1995. 50 wkts (1): 58 (1999). BB 7-70 v Hants (Chester-le-St) 2003. LO HS 32 v Middlesex (Lord's) 1996 (SL). LO BB 6-31 v Derbys (Derby) 2000 (NL). T20 HS 17*. T20 BB 4-7.

MUCHALL, Gordon James (Durham S), b Newcastle upon Tyne, Northumb 2 Nov 1982. 6'0". Elder brother of P.B.Muchall. RHB, RM. Northumberland 1999. Debut (Durham) 2002; cap 2005. F-c Tours (E): NZ 2007-08; SL 2002-03 (ECB Acad), 2007-08. HS 219 v Kent (Canterbury) 2006, sharing Du record 6th wkt partnership of 249 with P.Mustard (*see below*). BB 3-26 v Yorks (Leeds) 2003. LO HS 101* v Yorks (Leeds) 2005 (NL). LO BB 1-15 (NL). T20 HS 64*. T20 BB 1-8.

MUCHALL, Paul Bernard (Durham S), b Newcastle upon Tyne, Northumb 17 Mar 1987. Younger brother of G.J.Muchall. RHB, RM. Durham 2nd XI 2006-08. Northumberland 2006-08. Development contract – awaiting 1st XI debut.

MUSTARD, Philip (Usworth CS), b Sunderland 8 Oct 1982. 5'11". LHB, WK. Debut (Durham) 2002. **LOI**: 10 (2007-08); HS 83 v NZ (Napier) 2007-08. HS 130 v Kent (Canterbury) 2006. LO HS 108 v Northants (Northampton) 2007 (FPT). IT20 HS 40. T20 HS 67*.

ONIONS, Graham (St Thomas More RC S, Blaydon), b Gateshead 9 Sep 1982. 6'1". RHB, RMF. Debut (Durham) 2004. MCC 2007-08. England Lions 2008. HS 41 v Yorks (Leeds) 2007. 50 wkts (1): 54 (2006). BB 8-101 v Warwks (Birmingham) 2007. LO HS 19 v Derbys (Derby) 2008 (FPT). LO BB 3-39 v Derbys (Derby) 2005 (NL). T20 HS 31. T20 BB 3-25.

PLUNKETT, Liam Edward (Nunthorpe SS; Teesside Tertiary C), b Middlesbrough, Yorks 6 Apr 1985. 6'3". RHB, RFM. Debut (Durham) 2003. Dolphins 2007-08. **Tests**: 9 (2005-06 to 2007); HS 44* v WI (Leeds) 2007; BB 3-17 v SL (Birmingham) 2006. **LOI**: 27 (2005-06 to 2007); HS 56 v P (Lahore) 2005-06; BB 3-24 v A (Sydney) 2006-07. F-c Tours: NZ 2008-09 (Eng A); I 2005-06; P 2005-06. HS 74* v Somerset (Stockton) 2005. 50 wkts (2); most – 51 (2005). BB 6-74 v Hants (Chester-le-St) 2004. LO HS 72 v Somerset (Chester-le-St) 2008 (P40). LO BB 4-15 v Essex (Chester-le-St) 2007 (FPT). IT20 HS – . IT20 BB 1-37. T20 HS 13*. T20 BB 3-16.

SMITH, William Rew (Bedford S; Collingwood C, Durham), b Luton, Beds 28 Sep 1982. 5'9". RHB, OB. Nottinghamshire 2002-06. Durham UCCE 2003-05; captain 2004-05. British U 2004-05. Durham debut 2007; captain 2009. Notts 2nd XI debut 1999 when aged 16y 309d. Bedfordshire 1999-2002. HS 201* v Surrey (Guildford) 2008. BB 3-34 DU v Leics (Leicester) 2005. CC BB 1-5 v Lancs (Chester-le-St) 2007. LO HS 103 v Worcs (Chester-le-St) 2007 (FPT). LO BB 1-6 v Derbys (Chester-le-St) 2008 (FPT). T20 HS 55. T20 BB 1-31.

STONEMAN, Mark Daniel (Whickham CS), b Newcastle upon Tyne, Northumb 26 Jun 1987. 5'11". LHB, RM. Debut (Durham) 2007. HS 101 v Sussex (Chester-le-St) 2007. LO HS 21 v Bangladesh A (Chester-le-St) 2008.

THORP, Callum David (Servite C, Tuart Hill, Perth), b Mount Lawley, Perth, Australia 11 Feb 1975. 6'3". British passport (English parents). RHB, RMF. W Australia 2002-03 to 2003-04. Durham debut 2005. HS 75 v Hants (Southampton) 2006. 50 wkts (1): 50 (2008). BB 7-88 v Kent (Canterbury) 2008. LO HS 52 v B (Chester-le-St) 2005. LO BB 6-17 v Scotland (Edinburgh) 2006 (CGT). T20 HS 13. T20 BB 2-32.

‡**TURNER, Karl** (Deerness Valley CS, Ushaw Moor), b Dryburn, Durham 29 Nov 1987. LHB, RM. Durham 2nd XI 2005-08. Development contract – awaiting 1st XI debut.

‡NQ**WARNER, David** Andrew, b Paddington, Sydney, NSW, Australia 27 Oct 1986. LHB, LBG. Debut NSW 2008-09. T20 contract for 2009. **LOI** (A): 6 (2008-09); HS 69 v SA (Sydney) 2008-09. HS 42 NSW v WA (Sydney) 2008-09 – on debut. LO HS 165* NSW v Tas (Sydney) 2008-09. IT20 HS 89 – on IT20 debut, becoming the first man to play for Australia before making f-c debut since 1877. T20 HS 89.

^{NQ}**WISEMAN, Paul** John (Auckland IT), b Takapuna, Auckland, New Zealand 4 May 1970. 6'1". RHB, OB. Auckland 1991-92 to 1992-93. Otago 1994-95 to 2000-01. Canterbury 2001-02 to 2005-06. Durham debut 2006. **Tests** (NZ): 25 (1998 to 2004-05); HS 36 v SA (Hamilton) 2003-04; BB 5-82 v SL (Colombo) 1997 98   on debut. **LOI** (NZ): 15 (1997-98 to 2003); HS 16 v SL (Colombo) 1998; BB 4-45 v Z (Nairobi) 2000-01. Tours (NZ): A 2004-05; SA 1997 (NZ Acad), 2004-05 (NZ A); I 1999-00, 2003-04; SL 1998, 2003, 2005-06 (NZ A); Z 1997-98, 2000-01; B 2004-05. HS 130 Canterbury v ND (Hamilton) 2005-06. Du HS 65 v DU (Chester-le-St) 2008. CC HS 60* v Surrey (Guildford) 2008. BB 9-13 Canterbury v CD (Christchurch) 2004-05. UK BB 5-65 v Hants (Chester-le-St) 2007. LO HS 65* Canterbury v Auckland (Christchurch) 2001-02. LO BB 4-45 (*see LOI*). T20 HS 0. T20 BB 2-20.

RELEASED/RETIRED
(Having made a County First-Class or List A appearance in 2008)

^{NQ}**McKENZIE, Neil** Douglas (King Edward VII HS; Rand Afrikaans U), b Johannesburg, South Africa 24 Nov 1975. 5'9½". Son of K.A.McKenzie (N-E Transvaal and Transvaal 1966-67 to 1986-87). RHB, RM. Transvaal/Gauteng 1994-95 to 1998-99. Northerns 1999-00 to 2003-04. Lions 2004-05 to date. Somerset 2007 (Kolpak registration). Durham 2008 (*part*). *Wisden 2008*. **Tests** (SA): 58 (2000 to 2008-09); HS 226 v B (Chittagong) 2007-08, sharing Test record 1st wkt partnership of 415 with G.C.Smith. BB – . **LOI** (SA): 64 (1999-00 to 2008-09): HS 131* v K (Cape Town) 2001-02. BB – . F-c Tours (SA): E 2003, 2008; A 2001-02, 2008-09; WI 2000-01; NZ 2003-04; I 2007-08; P 2003-04; SL 2000; Z 2001-02, 2004 (SA A); B 2003, 2007-08. HS 226 (*see Tests*). UK HS 138 SA v E (Lord's) 2008. CC HS 84 Sm v Glamorgan (Taunton) 2007. BB 2-13 Lions v Eagles (Kimberley) 2007-08. LO HS 131* (*see LOI*). LO BB 2-19 Gauteng v GW (Kimberley) 1997-98. IT20 HS 7*. T20 HS 85*. T20 BB – .

MAHOMED, Uzair (Woodhouse Grove S, Leeds), b Johannesburg, South Africa 20 Aug 1987. 5'8". RHB, OB. Durham Academy and 2nd XI 2005-08. Awaiting f-c debut. Northumberland 2006. LO HS 3 v Bangladesh A (Chester-le-St) 2008.

^{NQ}**MORKEL, Johannes** Albertus (*'Albie'*) (Hoërskool Vereeniging), b Vereeniging, Transvaal, South Africa 10 June 1981. 6'1". Brother of M.Morkel (*see YORKSHIRE*). LHB, RM. Easterns 1999-00 to 2003-04. Titans 2004-05 to date. **Tests** (SA): 1 (2008-09); HS 58 and BB 1-44 v A (Cape Town) 2008-09 – on debut. **LOI** (SA): 35 (2003-04 to 2008-09); HS 97 v Z (Harare) 2007; BB 4-29 v B (Dhaka) 2007-08. HS 204* Titans v WP (Paarl) 2004-05; Du HS 37 v Yorkshire (Leeds) 2008 – only f-c match for Du. BB 6-36 EP v GW (Kimberley) 1999-00. LO HS 97 (*see LOI*). LO BB 4-23 Easterns v Free State (Bloemfontein) 1999-00. IT20 HS 43. IT20 BB 2-12. T20 HS 71. T20 BB 4-30.

PARK, G.T. – *see DERBYSHIRE*.

^{NQ}**POLLOCK, Shaun** Maclean (Northwood HS; Durban U), b Port Elizabeth, South Africa 16 Jul 1973. Son of P.M.Pollock (EP and SA 1958-59 to 1971-72); nephew of R G Pollock (EP, Transvaal and SA 1960-61 to 1986-87). 6'3". RHB, RFM. Natal/KZ-Natal 1991-92 to 2003-04. Warwickshire 1996, 2002; cap 1996. Dolphins 2004-05 to 2007-08. Durham 2008 (T20 and one l-o only). **Tests** (SA): 108 (1995-96 to 2007-08, 26 as captain); HS 11 v SL (Pretoria) 2000-01; BB 7-87 v A (Adelaide) 1997-98. **LOI** (SA): 294 (1995-96 to 2007-08, 92 as captain); HS 90 v P (Multan) 2007-08; BB 6-35 v WI (E London) 1988-99. F-c Tours (SA) (C=captain): E 1998, 2003; A 1997-98, 2001-02C, 2005-06; WI 2000-01C, 2004-05 (*part*); NZ 1998-99, 2003-04; I 1999-00, 2004-05; P 1997-98, 2003-04; SL 1995 (SA U-24), 2000C, 2004, 2006; Z 1999-00, 2001-02C; B 2003. HS 150* Wa v Glamorgan (Birmingham) 1996. 50 wkts (0+1): 51 (1995-96). BB 7-33 KZ-Natal v Border (E London) 1995-96. UK BB 6-56 Wa v Middlesex (Lord's) 1996. LO HS 134* KZ-Natal v EP (Durban) 2003-04. LO BB 6-21 Wa v Leics (Birmingham) 1996 (BHC) – inc 4 wkts in 4 balls on Wa debut. IT20 HS 36*. IT20 BB 3-28. T20 HS 59. T20 BB 3-12.

M.M.Iqbal and G.M.Scott left the staff, without making a County First-Class or List A appearance in 2008.

DURHAM 2008

	Place	Won	Lost	Tied	Drew	No Result
County Championship (1st Division)	1st	6	3		6	1
All First-Class Matches		6	3		7	1
FP Trophy (North Division)	Semi-Finalist	6	4			
Pro40 League (1st Division)	3rd	4	3			1
Twenty/20 Cup (North Division)	Semi-Finalist	7	2	1		2

LV COUNTY CHAMPIONSHIP AVERAGES
BATTING AND FIELDING

Cap†		M	I	NO	HS	Runs	Avge	100	50	Ct/St
	W.R.Smith	12	20	2	201*	925	51.38	3	3	2
	M.J.Di Venuto	15	27	4	184	1058	46.00	2	7	16
2005	D.M.Benkenstein	14	22	4	110	783	43.50	1	7	5
	S.Chanderpaul	8	12	1	138	411	37.36	1	2	2
	L.E.Plunkett	7	9	2	68*	191	27.28	–	2	5
	P.J.Wiseman	15	21	2	60	414	21.78	–	2	1
	P.Mustard	15	23	1	92	479	21.77	–	4	56/2
	M.D.Stoneman	12	21	1	60*	429	21.45	–	3	4
	N.D.McKenzie	4	8	1	48	133	19.00	–	–	7
	P.D.Collingwood	2	4	1	44*	53	17.66	–	–	6
	B.W.Harmison	12	18	1	39	281	16.52	–	–	10
1999	S.J.Harmison	12	13	5	36*	121	15.12	–	–	1
	C.D.Thorp	12	15	4	29*	145	13.18	–	–	6
	G.Onions	5	8	1	28	80	11.42	–	–	3
	K.J.Coetzer	3	6	–	23	48	8.00	–	–	1
2005	A.M.Davies	11	14	6	19	63	7.87	–	–	1

Also batted: G.R.Breese (2 matches – cap 2005) 63, 121* (1 ct); M.E.Claydon (1) 40, 4; N.Killeen (1) 1 (1 ct); J.A.Morkel (1) 37 (2 ct); G.T.Park (1) 19, 2 (1 ct).

BOWLING

	O	M	R	W	Avge	Best	5wI	10wM
A.M.Davies	245.2	69	587	39	15.05	8- 24	4	2
C.D.Thorp	321.2	76	981	50	19.62	7- 88	3	–
S.J.Harmison	411.1	92	1341	60	22.35	6-122	2	–
G.Onions	110.4	27	386	16	24.12	5- 75	1	–
B.W.Harmison	113.3	21	437	16	27.31	4- 27	–	–
L.E.Plunkett	129.1	16	520	16	32.50	3- 49	–	–
P.J.Wiseman	193	42	610	16	38.12	4- 87	–	–

Also bowled:

| P.D.Collingwood | 17 | 3 | 62 | 5 | 12.40 | 3- 17 | – | – |

D.M.Benkenstein 25-7-60-1; G.R.Breese 7-1-22-1; S.Chanderpaul 4-0-19-0; M.E.Claydon 28-9-94-1; N.Killeen 25-7-50-3; G.T.Park 8-3-20-2.

The First-Class Averages (pp 136–153) give the records of Durham players in all first-class county matches (Durham's other opponents being Durham UCCE), with the exception of P.D.Collingwood and N.D.McKenzie, whose first-class figures for Durham are as above, and:

S.J.Harmison 13-14-5-36*-123-13.66-0-0-1ct. 429.1-105-1353-61-22.18-6/122-2-0.
G.Onions 6-9-1-36-116-14.50-0-0-3ct. 127.2-33-431-18-23.94-5/75-1-0.
† Durham abolished their capping system after 2005.

24

DURHAM RECORDS

FIRST-CLASS CRICKET

Highest Total	For	645-6d		v	Middlesex	Lord's	2002
	V	810-4d		by	Warwicks	Birmingham	1994
Lowest Total	For	67		v	Middlesex	Lord's	1996
	V	56		by	Somerset	Chester-le-St[2]	2003
Highest Innings	For	273	M.L.Love	v	Hampshire	Chester-le-St[2]	2003
	V	501*	B.C.Lara	for	Warwicks	Birmingham	1994

Highest Partnership for each Wicket

1st	334*	S.Hutton/M.A.Roseberry	v	Oxford U	Oxford	1996
2nd	258	J.J.B.Lewis/M.L.Love	v	Notts	Chester-le-St[2]	2001
3rd	205	G.Fowler/S.Hutton	v	Yorkshire	Leeds	1993
4th	250	P.D.Collingwood/D.M.Benkenstein	v	Derbyshire	Derby	2005
5th	222	D.M.Benkenstein/G.R.Breese	v	Middlesex	Lord's	2006
6th	249	G.J.Muchall/P.Mustard	v	Kent	Canterbury	2006
7th	315	D.M.Benkenstein/O.D.Gibson	v	Yorkshire	Leeds	2006
8th	143	P.Mustard/L.E.Plunkett	v	Yorkshire	Leeds	2008
9th	127	D.G.C.Ligertwood/S.J.E.Brown	v	Surrey	Stockton	1996
10th	103	M.M.Betts/D.M.Cox	v	Sussex	Hove	1996

Best Bowling	For	10- 47	O.D.Gibson	v	Hampshire	Chester-le-St[2]	2007
(Innings)	V	9- 36	M.S.Kasprowicz	for	Glamorgan	Cardiff	2003
Best Bowling	For	14-177	A.Walker	v	Essex	Chelmsford	1995
(Match)	V	13-110	M.S.Kasprowicz	for	Glamorgan	Chester-le-St[2]	2003

Most Runs – Season	1536	W.Larkins	(av 37.46)	1992
Most Runs – Career	7854	J.J.B.Lewis	(av 31.41)	1997-2006
Most 100s – Season	6	P.D.Collingwood		2005
Most 100s – Career	14	J.E.Morris		1994-99
	14	P.D.Collingwood		1996-2005
Most Wkts – Season	80	O.D.Gibson	(av 20.75)	2007
Most Wkts – Career	518	S.J.E.Brown	(av 28.30)	1992-2002
Most Career W-K Dismissals	289	P.Mustard	(277 ct; 12 st)	2002-08
Most Career Catches in the Field	123	P.D.Collingwood		1996-2008

LIMITED-OVERS CRICKET

Highest Total	FPT	332-4		v	Worcs	Chester-le-St[2]	2007
	P40	319-3		v	Worcs	Worcester	2004
	T20	181-4		v	Lancashire	Manchester	2008
Lowest Total	FPT	82		v	Worcs	Chester-le-St[1]	1968
	P40	72		v	Warwicks	Birmingham	2002
	T20	98		v	Yorkshire	Chester-le-St[2]	2006
Highest Innings	FPT	138	M.J.Di Venuto	v	Derbyshire	Chester-le-St[2]	2008
	P40	131*	W.Larkins	v	Hampshire	Portsmouth	1994
	T20	67*	P.Mustard	v	Derbyshire	Chester-le-St[2]	2006
Best Bowling	FPT	7-32	S.P.Davis	v	Lancashire	Chester-le-St[1]	1983
	P40	6-31	N.Killeen	v	Derbyshire	Derby	2000
	T20	5-14	P.D.Collingwood	v	Derbyshire	Chester-le-St[2]	2008

[1] Chester-le-Street CC (Ropery Lane)   [2] Riverside Ground

ESSEX

Formation of Present Club: 14 January 1876
Inaugural First-Class Match: 1894
Colours: Blue, Gold and Red
Badge: Three Seaxes above Scroll bearing 'Essex'
County Champions: (6) 1979, 1983, 1984, 1986, 1991, 1992
Gillette/NatWest/C&G/FP Trophy Winners: (3) 1985, 1997, 2008
Benson and Hedges Cup Winners: (2) 1979, 1998
Pro 40/National League (Div 1) Winners: (2) 2005, 2006
Sunday League Winners: (3) 1981, 1984, 1985
Twenty20 Cup Winners: (0); best – Semi-Finalist 2006

Chief Executive: David E.East, County Ground, New Writtle Street, Chelmsford CM2 0PG • Tel: 01245 252420 • Fax: 01245 254030 • Email: administration.essex@ecb.co.uk • Web: www.essexcricket.org.uk

First Team Coach: A.P.Grayson. **Batting Coach:** G.A.Gooch. **Seam Bowling Coach:** G.Welch. **Captain:** M.L.Pettini. **Vice-Captain:** J.S.Foster. **Overseas Player:** Danish Kaneria. **2009 Beneficiary:** none. **Head Groundsman:** Stuart Kerrison. **Scorer:** A.E. (Tony) Choat. ‡ New registration. NQ Not qualified for England.

AHMED, Jahid Sheikh (St Peter's HS, Burnham-on-Crouch; East London U), b Chelmsford 20 Feb 1986. 5'11". RHB, RMF. Debut (Essex) 2005. MCC YC 2004. HS 16* and BB 3-42 v Glos (Bristol) 2008. LO HS 1* v Hants (Southampton) 2007 (P40). LO BB 4-32 v SL (Chelmsford) 2006. T20 HS – . T20 BB 1-25.

BOPARA, Ravinder Singh (Brampton Manor S; Barking Abbey Sports C), b Newham, London 4 May 1985. 5'8". RHB, RMF. Debut (Essex) 2002; cap 2005. MCC 2006, 2008. **YC 2008**. **Tests:** 4 (2007-08 to 2008-09); HS 104 v WI (Bridgetown) 2008-09; BB 1-39 v SL (Galle) 2007-08. **LOI:** 33 (2006-07 to 2008-09); HS 60 v I (Kanpur) 2008-09. BB 2-43 v Canada (Gros Islet, St Lucia) 2006-07. F-c Tours: WI 2008-09; SL 2007-08. 1000 runs (1): 1256 (2008). HS 229 v Northants (Chelmsford) 2007. BB 5-75 v Surrey (Chelmsford) 2006. LO HS 201* v Leics (Leicester) 2008 (FPT) – Ex record l-o score. LO BB 4-52 v Derbys (Derby) 2008 (P40). IT20 HS 13. T20 HS 83. T20 BB 3-18.

CHAMBERS, Maurice Anthony (Homerton TC; Sir George Monoux C), b Port Antonio, Portland, Jamaica 14 Sep 1987. 6'3". RHB, RFM. Debut (Essex) 2005. No f-c appearances 2006-07 – stress fracture of the back. MCC YC 2004. HS 7 and BB 3-37 v NZ (Chelmsford) 2008. CC HS 2* v Derbys (Chelmsford) 2005 – on debut. CC BB 2-29 v Glamorgan (Cardiff) 2008. LO HS 1* v Leics (Leicester) 2008 (P40). LO BB 1-26 v Yorkshire (Chelmsford) 2008. T20 HS 10*. T20 BB 3-31.

CHOPRA, Varun (Ilford County HS), b Barking 21 Jun 1987. 6'1". RHB, LB. Debut (Essex) 2006. HS 155 v Glos (Bristol) 2008. Scored 106 v Glos (Chelmsford) 2006 – on CC debut. BB – . LO HS 102 v Middlesex (Chelmsford) 2007 (FPT). T20 HS 18.

COOK, Alastair Nathan (Bedford S), b Gloucester 25 Dec 1984. 6'3". LHB, OB. Debut (Essex) 2003; cap 2005. MCC 2004-07. Essex 2nd XI debut 2000 when aged 15y 235d. England U19 captain 2003-04. YC 2005. **ECB central contract 2008-09. Tests**: 41 (2005-6 to 2008-09); HS 139* v WI (Bridgetown) 2008-09. Scored 60 and 104* v I (Nagpur) 2005-06 on debut. Third, after D.G.Bradman and S.R.Tendulkar, to score seven Test hundreds before his 23rd birthday. Second, after M.A.Taylor, to score 1000 runs in the calendar year of his debut. BB – . **LOI**: 23 (2006 to 2008-09); HS 102 v I (Southampton) 2007. F-c Tours: A 2006-07; WI 2005-06 (Eng A), 2008-09; NZ 2007-08; I 2005-06, 2008-09; SL 2004-05 (Eng A), 2007-08. 1000 runs (3); most – 1466 (2005). HS 195 v Northants (Northampton) 2005. Scored 214 v Australians (Chelmsford) 2005 in 2-day non-f-c match. BB 3-13 v Northants (Chelmsford) 2005. LO HS 125 v Surrey (Croydon) 2007 (FPT). BB – . IT20 HS 15. T20 HS 15.

[NQ]**DANISH** Parabha Shanker **KANERIA** (St Patrick's HS; Government Islamia C), b Karachi, Pakistan 16 Dec 1980. 6'1". Cousin of Anil Dalpat (Pakistan) and second Hindu to represent Pakistan. RHB, LBG. Debut (PNSC) 1998 99. Karachi Whites/Blues/Harbour 1998-99 to 2006-07. Habib Bank 2000-01 to date. Essex 2004-05, 2007; cap 2004. Sind 2007-08. **Tests** (P): 53 (2000-01 to 2008-09); HS 29 v E (Leeds) 2006; BB 7-77 v B (Dhaka) 2001-02. **LOI** (P): 18 (2001-02 to 2006-07); HS 6*; BB 3-31 v NZ (Dambulla) 2003. F-c Tours (P): E 2006; A 2004-05; SA 2006-07; WI 2004-05; NZ 2003-04; I 2004-05, 2007-08; SL 2001 (Pak A), 2005-06; B 2001-02; K 2000 (Pak A). HS 65 v Notts (Nottingham) 2007. 50 wkts (2+1); most – 74 (2007). BB 8-59 (13-81 match) Habib Bank v Sui Southern Gas (Karachi) 2008-09. UK BB 7-65 (13-186 match) v Yorks (Chelmsford) 2004. LO HS 33* v Sussex (Arundel) 2007 (FPT). LO BB 5-21 Habib Bank v Customs (Karachi) 2005-06. T20 HS 7*. T20 BB 4-22.

[NQ]**FLOWER, Grant** William (St George's C), b Salisbury, Rhodesia 20 Dec 1970. 5'10". Younger brother of A. Flower (Mashonaland, Essex, S Australia and Zimbabwe 1986-87 to 2006). RHB, SLA. Debut (Zimbabwe) 1989-90. Mashonaland U24/Young Mashonaland 1993-94 to 1995-96. Mashonaland 1994-95 to 2003-04. MCC 1996-97. Leicestershire 2002 (one match); cap 2002. Essex debut/cap 2005 (Kolpak registration). **Tests** (Z): 67 (1992-93 to 2003-04); HS 201* v P (Harare) 1994-95 sharing with A.Flower in fourth-wicket partnership of 269, the highest stand between brothers in Test cricket; BB 4-41 (8-104 match) v B (Chittagong) 2001-02. **LOI** (Z): 219 (1992-93 to 2003-04, 1 as captain); HS 142* v B (Bulawayo) 2000-01; BB 4-32 v K (Dhaka) 1998-99. F-c Tours (Z): E 1990, 2000; A 1994-95; SA 1999-00; WI 1999-00; NZ 1995-96, 1997-98, 2000-01; I 1992-93, 2000-01, 2001-02; P 1993-94, 1996-97, 1998-99; SL 1996-97, 1997-98, 2001-02; B 2001-02. HS 243* Mashonaland v Matabeleland (Harare) 1996-97. UK HS 203 v Northants (Chelmsford) 2007. BB 7-31 Z v Lahore (Lahore) 1998-99. UK BB 4-66 Le v Warwks (Birmingham) 2002. Ex BB 3-28 v Glos (Bristol) 2006. LO HS 148* Mashonaland v Midlands (Kwekwe) 2002-03. LO BB 4-32 (see LOI). T20 HS 40. T20 BB 3-20.

FOSTER, James Savin (Forest S, Snaresbrook; Collingwood C, Durham U), b Whipps Cross 15 Apr 1980. 6'0". RHB, WK. British U 2000-01. Essex debut 2000; cap 2001. Durham UCCE 2001. MCC 2004, 2008. **Tests**: 7 (2001-02 to 2002-03); HS 48 v I (Bangalore) 2001-02. **LOI**: 11 (2001-02); HS 13 v I (Bombay) 2001-02. F-c Tours: A 2002-03; WI 2000-01 (Eng A); NZ 2001-02; I 2001-02, 2007-08 (Eng A). 1000 runs (1): 1037 (2004). HS 212 v Leics (Chelmsford) 2004. BB 1-122 v Northants (Northampton) 2008 – in contrived circumstances. LO HS 69* v Hants (Chelmsford) 2007 (FPT). T20 HS 62*.

GALLIAN, Jason Edward Riche (Pittwater House S, Sydney; Keble C, Oxford), b Manly, Sydney, Australia 25 Jun 1971. Qualified for England 1994. 6'0". RHB, RM. Lancashire 1990-97, taking wicket of D.A.Hagan (OU) with his first ball; cap 1994. Oxford U 1992-93; blue 1992-93; captain 1993. Combined U 1992-93. Nottinghamshire 1998-2007; cap 1998; captain 1998 (*part*) to 2004; benefit 2005. Essex debut 2008; cap 2008. Captained Australia YC v England YC 1989-90, scoring 158* in 1st 'Test'. **Tests**: 3 (1995 to 1995-96); HS 28 v SA (Pt Elizabeth) 1995-96. F-c Tours: A 1996-97 (Eng A); WI 1995-96 (La); SA 1995-96 (*part*); I 1994-95 (Eng A); P 1995-96 (Eng A). 1000 runs (6); most – 1220 (2005). HS 312 La v Derbys (Manchester) 1996 (record score at Old Trafford). Ex HS 171 v Northants (Chelmsford) 2008 – on Ex CC debut. BB 6-115 La v Surrey (Southport) 1996. Ex BB – . LO HS 134 La v Notts (Manchester) 1995 (BHC). LO BB 5-15 La v Minor C (Leek) 1995 (BHC). T20 HS 62.

MASTERS, David Daniel (Fort Luton HS; Mid Kent CHE), b Chatham, Kent 22 Apr 1978. Son of K.D.Masters (Kent 1983-84). 6'4". RHB, RMF. Kent 2000-02. Leicestershire 2003-07; cap 2007. Essex debut 2008. HS 119 Le v Sussex (Hove) 2003. Ex HS 27 v Middlesex (Lord's) 2008. BB 6-24 v Leics (Chelmsford) 2008. LO HS 39 Le v Glos (Cheltenham) 2006 (P40). LO BB 5-17 v Surrey (Oval) 2008 (FPT). T20 HS 14. T20 BB 3-7.

‡**MAUNDERS, John** Kenneth (Ashford HS; Spelthorne C), b Ashford, Middlesex 4 Apr 1981. 5'10". LHB, RM. Middlesex 1999 (one non-CC match); 2nd XI debut aged 16 years 19 days. Leicestershire 2003-07. Essex debut 2008. Shropshire 2008. HS 180 Le v Glos (Cheltenham) 2006. Ex HS 105 v Warwks (Chelmsford) 2008. BB 4-15 Le v Worcs (Worcester) 2006. LO HS 109* Le v Derbys (Leicester) 2007 (FPT). LO BB 2-16 Le v Warwks (Birmingham) 2005 (CGT). T20 HS 10. T20 BB 2-14.

MICKELBURGH, Jaik Charles (Bungay HS), b Norwich, Norfolk 30 Mar 1990. RHB, RM. Norfolk 2007. Debut (Essex) 2008. Essex 2nd XI debut aged 16 years 160 days. HS 72 v Warwks (Chelmsford) 2008. BB – .

MIDDLEBROOK, James Daniel (Pudsey Crawshaw S), b Leeds, Yorks 13 May 1977. 6'1". RHB, OB. Yorkshire 1998-2001. Essex debut 2002; cap 2003. HS 127 v Middlesex (Lord's) 2008. 50 wkts (1): 56 (2003). BB 6-82 (10-170 match) Y v Hants (Southampton) 2000 – including 4 wickets in 5 balls. Ex BB 6-123 v Kent (Chelmsford) 2003. Hat-trick v Kent (Canterbury) 2003. LO HS 47 v Worcs (Worcester) 2004 (CGT). LO BB 4-27 v Somerset (Taunton) 2006 (CGT). T20 HS 43. T20 BB 3-13.

NAPIER, Graham Richard (The Gilberd S, Colchester), b Colchester 6 Jan 1980. 5'9½". RHB, RM. Debut (Essex) 1997; cap 2003. MCC 2004. Wellington 2008-09. F-c Tour (Eng A): I 2003-04. HS 125 v Notts (Chelmsford) 2007. BB 6-103 v Glamorgan (Southend) 2008. LO HS 79 Essex CB v Lancs CB (Chelmsford) 2000 (NWT). LO BB 6-29 v Worcs (Chelmsford) 2001 (NL). T20 HS 152* v Sussex (Chelmsford) 2008 – record T20 Cup score (58b, 10 fours, 16 sixes); 2nd highest score in all T20. T20 BB 4-10 v Northants (Chelmsford) 2008 – record Ex analysis.

PALLADINO, Antonio Paul (Cardinal Pole SS; Anglia Polytechnic U), b Tower Hamlets, London 29 Jun 1983. 6'0". RHB, RMF. Cambridge UCCE 2003-05. Essex debut 2003. HS 41 v Notts (Nottingham) 2004. BB 6-41 v Kent (Canterbury) 2003. LO HS 16 Essex CB v Essex (Chelmsford) 2003. LO BB 3-32 v Glamorgan (Chelmsford) 2003 (NL). T20 HS 1*. T20 BB 2-3.

PETTINI, Mark Lewis (Comberton Village C; Hills Road SFC, Cambridge; Cardiff U), b Brighton, Sussex 7 Aug 1983. RHB, RM. 5'10". Debut (Essex) 2001; cap 2006; captain 2007 (*part*) to date. MCC 2005. 1000 runs (1): 1218 (2006). HS 208* v Derbys (Chelmsford) 2006. BB – . LO 144 v Surrey (Oval) 2007 (FPT). T20 HS 66.

PHILLIPS, Timothy James (Felsted S; St Hild & St Bede C, Durham U), b Cambridge 13 Mar 1981. 6'1". LHB, SLA. Essex 1999, 2001-02, 2005 to date; cap 2006. Durham UCCE 2001-02. HS 89 v Worcs (Worcester) 2005. BB 5-41 v Derbys (Chelmsford) 2006. LO HS 24* v Lancs (Manchester) 2005 (CGT). LO BB 5-34 v Lancs (Chelmsford) 2006 (P40). T20 HS 31. T20 BB 2-11.

NQTen DOESCHATE, Ryan Neil (Fairbairn C; Cape Town U), b Port Elizabeth, South Africa 30 Jun 1980. 5'10½". RHB, RMF. Debut (Essex) 2003; cap 2006. EU passport – Dutch ancestry. Netherlands 2005 to date. **LOI** (Ne): 19 (2006 to 2008); HS 109* v Bermuda (Nairobi) 2006-07; BB 4-31 v Canada (Nairobi) 2006-07. F-c Tours (Ne): SA 2006-07, 2007-08; K 2005-06; Ireland 2005. HS 259* and BB 6-20 (9-112 match) Netherlands v Canada (Pretoria) 2006. Ex HS 148 v Glamorgan (Chelmsford) 2007. Ex BB 6-57 v NZ (Chelmsford) 2008. CC BB 5-58 v Leics (Chelmsford) 2008. LO HS 109* (*see LOI*). LO BB 5-50 v Glos (Bristol) 2007 (FPT). IT20 HS 56. IT20 BB 3-23. T20 HS 56. T20 BB 4-24.

‡WALKER, Matthew Jonathan (King's S, Rochester), b Gravesend, Kent 2 Jan 1974. Grandson of Jack Walker (Kent 1949). 5'8". LHB, RM. Kent 1992-93 (Z tour) to 2008; UK debut 1994; cap 2000; benefit 2008. F-c Tour: Z 1992-93 (K). 1000 runs (3); most – 1419 (2006). HS 275* K v Somerset (Canterbury) 1996. BB 2-21 K v Middlesex (Canterbury) 2004. LO HS 117 K v Warwks (Canterbury) 1997 (BHC). LO BB 4-24 K v Yorks (Leeds) 2001 (NL). T20 HS 58*.

WESTFIELD, Mervyn Simon (Barking C), b Romford 5 May 1988. 6'1". RHB, RFM. Debut (Essex) 2005. No 1st XI appearances in 2008. England U19s 2006-07. HS 32 v and BB 4-72 v Somerset (Southend) 2006. LO HS 4* (P40). LO BB – .

WESTLEY, Thomas (Linton Village C; Hills Road SFC), b Cambridge 13 March 1989. 6'2". RHB, OB. Debut (Essex) 2007. MCC 2007. Essex 2nd XI debut 2004 when aged 15 years 88 days. Cambridgeshire 2005. HS 93* v Derbys (Derby) 2008. BB 1-19 v NZ (Chelmsford) 2008. CC BB – . LO HS 36 v Worcs (Chelmsford) 2007 (P40).

WHEATER, Adam (Millfield S), b Whipps Cross 13 Feb 1990. RHB, WK. Debut (Essex) 2008. Essex 2nd XI debut when aged 16 years 190 days. HS 22 v Derbys (Derby) 2008 – on CC debut.

WRIGHT, Christopher Julian Clement (Eggars S, Alton; Anglia Ruskin U), b Chipping Norton, Oxon 14 Jul 1985. 6'3". RHB, RFM. Cambridge UCCE 2004-05. Middlesex 2004-07. Tamil Union 2005-06. Essex debut 2008. HS 76 CU v Essex (Cambridge) 2005. CC HS 71* v Middlesex (Chelmsford) 2008. BB 6-22 v Leics (Leicester) 2008. LO HS 23 v Kent (Chelmsford) 2008 (FPT). LO BB 3-3 v Northants (Southend) 2008. T20 HS 1*. T20 BB 2-24.

RELEASED/RETIRED
(Having made a County First-Class or List A appearance in 2008)

DEXTER, N.J. – *see MIDDLESEX.*

NEL, A. – *see SURREY.*

TUDOR, A.J. – *see SURREY.*

ESSEX 2008
RESULTS SUMMARY

	Place	Won	Lost	Tied	Drew	No Result
County Championship (2nd Division)	5th	5	6		5	
All First-Class Matches		5	7		6	
FP Trophy (South East Division)	**Winners**	7	3			1
Pro40 League (2nd Division)	1st	6	1		1	
Twenty/20 Cup (South Division)	Semi-Finalist	7	4	1		

LV COUNTY CHAMPIONSHIP AVERAGES
BATTING AND FIELDING

Cap		M	I	NO	HS	Runs	Avge	100	50	Ct/St
2005	R.S.Bopara	12	21	3	150	1162	64.55	4	6	11
2001	J.S.Foster	15	22	4	132*	912	50.66	3	4	53/1
	J.K.Maunders	3	5	–	105	217	43.40	1	1	–
	J.C.Mickleburgh	3	4	–	72	150	37.50	–	2	3
2005	A.N.Cook	3	6	–	95	217	36.16	–	1	1
2006	R.N.ten Doeschate	15	21	2	118	675	35.52	1	4	10
2006	M.L.Pettini	16	25	4	92	674	32.09	–	6	9
	V.Chopra	10	16	1	155	434	28.93	1	1	12
2008	J.E.R.Gallian	15	27	–	171	700	25.92	1	4	22
	T.Westley	7	13	2	93*	271	24.63	–	2	4
	A.J.Tudor	4	8	1	68	169	24.14	–	1	–
2003	J.D.Middlebrook	12	16	2	75	335	23.92	–	1	4
	N.J.Dexter	3	5	1	71*	85	21.25	–	1	3
2003	G.R.Napier	7	8	–	76	164	20.50	–	1	–
	C.J.C.Wright	10	12	3	71*	181	20.11	–	1	4
2005	G.W.Flower	5	7	–	39	87	12.42	–	–	3
2004	Danish Kaneria	9	14	3	22	123	11.18	–	–	5
	A.P.Palladino	5	9	3	22*	66	11.00	–	–	5
2008	D.D.Masters	13	17	3	27	147	10.50	–	–	3

Also batted: J.S.Ahmed (1 match) 16*; M.A.Chambers (2) 0*, 0, 0*; A.Nel (3 – cap 2008) 0*, 4; T.J.Phillips (2 – cap 2006) 11, 4, 16 (2 ct); A.J.Wheater (1) 22 (2 ct).

BOWLING

	O	M	R	W	Avge	Best	5wI	10wM
Danish Kaneria	315.2	65	852	40	21.30	7-157	4	–
D.D.Masters	428.3	146	962	40	24.05	6- 24	2	–
R.N.ten Doeschate	250.5	37	893	36	24.80	5- 58	1	–
A.P.Palladino	125.5	41	326	13	25.07	4- 29	–	–
G.R.Napier	172.5	35	567	22	25.77	6-103	1	–
C.J.C.Wright	232.5	55	770	29	26.55	6- 22	1	–
J.D.Middlebrook	310.2	50	972	31	31.35	5- 69	1	–
R.S.Bopara	227.5	39	797	25	31.88	4- 33	–	–
A.Nel	129	28	341	10	34.10	3- 38	–	–

Also bowled:

J.S.Ahmed	34.4	5	127	5	25.40	3- 42	–	–
M.A.Chambers	32.2	4	135	5	27.00	2- 29	–	–
A.J.Tudor	107	17	378	7	54.00	3- 46	–	–

V.Chopra 1.4-0-14-0; G.W.Flower 21-1-69-2; J.S.Foster 12-0-122-1; J.E.R.Gallian 4-0-12-0; J.C.Mickleburgh 4-0-11-0; M.L.Pettini 12-0-129-0; T.J.Phillips 7-1-32-0; T.Westley 11-1-39-0.

The First-Class Averages (pp 136–153) give the records of Essex players in all first-class county matches (Essex's other opponents being the New Zealanders and Cambridge UCCE), with the exception of N.J.Dexter and A.Nel, whose first-class figures for Essex are as above, and:

R.S.Bopara 13-23-3-150-1237-61.85-4-7-11ct. 243.5-44-848-27-31.40-4/33-0-0.
A.N.Cook 4-8-0-95-289-36.12-0-2-1ct. Did not bowl.
J.S.Foster 16-25-5-132*-925-46.25-3-4-55ct-1st. 12-0-122-1-122.00-0-0.
A.J.Tudor 6-10-1-68-228-25.33-0-1-1ct. 149-26-551-9-61.22-3/46-0-0.

30

ESSEX RECORDS

FIRST-CLASS CRICKET

Highest Total	For 761-6d		v	Leics	Chelmsford	1990
	V 803-4d		by	Kent	Brentwood	1934
Lowest Total	For 30		v	Yorkshire	Leyton	1901
	V 14		by	Surrey	Chelmsford	1983
Highest Innings	For 343*	P.A.Perrin	v	Derbyshire	Chesterfield	1904
	V 332	W.H.Ashdown	for	Kent	Brentwood	1934

Highest Partnership for each Wicket

1st	316	G.A.Gooch/P.J.Prichard	v	Kent	Chelmsford	1994
2nd	403	G.A.Gooch/P.J.Prichard	v	Leics	Chelmsford	1990
3rd	347*	M.E.Waugh/N.Hussain	v	Lancashire	Ilford	1992
4th	314	Salim Malik/N.Hussain	v	Surrey	The Oval	1991
5th	316	N.Hussain/M.A.Garnham	v	Leics	Leicester	1991
6th	206	J.W.H.T.Douglas/J.O'Connor	v	Glos	Cheltenham	1923
	206	B.R.Knight/R.A.G.Luckin	v	Middlesex	Brentwood	1962
7th	261	J.W.H.T.Douglas/J.Freeman	v	Lancashire	Leyton	1914
8th	263	D.R.Wilcox/R.M.Taylor	v	Warwicks	Southend	1946
9th	251	J.W.H.T.Douglas/S.N.Hare	v	Derbyshire	Leyton	1921
10th	218	F.H.Vigar/T.P.B.Smith	v	Derbyshire	Chesterfield	1947

Best Bowling	For 10- 32	H.Pickett	v	Leics	Leyton	1895
(Innings)	V 10- 40	E.G.Dennett	for	Glos	Bristol	1906
Best Bowling	For 17-119	W.Mead	v	Hampshire	Southampton	1895
(Match)	V 17- 56	C.W.L.Parker	for	Glos	Gloucester	1925

Most Runs – Season	2559	G.A.Gooch	(av 67.34)	1984
Most Runs – Career	30701	G.A.Gooch	(av 51.77)	1973-97
Most 100s – Season	9	J.O'Connor		1929, 1934
	9	D.J.Insole		1955
Most 100s – Career	94	G.A.Gooch		1973-97
Most Wkts – Season	172	T.P.B.Smith	(av 27.13)	1947
Most Wkts – Career	1610	T.P.B.Smith	(av 26.68)	1929-51
Most Career W-K Dismissals	1231	B.Taylor	(1040 ct; 191 st)	1949-73
Most Career Catches in the Field	519	K.W.R.Fletcher		1962-88

LIMITED-OVERS CRICKET

Highest Total	FPT	391-5		v	Surrey	The Oval	2008
	P40	316-4		v	Glamorgan	Chelmsford	2004
	T20	242-3		v	Sussex	Chelmsford	2008
Lowest Total	FPT	57		v	Lancashire	Lord's	1996
	P40	69		v	Derbyshire	Chesterfield	1974
	T20	99		v	Kent	Chelmsford	2007
Highest Innings	FPT	201*	R.S.Bopara	v	Leics	Leicester	2008
	P40	176	G.A.Gooch	v	Glamorgan	Southend	1983
	T20	152*	G.R.Napier	v	Sussex	Chelmsford	2008
Best Bowling	FPT	5- 8	J.K.Lever	v	Middlesex	Westcliff	1972
		5- 8	G.A.Gooch	v	Cheshire	Chester	1995
	P40	8-26	K.D.Boyce	v	Lancashire	Manchester	1971
	T20	4-10	G.R.Napier	v	Northants	Chelmsford	2008

GLAMORGAN

GlamorganCricket
CricedMorgannwg

Formation of Present Club: 6 July 1888
Inaugural First-Class Match: 1921
Colours: Blue and Gold
Badge: Gold Daffodil
County Champions: (3) 1948, 1969, 1997
Gillette/NatWest/C&G/FP Trophy Winners: (0); best – Finalist 1977
Benson and Hedges Cup Winners: (0); best – Finalist 2000
Pro 40/National League (Div 1) Winners: (2) 2002, 2004
Sunday League Winners: (1) 1993
Twenty20 Cup Winners: (0); best – Semi-Finalist 2004

Executive Chairman: R. Paul Russell, SWALEC Stadium, Cardiff, CF11 9XR • Tel: 0871 282 3401 • Fax: 0871 282 3405 • email: info@glamorgancricket.co.uk • Web: www.glamorgancricket.com

Cricket Director: M.P.Maynard. **Bowling Coach:** S.L.Watkin. **Captain:** J.W.M.Dalrymple. **Vice-Captain:** M.A.Wallace. **Overseas Player:** M.J.Cosgrove/H.H.Gibbs. **2009 Beneficiary:** A.G.Wharf. **Head Groundsman:** Keith Exton. **Scorer:** Andrew K.Hignell. ‡ New registration. NQ Not qualified for England.

ASHLING, Christopher Paul (UWIC), b Manchester 26 Nov 1988. RHB/RFM. Lancashire 2nd XI 2005-07. Cardiff UCCE 2008. Wales MC 2008. Awaiting f-c debut.

BRAGG, William David (Rougemont S, Newport; UWIC), b Newport, Monmouthshire 24 Oct 1986. 5'9". LHB, WK. Debut (Glamorgan) 2007. No f-c appearances in 2008. Wales MC 2004-08. HS 24 v Somerset (Taunton) 2007 – on debut. LO HS 41* Wales MC v Notts (Swansea) 2005.

NQ**COSGROVE, Mark** James, b Elizabeth, Adelaide, S Australia 14 Jun 1984. 5'10". LHB/RM. S Australia 2002-03 to date. Glamorgan 2006 – scoring 114 v Derbys (Cardiff) on debut. **LOI** (A): 3 (2005-06 to 2006-07); HS 74 v B (Fatullah) 2005-06 – on debut; BB 1-1 v WI (Kuala Lumpur) 2006-07. HS 233 v Derbys (Derby) 2006. BB 3-3 S Aus v Tas (Adelaide) 2006-07. Gm BB 1-8 (twice). LO HS 121 S Aus v WA (Perth) 2005-06. LO BB 2-21 S Aus v Q (Brisbane) 2005-06. T20 HS 50*. T20 BB 1-22.

COSKER, Dean Andrew (Millfield S), b Weymouth, Dorset 7 Jan 1978. 5'11". RHB, SLA. Debut (Glamorgan) 1996; cap 2000. F-c Tours (Eng A): SA 1998-99; SL 1997-98; Z 1998-99; K 1997-98. HS 52 v Glos (Bristol) 2005. BB 6-140 v Lancs (Colwyn Bay) 1998. LO HS 39* v Hants (Swansea) 2007 (FPT). LO BB 5-54 v Essex (Chelmsford) 2003 (NL). T20 HS 10*. T20 BB 3-18.

CROFT, Robert Damien Bale (St John Lloyd Catholic CS, Llanelli; Neath Tertiary C; W Glamorgan IHE), b Morriston, Swansea 25 May 1970. 5'10½". RHB, OB. Debut (Glamorgan) 1989; cap 1992; benefit 2000; captain 2003 to 2006 (*part*). MCC 1996. **Tests:** 21 (1996 to 2001); HS 37* v SA (Manchester) 1998; BB 5-95 v NZ (Christchurch) 1996-97. **LOI:** 50 (1996 to 2001); HS 32 v SL (Perth) 1998-99; BB 3-51 v SA (Oval) 1998. F-c Tours: A 1998-99; SA 1993-94 (Eng A), 1995-96 (Gm); WI 1991-92 (Eng A), 1997-98; NZ 1996-97; SL 2000-01, 2003-04; Z 1990-91 (Gm), 1994-95 (Gm), 1996-97. HS 143 v Somerset (Taunton) 1995. 50 wkts (9); most – 76 (1996). Took 1,000th f-c wicket 2007. BB 8-66 (14-169 match) v Warwks (Swansea) 1992. LO HS 143 v Lincs (Lincoln) 2004 (CGT). LO BB 6-20 v Worcs (Cardiff) 1994 (SL). T20 HS 62*. T20 BB 3-12.

DALRYMPLE, James William Murray (Radley C; St Peter's C, Oxford), b Nairobi, Kenya 21 Jan 1981. Brother of S.H.Dalrymple (Oxford U 2002-04). 5'11". RHB, OB. Oxford UCCE/U 2001-03; captain 2002; blue 2001-02-03. British U 2001-02. Middlesex 2001-07; cap 2004. Glamorgan debut 2008; captain 2009. **LOI**: 27 (2006 to 2006-07); HS 67 v SL (Lord's) 2006; BB 2-5 v I (Jaipur) 2006-07. F-c Tour (Eng A): WI 2005-06. HS 244 M v Surrey (Oval) 2004. Gm HS 106 v Middlesex (Colwyn Bay) 2008. BB 5-49 OU v CU (Cambridge) 2003. CC BB 4-53 M v Hants (Southgate) 2005. Gm BB 2-23 v Derbys (Cardiff) 2008. LO HS 107 M v Glamorgan (Lord's) 2004 (CGT). LO BB 4-14 M v Essex (Southgate) 2001 (NL). IT20 HS 32. IT20 BB 1-10. T20 HS 61. T20 BB 2-8.

^{NQ}**GIBBS, Herschelle** Herman, b Green Point, Cape Town, South Africa 23 Feb 1974. RHB/RM. Western Province 1990-91 to 2004-05. Cape Cobras 2005-06 to date. Glamorgan 2008 T20 only. **Tests** (SA): 90 (1996-97 to 2007-08); HS 228 v P (Cape Town) 2002-03. BB – . **LOI** (SA): 239 (1996-97 to 2008-09); HS 175 v A (Johannesburg) 2005-06 in total of 438-9 – highest ever LO run chase. F-c Tours (SA): E 1995 (SA A), 2003; A 1997-98, 2001-02, 2005-06; WI 2000-01, 2004-05; NZ 1998-99, 2003-04; I 1996-97, 1999-00; P 2003-04, 2007-08; SL 2004, 2006; Z 2001-02; B 2003. HS (*see Tests*). BB 2-14 SA A v Somerset (Taunton) 1996. LO HS 175 (*see LOI*). LO BB 1-16 SA A v Essex (Chelmsford) 1996. IT20 HS 90*. T20 HS 98.

HARRIS, James Alexander Russell (Pontardulais CS; Gorseinon C), b Morriston 16 May 1990. 6'0". RHB, RFM. Debut (Glamorgan) 2007 – aged 16 years 351 days – youngest Glamorgan player to take a first-class wicket. Glamorgan 2nd XI debut 2005 when aged 14 years 353 days. Wales MC 2005-08. England U19s 2007 to 2008. HS 87* v Notts (Swansea) 2007. BB 7-66 (12-118) v Glos (Bristol) 2007 – youngest (17 years 3 days) to take 10 wickets in any CC match. LO HS 15 v Northants (Northampton) 2008 (P40). LO BB 4-48 v Kent (Canterbury) 2008 (P40). T20 HS 8. T20 BB 3-41.

HARRISON, David Stuart (W Monmouth CS; Usk C, Pontypool), b Newport, Monmouthshire 30 Jul 1981. Elder brother of A.J.Harrison (Glamorgan 2005-06); son of S.C.Harrison (Glamorgan 1971-77). 6'4". RHB, RMF. Debut (Glamorgan) 1999; cap 2006. No appearances 2007. MCC 2005. HS 88 v Essex (Chelmsford) 2004. 50 wkts (1): 57 (2004). BB 5-48 v Somerset (Swansea) 2004. LO HS 37* and LO BB 5-26 v Yorks (Leeds) 2002 (NL). T20 HS 4. T20 BB 2-17.

JONES, Alexander John (Cowbridge CS), b Bridgend 10 Nov 1988. RHB, LM. Glamorgan 2nd XI 2008. Wales MC 2008. Awaiting f-c debut.

‡^{NQ}**KRUGER, Garnett** John-Peter (Gelvandale HS; Russel Road C), b Port Elizabeth, South Africa 5 Jan 1977. RHB, RMF. E Province 1997-98 to 2002-03. Gauteng 2003-04. Lions 2004-05 to date. Leicestershire 2007-08 (Kolpak registration). **LOI** (SA): 3 (2005-06); HS 0*; BB 1-43 v A (Brisbane) 2005-06 – on debut. F-c Tours (SA A): WI 2000-01; SL 2005-06; Z 2004. HS 58 South Africa A v Windward Is (Kingstown) 2000-01. UK HS Le 15 v Derbys (Leicester) 2007. BB 8-112 Lions v Dolphins (Durban) 2005-06. UK BB 5-62 Le v Glos (Leicester) 2008. LO HS 20* EP v WP (Cape Town) 2002-03. LO BB 6-23 EP v NW (Port Elizabeth) 1999-00. IT20 HS 3. IT20 BB – . T20 HS 12*. T20 BB 3-32.

MAYNARD, Thomas Lloyd (Millfield S; Whitchurch HS, Cardiff), b Cardiff 25 Mar 1989. Son of M.P.Maynard (Glamorgan and England 1985-2005). 6'3". RHB, OB. Wales MC 2006-08. HS 26 v Leics (Cardiff) 2008. BB – . LO HS 71 v Glos (Colwyn Bay) 2007 (FPT). T20 HS 11.

O'SHEA, Michael Peter (Barry CS; Millfield S), b Cardiff 4 Sep 1987. 5'11". RHB, OB. Debut (Glamorgan) 2005; no f-c appearances 2006, 2008. Wales MC 2005-08. England U19s 2004-05 to 2006. HS 24 v Kent (Canterbury) 2005. LO HS 49 v Durham (Chester-le-St) 2007 (P40). LO BB 2-37 v Hants (Swansea) 2007 (FPT).

OWEN, William Thomas (Prestatyn HS; UWIC), b St Asaph, Flintshire 2 Sep 1988. 6'0". RHB, RMF. Debut (Glamorgan) 2007. Wales MC 2007-08. HS – v Glos (Cardiff) 2007 – only 1st XI appearance.

POWELL, Michael John (Crickhowell SS; Pontypool CFE), b Abergavenny, Monmouthshire 3 Feb 1977. 6'1". RHB, OB, occ WK. Debut (Glamorgan) 1997 scoring 200* v OU (Oxford); cap 2000. 1000 runs (5); most – 1327 (2006). HS 299 v Glos (Cheltenham) 2006 – record score for Glamorgan in England. BB 2-39 v OU (Oxford) 1999. CC BB – . LO HS 114* v Hants (Cardiff) 2008 (FPT). LO BB 1-26 (CGT). T20 HS 68*.

REES, Gareth Peter (Coedcae CS; Bath U), b Swansea 8 Apr 1985. 6'1". LHB, LM. Wales MC 2003-05. Debut (Glamorgan) 2006. 1000 runs (1): 1088 (2008). HS 140 v Leics (Cardiff) 2008. LO HS 63 v Durham (Chester-le-St) 2007 (P40).

SHANTRY, Adam John (Priory S; Shrewsbury SFC), b Bristol 13 Nov 1982. 6'2½". Son of B.K.Shantry (Gloucestershire 1978 79). LHB, LFM. Northamptonshire 2003-04. Warwickshire 2006-07. Glamorgan debut 2008. Shropshire 2001. HS 38* Nh v Somerset (Northampton) 2003 – on CC debut (also took 3-8 including 3 wkts in 5 balls). Gm HS 16 and CC/Gm BB 5-52 (10-129 match) v Warwks (Birmingham) 2008. BB 5-49 Wa v West Indies A (Birmingham) 2006. LO HS 15 Nh CB v Yorks CB (Northampton) 2002 (CGT). LO BB 5-37 Nh v NZ (Northampton) 2004. T20 HS – . T20 BB – .

WALLACE, Mark Alexander (Crickhowell HS), b Abergavenny, Monmouthshire 19 Nov 1981. 5'9". LHB, WK. Debut (Glamorgan) 1999; cap 2003. F-c Tour (ECB Acad): SL 2002-03. HS 128 v Glos (Bristol) 2007. LO HS 85 v Surrey (Cardiff) 2008 (P40). T20 HS 35*.

WATERS, Huw Thomas (Llantaram CS; Monmouth S), b Cardiff 26 Sep 1986. 6'2". RHB, RMF. Debut (Glamorgan) 2005. Wales MC 2004-07. HS 34 v Kent (Canterbury) 2005. BB 5-86 v Somerset (Taunton) 2006. LO HS 8 v Hants (Swansea) 2007 (FPT). LO BB 3-47 v Durham (Chester-le-St) 2007 (P40).

WATKINS, Ryan Edward (Pontllanfraith CS; Cross Keys TC), b Abergavenny, Monmouthshire 9 Jun 1983. 6'0". LHB, RM. Debut (Glamorgan) 2005. Wales MC 2004-06. HS 87 v Essex (Cardiff) 2006. BB 4-40 v Worcs (Worcester) 2006. LO HS 39 v Derbys (Derby) 2007 (P40). LO BB 2-25 v Warwks (Colwyn Bay) 2006 (P40). T20 HS 6*. T20 BB 3-33.

WHARF, Alexander George (Buttershaw Upper S; Thomas Danby C), b Bradford, Yorks 4 Jun 1975. 6'5". RHB, RMF. Yorkshire 1994-97. Nottinghamshire 1998-99. Glamorgan debut 2000, scoring 100* v OU (Oxford); cap 2000; benefit 2009. **LOI**: 13 (2004 to 2004-05); HS 9; BB 4-24 v Z (Harare) 2004-05. F-c Tour (Eng A): WI 2005-06. HS 128* v Glos (Bristol) 2007. 50 wkts (1): 52 (2003). BB 6-59 v Glos (Bristol) 2005. LO HS 72 v Lancs (Manchester) 2004 (NL). LO BB 6-5 v Kent (Cardiff) 2004 (NL). T20 HS 19. T20 BB 4-39.

WRIGHT, Ben James (Cowbridge CS), b Preston, Lancs 5 Dec 1987. 5'9". RHB, RM. Debut (Glamorgan) 2006. No f-c appearances in 2008. HS 108 v Leics (Leicester) 2007. BB 1-14 v Essex (Chelmsford) 2007. LO HS 61 v Middlesex (Lord's) 2007 (FPT). LO BB – . T20 HS 35*.

[NQ]**GILLESPIE, Jason** Neil (Cabra C, Adelaide), b Darlinghurst, Sydney, Australia 19 April 1975. 6'5". RHB, RFM. S Australia 1994-95 to 2007-08. Yorkshire 2006-07; cap 2007. Glamorgan 2008. *Wisden* 2001. **Tests** (A): 71 (1996-97 to 2005-06); HS 201* v B (Chittagong) 2005-06 (as a night-watchman in probably his final Test innings); BB 7-37 v E (Leeds) 1997. **LOI** (A): 97 (1996 to 2005); HS 44* v WI (Adelaide) 2004-05; BB 5-22 v P (Nairobi) 2002. F-c Tours (A): E 1997, 2001, 2005; SA 1996-97, 2001-02; WI 1998-99, 2002-03; NZ 2004-05; I 2000-01, 2004-05; P 2007-08 (Aus A); SL 1999, 2002-03 (v P), 2003-04; B 2005-06; Scotland/Ireland 1998 (Aus A). HS 201* (*see Tests*). UK HS 123* Y v Surrey (Oval) 2007, sharing in Yorkshire record 9th wicket partnership of 246 with T.T.Bresnan. Gm HS 52 v Warwks (Cardiff) 2008. 50 wkts (0+1): 51 (1995-96). BB 8-50 S Aus v NSW (Sydney) 2001-02. UK BB 7-37 A v E (Leeds) 1997. CC BB 6-37 v Durham (Chester-le-St) 2006. Gm BB 4-32 v Essex (Southend) 2008. LO HS 44* (*see LOI*). LO BB 5-13 Gm v Warwks (Cardiff) 2008. IT20 HS 24. IT20 BB 1-49. T20 HS 24. T20 BB 2-19.

GRANT, Richard Neil (Cefn Saeson CS; Neath Port Talbot C), b Neath 5 Jun 1984. 5'10". RHB, RM. Glamorgan 2005-08. HS 79 v Northants (Colwyn Bay) 2007. BB 1-7 v Somerset (Taunton) 2007. LO HS 45 v Kent (Cardiff) 2006 (CGT). LO BB 2-21 v West Indies A (Ebbw Vale) 2006. T20 HS 77. T20 BB 4-38.

HEMP, David Lloyd (Olchfa CS; Millfield S; W Glamorgan C; Birmingham U), b Hamilton, Bermuda 8 Nov 1970. UK resident since 1976. 6'0". LHB, RM. Glamorgan 1991-96, 2002-08; cap 1994; captain 2006 (*part*) to date; benefit 2007. Warwickshire 1997-2001; cap 1997. Bermuda 2006-07. Free State (List A only) 1997-98. Wales MC 1992-93. **LOI** (Bermuda): 20 (2006-07 to 2007-08); HS 76* v I (Port-of-Spain) 2006-07; BB 1-25 v K (Mombasa) 2006-07 – on debut. F-c Tours (Bermuda): SA 1995-96 (Gm), 2006-07; I 1994-95 (Eng A); Z 1994-95 (Gm); K 2006-07, 2007-08; UAE 2007-08. 1000 runs (6); most – 1452 (1994). HS 247* Bermuda v Holland (Pretoria) 2006-07. CC HS 186* Wa v Worcs (Birmingham) 2001. Gm HS 171* v Kent (Canterbury) 2005. BB 3-23 v South Africa A (Cardiff) 1996. CC BB 2-29 Wa v Glos (Birmingham) 2000. LO HS 121 v Comb U (Cardiff) 1995 (BHC). LO BB 4-32 Wa v Minor C (Lakenham) 1998 (BHC). IT20 HS 20. T20 HS 74.

WOOD, Matthew James (Shelley HS & SFC), b Huddersfield, Yorks 6 Apr 1977. 5'9". RHB, OB. Yorkshire 1997-2007; cap 2001. Glamorgan 2008. MCC 1999-00. F-c Tour (MCC): B 1999-00. 1000 runs (4); most – 1432 (2003). HS 207 Y v Somerset (Taunton) 2003. Gm HS 83* v Glos (Bristol) 2008. BB 1-4 Y v Somerset (Leeds) 2003. LO HS 160 Y v Devon (Exmouth) 2004 (CGT). LO BB 3-45 Y v Cambs (March) 2003 (CGT). T20 HS 96*. T20 BB 1-11.

K.D.Tudge left the staff, without making a County First-Class or List A appearance in 2008.

GLAMORGAN 2008

RESULTS SUMMARY

	Place	Won	Lost	Tied	Drew	No Result
County Championship (2nd Division)	8th	3	5		7	1
All First-Class Matches		3	5		8	1
FP Trophy (South West Division)	5th	1	4			3
Pro40 League (2nd Division)	3rd	5	3			
Twenty/20 Cup (Midlands/West/Wales Division)	Quarter-Finalist	3	4			4

LV COUNTY CHAMPIONSHIP AVERAGES

BATTING AND FIELDING

Cap		M	I	NO	HS	Runs	Avge	100	50	Ct/St
	G.P.Rees	15	26	1	140	989	39.56	3	5	17
2000	M.J.Powell	15	24	3	120	672	32.00	1	3	15
1994	D.L.Hemp	14	24	3	104	659	31.38	1	5	10
	J.W.M.Dalrymple	15	23	–	106	671	29.17	1	5	8
2003	M.A.Wallace	15	22	–	72	630	28.63	–	4	31/5
1992	R.D.B.Croft	14	19	3	89*	393	24.56	–	1	2
	J.A.R.Harris	5	9	2	46	167	23.85	–	–	–
	J.N.Gillespie	13	20	5	52	332	22.13	–	1	4
	R.N.Grant	6	11	–	75	239	21.72	–	2	5
2000	A.G.Wharf	9	12	2	51*	206	20.60	–	1	3
2006	D.S.Harrison	13	17	2	64*	299	19.93	–	2	2
	M.J.Wood	6	10	1	83*	179	19.88	–	1	4
	R.E.Watkins	5	8	2	33	90	15.00	–	–	2
2000	D.A.Cosker	8	13	2	42	160	14.54	–	–	4
	T.L.Maynard	5	7	–	26	82	11.71	–	–	5
	A.J.Shantry	7	9	4	16	32	6.40	–	–	3

BOWLING

	O	M	R	W	Avge	Best	5wI	10wM
A.J.Shantry	183.2	50	545	30	18.16	5-52	2	1
R.D.B.Croft	486.4	119	1217	39	31.20	5- 6	1	–
J.A.R.Harris	109.2	25	362	11	32.90	3-40	–	–
D.A.Cosker	186.2	25	656	19	34.52	5-81	1	–
J.N.Gillespie	348.5	107	902	24	37.58	4-32	–	–
D.S.Harrison	349.4	65	1132	29	39.03	4-49	–	–
A.G.Wharf	177.2	14	855	20	42.75	3-10	–	–
Also bowled:								
R.E.Watkins	101.2	16	396	7	56.57	3-76	–	–
J.W.M.Dalrymple	96	9	369	6	61.50	2-23	–	–
R.N.Grant 17-4-44-1.								

The First-Class Averages (pp 136–153) give the records of Glamorgan players in all first-class county matches (Glamorgan's other opponents being Oxford UCCE).

GLAMORGAN RECORDS

FIRST-CLASS CRICKET

Highest Total	For 718-3d			v	Sussex	Colwyn Bay	2000
	V 712			by	Northants	Northampton	1998
Lowest Total	For 22			v	Lancashire	Liverpool	1924
	V 33			by	Leics	Ebbw Vale	1965
Highest Innings	For 309*	S.P.James		v	Sussex	Colwyn Bay	2000
	V 322*	M.B.Loye		for	Northants	Northampton	1998

Highest Partnership for each Wicket

1st	374	M.T.G.Elliott/S.P.James	v	Sussex	Colwyn Bay	2000
2nd	252	M.P.Maynard/D.L.Hemp	v	Northants	Cardiff	2002
3rd	313	D.E.Davies/W.E.Jones	v	Essex	Brentwood	1948
4th	425*	A.Dale/I.V.A.Richards	v	Middlesex	Cardiff	1993
5th	264	M Robinson/S.W.Montgomery	v	Hampshire	Bournemouth	1949
6th	230	W.E.Jones/B.L.Muncer	v	Worcs	Worcester	1953
7th	211	P.A.Cottey/O.D.Gibson	v	Leics	Swansea	1996
8th	202	D.Davies/J.J.Hills	v	Sussex	Eastbourne	1928
9th	203*	J.J.Hills/J.C.Clay	v	Worcs	Swansea	1929
10th	143	T.Davies/S.A.B.Daniels	v	Glos	Swansea	1982

Best Bowling	For	10- 51	J.Mercer	v	Worcs	Worcester	1936
(Innings)	V	10- 18	G.Geary	for	Leics	Pontypridd	1929
Best Bowling	For	17-212	J.C.Clay	v	Worcs	Swansea	1937
(Match)	V	16- 96	G.Geary	for	Leics	Pontypridd	1929

Most Runs – Season	2276	H.Morris	(av 55.51)	1990
Most Runs – Career	34056	A.Jones	(av 33.03)	1957-83
Most 100s – Season	10	H.Morris		1990
Most 100s – Career	54	M.P.Maynard		1985-2005
Most Wkts – Season	176	J.C.Clay	(av 17.34)	1937
Most Wkts – Career	2174	D.J.Shepherd	(av 20.95)	1950-72
Most Career W-K Dismissals	933	E.W.Jones	(840 ct; 93 st)	1961-83
Most Career Catches in the Field	656	P.M.Walker		1956-72

LIMITED-OVERS CRICKET

Highest Total	FPT	429		v	Surrey	The Oval	2002
	P40	305-6		v	Worcs	Cardiff	2001
	T20	206-6		v	Somerset	Taunton	2006
Lowest Total	FPT	76		v	Northants	Northampton	1968
	P40	42		v	Derbyshire	Swansea	1979
	T20	113		v	Warwicks	Birmingham	2003
Highest Innings	FPT	162*	I.V.A.Richards	v	Oxfordshire	Swansea	1993
	P40	155*	J.H.Kallis	v	Surrey	Pontypridd	1999
	T20	116*	I.J.Thomas	v	Somerset	Taunton	2004
Best Bowling	FPT	5-13	R.J.Shastri	v	Scotland	Edinburgh	1988
	P40	7-16	S.D.Thomas	v	Surrey	Swansea	1998
	T20	4-38	R.N.Grant	v	Worcs	Worcester	2005

GLOUCESTERSHIRE

Formation of Present Club: 1871
Inaugural First-Class Match: 1870
Colours: Blue, Gold, Brown, Silver, Green and Red
Badge: Coat of Arms of the City and County of Bristol
County Champions (since 1890): (0); best – 2nd 1930, 1931, 1947, 1959, 1969, 1986
Gillette/NatWest/C&G/FP Trophy Winners: (5) 1973, 1999, 2000, 2003, 2004
Benson and Hedges Cup Winners: (3) 1977, 1999, 2000
Pro 40/National League (Div 1) Winners: (1) 2000
Sunday League Winners: (0); best – 2nd 1988
Twenty20 Cup Winners: (0); best – Finalist 2007

Chief Executive: Tom E.M.Richardson, County Ground, Nevil Road, Bristol BS7 9EJ • Tel: 0117 910 8000 • Fax: 0117 924 1193 • Email: info@gloscc.co.uk • Web: www.gloscc.co.uk

Director of Cricket: J.G.Bracewell. **Captain:** A.P.R.Gidman. **Vice-Captain:** tbc. **Overseas Player:** J.E.C.Franklin. **2009 Beneficiary:** C.G.Taylor. **Head Groundsman:** Sean Williams. **Scorer:** Keith T.Gerrish. ‡ New registration. ^{NQ} Not qualified for England.

Gloucestershire revised their capping policy in 2004 and now award players with their County Caps when they make their first-class debut.

ADSHEAD, Stephen John (Bridley Moor HS, Redditch), b Redditch 29 Jan 1980. 5'9". RHB, WK. Herefordshire 1999. Leicestershire 2000 (one non-CC match). Worcestershire 2003 (2 matches). Gloucestershire debut/cap 2004. HS 148* v Surrey (Oval) 2005. LO HS 77* Shropshire v Northumb (Oswestry) 2003 (CGT). T20 HS 81.

ALI, Kadeer (Handsworth GS), b Moseley, Birmingham 7 Mar 1983. 6'1". Brother of M.M.Ali (*see WORCESTERSHIRE*), cousin of Kabir Ali (*see WORCESTERSHIRE*). RHB, RM/LB. Worcestershire 2000-04. Gloucestershire debut/cap 2005. F-c Tour (Eng A): I 2003-04. HS 161 v Northants (Bristol) 2008. BB 1-4 v Glamorgan (Bristol) 2005. LO HS 114 v Hants (Southampton) 2007 (P40). LO BB 1-4 Wo v Worcs CB (Worcester) 2003 (CGT). T20 HS 53.

BANERJEE, Vikram (King Edward's S, Birmingham; Downing C, Cambridge), b Bradford, Yorks 20 Mar 1984. 6'0". LHB, SLA. Cambridge UCCE/U 2004-06; blue 2004-05-06. Gloucestershire debut/cap 2006. HS 29 CU v OU (Cambridge) 2005. Gs HS 15 v Worcs (Cheltenham) 2008. BB 4-38 v Northants (Gloucester) 2007.

BROWN, David Owen (Queen Elizabeth GS, Blackburn; Collingwood C, Durham U), b Burnley, Lancs 8 Dec 1982. Younger brother of M.J.Brown (*see SURREY*). RHB, RM. 6'0". Durham UCCE 2003-05. British U 2005. Gloucestershire debut/cap 2006. HS 83 v Worcs (Cheltenham) 2008. BB 5-38 v Derbys (Derby) 2008. LO HS 63* v Surrey (Bristol) 2006 (CGT) – on debut. LO BB 3-29 v Glamorgan (Colwyn Bay) 2007 (FPT). T20 HS 36. T20 BB 1-11.

DAWSON, Richard Kevin James (Batley GS; Exeter U), b Doncaster, Yorks 4 Aug 1980. 6'3". RHB, OB. British U 2000. Yorkshire 2001-06; cap 2004. MCC 2002. Northamptonshire 2007. Gloucestershire debut/cap 2008. Devon 1999-2000. **Tests:** 7 (2001-02 to 2002-03); HS 19* v A (Perth) 2002-03; BB 4-134 v I (Chandigarh) 2001-02 – on debut. F-c Tours: A 2002-03; NZ 2001-02; I 2001-02; SL 2002-03 (ECB Acad), 2004-05 (Eng A). HS Y v Kent (Canterbury) 2002. Gs HS 40 v Essex (Bristol) 2008. BB 6-82 Y v Glamorgan (Scarborough) 2001. Gs BB 1-113 v Derbys (Derby) 2008. LO HS 41 Y v Leics (Scarborough) 2002 (NL). LO BB 4-13 Y v Derbys (Derby) 2002 (BHC). T20 HS 22. T20 BB 3-24.

‡**NQFRANKLIN, James** Edward Charles (Wellington C; Victoria U), Wellington, New Zealand 7 Nov 1960. 6'4½". LHB, LFM. Wellington 1999-99 to date. Gloucestershire debut/cap 2004. Glamorgan 2006. **Tests** (NZ): 23 (2000-01 to 2008-09); HS 122* v SA (Cape Town) 2006-07; BB 6-119 v A (Auckland) 2004-05. Hat-trick v B (Dhaka) 2004-05. **LOI** (NZ): 65 (2000-01 to 2006-07); HS 45* v SL (Queenstown) 2006-07; BB 5-42 v E (Chester-le-St) 2004. F-c Tours (NZ): E 2004; A 2004-05; SA 2004-05 (NZ A), 2005-06; Z 2005; B 2004-05. HS 219 Wellington v Auckland (Auckland) 2008-09. UK/CC HS 94 Gm v Glos (Cheltenham) 2006. Gs HS 44 v Middlesex (Lord's) 2004. BB 7-30 Wellington v CD (Wellington) 2005-06. UK/Gs BB 7-60 v Lancs (Cheltenham) 2004. LO HS 87* Wellington v Otago (Invercargill) 2008-09. LO BB 5-42 (see LOI). IT20 HS 20. IT20 BB 3-23. T20 HS 69*. T20 BB 3-23.

GIDMAN, Alex Peter Richard (Wycliffe C), b High Wycombe, Bucks 22 Jun 1981. Elder brother of W.R.S.Gidman (see DURHAM). 6'3". RHB, RM. Debut (Gloucestershire) 2002; cap 2004. MCC YC 2001. MCC 2004, 2007. Otago 2007-08. F-c Tours (Eng A): SL 2004-05. Appointed captain of Eng A tour to India 2003-04 but withdrew because of hand injury. 1000 runs (3); most – 1244 (2006). HS 142 v Surrey (Bristol) 2005. BB 4-47 v Glamorgan (Cardiff) 2005. LO HS 105 v Hampshire (Southampton) 2008 (FPT). LO BB 5-42 Eng A v Bangladesh A (Mirpur) 2006-07. T20 HS 61. T20 BB 2-24.

GITSHAM, Matthew Thomas (Queen's C, Taunton; C of St Mark and St John, Plymouth), b Truro, Cornwall 1 Feb 1982. 5'10". RHB, LB. Debut (Gloucestershire) 2008; cap 2008. Somerset Cricket Board 1999-2001. Buckinghamshire 2006. Gloucestershire 2nd XI 2007-08. HS 35* v LU (Bristol) 2008 – on debut. CC HS 11 v Warwks (Gloucester) 2008. BB 1-12 v Worcs (Worcester) 2008. LO HS 15 v Somerset CB v Wales MC (North Perrott) 2001 (CGT).

HODNETT, Grant Phillip (Durban Preparatory HS; Northwood HS), b Johannesburg, South Africa 17 Aug 1982. 6'4". RHB, LB. Debut (Gloucestershire) 2005; cap 2005 (Kolpak registration). HS 168 v Derbys (Bristol) 2007. BB 2-91 v LU (Bristol) 2008. CC BB – . LO HS 50 v Somerset (Bristol) 2007 (FPT).

NQIRELAND, Anthony John (Plumtree HS), b Masvingo, Zimbabwe 30 Aug 1984. RHB, RM. Midlands 2002-03 to 2004-05. Gloucestershire debut/cap 2007 (Kolpak registration). **LOI** (Z): 26 (2005-06 to 2006-07); HS 8* v K (Bulawayo) 2005-06; BB 3-41 v B (Harare) (twice) – 2006 and 2006-07. HS 16* v Middlesex (Bristol) 2008. BB 7-36 Zimbabwe A v Bangladesh A (Mirpur) 2006-07. Gs BB 3-33 v Derbys (Bristol) 2008. LO HS 17 Midlands v Matabeleland (Harare) 2005-06. LO BB 4-16 Zimbabwe A v Kenya (Harare) 2005-06. T20 HS 2*. IT20 BB 1-33. T20 HS 8*. T20 BB 3-10.

KIRBY, Steven Paul (Elton HS; Bury C), b Ainsworth, nr Bolton, Lancs 4 Oct 1977. 6'3½". RHB, RFM. Leicestershire staff 1998 – no f-c appearances. Yorkshire 2001-04, debut as sub for M.J.Hoggard (England duty) taking 7-50; cap 2003. Gloucestershire debut/cap 2005. MCC 2008. F-c Tour (Eng A): I 2003-04 (*part*). HS 57 Y v Hants (Leeds) 2002. Gs HS 37 v Northants (Northampton) 2007. 50 wkts (1): 67 (2003). BB 8-80 (13-154 match) Y v Somerset (Taunton) 2003. Gs BB 5-41 v Essex (Southend) 2007. LO HS 15 Y v Leics (Leicester) 2003 (NL). LO BB 5-36 v Middlesex (Lord's) 2007 (FPT). T20 HS 3*. T20 BB 2-15.

LEWIS, Jonathan (Churchfields S, Swindon; Swindon C), b Aylesbury, Bucks 26 Aug 1975. 6'2". RHB, RMF. Debut (Gloucestershire) 1995; cap 1998; captain 2006-08; benefit 2007. MCC 2005. Wiltshire 1993, 1995. Northamptonshire staff 1994. **Tests**: 1 (2006); HS 20 and BB 3-68 v SL (Nottingham) 2006. **LOI**: 13 (2005 to 2007); HS 17 v I (Leeds) 2007; BB 4-36 v A (Brisbane) 2006-07. F-c Tours (Eng A): WI 2000-01; SL 2004-05. HS 62 v Worcs (Cheltenham) 1999. 50 wkts (6); most – 74 (2003). BB 8-95 v Z (Gloucester) 2000. CC BB 7-38 (10-75 match) v Somerset (Bristol) 2006. Hat-trick v Notts (Nottingham) 2000. LO HS 40 and LO BB 5-19 v Hants (Southampton) 2005 (NL). IT20 HS 1. IT20 BB 4-24. T20 HS 43. T20 BB 4-24.

^{NQ}**MARSHALL, Hamish** John Hamilton (Mahurangi C, Warkworth; King C, Auckland), b Warkworth, New Zealand 15 Feb 1979. Twin brother of J.A.H.Marshall (ND and NZ 1997-98 to date). Irish passport. 5'9". RHB, RM. N Districts 1998-99 to date. Gloucestershire debut 2006 (scoring 102 v Worcs on UK debut); cap 2006; Kolpak registration 2008. Buckinghamshire 2003. **Tests** (NZ): 13 (2000-01 to 2005-06); HS 160 v SL (Napier) 2004-05. **LOI** (NZ): 65 (2003-04 to 2006-07); HS 101* v P (Faisalabad) 2003-04. F-c Tours (NZ): A 2004-05; SA 2000-01, 2005-06; Z 2005; B 2004-05. 1000 runs (1): 1218 (2006). HS 168 v Leics (Cheltenham) 2006. BB 1-6 ND v CD (Gisborne) 2006-07. Gs BB 1-9 v Leics (Leicester) 2007. LO HS 122 v Sussex (Hove) 2007 (P40). LO BB 1-14 ND v Otago (Dunedin) 2004-05. T20 HS 100.

^{NQ}**PORTERFIELD, William** Thomas Stuart, b Londonderry, Ireland 6 Sep 1984. LHB, OB. Debut (Ireland) 2006. MCC 2007. Gloucestershire debut/cap 2008. Captained Ireland in ICC Intercontinental Cup in Africa in 2008-09. F-c Tours (Ire): E 2007; Scot 2006; UAE 2006-07. **LOI** (Ire): 29 (2006 to 2008-09); HS 112* v Bermuda (Nairobi) 2006-07. HS 166 Ireland v Bermuda (Dublin) 2007. Gs HS 93 v Glamorgan (Cardiff) 2008. BB 1-57 v LU (Bristol) 2008. LO HS 112* (*see LOI*). IT20 HS 7. T20 HS 62.

SAXELBY, Ian David (Oakham S), b Nottingham 22 May 1989. 6'2". RHB, RMF. Nephew of K.Saxelby (Nottinghamshire 1978-90) and M.Saxelby (Notts, Durham and Derbys 1989-2000). Debut (Gloucestershire) 2008; cap 2008. Nottinghamshire 2nd XI 2006-08. England U19s 2008. HS 11* and BB 1-64 v Middlesex (Bristol) 2008 – on debut.

SNELL, Stephen David (Sandown HS), b Winchester, Hampshire 27 Feb 1983. 6'0". RHB, WK. Debut (Gloucestershire)/cap 2005. MCC YC 2002-04. HS 127 v Worcs (Worcester) 2008. LO HS 17 v Glamorgan (Cardiff) 2005 (NL).

SPEARMAN, Craig Murray (Kelston HS, Auckland; Massey U, Palmerston North), b Auckland, New Zealand 4 Jul 1972. RHB. Auckland 1993-94 to 1994-95. Central Districts 1996-97 to 2003-04. Gloucestershire debut/cap 2002; benefit 2008. Qualified for England 2005. **Tests** (NZ): 19 (1995-96 to 2000-01); HS 112 v Z (Auckland) 1995-96. **LOI** (NZ): 51 (1995-96 to 2000-01); HS 86 v Z (Harare) 2000-01. F-c Tours (NZ): SA 2000-01; WI 1995-96; I 1999-00; P 1996-97; SL 1998; Z 1997-98, 2000-01. 1000 runs (3); most – 1462 (2004). HS 341 v Middlesex (Gloucester) 2004 – record Gloucestershire score. BB 1-37 CD v Wellington (New Plymouth) 1999-00. LO HS 153 v Warwks (Gloucester) 2003 (NL). LO BB – . T20 HS 88.

STAYT, Thomas Patrick (Lavington S, Market Lavington; St Augustine's C, Trowbridge; Exeter U), b Salisbury, Wilts 20 Jan 1986. 6'2". RHB, RMF. Debut (Gloucestershire) 2007; cap 2007. No f-c appearances in 2008. HS 6 v Middlesex (Bristol) 2007. BB 3-51 v Middlesex (Lord's) 2007 – on debut. LO HS – . LO BB – .

TAYLOR, Christopher Glyn (Colston's Collegiate S), b Southmead, Bristol 27 Sep 1976. 5'7". RHB, OB. Debut (Gloucestershire) 2000, scoring 104 v Middlesex – first to score a hundred at Lord's in a Championship match on his first-class debut; cap 2001; captain 2004-05. 1000 runs (2); most – 1101 (2008). HS 196 v Notts (Nottingham) 2001. BB 4-52 v Northants (Northampton) 2007. LO HS 93 v Warwks (Bristol) 2002 (BHC). LO BB 2-5 v Northants (Northampton) 2004 (NL). T20 HS 83.

THOMPSON, Jackson Gladwin (St Benedict's C; Gloucestershire U), b Nasik, Maharashtra, India 7 Feb 1986. 6'3". LHB, OB. Debut (Gloucestershire) 2007; cap 2007. Oxfordshire 2007. No f-c or List A appearances in 2008. HS 21 v Middlesex (Bristol) 2007 – on debut. LO HS 7 v Glamorgan (Colwyn Bay) 2007 (FPT). T20 HS 22.

WOODMAN, Robert James (Castle S, Taunton; Richard Huish C), b Taunton, Somerset 12 Oct 1986. 5'11". LHB, LMF. Somerset 2005. Gloucestershire debut/cap 2008. Devon 2006-07. HS 46* Sm v Worcs (Worcester) 2005 – on debut. Gs HS 13 and BB 4-65 v Essex (Bristol) 2008. LO HS 14 MCC v Bangladesh A (Durham) 2008. LO BB 1-38 Sm v Durham (Taunton) 2005. T20 HS 1*. T20 BB 2-37.

RELEASED/RETIRED
(Having made a County First-Class or List A appearance in 2008)

FISHER, I.D. – see WORCESTERSHIRE.

GREENIDGE, Carl Gary (Lodge S and St Michael S, Barbados; Heathcote S, Chingford; W Hatch HS; City of Westminster C), b Basingstoke, Hants 20 Apr 1978. Son of C.Gordon Greenidge (Hampshire, Barbados and West Indies 1970-92). 5'10". RHB, RMF. MCC YC 1998. Surrey 1999-2000. Northamptonshire 2002-04. Gloucestershire 2005-08; cap 2005. HS 46 Nh v Derbys (Derby) 2002. Gs HS 27 v Derbys (Derby) 2007. 50 wkts (1): 53 (2002). BB 6-40 Nh v Durham (Chester-le-St) 2002. Gs BB 5-54 v Leics (Leicester) 2007. LO HS 29 v Glamorgan (Colwyn Bay) 2007 (FPT). LO BB 4-15 v Ireland (Dublin) 2007 (FPT). T20 HS 20. T20 BB 3-15.

HARDINGES, Mark Andrew (Malvern C; Bath U), b Gloucester 5 Feb 1978. 6'1". RHB, RMF. Gloucestershire 1999-2008; cap 2004. British U 2000. HS 172 v OU (Oxford) 2002. CC HS 107* v Essex (Chelmsford) 2006. BB 5-51 v Kent (Maidstone) 2005. LO HS 111* v Lancs (Manchester) 2005 (NL). LO BB 4-19 v Salop (Shrewsbury) 2002 (CGT). T20 HS 94*. T20 BB 4-30.

HARRIS, A.J. – see LEICESTERSHIRE.

NORTH, M.J. – see HAMPSHIRE.

RUDGE, William Douglas (Clifton C), b Southmead, Bristol 15 Jul 1983. 6'4". RHB, RM. Gloucestershire 2005-08; cap 2005. HS 19* v Loughborough UCCE (Bristol) 2008. CC HS 15 v Surrey (Oval) 2005. BB 3-46 v Bangladesh A (Bristol) 2005 – on debut. CC BB 3-75 v Middlesex (Bristol) 2005. LO HS 4 v Sussex (Arundel) 2006 (CGT). LO BB 4-57 v Notts (Cheltenham) 2008. T20 HS 9*. T20 BB 3-37.

GLOUCESTERSHIRE 2008

RESULTS SUMMARY

	Place	Won	Lost	Tied	Drew	No Result
County Championship (2nd Division)	9th		5		11	
All First-Class Matches		1	5		11	
FP Trophy (South West Division)	Quarter-Finalist	4	2			3
Pro40 League (1st Division)	5th	3	3			2
Twenty/20 Cup (Midlands/West/Wales Division)	6th	1	5	1		3

LV COUNTY CHAMPIONSHIP AVERAGES
BATTING AND FIELDING

Cap†		M	I	NO	HS	Runs	Avge	100	50	Ct/St
2007	M.J.North	12	20	2	104	900	50.00	1	8	13
2005	S.D.Snell	15	23	4	127	879	46.26	1	8	35/1
2001	C.G.Taylor	16	28	4	137	1076	44.83	2	8	6
2004	M.A.Hardinges	6	9	2	82	268	38.28	–	2	4
2005	Kadeer Ali	12	22	–	161	791	35.95	3	2	7
2006	D.O.Brown	8	13	3	83	348	34.80	–	3	3
2008	W.T.S.Porterfield	12	22	–	93	718	32.63	–	7	7
2006	H.J.H.Marshall	16	29	1	121	850	30.35	2	5	6
2008	R.K.J.Dawson	5	7	1	40	132	22.00	–	–	3
2002	C.M.Spearman	5	9	1	95	173	21.62	–	1	2
2004	A.P.R.Gidman	12	21	2	68	378	19.89	–	1	2
1998	J.Lewis	14	20	5	51	253	16.86	–	1	1
2005	S.P.Kirby	12	16	5	28	80	7.27	–	–	3
2008	M.T.Gitsham	3	5	1	11	23	5.75	–	–	1
2006	V.Banerjee	5	6	1	15	22	4.40	–	–	1
2007	A.J.Ireland	9	13	6	16*	30	4.28	–	–	3

Also batted: S.J.Adshead (1 match – cap 2004) 47 (9 ct); A.J.Harris (1 – cap 2008) 0; G.P.Hodnett (2 – cap 2005) 13, 3, 1 (3 ct); O.J.Newby (4 – cap 2008) 5, 13, 5; W.D.Rudge (1 – cap 2005) 7*; I.D.Saxelby (3 – cap 2008) 8, 11* (1 ct), 1; D.H.Wigley (1 – cap 2008) 9; R.J.Woodman (1 – cap 2008) 2, 13.

BOWLING

	O	M	R	W	Avge	Best	5wI	10wM
D.O.Brown	104.3	22	400	15	26.66	5-38	1	–
J.Lewis	392.5	123	1009	35	28.82	5-64	1	–
S.P.Kirby	370.1	84	1110	36	30.83	5-60	1	–
M.A.Hardinges	99.3	22	366	10	36.60	2-13	–	–
A.J.Ireland	218.1	39	846	23	36.78	3-33	–	–
M.J.North	191	29	585	13	45.00	3-57	–	–
Also bowled:								
A.P.R.Gidman	54	4	191	6	31.83	2-36	–	–
O.J.Newby	54.1	9	250	7	35.71	5-69	1	–
V.Banerjee	120.4	21	451	6	75.16	3-31	–	–

R.K.J.Dawson 87-13-346-1; M.T.Gitsham 88.3-15-249-3; A.J.Harris 12-1-54-0; G.P.Hodnett 10-0-41-0; H.J.H.Marshall 62-12-204-1; W.R.Rudge 29-5-130-4; I.D.Saxelby 47-8-218-2; C.G.Taylor 43-2-165-2; D.H.Wigley 21-3-99-1; R.J.Woodman 11.3-0-65-4.

The First-Class Averages (pp 136–153) give the records of Gloucestershire players in all first-class county matches (Gloucestershire's other opponents being Loughborough UCCE), with the exception of A.J.Harris, S.P.Kirby, O.J.Newby and D.H.Wigley, whose first-class figures for Gloucestershire are as above.

† Gloucestershire revised their capping policy in 2004 and now award players with their County Caps when they make their first-class debut.

GLOUCESTERSHIRE RECORDS

FIRST-CLASS CRICKET

Highest Total	For 695-9d		v	Middlesex	Gloucester	2004
	V 774-7d		by	Australians	Bristol	1948
Lowest Total	For 17		v	Australians	Cheltenham	1896
	V 12		by	Northants	Gloucester	1907
Highest Innings	For 341	C.M.Spearman	v	Middlesex	Gloucester	2004
	V 319	C.J.L.Rogers	for	Northants	Northampton	2006

Highest Partnership for each Wicket

1st	395	D.M.Young/R.B.Nicholls	v	Oxford U	Oxford	1962
2nd	256	C.T.M.Pugh/T.W.Graveney	v	Derbyshire	Chesterfield	1960
3rd	336	W.R.Hammond/B.H.Lyon	v	Leics	Leicester	1933
4th	321	W.R.Hammond/W.L.Neale	v	Leics	Gloucester	1937
5th	261	W.G.Grace/W.O.Moberley	v	Yorkshire	Cheltenham	1876
6th	320	G.L.Jessop/J.H.Board	v	Sussex	Hove	1903
7th	248	W.G.Grace/E.L.Thomas	v	Sussex	Hove	1896
8th	239	W.R.Hammond/A.E.Wilson	v	Lancashire	Bristol	1938
9th	193	W.G.Grace/S.A.P.Kitcat	v	Sussex	Bristol	1896
10th	131	W.R.Gouldsworthy/J.G.Bessant	v	Somerset	Bristol	1923

Best Bowling	For 10-40	E.G.Dennett		v	Essex	Bristol	1906
(Innings)	V 10-66	A.A.Mailey		for	Australians	Cheltenham	1921
	10-66	K.Smales		for	Notts	Stroud	1956
Best Bowling	For 17-56	C.W.L.Parker		v	Essex	Gloucester	1925
(Match)	V 15-87	A.J.Conway		for	Worcs	Moreton-in-M	1914

Most Runs – Season		2860	W.R.Hammond	(av 69.75)		1933
Most Runs – Career		33664	W.R.Hammond	(av 57.05)		1920-51
Most 100s – Season		13	W.R.Hammond			1938
Most 100s – Career		113	W.R.Hammond			1920-51
Most Wkts – Season		222	T.W.J.Goddard	(av 16.80)		1937
		222	T.W.J.Goddard	(av 16.37)		1947
Most Wkts – Career		3170	C.W.L.Parker	(av 19.43)		1903-35
Most Career W-K Dismissals		1054	R.C.Russell	(950 ct; 104 st)		1981-2004
Most Career Catches in the Field		719	C.A.Milton			1948-74

LIMITED-OVERS CRICKET

Highest Total	FPT	401 7		v	Bucks	Wing	2003
	P40	344-6		v	Northants	Cheltenham	2001
	T20	227-4		v	Somerset	Bristol	2006
Lowest Total	FPT	82		v	Notts	Bristol	1987
	P40	49		v	Middlesex	Bristol	1978
	T20	93		v	Worcs	Bristol	2008
Highest Innings	FPT	177	A.J.Wright	v	Scotland	Bristol	1997
	P40	153	C.M.Spearman	v	Warwicks	Gloucester	2003
	T20	100*	I.J.Harvey	v	Warwicks	Birmingham	2003
Best Bowling	FPT	6-21	C.A.Walsh	v	Kent	Bristol	1990
		6-21	C.A.Walsh	v	Cheshire	Bristol	1992
	P40	6-52	J.N.Shepherd	v	Kent	Bristol	1983
	T20	4-22	I.D.Fisher	v	Somerset	Bristol	2004

HAMPSHIRE

Formation of Present Club: 12 August 1863
Inaugural First-Class Match: 1864
Colours: Blue, Gold and White
Badge: Tudor Rose and Crown
County Champions: (2) 1961, 1973
Gillette/NatWest/C&G/FP Trophy Winners: (2) 1991, 2005
Benson and Hedges Cup Winners: (2) 1988, 1992
Pro 40/National League (Div 1) Winners: (0); best – 2nd 2008
Sunday League Winners: (3) 1975, 1978, 1986
Twenty20 Cup Winners: (0) – best Quarter-Finalist 2004

Chairman and CEO: Rod Bransgrove, The Rose Bowl, Botley Road, West End, Southampton SO30 3XH • Tel: 023 8047 2002 • Fax: 023 8047 2122 • Email: enquiries@rosebowlplc.com • Web: www.rosebowlplc.com

Cricket Secretary and Director of Rose Bowl Plc: T.M.Tremlett. **First XI Manager**: G.W.White. **Captain**: A.D.Mascarenhas. **Vice-Captain**: N.Pothas. **Overseas Players**: M.J.North and Imran Tahir. **2009 Beneficiary**: None. **Head Groundsman**: Nigel Gray. **Scorer**: A.E. (Tony) Weld. ‡ New registration. [NQ]Not qualified for England.

ADAMS, James Henry Kenneth (Sherborne S; University C, London; Loughborough U), b Winchester 23 Sep 1980. 6'2". LHB, LM. British U 2002-04. Hampshire debut 2002; cap 2006. Loughborough UCCE 2003-04 – scoring 107 v Somerset (Taunton) on debut. Dorset 1998. 1000 runs (1): 1173 (2006). HS 262* v Notts (Nottingham) 2006. BB 2-16 v Durham (Chester-le-St) 2004. LO HS 90 v Durham (Southampton) 2008 (P40). LO BB 1-34 v Essex (Chelmsford) 2007 (FPT). T20 HS 17*.

BALCOMBE, David John (St John's S, Leatherhead; St Hild & St Bede C, Durham), b City of London 24 Dec 1984. 6'4". RHB, RFM. Durham UCCE 2005-07. British U 2006. Hampshire debut 2007. HS 73 DU v Leics (Leicester) 2005. H HS 29 v Kent (Southampton) 2007. BB 5-112 DU v Durham (Durham) 2005. H BB 3-58 v Yorks (Leeds) 2007. LO HS 2 v Lancs (Manchester) 2007 (P40). LO BB 2-39 v Somerset (Taunton) 2008. T20 HS 3. T20 BB – .

BENHAM, Christopher Charles (Yately CS; Loughborough U), b Frimley, Surrey 24 Mar 1983. 6'1". RHB, RM/OB. Loughborough UCCE 2004. Hampshire debut 2004. HS 95 v Warwks (Southampton) 2006. LO HS 158 v Glamorgan (Southampton) 2006. T20 HS 59.

BURROWS, Thomas George (Reading GS; Southampton Solent U), b Wokingham, Berkshire 5 May 1985. 5'8". RHB, WK. Debut (Hampshire) 2005. Berkshire 2001-03. HS 42 v Kent (Canterbury) 2005 – on debut. LO HS 16 v West Indies A (Southampton) 2006. T20 HS – .

CARBERRY, Michael Alexander (St John Rigby Catholic C), b Croydon, Surrey 29 Sep 1980. 6'0". LHB, OB. Surrey 2001-02. Kent 2003-05. Hampshire debut/cap 2006. MCC 2008. F-c Tour (Eng A): B 2006-07. 1000 runs (1): 1067 (2007). HS 192* v Warwks (Southampton) 2007. BB 2-85 v Durham (Chester-le-St) 2006. LO HS 88 v Surrey (Croydon) 2006 (CGT). LO BB (K) 1-21 (NL). T20 HS 90.

‡**CORK, Dominic** Gerald (St Joseph's C, Stoke-on-Trent; Newcastle CFE), b Newcastle-under-Lyme, Staffs 7 Aug 1971. 6'2". RHB, RFM. Derbyshire 1990-2003; cap 1993; captain 1998-2003; benefit 2001. Lancashire 2004-08; cap 2004. *Wisden* 1995. PCA 1995. Staffordshire 1989-90. **Tests**: 37 (1995 to 2002); HS 59 v NZ (Auckland) 1996-97; BB 7-43 v WI (Lord's) 1995 – on debut (record England analysis by Test match debutant); hat-trick v WI (Manchester) 1995 – the first in Test history to occur in the opening over of a day's play. **LOI**: 32 (1992 to 2002-03); HS 31* v NZ (Napier) 1996-97; BB 3-27 v WI (Lord's) 1995. F-c Tours: A 1992-93 (Eng A), 1998-99; SA 1993-94 (Eng A), 1995-96; WI 1991-92 (Eng A); NZ 1996-97; I 1994-95 (Eng A); P 2000-01 (*part*). HS 200* De v Durham (Derby) 2000. 50 wkts (7); most – 90 (1995). BB 9-43 (13-93 match) De v Northants (Derby) 1995. Took 8-53 before lunch on his 20th birthday for De v Essex (Derby) 1991. 2 hat-tricks: 1994 and 1995 (*see* Tests). LO HS 93 De v Derbys CB (Derby) 2000 (NWT). LO BB 6-21 De v Glamorgan (Chesterfield) 1997 (SL). T20 HS 28. T20 BB 4-16.

CRAWLEY, John Paul (Manchester GS; Trinity C, Cambridge), b Maldon, Essex 21 Sep 1971. Younger brother of M.A.Crawley (Oxford U, Lancs and Notts 1987-94) and P.M.Crawley (Cambridge U 1992). 6'1". RHB, RM, occ WK. Lancashire 1990-2001; cap 1994; captain 1999-2001. Cambridge U 1991-93; blue 1991-92-93; captain 1992-93. Hampshire debut/cap 2002; captain 2003; benefit 2007. YC 1994. **Tests**: 37 (1994 to 2002-03); HS 156* v SL (Oval) 1998. **LOI**: 13 (1994-95 to 1998-99); HS 73 v Z (Harare) 1996-97. F-c Tours: A 1994-95, 1998-99, 2002-03; SA 1993-94 (Eng A), 1995-96; WI 1995-96 (La), 1997-98, 2000-01 (Eng A); NZ 1996-97; Z 1996-97. 1000 runs (10); most – 1851 (1998). HS 311* v Notts (Southampton) 2005. BB 1-7 v Surrey (Oval) 2005. LO HS 114 La v Notts (Manchester) 1995 (BHC). T20 HS 23.

DAWSON, Liam Andrew (John Bentley S, Calne), b Swindon, Wilts 1 Mar 1990. 5'8". RHB, SLA. Debut (Hampshire) 2007. Wiltshire 2006-07. HS 100 v Notts (Nottingham) 2008. BB 2-32 v Surrey (Oval) 2008. LO HS 45 and BB 4-45 v Middlesex (Lord's) 2008 (P40). T20 HS 11*. T20 BB 1-14.

^{NQ}**ERVINE, Sean** Michael (Lomagundi C, Chinhoyi), b Harare, Zimbabwe 6 Dec 1982. Elder brother of C.R.Ervine (Midlands 2003-04 to 2004-05); son of R.M.Ervine (Rhodesia 1977-78); grandson of M.A.Den (Rhodesia 1935-36); nephew of N.B.Ervine (Rhodesia 1977-78) and G.M.Den (Rhodesia and Eastern Province 1963-64 to 1969-70). Irish passport. 6'2". LHB, RM. CFX Academy 2000-01 to 2001. Midlands 2001-02 to 2003-04. Hampshire debut/cap 2005 (Kolpak registration). Western Australia 2006-07 to 2007-08. **Tests** (Z): 5 (2003 to 2003-04); HS 86 v B (Harare) 2003-04; BB 4-146 v A (Perth) 2003-04. **LOI** (Z): 42 (2001-02 to 2003-04); HS 100 v I (Adelaide) 2003-04; BB 3-29 v P (Sharjah) 2001-02. F-c Tours (Z): E 2003; A 2003-04. HS 126 Midlands v Manicaland (Mutare) 2002-03. H HS 103* v Lancs (Manchester) 2007. BB 6-82 Midlands v Mashonaland (Kwekwe) 2002-03. H BB 5-60 v Glamorgan (Cardiff) 2005. LO HS 134* WA v S Aus (Adelaide) 2007-08. LO BB 5-50 v Glamorgan (Cardiff) 2005 (CGT). T20 HS 56*. T20 BB 3-18.

GRIFFITHS, David Andrew (Sandown HS, IOW), b Newport, IOW 10 Sep 1985. 6'1". LHB, RFM. Debut (Hampshire) 2006. HS 31* v Surrey (Southampton) 2007. BB 4-46 v Durham (Chester-le-St) 2007 – on CC debut. LO HS 3* v Worcs (Worcester) 2008 (FPT). LO BB 1-53 v Glam (Cardiff) 2008. T20 HS 4*. T20 BB 3-13.

HOWELL, Benny Alexander Cameron (The Oratory S), b Bordeaux, France 5 Oct 1988. Son of J.B.Howell (Warwickshire 2nd XI 1978). 5'11". RHB, RM. Awaiting f-c debut. Hampshire 2nd XI 2005-08. Berkshire 2007.

IMRAN TAHIR, Mohammad (Government Pakistan Angels HS and MAO College, Lahore), b Lahore, Pakistan 4 Jun 1979. 5'11". RHB, LB. Lahore City 1996-97 to 1997-98. WAPDA 1998-99. REDCO 1999-00. Lahore Whites 2000-01. Sui Northern Gas Pipelines 2001-02 to 2003-04. Sialkot 2002-03. Middlesex 2003. Lahore Blues 2004-05. PIA 2004-05 to 2006-07. Lahore Ravi 2005-06. Yorkshire (1 match) 2007. Titans 2007-08 to date. Hampshire debut 2008. Staffordshire 2004-05. Qualified for SA on 1 Apr 2009. F-c Tour (Pak A): SL 2004-05. HS 48 REDCO v KRL (Rawalpindi) 1999-00. UK HS M v Kent (Canterbury) 2003. H HS 24* v Notts (Nottingham) 2008. 50 wkts (0+1): 74 (2004-05). BB 8-76 REDCO v Karachi Blues (Lahore) 1999-00. UK BB 7-66 (12-189 match) H v Lancs (Manchester) 2008 – on debut. LO HS 41* Staffs v Lancs (Stone) 2004 (CGT). LO BB 5-27 v Sussex (Southampton) 2008 (P40). T20 HS 13. T20 BB 3-13.

LUMB, Michael John (St Stithians C, Johannesburg), b Johannesburg, South Africa 12 Feb 1980. Son of R.G.Lumb (Yorkshire 1970-84); nephew of A.J.S.Smith (SAU and Natal 1972-73 to 1983-84). 6'0". LHB, RM. Yorkshire 2000-06; ECB qualified and CC debut 2001; cap 2003. Hampshire debut 2007. F-c Tour (Eng A): I 2003-04. 1000 runs (1): 1038 (2003). HS 144 Y v Middlesex (Southgate) 2006. H HS 107 v Somerset (Southampton) 2008. BB 2-10 Y v Kent (Canterbury) 2001. H BB – . LO HS 108 v Sussex (Hove) 2007 (P40). T20 HS 84*. T20 BB 3-32.

MASCARENHAS, Adrian Dimitri (Trinity C, Perth, Australia), b Hammersmith, London 30 Oct 1977. 6'2". RHB, RMF. Resident in Australia 1979-96. RHB, RMF. Debut (Hampshire) 1996, taking 6-88 v Glamorgan (Southampton); took 16 wickets in first two CC matches; cap 1998; benefit 2007; captain 2008 to date. Dorset 1996. **LOI:** 11 (2007 to 2008); HS 52 v I (Bristol) 2007; hit sixes off five successive balls from Yuvraj Singh v I (Oval) 2007; BB 3-23 v I (Lord's) 2007. HS 131 v Kent (Canterbury) 2006. 50 wkts (1): 56 (2004). BB 6-25 v Derbys (Southampton) 2004. LO HS 79 v Worcs (Southampton) 1999 (NL) and 79 v Kent (Canterbury) 2004 (NL). LO BB 5-27 v Glos (Southampton) 2002 (NL). IT20 HS 31. IT20 BB 3-18. T20 HS 52. T20 BB 5-14.

MORGAN, Christopher George Wakefield (Portsmouth GS) b Portsmouth 28 Oct 1989. 5'11". RHB, SLA. Hampshire 2nd XI 2008. Awaiting 1st XI debut.

‡[NQ]**NORTH, Marcus** James (Kent Street Sr HS), b Pakenham, Melbourne, Australia 28 Jul 1979. 6'1". LHB, OB. Debut (Aus Academy in Zim) 1998-99. W Australia 1999-00 to date; captain 2007-08 to date. Durham 2004. Lancashire 2005. Derbyshire 2006. Gloucestershire 2007-08; cap 2007. **Tests** (A): 2 (2008-09); HS 117 and BB 1-29 v SA (Johannesburg) 2008-09 – on debut. F-c Tours (Aus): SA 2008-09; P 2005-06 (Aus A); Z 1998-99 (Aus Acad). 1000 runs (0+1): 1074 (2003-04). HS 239* WA v Vic (Perth) 2006-07. UK HS 219 Du v Glamorgan (Cardiff) 2004. BB 6-69 A v SAB President's XI (Potchefstroom) 2008-09. UK BB 4-16 Du v Durham UCCE (Chester-le-St) 2004 – on Du debut. CC BB 3-53 Gs v Leics (Bristol) 2007. LO HS 134* WA v Q (Perth) 2004-05. LO BB 4-26 Durham CB v Bucks (Beaconsfield) 2001 (CGT). T20 HS 59. T20 BB 2-19.

‡**PARSONS, Thomas** William (Maidstone GS; Rutherford Hall, Loughborough U), b Melbourne, Australia 2 May 1987. 6'3". RHB, RFM. Loughborough UCCE 2007-08. Kent 2007 – l-o only, no f-c appearances. HS 12 LU v Worcs (Kidderminster) 2008. BB 3-70 LU v Worcs (Worcester) 2007 – on debut. LO HS – and BB 2 41 K v Sri Lanka A (Canterbury) 2007.

PIETERSEN, Kevin Peter (Maritzburg C; Natal U), b Pietermaritzburg, South Africa 27 Jun 1980. British passport (English mother) – qualified for England Oct 2004. 6'4". RHB, OB. MBE 2005. *Wisden* 2005. Natal/KwaZulu-Natal 1997-98 to 1999-00. Nottinghamshire 2001-04; cap 2002. MCC 2004. Hampshire debut/cap 2005 (no f-c appearances 2006-07). **ECB central contract 2008-09. Tests**: 50 (2005 to 2008-09, 3 as captain); HS 226 v WI (Leeds) 2007; BB 1-0 v SA (Lord's) 2008. **LOI**: 87 (2004-05 to 2008-09, 10 as captain); HS 116 v SA (Pretoria) 2004-05; scored 454 runs (av 151.33) in 7-match series, including fastest England 100 off 69 balls (E London), v SA 2004-05; BB 2-22 v SA (Leeds) 2008. F-c Tours: A 2006-07; WI 2008-09; NZ 2007-08; I 2003-04 (Eng A), 2005-06, 2008-09 (Captain); P 2005-06; SL 2007-08. 1000 runs (3); most – 1546 (2003). HS 254* Nt v Middlesex (Nottingham) 2002. H HS 126 v Glamorgan (Southampton) 2005. BB 4-31 Nt v DU (Nottingham) 2003. CC BB 3-72 Nt v Hants (Nottingham) 2004. H BB – . LO HS 147 Nt v Somerset (Taunton) 2002 (NL). LO BB 3-14 Nt v Middlesex (Lord's 2004 (NL). IT20 HS 79. T20 HS 79. T20 BB 3-33.

POTHAS, Nic (King Edward VII S; Rand Afrikaans U), b Johannesburg, South Africa 18 Nov 1973. ECB qualified – EU (Greek) passport. 6'3". RHB, WK, occ RM. Transvaal 1993-94 to 1996-97. Gauteng 1997-98 to 2000-01. Hampshire debut 2002; cap 2003. **LOI** (SA): 3 (2000-01); HS 24 v P (Singapore) 2000 – on debut. F-c Tours: SA: E 1996 (SA A); WI 2000 (SA A); SL 1998. HS 165 Gauteng v KZ-Natal (Johannesburg) 1998-99. H HS 146* v Worcs (Worcester) 2003. BB 1-16 v Middlesex (Lord's) 2006. Held 7 catches in an innings v Lancs (Manchester) 2006. LO HS 114* v Glamorgan (Cardiff) 2005 (CGT). T20 HS 59.

RIAZUDDIN, Hamza (Bradfield C) b Chelsea, London 19 Dec 1989. 5'11". RHB, RMF. HS 4 and BB 1-21 v Somerset (Taunton) 2008 – on debut. Berkshire 2008. LO HS – . BB 1-15 v Worcs (Southampton) 2008 (FPT). T20 HS 0*. T20 BB 1-23.

TAYLOR, Billy Victor (Bitterne Park S, Southampton), b Southampton 11 Jan 1977. Younger brother of J.L.Taylor (Wiltshire 1998-2002). 6'3". LHB, RMF. Sussex 1999-2003. Hampshire debut 2004; cap 2006. No f-c appearances 2007-08. Wiltshire 1996-98. HS 40 v Essex (Southampton) 2004. BB 6-32 v Middlesex (Southampton) 2006 (inc hat-trick). LO HS 21* Sx v Notts (Cleethorpes) 1999 (NL). LO BB 5-28 Sx v Middlesex (Lord's) 2002 (BHC). T20 HS 12*. T20 BB 2-9.

TOMLINSON, James Andrew (Harrow Way S, Andover; Cardiff U), b Winchester 12 Jun 1982. 6'1". LHB, LMF. British U 2002-03. Hampshire debut 2002; cap 2008. Wiltshire 2001. HS 35* v Lancs (Southampton) 2008. 50 wkts (1): 67 (2008). BB 8-46 (10-194 match) v Somerset (Taunton) 2008. LO HS 6 (NL). LO BB 4-47 v Glamorgan (Southampton) 2006 (CGT). T20 HS 5. T20 BB 1-20.

TREMLETT, Christopher Timothy (Thornden S, Chandler's Ford; Taunton's C, Southampton), b Southampton 2 Sep 1981. Son of T.M.Tremlett (Hampshire 1976-91); grandson of M.F.Tremlett (Somerset, CD and England 1947-60). 6'7". RHB, RMF. Debut (Hampshire) v NZ A (Portsmouth) 2000, taking wicket of M.H.Richardson with his first ball; cap 2004. **Tests**: 3 (2007); HS 25* v I (Oval) 2007; BB 3-12 v I (Nottingham) 2007. **LOI**: 9 (2005 to 2008); HS 19* v I (Birmingham) 2007; BB 4-32 v B (Nottingham) 2005 – on debut (hat-trick ball hit stump without dislodging bails). F-c Tour (ECB Acad): SL 2002-03. HS 64 v Glos (Southampton) 2005. BB 6-44 v Sussex (Hove) 2005. Hat-trick v Notts (Nottingham) 2005. LO HS 38* v Cheshire (Alderley Edge) 2004 (CGT). LO BB 4-25 v Essex (Southend) 2002 (NL). IT20 HS – . IT20 BB 2-45.T20 HS 13. T20 BB 4-25.

VINCE, James Michael (Warminster S) b Cuckfield, Sussex 14 Mar 1991. 6'2". RHB, RM. Hampshire 2nd XI 2006-08. Wiltshire 2007-08. Awaiting 1st XI debut.

RELEASED/RETIRED
(Having made a County First-Class or List A appearance in 2008)

[NQ]**BOND, Shane** Edward (Papanui HS, Canterbury; Lincoln U), b Christchurch, NZ 7 Jun 1975. 6'2". RHB, RF. Canterbury 1996-97 to 2006-07. Warwickshire 2002. Hampshire 2008. **Tests** (NZ): 17 (2001-02 to 2007-08); HS 41* v Z (Harare) 2005; BB 6-51 v Z (Bulawayo) 2005. **LOI** (NZ): 67 (2001-02 to 2006-07); HS 31* v I (Auckland) 2002-03; BB 6-19 v I (Bulawayo) 2005. F-c Tours (NZ): E 2004; A 2001-02; SA 2005-06, 2007-08; WI 2002; SL 2003; Z 2005-06. HS 100 Canterbury v ND (Christchurch) 2004-05. UK HS 29* Wa v Somerset (Taunton) 2002. H HS 11 v Durham (Chester-le-Street) 2008. BB 7-66 H v Sussex (Southampton) 2008 – on Hampshire debut. LO HS 40 Canterbury v Wellington (Christchurch) 2002-03. LO BB 6-19 (see LOI). IT20 HS 8*. IT20 BB 2-12. T20 HS 29. T20 BB 4-19.

BROWN, Michael James (Queen Elizabeth GS, Blackburn; Collingwood C, Durham U), b Burnley, Lancs 9 Feb 1980. 6'0" Elder brother of D.O.Brown (see GLOUCESTERSHIRE). RHB, OB. Middlesex 1999-2003. Durham UCCE 2001-02. British U 2001-02. Hampshire 2004-08; 2007. 1000 runs (1): 1078 (2007). HS 133 v LU (Southampton) 2006. CC HS 126* v Durham (Chester-le-St) 2007. LO HS 96* v Worcs (Southampton) 2008 (FPT). T20 HS 44.

LAMB, Gregory Arthur (Lomagundi C, Chinhoyi; Guildford C, Surrey), b Harare, Zimbabwe 4 Mar 1980. 5'11". RHB, RM/OB. Debut (ZCU President's XI) 1998-99. ZC/CFX Academy 1998-99 to 1999-00. Mashonaland 2000-01. Hampshire 2004-08. F-c Tour (Zim A): SL 1999-00. HS 100* CFX Academy v Manicaland (Mutare) 1999-00. H HS 94 v Derbys (Derby) 2004 – on UK debut. BB 7-73 CFX Academy v Midlands (Kwekwe) 1999-00. H BB 2-30 v Middlesex (Southgate) 2005. LO HS 100* v Northants (Southampton) 2005 (NL). LO BB 4-38 v Yorks (Leeds) 2006 (P40). T20 HS 67. T20 BB 4-28.

LATOUF, Kevin John (Millfield S; Barton Peveril C), b Pretoria, South Africa 7 Sep 1985. 5'10". RHB, RM. Hampshire 2006. HS 29 v LU (Southampton) 2006 – on only f-c appearance. LO HS 25 v Surrey (Oval) 2005 (CGT) on 1st XI debut.

R.K.Morris left the staff, without making a County First-Class or List A appearance in 2008.

COUNTY BENEFITS AWARDED FOR 2009

Derbyshire	–
Durham	B.Hunt
Essex	–
Glamorgan	A.G.Wharf
Gloucestershire	C.G.Taylor
Hampshire	–
Kent	M.J.Saggers
Lancashire	G.Keedy
Leicestershire	–
Middlesex	A.J.Strauss
Northamptonshire	–
Nottinghamshire	C.M.W.Read
Somerset	A.R.Caddick (Testimonial)
Surrey	J.N.Batty
Sussex	M.W.Goodwin
Warwickshire	T.Frost
Worcestershire	B.F.Smith
Yorkshire	A.McGrath

HAMPSHIRE 2008

RESULTS SUMMARY

	Place	Won	Lost	Tied	Drew	No Result
County Championship (1st Division)	3rd	5	4		7	
All First-Class Matches		5	4		7	
FP Trophy (South West Division)	4th	3	4			1
Pro40 League (1st Division)	2nd	4	2			2
Twenty/20 Cup (South Division)	4th	5	4	1		

LV COUNTY CHAMPIONSHIP AVERAGES

BATTING AND FIELDING

Cap		M	I	NO	HS	Runs	Avge	100	50	Ct/St
2003	N.Pothas	14	23	5	137*	963	53.50	3	3	45/1
2007	M.J.Brown	14	26	3	104*	940	40.86	1	6	10
2008	M.J.Lumb	16	27	2	107	818	32.72	1	6	17
1998	A.D.Mascarenhas	15	24	2	99	673	30.59	–	3	8
	C.C.Benham	8	13	–	89	374	28.76	–	3	9
2006	M.A.Carberry	14	26	3	92	658	28.60	–	4	5
2005	S.M.Ervine	13	22	1	94*	587	27.95	–	5	19
2002	J.P.Crawley	9	16	1	104	416	27.73	1	2	3
	L.A.Dawson	5	8	1	100*	193	27.57	1	–	–
	Imran Tahir	7	8	4	24*	85	21.25	–	–	3
	G.A.Lamb	9	15	2	54*	272	20.92	–	1	7
2004	C.T.Tremlett	12	17	1	60	276	17.25	–	3	6
2006	J.H.K.Adams	7	12	–	50	206	17.16	–	1	10
2008	J.A.Tomlinson	16	20	10	35*	145	14.50	–	–	4
	D.J.Balcombe	6	10	3	20*	85	12.14	–	–	1
	S.E.Bond	4	5	–	17	33	6.60	–	–	–

Also batted: T.G.Burrows (2 matches) 13*, 4*, 13 (8 ct); D.A.Griffiths (1) 4; M.Hayward (1) 7, 17*; R.K.Kleinveldt (1) 16, 4; K.P.Pietersen (1 – cap 2005) 100; H.Riazuddin (1) 4.

BOWLING

	O	M	R	W	Avge	Best	5wI	10wM
Imran Tahir	258.2	58	734	44	16.68	7-66	3	1
S.E.Bond	99.1	15	365	19	19.21	7-66	2	–
A.D.Mascarenhas	394.4	132	977	41	23.82	6-67	2	–
J.A.Tomlinson	464.2	90	1659	67	24.76	8-46	4	1
C.T.Tremlett	356.2	90	999	27	37.00	5-67	1	–
Also bowled:								
L.A.Dawson	57.1	12	213	6	35.50	2-32	–	–
D.J.Balcombe	113.1	20	412	9	45.77	2- 1	–	–
S.M.Ervine	124	12	499	9	55.44	4-42	–	–
G.A.Lamb	140.4	21	571	8	71.37	2-69	–	–

J.H.K.Adams 12-1-42-0; M.A.Carberry 13-1-31-0; D.A.Griffiths 42-8-178-2; M.Hayward 25.1-4-101-3; R.K.Kleinveldt 9-1-42-1; K.P.Pietersen 4-0-16-0; H.Riazuddin 29-5-99-1.

Hampshire played no first-class fixtures outside the County Championship in 2008. The First-Class Averages (pp 136–153) give the records of Hampshire players in all first-class county matches, with the exception of M.A.Carberry, K.P.Pietersen and C.T.Tremlett, whose first-class figures for Hampshire are as above.

HAMPSHIRE RECORDS

FIRST-CLASS CRICKET

Highest Total	For 714-5d		v	Notts	Southampton	2005
	V 742		by	Surrey	The Oval	1909
Lowest Total	For 15		v	Warwicks	Birmingham	1922
	V 23		by	Yorkshire	Middlesbrough	1965
Highest Innings	For 316	R.H.Moore	v	Warwicks	Bournemouth	1937
	V 303*	G.A.Hick	for	Worcs	Southampton	1997

Highest Partnership for each Wicket

1st	347	V.P.Terry/C.L.Smith	v	Warwicks	Birmingham	1987
2nd	321	G.Brown/E.I.M.Barrett	v	Glos	Southampton	1920
3rd	344	G.Brown/C.P.Mead	v	Yorkshire	Portsmouth	1927
4th	263	R.E.Marshall/D.A.Livingstone	v	Middlesex	Lord's	1970
5th	235	G.Hill/D.F.Walker	v	Sussex	Portsmouth	1937
6th	411	R.M.Poore/E.G.Wynyard	v	Somerset	Taunton	1899
7th	325	G.Brown/C.H.Abercrombie	v	Essex	Leyton	1913
8th	257	N.Pothas/A.J.Bichel	v	Glos	Cheltenham	2005
9th	230	D.A.Livingstone/A.T.Castell	v	Surrey	Southampton	1962
10th	192	H.A.W.Bowell/W.H.Livsey	v	Worcs	Bournemouth	1921

Best Bowling	For 9- 25	R.M.H.Cottam	v	Lancashire	Manchester	1965
(Innings)	V 10- 46	W.Hickton	for	Lancashire	Manchester	1870
Best Bowling	For 16- 88	J.A.Newman	v	Somerset	Weston-s-Mare	1927
(Match)	V 17-103	W.Mycroft	for	Derbyshire	Southampton	1876

Most Runs – Season	2854	C.P.Mead	(av 79.27)	1928
Most Runs – Career	48892	C.P.Mead	(av 48.84)	1905-36
Most 100s – Season	12	C.P.Mead		1928
Most 100s – Career	138	C.P.Mead		1905-36
Most Wkts – Season	190	A.S.Kennedy	(av 15.61)	1922
Most Wkts – Career	2669	D.Shackleton	(av 18.23)	1948-69
Most Career W-K Dismissals	700	R.J.Parks	(630 ct/70 st)	1980-92
Most Career Catches in the Field	629	C.P.Mead		1905-36

LIMITED-OVERS CRICKET

Highest Total	FPT	371-4		v	Glamorgan	Southampton	1975
	P40	353-8		v	Middlesex	Lord's	2005
	T20	225-2		v	Middlesex	Southampton	2006
Lowest Total	FPT	75		v	Essex	Chelmsford	2007
	P40	43		v	Essex	Basingstoke	1972
	T20	85		v	Essex	Southampton	2008
Highest Innings	FPT	177	C.G.Greenidge	v	Glamorgan	Southampton	1975
	P40	172	C.G.Greenidge	v	Surrey	Southampton	1987
	T20	97*	S.R.Watson	v	Kent	Southampton	2004
Best Bowling	FPT	7-30	P.J.Sainsbury	v	Norfolk	Southampton	1965
	P40	6-20	T.E.Jesty	v	Glamorgan	Cardiff	1975
	T20	5-14	A.D.Mascarenhas	v	Sussex	Hove	2004

KENT

Formation of Present Club: 1 March 1859
Substantial Reorganisation: 6 December 1870
Inaugural First-Class Match: 1864
Colours: Maroon and White
Badge: White Horse on a Red Ground
County Champions: (6) 1906, 1909, 1910, 1913, 1970, 1978
Joint Champions: (1) 1977
Gillette/NatWest/C&G/FP Trophy Winners: (2) 1967, 1974
Benson and Hedges Cup Winners: (3) 1973, 1976, 1978
Pro 40/National League (Div 1) Winners: (1) 2001
Sunday League Winners: (4) 1972, 1973, 1976, 1995
Twenty20 Cup Winners: (1) 2007

Chief Executive: Paul E.Millman, St Lawrence Ground, Canterbury, CT1 3NZ • Tel: 01227 456886 • Fax: 01227 762168 • Email: kent@ecb.co.uk • Web: www.kentccc.com

Director of Cricket: G.Ford. **Captain:** R.W.T.Key. **Vice-Captain:** tba. **Overseas Player:** Yasir Arafat. **2009 Beneficiary:** M.J.Saggers. **Grounds Co-ordinator:** Andy Peirson. **Scorer:** Jack C.Foley. ‡ New registration. ^{NQ} Not qualified for England.

^{NQ}**AZHAR MAHMOOD** SAGAR (F.G. No. 1 HS, Islamabad), b Rawalpindi, Pakistan 28 Feb 1975. 5'11". RHB, RFM. Islamabad 1993-94 to 1997-98, 2001-02 to 2006-07. United Bank 1995-96 to 1996-97. Rawalpindi 1998-99 to 2004-05. MCC 2001. PIA 2001-02. Surrey 2002-07; cap 2004. Habib Bank 2006-07. Kent debut 2008 (British passport holder) scoring 116 v Notts (Canterbury); cap 2008. **Tests** (P): 21 (1997-98 to 2001); HS 136 v SA (Johannesburg) 1997-98; BB 4-50 v E (Lord's) 2001. Scored 128* and 50* v SA (Rawalpindi) 1997-98 on debut. **LOI** (P): 143 (1996-97 to 2006-07); HS 67 v I (Adelaide) 1999-00; BB 6-18 v WI (Sharjah) 1999-00. F-c Tours (P): E 1997 (Pak A), 2001; A 1999-00; SA 1997-98; I 1998-99; SL 2000; Z 1997-98. HS 204* Sy v Middlesex (Oval) 2005. K HS 116 (*see above*). 50 wkts (0+1): 59 (1996-97). BB 8-61 Sy v Lancs (Oval) 2002. K BB 6-55 v Yorkshire (Canterbury) 2008. LO HS 101* Sy v Glamorgan (Oval) 2006 (CGT). LO BB 6-18 (*see LOI*). T20 HS 65*. T20 BB 4-20.

BLAKE, Alexander James (Hayes SS), b Farnborough 25 Jan 1989. 6'3". LHB, RMF. Debut (Kent) 2008 – awaiting CC debut. Kent 2nd XI debut 2005. England U19s 2006-07 to 2009. HS – and BB-v NZ (Canterbury) 2008. LO HS 11* v Surrey (Canterbury) 2007 (P40). LO BB 1-25 v Glamorgan (Cardiff) 2007 (P40).

‡^{NQ}**CLARK, Stuart** Rupert (Woolooware HS; Sydney U), b Caringbah, Sydney, Australia 28 Sep 1975. 6'5". RHB, RFM. NSW 1997-98 to date. Middlesex 2004-05. Hampshire 2007; cap 2007. **Tests** (A): 22 (2005-06 to 2008-09); HS 39 v E (Brisbane) 2006-07; BB 5-32 v WI (Kingston) 2008. **LOI** (A): 35 (2005-06 to 2008-09); HS 16* v SA (Durban) 2005-06; BB 4-54 v NZ (Sydney) 2006-07. F-c Tours (A): SA 2005-06; WI 2008; I 2008-09; P 2005-06 (Aus A); B 2005-06. HS 62 NSW v S Aus (Adelaide) 2006-07. UK HS 34 M v Northants (Northampton) 2004 – on debut. BB 8-58 NSW v WA (Perth) 2006-07, inc hat-trick. UK BB 7-82 H v Lancashire (Southampton) 2007. LO HS 26* M v Sussex (Hove) 2004 (NL). LO BB 6-27 H v Surrey (Southampton) 2007. IT20 HS – . IT20 BB 4-20. T20 HS – . T20 BB 4-20.

‡**COLES, Matthew** Thomas, b Maidstone 26 May 1990. LHB, RM. Kent 2nd XI debut 2007. Awaiting f-c debut.

51

COOK, Simon James (Matthew Arnold S), b Oxford 15 Jan 1977. 6'4". RHB, RMF. Middlesex 1999-2004; cap 2003. Kent debut 2005; cap 2007. HS 93* M v Notts (Lord's) 2001. K HS 71 v Yorks (Leeds) 2006. BB 8-63 M v Northants (Northampton) 2002. K BB 6-35 v Sussex (Canterbury) 2007. LO HS 67* M v Durham (Lord's) 2003 (NL). LO BB 6-37 M v Leics (Leicester) 2004 (NL). T20 HS 25*. T20 BB 3-14.

DENLY, Joseph Liam (Chaucer TC), b Canterbury 16 Mar 1986. 6'0". RHB, LB. Debut (Kent) 2004; cap 2008. F-c Tours (Eng A): NZ 2008-09; I 2007-08. 1000 runs (1): 1003 (2007). HS 149 v Somerset (Tunbridge Wells) 2008. BB 2-13 v Surrey (Canterbury) 2007. LO HS 102* v Ireland (Belfast) 2007 (FPT). T20 HS 91.

DIXEY, Paul Garrod (King's S, Canterbury; Hatfield C, Durham U), b Canterbury 2 Nov 1987. 5'8". RHB, WK. Debut (Kent) 2005; awaiting CC debut – no f-c appearances 2007-08. MCC 2007. Durham UCCE 2007-08. HS 31 DU v Lancashire (Durham) 2008. K HS 24 v Bangladesh A (Canterbury) 2005 – on debut. LO HS – v Sri Lanka A (Canterbury) 2007.

‡FERLEY, Robert Steven (King Edward VII HS; Sutton Valence S; Grey C, Durham U), b Norwich, Norfolk 4 Feb 1982. 5'8". RHB, SLA. Durham UCCE 2001-03. British U 2001-03. Kent 2003-06. Nottinghamshire 2007-08. Norfolk 1998. HS 78* DU v Durham (Chester-le-St) 2003. CC HS 43* Nt v Essex (Chelmsford) 2007 – on Notts debut. K HS 29 v Surrey (Canterbury) 2004. BB 6-136 v Middlesex (Canterbury) 2006. LO HS 42 v Lancs (Manchester) 2004 (NL). LO BB 4-33 v Yorks (Scarborough) 2006 (P40). T20 HS 16*. T20 BB 3-17.

GOODMAN, James Elliot (St Olave's GS), b Farnborough 19 Nov 1990. 5'10". RHB, RM. Kent l-o debut 2007 – awaiting f-c debut. Kent 2nd XI debut 2006. England U19s 2007-08 to 2008. LO HS – v Sri Lanka A (Canterbury) 2007.

‡HEMPHREY, Charlie Richard (Harvey GS), b Doncaster, Yorkshire 31 Aug 1989. RHB, OB. Kent 2nd XI debut 2005. Awaiting f-c debut.

‡HOCKLEY, James Bernard (Kelsey Park S, Beckenham), b Beckenham 16 Apr 1979. 6'2". RHB, OB. Kent 1998-2002. HS 74 v Z (Canterbury) 2000. CC HS 46 v Surrey (Canterbury) 2002. BB 1-21 v Glamorgan (Maidstone) 2001. LO HS 121 v Warwks (Canterbury) 2002 (CGT). LO BB 1-35 v Norfolk (Horsford) 2002 (CGT).

ILES, James Alexander (Maidstone GS), b Chatham 11 Feb 1990. 6'4". RHB, RMF. Debut (Kent) 2006; no f-c appearances 2007-08; awaiting CC debut. HS – and BB 1-27 v CU (Cambridge) 2006. LO HS – and BB 1-27 v Sri Lanka A (Canterbury) 2007.

JONES, Geraint Owen (Harristown State HS, Toowoomba and MacGregor State HS, Brisbane, Australia), b Kundiawa, Papua New Guinea 14 Jul 1976. Welsh parents. 5'10". RHB, WK. Debut (Kent) 2001; cap 2003. MBE 2005. **Tests**: 34 (2003-04 to 2006-07); HS 100 v NZ (Leeds) 2004. **LOI**: 49 (2004 to 2006); HS 80 v Z (Bulawayo) 2004-05. F-c Tours: A 2006-07; SA 2004-05; WI 2003-04; I 2005-06; P 2005-06; SL 2003-04. HS 108* v Essex (Chelmsford) 2003. LO HS 86 v Surrey (Oval) 2008. IT20 HS 19. T20 HS 28.

JOSEPH, Robert ('Robbie') Hartman (Sutton Valence S; St Mary's C, Twickenham), b Antigua 20 Jan 1982. Resided in England since 1997. 6'1". RHB, RFM. Debut (First-Class Counties XI v NZ) 2000. Kent debut 2004. Leeward Is 2008-09. F-c Tour (Eng A): NZ 2008-09. HS 36* v Sussex (Hove) 2007. 50 wkts (1): 55 (2008). BB 6-32 (9-62 match) v Durham (Chester-le-Street) 2008. LO HS 15 v (Canterbury) 2005 (NL). LO BB 5-13 v Derbys (Canterbury) 2008 (P40). T20 HS 1*. T20 BB 2-24.

NQKEMP, Justin Miles (Queens C; Port Elizabeth U), b Queenstown, Cape Province, South Africa 2 Oct 1977. Son of J.W.Kemp (Border 1975-76 to 1976-77); grandson of J.M.Kemp (Border 1947-48). RHB, RFM. E Province 1996-97 to 2002-03. Worcestershire 2003. Northerns 2003-04 to 2004-05. Titans 2004-05 to 2006-07. Kent 2005-06; cap 2006. Cape Cobras 2007-08. **Tests** (SA): 4 (2000-01 to 2005-06); HS 55 v A (Perth) 2005-06; BB 3-33 v SL (Pretoria) 2000-01 on debut. **LOI** (SA): 79 (2000-01 to 2007-08); HS 100* v I (Cape Town) 2006-07; BB 3-20 v I (Durban) 2001-02. F-c Tours (SA): A 2002-03 (SA A), 2005-06; WI 2000 (SA A), 2000-01; Z 1998-99 (SA Acad). HS 188 EP v North West (Port Elizabeth) 2000-01. CC HS 124* v Yorks (Canterbury) 2006. BB 6-56 EP v Border (Port Elizabeth) 2000-01. CC BB 5-48 Wo v Glamorgan (Cardiff) 2003 – on Worcs debut. K BB 3-53 v Middlesex (Lord's) 2005. LO HS 107* Northerns v GW (Centurion) 2003-04. LO BB 6-20 EP v FS (Port Elizabeth) 2000-01. IT20 HS 89*. IT20 BB – . T20 HS 89*. T20 BB 3-19.

KEY, Robert William Trevor (Colfe's S), b East Dulwich, London 12 May 1979. 6'1". RHB, RM/OB. Debut (Kent) 1998; cap 2001, captain 2006 to date. MCC 2002-04. *Wisden* 2004. **Tests**: 15 (2002 to 2004-05); HS 221 v WI (Lord's) 2004. **LOI**: 5 (2003 to 2004); HS 19 v WI (Lord's) 2004. F-c Tours: A 2002 03; SA 1998-99 (Eng A), 2004-05; NZ 2008-09 (Eng A – captain); SL 2002-03 (ECB Acad); Z 1998-99 (Eng A). 1000 runs (5); most – 1896 (2004). HS 221 (*see Tests*). K HS 199 v Surrey (Oval) 2004. BB – . LO HS 120* v Essex (Canterbury) 2008 (P40). T20 HS 68*.

KHAN, Amjad (Skolenpa Duevej, Denmark), b Copenhagen, Denmark 14 Oct 1980. 6'0". RHB, RFM. Debut (Kent) 2001. Denmark 1998-2000. Qualified for England Dec 2006. Missed 2007 season following reconstructive knee surgery. **Tests**: 1 (2008-09); HS- and BB 1-111 v WI (Port of Spain) 2008-09. F-c Tours: WI 2008-09 (part); NZ 2008-09 (Eng A – part). HS 78 v Middlesex (Lord's) 2003. 50 wkts (2); most – 63 (2002). BB 6-52 v Yorks (Canterbury) 2002. LO HS 65* Denmark v Ireland (Harare) 1999-00. LO BB 4-26 v Leics (Leicester) 2003 (NL). IT20 HS 2. IT 20 BB 2-34. T20 HS 15. T20 BB 3-11.

LEE, Warren Wain (Eaglesfield S, Shooters Hill), b New Delhi, India 28 Jul 1987. RHB, RM. Kent 2nd XI debut 2005. Middlesex 2nd XI 2008. Surrey 2nd XI 2008. Awaiting 1st XI debut.

NQMcLAREN, Ryan (Grey C, Bloemfontein, Free State U), b Kimberley, South Africa 9 Feb 1983. 6'4". Son of P.McLaren (GW 1977-78 to 1994-95). Nephew of Keith McLaren (GW 1971-72 to 1984-85). Cousin of A.P.McLaren (GW 1998-99 to date, Eagles 2007-08). LHB, RMF. Free State 2003-04 to 2004-05. Eagles 2004-05 to date. Kent debut 2007 (Kolpak registration); cap 2007. HS 140 Eagles v Warriors (Bloemfontein) 2005-06. K HS 65* v Durham (Canterbury) 2008. 50 wkts (2); most – 54 (2006-07). BB 8-38 Eagles v Cape Cobras (Stellenbosch) 2006-07. K BB 6-75 v Notts (Nottingham) 2008. LO HS 82* Eagles v Dolphins (Durban) 2007-08. LO BB 5-46 v Surrey (Oval) 2008 (FPT). T20 HS 46*. T20 BB 3-22.

NORTHEAST, Sam Alexander (Harrow S), b Ashford 16 Oct 1989. 5'11". RHB, OB. Debut (Kent) 2007. No 1st XI appearances in 2008. England U19s 2006-07 to 2008-09. HS 5 v Durham (Canterbury) 2007 – on debut. LO HS – v Sri Lanka A (Canterbury) 2007.

SAGGERS, Martin John (Springwood HS, King's Lynn; Huddersfield U), b King's Lynn, Norfolk 23 May 1972. 6'2". RHB, RMF. Durham 1996-98. Kent debut 1999; cap 2001; benefit 2009. MCC 2004. Essex 2007 (on loan). Norfolk 1995-96. **Tests**: 3 (2003-04 to 2004); HS 1 and BB 2-29 v B (Chittagong) 2003-04 on debut. F-c Tour: B 2003-04. HS 64 v Worcs (Canterbury) 2004. 50 wkts (4); most – 83 (2002). BB 7-79 v Durham (Chester-le-St) 2000. LO HS 34* Minor C v Leics (Jesmond) 1996 (BHC). LO BB 5-22 v Glos (Canterbury) 2001 (NL). T20 HS 5. T20 BB 2-14.

STEVENS, Darren Ian (Hinckley C), b Leicester 30 Apr 1976. 5'11". RHB, RM. Leicestershire 1997-2004; cap 2002. MCC 2002. Kent debut/cap 2005. F-c Tour (ECB Acad): SL 2002-03. 1000 runs (1): 1277 (2005). HS 208 v Glamorgan (Canterbury) 2005. BB 4-36 v Yorks (Canterbury) 2006. LO HS 133 Le v Northumb (Jesmond) 2000 (NWT). LO BB 5-32 v Scotland (Edinburgh) 2005 (NL). T20 HS 69. T20 BB 4-14.

TREDWELL, James Cullum (Southlands Community CS, New Romney), b Ashford 27 Feb 1982. 6'0". LHB, OB. Debut (Kent) 2001; cap 2007. MCC 2004, 2008. F-c Tour (Eng A): I 2003-04 (captain). HS 123* v NZ (Canterbury) 2008. CC HS 116* v Yorks (Tunbridge Wells) 2007. BB 6-47 v Surrey (Canterbury) 2007. LO HS 88 v Surrey (Oval) 2007. LO BB 4-16 v Scotland (Canterbury) 2005 (NL). T20 HS 34. T20 BB 4-21.

^NQ^**VAN JAARSVELD, Martin** (Warmbaths S; Pretoria U), b Klerksdorp, South Africa 18 Jun 1974. 6'2". RHB, OB. N Transvaal/Northerns 1994-95 to 2003-04. Northamptonshire 2004. Titans 2004-05 to date. Kent debut/cap 2005 (Kolpak registration) scoring 118 and 111 v Warwicks (Canterbury) – second player after C.W.G.Bassano (Derbyshire) to score two hundreds on a county debut. **PCA 2008. Tests** (SA): 9 (2002-03 to 2004-05); HS 73 v WI (Johannesburg) 2003-04. **LOI** (SA): 11 (2002-03 to 2004); HS 45 v E (Birmingham) 2003; BB 1-0. Took wickets with his first and third balls in LOI. F-c Tours (SA): A 2002-03 (SA A); NZ 2003-04; I 2004-05; SL 1998-99 (SA A), 2004; Z 1998-99 (SA Acad). 1000 runs (4+1); most – 1268 (2001-02). HS 262* v Glamorgan (Cardiff) 2005. BB 5-33 v Surrey (Oval) 2008. LO HS 132* Titans v Eagles (Bloemfontein) 2008-09. LO BB 3-13 Titans v Cape Cobras (Centurion) 2008-09. T20 HS 76*. T20 BB 2-19.

RELEASED/RETIRED
(Having made a County First-Class or List A appearance in 2008)

DEXTER, N.J. – *see MIDDLESEX.*

YASIR ARAFAT – *see SUSSEX.*

WALKER, M.J. – *see ESSEX.*

D.J.Chambers, T.W.Parsons left the staff, without making a County First-Class or List A appearance in 2008.

KENT 2008

RESULTS SUMMARY

	Place	Won	Lost	Tied	Drew	No Result
County Championship (1st Division)	8th	4	6		6	
All First-Class Matches		4	6		7	
FP Trophy (South East Division)	Finalist 7	3				1
Pro40 League (2nd Division)	4th	4	2		2	
Twenty/20 Cup (South Division)	Finalist 8	5				

LV COUNTY CHAMPIONSHIP AVERAGES

BATTING AND FIELDING

Cap		M	I	NO	HS	Runs	Avge	100	50	Ct/St
2008	Azhar Mahmood	6	8	2	116	306	51.00	1	1	4
2005	M.van Jaarsveld	16	27	3	133	1150	47.91	4	7	28
	N.J.Dexter	6	8	–	105	265	33.12	1	1	3
2001	R.W.T.Key	14	24	2	157	686	31.18	1	4	5
2008	J.L.Denly	16	29	–	149	893	30.79	2	4	6
2003	G.O.Jones	16	26	4	106	668	30.36	1	3	63/3
2007	Yasir Arafat	12	19	5	90*	395	28.21	–	2	1
2006	J.M.Kemp	10	17	1	102	412	25.75	1	3	16
2007	R.McLaren	15	23	3	65*	464	23.20	–	2	6
2005	D.I.Stevens	13	21	1	127	463	23.15	1	1	9
2007	J.C.Tredwell	16	27	2	68	443	17.72	–	3	19
2001	M.J.Saggers	10	16	7	33	101	11.22	–	–	1
2000	M.J.Walker	5	10	1	23	94	10.44	–	–	–
	R.H.Joseph	15	18	5	23*	118	9.07	–	–	1
	A.Khan	6	7	1	21*	46	7.66	–	–	1

BOWLING

	O	M	R	W	Avge	Best	5wI	10wM
Azhar Mahmood	147	28	404	21	19.23	6-55	2	–
M.van Jaarsveld	77	12	220	11	20.00	5-33	1	–
A.Khan	145.1	36	433	21	20.61	3-10	–	–
R.McLaren	389.4	81	1150	49	23.46	6-75	2	–
R.H.Joseph	419.1	87	1433	55	26.05	6-32	2	–
Yasir Arafat	317.4	62	1105	38	29.07	6-86	1	–
D.I.Stevens	123	26	322	10	32.20	4-70	–	–
M.J.Saggers	265.5	63	857	24	35.70	4-26	–	–
J.C.Tredwell	358.4	58	1224	24	51.00	3-35	–	–

Also bowled: J.L.Denly 14-2-47-0; N.J.Dexter 2-0-9-0; R.W.T.Key 2-1-2-0; M.J.Walker 9-1-40-1.

The First-Class Averages (pp 136–153) give the records of Kent players in all first-class county matches (Kent's other opponents being the New Zealanders), with the exception of:
N.J.Dexter 7-8-0-105-265-33.12-1-1-3ct. 2-0-9-0.
R.W.T.Key 15-25-3-178*-864-39.27-2-4-5ct. 2-1-2-0.
J.C.Tredwell 17-28-3-123*-566-22.64-1-3-19ct. 364.4-63-1226-24-51.08-3/35-0-0.

KENT RECORDS

FIRST-CLASS CRICKET

Highest Total	For 803-4d		v	Essex	Brentwood	1934
	V 676		by	Australians	Canterbury	1921
Lowest Total	For 18		v	Sussex	Gravesend	1867
	V 16		by	Warwicks	Tonbridge	1913
Highest Innings	For 332	W.H.Ashdown	v	Essex	Brentwood	1934
	V 344	W.G.Grace	for	MCC	Canterbury	1876

Highest Partnership for each Wicket

1st	300	N.R.Taylor/M.R.Benson	v	Derbyshire	Canterbury	1991
2nd	366	S.G.Hinks/N.R.Taylor	v	Middlesex	Canterbury	1990
3rd	323	R.W.T.Key/M.van Jaarsveld	v	Surrey	Tunbridge W	2005
4th	368	P.A.de Silva/G.R.Cowdrey	v	Derbyshire	Maidstone	1995
5th	277	F.E.Woolley/L.E.G.Ames	v	New Zealand	Canterbury	1931
6th	315	P.A.de Silva/M.A.Ealham	v	Notts	Nottingham	1995
7th	248	A.P.Day/E.Humphreys	v	Somerset	Taunton	1908
8th	177	G.O.Jones/Yasir Arafat	v	Warwicks	Canterbury	2007
9th	171	M.A.Ealham/P.A.Strang	v	Notts	Nottingham	1997
10th	235	F.E.Woolley/A.Fielder	v	Worcs	Stourbridge	1909

Best Bowling	For	10- 30	C.Blythe	v	Northants	Northampton	1907
(Innings)	V	10- 48	C.H.G.Bland	for	Sussex	Tonbridge	1899
Best Bowling	For	17- 48	C.Blythe	v	Northants	Northampton	1907
(Match)	V	17-106	T.W.J.Goddard	for	Glos	Bristol	1939

Most Runs – Season	2894	F.E.Woolley	(av 59.06)	1928
Most Runs – Career	47868	F.E.Woolley	(av 41.77)	1906-38
Most 100s – Season	10	F.E.Woolley		1928, 1934
Most 100s – Career	122	F.E.Woolley		1906-38
Most Wkts – Season	262	A.P.Freeman	(av 14.74)	1933
Most Wkts – Career	3340	A.P.Freeman	(av 17.64)	1914-36
Most Career W-K Dismissals	1253	F.H.Huish	(901 ct/352 st)	1895-1914
Most Career Catches in the Field	773	F.E.Woolley		1906-38

LIMITED-OVERS CRICKET

Highest Total	FPT	384-6		v	Berkshire	Finchampstead	1994
	P40	327-6		v	Leics	Canterbury	1993
	T20	204-5		v	Essex	Beckenham	2008
Lowest Total	FPT	60		v	Somerset	Taunton	1979
	P40	83		v	Middlesex	Lord's	1984
	T20	91		v	Surrey	The Oval	2006
Highest Innings	FPT	136*	C.L.Hooper	v	Berkshire	Finchampstead	1994
	P40	146	A.Symonds	v	Lancs	Tunbridge Wells	2004
	T20	112	A.Symonds	v	Middlesex	Maidstone	2004
Best Bowling	FPT	8-31	D.L.Underwood	v	Scotland	Edinburgh	1987
	P40	6- 9	R.A.Woolmer	v	Derbyshire	Chesterfield	1979
	T20	4-14	D.I.Stevens	v	Essex	Chelmsford	2007

LANCASHIRE

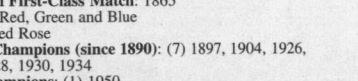

Formation of Present Club: 12 January 1864
Inaugural First-Class Match: 1865
Colours: Red, Green and Blue
Badge: Red Rose
County Champions (since 1890): (7) 1897, 1904, 1926, 1927, 1928, 1930, 1934
Joint Champions: (1) 1950
Gillette/NatWest/C&G/FP Trophy Winners: (7) 1970, 1971, 1972, 1975, 1990, 1996, 1998
Benson and Hedges Cup Winners: (4) 1984, 1990, 1995, 1996
Pro 40/National League (Div 1) Winners: (1) 1999.
Sunday League Winners: (4) 1969, 1970, 1989, 1998
Twenty20 Cup Winners: (0); best – Finalist 2005

Chief Executive: Jim Cumbes, Old Trafford, Manchester M16 0PX • Tel: 0161 282 4000 • Fax: 0161 282 4100 • Email: enquiries@lccc.co.uk • Web: www.lccc.co.uk

Director of Cricket: M.Watkinson. **Head Coach**: Peter Moores. **Captain**: G.Chapple. **Vice-Captain**: none. **Overseas Players**: V.V.S.Laxman and A.G.Prince. **2009 Beneficiary**: G.Keedy. **Head Groundsman**: Matthew Merchant. **Scorer**: Alan West. ‡ New registration. NQ Not qualified for England.

ANDERSON, James Michael (St Theodore RC HS and SFC, Burnley), b Burnley 30 Jul 1982. 6'2". LHB, RFM. Debut (Lancashire) 2002; cap 2003. YC 2003. *Wisden* 2008. **ECB central contract 2008-09**. Tests: 35 (2003 to 2008-09); HS 34 v SA (Leeds) 2008; BB 7-43 v NZ (Nottingham) 2008. LOI: 101 (2002-03 to 2008-09); HS 15 v A (Jaipur) 2006-07; BB 4-23 v I (Southampton) 2007. Hat-trick v P (Oval) 2003 – 1st for Eng in 373 LOI. F-c Tours: A 2006-07; SA 2004-05; WI 2003-04, 2005-06 (Eng A) (*part*), 2008-09; NZ 2007-08; I 2005-06 (*part*), 2008-09; SL 2003-04, 2007-08. HS 37* v Durham (Manchester) 2005. 50 wkts (2); most – 60 (2005). BB 7-43 (*see Tests*); La BB 6-23 v Hants (Southampton) 2002. Hat-trick (Lancs) 2003. LO HS 15 (*see LOI*). LO BB 4-23 (*see LOI*). IT20 HS 1*. IT20 BB 2-24. T20 HS 16. T20 BB 2-24.

BROWN, Karl Robert (Hesketh Fletcher HS, Atherton), b Bolton 17 May 1988. 5'10". RHB, RMF. Debut (Lancashire) 2006. HS 40 v Kent (Liverpool) 2008. BB – . LO HS 41 v Notts (Nottingham) 2008 (P40).

CHAPPLE, Glen (West Craven HS; Nelson & Colne C), b Skipton, Yorks 23 Jan 1974. 6'1". RHB, RFM. Debut (Lancashire) 1992; cap 1994; benefit 2004; captain 2009. **LOI**: 1 (2006); HS 14 and BB – v Ireland (Belfast) 2006. F-c Tours (Eng A): A 1996-97; WI 1995-96 (La); I 1994-95. HS 155 v Somerset (Manchester) 2001. Scored 100 off 27 balls in contrived circumstances v Glamorgan (Manchester) 1993. 50 wkts (4); most – 55 (1994). BB 7-53 v Durham (Blackpool) 2007. LO HS 81* v Derbys (Manchester) 2002 (CGT). LO BB 6-18 v Essex (Lord's) 1996 (NWT). T20 HS 55*. T20 BB 2-13.

CHEETHAM, Steven Philip (Bury GS; Holy Cross SFC), b Oldham 5 Sep 1987. 6'5". RHB, RFM. Debut (Lancashire) 2007. Awaiting CC debut; no f-c appearances in 2008. HS – and BB 1-44 v DU (Durham) 2007. LO HS 3* v Derbys (Derby) 2008. LO BB 3-25 v Bangladesh A (Alderley Edge) 2008.

CHILTON, Mark James (Manchester GS; Durham U), b Sheffield, Yorks 2 Oct 1976. 6'3". RHB, RM. Debut (Lancashire) 1997; cap 2002; captain 2005-07. British U 1998. 1000 runs (1): 1154 (2003). HS 131 v Kent (Manchester) 2006. BB 1-1 (*twice*). LO HS 115 v Surrey (Croydon) 2004 (NL). LO BB 5-26 Brit U v Sussex (Cambridge) 1997 (BHC). T20 HS 38.

CROFT, Steven John (Highfield HS, Blackpool; Myerscough C), b Blackpool 11 Oct 1984. 5'10". RHB, RMF. Debut (Lancashire) 2005. Auckland 2008-09. HS 122 v Notts (Manchester) 2008. BB 4-51 v Notts (Nottingham) 2008. LO HS 70 v Hampshire (Southampton) 2008 (P40). LO BB 4-24 v Scotland (Manchester) 2008 (FPT). T20 HS 49. T20 BB 3-6.

CROSS, Gareth David (Moorside S; Eccles C), b Bury 20 Jun 1984. 5'9". RHB, RMF, WK. Debut (Lancashire) 2005. No f-c appearances in 2008. HS 72 v Kent (Canterbury) 2006. LO HS 76 v Warwks (Birmingham) 2007 (P40). T20 HS 62.

NQDu PLESSIS, Francois (Affies BS, Pretoria), b Pretoria, South Africa 13 Jul 1984. 6'0". RHB, LB. Northerns 2003-04 to 2005-06. Titans 2005-06 to date. Lancashire debut 2008 (Kolpak registration). HS 176 Titans v Lions (Centurion) 2008-09. La HS 57 v Hampshire (Manchester) 2008. BB 4-39 Northerns v Free State (Pretoria) 2004-05. La BB 3-61 v Yorkshire (Manchester) 2008. LO HS 114* Titans v Eagles (Bloemfontein) 2008-09. LO BB 4-47 Northerns v Easterns (Pretoria) 2005-06. T20 HS 76. T20 BB 3-24.

FLINTOFF, Andrew (Ribbleton Hall HS), b Preston 6 Dec 1977. 6'4". RHB, RF. Debut (Lancashire) 1995; cap 1998; benefit 2006. YC 1998. *Wisden* 2003. PCA 2004, 2005. MBE 2005. BBC Sports Personality of 2005. **ECB central contract 2008-09. Tests**: 75 (1998 to 2008-09, 11 as captain); HS 167 v WI (Birmingham) 2004; BB 5-58 v WI (Bridgetown) 2003-04. **LOI**: 138 (1998-99 to 2008-09, 14 as captain); HS 123 v WI (Lord's) 2004; BB 5-56 v I (Bristol) 2007. F-c Tours (Eng) (C=Captain): A 2002-03 (*part*), 2006-07C; SA 1998-99 (Eng A), 1999-00, 2004-05; WI 2003-04, 2008-09; NZ 2001-02; I 2001-02, 2005-06C, 2008-09; P 2000-01 (*part*), 2005-06; SL 1997-98 (Eng A), 2003-04; Z 1998-99 (Eng A); K 1997-98 (Eng A). HS 167 (*see Tests*). La HS 160 v Yorks (Manchester) 1999. BB 5-24 v Hants (Southampton) 1999. LO HS 143 (off 66 balls) v Essex (Chelmsford) 1999 (NL). LO BB 5-56 (*see LOI*). IT20 HS 31. IT20 BB 2-23. T20 HS 85. T20 BB 4-12 v Durham (Chester-le-St) 2008 – La record.

HOGG, Kyle William (Saddleworth HS), b Birmingham, Warwks 2 Jul 1983. Son of W.Hogg (Lancashire and Warwickshire 1976-83); grandson of S.Ramadhin (Trinidad, Lancashire and West Indies 1949-50 to 1965). 6'4". LHB, RFM. Debut (Lancashire) 2001. Otago 2006-07. Worcestershire 2007 (on loan). Nottinghamshire 2007 (on loan). F-c Tour (ECB Acad): SL 2002-03. HS 71 Otago v CD (Napier) 2006-07. La HS 70 v Middlesex (Lord's) 2006. BB 5-48 v Leics (Manchester) 2002 – on CC debut. LO HS 66* v Scotland (Manchester) 2008 (FPT). LO BB 4-20 v Hants (Southampton) 2002 (NL). T20 HS 44. T20 BB 2-10.

HORTON, Paul James (St Margaret's HS, Liverpool), b Sydney, Australia 20 Sep 1982. 5'10". RHB, RM. UK resident since 1997. Debut (Lancashire) 2003; cap 2007. 1000 runs (2); most – 1116 (2007). HS 152 v Hants (Manchester) 2007 and 152 v Yorkshire (Leeds) 2008. LO HS 56 v Sussex (Hove) 2008 (P40). T20 HS 11.

KEEDY, Gary (Garforth CS), b Wakefield, Yorks 27 Nov 1974. 6'0". LHB, SLA. Yorkshire 1994 (one match). Lancashire debut 1995; cap 2000; benefit 2009. F-c Tour: WI 1995-96 (La). HS 64 v Sussex (Hove) 2008. 50 wkts (3); most – 72 (2004). BB 7-95 (14-227 match) v Glos (Manchester) 2004. LO HS 33 v Derbys (Derby) 2008. LO BB 5-30 v Sussex (Manchester) 2000 (NL). T20 HS 9*. T20 BB 4-15.

‡**KERRIGAN, Simon** Christopher, b Preston, 10 May 1989. RHB, SLA. Lancashire 2nd XI 2007-08. Awaiting 1st XI debut.

‡**NQLAXMAN, Vangipurapu** Venkata Sai (*'VVS'*), b Hyderabad, India 1 Nov 1974. 6'1". RHB, OB. Hyderabad 1992-93 to date. South Zone 1994-95 to date. Lancashire 2007. Otago 2008-09. *Wisden* 2001. **Tests** (I): 102 (1996-97 to 2008-09); HS 281 v A (Calcutta) 2000-01; BB 1-2 v P (Calcutta) 2007-08. **LOI** (I): 86 (1997-98 to 2006-07); HS 131 v Z (Adelaide) 2003-04; BB – . F-c Tours (I): E 2002, 2007; A 1999-00, 2003-04, 2007-08; SA 1996-97, 2001-02, 2006-07; WI 1996-97, 2001-02, 2002-03 (Ind A – Capt), 2006; NZ 1998-99, 2002-03, 2008-09; P 2003-04, 2005-06; SL 1998-99, 2008; Z 2001, 2005-06; B 2004-05. 1000 runs (0+4); most – 1432 (1999-00). HS 353 Hyderabad v Karnataka (Bangalore) 1999-00. La HS 103 v Warwks (Manchester) 2007. BB 3-11 Hyderabad v Railways (Delhi) 1999-00. La BB – . LO HS 131 (*see LOI*). LO BB 2-42 Hyderabad v Tamil Nadu (Madras) 2000-01. T20 HS 52.

LOYE, Malachy Bernhard (Moulton S), b Northampton 27 Sep 1972. 6'2". RHB, OB. Northamptonshire 1991-2002; cap 1994. PCA 1998. Lancashire 2007-08. Lancashire debut – scoring 126 v Surrey (Oval) and 113 v Notts (Manchester) in his first two innings; cap 2003; benefit 2008. Auckland 2006-07. **LOI**: 7 (2006-07); HS 45 v A (Sydney) 2006-07. F-c Tours (Eng A): SA 1993-94, 1998-99; Z 1994-95 (Nh), 1998-99. 1000 runs (6); most – 1296 (2006). HS 322* Nh v Glamorgan (Northampton) 1998 – record Northants score until 2001. La HS 200 v Durham (Chester-le-St) 2005. BB 1-8 v Kent (Blackpool) 2003. LO HS 127 v Durham (Manchester) 2006 (CGT). T20 HS 100.

MAHMOOD, Sajid Iqbal (North C, Bolton), b Bolton 21 Dec 1981. 6'4". RHB, RF. Debut (Lancashire) 2002; cap 2007. MCC 2005. **Tests**: 8 (2006 to 2006-07); HS 34 and BB 4-22 v P (Leeds) 2006. **LOI**: 25 (2004 to 2006-07); HS 22* v P (Birmingham) 2006; BB 4-50 v SL (North Shore, Antigua) 2006-07. F-c Tours (Eng A): A 2006-07 (Eng); WI 2005-06; NZ 2008-09; I 2003-04; SL 2004-05. HS 94 v Sussex (Manchester) 2004. BB 5-37 v DU (Durham) 2003. CC BB 5-52 v Sussex (Liverpool) 2006. LO HS 29 v Staffs (Stone) 2004 (CGT). LO BB 5-16 v Sri Lanka A (Liverpool) 2007. IT20 HS 0*. IT20 BB 1-34. T20 HS 21. T20 BB 3-12.

MULLANEY, Steven John (St Mary's RC S, Astley), b Warrington, Cheshire 19 Nov 1986. 5'9". RHB, RM. Debut (Lancashire) 2006. HS 165* v DU (Durham) 2007. CC HS 15 v Notts (Nottingham) 2008. LO HS 12 v Notts (Nottingham) 2007 (FPT). LO BB 3-13 v Derbys (Derby) 2007 (FPT). T20 HS 5.

NEWBY, Oliver James (Ribblesdale HS; Myerscough C), b Blackburn 26 Aug 1984. 6'5". RHB, RMF. Debut (Lancashire) 2003. Nottinghamshire 2005 (on loan). Gloucestershire (on loan); cap 2008. HS 38* Nt v Kent (Nottingham) 2005 – on Notts debut. La HS 26 v Warwks (Manchester) 2007. BB 5-69 Gs v Northants (Bristol) 2008. La BB 4-58 v Notts (Manchester) 2006. LO HS 7* (NL). LO BB 2-37 v Glos (Manchester) 2004 (NL). T20 HS 6*. T20 BB 2-34.

PARRY, Stephen David (Audenshaw HS), b Manchester 12 Jan 1986. 5'11". RHB, SLA. Debut (Lancashire) 2007 taking 5-23 v Durham UCCE (Durham). Awaiting CC debut; no 1st XI appearances in 2008. Cumberland 2005-06. HS – and BB 5-23 (*see above*).

‡**NQPRINCE, Ashwell** Gavin (St Thomas Senior SS, UPE), b 28 May 1977. LHB, OB. Debut Eastern Province 1995-96 to 1997-98. Western Province 1997-98 to 2003-04. Western Province Boland 2004-05. Cape Cobras 2005-06 to 2007-08. Nottinghamshire 2008. Warriors 2008-09. **Tests** (SA): 48 (2001-02 to 2008-09, 2 as captain); HS 162* v B (Centurion) 2008-09; BB 1-2 v NZ (Cape Town) 2006. **LOI** (SA): 49 (2002-03 to 2007); HS 89* v WI (Port of Spain) 2005; BB – . F-c Tours (SA): E 2008; A 2005-06; WI 2000 (SA A), 2005; I 2007-08; P 2007-08; SL 2006; Z 2007 (SA A); B 2007-08. HS 254 Warriors v Titans (Centurion) 2008-09; CC HS 57 Nt v Hampshire (Nottingham) 2008. BB 2-11 SA v Middlesex (Uxbridge) 2008; CC BB – . LO HS 89* (*see LOI*). LO BB – . IT20 HS 5. T20 HS 46. T20 BB – .

‡**SHANKAR, Adrian** (Bedford S; Queens C, Cambridge U), b Ascot, Berks 7 May 1982. RHB, OB. Cambridge U 2002-05; blue 2002-03-04-05. Bedfordshire 2000-06. Awaiting La 1st XI debut. HS 143 CU v OU (Oxford) 2002. LO HS 27 Beds v Sussex (Luton) 2005.

SMITH, Thomas Christopher (Parkland HS, Chorley; Runshaw C, Leyland), b Liverpool 26 Dec 1985. 6'3". LHB, RMF. Debut (Lancashire) 2005. Leicestershire (on loan) 2008. F-c Tour (Eng A): B 2006-07. HS 63 Le v Warwicks (Leicester) 2008. La HS 49 v Hants (Southampton) 2006. BB 4-57 v Yorks (Leeds) 2008. LO HS 52 Le v Yorkshire (Leeds) 2008 (P40). LO BB 3-8 v Leics (Manchester) 2006 (CGT). T20 HS 21. T20 BB 3-15.

SUTTON, Luke David (Millfield S; Durham U), b Keynsham, Somerset 4 Oct 1976. 5'11". RHB, WK. Somerset 1997-98. Derbyshire 2000-05; cap 2002; captain 2004-05. Lancashire debut 2006; cap 2007. HS 151* v Yorks (Manchester) 2006. LO HS 83 De v Lancs (Derby) 2003 (NL). T20 HS 61*.

RELEASED/RETIRED
(Having made a County First-Class or List A appearance in 2008)

CORK, D.G – *see HAMPSHIRE*.

NQHODGE, Bradley John (St Bede's C, Mentone; Deakin U), b Sandringham, Victoria, Australia 29 Dec 1974. 5'8". RHB, OB. Victoria 1993-94 to date. Durham 2002. Leicestershire 2003-04; cap 2003; captain 2004 (*part*). Lancashire 2005-08; cap 2006. **Tests** (A): 6 (2005-06 to 2008); HS 203* v SA (Perth) 2005-06. BB – . **LOI** (A): 25 (2005-06 to 2007-08); HS 123 v Holland (Basseterre, St Kitts) 2006-07; BB 1-17 v Scotland (Basseterre) 2006-07. F-c Tours (A): I 2004-05; WI 2008; P 2005-06 (Aus A); Z 1998-99 (Aus Acad). 1000 runs (2+3); most – 1548 (2004). HS 302* (Le) v Notts (Nottingham) 2003. La HS 161 v Middlesex (Lord's) 2006. BB 4-17 Aus A v WI (Hobart) 2000-01. CC BB 3-21 v Warwks (Birmingham) 2006. LO HS 164 Aus A v SA A (Perth) 2002-03. LO BB 5-28 Aus A v SA A (Canberra) 2002-03. IT20 HS 36. IT20 BB – . T20 HS 106. T20 BB 4-17.

LAW, Stuart Grant (Craigslea State HS), b Herston, Brisbane, Australia 18 Oct 1968. 6'1". RHB, RM/LBG. Queensland 1988-89 to 2003-04; captain 1994-95 to 1996-97, 1999-00 to 2001-02. Essex 1996-2001; cap 1996. Lancashire 2002-08; cap 2002; benefit 2007; captain 2008. Wisden 1997. PCA 1999. British Citizenship after 2004 season. **Tests** (A): 1 (1995-96); HS 54* v SL (Perth) 1995-96. **LOI** (A): 54 (1994-95 to 1998-99); HS 110 v Z (Hobart) 1994-95; BB 2-22 v P (Sydney) 1996-97. F-c Tours: E 1995 (Young A); Z 1991-92 (Aus B). 1000 runs (9+2); most – 1833 (1999). HS 263 Ex v Somerset (Chelmsford) 1999. La HS 236* v Warwks (Manchester) 2003. BB 5-39 Q v Tasmania (Brisbane) 1995-96. CC BB 3-27 Ex v Worcs (Chelmsford) 1997. La BB 1-24 v Yorks (Manchester) 2002. LO HS 163 Young A v Surrey (Oval) 1995. LO BB 5-26 Q v SL (Cairns) 1995-96. T20 HS 101.

RELEASED/RETIRED continued on p 66

LANCASHIRE 2008

RESULTS SUMMARY

	Place	Won	Lost	Tied	Drew	No Result
County Championship (1st Division)	5th	5	2		8	1
All First-Class Matches		5	2		9	1
FP Trophy (North Division)	4th	3	3			2
Pro40 League (1st Division)	8th	1	3			4
Twenty/20 Cup (North Division)	Quarter-Finalist	6	4			1

LV COUNTY CHAMPIONSHIP AVERAGES

BATTING AND FIELDING

Cap		M	I	NO	HS	Runs	Avge	100	50	Ct/St
2007	P.J.Horton	15	25	2	152	966	42.00	2	7	10
2002	S.G.Law	13	21	2	158*	704	37.05	1	4	11
	S.J.Croft	12	18	1	122	582	34.23	1	3	3
2002	M.J.Chilton	6	10	–	102	287	28.70	1	1	1
2007	L.D.Sutton	15	21	4	55	461	27.11	–	1	54/2
1994	G.Chapple	11	13	2	52*	288	26.18	–	1	4
	L.Vincent	6	12	1	83	272	24.72	–	2	6
	F.du Plessis	11	18	1	57	398	23.41	–	3	4
1998	A.Flintoff	5	8	2	62*	132	22.00	–	1	5
	K.R.Brown	3	4	1	40	55	18.33	–	–	1
2000	G.Keedy	13	18	4	64	243	17.35	–	1	2
2004	D.G.Cork	9	11	1	43	162	16.20	–	–	5
2003	I.J.Sutcliffe	7	11	–	50	164	14.90	–	1	3
2003	M.B.Loye	9	14	–	61	164	11.71	–	1	6
2007	S.I.Mahmood	12	15	4	33	113	10.27	–	–	3
	O.J.Newby	6	4	2	2	3	1.50	–	–	3

Also batted: J.M.Anderson (2 matches – cap 2003) 1*, 0, 0 (2 ct); B.J.Hodge (2 – cap 2006) 43*, 1 (1 ct); K.W.Hogg (1) 0, 33; S.J.Marshall (1) 29*; Moh'd Yousuf Youhana (2) 3, 40, 205*; S.J.Mullaney (1) 0, 15; T.C.Smith (3) 0, 13*, 29 (1 ct).

BOWLING

	O	M	R	W	Avge	Best	5wI	10wM
J.M.Anderson	56.5	15	142	11	12.90	5-46	1	–
G.Chapple	332.5	93	861	42	20.50	6-40	2	–
A.Flintoff	140.1	41	336	13	25.84	4-21	–	–
D.G.Cork	203	48	552	20	27.60	3-33	–	–
O.J.Newby	139.4	21	543	18	30.16	4 72	–	–
S.I.Mahmood	322.5	66	1147	35	32.77	5-76	1	–
S.J.Croft	154	24	557	16	34.81	4-51	–	–
G.Keedy	421.3	85	1157	28	41.32	5-56	1	–
F.du Plessis	110	11	341	7	48.71	3-61	–	–

Also bowled:

	O	M	R	W	Avge	Best		
T.C.Smith	79	21	195	7	27.85	3-28		

B.J.Hodge 10-2-26-2; K.W.Hogg 7-2-33-1; S.J.Marshall 38-5-159-2; S.J.Mullaney 5-2-19-0.

The First-Class Averages (pp 136–153) give the records of Lancashire players in all first-class county matches (Lancashire's other opponents being Durham UCCE), with the exception of A.Flintoff and O.J.Newby, whose first-class figures for Lancashire are as above, and:
J.M.Anderson 3-3-1-1*-1-0.50-0-0-3ct. 70.5-21-155-15-10.33-5/46-1-0.
T.C.Smith 4-4-2-29-67-33.50-0-0-3ct. 93-23-250-11-22.72-3/28-0-0.

LANCASHIRE RECORDS

FIRST-CLASS CRICKET

Highest Total	For 863		v	Surrey	The Oval	1990
	V 707-9d		by	Surrey	The Oval	1990
Lowest Total	For 25		v	Derbyshire	Manchester	1871
	V 22		by	Glamorgan	Liverpool	1924
Highest Innings	For 424	A.C.MacLaren	v	Somerset	Taunton	1895
	V 315*	T.W.Hayward	for	Surrey	The Oval	1898

Highest Partnership for each Wicket

1st	368	A.C.MacLaren/R.H.Spooner	v	Glos	Liverpool	1903
2nd	371	F.B.Watson/G.E.Tyldesley	v	Surrey	Manchester	1928
3rd	364	M.A.Atherton/N.H.Fairbrother	v	Surrey	The Oval	1990
4th	358	S.P.Titchard/G.D.Lloyd	v	Essex	Chelmsford	1996
5th	360	S.G.Law/C.L.Hooper	v	Warwicks	Birmingham	2003
6th	278	J.Iddon/H.R.W.Butterworth	v	Sussex	Manchester	1932
7th	248	G.D.Lloyd/I.D.Austin	v	Yorkshire	Leeds	1997
8th	158	J.Lyon/R.M.Ratcliffe	v	Warwicks	Manchester	1979
9th	142	L.O.S.Poidevin/A.Kermode	v	Sussex	Eastbourne	1907
10th	173	J.Briggs/R.Pilling	v	Surrey	Liverpool	1885

Best Bowling	For	10-46	W.Hickton	v	Hampshire	Manchester	1870
(Innings)	V	10-40	G.O.B.Allen	for	Middlesex	Lord's	1929
Best Bowling	For	17-91	H.Dean	v	Yorkshire	Liverpool	1913
(Match)	V	16-65	G.Giffen	for	Australians	Manchester	1886

Most Runs – Season	2633	J.T.Tyldesley	(av 56.02)		1901
Most Runs – Career	34222	G.E.Tyldesley	(av 45.20)		1909-36
Most 100s – Season	11	C.Hallows			1928
Most 100s – Career	90	G.E.Tyldesley			1909-36
Most Wkts – Season	198	E.A.McDonald	(av 18.55)		1925
Most Wkts – Career	1816	J.B.Statham	(av 15.12)		1950-68
Most Career W-K Dismissals	925	G.Duckworth	(635 ct/290 st)		1923-38
Most Career Catches in the Field	556	K.J.Grieves			1949-64

LIMITED-OVERS CRICKET

Highest Total	FPT	381-3		v	Herts	Radlett	1999
	P40	310-7		v	Somerset	Taunton	2003
	T20	217-4		v	Surrey	The Oval	2005
Lowest Total	FPT	59		v	Worcs	Worcester	1963
	P40	68		v	Yorkshire	Leeds	2000
		68		v	Surrey	The Oval	2002
	T20	91		v	Derbyshire	Manchester	2003
Highest Innings	FPT	162*	A.R.Crook	v	Bucks	Wormsley	2005
	P40	143	A.Flintoff	v	Essex	Chelmsford	1999
	T20	102*	L.Vincent	v	Derbyshire	Manchester	2008
Best Bowling	FPT	6-18	G.Chapple	v	Essex	Lord's	1996
	P40	6-25	G.Chapple	v	Yorkshire	Leeds	1998
	T20	4-12	A.Flintoff	v	Durham	Chester-le-St	2008

LEICESTERSHIRE

Formation of Present Club: 25 March 1879
Inaugural First-Class Match: 1894
Colours: Dark Green and Scarlet
Badge: Gold Running Fox on Green Ground
County Champions: (3) 1975, 1996, 1998
Gillette/NatWest/C&G/FP Trophy Winners: (0); best –
Finalist 1992, 2001
Benson and Hedges Cup Winners: (3) 1972, 1975, 1985
Pro 40/National League (Div 1) Winners: (0); best – 2nd
2001
Sunday League Champions: (2) 1974, 1977
Twenty20 Cup Winners: (2) 2004, 2006

Chief Executive: David Smith, County Ground, Grace Road, Leicester LE2 8AD • Tel:
0871 282 1879 • Fax: 0871 282 1873 • Email: enquiries@leicestershireccc.co.uk • Web:
www.leicestershireccc.co.uk

Senior Coach: Tim Boon. **Head Coach/Academy Director:** Phil Whitticase. **Captain:**
P.A.Nixon. **Vice-Captain:** tba. **Overseas Players:** I.E.O'Brien. **2009 Beneficiary:** none.
Head Groundsman: Andy Whiteman. **Scorer:** Graham A.York. ‡ New registration. NQ Not
qualified for England.

NQACKERMAN, Hylton Deon ('**HD**') (Rondebosch BHS), b Cape Town, South Africa
14 Feb 1973. 5'11". Son of H.M.Ackerman (Border, NE Transvaal, Northants, Natal, W
Province 1963-64 to 1981-82). RHB, RM. W Province 1993-94 to 2002-03. Gauteng
2003-04. Lions 2004-05. Leicestershire debut/captain/cap 2005 (Kolpak registration). Cape
Cobras 2005-06. Warriors 2006-07 to 2007-08. Dolphins 2008-09. **Tests** (SA): 4 (1997-98);
HS 57 v P (Durban) 1997-98 – on debut. F-c Tours (SA): E 1996 (SA A); A 1995-96 (WP);
SL 1995 (SA U-24), 1998; Z 1996-97 (WP). 1000 runs (3+1); most – 1808 (2006). HS 309*
v Glamorgan (Cardiff) 2006 – Le record f-c score. BB – . LO HS 139 v Northants
(Northampton) 2008 (FPT). BB – . T20 HS 87.

ALLENBY, James (Christ Church GS, Perth), b Perth, W Australia 12 Sep 1982. 6'0".
RHB, RM. Debut (Leicestershire) 2006. Western Australia (T20) 2006-07. HS 138* v
Bangladesh A (Leicester) 2008. CC HS 103* v Essex (Leicester) 2006. BB 5-125 v Glos
(Bristol) 2007 – his first five f-c wickets. LO HS 91* v Middlesex (Lord's) 2007 (P40). LO
BB 5-43 v Derbys (Leicester) 2007 (FPT). T20 HS 64. T20 BB 5-21 v Lancashire
(Manchester) 2008 – Le record T20 analysis and inc 4 wkts in 4 balls.

BOYCE, Matthew Andrew Golding (Oakham S; Nottingham U), b Cheltenham, Glos
13 Aug 1985. 5'9". LHB, RM. Debut (Leicestershire) 2006. HS 106 v Warwks (Birmingham) 2008. BB – . LO HS 59 v Essex (Leicester) 2008 (P40). T20 HS 31.

‡BUCK, Nathan Liam (Newbridge HS; Ashby S), b Leicester 26 Apr 1991. 6'2" RHB,
RMF. Leicestershire 2nd XI debut 2007. England U19s 2008-09. Awaiting 1st XI debut.

CLIFF, Samuel James (Colonel Frank Seely S, Calverton, Notts), b Nottingham 3 Oct
1987. 6'2". RHB, RMF. Debut (Leicestershire) 2007. HS 15 and BB 4-42 v Derbys
(Leicester) 2008. LO HS 0*. LO BB 4-26 v Derbys (Leicester) 2008 (P40). T20 HS – . T20
BB 1-24.

COBB, Joshua James (Oakham S), b Leicester 17 Aug 1990. 5'11½". Son of R.A.Cobb
(Leics and N Transvaal 1980-89). RHB, LB. Debut (Leicestershire) 2007. England U19s
2008-09. HS 148* v Middlesex (Lord's) 2008. BB 2-11 v Glos (Leicester) 2008. LO HS 28
v Derbys (Leicester) 2008 (P40). T20 HS 2*.

63

NQDIPPENAAR, Hendrik Human ('Boeta') (Grey C, Bloemfontein; UNISA), Kimberley, South Africa 14 Jun 1977. 5'10½". RHB, OB. Free State 1995-96 to 2003-04. Eagles 2004-05 to date. Leicestershire debut/cap 2008. Kolpak registration 2009. **Tests** (SA): 38 (1999-00 to 2006-07); HS 177* v B (Chittagong) 2002-03. **LOI** (SA): 101 (1999-00 to 2007); HS 125* v SL (Adelaide) 2005-06. F-c Tours (SA): C=Captain): E 2003; A 2001-02; WI 1996-97 (FS), 2000-01, 2004-05; I 2004-05, 2007-08C (SA A); P 2003-04; SL 2004, 2006; Z 1999-00, 2001-02, 2007C (SA A); B 2003. 1000 runs (0+1): 1070 (1998-99). HS 250* Eagles v Warriors (Kimberley) 2006-07. Le HS 84* v Derbys (Leicester) 2008. BB – . LO HS 125* (*see LOI*). LO BB – . IT20 HS 1. T20 HS 53.

NQDu TOIT, Jacques (Elspark S; Oosterlig C; Pretoria U), b Port Elizabeth, South Africa 2 Jan 1980. RHB, RMF. Easterns 1998-99 to 2004-05. Leicestershire debut 2008 (Kolpak registration). HS 103 v Northants (Leicester) 2008. BB 3-31 v Glos (Leicester) 2008. LO HS 144 v Glamorgan (Colwyn Bay) 2008 (P40). LO BB 2-30 Easterns v KZ-Natal (Benoni) 2004-05. T20 HS 25. T20 BB 2-15.

‡HARRIS, Andrew James (Hadfield CS; Glossopdale Community C), b Ashton-under-Lyne, Lancs 26 Jun 1973. 6'1". RHB, RM. Derbyshire 1994-99; cap 1996. Nottinghamshire 2000-08; cap 2000; benefit 2008. Gloucestershire (1 match) 2008. Worcestershire (2 matches) 2008. F-c Tour (Eng A): A 1996-97. HS 41* v Northants (Northampton) 2002. Dismissed 'Timed Out' v DU (Nottingham) 2003 – third instance in f-c cricket. 50 wkts (2); most – 67 (2002). BB 7-54 (11-122 match) v Northants (Nottingham) 2002. LO HS 34 v Durham (Nottingham) 2006 (CGT). LO BB 5-35 v Hants (Nottingham) 2000 (NL). T20 HS 6. T20 BB 2-13.

NQHENDERSON, Claude William (Worcester HS), b Worcester, Cape Province South Africa 14 Jun 1972. Elder brother of J.M.Henderson (Boland, Transvaal, North West, Free Ste and Eagles 1994-95 to 2005-06). 6'1½". RHB, SLA. Boland 1990-91 to 1997-98. W Province 1998-99 to 2003-04. Leicestershire debut/cap 2004 (the first Kolpak registration). Lions 2006-07 to 2007-08. Cape Cobras 2008-09. **Tests** (SA): 7 (2001-02 to 2002-03); HS 30 and BB 4-116 v A (Adelaide) 2001-02. **LOI** (SA): 4 (2001-02); HS – ; BB 4-17 v Z (Harare) 2001-02. F-c Tours (SA): A 2001-02; SL 1998 v Z) 2001-02. HS 81 v Glos (Leicester) 2007. BB 7-57 Boland v EP (Paarl) 1994-95. Le BB 7-74 v Durham (Leicester) 2004. LO HS 45 Lions v Eagles (Johannesburg) 2006-07. LO BB 6-29 Boland v Easterns (Paarl) 1997-98. T20 HS 16. T20 BB 3-23.

MALIK, Muhammad Nadeem (Wilford Meadows CS; Bilborough C), b Nottingham 6 Oct 1982. 6'5". RHB, RFM. Nottinghamshire 2001-03, 2007 – on loan. Worcestershire 2004-07. Leicestershire debut 2008, taking 5-51 (8-119 match) v Middlesex (Leicester). Notts 2nd XI debut 1999 when aged 16y 337d. HS 41 v Essex (Leicester) 2008. BB 6-46 v Essex (Chelmsford) 2008. LO HS 11 Nt v Worcs (Nottingham) 2002 (NL). LO BB 4-42 Wo v Sussex (Worcester) 2004 (NL). T20 HS 3*. T20 BB 4-16.

NAIK, Jigar Kumar Hakumatrai (Rushey Mead SS; Gateway SFC; Nottingham Trent U; Loughborough U), b Leicester 10 Aug 1984. 6'2". RHB, OB. Debut (Leicestershire) 2006. Loughborough UCCE 2007. HS 15 LU v Yorks (Leeds) 2007. Le HS 15 and CC BB 1-58 v Middlesex (Southgate) 2007. BB 3-70 v Bangladesh A (Leicester) 2008. LO HS 13 v Surrey (Oval) 2008 (P40). LO BB 3-24 v Glamorgan (Leicester) 2007 (P40). T20 HS 3*. T20 BB 1-18.

NEW, Thomas James (Quarrydale S), b Sutton in Ashfield, Notts 18 Jan 1985. 5'10". LHB, RM, WK. Debut (Leicestershire) 2004. Derbyshire 2008 – on loan. HS 125 v OU (Oxford) 2007. CC HS 109 v Middlesex (Leicester) 2008. BB 2-18 v Glos (Leicester) 2007. LO HS 68 v Northants (Oakham) 2006 (CGT). T20 HS 18.

NIXON, Paul Andrew (Ullswater HS, Penrith), b Carlisle, Cumberland 21 Oct 1970. 6'0". LHB, WK, occ RM. Leicestershire 1989-99, 2003 to date; cap 1994; benefit 2007; captain 2007 (*part*) to date. MCC 1999-00. Kent 2000-02; cap 2000. Cumberland 1987. **LOI**: 19 (2006-07); HS 49 v NZ (Perth) 2006-07. F-c Tours: SA 1996-97 (Le); I 1994-95 (Eng A); P 2000-01; B 1999-00 (MCC). 1000 runs (1): 1046 (1994). HS 144* v Northants (Northampton) 2006. LO HS 101 v Sri Lanka A (Galle) 1998-99. IT20 HS 65. T20 HS 65.

‡^{NQ}**O'BRIEN, Iain** Edward, b Lower Hutt, Wellington, New Zealand 10 Jul 1976. RHB, RFM. Wellington 2000-01 to date. **Tests** (NZ): 14 (2004-05 to 2008-09); HS 14* v SA (Johannesburg) 2007-08; BB 6-75 v WI (Napier) 2008-09. **LOI** (NZ): 10 (2007-08 to 2008-09); HS 3* v I (Napier) 2008-09; BB 3-68 v A (Sydney) 2008-09. F-c Tours (NZ): E 2008; A 2008-09; SA 2007-08; SL 2005-06 (NZ A); B 2008-09. HS 44 Wellington v Canterbury (Wellington) 2006-07. BB 8-55 (13-117 match) Wellington v Auckland (Wellington) 2006-07. LO HS 19* Wellington v Canterbury (Christchurch) 2008-09. LO BB 5-35 Wellington v CD (Wellington) 2004-05. IT20 HS – . IT20 BB 2-30. T20 HS 1*. T20 BB 3-21.

POPE, Joel Ian (Whitton S), b Ashford, Middlesex 23 Oct 1988. Nephew of B.J.M.Scott (*see MIDDLESEX*). 5'6". RHB, WK. Middlesex 2nd XI 2006. MCC YC 2007. Leicestershire 2nd XI debut 2007. Awaiting f-c debut. LO HS 9 v Derbys (Leicester) 2008 (P40) – on debut.

SMITH, Gregory Philip (Oundle S; St Hild & St Bede C, Durham U), b Leicester 16 Nov 1988. 6'0". RHB, LBG. Debut (Leicestershire) 2008. England U19s 2008. HS 54 v Derbys (Leicester) 2008. BB 1-64 v Glos (Leicester) 2008. LO HS 58 v Surrey (Oval) 2008 (P40).

TAYLOR, James William (Shrewsbury S), b Nottingham 6 Jan 1990. 5'5". RHB, LB. Debut (Leicestershire) 2008. Worcs 2nd XI 2006-07. Shropshire 2007. England U19s 2007-08 to 2008-09. HS 51 v Bangladesh A (Leicester) 2008. CC HS 8 v Worcs (Worcester) 2008. LO HS 43* v Derbys (Leicester) 2008 (P40). T20 HS 22.

‡**WYATT, Alexander** Charles Frederick (Oakham S), b Roehampton 23 Jul 1990. 6'7". RHB, RMF. Awaiting f-c debut. Leicestershire 2nd XI debut 2007.

RELEASED/RETIRED
(Having made a County First-Class or List A appearance in 2008)

CUMMINS, R.A.G. – *see NORTHAMPTONSHIRE*.

^{NQ}**Du PREEZ, Dillon** (HTS Louis Botha), b Queenstown, Cape Province, South Africa 8 Nov 1981. RHB, RMF. Free State 2003-04 to 2005-06. Eagles 2004-05 to date. Leicestershire 2008 (Kolpak registration). HS 122 Eagles v Cape Cobras (Cape Town) 2007-08. Le HS 22 v Glamorgan (Cardiff) 2008. BB 7-108 Eagles v Titans (Benoni) 2007-08. Le BB 5-48 v Glamorgan (Leicester) 2008. LO HS 107* v Yorkshire (Leeds) 2008. LO BB 4-22 Eagles v Warriors (Port Elizabeth) 2007-08. T20 HS 40*. T20 BB 3-25.

KRUGER, G.J-P. – *see GLAMORGAN*.

^{NQ}**LAWSON, Jermaine** Jay Charles, b Spanish Town, St Catherine, Jamaica 13 Jan 1982. 6'8". RHB, RFM. Jamaica 2001-02 to date. Leicestershire 2008. **Tests** (WI): 13 (2002-03 to 2005-06; HS 14 and BB 7-78 v A (St John's) 2002-03. Took 6-3 v B (Dhaka) 2002-03. Hat-trick v B (Bridgetown) 2002-03. **LOI** (WI): 13 (2001-02 to 2005); HS 8 v SL (Dambulla) 2005; BB 4-57 v I (Vijawada) 2002-03. F-c Tours (WI): E 2002 (WI A), 2004; A 2005-06; I 2002-03; SL 2005; B 2002-03. HS 35 v Northants (Leicester) 2008. BB 7-78 (*see Tests*). Le BB 1-41 v Middlesex (Leicester) 2008. LO HS 8 (*see LOI*). LO BB 5-66 Jamaica v Barbados (Kingston) 2006-07. T20 HS – . T20 BB 3-29.

MALCOLM-HANSEN, Richard Johan Anders, b Farnborough, Kent 22 Apr 1986. RHB, OB. Loughborough UCCE 2007-08. Leicestershire 2008. Kent 2nd XI 2003-07. Denmark 2005 to 2007-08. HS 93 LU v Surrey (Oval) 2008. Le HS 20* v Glos (Cheltenham) 2008. BB 1-40 LU v Worcs (Kidderminster) 2008. CC BB – . LO HS 71 Denmark v Uganda (Muckamore) 2005. LO BB 3-38 v Bermuda (Greenisland) 2005.

NEW, T.J. – *see DERBYSHIRE.*

ROWE, Daniel Thomas (Archbishop McGrath S; Glamorgan U, Cardiff), b Ogwr, Glamorgan 22 Mar 1984. 6'0". RHB, RM. Leicestershire 2006-08. Cardiff UCCE 2004-06 (not f-c). HS 85 v Essex (Leicester) 2007. BB 5-61 v OU (Oxford) 2007. CC BB 2-27 v Essex (Leicester) 2007. LO HS 17 v Warwks (Leicester) 2008 (P40). LO BB 1-26 v Derbys (Leicester) 2006 (P40). T20 HS 11*. T20 BB 1-26.

SNAPE, Jeremy Nicholas (Denstone C; Durham U), b Stoke-on-Trent, Staffs 27 Apr 1973. 5'8½". RHB, OB. Northamptonshire 1992-97. Combined U 1993-94. Gloucestershire 1999-2002; cap 1999. Leicestershire 2003-06; cap 2006; captain 2006-07 (*part*). No f-c appearances 2007. Limited-Overs contract 2008. **LOI**: 10 (2001-02 to 2002-03); HS 38 v I (Madras) 2001-02; BB 3-43 v Z (Bulawayo) 2001-02. F-c Tour: Z 1994-95 (Nh). HS 131 Gs v Sussex (Cheltenham) 2001. Le HS 90 v Derbys (Leicester) 2006. BB 5-65 Nh v Durham (Northampton) 1995. Le BB 3-108 v Surrey (Leicester) 2003. LO HS 104* Gs v Notts (Nottingham) 2001 (NL). LO BB 5-32 Nh v Leics (Northampton) 1997 (BHC). IT20 HS 7. IT20 BB – . T20 HS 47*. T20 BB 4-22 – took 3-6, including T20 hat-trick, v Yorks (Leicester) 2007.

E.J.Foster and H.F.Gurney left the staff, without making a County First-Class or List A appearance in 2008.

LANCASHIRE RELEASED/RETIRED (continued from p 60)

MARSHALL, Simon James (Birkenhead S; Pembroke C, Cambridge), b Arrowe Park, Wirral, Cheshire 20 Sep 1982. 6'3". RHB, LB. Cambridge U 2002-04; blue 2002-03-04. British U 2004. Lancashire 2005-08. Cheshire 2001-03. Hockey blue. HS 126* CU v OU (Cambridge) 2003. La HS 35* v OU (Oxford) 2005. CC HS 29* v Somerset (Manchester) 2008. BB 6-128 CU v Essex (Cambridge) 2002. La BB 2-23 v OU (Oxford) 2005 – on La debut. CC BB 1-8. LO HS 22 v Warwks (Manchester) 2007 (FPT). LO BB 3-36 v Durham (Manchester) 2006 (CGT) and 3-36 v Warwks (Birmingham) 2007 (P40). T20 HS 47. T20 BB 4-20.

SUTCLIFFE, Iain John (Leeds GS; Queen's C, Oxford), b Leeds, Yorks 20 Dec 1974. 6'2". LHB, occ LB. Oxford U 1994-96; blue 1995-96; boxing blue 1993-94. Leicestershire 1995-2002; cap 1997. Combined/British U 1995-96. Lancashire 2003-08; cap 2003. Northamptonshire 2007 (on loan). F-c Tour (Le): SA 1996-97. 1000 runs (3); most – 1088 (2002). HS 203 Le v Glamorgan (Cardiff) 2001. La HS 159 v Warwks (Blackpool) 2006. BB 2-21 OU v CU (Lord's) 1996. CC BB (Le) 1-7. La BB 1-11. LO HS 105* Le v Notts (Nottingham) 1998 (BHC). T20 HS 4.

[NQ]**YOUSUF YOUHANA, Mohammad,** b Lahore, Pakistan 27 Aug 1974. RHB. Debut 1996-97. Bahawalpur 1996-97. Lahore 1997-98 to 2003-04. WAPDA 1997-98 to 2006-07. PIA 2001-02. Punjab 2007-08. Lancashire 2008. *Wisden* 2007. **Tests** (P): 79 (1997-98 to 2007-08, 3 as captain); HS 223 v E (Lahore) 2005-06. BB – . **LOI** (P): 262 (1997-98 to 2008, 4 as captain); HS 141* v Z (Bulawayo) 2000-01; BB 1-0 v Z (Kingston) 2006-07. Tours (P): E 2001, 2006; A 1999-00, 2004-05; WI 1999-00, 2004-05; SA 1997-98, 2002-03, 2006-07; NZ 2000-01, 2003-04; I 1998-99, 2004-05, 2007-08; SL 2000-01, 2006; Z 1997-98, 2002-03; B 2001-02. HS 223 (*see Tests*). La HS 205* v Yorkshire (Leeds) 2008. LO HS 141* (*see LOI*). LO BB 1-0 (*see LOI*). IT20 HS 20. T20 HS 30. T20 BB – .

LEICESTERSHIRE 2008

RESULTS SUMMARY

	Place	Won	Lost	Tied	Drew	No Result
County Championship (2nd Division)	7th	3	4		9	
All First-Class Matches		3	4		10	
FP Trophy (Midlands Division)	Quarter-Finalist	5	3			1
Pro40 League (2nd Division)	7th	1	4	1		2
Twenty/20 Cup (North Division)	6th	2	7			1

LV COUNTY CHAMPIONSHIP AVERAGES

BATTING AND FIELDING

Cap		M	I	NO	HS	Runs	Avge	100	50	Ct/St
	J.J.Cobb	7	10	3	148*	419	59.85	1	2	5
2005	H.D.Ackerman	16	26	3	199	1302	56.60	6	3	12
1994	P.A.Nixon	16	24	6	106*	954	53.00	1	6	53/1
	T.C.Smith	5	8	1	63	228	32.57	–	1	3
	M.A.G.Boyce	16	25	1	106	648	27.00	1	4	2
	J.du Toit	10	16	–	103	399	24.93	1	1	6
2008	H.H.Dippenaar	11	17	1	84*	383	23.93	–	3	19
	J.Allenby	16	22	2	72*	448	22.40	–	3	16
2004	C.W.Henderson	16	21	4	66	349	20.52	–	4	2
	G.P.Smith	5	9	–	54	180	20.00	–	1	2
	T.J.New	9	15	–	109	258	17.20	1	–	10
	D.du Preez	10	13	3	22	122	12.20	–	–	1
	M.N.Malik	15	20	5	41	178	11.86	–	–	2
	G.J.P.Kruger	10	12	1	7	39	3.54	–	–	1
	J.W.A.Taylor	3	4	–	8	13	3.25	–	–	4

Also batted: S.J.Cliff (2 matches) 8, 1, 15; R.A.G.Cummins (2) 22, 22 (2 ct); L.M.Daggett (1) 8*; J.J.C.Lawson (2) 0, 35 (1 ct); R.J.A.Malcolm-Hansen (2) 1, 20*; D.T.Rowe (2) 1, 1.

BOWLING

	O	M	R	W	Avge	Best	5wI	10wM
D.du Preez	272.3	73	730	32	22.81	5-48	1	–
J.Allenby	267.4	68	729	26	28.03	4-40	–	–
G.J.P.Kruger	300.1	59	970	32	30.31	5-47	2	–
C.W.Henderson	545.3	158	1294	41	31.56	5-39	1	–
M.N.Malik	466.5	86	1475	42	35.11	6-46	3	–
T.C.Smith	153.2	40	424	11	38.54	3-49	–	–
Also bowled:								
S.J.Cliff	51.3	16	152	8	19.00	4-42	–	–
R.A.G.Cummins	84.2	16	268	7	38.28	3-73	–	–

M.A.G.Boyce 6-0-61-0; J.J.Cobb 19-3-85-4; L.M.Daggett 23-4-82-3; J.du Toit 18-1-83-4; J.J.C.Lawson 38-6-188-2; R.J.A.Malcolm-Hansen 18-7-45-0; T.J.New 2-0-7-1; P.A.Nixon 5-0-41-0; D.T.Rowe 32-6-160-2; G.P.Smith 5-0-64-1.

The First-Class Averages (pp 136–153) give the records of Leicestershire players in all first-class county matches (Leicestershire's other opponents being Bangladesh A), with the exception of L.M.Daggett and R.J.A.Malcolm-Hansen, whose first-class figures for Leicestershire are as above, and:
   T.J.New 10-17-2-109-349-23.26-1-0-14ct. 2-0-7-1-7.00-1/7-0-0.
   T.C.Smith 6-8-1-63-228-32.57-0-1-4ct. 173.2-44-497-13-38.23-3/49-0-0.

LEICESTERSHIRE RECORDS

FIRST-CLASS CRICKET

Highest Total	For 701-4d		v	Worcs	Worcester	1906
	V 761-6d		by	Essex	Chelmsford	1990
Lowest Total	For 25		v	Kent	Leicester	1912
	V 24		by	Glamorgan	Leicester	1971
	24		by	Oxford U	Oxford	1985
Highest Innings	For 309*	H.D.Ackerman	v	Glamorgan	Cardiff	2006
	V 341	G.H.Hirst	for	Yorkshire	Leicester	1905

Highest Partnership for each Wicket

1st	390	B.Dudleston/J.F.Steele	v	Derbyshire	Leicester	1979
2nd	289*	J.C.Balderstone/D.I.Gower	v	Essex	Leicester	1981
3rd	436*	D.L.Maddy/B.J.Hodge	v	L'boro UCCE	Leicester	2003
4th	290*	P.Willey/T.J.Boon	v	Warwicks	Leicester	1984
5th	322	B.F.Smith/P.V.Simmons	v	Notts	Worksop	1998
6th	284	P.V.Simmons/P.A.Nixon	v	Durham	Chester-le-St	1996
7th	219*	J.D.R.Benson/P.Whitticase	v	Hampshire	Bournemouth	1991
8th	172	P.A.Nixon/D.J.Millns	v	Lancashire	Manchester	1996
9th	160	R.T.Crawford/W.W.Odell	v	Worcs	Leicester	1902
10th	228	R.Illingworth/K.Higgs	v	Northants	Leicester	1977

Best Bowling	For 10- 18	G.Geary	v	Glamorgan	Pontypridd	1929
(Innings)	V 10- 32	H.Pickett	for	Essex	Leyton	1895
Best Bowling	For 16- 96	G.Geary	v	Glamorgan	Pontypridd	1929
(Match)	V 16-102	C.Blythe	for	Kent	Leicester	1909

Most Runs – Season		2446	L.G.Berry	(av 52.04)	1937
Most Runs – Career		30143	L.G.Berry	(av 30.32)	1924-51
Most 100s – Season		7	L.G.Berry		1937
		7	W.Watson		1959
		7	B.F.Davison		1982
Most 100s – Career		45	L.G.Berry		1924-51
Most Wkts – Season		170	J.E.Walsh	(av 18.96)	1948
Most Wkts – Career		2131	W.E.Astill	(av 23.18)	1906-39
Most Career W-K Dismissals		905	R.W.Tolchard	(794 ct/111 st)	1965-83
Most Career Catches in the Field		426	M.R.Hallam		1950-70

LIMITED-OVERS CRICKET

Highest Total	FPT	406-5		v	Berkshire	Leicester	1996
	P40	344-4		v	Durham	Chester-le-St	1996
	T20	221-3		v	Yorkshire	Leeds	2004
Lowest Total	FPT	56		v	Northants	Leicester	1964
	P40	36		v	Sussex	Leicester	1973
	T20	97-9 (20)		v	Durham	Leicester	2004
		105		v	Lancashire	Leicester	2008
Highest Innings	FPT	201	V.J.Wells	v	Berkshire	Leicester	1996
	P40	154*	B.J.Hodge	v	Sussex	Horsham	2004
	T20	111	D.L.Maddy	v	Yorkshire	Leeds	2004
Best Bowling	FPT	6-16	C.M.Willoughby	v	Somerset	Leicester	2005
	P40	6-17	K.Higgs	v	Glamorgan	Leicester	1973
	T20	5-21	J.Allenby	v	Lancashire	Manchester	2008

MIDDLESEX

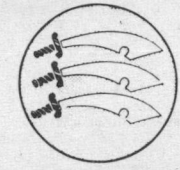

Formation of Present Club: 2 February 1864
Inaugural First-Class Match: 1864
Colours: Blue
Badge: Three Seaxes
County Champions (since 1890): (10) 1903, 1920, 1921, 1947, 1976, 1980, 1982, 1985, 1990, 1993
Joint Champions: (2) 1949, 1977
Gillette/NatWest/C&G/FP Trophy Winners: (4) 1977, 1980, 1984, 1988
Benson and Hedges Cup Winners: (2) 1983, 1986
Pro 40/National League (Div 1) Winners: (0); best – 1st (Div 2) 2004
Sunday League Winners: (1) 1992
Twenty20 Cup Winners: (1) 2008

Secretary: Vincent J.Codrington, Lord's Cricket Ground, London NW8 8QN • Tel: 020 7289 1300 • Fax: 020 7289 5831 • Email: enquiries@middlesexccc.com • Web: www.middlesexccc.com

Head Coach: Toby A.Radford. **Assistant Coach:** Richard J.Scott. **Captain:** S.D.Udal. **Vice-Captain:** E.C.Joyce. **Overseas Player:** P.J.Hughes and M.Kartik. **2009 Beneficiary:** A.J.Strauss. **Head Groundsman:** Mick Hunt. **Scorer:** Don K.Shelley. ‡ New registration. NQ Not qualified for England.

NQBERG, Gareth Kyle (South African College S), b Cape Town, South Africa 18 Jan 1981. 6'0". RHB, RMF. Debut (Middlesex) 2008. Western Province Academy (1999-00) and WP B (2001-02 to 2002-03). Northants 2nd XI 2004. Middlesex 2nd XI 2007 (Kolpak registration). HS 35 and BB 3-38 v Essex (Lord's) 2008. LO HS 65 v Surrey (Lord's) 2008 (FPT). LO BB 4-50 v Surrey (Oval) 2008.

COMPTON, Nicholas Richard Denis (Harrow S; Durham U), b Durban, South Africa 26 Jun 1983. 6'1". Son of R.Compton (Natal 1978-79 to 1980-81). Grandson of D.C.S.Compton (Middlesex, England, Holkar, Europeans, Commonwealth and Cavaliers 1936-64); great-nephew of L.H.Compton (Middlesex 1938-56). RHB, OB. Debut (Middlesex) 2004; cap 2006. MCC 2007. F-c Tour (Eng A): B 2006-07. 1000 runs (1): 1315 (2006). HS 190 v Durham (Lord's) 2006. BB 1-94 v Sussex (Southgate) 2007. LO HS 110* v Sussex (Lord's) 2007 (FPT). LO BB – . T20 HS 50*.

‡NQDEXTER, Neil John (Northwood HS; Varsity C; U of South Africa), b Johannesburg, South Africa 21 Aug 1984. 6'0". RHB, RM. Kent 2005-08. Essex 2008. HS 131* K v Notts (Canterbury) 2006. BB 2-40 K v Lancs (Manchester) 2006. LO HS 135* K v Glamorgan (Cardiff) 2006 (CGT). LO BB 3-17 K v Leics (Canterbury) 2006 (P40). T20 HS 46. T20 BB 3-27.

EVANS, Daniel (Brierton CS, Hartlepool), b Hartlepool, Co Durham 24 Jul 1987. 6'5". RHB, RFM. Debut (Middlesex) 2007. Durham 2nd XI 2004-06. HS 12* v Worcs (Lord's) 2008. BB 6-35 v Essex (Chelmsford) 2008. LO HS – . LO BB 3-36 v Surrey (Oval) 2008.

FINN, Steven Thomas (Parmiter's S, Garston), b Watford, Herts 4 Apr 1989. 6'5½". RHB, RFM. Debut (Middlesex) 2005. HS 26 v Worcs (Kidderminster) 2008. BB 4-51 v Glos (Bristol) 2007. LO HS 4 v Hampshire (Lord's) 2008 (P40). LO BB 3-23 v Somerset (Taunton) 2007 (P40). T20 HS 6*. T20 BB 3-22

GODLEMAN, Billy Ashley (Islington Green S), b Islington, London 11 Feb 1989. 6'3". LHB, LB. Debut (Middlesex) 2005. HS 113* v Somerset (Taunton) 2007 – on CC debut. BB – . LO HS 48 v Worcs (Kidderminster) 2008 (P40). T20 HS 69.

NOHENDERSON, Tyron (Durban HS), b Durban, Natal, South Africa 1 Aug 1974. Grandson of J.K.Henderson (N.E.Transvaal 1950-51). Great nephew of W.A.Henderson (N.E.Transvaal 1937-38 to 1946-47). 6'2". RHB, RFM. Border 1998-99 to 2003-04. Warriors 2004-05 to 2005-06. Kent 2006. Lions 2006-07. Cape Cobras 2007-08. Boland 2007-08. Middlesex 2008 – awaiting f-c debut; cap 2008 (Kolpak registration). Berkshire 2002-03. F-c Tours (SA A): SL 2005-06; Ire/Scot 1999 (SA Acad). HS 81 Border v Gauteng (Johannesburg) 1999-00. UK HS 59 K v Hampshire (Canterbury) 2006. BB 7-67 (10-115 match) Boland v WP (Paarl) 2007-08. UK BB 5-44 SA Acad v Scotland (Linlithgow) 1999. CC BB 4-29 K v Lancashire (Canterbury) 2006. LO HS 126* Border v GW (Kimberley) 2003-04. LO BB 5-5 Border v WP (E London) 1998-99. IT20 HS 0. IT20 BB – . T20 HS 85. T20 BB 4-29.

‡HOUSEGO, Daniel Mark (Oratory S, Reading), b Windsor, Berkshire 12 Oct 1988. RHB, LB. Debut (Middlesex) 2008. Middlesex 2nd XI debut 2005. Berkshire 2006. England U19s 2007. HS 36 v Derbys (Derby) 2008 – on debut. T20 HS 18.

‡NOHUGHES, Phillip Joel, Macksville NSW, Australia 30 Nov 1988. LHB. NSW 2007-08 to date. Joins Middlesex for part of 2009. **Tests** (A): 3 (2008-09); HS 160 v SA (Durban) 2008-09 – in his 2nd Test, also scored 115 in same match. F-c Tours (A): Sa 2008-09; I 2008-09 (Aus A). HS 198 NSW v S Australia (Adelaide) 2007-08. LO HS 68 NSW v Victoria (Melbourne) 2007-08 – on l-o debut. T20 HS 80*.

NOKARTIK, Murali (educated in New Delhi), b Madras, India 11 Sep 1976. 6'0". LHB, SLA. Railways 1996-97 to date. Central Zone 1997-98 to date. Lancashire 2005-06. Middlesex debut/cap 2007. **Tests** (I): 8 (1999-00 to 2004-05); HS 43 v B (Dhaka) 2000-01; BB 4-44 v A (Bombay) 2004-05. **LOI** (I): 37 (2001-02 to 2007-08); HS 32* v A (Perth) 2003-04; BB 6-27 v A (Bombay) 2007-08. F-c Tours (Ind A): E 2003; A 2003-04 (Ind); SA 2001-02; WI 1999-00, 2002-03; P 1997-98; SL 2002; B 2000-01 (Ind). HS 96 Railways v Rest of India (Delhi) 2005-06. CC HS 44 v Warwks (Uxbridge) 2008. 50 wkts (1): 51 (2007). BB 9-70 Rest of India v Bombay (Bombay) 2000-01. CC BB 6-21 v Glamorgan (Lord's) 2007. LO HS 44 Railways v Rajasthan (Indore) 2008-09. LO BB 6-27 (see LOI). IT20 HS – . IT20 BB – . T20 HS 1*. T20 BB 5-13.

‡LONDON, Adam Brian, b Ashford 12 Oct 1988. LHB, OB. Middlesex 2nd XI debut 2006 – awaiting 1st XI debut.

MALAN, Dawid Johannes (Paarl HS), b Roehampton, Surrey 3 Sep 1987. Son of D.J.Malan (WP B and Transvaal B 1978-79 to 1981-82). LHB, LB. Boland 2005-06. MCC YC 2006-07. Middlesex debut 2008. HS 132* and BB 2-26 v Northants (Uxbridge) 2008 – on M debut. LO HS 42 Boland v EP (Port Elizabeth) 005-06. LO BB 1-24 v Worcs (Kidderminster) 2008. T20 HS 103 v Lancashire (Oval) 2008 – record M score. T20 BB 2-11.

NOMORGAN, Eoin Joseph Gerard (Catholic University S), b Dublin, Ireland 10 Sep 1986. 6'0". LHB, RM. British passport. Ireland 2004 to date. Middlesex debut 2006; cap 2008. **LOI** (Ire): 21 (2006 to 2007-08); HS 115 v Canada (Nairobi) 2006-07. F-c Tours (Ire): NZ 2008-09 (Eng A); Namibia 2005-06; UAE 2006-07. 1000 runs (1): 1085 (2008). HS 209* Ire v UAE (Abu Dhabi) 2006-07. CC HS 137* v Glos (Bristol) 2008. BB 2-24 v Notts (Lord's) 2007. LO HS 115 (see LOI). LO BB – . T20 HS 66.

MURTAGH, Timothy James (John Fisher S; St Mary's C), b Lambeth, London 2 Aug 1981. Elder brother of C.P.Murtagh (see SURREY); nephew of A.J.Murtagh (Hampshire and E Province 1973-77). 6'0". LHB, RFM. British U 2000-03. Surrey 2001-06. Middlesex debut 2007; cap 2008. HS 74* Sy v Middlesex (Oval) 2004 and 74* Sy v Warwks (Croydon) 2005. M HS 49 v OU (Oxford) 2008. 50 wkts (1): 64 (2008). BB 7-95 v Glamorgan (Lord's) 2008. LO HS 35* v Surrey (Lord's) 2008 (FPT). LO BB 4-14 Sy v Derbys (Derby) 2005 (NL). T20 HS 40*. T20 BB 6-24 Sy v Middlesex (Lord's) 2005 – Sy record and 2nd best UK figs.

NASH, David Charles (Sunbury Manor S; Malvern C), b Chertsey, Surrey 19 Jan 1978. 5'8". RHB, occ LB, WK. Debut (Middlesex) 1997; cap 2000; benefit 2007. F-c Tour (Eng A): SL 1997-98. HS 114 v Somerset (Lord's) 1998. BB 1-8 v Essex (Chelmsford) 1997. LO HS 67 v Sussex (Lord's) 2002 (BHC).

RICHARDSON, Alan (Alleyne's HS, Stone; Stafford CFE; Durham U), b Newcastle-under-Lyme, Staffs 6 May 1975. 6'2". RHB, RMF. Derbyshire 1995 (one match). Warwickshire 1999-2004; cap 2002. Middlesex debut/cap 2005, taking 7-113 v Notts (Lord's) on debut. Staffordshire 1996-98. Minor Counties 1998. HS 91 Wa v Hants (Birmingham) 2002 – adding 214 for 10th wicket with N.V.Knight. M HS 26 v Leics (Lord's) 2008. 50 wkts (1): 57 (2005). BB 8-46 Wa v Sussex (Birmingham) 2002. M BB 7-113 (*see above*). LO HS 21* v Lancs (Lord's) 2005 (NL). LO BB 5-35 Wa v Staffs (Stone) 2002 (CGT). T20 HS 6*. T20 BB 3-13.

‡**ROBSON, Sam** David, b Paddington, Sydney, NSW, Australia 1 Jul 1989. RHB, LBG. Middlesex 2nd XI debut 2008. Australia U19s 2007 to 2007-08. Awaiting f-c debut. LO HS 21 v Worcs (Kidderminster) 2008 – only game.

SCOTT, Ben James Matthew (Whitton S, Richmond; Richmond C), b Isleworth, Middlesex 4 Aug 1981. Uncle of J.I.Pope (*see LEICESTERSHIRE*). 5'8". RHB, WK. Surrey 2003. Middlesex debut 2004; cap 2007. MCC YC 2000. F-c Tour (Eng A): NZ 2008-09. HS 164* v Northants (Uxbridge) 2008. BB – . LO HS 73* v Surrey (Southgate) 2006 (CGT). T20 HS 32*.

SHAH, Owais Alam (Isleworth & Syon S), b Karachi, Pakistan 22 Oct 1978. 6'0". RHB, OB. Debut (Middlesex) 1996; cap 2000; captain 2004 (*part*); benefit 2008. MCC 2002-08. YC 2001. **Tests**: 6 (2005-06 to 2008-09); HS 88 v I (Bombay) 2005-06. **LOI**: 52 (2001 to 2008-09); HS 107* v India (Oval) 2007; BB 1-18 v SL (Colombo) 2007-08. F-c Tours (Eng A): A 1996-97; WI 2005-06 (*part*), 2008-09 (Eng); I 2005-06 (Eng – *part*); SL 1997-98, 2004-05, 2007-08 (Eng). 1000 runs (8); most – 1728 (2005). HS 203 v Derbys (Southgate) 2001. BB 3-33 v Glos (Bristol) 1999. LO HS 134 v Sussex (Arundel) 1999 (NL). LO BB 2-2 v Glamorgan (Cardiff) 1998 (BHC). IT20 HS 55*. T20 HS 79. T20 BB 1-10.

SILVERWOOD, Christopher Eric Wilfred (Garforth CS), b Pontefract, Yorks 5 Mar 1975. 6'1". RHB, RFM. Yorkshire 1993-2005; cap 1996; benefit 2004. MCC 1996. Middlesex debut/cap 2006. YC 1996. **Tests**: 6 (1996-97 to 2002-03); HS 10 v A (Perth) 2002-03; BB 5-91 v SA (Cape Town) 1999-00. **LOI**: 7 (1996-97 to 2001-02); HS 12 v NZ (Auckland) 1996-97; BB 3-43 v Z (Bulawayo) 2001-02. F-c Tours: A 2002-03 (*part*); SA 1999-00 (*part*); WI 1997-98, 2000-01 (Eng A); NZ 1996-97; Z 1995-96 (Y), 1996-97. M HS 80 Y v Durham (Chester-le-St) 2005. M HS 50 v Sussex (Horsham) 2006. 50 wkts (3); most – 63 (2006). BB 7-93 (12-148 match) Y v Kent (Leeds) 1997. M BB 6-49 v Somerset (Leeds) 2007. LO HS 61 Y v Northants (Northampton) 2002 (CGT). LO BB 5-28 Y v Scot (Leeds) 1996 (BHC). T20 HS 13*. T20 BB 2-22.

SIMPSON, John Andrew, b Bury, Lancs 13 Jul 1988. LHB, WK. Lancashire 2nd XI 2004-07. Durham 2nd XI 2007. Nottinghamshire 2nd XI 2007-08. Middlesex 2nd XI 2008. Cumberland 2007. MCC YCs 2008. England U19s 2004-05 to 2006. Awaiting 1st XI debut.

STRAUSS, Andrew John (Radley C; Durham U), b Johannesburg, South Africa 2 Mar 1977. 5'11". LHB, LM. Debut (Middlesex) 1998; cap 2001; captain 2002 (*part*) to 2004 (*part*); benefit 2009. MCC 2002. Northern Districts 2007-08. Oxfordshire 1996. British U (List A) 1997-98. *Wisden* 2004. MBE 2005. **ECB central contract 2008-09. Tests**: 60 (2004 to 2008-09, 10 as captain); HS 177 v NZ (Napier) 2007-08. Scored 112 & 83 (run out) v NZ (Lord's) on debut and 126 & 94* v SA (Pt Elizabeth) 2004-05 on his debut overseas. **LOI**: 78 (2003-04 to 2006-07, 13 as captain); HS 152 v B (Nottingham) 2005. BB – . F-c Tours (C=captain): A 2006-07; SA 2004-05; WI 2008-09(C); NZ 2007-08; I 2005-06, 2008-09; P 2005-06. 1000 runs (4); most – 1529 (2003). HS 177 (*see Tests*). M HS 176 v Durham (Lord's) 2001. BB 1-16 v Notts (Lord's) 2007. LO HS 163 v Surrey (Oval) 2008 (FPT). BB – . IT20 HS 33. T20 HS 60.

‡**TOOR, Kabir** Singh (John Lyon S, Harrow), b Watford, Herts 30 Apr 1990. RHB, LB. Middlesex 2nd XI debut 2006, when aged 16 years 87 days. Awaiting 1st XI debut.

UDAL, Shaun David (Cove CS), b Cove, Farnborough, Hants 18 Mar 1969. Grandson of G.F.U.Udal (Middlesex and RAF 1932; Leics 1946); great great grandson of J.S.Udal (MCC 1871-75; Fiji 1894-95). 6'2". RHB, OB. Hampshire 1989-2007; cap 1992; benefit 2002. Middlesex debut/cap 2008; captain 2009. **Tests**: 4 (2005-06); HS 33* v P (Faisalabad) 2005-06; BB 4-14 v I (Bombay) 2005-06. **LOI**: 11 (1994 to 2005-06); HS 11* v Z (Brisbane) 1994-95; BB 2-37 v A (Sydney) 1994-95. F-c Tours: A 1994-95; I 2005-06; P 1995-96 (Eng A); 2005-06. HS 117* H v Warwks (Southampton) 1997. M HS 91 v Worcs (Lord's) 2008. 50 wkts (7); most – 74 (1993). BB 8-50 H v Sussex (Southampton) 1992. M BB 5-36 v Northants (Northampton) 2008. LO HS 78 H v Surrey (Guildford) 1997 (SL). LO BB 5-43 H v Surrey (Oval) 1998 (SL). T20 HS 40*. T20 BB 3-19.

WILLIAMS, Robert Edward Morgan (Marlborough C; St Mary's C, Durham U); b Pembury, Kent 19 Jan 1987. 6'0". RHB, RMF. Durham UCCE 2007-08. MCC 2007. Middlesex debut 2007; no 1st XI appearances in 2008. HS 15 and M BB 5-112 v Essex (Chelmsford) 2007 – on M debut. BB 5-70 DU v Lancs (Durham) 2007. LO HS – and BB – v Derbys (Lord's) 2007 (P40).

RELEASED/RETIRED

(Having made a County First-Class or List A appearance in 2008)

BURTON, David Alexander (Sacred Heart RC SS; Lambeth C), b Dulwich, London 23 Aug 1985. 5'11". RHB, RMF. Gloucestershire 2006; cap 2006. Middlesex 2008. MCC YC 2006. HS 52* Gs v Glamorgan (Cardiff) 2006 – on debut. BB 1-97 v SA (Uxbridge) 2008. T20 HS – . T20 BB 1-17.

JOYCE, E.C. – *see SUSSEX.*

NQ**NANNES, Dirk** Peter (Wesley C and Monash U, Melbourne), b Mount Waverley, Victoria, Australia 16 May 1976. 6'3". RHB, LFM. Victoria 2005-06 to date. Middlesex 2008; cap 2008. Dutch passport. HS 31* Vic v S Australia (Adelaide) 2007-08. M HS 5 and BB 6-32 v Worcs (Kidderminster) 2008. LO HS 5* v Somerset (Lord's) 2008. LO BB 4-38 v Worcs (Kidderminster) 2008 (P40). T20 HS 5*. T20 BB 4-11.

PEPLOE, Christopher Thomas (Twyford C of E HS; Surrey U, Roehampton), b Hammersmith, London 26 Apr 1981. 6'4". LHB, SLA. MCC YC 2002-03. Middlesex 2003-08. HS 46 v Lancs (Lord's) 2006. BB 4-31 v Yorks (Southgate) 2006. LO HS 14* v Hants (Southampton) 2005 (NL). LO BB 4-38 v Glamorgan (Cardiff) 2005 (NL). T20 HS 7. T20 BB 3-35.

NQ**PHILANDER, Vernon** Darryl, b Bellville, Cape Province, South Africa 24 Jun 1985. RHB, RMF. Western Province 2003-04 to 2005-06. WP Boland 2004-05. Cape Cobras 2005-06 to date. Middlesex 2008. Devon 2004. **LOI** (SA): 7 (2007 to 2008); HS 23 v E (Leeds) 2008; BB 4-12 v Ireland (Belfast) 2007 – on debut. HS 168 WP v GW (Kimberley) 2004-05. M HS 30 and BB 3-45 v Essex (Chelmsford) 2008 – on debut. BB 7-64 Cape Cobras v Lions (Potchefstroom) 2007-08. LO HS 76* Cape Cobras v Warriors (Cape Town) 2006-07. LO BB 4-12 (*see LOI*). IT20 HS 6. IT20 BB 2-23. T20 HS 56*. T20 BB 3-17.

SMITH, Edward Thomas (Tonbridge S; Peterhouse, Cambridge), b Pembury, Kent 19 Jul 1977. 6'2". RHB, RM. Cambridge U 1996-98, scoring 101 v Glamorgan (Cambridge) on debut; blue 1996-97 (*injured 1998*). Kent 1996-2004; cap 2001. Middlesex debut/cap 2005; captain 2007-08. British U 1998. **Tests**: 3 (2003); HS 64 v SA (Nottingham) 2003 on debut. F-c Tour (Eng A): I 2003-04. 1000 runs (8): most – 1534 (2003). Scored 135, 0, 149, 113, 203 and 108 in successive f-c innings 2003. HS 213 K v Warwks (Canterbury) 2003. M HS 166 v Warwks (Lord's) 2006. BB 1-60 (off 5 overs) v Sussex (Southgate) 2006. LO HS 122 K v Glamorgan (Maidstone) 2003 (NL). T20 HS 85.

MIDDLESEX 2008

RESULTS SUMMARY

	Place	Won	Lost	Tied	Drew	No Result
County Championship (2nd Division)	3rd	4	5		7	
All First-Class Matches		4	5		9	
FP Trophy (South East Division)	3rd	3	3			2
Pro40 League (1st Division)	9th	2	5			1
Twenty/20 Cup (South Division)	**Winners**	11	2			

LV COUNTY CHAMPIONSHIP AVERAGES
BATTING AND FIELDING

Cap		M	I	NO	HS	Runs	Avge	100	50	Ct/St
2000	D.C.Nash	3	6	2	96	251	62.75	–	3	9
2001	A.J.Strauss	8	15	1	172	748	53.42	2	3	9
2008	E.J.G.Morgan	15	27	6	137*	915	43.57	2	4	18
2008	S.D.Udal	13	19	6	91	556	42.76	–	4	1
2000	O.A.Shah	12	22	1	144	894	42.57	3	5	13
2007	B.J.M.Scott	13	20	2	164*	747	41.50	1	7	45/3
2002	E.C.Joyce	15	26	1	101	941	37.64	1	7	11
	D.J.Malan	9	15	2	132*	489	37.61	1	3	3
2005	E.T.Smith	5	9	–	85	309	34.33	–	3	1
	B.A.Godleman	23	–	106	658	28.60	1	3	5	
	G.K.Berg	3	5	–	35	118	23.60	–	–	1
2007	M.Kartik	7	10	2	44	161	20.12	–	–	9
2008	T.J.Murtagh	16	24	3	44	353	16.80	–	–	4
	D.M.Housego	2	4	–	36	66	16.50	–	–	–
	V.D.Philander	3	6	1	30	77	15.40	–	–	1
2005	A.Richardson	8	8	2	26	79	13.16	–	–	3
	S.T.Finn	12	15	5	26*	87	8.70	–	–	5
	D.Evans	9	13	3	12*	45	4.50	–	–	1
2006	N.R.D.Compton	3	6	–	14	19	3.16	–	–	2
2008	D.P.Nannes	5	4	–	5	8	2.00	–	–	2

Also batted: C.E.W.Silverwood (2 matches – cap 2006) 21*, 33*, 16 (1 ct).

BOWLING

	O	M	R	W	Avge	Best	5wI	10wM
D.P.Nannes	107.4	20	393	20	19.65	6- 32	1	–
A.Richardson	241.5	63	607	26	23.34	5- 34	1	–
T.J.Murtagh	489.5	84	1692	64	26.43	7- 95	3	1
V.D.Philander	108.5	27	277	10	27.70	3- 45	–	–
D.Evans	220.3	44	895	28	31.96	6- 35	2	–
M.Kartik	224	60	545	16	34.06	4-101	–	–
S.D.Udal	351.2	67	1102	31	35.54	5- 36	1	–
S.T.Finn	286.2	45	1050	25	42.00	4- 80	–	–

Also bowled:
G.K.Berg	52	13	171	5	34.20	3- 38		

D.J.Malan 42.2-6-135-4; B.J.M.Scott 0.3-0-1-0; O.A.Shah 20.4-89-1; C.E.W.Silverwood 47.2-5-144-4; A.J.Strauss 1-0-5-0.

The First-Class Averages (pp 136–153) give the records of Middlesex players in all first-class county matches (Middlesex's other opponents being the South Africans and Oxford UCCE), with the exception of O.A.Shah, whose first-class figures for Middlesex are as above, and:

E.C.Joyce 16-27-1-101-961-36.96-1-7-11ct. Did not bowl.
M.A.K.Lawson 1 (did not bat) 0ct. 16-0-83-0.
A.J.Strauss 9-16-1-172-777-51.80-2-3-9ct. 1-0-5-0.

MIDDLESEX RECORDS

FIRST-CLASS CRICKET

Highest Total	For 642-3d		v	Hampshire	Southampton	1923
	V 850-7d		by	Somerset	Taunton	2007
Lowest Total	For 20		v	MCC	Lord's	1864
	V 31		by	Glos	Bristol	1924
Highest Innings	For 331*	J.D.B.Robertson	v	Worcs	Worcester	1949
	V 341	C.M.Spearman	for	Glos	Gloucester	2004

Highest Partnership for each Wicket

1st	372	M.W.Gatting/J.L.Langer	v	Essex	Southgate	1998
2nd	380	F.A.Tarrant/J.W.Hearne	v	Lancashire	Lord's	1914
3rd	424*	W.J.Edrich/D.C.S.Compton	v	Somerset	Lord's	1948
4th	325	J.W.Hearne/E.H.Hendren	v	Hampshire	Lord's	1919
5th	338	R.S.Lucas/T.C.O'Brien	v	Sussex	Hove	1895
6th	270	J.D.Carr/P.N.Weekes	v	Glos	Lord's	1994
7th	271*	E.H.Hendren/F.T.Mann	v	Notts	Nottingham	1925
8th	182*	M.H.C.Doll/H.R.Murrell	v	Notts	Lord's	1913
9th	160*	E.H.Hendren/T.J.Durston	v	Essex	Leyton	1927
10th	230	R.W.Nicholls/W.Roche	v	Kent	Lord's	1899

Best Bowling	For 10- 40	G.O.B.Allen	v	Lancashire	Lord's	1929
(Innings)	V 9- 38	R.C.R.Glasgow†	for	Somerset	Lord's	1924
Best Bowling	For 16-114	G.Burton	v	Yorkshire	Sheffield	1888
(Match)	16-114	J.T.Hearne	v	Lancashire	Manchester	1898
	V 16-100	J.E.B.B.P.Q.C.Dwyer	for	Sussex	Hove	1906

Most Runs – Season	2669	E.H.Hendren	(av 83.41)	1923
Most Runs – Career	40302	E.H.Hendren	(av 48.81)	1907-37
Most 100s – Season	13	D.C.S.Compton		1947
Most 100s – Career	119	E.H.Hendren		1907-37
Most Wkts – Season	158	F.J.Titmus	(av 14.63)	1955
Most Wkts – Career	2361	F.J.Titmus	(av 21.27)	1949-82
Most Career W-K Dismissals	1223	J.T.Murray	(1024 ct/199 st)	1952-75
Most Career Catches in the Field	561	E.H.Hendren		1907-37

LIMITED-OVERS CRICKET

Highest Total	FPT	315-6	v	Surrey	The Oval	2008
	P40	337-5	v	Somerset	Southgate	2003
	T20	210-6	v	Hampshire	Southampton	2005
Lowest Total	FPT	41	v	Essex	Westcliff	1972
	P40	23	v	Yorkshire	Leeds	1974
	T20	108	v	Sussex	Richmond	2006
Highest Innings	FPT	163	A.J.Strauss	v	Surrey	The Oval	2008
	P40	147*	M.R.Ramprakash	v	Worcs	Lord's	1990
	T20	103	D.J.Malan	v	Lancashire	The Oval	2008
Best Bowling	FPT	6-15	W.W.Daniel	v	Sussex	Hove	1980
	P40	6- 6	R.W.Hooker	v	Surrey	Lord's	1969
	T20	5-13	M.Kartik	v	Essex	Lord's	2007

† R.C.Robertson-Glasgow

NORTHAMPTONSHIRE

Formation of Present Club: 31 July 1878
Inaugural First-Class Match: 1905
Colours: Maroon
Badge: Tudor Rose
County Champions: (0); best – 2nd 1912, 1957, 1965, 1976
Gillette/NatWest/C&G/FP Trophy Winners: (2) 1976, 1992
Benson and Hedges Cup Winners: (1) 1980
Pro 40/National League (Div 1) Winners: (0); best – 2nd 2006, 2007
Sunday League Winners: (0); best – 3rd 1991
Twenty20 Cup Winners: (0); best – Quarter-Finalist 2005, 2006, 2007, 2008

Chief Executive: Mark J.Tagg, County Ground, Wantage Road, Northampton, NN1 4TJ • Tel: 01604 514455 • Fax: 01604 609288 • Email: post@nccc.co.uk • Web: www.nccc.co.uk

First XI Coach: David J.Capel. **Captain**: N.Boje. **Vice-Captain**: none. **Overseas Player**: none. **2009 Beneficiary**: none. **Head Groundsman**: Paul Marshall. **Scorer**: A.C. (Tony) Kingston. ‡ New registration. NQNot qualified for England.

BAILEY, Shaun Peter ('Bud') (Hockham S; Wayland Community HS), b Norwich, Norfolk 19 Feb 1990. 6'7". RHB, RFM. Debut (Northamptonshire) 2008. Norfolk 2007. HS 15 and BB 2-119 v Essex (Chelmsford) 2008 – on debut.

NQ**BOJE, Nico ('Nicky')** (Grey C, Bloemfontein), b Bloemfontein, South Africa 20 Mar 1973. 5'10". Brother of E.H.L.Boje (OFS 1989-1990 to 1990-91). LHB, SLA. (Orange) Free State 1990-91 to 2001-02. Nottinghamshire 2002. Eagles 2004-05 to 2006-07. Northamptonshire debut 2007 (Kolpak registration); cap 2008; captain 2008 to date. **Tests** (SA): 43 (1999-00 to 2006); HS 85 v I (Bangalore) 1999-00; BB 5-62 v SL (Colombo) 2000-01. **LOI** (SA): 113 (1995-96 to 2005-06); HS 129 v NZ (Pretoria) 2000-01; BB 5-21 v A (Cape Town) 2001-02. **Tours** (SA): E 1996 (SA A); A 2001-02, 2002-03 (SA A), 2005-06; WI 2000-01, 2004-05; NZ 1998-99, 2003-04; I 1996-97, 1999-00; SL 1995 (SA U-24), 1998 (SA A), 2000, 2004, 2006; Z 1994-95. HS 226* v Worcs (Northampton) 2008. BB 8-93 Eagles v Dolphins (Durban) 2005-06. Nh BB 6-110 v Leics (Leicester) 2007. LO HS 129 (*see LOI*). LO BB 5-21 (*see LOI*). IT20 HS . IT20 BB 1-27. T20 IIS 58*. T20 BB 3-31.

CROOK, Steven Paul (Rostrevor C; Magill U), b Modbury, S Australia 28 May 1983. Younger brother of A.R.Crook. 5'11". RHB, RFM. British passport. Lancashire 2003-05. Northamptonshire debut 2005 (while on loan from Lancashire). Aus Academy 2001-02. HS 97 v Yorks (Northampton) 2005. BB 4-56 v Essex (Northampton) 2007. LO HS 23 v Glamorgan (Cardiff) 2006 (P40). LO BB 4-20 v Sussex (Northampton) 2006 (P40). T20 HS 27. T20 BB 2-24.

‡**CUMMINS, Ryan** Anthony Gilbert (Wallington CGS; Loughborough U), b Sutton, Surrey 14 Apr 1984. Great-grandson of G.M.Reay (Surrey 1913-23). 6'4". RHB, RM. Loughborough UCCE 2003-05. Leicestershire 2005-08. HS 34* v OU (Oxford) 2007. CC HS 26* Le v Glos (Leicester) 2007. BB 5-60 Le v Northants (Leicester) 2007. LO HS 10 Le v Warwks (Birmingham) 2007 (FPT). LO BB 3-21 Le v Warwks (Birmingham) 2008 (FPT). T20 HS – . T20 BB – .

‡**DAGGETT, Lee** Martin (Woodhey HS, and Holy Cross C, Bury; Durham U) b Bury, Lancs 1 Oct 1982. 6'0". RHB, RFM. Durham UCCE 2003-05. British U 2004. Warwickshire 2006-08. Leicestershire 2008. HS 33 Wa v Durham (Chester-le-St) 2007. BB 8-94 DU v Durham (Chester-le-St) 2004. CC BB 6-30 Wa v Durham (Birmingham) 2006. LO HS 5* (twice – CGT, P40). LO BB 2-33 Wa v Essex (Birmingham) 2006 (P40). T20 HS – . T20 BB 1-13.

ᴺᵠ**HALL, Andrew** James (Alberton HS), b Alberton, Johannesburg, South Africa 31 Jul 1975. 6'0". RHB, RFM. Transvaal/Gauteng 1995-96 to 2000-01. Easterns 2001-02 to 2003-04. Worcestershire 2003-04. Lions 2004-05 to 2005-06. Kent 2005-07; cap 2005. Northamptonshire debut 2008 (Kolpak registration). Durham CB 1999. Suffolk 2002. **Tests** (SA): 21 (2001-02 to 2006-07); HS 163 v I (Kanpur) 2004-05; BB 3-1 v SL (Johannesburg) 2002-03. **LOI** (SA): 88 (1998-99 to 2007); HS 81 v SL (Galle) 2000-01; BB 5-18 v E (Bridgetown) 2006-07. F-c Tours (SA): E 2003; WI 2004-05; I 2004-05; SL 2006; Z 1995-96 (Transvaal B), 2007-08 (SA A). HS 163 (*see Tests*). UK HS 133 K v Glamorgan (Canterbury) 2005. Nh HS 58 v Glos (Bristol) 2008. BB 6-77 (11-99 match) Easterns v WP (Port Elizabeth) 2002-03. UK BB 5-59 K v Surrey (Croydon) 2007. Nh BB 5-81 v Derbyshire (Chesterfield) 2008. LO HS 129* Gauteng v Border (E London) 1999-00. LO BB 5-18 (*see LOI*). IT20 HS 11. IT20 BB 3-22. T20 HS 66* and T20 BB 6-21 v Worcs (Northampton) 2008 (Nh record T20 bowling, and 1st man in UK to score 50 and take 5 wkts in a game).

HOWGEGO, Benjamin Henry Nicholas ('**Ben**') (King's S, Ely; Stowe S; Exeter U), b King's Lynn, Norfolk 3 Mar 1988. 5'11". LHB, RM. Debut (Northamptonshire) 2008. Northamptonshire 2nd XI 2005-08. HS 15 v Glos (Bristol) 2008 – on debut.

LUCAS, David Scott (Djanogly CTC, Nottingham), b Nottingham 19 Aug 1978. 6'2". RHB, LMF. Nottinghamshire 1999-2002. Yorkshire 2005. Northamptonshire debut 2007. Lincolnshire 2006. HS 49 Nt v DU (Nottingham) 2002. CC HS 46* Nt v Middlesex (Nottingham) 2000. Nh HS 37 v Derbys (Derby) 2007. BB 5-30 v Glos (Northampton) 2008. LO HS 32 v Derbys (Derby) 2005 (NL). LO BB 4-27 Nt v Derbys (Derby) 2000 (NL). T20 HS 5*. T20 BB 2-37.

NELSON, Mark Anthony George (Lord Grey S, Milton Keynes; Stowe S), b Milton Keynes, Bucks 24 Sep 1986. 5'11". LHB, RM. Debut (Northamptonshire) 2007. HS 42 v Warwks (Birmingham) 2008. BB 2-62 v Middlesex (Northampton) 2007 – on debut. LO HS 26 v Durham (Northampton) 2007 (FPT). LO BB 1-26 v Derbyshire (Northampton) 2008 (P40).

O'BRIEN, Niall John (Marian C, Dublin), b Dublin, Ireland 8 Nov 1981. 5'6". Son of B.A.O'Brien (Ireland 1966-81); elder brother of K.J.O'Brien (Ireland 2006 to 2008-09). LHB, WK. Kent 2004-06. Ireland 2005-06 to 2008-09. Northamptonshire debut 2007. **LOI** (Ire): 29 (2006 to 2008-09); HS 72 v Scotland (Belfast) 2007. HS 176 Ireland v UAE (Windhoek) 2005. Nh HS 168 v Glamorgan (Northampton) 2008. BB 1-4 K v CU (Cambridge) 2006 – his only f-c spell. LO HS 95 v Leics (Northampton) 2008. IT20 HS 22. T20 HS 69.

PANESAR, Mudhsuden Singh ('*Monty*') (Stopsley HS; Bedford Modern S; Loughborough U), b Luton, Beds 25 Apr 1982. 6'0". LHB, SLA. Debut (Northamptonshire) 2001; cap 2006. British U 2002-05. Loughborough UCCE 2004. MCC 2006. Bedfordshire 1998-99. *Wisden* 2007. **ECB central contract 2008-09. Tests**: 38 (2005-06 to 2008-09); HS 26 v SL (Nottingham) 2006; BB 6-37 v NZ (Manchester) 2008. **LOI**: 26 (2006-07 to 2007-08); HS 13 v WI (Nottingham) 2007, BB 3-25 v B (Bridgetown) 2006-07. F-c Tours: A 2006-07; WI 2008-09; NZ 2007-08; I 2005-06, 2008-09; SL 2002-03 (ECB Acad), 2007-08. HS 39* v Worcs (Northampton) 2005. 50 wkts (3); most – 71 (2006). BB 7-181 v Essex (Chelmsford) 2005. LO HS 17* v Leics (Northampton) 2008 (FPT). LO BB 5-20 ECB Acad v SL Acad XI (Colombo) 2002-03. IT20 HS 1. IT20 BB 2-40. T20 HS 3*. T20 BB 2-22.

PETERS, Stephen David (Coopers Coborn & Co S), b Harold Wood, Essex 10 Dec 1978. 5'11". RHB, occ LB. Essex 1996-2001, scoring 110 and 12* v CU (Cambridge) on debut. Worcestershire 2002-05. Northamptonshire debut 2006; cap 2007. 1000 runs (2); most – 1177 (2003). HS 178 v Essex (Northampton) 2006. BB 1-19 Ex v OU (Chelmsford) 1999. LO HS 107 v Yorks (Leeds) 2007 (FPT). T20 HS 26*.

SALES, David John Grimwood (Caterham S; Cumnor House S), b Carshalton, Surrey 3 Dec 1977. 6'0". RHB, RM. Debut (Northamptonshire) 1996 v Worcs (Kidderminster) scoring 0 and 210* – record Championship score on f-c debut; youngest (18 years 237 days) to score 200 in a Championship match; cap 1999; captain 2004-07; benefit 2007. Wellington 2001-02. F-c Tours (Eng A): NZ 1999-00; SL 1997-98; K 1997-98; B 1999-00. Sustained severe knee injury prior to start of England A tour of WI 2000-01 – no f-c appearances 2001. 1000 runs (6); most – 1384 (2007). HS 303* v Essex (Northampton) 1999 – youngest Englishman (21 years 240 days) to score a f-c 300. BB 4-25 v SL A (Northampton) 1999. CC BB 2-7 v Yorks (Scarborough) 1999. LO HS 161 v Yorks (Northampton) 2006 (CGT). T20 HS 78*. T20 BB 1-10.

[NQ]**VAN DER WATH, Johannes** Jacobus (Ermelo HS), b Newcastle, Natal, South Africa 10 Jan 1978. RHB, RFM. Easterns 1996-97. Free State 1997-98 to 2003-04. Eagles 2004-05 to 2006-07. Sussex 2005. Northamptonshire debut 2007. Kolpak registration 2008. **LOI** (SA): 10 (2005-06 to 2007-08); HS 37* v A (Sydney) 2005-06; BB 2-21 v SA (Melbourne) 2005-06 – on debut. F-c Tour (SA A): SL 2005-06. HS 113* FS v KZ-Natal (Bloemfontein) 2001-02. UK HS 94 v Essex (Northampton) 2007. BB 7-60 (12-128 match) v Middlesex (Uxbridge) 2008. LO HS 91 FS v GW (Bloemfontein) 2000-01. LO BB 4-31 SA A v NZ (Potchefstroom) 2005-06. IT20 HS 21. IT20 BB 2-31. T20 HS 48*. T20 BB 2-8.

WAKELY, Alexander George (Bedford S), b Hammersmith, London 3 Nov 1988. 6'2". RHB, OB. Debut (Northamptonshire) 2007. Bedfordshire 2004-05. Northamptonshire 2nd XI debut when aged 15 years 295 days. HS 66 and BB 2-62 v Somerset (Taunton) 2007 – on debut. LO HS 14 and BB 2-14 v Lancs (Northampton) 2007 (P40).

[NQ]**WESSELS, Mattheus Hendrik ('*Riki*')** (Woodridge C, Pt Elizabeth; Northampton U), b Marogudoore, Queensland, Australia 12 Nov 1985. Left Australia when 2 months old. Son of K.C.Wessels (OFS, Sussex, WP, NT, Q, EP, GW, Australia and South Africa 1973-74 to 1999-00). 5'11". RHB, WK. MCC 2004. Northamptonshire debut 2005 (Kolpak registration). Nondescripts (Sri Lanka) 2007-08. HS 107 v Durham (Chester-le-St) 2005. BB – . LO HS 100 v Surrey (Oval) 2008. T20 HS 49*.

WHITE, Graeme Geoffrey (Stowe S), b Milton Keynes, Bucks 18 Apr 1987. 5'11". RHB, SLA. Debut (Northamptonshire) 2006. HS 65 and CC BB 1-18 v Glamorgan (Colwyn Bay) 2007. BB 2-35 v CU (Cambridge) 2007. LO HS 14 v Middlesex (Southgate) 2007 (P40). LO BB 2-44 v Worcs (Kidderminster) 2007 (P40). T20 HS – . T20 BB 1-10.

WHITE, Robert Allan (Stowe S; Durham U; Loughborough U), b Chelmsford, Essex 15 Oct 1979. 5'11". RHB, LB. Debut (Northamptonshire) 2000; cap 2008. Loughborough UCCE 2003. British U 2003. 1000 runs (1): 1037 (2008). HS 277 and BB 2-30 v Glos (Northampton) 2002 – highest maiden f-c hundred in UK; included 107 before lunch on first day. LO HS 111 v Warwks (Northampton) 2008 (FPT). LO BB 2-18 v Sussex (Northampton) 2002 (NL). T20 HS 94*.

WIGLEY, David Harry (St Mary's RCS, Menston, Ilkley; Loughborough U), b Bradford, Yorks 26 Oct 1981. 6'4". RHB, RFM. Yorkshire 2002 (one match). Loughborough UCCE 2003-04. British U 2004. Worcestershire 2003, 2005. Northamptonshire debut 2006. Gloucestershire 2008; cap 2008 (1 match). HS 70 v Middlesex (Northampton) 2007. BB 5-77 v P (Northampton) 2006. CC BB 4-43 v Worcs (Worcester) 2008. LO HS 10 v Middlesex (Southgate) 2007 (P40). LO BB 4-37 Wo v Leics (Worcester) 2004 (NL). T20 HS 1. T20 BB 1-8.

RELEASED/RETIRED
(Having made a County First-Class or List A appearance in 2008)

BROWN, J.F. – *see NOTTINGHAMSHIRE.*

CROOK, Andrew Richard (Rostrevor C), b Modbury, S Australia 14 Oct 1980. 6'4". Elder brother of S.P.Crook (*see above*). RHB, OB. British passport. S Australia 1998-99 (one match). Aus Academy 1999-2000. Lancashire 2004-05. Northamptonshire 2007-08. HS 88 La v OU (Oxford) 2005. Nh HS 72 v Leics (Leicester) 2007. BB 3-71 La v Essex (Manchester) 2005. Nh BB 1-5 v New Zealanders (Northampton) 2008. LO HS 162* La v Bucks (Wormsley) 2005 (Lancs CGT record). LO BB 3-32 La v Hants (Manchester) 2005. T20 HS 15. T20 BB 2-25.

NQKLUSENER, Lance (Durban HS), b Durban, South Africa 4 Sep 1971. 5'10". LHB, RM/OB. Natal/KwaZulu-Natal 1993-94 to 2003-04. Nottinghamshire 2002. Middlesex 2004. Dolphins 2004-05 to 2006-07. Northamptonshire 2006-08; cap 2006 (Kolpak registration). *Wisden* 1999. **Tests** (SA): 49 (1996-97 to 2004); HS 174 v E (Pt Elizabeth) 1999-00; BB 8-64 v I (Calcutta) 1996-97 – on debut. **LOI** (SA): 171 (1995-96 to 2004); HS 103* v NZ (Auckland) 1998-99; BB 6-49 v SL (Lahore) 1997-98. F-c Tours (SA): E 1996 (SA A), 1998; A 1997-98, 2001-02; WI 2000-01; NZ 1998-99; I 1996-97, 1999-00; P 1997-98; SL 1995 (SA U-24), 2000, 2004; Z 1999-00, 2001-02. 1000 runs (3); most – 1251 (2006 – inc 6 hundreds). HS 202* v Glam (Northampton) 2008. BB 8-34 Natal v WP (Durban) 1995-96. CC BB 6-69 v Leics (Oakham) 2006. LO HS 142* SA v Northants (Northampton) 1998. LO BB 6-49 (*see LOI*). T20 HS 111*. T20 BB 2-8.

LOGAN, Richard James (Wolverhampton GS), b Stone, Staffs 28 Jan 1980. 6'1". RHB, RMF. Northamptonshire 1999-2000, 2007-08. Nottinghamshire 2001-04. Hampshire 2005-06. HS 37* Nt v Hants (Nottingham) 2001. Nh HS 24 v Essex (Ilford) 2000. BB 6-93 Nt v Derbys (Nottingham) 2001. Nh BB 5-61 v Middlesex (Northampton) 2000. LO HS 28* H v Northants (Northampton) 2005 (NL). LO BB 5-24 Nt v Suffolk (Mildenhall) 2001 (CGT). T20 HS 11*. T20 BB 5-26.

NQLOUW, Johann (Fraserburg HS; Port Elizabeth U), b Cape Town, South Africa 12 Apr 1979. 6'2". RHB, RFM. Griqualand West 2000-01 to 2002-03. Eastern Province 2003-04. Northamptonshire 2004-05, 2008 (Kolpak registration). Dolphins 2004-05 to date. Eagles 2005-06. Middlesex 2006. **LOI** (SA): 3 (2008-09); HS 23 v B (Potchefstroom) 2008-09; BB 1-45 v B (Benoni) 2008-09. HS 124 EP v Boland (Pt Elizabeth) 2003-04. UK HS 82 v New Zealanders (Northampton) 2008. CC HS 67* v Worcs (Northampton) 2008. 50 wkts (1): 60 (2004). BB 6-51 v Essex (Northampton) 2005. LO HS 72 GW v Northerns (Kimberley) 2000-01. LO BB 5-27 Nh v Warwks (Northampton) 2004 (NL). T20 HS 21*. T20 BB 4-18.

R.J.Browning left the staff, without making a County First-Class or List A appearance in 2008.

NORTHAMPTONSHIRE 2008

RESULTS SUMMARY

	Place	Won	Lost	Tied	Drew	No Result
County Championship (2nd Division)	4th	3	3		10	
All First-Class Matches		3	3		11	
FP Trophy (Midlands Division)	3rd	4	2			2
Pro40 League (2nd Division)	9th		6			2
Twenty/20 Cup (Midlands/West/Wales Division)	Quarter-Finalist	6	4			1

LV COUNTY CHAMPIONSHIP AVERAGES

BATTING AND FIELDING

Cap		M	I	NO	HS	Runs	Avge	100	50	Ct/St
2006	L.Klusener	14	20	5	202*	1095	73.00	2	9	3
1999	D.J.G.Sales	16	25	3	173	1120	50.90	3	4	14
	J.Louw	6	7	3	67*	199	49.75	–	1	1
2008	R.A.White	15	25	4	132*	1037	49.38	3	6	11
	N.J.O'Brien	13	20	1	168	857	45.10	2	4	40/3
2007	S.D.Peters	15	24	3	130*	888	42.28	3	4	13
2008	N.Boje	13	17	1	226*	644	40.25	2	1	9
	S.P.Crook	4	6	–	63	223	37.16	–	2	–
	A.J.Hall	10	9	1	58	257	32.12	–	2	19
	M.H.Wessels	13	19	1	95	576	32.00	–	6	13/2
	J.J.van der Wath	11	10	3	75*	148	21.14	–	1	–
2006	M.S.Panesar	7	8	4	30*	72	18.00	–	–	2
	A.G.Wakely	4	6	–	53	95	15.83	–	1	2
	D.S.Lucas	15	15	4	35	104	9.45	–	–	3
	D.H.Wigley	7	9	4	18*	41	8.20	–	–	2
2000	J.F.Brown	9	6	1	13	35	7.00	–	–	1

Also batted: S.P.Bailey (1 match) 3, 15 (1 ct); B.H.Howgego (1) 15, 1*; M.A.G.Nelson (2) 42, 9, 0.

BOWLING

	O	M	R	W	Avge	Best	5wI	10wM
J.J.van der Wath	274.4	62	869	43	20.20	7- 60	3	1
A.J.Hall	173.4	40	535	24	22.29	5- 81	1	–
N.Boje	400.5	88	1194	33	36.18	4- 26	–	–
D.S.Lucas	391.4	71	1392	35	39.77	5- 30	1	–
J.Louw	154	32	489	12	40.75	3- 77	–	–
D.H.Wigley	150.4	25	590	14	42.14	4- 43	–	–
M.S.Panesar	270.4	45	868	18	48.22	5-143	1	–
Also bowled:								
J.F.Brown	243.4	51	717	9	79.66	2- 33	–	–
L.Klusener	183.2	43	638	6	106.33	1- 21	–	–

S.P.Bailey 26-2-127-3; S.P.Crook 73.3-17-286-1; M.A.G.Nelson 8-0-62-0; A.G.Wakely 1-0-4-0; M.H.Wessels 2-0-13-0.

The First-Class Averages (pp 136–153) give the records of Northamptonshire players in all first-class county matches (Northamptonshire's other opponents being the New Zealanders), with the exception of M.S.Panesar, whose first-class figures for Northamptonshire are as above, and:

D.H.Wigley 8-10-4-18*-51-8.50-0-0-2ct. 187-35-745-23-32.39-5/78-1-0.

NORTHAMPTONSHIRE RECORDS

FIRST-CLASS CRICKET

Highest Total	For 781-7d		v	Notts	Northampton	1995
	V 673-8d		by	Yorkshire	Leeds	2003
Lowest Total	For 12		v	Glos	Gloucester	1907
	V 33		by	Lancashire	Northampton	1977
Highest Innings	For 331*	M.E.K.Hussey	v	Somerset	Taunton	2003
	V 333	K.S.Duleepsinhji	for	Sussex	Hove	1930

Highest Partnership for each Wicket

1st	375	R.A.White/M.J.Powell	v	Glos	Northampton	2002
2nd	344	G.Cook/R.J.Boyd-Moss	v	Lancashire	Northampton	1986
3rd	393	A.Fordham/A.J.Lamb	v	Yorkshire	Leeds	1990
4th	370	R.T.Virgin/P.Willey	v	Somerset	Northampton	1976
5th	401	M.B.Loye/D.Ripley	v	Glamorgan	Northampton	1998
6th	376	R.Subba Row/A.Lightfoot	v	Surrey	The Oval	1958
7th	293	D.J.G.Sales/D.Ripley	v	Essex	Northampton	1999
8th	164	D.Ripley/N.G.B.Cook	v	Lancashire	Manchester	1987
9th	156	R.Subba Row/S.Starkie	v	Lancashire	Northampton	1955
10th	148	B.W.Bellamy/J.V.Murdin	v	Glamorgan	Northampton	1925

Best Bowling	For 10-127	V.W.C.Jupp	v	Kent	Tunbridge W	1932
(Innings)	V 10- 30	C.Blythe	for	Kent	Northampton	1907
Best Bowling	For 15- 31	G.E.Tribe	v	Yorkshire	Northampton	1958
(Match)	V 17- 48	C.Blythe	for	Kent	Northampton	1907

Most Runs – Season	2198	D.Brookes	(av 51.11)	1952
Most Runs – Career	28980	D.Brookes	(av 36.13)	1934-59
Most 100s – Season	8	R.A.Haywood		1921
Most 100s – Career	67	D.Brookes		1934-59
Most Wkts – Season	175	G.E.Tribe	(av 18.70)	1955
Most Wkts – Career	1102	E.W.Clark	(av 21.26)	1922-47
Most Career W-K Dismissals	810	K.V.Andrew	(653 ct/157 st)	1953-66
Most Career Catches in the Field	469	D.S.Steele		1963-84

LIMITED-OVERS CRICKET

Highest Total	FPT	360-2		v	Staffs	Northampton	1990
	P40	319-7		v	Scotland	Northampton	2003
	T20	224-5		v	Glos	Milton Keynes	2005
Lowest Total	FPT	62		v	Leics	Leicester	1974
	P40	41		v	Middlesex	Northampton	1972
	T20	102-9 (20)		v	Warwicks	Milton Keynes	2008
Highest Innings	FPT	161	D.J.G.Sales	v	Yorkshire	Northampton	2006
	P40	172*	W.Larkins	v	Warwicks	Luton	1983
	T20	111*	L.Klusener	v	Worcs	Kidderminster	2007
Best Bowling	FPT	7-10	C.Pietersen	v	Denmark	Brondby	2005
	P40	7-39	A.Hodgson	v	Somerset	Northampton	1976
	T20	6-21	A.J.Hall	v	Worcs	Northampton	2008

NOTTINGHAMSHIRE

Formation of Present Club: March/April 1841
Substantial Reorganisation: 11 December 1866
Inaugural First-Class Match: 1864
Colours: Green and Gold
Badge: Badge of City of Nottingham
County Champions (since 1890): (5) 1907, 1929, 1981, 1987, 2005
Gillette/NatWest/C&G/FP Trophy Winners: (1) 1987
Benson and Hedges Cup Winners: (1) 1989
Pro 40/National League (Div 1) Winners: (0); best – 2nd 2007
Sunday League Winners: (1) 1991
Twenty20 Cup Winners: (0); best – Finalist 2006

Chief Executive: Derek Brewer, Trent Bridge, Nottingham NG2 6AG • Tel: 0115 982 3000 • Fax: 0115 945 5730 • Email: administration@nottsccc.co.uk • Webs: www.nottsccc.co.uk • www.trentbridge.co.uk

Director of Cricket: Mick Newell. **Club Coach**: Paul Johnson. **Captain**: C.M.W.Read. **Vice-Captain**: none. **Overseas Player**: A.C.Voges. **2009 Beneficiary**: C.M.W.Read. **Head Groundsman**: Steve Birks. **Scorer**: L. Brian Hewes. ‡ New registration. NQ Not qualified for England.

NQ**ADAMS, Andre** Ryan (Westlake BHS, Auckland), b Mangere, Auckland, New Zealand 17 Jul 1975. 5'9". RHB, RMF. Auckland 1997-98 to 2007-08. Essex 2004-06, scoring 124 on debut (*see below*); cap 2004. Nottinghamshire debut/cap 2007 (Kolpak registration). Herefordshire 2001. **Tests** (NZ): 1 (2001-02); HS 11 and BB 3-44 v E (Auckland) 2001-02 – on debut. **LOI** (NZ): 41 (2000-01 to 2006-07); HS 45 v P (Rawalpindi) 2001-02; BB 5-22 v I (Queenstown) 2002-03. HS 124 Ex v Leics (Leicester) 2004 (91 balls, 7 sixes, 13 fours; 100 off 80 balls) on UK debut. Nt HS 58 v Surrey (Nottingham) 2008. BB 6-25 Auckland v Wellington. UK BB 5-60 Ex v Durham (Southend) 2005. Nt BB 4-39 v Somerset (Taunton) 2008. Hat-trick Ex v Somerset (Taunton) 2005. LO HS 90* N Is Selection XI v SL (New Plymouth) 2000-01. LO BB 5-7 Auckland v ND (Auckland) 1999-00. T20 HS 54*. T20 BB 3-35.

BROAD, Stuart Christopher John (Oakham S), b Nottingham 24 Jun 1986. 6'5". LHB, RFM. Son of B.C.Broad (Glos, Notts, OFS and England 1979-94). Debut (Leicestershire) 2005; cap 2007. Nottinghamshire debut 2008. YC 2006. **ECB central contract 2008-09. Tests**: 15 (2007-08 to 2008-09); HS 76 v SA (Lord's) 2008; BB 5-85 v WI (Kingston) 2008-09. **LOI**: 42 (2006 to 2008-09); HS 45* v I (Manchester) 2007; BB 5-23 v SA (Nottingham) 2008. F-c Tours: WI 2005-06 (Eng A), 2008-09; NZ 2007-08; I 2008-09; SL 2007-08; B 2006-07 (Eng A). HS 91* and BB 5-67 Le v Derbys (Leicester) 2007. Nt HS 53 v Yorks (Leeds) 2008 – on Nt debut; Nt BB 4-39 v Durham (Nottingham) 2008. LO HS 45* (*see LOI*). LO BB 4-51 (*see LOI*). IT20 HS 6. IT20 BB 3-37. T20 HS 9*. T20 BB 3-13.

‡**BROWN, Alistair** Duncan (Caterham S), b Beckenham, Kent 11 Feb 1970. 5'10". RHB, OB, occ WK. Surrey 1992-2008; cap 1994; benefit 2002. TCCB XI 1996. Walter Lawrence Trophy for fastest f-c hundred 1998. **LOI**: 16 (1996 to 2001); HS 118 v I (Manchester) 1996. 1000 runs (8); most – 1382 (1993). HS 295* Sy v Leics (Oakham) 2000 – record score (all levels) in Rutland. BB 3-25 Sy v Somerset (Guildford) 2006. LO HS 268 Sy v Glamorgan (Oval) 2002 (CGT) – world record l-o score (160 balls, 12 sixes, 30 fours). LO BB 3-39 Sy v Notts (Nottingham) 2000 (NL). T20 HS 83.

‡BROWN, Jason Fred (St Margaret Ward HS & SFC), b Newcastle-under-Lyme, Staffs 10 Oct 1974. 6'0". RHB, OB. Northamptonshire 1996-2008; cap 2000; benefit 2008. Staffordshire 1994-95. F-c Tours: WI 2000-01 (part) (Eng A); SL 2000-01 (no f-c). HS 38 Nh v Hants (Northampton) 2003. 50 wkts (3); most – 66 (2003). BB 7-69 Nh v Durham (Chester-le-St) 2003. LO HS 16 Nh v Lancs (Manchester) 2002 (NL). LO BB 5-19 Nh v Cambs (Northampton) 2004 (CGT). T20 HS 13*. T20 BB 5-27.

‡CARTER, Andrew (Lincoln C), b Lincoln 27 Aug 1988. RHB, RM. Nottinghamshire 2nd XI debut 2006. Lincolnshire 2007-08.

EALHAM, Mark Alan (Stour Valley SS, Chartham), b Willesborough, Ashford, Kent 27 Aug 1969. Son of A.G.E.Ealham (Kent 1966-82). 5'9". RHB, RMF. Kent 1989-2003; cap 1992; benefit 2003. Nottinghamshire debut/cap 2004. Lawrence Trophy (fastest f-c hundred of 2006 – 45 balls v MCC at Lord's). **Tests**: 8 (1996 to 1998); HS 53* v A (Birmingham) 1997; BB 4-21 v I (Nottingham) 1996. **LOI**: 64 (1996 to 2001); HS 45 v WI (Bridgetown) 1997-98; BB 5-15 v Z (Kimberley) 1999-00 – Eng record (then). F-c Tours: A 1996-97 (Eng A); SA 1999-00 (part); SL 1997-98; Z 1992-93 (K); K 1997-98. 1000 runs (1): 1055 (1997). HS 153* K v Northants (Canterbury) 2001. Nt HS 139 v Leics (Leicester) 2004. BB 8-36 (10-74 match) K v Warwks (Birmingham) 1996. 50 wkts (1): 56 (2005). Nt BB 7-59 (10-76 match) v Yorks (Nottingham) 2008. LO HS 112 K v Derbys (Maidstone) 1995 (off 44 balls – SL record). LO BB 6-53 K v Hants (Basingstoke) 1993 (SL). T20 HS 91. T20 BB 3-21.

FLETCHER, Luke Jack (Henry Mellish S, Nottingham), b Nottingham 18 Sep 1988. 6'6". RHB, RMF. Debut (Nottinghamshire) 2008 – awaiting CC debut. Nottinghamshire 2nd XI debut 2007. HS – and BB 1-70 v OU (Oxford) 2008. LO HS 2* v Leics (Nottingham) 2008 (FPT). LO BB 2-41 v Ireland (Nottingham) 2008 (FPT).

FOOTITT, Mark Harold Alan (Carlton le Willows S; West Notts C), b Nottingham 25 Nov 1985. 6'2". RHB, LFM. Debut (Nottinghamshire) 2005. MCC 2006. No f-c appearances in 2008. HS 19* v Hants (Southampton) 2005. BB 5-45 v West Indies A (Nottingham) 2006. CC BB 5-59 v Essex (Nottingham) 2007. LO HS – and BB – Nt v Oxon (Oxford) 2001 (CGT). T20 HS – . T20 BB – .

FRANKS, Paul John (Southwell Minster CS), b Mansfield 3 Feb 1979. 6'2". LHB, RMF. Debut (Nottinghamshire) 1996; cap 1999; benefit 2007. Canterbury 2002-03. YC 2000. **LOI**: 1 (2000); HS 4 v WI (Nottingham) 2000. F-c Tours (Eng A): SA 1998-99; WI 2000-01; NZ 1999-00; SL 2004-05; B 1999-00. HS 123* v Leics (Leicester) 2003. 50 wkts (2); most – 63 (1999). BB 7-56 v Middlesex (Lord's) 2000. Hat-trick v Warwks (Nottingham) 1997. LO HS 84* v Lincs (Lincoln) 2003 (CGT). LO BB 6-27 v Durham (Chester-le-St) 2000 (NL). T20 HS 29*. T20 BB 2-12.

HALES, Alexander Daniel (Chesham S), b Hillingdon, Middlesex 3 Jan 1989. RHB, RM, occ WK. Buckinghamshire 2006-07. MCC YC 2006-07. Nottinghamshire 2nd XI. Debut (Nottinghamshire) 2008. HS – . LO HS – .

JEFFERSON, William Ingleby (Beeston Hall S, Norfolk; Oundle S; St Hild & St Bede C, Durham U), b Derby 25 Oct 1979. Son of R.I.Jefferson (Cambridge U and Surrey 1961-66); grandson of J.Jefferson (Army 1919, Comb Services 1922). 6'10". RHB, RMF. British U 2000-02. Essex 2000-06; cap 2002. Durham UCCE 2001-02. Nottinghamshire debut 2007. Scored 50 and 65 in first two l-o innings. F-c Tour (Eng A): B 2006-07. 1000 runs (1): 1555 (2004). HS 222 Ex v Hants (Southampton) 2004. Nt HS 98 v OU (Oxford) 2008. Nt CC HS 80 v Sussex (Hove) 2008. BB 1-16 Ex v Yorks (Leeds) 2005. LO HS 132 Ex v Essex CB (Chelmsford) 2003 (CGT). LO BB 2-9 Ex v Worcs (Worcester) 2005 (NL). T20 HS 51.

PATEL, Samit Rohit (Worksop C), b Leicester 30 Nov 1984. 5'8". Elder brother of A.Patel (*see DERBYSHIRE*). RHB, SLA. Debut (Nottinghamshire) 2002; cap 2008. Notts 2nd XI debut 1999 when aged 14 years 274 days. **LOI:** 11 (2008 to 2008-09); HS 31 and BB 5-41 v SA (Oval) 2008. F-c Tour: NZ 2008-09 (Eng A). HS 176 v Glos (Nottingham) 2007. BB 4-68 v DU (Durham) 2007. CC BB 3-39 v Derbys (Chesterfield) 2007. LO HS 114 v Durham (Chester-le-Street) 2008 (FPT). LO BB 3-19 v Warwks (Nottingham) 2008 (FPT). T20 HS 84*. T20 BB 3-11.

PATTINSON, Darren John, b Grimsby, Lincs 2 Sep 1979. Elder brother of J.L.Pattinson (Victoria 2008-09). RHB, RFM. Victoria 2006-07 to date. Nottinghamshire debut 2008 taking 5-22 (8-85 match) v Kent (Canterbury). **Tests:** 1 (2008); HS 13 and BB 2-95 v SA (Leeds) 2008. HS 39* Victoria v Tasmania (Hobart) 2008-09. UK/Nt HS 33 v Kent (Canterbury) 2008 – on UK debut; BB 6-30 v Lancs (Nottingham) 2008. LO HS 13* v Lancs (Nottingham) 2008. LO BB 4-29 v Warwks (Nottingham) 2008. T20 HS 4*. T20 BB 3-18.

READ, Christopher Mark Wells (Torquay GS; Bath U), b Paignton, Devon 10 Aug 1978. 5'8". RHB, WK. Gloucestershire (1-o only) 1997. Debut 1997-98 for England A in Kenya. Nottinghamshire debut 1998; cap 1999; captain 2008 to date; benefit 2009. MCC 2002. Devon 1995-97. **Tests:** 15 (1999 to 2006-07); HS 55 v P (Leeds) 2006. Made six dismissals twice in successive innings 2006-07 to establish an Ashes record. **LOI:** 36 (1999-00 to 2006-07); HS 30* v SA (Manchester) 2003. F-c Tours: A 2006-07; SA 1998-99 (Eng A), 1999-00; WI 2000-01 (Eng A), 2003-04, 2005-06 (Eng A); SL 1997-98 (Eng A), 2002-03 (ECB Acad), 2003-04; Z 1998-99 (Eng A); B 2003-04; K 1997-98 (Eng A). 1000 runs (1): 1001 (2007). HS 240 v Essex (Chelmsford) 2007. LO HS 135 v Durham (Nottingham) 2006 (CGT). IT20 HS 13. T20 HS 48*.

SHAFAYAT, Bilal Mustapha (Greenwood Dale; Nottingham Bluecoat SFC), b Nottingham 10 Jul 1984. 5'7". RHB, RMF. Nottinghamshire 2001-04, 2007 to date. National Bank of Pakistan 2004-05. Northamptonshire 2005-06. Pakistan Customs 2007-08 to date. Captained Eng U-19 tour of Australia 2002-03. F-c Tour (Eng A): I 2003-04. 1000 runs (1): 1058 (2005). HS 161 Nh v Derbys (Derby) 2005. Nt HS 118 v Sussex (Hove) 2008. BB 2-25 Nh v P (Northampton) 2006. Nt BB 1-22 v DU (Nottingham) 2003. CC BB 1-24 v Essex (Chelmsford) 2007. LO HS 104 v Northants (Northampton) 2007 (FPT). LO BB 4-33 Nh v Worcs (Worcester) 2005 (NL). T20 HS 40. T20 BB 2-13.

SHRECK, Charles Edward (Truro S), b Truro, Cornwall 6 Jan 1978. 6'7". RHB, RFM. Debut (Nottinghamshire) 2003; cap 2006. Wellington 2005-06 to date. MCC 2008. Cornwall 1997-2002. HS 19 v Essex (Chelmsford) 2003. 50 wkts (2); most – 61 (2006, 2008). BB 8-31 (12-129 match) v Middlesex (Nottingham) 2006. Hat-trick v Middlesex (Lord's) 2006. LO IIS 9* Wellington v CD (Palmerston N) 2005-06. LO BB 5-19 Cornwall v Worcs (Truro) 2002 (CGT). Took 5-35 v Worcs (Nottingham) 2002 (NL) – on 1st XI debut. T20 HS 6*. T20 BB 4-22.

SIDEBOTTOM, Ryan Jay (King James's GS, Almondbury), b Huddersfield, Yorks 15 Jan 1978. Son of A.Sidebottom (Yorks, OFS and England 1973-91). 6'3". LHB, LFM. Yorkshire 1997-2003; cap 2000. Nottinghamshire debut/cap 2004. **ECB central contract 2008-09.** **Tests:** 21 (2001 to 2008-09); HS 31 v SL (Kandy) 2007-08; BB 7-47 v NZ (Napier) 2007-08. Hat-trick v NZ (Hamilton) 2007-08. LOI: 16 (2001-02 to 2008); HS 15 v WI (Birmingham) 2007; BB 3-19 v SL (Dambulla) 2007-08. F-c Tours: WI 2000-01 (Eng A), 2008-09; NZ 2007-08; SL 2007-08. HS 54 Y v Glamorgan (Cardiff) 1998. Nt HS 33 v Durham (Chester-le-St) 2006. 50 wkts (2); most – 50 (2005, 2006). BB 7-97 Y v Derbys (Leeds) 2003. Nt BB 5-22 v Kent (Nottingham) 2006. LO HS 32 v Middlesex (Nottingham) 2005 (NL). LO BB 6-40 Y v Glamorgan (Cardiff) 1998 (SL). IT20 HS 5*. IT20 and T20 BB 3-16. T20 HS 12*.

SWANN, Graeme Peter (Sponne SS, Towcester), b Northampton 24 Mar 1979. Son of R.Swann (Northumberland 1969-72; Bedfordshire 1988-95); younger brother of A.J.Swann (Northamptonshire and Lancashire 1996-2004). 6'0". RHB, OB. Northamptonshire 1998-2004; cap 1999. Nottinghamshire debut/cap 2005. MCC 2005. Bedfordshire 1996. **Tests**: 5 (2008-09); HS 20* and BB 5-57 (8-149 match) v WI (St John's) 2008-09. **LOI**: 15 (1999-00 to 2008-09); HS 34 v SL (Dambulla) 2007-08; BB 4-34 v SL (Dambulla) 2007-08. F-c Tours: SA 1998-99 (Eng A), 1999-00; WI 2000-01 (Eng A *part*), 2008-09; I 2008-09; SL 2004-05 (Eng A), 2007-08 (no f-c matches); Z 1998-99 (Eng A). HS 183 Nh v Glos (Bristol) 2002 – including 114 before lunch on third day. Nt HS 97 v Essex (Chelmsford) 2007. 50 wkts (1): 57 (1999). BB 7-33 Nh v Derbys (Northampton) 2003. Nt BB 7-100 v Glamorgan (Swansea) 2007. LO HS 83 Nh v Leics (Northampton) 2001 (NL). LO BB 5-17 v Glos (Nottingham) 2007 (P40). IT20 HS 15*. IT20 BB 2-21. T20 HS 62. T20 BB 3-16.

VOGES, Adam Charles (Edith Cowan U, Perth), b Perth, Australia 4 Oct 1979. 6'0". RHB, SLC. W Australia 2002-03 to date. Hampshire (l-o) 2007. Nottinghamshire debut/cap 2008. **LOI** (A): 1 (2006-07); HS 16* and BB – v NZ (Hamilton) 2006-07 – on debut. F-c Tour (Aus A): P 2007-08. HS 180 WA v Tas (Hobart) 2007-08. Nt HS 77 v OU (Oxford) 2008. CC HS 69* v Lancs (Nottingham) 2008. BB 4-92 WA v S Aus (Adelaide) 2006-07. Nt BB 3-21 v Durham (Nottingham) 2008. LO HS 100* WA v NSW (Sydney) 2004-05. LO BB 3-33 WA v Tas (Perth) 2007-08. IT20 HS 26. IT20 BB 2-5. T20 HS 74*. T20 BB 2-4.

WAGH, Mark Anant (King Edward's S, Birmingham; Keble C, Oxford), b Birmingham, Warwks 20 Oct 1976. 6'2". RHB, OB. Oxford U 1996-98; blue 1996-97-98; captain 1997. Warwickshire 1997-2006; cap 2000. British U 1996-1998. Mashonaland A 1998-99. Nottinghamshire debut/cap 2007. Zimbabwe CA (List A) 1998-99. 1000 runs (6); most – 1310 (2007). HS 315 Wa v Middlesex (Lord's) 2001. Nt HS 152 v Northants (Northampton) 2007. BB 7-222 Wa v Lancs (Birmingham) 2003. Nt BB 2-6 v Somerset (Taunton) 2007. LO HS 102* Wa v Kent (Birmingham) 2004 (NL). LO BB 4-35 Wa v Glamorgan (Birmingham) 2004 (NL). T20 HS 56. T20 BB 2-16.

WOOD, Matthew James (Exmouth Community C; Exeter U), b Exeter, Devon 30 Sep 1980. 5'11". RHB, OB. Somerset 2001-07; cap 2005. Nottinghamshire debut 2008. MCC 2007. Devon 1998-2004. 1000 (1): 1058 (2005). HS 297 Sm v Yorks (Taunton) 2005. Nt HS 98 v Sussex (Hove) 2008. LO HS 129 Sm v Yorks (Taunton) 2005 (NL). T20 HS 94.

RELEASED/RETIRED
(Having made a County First-Class or List A appearance in 2008)

HARRIS, A.J. – *see LEICESTERSHIRE*.

FERLEY, R.S. – *see KENT*.

PRINCE, A.G. – *see LANCASHIRE*.

D.Alleyne, G.D.Clough, D.J.Hussey and J.A.Mierkalns left the staff, without making a County First-Class or List A appearance in 2008.

NOTTINGHAMSHIRE 2008

RESULTS SUMMARY

	Place	Won	Lost	Tied	Drew	No Result
County Championship (1st Division)	2nd	5	3		7	1
All First-Class Matches		6	3		7	1
FP Trophy (Midlands Division)	Quarter-Finalist	4	3			2
Pro40 League (1st Division)	4th	4	4			
Twenty/20 Cup (North Division)	4th	4	5			1

LV COUNTY CHAMPIONSHIP AVERAGES

BATTING AND FIELDING

Cap		M	I	NO	HS	Runs	Avge	100	50	Ct/St
2008	S.R.Patel	13	21	3	135	970	53.88	2	7	7
2007	M.A.Wagh	15	24	2	141	1033	46.95	2	8	3
1999	C.M.W.Read	15	20	4	142	673	42.06	1	4	52/2
	B.M.Shafayat	9	14	2	118	476	39.66	2	1	7
2005	G.P.Swann	12	15	1	82	523	37.35	–	4	15
2008	A.C.Voges	11	19	3	69*	550	34.37	–	3	11
2008	A.G.Prince	4	4	–	57	123	30.75	–	1	1
	M.J.Wood	13	20	1	98	524	27.57	–	4	4
1999	P.J.Franks	7	11	2	52	245	27.22	–	1	5
2004	M.A.Ealham	14	17	1	130*	329	20.56	1	–	9
	S.C.J.Broad	3	4	–	53	77	19.25	–	1	1
	W.I.Jefferson	12	20	1	80	344	18.10	–	1	18
2007	A.R.Adams	8	11	1	58	133	13.30	–	1	4
2008	D.J.Pattinson	12	12	–	33	118	9.83	–	–	1
2006	C.E.Shreck	15	17	11	3*	9	1.50	–	–	6

Also batted: R.S.Ferley (1 match) 26* (1 ct); R.J.Sidebottom (2 – cap 2004) 1, 11*, 1. A.D.Hales (1) did not bat.

BOWLING

	O	M	R	W	Avge	Best	5wI	10wM
A.R.Adams	230.4	64	594	31	19.16	4-39	–	–
R.J.Sidebottom	87	26	208	10	20.80	5-55	1	–
S.C.J.Broad	101.2	26	337	16	21.06	4-39	–	–
D.J.Pattinson	356.1	80	1159	47	24.65	6-30	4	–
G.P.Swann	306.5	59	793	30	26.43	4-25	–	–
C.E.Shreck	572.3	147	1663	58	28.67	5-40	2	–
M.A.Ealham	362.4	102	887	30	29.56	7-59	1	1
S.R.Patel	167.3	38	449	12	37.41	2-26	–	–
P.J.Franks	156	30	573	12	47.75	2-25	–	–

Also bowled: R.S.Ferley 55.1-9-136-2; A.G.Prince 7-0-38-0; C.M.W.Read 4-0-20-0; B.M.Shafayat 17-1-59-0; A.C.Voges 13-4-25-3; M.A.Wagh 9-4-11-0.

The First-Class Averages (pp 136–153) give the records of Nottinghamshire players in all first-class county matches (Nottinghamshire's other opponents being Oxford UCCE), with the exception of D.J.Pattinson, A.G.Prince, C.E.Shreck and R.J.Sidebottom, whose first-class figures for Nottinghamshire are as above, and:

    S.C.J.Broad 4-4-0-53-77-19.25-0-1-2ct. 119.2-30-394-17-23.17-4/39-0-0.

    G.P.Swann 13-16-2-82-525-37.50-0-4-15ct. 325.5-66-865-32-27.03-4/25-0-0.

NOTTINGHAMSHIRE RECORDS

FIRST-CLASS CRICKET

Highest Total	For	791		v	Essex	Chelmsford	2007
	V	781-7d		by	Northants	Northampton	1995
Lowest Total	For	13		v	Yorkshire	Nottingham	1901
	V	16		by	Derbyshire	Nottingham	1879
		16		by	Surrey	The Oval	1880
Highest Innings	For	312*	W.W.Keeton	v	Middlesex	The Oval	1939
	V	345	C.G.Macartney	for	Australians	Nottingham	1921

Highest Partnership for each Wicket

1st	406*	D.J.Bicknell/G.E.Welton	v	Warwicks	Birmingham	2000
2nd	398	A.Shrewsbury/W.Gunn	v	Sussex	Nottingham	1890
3rd	367	W.Gunn/J.R.Gunn	v	Leics	Nottingham	1903
4th	361	A.O.Jones/J.R.Gunn	v	Essex	Leyton	1905
5th	359	D.J.Hussey/C.M.W.Read	v	Essex	Nottingham	2007
6th	372*	K.P.Pietersen/J.E.Morris	v	Derbyshire	Derby	2001
7th	301	C.C.Lewis/B.N.French	v	Durham	Chester-le-St	1993
8th	220	G.F.H.Heane/R.Winrow	v	Somerset	Nottingham	1935
9th	170	J.C.Adams/K.P.Evans	v	Somerset	Taunton	1994
10th	152	E.B.Alletson/W.Riley	v	Sussex	Hove	1911
	152	U.Afzaal/A.J.Harris	v	Worcs	Nottingham	2000

Best Bowling	For	10-66	K.Smales	v	Glos	Stroud	1956
(Innings)	V	10-10	H.Verity	for	Yorkshire	Leeds	1932
Best Bowling	For	17-89	F.C.L.Matthews	v	Northants	Nottingham	1923
(Match)	V	17-89	W.G.Grace	for	Glos	Cheltenham	1877

Most Runs – Season	2620	W.W.Whysall	(av 53.46)	1929
Most Runs – Career	31592	G.Gunn	(av 35.69)	1902-32
Most 100s – Season	9	W.W.Whysall		1928
	9	M.J.Harris		1971
	9	B.C.Broad		1990
Most 100s – Career	65	J.Hardstaff jr		1930-55
Most Wkts – Season	181	B.Dooland	(av 14.96)	1954
Most Wkts – Career	1653	T.G.Wass	(av 20.34)	1896-1920
Most Career W-K Dismissals	957	T.W.Oates	(733 ct/224 st)	1897-1925
Most Career Catches in the Field	466	A.O.Jones		1892-1914

LIMITED-OVERS CRICKET

Highest Total	FPT	344-6		v	Northumb	Jesmond	1994
	P40	329-6		v	Derbyshire	Nottingham	1993
	T20	213-6		v	Northants	Nottingham	2006
Lowest Total	FPT	123		v	Yorkshire	Scarborough	1969
	P40	66		v	Yorkshire	Bradford	1969
	T20	91		v	Lancashire	Manchester	2006
Highest Innings	FPT	149*	D.W.Randall	v	Devon	Torquay	1988
	P40	167*	P.Johnson	v	Kent	Nottingham	1993
	T20	91	M.A.Ealham	v	Yorkshire	Nottingham	2004
Best Bowling	FPT	6-10	K.P.Evans	v	Northumb	Jesmond	1994
	P40	6-12	R.J.Hadlee	v	Lancashire	Nottingham	1980
	T20	5-26	R.J.Logan	v	Lancashire	Nottingham	2003

SOMERSET

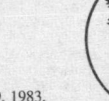

Formation of Present Club: 18 August 1875
Inaugural First-Class Match: 1882
Colours: Black, White and Maroon
Badge: Somerset Dragon
County Champions: (0); best – 2nd (Div 1) 2001
Gillette/NatWest/C&G/FP Trophy Winners: (3) 1979, 1983, 2001
Benson and Hedges Cup Winners: (2) 1981, 1982
Pro 40/National League (Div 1) Winners: (0); best – 4th 2001
Sunday League Winners: (1) 1979
Twenty20 Cup Winners: (1) 2005

Chief Executive: Richard A.Gould, County Ground, Taunton TA1 1JT • Tel: 0845 337 1875 • Fax: 01823 332395 • Email: enquiries@somersetcountycc.co.uk • Web: www.somerset countycc.co.uk

Director of Cricket: Brian C.Rose. **Head Coach**: Andy Hurry. **Captain**: J.L.Langer. **Vice-Captain**: M.E.Trescothick. **Overseas Player**: J.L.Langer. **2009 Beneficiary**: A.R.Caddick. **Head Groundsman**: Phil Frost. **Scorer**: Gerald A.Stickley. ‡ New registration. ^{NQ} Not qualified for England.

^{NQ}**BANKS, Omari** Ahmed Clement (Albena Lake Hodge CS), b Road Bay, Antigua 17 Jul 1982. 6'4". RHB, OB. Leeward Islands 2000-01 to date. Leicestershire 2001 (1 match – v Pakistanis). Carib Beer XI 2002-03 to 2003-04. Somerset 2008, l-o and T20 only – awaiting CC debut. **Tests** (WI): 10 (2002-03 to 2005): HS 50* v SL (Gros Islet, St Lucia) 2003; BB 4-87 v B (Kingston) 2004. **LOI** (WI): 5 (2002-03 to 2005): HS 33 and BB 2-24 v SL (Colombo) 2005. F-c **Tours** (WI): E 2004, 2006 (WI A); SL 2005; Z 2003-04. HS 108 Leeward Is v Jamaica (Basseterre) 2008-09. BB 7-70 Leeward Is v Jamaica (Molyneux, St Kitts) 2000-01. LO HS 77* Rest of Leeward Is v Canada (Kingston) 2003-04. LO BB 4-23 Rest of Leeward Is v N Windward Is (Kingston) 2001-02. T20 HS 50*. T20 BB 1-30.

‡**BURKE, Justin** Conrad, b Bristol, Glos 20 Jun 1975. RHB, RM. Somerset 2nd XI 1995. Awaiting 1st XI debut.

‡**BUTTLER, Joseph** Charles (*'Jos'*), b Taunton 8 Sep 1990. RHB, WK. Somerset 2nd XI debut 2007. Awaiting 1st XI debut.

CADDICK, Andrew Richard (Papanui HS), b Christchurch, NZ 21 Nov 1968. Son of English emigrants – qualified for England 1992. 6'5". RHB, RFM. Debut (Somerset) 1991; cap 1992; benefit 1999, 2009. Represented NZ in 1987-88 Youth World Cup. *Wisden* 2000. **Tests**: 62 (1993 to 2002-03); HS 49* v A (Birmingham) 2001; BB 7-46 v SA (Durban) 1999-00. **LOI**: 54 (1993 to 2002-03); HS 36 v A (Oval) 2001; BB 4-19 v SA (Johannesburg) 1999-00. F-c **Tours**: A 1992-93 (Eng A), 2002-03; SA 1999-00; WI 1993-94, 1997-98; NZ 1996-97, 2001-02; P 2000-01; SL 2000-01; Z 1996-97. HS 92 v Worcs (Worcester) 1995. 50 wkts (12) inc 100 (1): 105 (1998). BB 9-32 (12-120 match) v Lancs (Taunton) 1993. LO HS 39 v Hants (Taunton) 1996 (SL). LO BB 6-30 v Glos (Taunton) 1992 (NWT). T20 HS 0. T20 BB 2-12.

NQDE BRUYN, Zander (Helpmekaar HS; Randburg HS; Rand Afrikaans U, Jo'burg), b Johannesburg, South Africa 5 Jul 1975. 6'0". RHB, RMF. Transvaal B 1995-96 to 1996-97. Gauteng 1996-97 to 2001-02. Easterns 2002-03 to 2005-06. Titans 2004-05 to 2005-06. Worcestershire 2005. Warriors 2006-07 to date. Somerset debut 2008 (Kolpak registration); cap 2008. **Tests** (SA): 3 (2004-05); HS 83 v I (Kanpur) 2004-05 – on debut; BB 2-32 v I (Calcutta) 2004-05. F-c Tours (SA): I 2004-05; SL 2005-06 (SA A). 1000 runs (0+1): 1048 (2003-04). HS 266* Easterns v GW (Kimberley) 2003-04. UK HS 161 Wo v Somerset (Worcester) 2005. Sm HS 120 and UK BB 2-19 v Durham (Chester-le-St) 2008. BB 7-67 Warriors v Titans (Pt Elizabeth) 2007-08. LO HS 113* Surrey CB v Hunts (Cheam) 2001. LO BB 5-44 Easterns v WP (Cape Town) 2003-04. T20 HS 76*. T20 BB 4-18.

‡DIBBLE, Adam John, b Exeter, Devon 9 Mar 1991. RHB, RMF. Somerset 2nd XI debut 2006, aged 15 years 103 days. Awaiting 1st XI debut.

DURSTON, Wesley John (Millfield S; University C, Worcester), b Taunton 6 Oct 1980. 5'10". RHB, OB. Debut (Somerset) 2002. HS 146* v Derbys (Derby) 2005. BB 3-23 v SL A (Taunton) 2004. CC BB 2-31 v Surrey (Bath) 2006. LO HS 62* v Yorks (Taunton) 2006 (P40). LO BB 3-44 v Surrey (Taunton) 2006 (P40). T20 HS 34. T20 BB 3-25.

EDWARDS, Neil James (Cape Cornwall CS; Richard Huish C), b Treliske, Truro, Cornwall 14 Oct 1983. 6'3". LHB, RM. Debut (Somerset) 2002. Cornwall 2000-06. 1000 runs (1): 1251 (2007). HS 212 v LU (Taunton) 2007. CC HS 160 v Hants (Taunton) 2003. BB 1-16 v Derbys (Taunton) 2004. LO HS 65 v Yorks (Taunton) 2006 (P40). T20 HS 1.

GAZZARD, Carl Matthew (Mounts Bay CS, Penzance; Richard Huish C), b Penzance, Cornwall 15 Apr 1982. 6'0". RHB, WK. Debut (Somerset) 2002. Cornwall 1998-2001. HS 74 v Worcs (Worcester) 2005. LO HS 157 v Derbys (Derby) 2004 (NL). T20 HS 39.

HILDRETH James Charles (Millfield S), b Milton Keynes, Bucks 9 Sep 1984. 5'10", RHB, RMF. Debut (Somerset) 2003; cap 2007. 1000 runs (1): 1270 (2007). HS 227* v Northants (Taunton) 2006. BB 2-39 v Hants (Taunton) 2004. LO HS 122 v Derbys (Derby) 2006 (P40). LO BB 2-26 v Worcs (Worcester) 2008 (FPT). T20 HS 71. T20 BB 3-24.

‡JONES, Chris Robert, b Harold Wood, Essex 5 Nov 1990. RHB. Dorset 2007-08. Awaiting 1st XI debut.

JONES, Philip Steffan (Stradey CS, Llanelli; Neath TC; Loughborough U; Homerton C, Cambridge), b Llanelli, Carms, Wales 9 Feb 1974. 6'2". RHB, RMF. Cambridge U 1997; blue 1997. Somerset 1997-2003, 2007 to date; cap 2001. Northamptonshire 2004-05. Derbyshire 2006. Wales MC 1994-97. HS 114 v Leics (Leicester) 2007. 50 wkts (2); most – 59 (2001, 2006). BB 6-25 De v Glamorgan (Cardiff) 2006. Sm BB 6-61 v Leics (Taunton) 2007. LO HS 42 v Glamorgan (Taunton) 2008 (FPT). LO BB 6-56 Nh v Ire (Clontarf) 2004 (CGT). T20 HS 24*. T20 BB 3-26.

NQKIESWETTER, Craig (Diocesan C; Millfield S), b Johannesburg, South Africa 18 Nov 1987. 6'1". RHB, WK. Debut (Somerset) 2007 (Kolpak registration). Represented South Africa in U19 World Cup 2006. HS 93 v Glamorgan (Taunton) 2007. LO HS 121 v Glos (Taunton) 2008 (P40). T20 HS 48.

NQLANGER, Justin Lee (Aquinas C; U of WA), b Perth, Australia 21 Nov 1970. Nephew of R.S.Langer (W Australia 1973-74 to 1981-82). 5'8". LHB, RM. W Australia 1991-92 to 2007-08. Middlesex 1998-2000; cap 1998; captain 2000. Somerset debut 2006; cap 2007; captain 2007 to date. *Wisden* 2000. **Tests** (A): 104 (1992-93 to 2006-07); HS 250 v E (Melbourne) 2002-03. **LOI**: 8 (1993-94 to 1997); HS 36 v I (Sharjah) 1993-94. F-c Tours (A): E 1995 (Young A), 1997, 2001, 2005; SA 1996-97, 2001-02, 2005-06; WI 1994-95, 1998-99, 2002-03; NZ 1992-93, 1999-00, 2004-05; I 2000-01, 2004-05; P 1994-95, 1998-99, 2002-03 (*in UAE*); SL 1999, 2002-03 (*v P*), 2003-04; Z 1999-00. 1000 runs (5+6); most – 1472 (2000). HS 342 v Surrey (Guildford) 2006 – Somerset record f-c score. Scored 315 v Middlesex (Taunton) 2007 in his next CC innings. BB 2-17 Aus A v SA A (Brisbane) 1997-98. UK BB 1-10 M v Northants (Northampton) 1998. LO HS 146 WA v S Aus (Perth) 1999-00 (MM). LO BB 3-51 v Surrey (Guildford) 1998 (SL). T20 HS 97.

LETT, Robin Jonathan Hugh (Millfield S; Oxford Brookes U), b Westminster, London 23 Dec 1986. Grandson of P.H.Jaques (Leicestershire 1949). 6'2". RHB, RM. Debut (Somerset) 2006 – summer contract; no 1st XI appearances in 2008. Oxford UCCE 2007-08. HS 57 OU v Glamorgan (Oxford) 2007. Sm HS 50 v Glamorgan (Taunton) 2006 – on debut.

MUNDAY, Michael Kenneth (Truro S, Cornwall; Corpus Christi C, Oxford), b Nottingham 22 Oct 1984. 5'7½". RHB, LB. Oxford U 2003-06, blue 2003-04-05-06. Somerset debut 2005. Cornwall 2001-08. HS 21 v Lancashire (Manchester) 2008. BB 8-55 (10-65 match) v Notts (Taunton) 2007. LO HS – and BB 1-39 Cornwall v Sussex (Truro) 2001 (CGT).

PHILLIPS, Ben James (Langley Park S and SFC, Beckenham), b Lewisham, London 30 Sep 1974. 6'6". RHB, RFM. Kent 1996-98. Northamptonshire 2002-06; cap 2005. Joined Somerset staff 2007 but injury prevented his appearing for 1st XI. HS 100* K v Lancs (Manchester) 1997. Sm HS 53* v Kent (Taunton) 2008. BB 6-29 Nh v CU (Cambridge) 2006. CC BB 5-47 K v Sussex (Horsham) 1997. Sm BB 3-34 v Sussex (Taunton) 2008. LO HS 44* Nh v Kent (Canterbury) 2004 (NL). LO BB 4-25 K v Northants (Canterbury) 2000 (NL). T20 HS 41*. T20 BB 4-18.

‡STIFF, David Alexander (Batley GS; Wakefield C), Dewsbury, Yorks 20 Oct 1984. RHB, RFM. Kent 2004-06. Yorkshire 2nd XI 2001-03. Signed for Leicestershire in 2007 – no 1st XI appearances. HS 18 and CC BB 2-58 K v Lancashire (Tunbridge W) 2004. BB K v NZ (Canterbury) 2004. LO HS-and BB 1-27 Yorks CB v Glos CB (Bristol) 2001 (CGT).

NQSUPPIAH, Arul Vivasvan (Exeter U), b Kuala Lumpur, Malaysia 30 Aug 1983. Son of R.Suppiah (Kuala Lumpur). Brother of R.V.Suppiah (Malaysia 1997-98 to 2006; f-c 2004). 6'0". RHB, SLA. Somerset debut (Somerset) 2002 (Kolpak registration). Malaysia 2000-01 to 2005 (*not f-c*). Devon 2003-05. HS 123 v Derbys (Derby) 2005. BB 3-46 v WI A (Taunton) 2002. CC BB 2-36 v Leics (Leicester) 2004. LO HS 79 v Derbys (Derby) 2005 (NL). LO BB 4-39 v Surrey (Oval) 2006 (CGT). T20 HS 32*. T20 BB 3-36.

NQTHOMAS, Alfonso Clive (Ravensmead SS; Parow HS), b Cape Town, South Africa 9 Feb 1977. RHB, RFM. W Province 1998-99. North West 2000-01 to 2002-03. Northerns 2003-04 to 2005-06. Titans 2004-05 to 2007-08. Warwickshire 2007. Dolphins 2007-08 to date (no f-c apps). Somerset debut 2008; cap 2008. F-c Tour (SA A): Z 2004. HS 119* North West v Northerns (Pretoria) 2002-03. UK HS 43 v Hampshire (Southampton) 2008. BB 7-54 Titans v Cape Cobras (Cape Town) 2005-06. UK BB 5-46 v Yorkshire (Taunton) 2008. LO HS 27* Titans v WP Boland (Cape Town) 2004-05. LO BB 4-31 Northerns v Gauteng (Pretoria) 2003-04. IT20 HS – . IT20 BB 3-25. T20 HS 27. T20 BB 4-27.

TREGO, Peter David (Wyvern CS, W-s-M), b Weston-super-Mare 12 Jun 1981. 6'0". RHB, RMF. Somerset 2000-02, 2006 to date; cap 2007; 2nd XI debut 1997 when aged 16 years 20 days. Kent 2003. Middlesex 2005. Herefordshire 2005. HS 140 v West Indies A (Taunton) 2002. CC HS 135 v Derbys (Taunton) 2006. BB 6-59 M v Notts (Nottingham) 2005. Sm BB 4-49 v Leics (Leicester) 2007. LO HS 78 v Middlesex (Lord's) 2007 (FPT). BB 5-44 v Kent (Canterbury) 2007 (P40). T20 HS 79. T20 BB 2-17.

TRESCOTHICK, Marcus Edward (Sir Bernard Lovell S), b Keynsham 25 Dec 1975. 6'2". LHB, RM, occ WK. Debut (Somerset) 1993; cap 1999; joint captain 2002; benefit 2008. PCA 2000. *Wisden* 2004. MBE 2005. **Tests**: 76 (2000 to 2006, 2 as captain); HS 219 v SA (Oval) 2003; BB 1-34 v P (Karachi) 2000-01. **LOI**: 123 (2000 to 2006, 10 as captain); HS 137 v P (Lord's) 2001; BB 2-7 v Z (Manchester) 2000. F-c Tours: A 2002-03; SA 2004-05; WI 2003-04; NZ 1999-00 (Eng A), 2001-02; I 2001-02, 2005-06 (*part*); P 2000-01, 2005-06; SL 2000-01, 2003-04; B 1999-00 (Eng A), 2003-04. 1000 runs (2); most – 1343 (2007). HS 284 v Northants (Northampton) 2007. BB 4-36 (inc hat-trick) v Young A (Taunton) 1995. CC BB 4-82 v Yorks (Leeds) 1998. Hat-trick 1995. LO HS 184 v Glos (Taunton) 2008 (P40) – record Sm L-o score. LO BB 4-50 v Northants (Northampton) 2000 (NL). T20 HS 107.

TURNER, Mark Leif (Thornhill CS), b Sunderland, Co Durham 23 Oct 1984. 5'11". RHB, RMF. Durham 2005-06. Somerset debut 2007. HS 57 v Derbys (Taunton) 2007. BB 4-30 v LU (Taunton) 2007. CC BB 3-53 v Lancashire (Manchester) 2008. LO BB 11* v Essex (Chelmsford) 2007 (FPT). LO HS 3-39 v Lancashire (Liverpool) 2008 (P40). T20 HS 7. T20 BB 2-22.

WALLER, Maximilian Thomas Charles (Millfield S; Bournemouth U), b Salisbury, Wiltshire 3 March 1988. 6'0". RHB, LB. Somerset 2nd XI debut 2006. Dorset 2007-08. Awaiting 1st XI appearance.

[NQ]**WILLOUGHBY, Charl** Myles (Wynberg BHS; Stellenbosch U), b Cape Town, South Africa 3 Dec 1974. 6'2". LHB, LMF. Boland 1994-95 to 1999-00. W Province 2000-01 to 2003-04. MCC 2001, 2004. WP-Boland 2004-05. Leicestershire 2005 (Kolpak registration). Cape Cobras 2005-06 to 2006-07. Somerset debut 2006 (Kolpak); cap 2007. Berkshire 2000. **Tests** (SA): 2 (2003); HS – ; BB 1-47 v B (Chittagong) 2002-03 – on debut. **LOI** (SA): 3 (1999-00 to 2003); HS 0; BB 2-39 v P (Sharjah) 1999-00 – on debut. F-c Tours (SA): E 2003; WI 2000 (SA A); Z 1998-99 (SA Acad), 2004 (SA A); B 2003. HS 47 v Worcs (Taunton) 2006. 50 wkts (3+2); most – 66 (2006). BB 7-44 v Glos (Taunton) 2005. LO HS 12* v Middlesex (Bath) 2006 (CGT). LO BB 6-16 Le v Somerset (Leicester) 2005 (NL). T20 HS 11. T20 BB 4-9.

RELEASED/RETIRED
(Having made a County First-Class or List A appearance in 2008)

BLACKWELL, I.D. – *see DURHAM.*

FRANCIS, John Daniel (King Edward VI S, Southampton; Durham U; Loughborough U), b Bromley, Kent 13 Nov 1980. Younger brother of S.R.G.Francis (*see NOTTINGHAM-SHIRE*). 5'11". LHB, SLA. Hampshire 2001-03. British U 2002-03. Loughborough UCCE 2003. Somerset 2004-08. 1000 (1): 1062 (2005). HS 125* v Yorks (Leeds) 2005 – carrying bat. BB 1-1 H v Leics (Leicester) 2002. Sm BB 1-4 v Durham (Chester-le-St) 2004. LO HS 103* H v Northants (Southampton) 2002 (NL). T20 HS 49.

K.A.Parsons left the staff, without making a County First-Class or List A appearance in 2008.

SOMERSET 2008

RESULTS SUMMARY

	Place	Won	Lost	Tied	Drew	No Result
County Championship (1st Division)	4th	3	2		11	
All First-Class Matches		4	2		12	
FP Trophy (South West Division)	Quarter-Finalist 3	3				3
Pro40 League (1st Division)	6th		3	4	1	
Twenty/20 Cup (Midlands/West/Wales Division)	4th	3	4			3

LV COUNTY CHAMPIONSHIP AVERAGES

BATTING AND FIELDING

Cap		M	I	NO	HS	Runs	Avge	100	50	Ct/St
2008	Z.de Bruyn	15	23	2	120	988	47.04	3	5	7
1999	M.E.Trescothick	16	28	1	158	1258	46.59	3	8	19
2001	I.D.Blackwell	16	24	1	158	1006	43.73	3	7	6
2007	J.L.Langer	15	26	1	188	1083	43.32	3	7	15
2007	P.D.Trego	14	21	2	86	813	42.78	–	7	3
2007	J.C.Hildreth	16	28	2	158	804	30.92	1	4	7
	N.J.Edwards	6	11	–	99	298	27.09	–	2	7
	C.Kieswetter	15	24	4	67*	524	26.20	–	1	43/2
	B.J.Phillips	9	12	3	53*	181	20.11	–	1	3
2001	P.S.Jones	8	11	2	27*	175	19.44	–	–	
2008	A.C.Thomas	11	15	3	43	231	19.25	–	–	4
	W.J.Durston	3	4	1	21	54	18.00	–	–	1
1992	A.R.Caddick	8	11	3	35*	117	14.62	–	–	2
2007	C.M.Willoughby	16	17	11	18	70	11.66	–	–	1
	M.K.Munday	3	4	1	21	34	11.33	–	–	1

Also batted: J.D.Francis (1 match) 2, 9; C.M.Gazzard (1) 6; A.V.Suppiah (2) 26, 61, 19; M.L.Turner (1) 2, 1.

BOWLING

	O	M	R	W	Avge	Best	5wI	10wM
P.D.Trego	178.4	39	646	26	24.84	4- 52	–	
A.C.Thomas	253.2	52	817	30	27.23	5- 46	2	–
C.M.Willoughby	492	129	1366	49	27.87	4- 65	–	
P.S.Jones	206.2	36	749	26	28.80	5- 53	2	–
B.J.Phillips	207.1	47	627	18	34.83	3- 34	–	
A.R.Caddick	228	47	836	21	39.80	5-118	1	–
I.D.Blackwell	394	87	959	21	45.66	4- 74	–	
Also bowled:								
Z.de Bruyn	88.3	14	305	6	50.83	2- 19	–	–

W.J.Durston 34-2-88-0; N.J.Edwards 1-0-1-0; J.C.Hildreth 8-0-38-0; J.L.Langer 2-0-6-0; M.K.Munday 52.3-5-185-3; A.V.Suppiah 23-2-82-0; M.L.Turner 17-4-53-3.

The First-Class Averages (pp 136–153) give the records of Somerset players in all first-class county matches (Somerset's other opponents being the South Africans and Cambridge UCCE).

SOMERSET RECORDS

FIRST-CLASS CRICKET

Highest Total	For 850-7d		v	Middlesex	Taunton	2007
	V 811		by	Surrey	The Oval	1899
Lowest Total	For 25		v	Glos	Bristol	1947
	V 22		by	Glos	Bristol	1920
Highest Innings	For 342	J.L.Langer	v	Surrey	Guildford	2006
	V 424	A.C.MacLaren	for	Lancashire	Taunton	1895

Highest Partnership for each Wicket

1st	346	L.C.H.Palairet/H.T.Hewett	v	Yorkshire	Taunton	1892
2nd	290	J.C.W.MacBryan/M.D.Lyon	v	Derbyshire	Burton upon T	1924
3rd	319	P.M.Roebuck/M.D.Crowe	v	Leics	Taunton	1984
4th	310	P.W.Denning/I.T.Botham	v	Glos	Taunton	1980
5th	320	J.D.Francis/I.D.Blackwell	v	Durham UCCE	Taunton	2005
6th	265	W.E.Alley/K.E.Palmer	v	Northants	Northampton	1961
7th	279	R.J.Harden/G.D.Rose	v	Sussex	Taunton	1997
8th	172	I.V.A.Richards/I.T.Botham	v	Leics	Leicester	1983
	172	A.R.K.Pierson/P.S.Jones	v	N Zealanders	Taunton	1999
9th	183	C.H.M.Greetham/H.W.Stephenson	v	Leics	Weston-s-Mare	1963
	183	C.J.Tavaré/N.A.Mallender	v	Sussex	Hove	1990
10th	163	I.D.Blackwell/N.A.M.McLean	v	Derbyshire	Taunton	2003

Best Bowling	For 10- 49	E.J.Tyler	v	Surrey	Taunton	1895
(Innings)	V 10- 35	A.Drake	for	Yorkshire	Weston-s-Mare	1914
Best Bowling	For 16- 83	J.C.White	v	Worcs	Bath	1919
(Match)	V 17-137	W.Brearley	for	Lancashire	Manchester	1905

Most Runs – Season	2761	W.E.Alley	(av 58.74)	1961
Most Runs – Career	21142	H.Gimblett	(av 36.96)	1935-54
Most 100s – Season	11	S.J.Cook		1991
Most 100s – Career	49	H.Gimblett		1935-54
Most Wkts – Season	169	A.W.Wellard	(av 19.24)	1938
Most Wkts – Career	2165	J.C.White	(av 18.03)	1909-37
Most Career W-K Dismissals	1007	H.W.Stephenson	(698 ct/309 st)	1948-64
Most Career Catches in the Field	381	J.C.White		1909-37

LIMITED-OVERS CRICKET

Highest Total	FPT	413-4		v	Devon	Torquay	1990
	P40	377-9		v	Sussex	Hove	2003
	T20	250-3		v	Glos	Taunton	2006
Lowest Total	FPT	58		v	Middlesex	Southgate	2000
	P40	58		v	Essex	Chelmsford	1977
	T20	119-9 (20)		v	Glos	Taunton	2003
Highest Innings	FPT	162*	C.J.Tavaré	v	Devon	Torquay	1990
	P40	184	M.E.Trescothick	v	Glos	Taunton	2008
	T20	141*	C.L.White	v	Worcs	Worcester	2006
Best Bowling	FPT	8-66	S.R.G.Francis	v	Derbyshire	Derby	2004
	P40	6-24	I.V.A.Richards	v	Lancashire	Manchester	1983
	T20	4-15	A.W.Laraman	v	Worcs	Taunton	2004

SURREY

Formation of Present Club: 22 August 1845
Inaugural First-Class Match: 1864
Colours: Chocolate
Badge: Prince of Wales' Feathers
County Champions (since 1890): (18) 1890, 1891, 1892,
1894, 1895, 1899, 1914, 1952, 1953, 1954, 1955, 1956,
1957, 1958, 1971, 1999, 2000, 2002
Joint Champions: (1) 1950
Gillette/NatWest/C&G/FP Trophy Winners: (1) 1982
Benson and Hedges Cup Winners: (3) 1974, 1997, 2001
Pro 40/National League (Div 1) Winners: (1) 2003
Sunday League Winners: (1) 1996
Twenty20 Cup Winners: (1) 2003

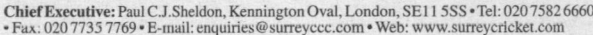

Chief Executive: Paul C.J.Sheldon, Kennington Oval, London, SE11 5SS • Tel: 020 7582 6660
• Fax: 020 7735 7769 • E-mail: enquiries@surreyccc.com • Web: www.surreycricket.com

Cricket Manager: Chris Adams. **Captain:** M.A.Butcher. **Vice-Captain:** tba. **Overseas
Players:** G.Elliott and A.Nel. **2009 Beneficiary:** J.N.Batty. **Head Groundsman:** W.H.
(Bill) Gordon. **Scorer:** Keith R.Booth. ‡ New registration. [NQ] Not qualified for England.

AFZAAL, Usman (Manvers Pierrepont CS; S Notts C), b Rawalpindi, Pakistan 9 Jun 1977.
6'0". LHB, SLA. Nottinghamshire 1995-2003; cap 2000. MCC 2002. Northamptonshire
2004-07; cap 2005. Surrey debut 2008. **Tests**: 3 (2001); HS 54 and BB 1-49 v A (Oval)
2001. F-c Tours: SA 1996-97 (Nt); WI 2000-01 (Eng A); NZ 2001-02. 1000 runs (6); most
– 1365 (2004). HS 168* Nh v Essex (Northampton) 2005. Sy HS 134* v Lancs (Oval) 2008
– on Sy CC debut. BB 4-101 Nt v Glos (Nottingham) 1998. Sy BB 2-62 v Yorkshire (Oval)
2008. LO HS 132 Nh v Yorks (Leeds) 2007 (FPT). LO BB 4-49 v Derbys (Chesterfield)
2008 (P40). T20 HS 64*. T20 BB 2-15.

BATTY, Jonathan Neil (Wheatley Park S, Oxon; Repton S; Durham U; Keble C, Oxford),
b Chesterfield, Derbys 18 Apr 1974. 5'10". RHB, WK. Comb U 1994-95. Oxford U 1996;
blue 1996. Surrey debut 1997; cap 2001; captain 2004; benefit 2009. Oxfordshire 1993-96.
Minor C 1996. 1000 runs (1): 1025 (2006). HS 168* v Essex (Chelmsford) 2003. BB 1-21 v
Lancs (Manchester) 2000. LO HS 158* v Hants (Oval) 2005 (CGT). T20 HS 59.

BENNING, James Graham Edward (Beacon S; Chesham S; Caterham S), b Mill Hill, N
London 4 May 1983. 6'0". RHB, RM. Debut (Surrey) 2003. Buckinghamshire 2000-01. HS
128 v OU (Oxford) 2004. CC HS 112 v Glos (Oval) 2006. BB 3-57 v Kent (Tunbridge
Wells) 2005. LO HS 189* v Glos (Bristol) 2006 (CGT). LO BB 4-43 v Leics (Oval) 2003
(NL). T20 HS 88. T20 BB 1-7.

‡BROWN, Michael James (Queen Elizabeth GS, Blackburn; Collingwood C, Durham U), b
Burnley, Lancs 9 Feb 1980. 6'0". Elder brother of D.O.Brown (*see GLOUCESTERSHIRE*).
RHB, OB. Middlesex 1999-2003. Hampshire 2004-08; cap 2007. Durham UCCE 2001-02.
British U 2001-02. 1000 runs (1): 1078 (2007). HS 133 Ha v LU (Southampton) 2006. CC
HS 126* Ha v Durham (Chester-le-St) 2007. LO HS 96* Ha v Worcs (Southampton) 2008
(FPT). T20 HS 44.

BUTCHER, Mark Alan (Trinity S; Archbishop Tenison's S, Croydon), b Croydon 23 Aug 1972. Son of A.R.Butcher (Surrey, Glamorgan and England 1972-92, 1998); brother of G.P.Butcher (Glamorgan and Surrey 1994-2001); nephew of I.P.Butcher (Leics and Glos 1980-90) and M.S.Butcher (Surrey 1982). 5'11". LHB, RM/OB. Debut (Surrey) 1992; cap 1996; captain 2005 to date; benefit 2005. **Tests**: 71 (1997 to 2004-05, 1 as captain); HS 173* v A (Leeds) 2001; BB 4-42 v A (Birmingham) 2001. F-c Tours: A 1996-97 (Eng A), 1998-99, 2002-03; SA 1999-00, 2004-05; WI 1997-98, 2003-04; NZ 2001-02; I 2001-02; SL 2003-04; B 2003-04. 1000 runs (8); most – 1604 (1996). HS 259 v Leics (Leicester) 1999. BB 5-86 v Lancs (Manchester) 2000. LO HS 139 v Kent (Canterbury) 2008 (FPT). LO BB 3-23 v Sussex (Oval) 1992 (SL). T20 HS 60.

[NQ]**COLLINS, Pedro** Tyrone (St James S), b Boscobelle, Barbados 12 Aug 1976. Half-brother of F.H.Edwards (Barbados & West Indies 2001-02 to date). 6'2". RHB, LFM. Barbados 1996-97 to date. Busta Cup XI 2001-02. Surrey debut 2008 (Kolpak registration). **Tests** (WI): 32 (1998-99 to 2006); HS 24 v I (Kingston) 2001-02; BB 6-53 v B (Kingston) 2004. **LOI** (WI): 30 (1999-00 to 2004-05); HS 10* v NZ (Wellington) 1999-00; BB 5-43 v A (Adelaide) 2004-05. F-c Tours (WI): E 2004; SA 1997-98 (WI A), 2007-08; NZ 1999-00; I 1998-99 (WI A), 2002-03; P (Sharjah) 2001-02; SL 2001-02; Z 2001; B 1998-99 (WI A), 1999-00, 2002-03; Kenya 2001. HS 25 Barbados v Trinidad (Pointe-a-Pierre) 2003-04. Sy HS 21 v Yorkshire (Leeds) 2008. 50 wkts (0+1): 54 (2003-04). BB 6-24 Barbados v Windward Is (Portsmouth, Dominica) 2006-07. Sy BB 4-111 v Yorkshire (Oval) 2008. LO HS 55* Barbados v Guyana (Georgetown) 2001-02. LO BB 7-11 Barbados v WI U-19 (Blairmont, Berbice) 2007-08. T20 HS 1. T20 BB 3-13.

[NQ]**DERNBACH, Jade** Winston (St John the Baptist S), b Johannesburg, South Africa 3 Mar 1986. 6'1½". RHB, RMF. Italian passport. UK resident since 1998. Debut (Surrey) 2003, when aged 17. HS 16* v Notts (Nottingham) 2008. BB 6-72 v Somerset (Croydon) 2008. LO HS 21 v Warwks (Birmingham) 2005 (NL). LO BB 5-31 v Derbys (Chesterfield) 2008 (P40). T20 HS 9. T20 BB 3-32.

‡[NQ]**ELLIOTT, Grant** David (St Stithians S) b Johannesburg, South Africa 21 Mar 1979. 6'1". RHB, RFM. Debut Transvaal B 1996-97. SA Academy 1998. Griqualand West 1999-00 to 2000-01. Gauteng 2001-02 to 2002-03. Wellington 2005-06 to date. Qualified for NZ in 2007. **Tests** (NZ): 3 (2007-08 to 2008-09); HS 9 and BB 1-15 v A (Brisbane) 2008-09. **LOI** (NZ): 21 (2008 to 2008-09); HS 115 v A (Sydney) 2008-09; BB 3-14 v Scotland (Aberdeen) 2008. F-c Tours (NZ): E 2008; A 2008-09; B 2008-09. HS 196* Wellington v Auckland (Wellington) 2007-08. BB Gauteng v Easterns (Johannesburg) 2002-03. LO HS 115 (*see LOI*). LO BB Wellington v Otago (Wellington) 2007-08. IT20 HS 23*. IT20 BB 1-11. T20 HS 57. T20 BB 2-25.

EVANS, Laurie John (Whitgift S; The John Fisher S; St Mary's C, Durham U), b Lambeth, London 12 Oct 1987. 6'0". RHB, RFM. Durham UCCE 2007. MCC 2007. Surrey 2nd XI debut 2005. Joined Surrey staff 2008. Awaiting Surrey 1st XI debut; no f-c appearances in 2008. HS 133* DU v Lancs (Durham) 2007.

HARINATH, Arun (Whitgift S; Loughborough U), b Sutton 26 Mar 1987. LHB, OB. Loughborough UCCE 2007. MCC 2007. Surrey 2nd XI debut 2003. Awaiting Sy 1st XI debut. Buckinghamshire 2007-08. HS 69 LU v Worcs (Worcester) 2007.

JORDAN, Christopher James (Comber Mere S, Barbados; Dulwich C), b Christ Church, Barbados 4 Oct 1988. 6'0". RHB, RFM. Debut (Surrey) 2007. HS 57 v Notts (Nottingham) 2008. BB 3-32 v Durham (Chester-le-St) 2008. LO HS 38 v Yorkshire (Guildford) 2008 (P40). LO BB 3-28 v Yorks (Scarborough) 2007 (P40). T20 HS 31. T20 BB 1-23.

KING, Simon James (Warlingham S; John Fisher S), b Warlingham 4 Sep 1987. RHB, OB. Surrey 2nd XI debut 2005. Awaiting 1st XI debut.

94

MEAKER, Stuart Christopher (Cranleigh S), b Durban, South Africa 21 Jan 1989. Moved to UK in 2001. 6'1". RHB, RFM. Debut (Surrey) 2008. England U-19 2007-08. Surrey 2nd XI debut 2007. HS 16 and BB 3-86 v Notts (Oval) 2008. LO HS – . LO BB1-57 v Leics (Oval) 2008.

MURTAGH, Christopher Paul (John Fisher S; Loughborough U), b Lambeth, S London 14 Oct 1984. Younger brother of T.J.Murtagh (*see MIDDLESEX*); nephew of A.J.Murtagh (Hampshire and E Province 1973-77). 5'10". RHB, OB. Loughborough UCCE 2005-07. Surrey debut 2008. Surrey 2nd XI debut 2002. HS 107 LU v Yorks (Leeds) 2007. Sy HS 12 v Durham (Guildford) 2008. BB – . LO HS 74 v Leics (Oval) 2008 (P40). T20 HS 0.

NQMURTAZA HUSSAIN (Abbasia HS), b Bahawalpur, Pakistan 20 Dec 1974. British passport. 5'11". RHB, OB. Bahawalpur 1990-91 to 2001-02. Pakistan Automobiles Corp 1992-93 to 1993-94. United Bank 1994-95. PNSC 1995-96 to 1996-97. KRL 1997-98 to 1999-00. Islamabad 1998-99. Pakistan Customs 2004-05 to date. Surrey debut 2007. HS 117 Pakistan Customs v Attock Group (Karachi) 2006-07. Sy HS 56 v Yorkshire (Oval) 2008. 50 wkts (0+5), inc 100 wkts (1): 105 (1995-96). BB 9-54 Bahawalpur v Islamabad (Bahawalpur) 1995-96. Sy BB 4-126 v Lancashire (Oval) 2007. LO HS 85 KRL v Rawalpindi (Rawalpindi) 1998-99. LO BB 5-18 Bahawalpur v Lahore City (Bahawalpur) 1992-93.

‡NQNEL, Andre (Dr E.G.Jansen S, Boksburg), b Germiston, Transvaal, South Africa 15 Jul 1977. 6'4". RHB, RFM. Easterns 1996-97 to 2003-04. Northamptonshire 2003; cap 2003. Titans 2004-05. Essex 2005 (one match), 2007-08. Lions 2008-09. Gauteng 2008-09. Kolpak registration 2009. **Tests** (SA): 36 (2001-02 to 2008); HS 34 v WI (Port Elizabeth) 2007-08; BB 6-32 (10-88 match) v WI (Bridgetown) 2004-05. **LOI** (SA): 79 (2000-01 to 2008); HS 30* v NZ (Port Elizabeth) 2007-08; BB 5-45 v B (Providence, Guyana) 2006-07. F-c Tours (SA): E 2008; A 2005-06; WI 2000-01, 2004-05; NZ 2003-04; P 2003-04, 2007-08; SL 2006; Z 2001-02, 2007 (SA A); Ireland/Scotland 1999 (SA Acad). HS 56 South Africans v Bangladesh A (Worcester) 2008. CC HS 42 Nh v Glamorgan (Cardiff) 2003. BB 6-25 Easterns v Gauteng (Johannesburg) 2001-02. UK/CC BB 5-47 Nh v Glos (Gloucester) 2003. LO HS 58 Lions v Cape Cobras (Paarl) 2008-09. LO BB 6-27 Easterns v GW (Benoni) 2000-01. IT20 HS 0*. IT20 BB 2-19. T20 HS 12. T20 BB 2-13.

NEWMAN, Scott Alexander (Trinity S, Croydon; Coulsdon C; Brighton U), b Epsom 3 Nov 1979. 6'2". LHB, RM. Debut (Surrey) 2002 – scoring 99 v Hants (Oval) 2002; cap 2005. F-c Tour (Eng A): I 2003-04. 1000 runs (4); most – 1404 (2006). HS 219 (and 117) v Glamorgan (Oval) 2005. LO HS 106 v Essex (Oval) 2004 (NL). T20 HS 59.

ORMOND, James (St Thomas More S, Nuneaton), b Walsgrave, Coventry, Warwks 20 Aug 1977. 6'3". RHB, RFM. Leicestershire 1995-2001; cap 1999. Surrey debut 2002; cap 2003. Tests: 2 (2001 to 2001-02); HS 18 v A (Oval) 2001; BB 1-70. F-c Tours: NZ 2001-02; I 2001-02; SL 1997-98 (Eng A); K 1997-98 (Eng A). HS 64* v Hampshire (Southampton) 2008. 50 wkts (4); most – 52 (1999, 2004). BB 7-63 v Glamorgan (Cardiff) 2005. Hat-trick (4 wkts in 6 balls) v Middlesex (Guildford) 2003. LO HS 32 v Somerset (Taunton) 2005 (NL). LO BB 4-12 Le v Middlesex (Leicester) 1998 (SL). T20 HS 12*. T20 BB 5-26.

RAMPRAKASH, Mark Ravin (Gayton HS; Harrow Weald SFC), b Bushey, Herts 5 Sep 1969. 5'9". RHB, OB. Middlesex 1987-2000; cap 1990; captain 1997-99. Surrey debut 2001 – scoring 146 v Kent (Oval); cap 2002; joint Testimonial 2008. YC 1991. *Wisden* 2006. PCA 2006. **Tests**: 52 (1991 to 2001-02); HS 154 v WI (Bridgetown) 1997-98; BB 1-2 v WI (Georgetown) 1997-98. **LOI**: 18 (1991 to 2001-02); HS 51 v WI (Port-of-Spain) 1997-98; BB 3-28 v Z (Harare) 2001-02. F-c Tours: A 1994-95 (*part*), 1998-99; SA 1995-96; WI 1991-92 (Eng A), 1993-94, 1997-98; NZ 1991-92, 2001-02; I 1994-95 (Eng A), 2001-02; P 1990-91 (Eng A); SL 1990-91 (Eng A). 1000 runs (18, inc 2000 (3): 2258 (1995), 2278 (2006), 2026 (2207)). Averaged 103.54 in f-c matches 2006, the second-highest average by any batsman scoring 1000 runs in a season (105.28 in CC), setting world records by scoring 2000 runs in only 20 innings, posting scores of at least 150 in five successive matches and reaching double figures in each of his 24 innings. In 2007 he became the first to score 2000 f-c runs in a season and average over 100 (101.30) twice. Ten hundreds in a season (2): 1995, 2007. HS 301* v Northants (Oval) 2006. BB 3-32 M v Glamorgan (Lord's) 1998. Sy BB 2-35 v Northants (Northampton) 2004. LO HS 147* M v Worcs (Lord's) 1990 (SL). LO BB 5-38 M v Leics (Lord's) 1993 (SL). T20 HS 85*.

SCHOFIELD, Christopher Paul (Wardle HS), b Birch Hill, Rochdale, Lancs 6 Oct 1978. 6'2". LHB, LBG. Lancashire 1998-2004; cap 2002. Surrey debut 2006. **Tests**: 2 (2000); HS 57 v Z (Nottingham) 2000. BB – . F-c Tours (Eng A): WI 2000-01; NZ 1999-00; B 1999-00. HS 99 La v Warwks (Manchester) 2004. Sy HS 95 v Glos (Bristol) 2006. BB 6-120 Eng A v Bangladesh (Chittagong) 1999-00. Sy BB 5-52 v Hants (Southampton) 2007. LO HS 75* v Hants (Southampton) 2007 (FPT). LO BB 5-31 La v Derbys (Manchester) 2001 (NL). IT20 HS 9*. IT20 BB 2-15. T20 HS 27. T20 BB 4-12.

SPRIEGEL, Matthew Neil William (Whitgift S; Loughborough U), b Epsom 4 Mar 1987. 6'3". LHB, OB. Loughborough UCCE 2007-08; captain 2007-08. Surrey debut 2008. Surrey 2nd XI debut 2004. HS 51 v Notts (Nottingham) 2008. BB 2-28 v Hampshire (Oval) 2008. LO HS 54 v Kent (Oval) 2008 (P40). LO BB 1-17 v Leics (Oval) 2008 (P40). T20 HS 12. T20 BB 2-16.

TUDOR, Alex Jeremy (St Mark's S, Hammersmith; City of Westminster C), b West Brompton, London 23 Oct 1977. 6'5". RHB, RF. Surrey 1995-2004, 2008; cap 1999. Essex 2005-08. YC 1999. **Tests**: 10 (1998-99 to 2002-03); HS 99* v NZ (Birmingham) 1999 – record score by an England 'night-watchman'; BB 5-44 v A (Nottingham) 2001. **LOI**: 3 (2002); HS 6; BB 2-30 v I (Oval) 2002. F-c Tours: A 1998-99, 2002-03; SA 1999-00; WI 2000-01 (Eng A); P 2000-01. HS 144 Ex v Derbys (Chelmsford) 2008. Sy HS 116 v Essex (Oval) 2001. BB 7-48 v Lancs (Oval) 2000. LO HS 56 v Lancs (Croydon) 2004 (NL). LO BB 4-26 v Hants (Oval) 2000 (NL).

NQ**WALTERS, Stewart** Jonathan (Guildford GS, Perth, WA), b Mornington, Victoria, Australia 25 Jun 1983. 6'1". RHB, RM. Debut (Surrey) 2006. W Australia U-19 2001-02. HS 70 v Durham (Oval) 2007. BB 1-4 v Durham (Chester-le-St) 2007. LO HS 91 v Northants (Oval) 2008 (P40). LO BB 1-12 v Yorks (Scarborough) 2007 (P40). T20 HS 18. T20 BB – .

NQ**WATERS, Seren**, b Nairobi, Kenya 11 Apr 1990. RHB, LBG. British passport. Debut (Kenya) 2008-09. Surrey 2nd XI debut 2008. **LOI** (K): 9 (2008-09); HS 74 v SA (Kimberley) 2008-09; BB – . HS 75 Kenya v Ireland (Nairobi) 2008-09 – on debut. LO HS 74 (*see LOI*). LO BB – .

‡**WILSON, Gary** Craig (Methodist C, Belfast; Manchester Met), b Dundonald, N Ireland 5 Feb 1986. RHB, WK. Ireland 2005 to 2008. Ireland U-19 2003-04 to 2005-06. MCC YC 2005. Surrey 2nd XI debut 2006. Awaiting Surrey f-c debut. **LOI** (Ire): 9 (2007 to 2008-09); HS 51 v Scotland (Dublin) 2008. HS 27 Ireland v Netherlands (Rotterdam) 2008. LO HS 58 Ireland A v UAE (Abu Dhabi) 2006 – on List A debut.

RELEASED/RETIRED
(Having made a County First-Class or List A appearance in 2008)

BROWN, A.D. – *see NOTTINGHAMSHIRE.*

CLINTON, Richard Selvey (Colfes S), b Sidcup, Kent 1 Sep 1981. Son of G.S.Clinton (Kent and Surrey 1974-90); cousin of P.J.S.Clinton (OU 2004-06). 6'3". LHB, RM. Kent staff 1999-2000 – no f-c appearances. Essex 2001-02. Loughborough UCCE 2004-06. Surrey 2004-08. British U 2006. HS 108* LU v Essex (Chelmsford) 2006. Sy HS 105 v Kent (Tunbridge Wells) 2005. BB 2-30 Ex v A (Chelmsford) 2001. CC/Sy BB – . LO HS 56 Ex v Durham (Ilford) 2001 (NL). LO BB 2-16 v Staffs (Leek) 2005 (CGT).

FRYLINCK, Robert, b Durban, South Africa 27 Sep 1984. RHB, RM. KZ-Natal 2005-06 to 2007-08. Dolphins 2005-06. Surrey 2008, 1-o only (Kolpak registration). Gauteng 2008-09. Lions 2008-09. HS 100* KZ-Natal v Z U23s (Chatsworth) 2005-06. BB 6-94 KZ-Natal v WP (Chatsworth) 2005-06 – on debut. LO HS 82* KZ-Natal v Z U23s (Chatsworth) 2005-06. LO BB 5-39 KZ-Natal v Gauteng (Durban) 2004-05. T20 HS 29. T20 BB 3-18.

JEWELL, Thomas Melvin, b Reading, Berkshire 13 Jan 1991. RHB, RFM. Surrey 2008. Surrey 2nd XI debut 2007. HS – and BB 1-16 v LU (Oval) 2008 – on debut.

LEWIS, Clairmonte Christopher (Willesden HS, London), b Georgetown, Guyana 14 Feb 1968. 6'2½". RHB, RFM. Leicestershire 1987-91, 1998-2000; cap 1990. Nottinghamshire 1992-94; cap 1994. Surrey 1996-97 and 2008; cap 1996. No f-c appearances in 2008. **Tests:** 32 (1990 to 1996); HS 117 v I (Madras) 1992-93; BB 6-111 v WI (Birmingham) 1991. **LOI:** 53 (1989-90 to 1998); HS 33 v SA (Melbourne) 1991-92; BB 4-30 v SL (Ballarat) 1991-92. Tours: A 1990-91 (*part*), 1994-95 (*part*); WI 1989-90 (*part*), 1993-94; NZ 1991-92; I/SL 1992-93. HS 247 Nt v Durham (Chester-le-St) 1993. Sy HS 94 v Warwks (Oval) 1996. 50 wkts (2); most 56 (1990). BB 6-22 v OU (Oxford) 1988. CC BB 6-55 Le v Glam (Cardiff) 1990. Sy BB 5-25 v Leics (Oval) 1996. LO HS 116* v Kent (Canterbury) 1999 (NL). LO BB 5-19 v Staffs (Leicester) 1998 (NWT). T20 HS 2. T20 BB – .

^{NQ}**NICHOLSON, Matthew** James (Knox GS; Edith Cowan U, Perth), b St Leonards, Sydney, Australia 2 Oct 1974. 6'6". RHB, RFM. W Australia.1996-97 to 2002-03. NSW 2003-04 to 2007-08. Missed entire 1997-98 season (salmonella poisoning, glandular fever, Ross River fever, chronic fatigue syndrome). Registered as an overseas player by Sussex for 2005 but was unable to take up his contract because of injury. Northamptonshire 2006. Surrey 2007-08; cap 2007. **Tests** (A): 1 (1998-99); HS 9 and BB 3-56 v E (Melbourne) 1998-99. F-c Tour (A): Z 1999-00. HS 133 v Yorkshire (Oval) 2008. BB 7-62 Nh v Glos (Northampton) 2006. Sy BB 5-89 v Sussex (Hove) 2007. LO HS 57* v Leics (Leicester) 2007 (P40). LO BB 3-23 Nh v Middlesex (Northampton) 2006 (P40). T20 HS 20*. T20 BB 3-12.

SAKER, Neil Clifford (Raynes Park HS; Nescot C), b Tooting, London 20 Sep 1984. 6'4". RHB, RFM. Surrey 2003-08; no f-c appearances in 2008. HS 58* v Essex (Colchester) 2006. BB 5-76 v Lancs (Manchester) 2007. LO HS 22 v Glos (Bristol) 2006 (CGT). LO BB 4-43 v Kent (Canterbury) 2005 (NL). T20 HS 0. T20 BB 1-28.

SAQLAIN MUSHTAQ (Govt Muslim League HS, M.A.O. College, Lahore), b Lahore, Pakistan 29 Dec 1976. British passport (English wife); qualified for England from April 2008. Brother of Sibtain Mushtaq (Lahore 1988-89). 5'11". RHB, OB. Islamabad 1994-95 to 1997-98. PIA 1994-95 to 2003-04. Surrey 1997-2005, 2008; cap 1998. Lahore 2003-04. Sussex 2007. Ireland (not f-c) 2006. *Wisden* 1999. **Tests** (P): 49 (1995-96 to 2003-04); HS 101* v NZ (Christchurch) 2000-01; BB 8-164 v E (Lahore) 2000-01 (all eight wickets to fall). **LOI** (P): 169 (1995-96 to 2003-04); HS 37* v A (Brisbane) 1999-00; BB 5-20 v E (Rawalpindi) 2000-01, 2 hat-tricks. F-c Tours (P): E 1996, 2001; A 1995-96, 1996-97, 1999-00; SA 1997-98, 2002-03; WI 1999-00; NZ 2000-01; I 1998-99, SL 1996-97, 2002-03; Z 1997-98, 2002-03; B 1998-99, 2001-02. HS 101* (*see Tests*). UK HS 78 P v Northants (Northampton) 1996 – on UK debut. CC HS 69 Sy v Middlesex (Lord's) 2003. 50 wkts (5+1); most – 66 (2000). BB 8-65 (11-107 match) v Derbys (Oval) 1988. Took 7-11 (including 7-5 in 34 balls) v Derbys (Oval) 2000. Three hat-tricks, all for Surrey, 1997 and 1999 (2). LO HS 38* v Yorks (Leeds) 2001 (NL). LO BB 5-20 (*see LOI*). T20 HS 14. T20 BB 3-24.

NQSHOAIB AKHTAR (Elliott HS; Government C, Rawalpindi), b Rawalpindi, Pakistan 13 Aug 1975. 5'11½". RHB, RF. PIA 1994-95 to 1995-96. Rawalpindi 1994-95 to 1998-99. ADBP 1996-97 to 1997-98. Somerset (one match) 2001. KRL 2001-02 to date. Durham 2003-04. Worcestershire 2005. Federal Areas 2007-08 to date. Surrey 2008. **Tests** (P): 46 (1997-98 to 2007-08); HS 47 v I (Faisalabad) 2005-06; BB 6-11 v NZ (Lahore) 2001-02. **LOI** (P): 135 (1997-98 to 2008-09); HS 43 v E (Cape Town) 2002-03; BB 6-16 v NZ (Karachi) 2002-03. F-c Tours (P): E 1997 (Pak A), 2001; A 1999-00, 2004-05; SA 1997-98, 2006-07; NZ 2000-01; I 1998-99, 2007-08; SL 2002-03; Z 1997-98, 2002-03; B 1998-99, 2001-02. HS 59* KRL v PIA (Lahore) 2001-02. CC HS 46 Du v Somerset (Taunton) 2004. Sy HS 32 v Notts (Oval) 2008. BB 6-11 (*see Tests*). CC BB 6-47 Wo v Northants (Worcester) 2005 – on Wo debut. Sy BB 1-54 v Hampshire (Oval) 2008. LO HS 56 KRL v Habib Bank (Lahore) 2002-03. LO BB 6-16 (*see LOI*) and 6-16 Wo v Glos (Worcester) 2005 (NL). IT20 HS 1*. IT20 BB 2-11. T20 HS 14. T20 BB 5-23.

WARWICKSHIRE RELEASED/RETIRED (continued from p 110)

NQZONDEKI, Monde (Dale C), b King William's Town, Cape Province, South Africa 25 Jul 1982. 6'1". RHB, RF. Border 2001-02 to 2004-05. Warriors 2004-05. Cape Cobras 2005-06 to date. Warwickshire debut 2008. **Tests** (SA): 6 (2003 to 2008-09); HS 59 v E (Leeds) 2003 – on debut; BB 6-39 v Z (Pretoria) 2004-05. **LOI** (SA): 11 (2002-03 to 2008-09); HS 3* v P (Cape Town) 2002-03. BB 2-40 v Kenya (Kimberley) 2008-09. F-c Tours (SA): E 2003; A 2005-06; WI 2004-05; SL 2005-06 (SA A). HS 59 (*see Tests*). Wa HS 9 and BB 4-125 v Northants (Northampton) 2008 – on Wa debut. BB 6-39 (*see Tests*). LO HS 23 SA A v SL (Potchefstroom) 2002-03 and 23 SA A v SL A (Benoni) 2003-04. LO BB 6-37 SA A v SL A (Pretoria) 2003-04. IT20 HS 0. IT20 BB 1-41. T20 HS 1*. T20 BB 2-19.

SURREY 2008

LV COUNTY CHAMPIONSHIP AVERAGES

BATTING AND FIELDING

Cap		M	I	NO	HS	Runs	Avge	100	50	Ct/St
2002	M.R.Ramprakash	14	23	3	200*	1235	61.75	6	1	4
1996	M.A.Butcher	6	10	1	205	521	57.88	2	1	4
2007	M.J.Nicholson	9	12	3	133	453	50.33	1	1	4
	U.Afzaal	15	25	4	134*	959	45.66	2	7	6
2005	S.A.Newman	15	25	–	129	1044	41.76	2	8	8
1994	A.D.Brown	6	9	2	76*	252	36.00	–	2	4
2001	J.N.Batty	15	24	3	136*	609	29.00	2	3	34/4
	M.N.W.Spriegel	9	14	1	51	301	23.15	–	1	2
	Shoaib Akhtar	2	4	1	32	69	23.00	–	–	2
	J.G.E.Benning	5	8	–	69	159	19.87	–	1	1
	C.J.Jordan	8	9	2	57	123	17.57	–	1	2
1998	Saqlain Mushtaq	13	16	4	50	206	17.16	–	1	2
	Murtaza Hussain	4	7	2	56	83	16.60	–	1	1
	S.J.Walters	5	8	–	40	127	15.87	–	–	3
2003	J.Ormond	7	7	1	64*	84	14.00	–	1	4
1999	A.J.Tudor	3	5	–	30	48	9.60	–	–	–
	C.P.Schofield	2	4	–	20	36	9.00	–	–	1
	J.W.Dernbach	9	12	3	16*	78	8.66	–	–	2
	P.T.Collins	12	13	4	21	53	5.88	–	–	2
	C.P.Murtagh	3	5	–	12	28	5.60	–	–	2

Also batted: (1 match each): Abdul Razzaq 4, 0; L.J.Hodgson 63, 3 (2 ct); S.C.Meaker 16, 6.

BOWLING

	O	M	R	W	Avge	Best	5wI	10wM
Saqlain Mushtaq	380.3	53	1252	38	32.94	6- 50	3	–
J.W.Dernbach	194	26	784	23	34.08	6- 72	1	–
P.T.Collins	308.3	59	1121	27	41.51	4-111	–	–
J. Ormond	158.2	27	561	13	43.15	4- 90	–	–
C.J.Jordan	159	27	570	12	47.50	3- 32	–	–
M.J.Nicholson	189	37	625	11	56.81	3- 44	–	–
Also bowled:								
A.J.Tudor	52	12	185	5	37.00	2- 24	–	–
Murtaza Hussain	123.1	23	365	7	52.14	3- 82	–	–

Abdul Razzaq 24.1-5-77-3; U.Afzaal 104-15-395-4; J.G.E.Benning 29-6-103-1; A.D.Brown 6-3-5-0; L.J.Hodgson 9-1-58-0; S.C.Meaker 20.1-1-86-3; C.P.Schofield 39.4-5-143-1; Shoaib Akhtar 33-4-117-1; M.N.W.Spriegel 21-1-105-4; S.J.Walters 15-2-52-0.

The First-Class Averages (pp 136–153) give the records of Surrey players in all first-class county matches (Surrey's other opponents being Loughborough UCCE), with the exception of M.N.W.Spriegel and A.J.Tudor, whose full first-class figures for Surrey are as above.

SURREY RECORDS

FIRST-CLASS CRICKET

Highest Total	For 811		v	Somerset	The Oval	1899
	V 863		by	Lancashire	The Oval	1990
Lowest Total	For 14		v	Essex	Chelmsford	1983
	V 16		by	MCC	Lord's	1872
Highest Innings	For 357*	R.Abel	v	Somerset	The Oval	1899
	V 366	N.H.Fairbrother	for	Lancashire	The Oval	1990

Highest Partnership for each Wicket

1st	428	J.B.Hobbs/A.Sandham	v	Oxford U	The Oval	1926
2nd	371	J.B.Hobbs/E.G.Hayes	v	Hampshire	The Oval	1909
3rd	413	D.J.Bicknell/D.M.Ward	v	Kent	Canterbury	1990
4th	448	R.Abel/T.W.Hayward	v	Yorkshire	The Oval	1899
5th	318	M.R.Ramprakash/Azhar Mahmood	v	Middlesex	The Oval	2005
6th	298	A.Sandham/H.S.Harrison	v	Sussex	The Oval	1913
7th	262	C.J.Richards/K.T.Medlycott	v	Kent	The Oval	1987
8th	205	I.A.Greig/M.P.Bicknell	v	Lancashire	The Oval	1990
9th	168	E.R.T.Holmes/E.W.J.Brooks	v	Hampshire	The Oval	1936
10th	173	A.Ducat/A.Sandham	v	Essex	Leyton	1921

Best Bowling	For 10-43	T.Rushby	v	Somerset	Taunton	1921
(Innings)	V 10-28	W.P.Howell	for	Australians	The Oval	1899
Best Bowling	For 16-83	G.A.R.Lock	v	Kent	Blackheath	1956
(Match)	V 15-57	W.P.Howell	for	Australians	The Oval	1899

Most Runs – Season	3246	T.W.Hayward	(av 72.13)	1906
Most Runs – Career	43554	J.B.Hobbs	(av 49.72)	1905-34
Most 100s – Season	13	T.W.Hayward		1906
	13	J.B.Hobbs		1925
Most 100s – Career	144	J.B.Hobbs		1905-34
Most Wkts – Season	252	T.Richardson	(av 13.94)	1895
Most Wkts – Career	1775	T.Richardson	(av 17.87)	1892-1904
Most Career W-K Dismissals	1221	H.Strudwick	(1035 ct/186 st)	1902-27
Most Career Catches in the Field	605	M.J.Stewart		1954-72

LIMITED-OVERS CRICKET

Highest Total	FPT	496-4	v	Glos	The Oval	2007
	P40	375-4	v	Yorkshire	Scarborough	1994
	T20	224-5	v	Glos	Bristol	2006
Lowest Total	FPT	74	v	Kent	The Oval	1967
	P40	64	v	Worcs	Worcester	1978
	T20	94	v	Essex	Chelmsford	2008
Highest Innings	FPT	268	A.D.Brown	v	Glamorgan	The Oval	2002
	P40	203	A.D.Brown	v	Hampshire	Guildford	1997
	T20	88	J.G.E.Benning	v	Kent	The Oval	2006
Best Bowling	FPT	7-33	R.D.Jackman	v	Yorkshire	Harrogate	1970
	P40	7-30	M.P.Bicknell	v	Glamorgan	The Oval	1999
	T20	6-24	T.J.Murtagh	v	Middlesex	Lord's	2005

SUSSEX

Formation of Present Club: 1 March 1839
Substantial Reorganisation: August 1857
Inaugural First-Class Match: 1864
Colours: Dark Blue, Light Blue and Gold
Badge: County Arms of Six Martlets
County Champions: (3) 2003, 2006, 2007
Gillette/NatWest/C&G/FP Trophy Winners: (5) 1963, 1964, 1978, 1986, 2006
Benson and Hedges Cup Winners: (0); best – Semi-Finalist 1982, 1999
Pro 40/National League (Div 1) Winners: (1) 2008
Sunday League Winners: (1) 1982
Twenty20 Cup Winners: (0); best – Semi-Finalist 2007

Chief Executive: David Brooks, County Ground, Eaton Road, Hove BN3 3AN • Tel: 0844 264 0202 • Fax: 01273 771549 • Email: info@sussexcricket.co.uk • Web: www.sussexcricket.co.uk

Professional Cricket Manager: Mark A.Robinson. **Club Coach**: Mark J.G.Davis. **Captain**: M.H.Yardy. **Vice-Captain**: None. **Overseas Player**: Yasir Arafat. **2009 Beneficiary**: M.W.Goodwin. **Head Groundsman**: Andy Mackay. **Scorer**: M.J. (Mike) Charman. ‡ New registration. NQ Not qualified for England.

AGA, Ragheb Gul (Hillcrest S; Brighton U), b Nairobi, Kenya 10 Jul 1984. RHB, RMF. Kenya 2003-04 to 2005-06. Sussex debut 2008. **LOI** (Kenya): 2 (2004); HS 1 and BB 2-17 K v P (Birmingham) 2004. F-c Tours (K): WI 2003-04; Z 2005-06; UAE 2004-05. HS 43 K v Namibia (Nairobi) 2004-05. Sx HS 26 v Kent (Hove) 2008. BB 4-63 v Hants (Canterbury) 2008. LO HS 16 Kenya v India A (Nairobi) 2004. LO BB 4-14 Kenya v Zimbabwe A (Harare) 2005-06. T20 HS 28. T20 BB 2-32.

BEER, William Andrew Thomas (Reigate GS; Collyer's C, Horsham), b Crawley 8 Oct 1988. RHB, LB. Debut (Sussex) 2008. Sussex 2nd XI 2006-07. HS 6* and BB 1-18 v MCC (Lord's) 2008 – on debut. T20 HS 17*. T20 BB 2-32.

BROWN, Ben Christopher (Ardingly C), b Crawley 23 Nov 1988. RHB, WK. Debut (Sussex) 2007 – awaiting CC debut. No f-c appearances in 2008. HS 46 v Sri Lanka A (Hove) 2007 – on debut. LO HS 4 v Notts (Hove) 2007 (P40). T20 HS 6.

‡NQCOLLYMORE, Corey Dalanelo (Alexandra SS), b Boscobelle, Barbados 21 Dec 1977. 6'0". RHB, RFM. Barbados 1998-99 to date. Warwickshire 2003. Sussex debut 2008. **Tests** (WI): 30 (1998-99 to 2007); HS 16* v Z (Bulawayo) 2003-04 and v E (Chester-le-St) 2007; BB 7-57 v SL (Kingston) 2003. **LOI** (WI): 84 (1999 to 2006-07); HS 13* v India (Toronto) 1999; BB 5-51 v SL (Colombo) 2001-02. F-c tours (WI): E 2000, 2004, 2007; A 2005-06; SA 2003-04; P 2006-07; Z 2002, 2003-04; K 2000-01. HS 20 v Barbados v WI B (Bridgetown) 2002-03. LO HS 13* (*see LOI*). LO BB 5-27 for Barbados v Leeward Is (Weymouth) 2005-06. T20 HS 4. T20 BB 1-21.

NQGOODWIN, Murray William (Newton Moore HS, Bunbury, WA), b Salisbury, Rhodesia 11 Dec 1972. Younger brother of D.G.Goodwin (Zimbabwe 1986-87 to 1989-90). 5'9". Migrated to Australia in Nov 1986 and gained Australian citizenship in Sep 1997. Kolpak registration 2005 to date. RHB, LB. W Australia 1994-95 to 1996-97, 2000-01 to 2005-06. Mashonaland 1997-98 to 1998-99. Sussex debut/cap 2001. Warriors 2006-07. Holland 1997. **Tests** (Z): 19 (1997-98 to 2000); HS 166* v P (Bulawayo) 1997-98. **LOI** (Z): 71 (1997-98 to 2000); HS 112* v WI (Chester-le-St) 2000; BB 1-12 v SL (Sharjah) 1998-99. F-c Tours (Z): E 2000, SA 1999-00; WI 1999-00; NZ 1997-98; P 1998-99; SL 1997-98. 1000 runs (7+1); most – 1654 (2001). HS 335* (Sussex record) v Leics (Hove) 2003. BB 2-23 Z v Lahore City (Lahore) 1998-99. Sx BB – . LO HS 167 WA v NSW (Perth) 2000-01 (MC). LO BB 1-9 Mashonaland v Eng A (Harare) 1998-99. T20 HS 102*.

101

HAMILTON-BROWN, Rory James (Millfield S), b St John's Wood, London 3 Sep 1987. 6'0". RHB, OB. Surrey 2005. No f-c appearances 2006-07. Sussex debut 2008. HS 62 v Durham (Hove) 2008 – on CC debut. BB 2-54 v Surrey (Oval) 2008. LO HS 35 v Kent (Canterbury) 2008 (FPT). LO BB 3-28 Sy v Leics (Leicester) 2007 (P40). T20 HS 36. T20 BB 2-17.

HODD, Andrew John (Bexhill C), b Chichester 12 Jan 1984. 5'9". RHB, WK. Sussex 2003 (1 match), 2006-08. Surrey 2005 (one match). HS 123 v Yorks (Hove) 2007. LO HS 42 v Notts (Hove) 2007 (P40). T20 HS 16.

HOPKINSON, Carl Daniel (Brighton C), b Brighton 14 Sep 1981. 5'11". RHB, RM. Debut (Sussex) 2002; cap 2008. HS 106 v Hants (Arundel) 2008. BB 1-20 v LU (Hove) 2004. CC BB 1-35 v Warwks (Hove) 2002. LO HS 123* v Notts (Hove) 2007 (P40). LO BB 3-19 v Scot (Edinburgh) 2003 (NL). T20 HS 26*.

JOYCE, Edmund Christopher (Presentation C, Bray, Co Wicklow; Trinity C, Dublin), b Dublin, Ireland 22 Sep 1978. 5'11". Brother of four Ireland cricketers: Augustine (2000), Dominick (2004-06), Cecilia (2001-07) and Isobel, her twin (1999-2007). LHB, RM. Ireland 1997-98. Middlesex 1999-2008; cap 2002. Qualified for England 2005. MCC 2006, 2008. **LOI**: 17 (2006 to 2006-07); HS 107 v A (Sydney) 2006-07. F-c Tour (Eng A): WI 2005-06. 1000 runs (5); most – 1668 (2005). HS 211 Mx v Warwks (Birmingham) 2006. BB Mx 2-34 v CU (Cambridge) 2004. CC BB 1-4 Mx v Glamorgan (Cardiff) 2005. LO HS 115* Ireland v UAE (Belfast) 2005. LO BB 2-10 v Notts (Nottingham) 2003 (NL). IT20 HS 1. T20 HS 47.

KIRTLEY, Robert **James** (Clifton C), b Eastbourne 10 Jan 1975. 6'0". RHB, RFM. Debut (Sussex) 1995; cap 1998; benefit 2006. TCCB XI 1996. Mashonaland 1996-97. MCC 2002. **Tests**: 4 (2003 to 2003-04); HS 12 v SL (Colombo) 2003-04; BB 6-34 v SA (Nottingham) 2003 – on debut. **LOI**: 11 (2001-02 to 2003-04); HS 1 (twice); BB 2-33 v Z (Harare) 2001-02 on debut, and 2-33 v B (Dhaka) 2003-04. F-c Tours (Eng A): NZ 1999-00; SL 2003-04 (Eng); B 1999-00. HS 59 v Durham (Eastbourne) 1998. 50 wkts (7); most – 75 (2001). BB 7-21 v Hants (Southampton) 1999. Took 5-53 (7-88 match) for Mashonaland v Eng XI (Harare) 1996-97. LO HS 30* v Middlesex (Lord's) 2003 (CGT). LO BB 5-27 v Lancs (Lord's) 2006 (CGT Final). IT20 HS 2*. IT20 BB – . T20 HS 2*. T20 BB 4-22.

LEWRY, Jason David (Durrington HS, Worthing), b Worthing 2 Apr 1971. 6'2". LHB, LFM. Debut (Sussex) 1994; cap 1996; benefit 2002. F-c Tour: Z 1998-99 (Eng A). HS 72 v Surrey (Oval) 2004. 50 wkts (5); most – 62 (1998). BB 8-106 v Leics (Hove) 2003. 2 hat-tricks (1998, 2001). LO HS 16* v Yorks (Arundel) 2004 (NL). LO BB 4-29 v Somerset (Bath) 1995 (SL). T20 HS 8*. T20 BB 3-34.

LIDDLE, Christopher John (Nunthorpe CS), b Middlesbrough, Yorks 1 Feb 1984. 6'5". RHB, LFM. Leicestershire 2005. Sussex debut 2007. HS 53 v Worcs (Hove) 2007. BB 3-42 Le v Somerset (Leicester) 2006. Sx BB 2-43 v Sri Lanka A (Hove) 2007. LO HS 11 v Essex (Arundel) 2007 (FPT). LO BB 3-60 v Notts (Hove) 2007 (P40). T20 HS 10*. T20 BB 4-15.

MARTIN-JENKINS, Robin Simon Christopher (Radley C; Durham U), b Guildford, Surrey 28 Oct 1975. Son of C.D.A.Martin-Jenkins (Cricket Broadcaster and Writer). 6'5". RHB, RFM. Debut (Sussex) 1995; cap 2000; benefit 2008. British U 1996. 1000 runs (1): 1008 (2002). HS 205* v Somerset (Taunton) 2002. BB 7-51 v Leics (Horsham) 2002. LO HS 68* v Northants (Hove) 2003 (NL). LO BB 4-22 v Kent (Canterbury) 2002 (BHC). T20 HS 56*. T20 BB 4-20.

NASH, Christopher David (Collyer's SFC; Loughborough U), b Cuckfield 19 May 1983. 5'11". RHB, OB. Debut (Sussex) 2002 – no f-c appearances 2003-04; cap 2008. Loughborough UCCE 2003-04. British U 2004. HS 108 v Lancs (Manchester) 2008. BB 3-7 v Surrey (Oval) 2008. LO HS 82 v Warwks (Hove) 2006 (P40). LO BB 3-8 v Lancs (Hove) 2008 (P40). T20 HS 52.

PRIOR, Matthew James (Brighton C), b Johannesburg, South Africa 26 Feb 1982. 5'11". RHB, WK. Debut (Sussex) 2001; cap 2003. MCC 2005. **Tests**: 15 (2007 to 2008-09); HS 131* v WI (Port-of-Spain) 2008-09 (scored 126* v WI on debut – first instance while keeping wicket for England). **LOI**: 33 (2004-05 to 2008-09); HS 52 v WI (Birmingham) 2007. F-c Tours (Eng): WI 2008-09; I 2003-04 (Eng A), 2008-09; SL 2004-05 (Eng A), 2007-08; B 2006-07 (Eng A). 1000 runs (3); most – 1158 (2004). HS 201* v LU (Hove) 2004. CC HS 153* v Essex (Colchester) 2003. LO HS 144 v Warwks (Hove) 2005 (NL). T20 HS 73.

RAYNER, Oliver Philip (St Bede's S, Sussex), b Fallingbostel, W Germany, 1 Nov 1985. 6'5". RHB, OB. Debut (Sussex) 2006, scoring 101 v SL (Hove) – first hundred on debut for Sussex since 1920. CC HS 101 (*see above*). CC HS 23 v Kent (Hove) 2006. BB 5-49 v Hants (Arundel) 2008. LO HS 61 v Lancs (Hove) 2006 (P40). LO BB 2-31 v Durham (Chester-le-St) 2008 (P40). T20 HS 11. T20 BB 1-20.

SMITH, Dwayne Romel, b St Michael, Barbados, 12 Apr 1983. RHB, RM. Barbados 2001-02 to date. Sussex 2008, no f-c appearances. Kolpak registration. **Tests** (WI): 10 (2003-04 to 2005-06); HS 105* v SA (Cape Town) 2003-04 – on debut; BB 3-71 v NZ (Auckland) 2005-06. **LOI** (WI): 71 (2003-04 to 2007); HS 68 v SL (Dambulla) 2005; BB 5-45 v NZ (Auckland) 2005-06. F-c Tours (WI): E 2004; A 2005-06; SA 2003-04; NZ 2005-06; SL 2005. HS 155 Barbados v CCC (Crab Hill) 2008-09. BB 4-22 Barbados v Trinidad & Tobago (Pointe-à-Pierre) 2006-07. LO HS 96 Barbados v Windward Is (Georgetown) 2005-06. LO BB 5-45 (*see LOI*); IT20 HS 29. IT20 BB 3-24. T20 HS 72*. T20 BB 4-9.

SMITH, Thomas Michael John (Seaford Head Community C; Sussex Downs C), b Eastbourne 22 Aug 1987. 5'9". RHB, SLA. Debut (Sussex) 2007. Awaiting CC debut. No f-c appearances in 2008. HS 2 and BB 1-52 v Sri Lanka A (Hove) 2007 – on debut. LO HS 15 v Surrey (Hove) 2008 (FPT). BB 2-45 v Durham (Chester-le-St) 2006 (P40). T20 HS 3*. T20 BB – .

THORNELY, Michael Alistair (Brighton C), b Camden, London 19 Oct 1987. 6'1". RHB, RM. Debut (Sussex) 2007. HS 11 v Indians (Hove) 2007 – on debut. CC HS 6*. BB – . LO HS – 2007 (P40).

WRIGHT, Luke James (Belvoir HS; Ratcliffe C; Loughborough U), b Grantham, Lincs 7 Mar 1985. 5'11". Younger brother of A.S.Wright (Leicestershire 2001-02). RHB, RM. Leicestershire 2003 (one f-c match). Sussex debut 2004; cap 2007. **LOI**: 16 (2007 to 2008); HS 52 (off 38 balls) v NZ (Birmingham) 2008; BB 2-34 v NZ (Bristol) 2008. F-c Tour (Eng A): NZ 2008-09. HS 155* v MCC (Lord's) 2008. CC HS 61 v Warwks (Hove) 2007. BB 3-33 v Surrey (Hove) 2005. LO HS 125 v Glos (Hove) 2007 (P40). LO BB 4-12 v Middlesex (Hove) 2004 (NL). IT20 HS 30. IT20 BB 1-32. T20 HS 103*. T20 BB 3-17.

YARDY, Michael Howard (William Parker S, Hastings), b Pembury, Kent 27 Nov 1980. 6'0". LHB, LM/SLA. Debut (Sussex) 2000; cap 2005; captain 2009. **LOI**: 6 (2006 to 2007); HS 19 v WI (Birmingham) 2007; BB 3-24 v P (Nottingham) 2006 – on debut. F-c Tours (Eng A): WI 2005-06; I 2007-08 (captain); B 2006-07 (captain). 1000 (1): 1520 (2005). HS 257 (record Sussex score v touring team) and BB 5-83 v B (Hove) 2005. CC HS 179 v Middlesex (Lord's) 2005. CC BB 2-62 v Glamorgan (Swansea) 2005. LO HS 98* v Surrey (Oval) 2006 (CGT). LO BB 6-27 v Warwks (Birmingham) 2005 (NL). IT20 HS 24*. IT20 BB 1-20. T20 HS 68*. T20 BB 3-24.

‡**NQ**YASIR ARAFAT Satti (Gordon C, Rawalpindi), b Rawalpindi, Pakistan 12 Mar 1982. 5'9½". RHB, RMF. Rawalpindi 1997-98 to 2006-07. Pakistan Reserves 1999-00. KRL 2000-01 to date. National Bank 2005-06. Sussex 2006; cap 2006. Kent 2007-08; cap 2007. Scotland (not f-c) 2004-05. **Tests** (P): 3 (2007-08 to 2008-09); HS 50* v SL (Karachi) 2008-09; BB 5-161 v I (Bangalore) 2007-08 – on debut. **LOI** (P): 8 (1999-00 to 2007-08); HS 27 v SA (Chandigarh) 2006-07; BB 1-28. F-c Tours (P): I 2007-08; SL 2001 (Pak A), 2004-05 (Pak A). HS 122 K v Sussex (Canterbury) 2007. 50 wkts (0+4); most – 91 (2001-02). BB 9-35 KRL v SSGC (Rawalpindi) 2008-09. UK BB 6-86 K v Hants (Canterbury) 2008. LO HS 87 Rawalpindi v Bahawalpur (Karachi) 2000-01. LO BB 6-24 Pakistan A v England A (Colombo) 2004-05. IT20 HS 17. IT20 BB 1-31. T20 HS 49. T20 BB 4-17.

RELEASED/RETIRED
(Having made a County First-Class or List A appearance in 2008)

ADAMS, Christopher John (Repton S), b Whitwell, Derbyshire 6 May 1970. 6'0". RHB, RM/OB. Derbyshire 1988-97; cap 1992. Sussex 1998-2008; cap 1998; captain 1998-2008; benefit 2003. ACT (l-o) 1998-99. *Wisden* 2003. **Tests**: 5 (1999-00); HS 31 v SA (Cape Town) 1999-00; BB 1-42 v SA (Durban) 1999-00. **LOI**: 5 (1998 to 1999-00); HS 42 v SA (Cape Town) 1999-00. F-c Tour: SA 1999-00. 1000 runs (6); most – 1742 (1996). HS 239 De v Hants (Southampton) 1996. Sx HS 217 v Lancs (Manchester) 2002. BB 4-28 v Durham (Chester-le-St) 2001. LO HS 163 v Middlesex (Arundel) 1999 (NL). LO BB 5-16 v Middlesex (Hove) 1998 (SL). T20 HS 63.

NQHARRIS, Ryan James, b Nowra, NSW, Australia 11 Oct 1979. British passport. RHB, RFM. South Australia 2001-02 to 2007-08. Sussex debut v MCC 2008 scoring 19 and taking 4-36 on only appearance; contract terminated when he signed as home player for Queensland 2008-09. HS 74 S Aus v Vic (Melbourne) 2006-07. BB 7-108 S Aus v Tas (Adelaide) 2007-08. LO HS 39 S Aus v Vic (Traralgon) 2007-08. LO BB 5-58 S Aus v Vic (Adelaide) 2007-08. T20 HS 31. T20 BB 2-18.

NQMUSHTAQ AHMED (Mahmoodia HS, Sahiwal), b Sahiwal, Pakistan 28 Jun 1970. 5'5". RHB, LBG. Multan 1986-87, 1988-89, 1990-91. United Bank 1987-88 to 1995-96. Somerset 1993-95, 1997-98; cap 1993. Islamabad 1994-95. Lahore 1996-97 (City), 2000-01 (Blues). Peshawar 1998-99. National Bank 2001-02 to 2004-05. Surrey 2002 (2 matches). Sussex 2003-08; cap 2003. WAPDA 2005-06 to 2006-07. *Wisden* 1996. PCA 2003. **Tests** (P): 52 (1989-90 to 2003-04); HS 59 v SA (Rawalpindi) 1997-98; BB 7-56 (10-171 match) v NZ (Christchurch) 1995-96. **LOI** (P): 144 (1988-89 to 2003-04); HS 34* v SA (Colombo) 2000-01; BB 5-36 v I (Toronto) 1996-97. F-c Tours (P): E 1992, 1996; A 1989-90, 1991-92, 1992-93, 1995-96, 1996-97, 1999-00; SA 1997-98; WI 1992-93, 1999-00; NZ 1992-93, 1993-94, 1995-96, 2000-01; I 1998-99; SL 1994-95, 1996-97, 2000-01; Z 1997-98. HS 90* v Kent (Hove) 2005. 50 wkts (9+2) inc 100 (2): 103 (2003), 102 (2006). Took 1000th f-c wicket during 2004 season. BB 9-48 (13-132 match) v Notts (Nottingham) 2006. LO HS 41 Sm v Durham (Taunton) 1998 (SL). LO BB 7-24 Sm v Ireland (Taunton) 1997 (BHC). T20 HS 20*. T20 BB 5-11.

J.A.G.Green left the staff, without making a County First-Class or List A appearance in 2008.

SUSSEX 2008

RESULTS SUMMARY

	Place	Won	Lost	Tied	Drew	No Result
County Championship (1st Division)	6th	2	2		12	
All First-Class Matches		2	2		13	
FP Trophy (South East Division)	5th	1	4			3
Pro40 League (1st Division)	**1st**	5	1			2
Twenty/20 Cup (South Division)	5th	2	8			

LV COUNTY CHAMPIONSHIP AVERAGES

BATTING AND FIELDING

Cap		M	I	NO	HS	Runs	Avge	100	50	Ct/St
2001	M.W.Goodwin	16	25	2	184	1343	58.39	6	5	3
2003	M.J.Prior	13	19	1	133*	931	51.72	3	7	33
2005	M.H.Yardy	15	25	1	93	899	37.45	–	7	8
2008	C.D.Nash	16	28	4	108	857	35.70	2	4	2
2008	C.D.Hopkinson	16	25	3	106	736	33.45	1	4	11
2000	R.S.C.Martin-Jenkins	16	21	4	71*	552	32.47	–	5	4
	A.J.Hodd	3	4	–	81	99	24.75	–	1	7
1998	C.J.Adams	14	21	3	61	431	23.94	–	2	12
2007	L.J.Wright	11	16	2	58	316	22.57	–	1	7
	O.P.Rayner	11	13	4	22	159	17.66	–	–	8
	R.G.Aga	4	5	1	26	69	17.25	–	–	–
2008	Mohammad Sami	3	4	1	28*	38	12.66	–	–	–
	C.D.Collymore	9	12	5	20	57	8.14	–	–	2
2003	Mushtaq Ahmed	6	10	1	20	65	7.22	–	–	1
1996	J.D.Lewry	14	17	3	27	95	6.78	–	–	7
	M.A.Thornely	2	4	1	6*	13	4.33	–	–	2

Also batted: W.A.T.Beer (1 match) 0; R.J.Hamilton-Brown (2) 62, 7, 39; R.J.Kirtley (2 – cap 1998) 19, 0; C.J.Liddle (2) 4*, 4, 0.

BOWLING

	O	M	R	W	Avge	Best	5wI	10wM
C.D.Collymore	268.2	81	727	26	27.96	4-47	–	–
J.D.Lewry	381.5	66	1211	41	29.53	4-56	–	–
R.S.C.Martin-Jenkins	370.3	105	1010	31	32.58	3-36	–	–
O.P.Rayner	347.3	53	1042	31	33.61	5-49	2	–
Mushtaq Ahmed	226.1	32	777	19	40.89	5-83	1	–
L.J.Wright	161.1	23	682	11	62.00	2-46	–	–
Also bowled:								
R.G.Aga	53.5	12	212	8	26.50	4-63	–	–
Mohammad Sami	83	21	265	9	29.44	5-95	1	–

C.J.Adams 2-0-13-0; W.A.T.Beer 11-0-63-0; R.J.Hamilton-Brown 22.5-1-85-3; C.D.Hopkinson 2-0-16-0; R.J.Kirtley 42-7-130-2; C.J.Liddle 32-8-74-1; C.D.Nash 23.3-1-63-3; M.A.Thornely 4-0-25-0; M.H.Yardy 111.4-10-365-2.

The First-Class Averages (pp 136–153) give the records of Sussex players in all first-class county matches (Sussex's other opponents being the MCC), with the exception of:
M.J.Prior 14-21-1-133*-983-49.15-3-7-35ct-0st. Did not bowl.
L.J.Wright 12-18-3-155*-486-32.40-1-1-7ct. 179.3-30-718-12-59.83-2/46-0-0.

SUSSEX RECORDS

FIRST-CLASS CRICKET

Highest Total	For 705-8d		v	Surrey	Hastings	1902
	V 726		by	Notts	Nottingham	1895
Lowest Total	For 19		v	Surrey	Godalming	1830
	19		v	Notts	Hove	1873
	V 18		by	Kent	Gravesend	1867
Highest Innings	For 335*	M.W.Goodwin	v	Leics	Hove	2003
	V 322	E.Paynter	for	Lancashire	Hove	1937

Highest Partnership for each Wicket

1st	490	E.H.Bowley/J.G.Langridge	v	Middlesex	Hove	1933
2nd	385	E.H.Bowley/M.W.Tate	v	Northants	Hove	1921
3rd	385*	M.H.Yardy/M.W.Goodwin	v	Warwicks	Hove	2006
4th	326*	J.Langridge/G.Cox	v	Yorkshire	Leeds	1949
5th	297	J.H.Parks/H.W.Parks	v	Hampshire	Portsmouth	1937
6th	255	K.S.Duleepsinhji/M.W.Tate	v	Northants	Hove	1930
7th	344	K.S.Ranjitsinhji/W.Newham	v	Essex	Leyton	1902
8th	291	R.S.C.Martin-Jenkins/M.J.G.Davis	v	Somerset	Taunton	2002
9th	178	H.W.Parks/A.F.Wensley	v	Derbyshire	Horsham	1930
10th	156	G.R.Cox/H.R.Butt	v	Cambridge U	Cambridge	1908

Best Bowling (Innings)	For 10- 48	C.H.G.Bland	v	Kent	Tonbridge	1899
	V 9- 11	A.P.Freeman	for	Kent	Hove	1922
Best Bowling (Match)	For 17-106	G.R.Cox	v	Warwicks	Horsham	1926
	V 17- 67	A.P.Freeman	for	Kent	Hove	1922

Most Runs – Season	2850	J.G.Langridge	(av 64.77)	1949
Most Runs – Career	34150	J.G.Langridge	(av 37.69)	1928-55
Most 100s – Season	12	J.G.Langridge		1949
Most 100s – Career	76	J.G.Langridge		1928-55
Most Wkts – Season	198	M.W.Tate	(av 13.47)	1925
Most Wkts – Career	2211	M.W.Tate	(av 17.41)	1912-37
Most Career W-K Dismissals	1176	H.R.Butt	(911 ct/265 st)	1890-1912
Most Career Catches in the Field	779	J.G.Langridge		1928-55

LIMITED-OVERS CRICKET

Highest Total	FPT	384-9	v	Ireland	Belfast	1996
	P40	323-5	v	Leics	Horsham	2004
	T20	205-5	v	Hampshire	Hove	2007
Lowest Total	FPT	49	v	Derbyshire	Chesterfield	1969
	P40	59	v	Glamorgan	Hove	1996
	T20	67	v	Hampshire	Hove	2004
Highest Innings	FPT	158* M.W.Goodwin	v	Essex	Chelmsford	2006
	P40	163 C.J.Adams	v	Middlesex	Arundel	1999
	T20	103 L.J.Wright	v	Kent	Canterbury	2004
Best Bowling	FPT	6- 9 A.I.C.Dodemaide	v	Ireland	Downpatrick	1990
	P40	7-41 A.N.Jones	v	Notts	Nottingham	1986
	T20	5-11 Mushtaq Ahmed	v	Essex	Hove	2005

WARWICKSHIRE

Formation of Present Club: 8 April 1882
Substantial Reorganisation: 19 January 1884
Inaugural First-Class Match: 1894
Colours: Dark Blue, Gold and Silver
Badge: Bear and Ragged Staff
County Champions: (6) 1911, 1951, 1972, 1994, 1995, 2004
Gillette/NatWest/C&G/FP Trophy Winners: (5) 1966, 1968, 1989, 1993, 1995
Benson and Hedges Cup Winners: (2) 1994, 2002
Pro 40/National League (Div 1) Winners: (0); best – 3rd 2001, 2002
Sunday League Winners: (3) 1980, 1994, 1997
Twenty20 Cup Winners: (0); best – Finalist 2003

Chief Executive: Colin Povey, County Ground, Edgbaston, Birmingham, B5 7QU • Tel: 0121 446 4422 • Fax: 0121 446 4544 • Email: info@edgbaston.com • Web: www.edgbaston.com

Director of Coaching/First XI Coach: Ashley F.Giles. **Captain:** I.J.Westwood. **Vice-Captain:** tba. **Overseas Players:** M.Zondeki and C.S.Martin. **2009 Beneficiary:** T.Frost. **Head Groundsman:** Steve Rouse. **Scorer:** David E.Wainwright. ‡ New registration. NQ Not qualified for England.

‡**ALLIN, Thomas** William (Cardiff U), b Devon 27 Nov 1987. Son of A.W.Allin (Glamorgan 1976) and brother of M.L.Allin (Devon 2003). RHB, RMF. Devon 2007-08. Cardiff UCCE (not f-c) 2008. Warwickshire 2nd XI debut 2008. Summer contract 2009.

AMBROSE, Timothy Raymond (Merewether HS, NSW; TAFE C), b Newcastle, NSW, Australia 1 Dec 1982. ECB qualified – British/EU passport. 5'7". RHB, WK. Sussex 2001-05; cap 2003. Warwickshire debut 2006; cap 2007. NSW U17 1999-00. **Tests:** 11 (2007-08 to 2008-09); HS 102 v NZ (Wellington) 2007-08. LOI: 5 (2008); HS 6 v NZ (Oval) 2008. F-c Tours: WI 2008-09; NZ 2007-08. HS 251* v Worcs (Worcester) 2007. LO HS 135 v Durham (Birmingham) 2007 (FPT). IT 20 HS – . T20 HS 77.

ANYON, James Edward (Garstang HS; Preston C; Loughborough U), b Lancaster, Lancs 5 May 1983. 6'1". LHB, RFM. Loughborough U 2003-04. Warwickshire debut 2005. Cumberland 2003. HS 37* v Durham (Chester-le-St) 2007. BB 6-82 v Glamorgan (Cardiff) 2008. LO HS 12 v Worcs (Birmingham) 2006 (CGT). LO BB 3-6 v Notts (Nottingham) 2008 (FPT). T20 HS 8*. T20 BB 3-6.

‡**BARKER, Keith** Hubert Douglas, b Manchester 21 Oct 1986. Son of K.H.Barker (British Guiana 1960-61 to 1963-64). Played football for Blackburn Rovers and Rochdale. LHB, LM. Warwickshire 2nd XI debut 2008. Awaiting 1st XI debut.

BELL, Ian Ronald (Princethorpe C), b Walsgrave-on-Sowe 11 Apr 1982. 5'9". RHB, RM. Debut (Warwickshire) 1999; cap 2001. MCC 2004. YC 2004. MBE 2005. **ECB central contract 2008-09. Tests:** 46 (2004 to 2008-09); HS 199 v SA (Lord's) 2008; BB 1-33 v P (Faisalabad) 2005-06. **LOI:** 79 (2004-05 to 2008-09); HS 126 v I (Southampton) 2007; BB 3-9 v Z (Bulawayo) 2004-05 – taking a wicket with his third ball in LOI. F-c Tours: A 2006-07; WI 2000-01 (Eng A – *part*), 2008-09; NZ 2007-08; I 2005-06, 2008-09; P 2005-06; SL 2002-03 (ECB Acad), 2004-05, 2007-08. 1000 runs (2); most – 1714 (2004). Scored 480 runs (avge 80.00) in April 2005 – record f-c UK aggregate before May. HS 262* v Sussex (Horsham) 2004. BB 4-4 v Middlesex (Lord's) 2004. LO HS 137 v Yorks (Birmingham) 2005 (NL). LO BB 5-41 v Essex (Chelmsford) 2003 (NL). IT20 HS 60*. T20 HS 66*. T20 BB 1-12.

NQBOTHA, Anthony Greyvensteyn (Maritzburg C; Maritzburg Technikon), b Pretoria, South Africa 17 Nov 1976. 6'0". LHB, SLA. Natal/KwaZulu Natal 1995-96 to 1998-99. EP/Easterns 1999-00 to 2002-03. Derbyshire 2004-07 (cap 2004). Moved to Warwickshire in mid-season – debut 2007. HS 156* De v Yorks (Derby) 2005. Wa HS 62 v Glamorgan (Cardiff) 2008. 50 wkts (1): 55 (2007). BB 8-53 Natal B v Northerns B (Pretoria) 1997-98. CC BB 6-101 De v Somerset (Derby) 2007. Wa BB 4-77 v Worcs (Birmingham) 2008. LO HS 60* Easterns v EP (Benoni) 2001-02. LO BB 5-43 v Leics (Leicester) 2008. T20 HS 35. T20 BB 4-14.

CARTER, Neil Miller (Hottentots Holland HS; Cape Technicon), b Cape Town, South Africa 29 Jan 1975. British passport. 6'2". LHB, LFM. Boland 1999-00 to 2000-01. Warwickshire debut 2001; cap 2005. HS 103 v Sussex (Hove) 2002 – completed maiden hundred off 67 balls. BB 6-63 Boland v GW (Kimberley) 2000-01 and 6-63 v Sussex (Birmingham) 2006. LO HS 135 v Scot (Birmingham) 2006 (CGT). LO BB 5-31 v Durham (Birmingham) 2002 (NL). T20 HS 58. T20 BB 5-19.

‡CHOUDRY, Shaaiq Mohammed, b Rotherham, Yorkshire 3 Nov 1985. RHB, RMF. MCC 2007. Bradford/Leeds UCCE 2006-08 (not f-c). Warwickshire 2nd XI debut 2007. Joins staff 2009 – awaiting Warwickshire 1st XI debut. HS 54* and BB- MCC v West Indians (Durham) 2007.

CLARKE, Rikki (Broadwater SS; Godalming C), b Orsett, Essex 29 Sep 1981. 6'4". RHB, RFM. Surrey 2002-07, scoring 107* v CU (Cambridge) on debut; cap 2005. MCC 2006. Derbyshire cap/captain 2008. Warwickshire debut 2008. YC 2002. **Tests**: 2 (2003-04); HS 55 and BB 2-7 v B (Chittagong) 2003-04. **LOI**: 20 (2003 to 2006); HS 39 v P (Lord's) 2006; BB 2-28 v B (Dhaka) 2003-04. F-c Tours: WI 2003-04, 2005-06; SL 2002-03 (ECB Acad), 2004-05; B 2003-04. 1000 runs (1): 1027 (2006). HS 214 Sy v Somerset (Guildford) 2006. Wa HS 81 v Glamorgan (Birmingham) 2008. BB 4-21 Sy v Leics (Leicester) 2003. Wa BB 2-49 v Essex (Chelmsford) 2008. LO HS 98* Sy v Derbys (Derby) 2002 (NL). LO BB 4-49 Sy v Warwks (Birmingham) 2005 (NL). T20 HS 79*. T20 BB 3-11.

FROST, Tony (James Brinkley HS; Stoke-on-Trent C), b Stoke-on-Trent, Staffs 17 Nov 1975. 5'11". RHB, WK. Warwickshire 1997-2006, 2008 to date; cap 1999. 1000 runs (1): 1003 (2008). HS 242* v Essex (Chelmsford) 2008. LO HS 56 v Ireland (Belfast) (FPT). T20 HS 53.

‡JAVID, Ateeq, b Birmingham 15 Oct 1991. RHB, RM. Warwickshire 2nd XI debut 2008. Joins staff 2009 – awaiting 1st XI debut.

JOHNSON, Richard Matthew, b Solihull 1 Sep 1988. RHB, WK. Debut (Warwickshire) 2008. Herefordshire 2006. Warwickshire 2nd XI debut 2007. HS 72 v Cambridge U (Cambridge) 2008 – on debut. Awaiting CC debut. LO HS 20 v Northants (Birmingham) 2008 (FPT).

MacLEOD, Calum Scott (Hillpark S), b Glasgow, Scotland 15 Nov 1988. 6'1". RHB, RMF. Scotland 2007. Warwickshire debut 2008. **LOI** (Scot): 1 (2008); HS 10* v England (Edinburgh) 2008. HS – . BB 3-36 v Cambridge U (Cambridge) 2008. Awaiting CC debut. LO HS 10* (see LOI). LO BB 1-44 Scotland v Durham (Chester-le-St) 2008 (FPT).

MADDY, Darren Lee (Wreake Valley C), b Leicester 23 May 1974. 5'9". RHB, RM/OB. Leicestershire 1994-2006; cap 1996; benefit 2006. Warwickshire debut/cap 2007; captain 2007-08. **Tests**: 3 (1999 to 1999-00); HS 24 v SA (Durban) 1999-00; BB – . **LOI**: 8 (1998 to 1999-00); HS 53 v Z (Harare) 1999-00. F-c Tours (Eng A): SA 1996-97 (Le), 1998-99, 1999-00 (Eng); SL 1997-98; Z 1998-99; K 1997-98. 1000 runs (4); most – 1187 (2002). HS 229* Le v LU (Leicester) 2003. Scored 202 Eng A v Kenya (Nairobi) 1997-98. CC HS 162 Le v Durham (Darlington) 1998. Wa HS 148* v Kent (Canterbury) 2007. BB 5-37 Le v Hants (Southampton) 2002. Wa BB 5-63 v Durham (Chester-le-St) 2007. LO HS 167* Le v Scot (Edinburgh) 2006 (CGT). LO BB 4-16 Le v Somerset (Taunton) 2000 (NL). IT20 HS 50. IT20 BB 2-6. T20 HS 111. T20 BB 2-6.

MILLER, Andrew Stephen (St Cecilia's RC HS; Preston C), b Preston, Lancs 27 Sep 1987. 6'4". RHB, RMF. Debut (Warwickshire) 2008. Lancashire 2nd XI 2004-05. Warwickshire 2nd XI debut 2006. England U19s 2004-05 to 2007. HS 4* and BB 2-35 v Bangladesh A (Birmingham) 2008 – on debut (only f-c game).

‡ORD, James Edward (Loughborough U), b Birmingham 9 Nov 1987. RHB, OB. Warwickshire 2nd XI debut 2006. Loughborough UCCE 2007 (not f-c). Summer contract 2009.

‡PIOLET, Steffan Andrew, b Redhill, Surrey 8 Aug 1988. RHB, RM. Worcestershire 2nd XI 2006. Sussex 2nd XI 2006-08. Warwickshire 2nd XI debut 2008. Joins staff in 2009 – awaiting 1st XI debut.

POONIA, Navdeep Singh (Moseley Park S; Wolverhampton U), b Govan, Glasgow, Scotland 11 May 1986. 6'3". RHB, RM. Debut (Warwickshire) 2006. Scotland 2006 to date (no f-c appearances). **LOI** (Scot): 16 (2006 to 2008); HS 67 v Canada (Mombasa) 2007. HS 111 v Cambridge U (Cambridge) 2008. CC HS 50 v Worcs (Birmingham) 2008. LO HS 75 Scotland v Derbyshire (Derby) 2008 (FPT). IT20 HS 38*. T20 HS 38*.

NQRANKIN, William Boyd (Strabane GS; Harper Adams UC), b Londonderry, Co Derry, N Ireland 5 Jul 1984. 6'8". LHB, RMF. Brother of R.J.Rankin (Ireland U19 2003-04). Debut (Ireland) 2006-07. Middlesex summer contract 2004-05. Derbyshire 2007. Warwickshire debut 2008. **LOI** (Ireland): 14 (2006-07 to 2008-09) HS 7* v SL (St George's) 2006-07; BB 3-32 v P (Kingston) 2006-07. F-c Tour (Ire): SA/Kenya 2008-09. HS 12* v Glamorgan (Birmingham) 2008. BB 5-39 Ire v Namibia (Windhoek) 2008-09. CC BB 4-41 De v Middlesex (Derby) 2007. Wa BB 4-80 v Essex (Birmingham) 2008. LO HS 7* (*see LOI*). LO BB 3-32 (*see LOI*).

TAHIR, Naqaash Sarosh (Moseley S; Spring Hill C), b Birmingham 14 Nov 1983. 5'10", RHB, RFM. Debut (Warwickshire) 2004. HS 49 v Worcs (Worcester) 2004. BB 7-107 v Lancs (Blackpool) 2006. LO HS 13* v Leics (Oakham) 2008 (FPT). LO BB 2-47 v Notts (Nottingham) 2008 (FPT).

TROTT, Ian Jonathan Leonard (Rondebosch BHC; Stellenbosch U), b Cape Town, South Africa 22 Apr 1981. 6'0". RHB, RM. Boland 2000-01. W Province 2001-02. EU/British passport. Warwickshire debut 2003 scoring 134 v Sussex (Birmingham); cap 2005. Otago 2005-06. F-c Tours (Eng A): NZ 2008-09; I 2007-08. 1000 runs (4); most – 1240 (2008). HS 210 v Sussex (Birmingham) 2005. BB 7-39 v Kent (Canterbury) 2003. LO HS 125* v Northants (Birmingham) 2007 (FPT). LO BB 4-55 v Hants (Lord's) 2005 (CGT). IT20 HS 9. T20 HS 75*. T20 BB 2-19.

TROUGHTON, Jamie Oliver (*'Jim'*) (Trinity S; Leamington Spa; Birmingham U), b Camden, London 2 Mar 1979. Great-grandson of H.T.Crichton (Warwicks 1908). 5'11". LHB, SLA. Debut (Warwickshire) 2001. **LOI**: 6 (2003); HS 20 v P (Lord's) 2003. F-c Tour (ECB Acad): SL 2002-03. 1000 runs (1): 1067 (2002). HS 162 v Worcs (Worcester) 2007. BB 3-1 v CU (Cambridge) 2004. CC BB 2-26 v Lancs (Birmingham) 2006. LO HS 115* and BB 4-23 Warwks CB v Cumb (Millom) 2001 (CGT). T20 HS 57. T20 BB 2-10.

WESTWOOD, Ian James (Wheelers Lane S; Solihull SFC), b Birmingham 13 Jul 1982. 5'7½". LHB, OB. Debut (Warwickshire) 2003; cap 2008; captain 2009. HS 178 v West Indies A (Birmingham) 2006. CC HS 176 v Glamorgan (Cardiff) 2008. BB 2-46 v Kent (Birmingham) 2006. LO HS 65 v Northants (Northampton) 2008 (FPT). BB 1-28 Warwks CB v Cambs (March) 2001 (CGT). T20 HS 35*. T20 BB 3-29.

WOAKES, Christopher Roger (Barr Beacon Language S, Walsall), b Birmingham 2 March 1989. 6'2". RHB, RMF. Debut (Warwickshire) 2006. Herefordshire 2006-07. HS 64* v Cambridge U (Cambridge) 2008. CC HS 45 v Derbys (Birmingham) 2008. BB 6-68 (10-162 match) v Glamorgan (Birmingham) 2008. LO HS 31* v Glamorgan (Cardiff) 2008 (P40). LO BB 1-21 v Kent (Birmingham) 2008 (P40). T20 HS 2*. T20 BB 4-21.

RELEASED/RETIRED
(Having made a County First-Class or List A appearance in 2008)

DAGGETT, L.M. – *see NORTHAMPTONSHIRE.*

GROENEWALD, T.D. – *see DERBYSHIRE.*

HOLE, Stuart Mark (Bartholomew S, Eynsham), b Oxford 17 Jul 1985. 6'1". RHB, RM. Warwickshire 2007-08. Oxfordshire 2005-07. HS 24 v Yorkshire (Scarborough) 2007 – on debut. BB 2-29 v Cambridge U (Cambridge) 2008. CC BB – . LO HS-and BB 1-16 v Essex (Southend) 2007 (P40).

JAMES, Nicholas Alexander (King Edward VI S, Aston), b Sandwell, Birmingham 17 Sep 1986. 5'9". LHB, SLA. Warwickshire 2008. Staffordshire 2006-07. England U19 2005 to 2005-06. HS 34 and BB 1-6 v Cambridge U (Cambridge) 2008 – only f-c game. LO HS 30 v Worcs (Birmingham) 2006 (CGT) on Wa debut. LO BB 2-34 v Notts (Birmingham) 2006 (CGT). T20 HS 12*.

NQMARTIN, Christopher Stewart, b Christchurch, Canterbury, New Zealand 10 Dec 1974. RHB, RFM. Canterbury 1997-98 to 2004-05. South Island 1999-00. Auckland 2005-06 to date. Warwickshire debut 2008. **Tests** (NZ): 45 (2000-01 to 2008-09); HS 12* v B (Dunedin (2007-08); BB 6-54 v SL (Wellington) 2004-05. **LOI** (NZ): 20 (2000-01 to 2007-08); HS 3 v Z (Taupo) 2000-01; BB 3-62 v SL (Napier) 2005-06. F-c Tours (NZ): E 2000 (NZ A), 2004, 2008; A 2001-02, 2004-05, 2008-09; SA 2000-01, 2004-05 (NZ A), 2005-06, 2007-08; P 2001-02; SL 2005-06 (NZ A); Z 2005. HS 25 Canterbury v ND (Gisborne) 2001-02. Wa HS 0. BB 6-54 (*see Tests*). Wa BB 5-84 v Glos (Birmingham) 2008. LO HS 13 Auckland v CD (Auckland) 2005-06. LO BB 6-24 NZ A v SL A (Moratuwa) 2005-06. IT20 HS 5*. IT20 BB 2-14. T20 HS 5*. T20 BB 3-33.

PARKER, Luke Charles (Finham Park S; Oxford Brookes U), b Coventry 27 Sep 1983. 6'0". RHB, RM. Oxford UCCE 2004-06. British U 2005-06. Warwickshire debut 2005. MCC 2006. HS 140 OU v Durham (Oxford) 2006. Wa HS 73 v Notts (Birmingham) 2006. BB 2-37 v Glos (Oxford) 2005. LO HS 19 v Northants (Birmingham) 2008. T20 HS 18.

POWELL, Michael James (Lawrence Sheriff S, Rugby), b Bolton, Lancs 5 Apr 1975. 5'11". RHB, RM. Warwickshire 1996-2008; cap 1999; captain 2001-03; benefit 2008. Griqualand West 2001-02. MCC 2004. Otago 2005-06. F-c Tour (Eng A): WI 2000-01. 1000 runs (1): 1046 (2000). HS 236 v OU (Oxford) 2001. CC HS 146 v Glamorgan (Birmingham) 2005. BB 2-16 v OU (Oxford) 1998. CC BB 2-29 v Somerset (Taunton) 2002. LO HS 101* v Northants (Birmingham) 2002 (BHC). LO BB 5-40 v Kent (Canterbury) 2002 (CGT). T20 HS 44*.

SALISBURY, Ian David Kenneth (Moulton CS), b Northampton 21 Jan 1970. 5'11". RHB, LBG. Sussex 1989-96; cap 1991. TCCB XI 1996. Surrey 1997-2007; cap 1998; benefit 2007. Warwickshire 2008; cap 2008. MCC YC 1988. YC 1992. *Wisden* 1992. **Tests**: 15 (1992 to 2000-01); HS 50 v P (Manchester) 1992; BB 4-163 v WI (Georgetown) 1993-94. **LOI**: 4 (1992-93 to 1993-94); HS 5 and BB 3-41 v WI (Port-of-Spain) 1993-94. F-c Tours: WI 1991-92 (Eng A), 1993-94; I 1992-93; 1994-95 (Eng A); P 1990-91 (Eng A), 1995-96 (Eng A), 2000-01; SL 1990-91 (Eng A). Wa HS 103 Sy v Hants (Oval) 2007. Wa HS 81 v Middlesex (Birmingham) 2008. 50 wkts (7); most – 87 (1992). BB 8-60 (12-91 match) Sy v Somerset (Oval) 2000. Wa BB 6-100 v Essex (Chelmsford) 2008. LO HS 59* Sy v Glamorgan (Oval) 2004 (NL). LO BB 5-30 Sx v Leics (Leicester) 1992 (SL). T20 HS 20. T20 BB 3-14.

RELEASED/RETIRED continued on p 98

110

WARWICKSHIRE 2008

RESULTS SUMMARY

	Place	Won	Lost	Tied	Drew	No Result
County Championship (2nd Division)	1st	5			11	
All First-Class Matches		6			12	
FP Trophy (Midlands Division)	4th	2	4			2
Pro40 League (2nd Division)	6th	3	3			2
Twenty/20 Cup (Midlands/West/Wales Division)	Quarter-Finalist 6	2		1		2

LV COUNTY CHAMPIONSHIP AVERAGES

BATTING AND FIELDING

Cap		M	I	NO	HS	Runs	Avge	100	50	Ct/St
1999	T.Frost	13	18	6	242*	1003	83.58	2	4	26/2
2001	I.R.Bell	4	6	–	215	436	72.66	1	1	6
2005	I.J.L.Trott	16	25	5	181	1240	62.00	3	6	16
2007	T.R.Ambrose	7	10	3	156*	333	47.57	1	1	23
2002	J.O.Troughton	12	17	3	138*	581	41.50	1	4	9
2007	D.L.Maddy	13	21	2	138	678	35.68	2	3	9
2008	I.D.K.Salisbury	13	14	2	81	393	32.75	–	3	7
2005	N.M.Carter	13	14	–	84	430	30.71	–	4	3
2008	I.J.Westwood	11	17	–	176	506	29.76	1	2	5
1999	M.J.Powell	10	15	1	68*	360	25.71	–	2	5
	A.G.Botha	12	15	3	62	262	21.83	–	3	16
	C.R.Woakes	10	10	2	45	171	21.37	–	–	7
	N.S.Poonia	10	16	–	50	306	19.12	–	1	5
	N.Tahir	4	4	1	37	47	15.66	–	–	–
	M.Zondeki	4	5	3	9	21	10.50	–	–	–
	W.B.Rankin	5	6	3	12*	31	10.33	–	–	2
	J.E.Anyon	7	6	2	6	14	3.50	–	–	4

Also batted: R.Clarke (2 matches) 41, 0, 81 (6 ct); L.M.Daggett (2) 6, 17, 1; T.D.Groenewald (1) 0 (1 ct); C.S.Martin (6) 0, 0 (1 ct); L.C.Parker (1) 5, 20.

BOWLING

	O	M	R	W	Avge	Best	5wI	10wM
C.R.Woakes	287	77	864	42	20.57	6- 68	3	1
D.L.Maddy	152	37	438	17	25.76	4- 25	–	–
I.D.K.Salisbury	268.4	39	865	31	27.90	6-100	5	–
W.B.Rankin	86.3	9	362	12	30.16	4- 80	–	–
N.M.Carter	373.4	70	1278	41	31.17	6-100	2	–
J.E.Anyon	228.2	32	844	26	32.46	6- 82	1	–
C.S.Martin	159.1	27	580	16	36.25	5- 84	1	–
I.J.L.Trott	152.5	42	463	10	46.30	3- 44	–	–
A.G.Botha	244	55	676	14	48.28	4- 77	–	–

Also bowled:
L.M.Daggett | 91 | 18 | 322 | 8 | 40.25 | 3- 69 | – | – |
M.Zondeki | 96.2 | 17 | 381 | 9 | 42.33 | 4-125 | – | – |

R.Clarke 18-3-87-2; T.Frost 2-0-3-0; T.D.Groenewald 33-5-13-1-0; M.J.Powell 1-0-1-0; N.Tahir 137-32-418-4; J.O.Troughton 6-1-25-0; I.J.Westwood 2-0-2-0.

The First-Class Averages (pp 136–153) give the records of Warwickshire's players in all first-class county matches (Warwickshire's other opponents being Bangladesh A and Cambridge UCCE), with the exception of T.R.Ambrose, I.R.Bell, R.Clarke, C.S.Martin and M.Zondeki, whose first-class figures for Warwickshire are as above, and:
L.M.Daggett 4-4-0-17-24-6.00-0-0-0ct. 96.2-17-381-9-42.22-4/125-0-0.

WARWICKSHIRE RECORDS

FIRST-CLASS CRICKET

Highest Total	For 810-4d		v	Durham	Birmingham	1994
	V 887		by	Yorkshire	Birmingham	1896
Lowest Total	For 16		v	Kent	Tonbridge	1913
	V 15		by	Hampshire	Birmingham	1922
Highest Innings	For 501*	B.C.Lara	v	Durham	Birmingham	1994
	V 322	I.V.A.Richards	for	Somerset	Taunton	1985

Highest Partnership for each Wicket

1st	377*	N.F.Horner/K.Ibadulla	v	Surrey	The Oval	1960
2nd	465*	J.A.Jameson/R.B.Kanhai	v	Glos	Birmingham	1974
3rd	327	S.P.Kinneir/W.G.Quaife	v	Lancashire	Birmingham	1901
4th	470	A.I.Kallicharran/G.W.Humpage	v	Lancashire	Southport	1982
5th	322*	B.C.Lara/K.J.Piper	v	Durham	Birmingham	1994
6th	226	T.R.Ambrose/H.H.Streak	v	Worcs	Worcester	2007
7th	289*	I.R.Bell/T.Frost	v	Sussex	Horsham	2004
8th	228	A.J.W.Croom/R.E.S.Wyatt	v	Worcs	Dudley	1925
9th	154	G.W.Stephens/A.J.W.Croom	v	Derbyshire	Birmingham	1925
10th	214	N.V.Knight/A.Richardson	v	Hampshire	Birmingham	2002

Best Bowling	For 10-41	J.D.Bannister	v	Comb Servs	Birmingham	1959
(Innings)	V 10-36	H.Verity	for	Yorkshire	Leeds	1931
Best Bowling	For 15-76	S.Hargreave	v	Surrey	The Oval	1903
(Match)	V 17-92	A.P.Freeman	for	Kent	Folkestone	1932

Most Runs – Season	2417	M.J.K.Smith	(av 60.42)		1959
Most Runs – Career	35146	D.L.Amiss	(av 41.64)		1960-87
Most 100s – Season	9	A.I.Kallicharran			1984
	9	B.C.Lara			1994
Most 100s – Career	78	D.L.Amiss			1960-87
Most Wkts – Season	180	W.E.Hollies	(av 15.13)		1946
Most Wkts – Career	2201	W.E.Hollies	(av 20.45)		1932-57
Most Career W-K Dismissals	800	E.J.Smith	(662 ct/138 st)		1904-30
Most Career Catches in the Field	422	M.J.K.Smith			1956-75

LIMITED-OVERS CRICKET

Highest Total	FPT	392-5	v	Oxfordshire	Birmingham	1984
	P40	310-5	v	Lancs	Birmingham	2004
	T20	205-2	v	Northants	Birmingham	2005
		205-7	v	Glamorgan	Swansea	2005
Lowest Total	FPT	98	v	Leics	Leicester	1998
	P40	59	v	Yorkshire	Leeds	2001
	T20	115	v	Surrey	Nottingham	2003
Highest Innings	FPT	206	A.I.Kallicharran	v	Oxfordshire	Birmingham	1984
	P40	137	I.R.Bell	v	Yorkshire	Birmingham	2005
	T20	89	N.V.Knight	v	Worcs	Worcester	2003
Best Bowling	FPT	6-32	K.Ibadulla	v	Hampshire	Birmingham	1965
		6-32	A.I.Kallicharran	v	Oxfordshire	Birmingham	1984
	P40	6-15	A.A.Donald	v	Yorkshire	Birmingham	1995
	T20	5-19	N.M.Carter	v	Worcs	Birmingham	2005

WORCESTERSHIRE

Formation of Present Club: 11 March 1865
Inaugural First-Class Match: 1899
Colours: Dark Green and Black
Badge: Shield Argent a Fess between three Pears Sable
County Championships: (5) 1964, 1965, 1974, 1988, 1989
Gillette/NatWest/C&G/FP Trophy Winners: (1) 1994
Benson and Hedges Cup Winners: (1) 1991
Pro 40/National League (Div 1) Winners: (1) 2007
Sunday League Winners: (3) 1971, 1987, 1988
Twenty20 Cup Winners: (0); best – Quarter-Finalist 2004, 2007

Chief Executive: Mark S.Newton, County Ground, New Road, Worcester, WR2 4QQ • Tel: 01905 748474 • Fax: 01905 748005 • Email: admin@wccc.co.uk • Web: www.wccc.co.uk

Director of Cricket: Steve J.Rhodes. **Captain:** V.S.Solanki. **Vice-Captain:** G.J.Batty. **Overseas Player:** A.Knoffke. **2009 Beneficiary:** B.F.Smith. **Head Groundsman:** Tim Packwood. **Scorer:** Neil D.Smith. ‡ New registration. NQ Not qualified for England.

Worcestershire revised their capping policy in 2002 and now award players with their County Colours when they make their Championship debut.

‡AHMED, Mehraj, b Birmingham, Warwks 5 Jan 1989. RHB, RFM. Worcestershire 2nd XI debut 2006. Debut (Worcestershire) 2008 – awaiting CC debut. HS – and BB 1-28 v Loughborough U (Kidderminster) 2008 – on debut. LO HS – and BB 1-34 v Glamorgan (Worcester) 2008.

ALI, Kabir (Moseley CS and SFC), b Moseley, Birmingham, Warwks 24 Nov 1980. 6'0". Cousin of Kadeer Ali (*see GLOUCESTERSHIRE*) and M.M.Ali (*see below*). RHB, RMF. Debut (Worcestershire) 1999. Rajasthan 2006-07. **Tests:** 1 (2003); HS 9 and BB 3-80 v SA (Leeds) 2003 – on debut. **LOI:** 14 (2003 to 2006); HS 39* v P (Rawalpindi) 2005-06; BB 4-45 v I (Delhi) 2005-06. F-c Tours (Eng A): WI 2005-06; SL 2002-03 (ECB Acad). HS 84* v Durham (Stockton) 2003. 50 wkts (5); most – 71 (2002). BB 8-50 v Lancs (Manchester) 2007. Took 8-53 before lunch first day v Yorks (Scarborough) 2003. LO HS 92 v Essex (Worcester) 2003 (NL). LO BB 5-36 v Yorks (Leeds) 2002 (NL). T20 HS 49. T20 BB 4-44.

ALI, Moeen Munir (Moseley S), b Birmingham, Warwks 18 Jun 1987. Brother of Kadeer Ali (*see GLOUCESTERSHIRE*) and cousin of Kabir Ali (*see above*). 6'0". LHB, OB. Warwickshire 2005-06 having joined staff when aged 15. Worcestershire debut 2007. HS 92 v Loughborough U (Kidderminster) 2008. CC HS 85 v Sussex (Hove) 2007. BB 2-50 Wa v Lancs (Birmingham) 2006. Wo BB – . LO HS 100 v Northants (Kidderminster) 2006 (P40). LO BB 2-45 v Northants (Northampton) 2007 (FPT). T20 HS 26*. T20 BB – .

ANDREW, Gareth Mark (Ansford Community S; Richard Huish C), b Yeovil 27 Dec 1983. 6'0". LHB, RMF. Somerset 2003-05; 2nd XI debut 1999 when aged 15 years 247 days. Worcestershire debut 2008. HS 44 Sm v SL A (Taunton) 2004. Wo HS 38* v Middlesex (Lord's) 2008. BB 5-58 v Middlesex (Kidderminster) 2008. LO HS 33 Sm v Leics (Leicester) 2006 (P40). LO BB 4-48 Sm v Scot (Taunton) 2004 (NL). T20 HS 14. T20 BB 4-22.

BATTY, Gareth Jon (Bingley GS), b Bradford, Yorks 13 Oct 1977. Younger brother of J.D.Batty (Yorkshire and Somerset 1989-96). 5'11". RHB, OB. Yorkshire 1997. Surrey 1999-2001. Worcestershire debut 2002. **Tests**: 7 (2003-04 to 2005); HS 38 v SL (Kandy) 2003-04; BB 3-55 v SL (Galle) 2003-04. Took wicket with his third ball in Test cricket. **LOI**: 7 (2002-03 to 2005-06); HS 3 v A (Melbourne) 2002-03; BB 2-40 v WI (Gros Islet, St Lucia) 2003-04. F-c Tours: WI 2003-04, 2005-06; NZ 2008-09 (Eng A); SL 2002-03 (ECB Acad); SL 2003-04; B 2003-04. HS 133 v Surrey (Oval) 2004. 50 wkts (2); most – 60 (2003). BB 7-52 (10-113 match) v Northants (Northampton) 2004. LO HS 83* Sy v Yorks (Oval) 2001 (NL). LO BB 4-14 v Glamorgan (Cardiff) 2008 (P40). IT20 HS 4. IT20 BB – . T20 HS 87. T20 BB 3-38.

DAVIES, Steven Michael (King Charles I S, Kidderminster), b Bromsgrove 17 Jun 1986. 5'10". LHB, WK. Debut (Worcestershire) 2005. 2nd XI debut 2001 when 15 years 8 days. MCC 2006-07. F-c Tours (Eng A): NZ 2008-09; B 2006-07. 1000 runs (1): 1052 (2006). HS 192 v Glos (Bristol) 2006. LO HS 119 v Glos (Worcester) 2008 (P40). IT20 HS 27. T20 HS 30.

‡**FISHER, Ian** Douglas (Beckfoot GS, Bingley; Thomas Danby C, Leeds), b Bradford, Yorks 31 Mar 1976. 5'10½". LHB, SLA. Yorkshire 1995-96 (Y in Zim) to 2001. Gloucestershire 2002-08; cap 2004. F-c Tour: Z 1995-96 (Y). HS 103* Gs v Essex (Gloucester) 2002. BB 5-30 (10-123 match) Gs v Durham (Bristol) 2003. LO HS 37* Gs v Glamorgan (Colwyn Bay) 2007 (FPT). LO BB 3-18 Gs v Northants (Northampton) 2004 (NL). T20 HS 14. T20 BB 4-22.

IMRAN ARIF, b Kotli, Azad Kashmir, Pakistan 15 Jan 1984. UK passport 2009. RHB, RFM. Debut (Worcestershire) 2008. Sussex 2nd XI 2007. Hampshire 2nd XI. HS 5 v Middlesex (Lord's) 2008. BB 5-50 v Glamorgan (Worcester) 2008 – on debut. LO HS 16* v Durham (Worcester) 2008. LO BB 1-17 v Lancashire (Manchester) 2008 (P40).

JONES, Richard Alan (Grange HS and King Edward VI C, Stourbridge; Loughborough U), b Wordsley, Stourbridge 6 Nov 1986. 6'2". RHB, RMF. Worcestershire debut 2007. HS 24 and BB 3-37 v Loughborough U (Worcester) 2007. CC HS 11* v Warwks (Worcester) 2007. CC BB 2-125 v Sussex (Hove) 2008. LO HS 6 v Somerset (Taunton) 2008 (FPT). LO BB – .

JONES, Simon Philip (Coedcae CS; Millfield S), b Morriston, Swansea 25 Dec 1978. Son of I.J.Jones (Glamorgan and England 1960-68). 6'3½". LHB, RFM. Glamorgan 1998-2007; cap 2002. Worcestershire debut 2008. MCC 2002-04. MBE 2005. *Wisden* 2005. **Tests**: 18 (2002 to 2005); HS 44 v I (Lord's) 2002 – on debut; BB 6-53 v A (Manchester) 2005. **LOI**: 8 (2004-05 to 2005); HS 1; BB 2-43 v Z (Bulawayo) 2004-05 – on debut. F-c Tours: A 2002-03 (*part*); SA 2004-05; WI 2003-04; I 2003-04 (Eng A – *part*). HS 46 Gm v Yorks (Scarborough) 2001. Wo HS 25 v Glamorgan (Worcester) 2008. BB 6-45 Gm v Derbys (Cardiff) 2002. Wo BB 5-30 v Leics (Leicester) 2008. LO HS 26 Gm v Hants (Swansea) 2007 (FPT). LO BB 5-32 v Hampshire (Worcester) 2008 (FPT). T20 HS 11*. T20 BB 1-36.

‡**KAPIL, Aneesh** Worcestershire 2nd XI debut 2008. Summer contract 2009. Awaiting 1st XI debut.

NO**KERVEZEE, Alexei** Nicolaas, b Walvis Bay, Namibia 11 Sep 1989. RHB, OB. Netherlands 2005-08. Worcestershire debut 2008. Worcestershire 2nd XI debut 2007. **LOI** (Ne): 18 (2006 to 2007); HS 62 v Bermuda (Rotterdam) 2007; BB – . HS 98 Netherlands v Canada (King City, Ontario) 2007. Wa HS 41 v Loughborough U (Kidderminster) 2008. BB 1-14 Netherlands v Namibia (Windhoek) 2007-08. LO HS 62 (*see LOI*). LO BB – .

KNAPPETT, Joshua Philip Thomas (East Barnet S; Oxford Brookes U), b Westminster, London 15 Apr 1985. 6'0". RHB, occ RM, WK. Oxford UCCE 2004-06. British U 2005-06. Worcestershire debut 2007. No 1st XI appearances in 2008. HS 100* OU v Durham (Oxford) 2006. Wo HS 18 v Sussex (Hove) 2007 – on Wo debut.

‡**MANUEL, Jack** Kenneth (Wilnecote HS, Tamworth), b Sutton Coldfield, Warwks 13 Feb 1991. LHB, OB. Worcestershire 2nd XI debut 2008. Summer contract 2009. Awaiting 1st XI debut.

MASON, Matthew Sean (Mazenod C, Lesmurdie, WA), b Claremont, Perth, Australia 20 Mar 1974. British passport. 6'5". RHB, RFM. W Australia 1996-97 to 1997-98. Worcestershire debut 2002. HS 63 v Warwks (Worcester) 2004. 50 wkts (3); most – 53 (2003, 2005). BB 8-45 (10-117) v Glos (Worcester) 2006. LO HS 25 v Durham (Worcester) 2004 (NL). LO BB 4-34 v Surrey (Guildford) 2003 (NL). T20 HS 8*. T20 BB 3-42.

MITCHELL, Daryl Keith Henry (Prince Henry's HS; University C, Worcester), b Badsey, near Evesham 25 Nov 1983. 5'10". RHB, RM. Debut (Worcestershire) 2005. HS 134* v Glamorgan (Colwyn Bay) 2006. BB 3-50 v Sussex (Hove) 2007. LO HS 92 v Somerset (Taunton) 2008 (FPT). LO BB 4-42 v Lancs (Worcester) 2006 (CGT). T20 HS 31*. T20 BB 4-11 v Glos (Bristol) 2008 – Wo record.

MOORE, Stephen Colin (St Stithian's C, Johannesburg; Exeter U), b Johannesburg, South Africa 4 Nov 1980. 6'1". RHB, RM. Debut (Worcestershire) 2003. F-c Tour (Eng A): NZ 2008-09. 1000 runs (3); most – 1451 (2008). HS 246 v Derbys (Worcester) 2005. BB 1-13 v Lancs (Worcester) 2004. LO HS 105* v Leics (Leicester) 2006 (P40). LO BB 1-1 v Scotland (Worcester) 2004 (NL). T20 HS 53.

^{NQ}**NOFFKE, Ashley** Allan (Immanuel Lutheran C; Sunshine Coast U), b Nambour, Queensland, Australia 30 Apr 1977. 6'3". RHB, RFM. Debut (Aus CA in Zim) 1998-99. Queensland 1999-00 to date. Middlesex 2002-03; cap 2003. Durham 2005. Gloucestershire debut/cap 2007 – taking 6-68 (9-113 match) v Notts (Bristol). F-c Tours (A): E 2001 (part); WI 2002-03; I 2008-09 (Aus A); P 2007-08 (Aus A); Z 1998-99 (Aus CA). HS 114* Q v S Aus (Brisbane) 2003-04. UK HS 76 M v Worcs (Worcester) 2002. BB 8-24 (12-108 match) M v Derbys (Derby) 2002. LO HS 58 M v Sussex (Lord's) 2002 (BHC). LO BB 4-32 Q v Tasmania (Hobart) 2001-02. IT20 HS 0. IT20 BB 3-18. T20 HS 19. T20 BB 3-18.

‡**SHANNON, James** Norman K., b 12 Feb 1990 Ireland. RHB, OB Worcestershire 2nd XI debut 2008. Scholarship 2009. Awaiting 1st XI debut.

SMITH, Benjamin Francis (Kibworth HS), b Corby, Northants 3 Apr 1972. 5'9". RHB, RM. Leicestershire 1990-2001; cap 1995. MCC 1999-00. Central Districts 2000-01 to 2001-02. Worcestershire debut 2002; captain 2003 to 2004 (part). F-c Tours (Le): SA 1996-97; B 1999-00 (MCC). 1000 runs (8); most – 1546 (2005). HS 204 Le v Surrey (Oval) 1998. Wo HS 203 v Somerset (Taunton) 2006. BB 1-5 Le v Essex (Ilford) 1991. Wo BB 1-39 v Surrey (Oval) 2006. LO HS 115 Le v Somerset (Weston-s-M) 1995 (SL). LO BB 1-2 v Worcs CB (Worcester) 2003 (CGT). T20 HS 105.

SOLANKI, Vikram Singh (Regis S, Wolverhampton), b Udaipur, India 1 Apr 1976. 6'0". RHB, OB, occ WK. Debut (Worcestershire) 1995; cap 1998; captain 2005 to date; benefit 2007. Rajasthan 2006-07. F-c Tours (Eng A): SA 1998-99, 1999-00 (Eng – *part*); WI 2000-01, 2005-06 (Captain); NZ 1999-00; SL 2004-05; Z 1996-97 (Wo), 1998-99; B 1999-00. **LOI:** 51 (1999-00 to 2006); HS 106 v SA (Oval) 2003; BB 1-17 v SL (Leeds) 2006. 1000 runs (4); most – 1339 (1999). HS 270 v Glos (Cheltenham) 2008, sharing Wo 2nd wkt record partnership of 316 with S.C.Moore. BB 5-40 v Middlesex (Lord's) 2004. LO HS 164* v Worcs CB (Worcester) 2003 (CGT). LO BB 4-14 v Somerset (Taunton) 2006 (P40). IT20 HS 43. T20 HS 92. T20 BB 1-9.

‡**WHEELDON, David** Antony, b Staffordshire 12 Apr 1989. LHB, LB. Worcestershire 2nd XI debut 2006. Staffordshire 2006.

WHELAN, Christopher David (St Margaret's HS), b Liverpool, Lancs 8 May 1986. 6'2". RHB, RMF. Middlesex 2005-07. Worcestershire debut 2008. HS 58 v Middlesex (Kidderminster) 2008. BB 4-66 v Warwks (Worcester) 2008. LO HS 6 M v Sussex (Hove) 2004 (NL). LO BB 4-78 v NZ (Worcester) 2008. T20 HS 2. T20 BB 2-24.

RELEASED/RETIRED
(Having made a County First-Class or List A appearance in 2008)

FERNANDO, Congenige Randhi **Dilhara**, b Colombo, Sri Lanka 19 Jul 1979. RHB, RFM. SL Board 1997-98. Sinhalese Sports Club 1997-98 to date. Western Province 2003-04 to 2004-05. Worcestershire 2008 (1 match). **Tests** (SL): 33 (2000 to 2008-09); HS 36* v E (Colombo SSC) 2007-08; BB 5-42 v I (Galle) 2001. **LOI** (SL): 131 (2000-01 to 2008-09); HS 20 v E (Dambulla) 2007-08; BB 6-27 v E (Colombo RPS) 2007-08. F-c Tours (SL): E 2002; A 2007-08; SA 2000-01, 2002-03; I 2005-06; P 2004-05, 2008-09; Z 2008-09; B 2005-06, 2008-09. HS 42 and BB 6-29 SSC v Colts (Colombo CCC) 1999-00. Wo HS 11 and BB 1-27 v Middlesex (Kidderminster) 2008. LO HS 21* SL B v SL A (Moratuwa) 1998-99. LO BB 6-27 (*see LOI*). IT20 HS 21. IT20 BB 3-19. T20 HS 21. T20 BB 4-18.

HARRIS, A.J. – *see LEICESTERSHIRE*.

HICK, Graeme Ashley (Prince Edward HS, Salisbury), b Salisbury, Rhodesia 23 May 1966. 6'3". RHB, OB. Zimbabwe 1983-84 to 1985-86. Worcestershire 1984-2008; cap 1986; benefit 1999; captain 2000-02; testimonial 2006. N Districts 1987-88 to 1988-89. MCC 1988-1991. Queensland 1990-91. *Wisden* 1986. PCA 1988. Lawrence Trophy 1988. **Tests**: 65 (1991 to 2000-01); HS 178 v I (Bombay) 1992-93; BB 4-126 v NZ (Wellington) 1991-92. Took wicket with his third ball in Test cricket. **LOI**: 120 (1991 to 2000-01); HS 126* v SL (Adelaide) 1998-99; BB 5-33 v Z (Harare) 1999-00. F-c Tours: E 1985 (Z); A 1994-95, 1998-99 (*part*); SA 1995-96, 1999-00 (*part*); WI 1993-94; NZ 1991-92; I 1992-93; P 2000-01; SL 1983-84 (Z), 1992-93, 2000-01; Z 1990-91 (Wo), 1996-97 (Wo). 1000 runs (19+1), inc 2000 (3): 2004 (1986), 2713 (1988), 2347 (1990); youngest to score 2000 (1986). Scored 1019 runs before June 1988, including a record 410 runs in April. Fewest innings for 10,000 runs in county cricket (179). Youngest (24) to score 50 f-c hundreds. Second-youngest (32) to score 100 f-c hundreds. Scored 645 runs without being dismissed (UK record) in 1990. 100th f-c hundred for Worcestershire 2006. HS 405* (Worcs record and then second highest in UK f-c matches) v Somerset (Taunton) 1988. BB 5-18 v Leics (Worcester) 1995. LO HS 172* v Devon (Worcester) 1987 (NWT). LO BB 5-19 Eng v Pak A (Lahore) 1998-99. T20 HS 116* v Northants (Luton) 2004 – Wo record score.

ᴺᵠ**MAGOFFIN, Stephen** James (Indooroopilly HS and Curtin U, Perth), b Corinda, Queensland, Australia, 17 Dec 1979. 6'2". LHB, RFM. Western Australia 2004-05 to date. Surrey 2007 (one f-c match). Worcestershire 2008. HS 79 WA v Tas (Perth) 2008-09. Wo HS 33 v Derbys (Chesterfield) 2008. BB 8-47 WA v S Australia (Perth) 2005-06. Wo BB 4-49 v Northants (Northampton) 2008. LO HS 24* v Hampshire (Southampton) 2008. LO BB 4-58 Sy v Kent (Oval) 2007 (FPT). T20 HS 11*. T20 BB 2-15.

WORCESTERSHIRE 2008

RESULTS SUMMARY

	Place	Won	Lost	Tied	Drew	No Result
County Championship (2nd Division)	2nd	6	2		7	1
All First-Class Matches		6	2		8	1
FP Trophy (South West Division)	3rd	3	3			2
Pro40 League (1st Division)	7th	2	3	1		2
Twenty/20 Cup (Midlands/West/Wales Division)	5th	3	6			1

LV COUNTY CHAMPIONSHIP AVERAGES

BATTING AND FIELDING

Cap†		M	I	NO	HS	Runs	Avge	100	50	Ct/St
2003[c]	S.C.Moore	15	28	4	156	1288	53.66	5	6	8
1998	V.S.Solanki	15	25	1	270	1127	46.95	4	5	7
1986	G.A.Hick	11	18	3	149	689	45.93	2	2	25
2002[c]	B.F.Smith	15	24	1	99	1004	43.65	–	10	12
2005[c]	D.K.H.Mitchell	15	27	5	102	856	38.90	1	3	8
2005[c]	S.M.Davies	15	23	5	99*	698	38.77	–	4	68
2002[c]	G.J.Batty	14	19	5	66	393	28.07	–	3	6
2008[c]	C.D.Whelan	5	5	2	58	82	27.33	–	1	–
2008[c]	M.M.Ali	5	7	1	42*	117	19.50	–	–	–
2002[c]	Kabir Ali	11	15	2	46	236	18.15	–	–	3
2008[c]	G.M.Andrew	12	15	3	38*	199	16.58	–	–	5
2008[c]	S.P.Jones	9	11	4	25	97	13.85	–	–	–
2008[c]	S.J.Magoffin	7	9	2	33	85	12.14	–	–	–

Also batted: C.R.D.Fernando (1 match – 2008[c]) 11, 0; A.J.Harris (2 – 2008[c]) 1, 11*, 2*; Imran Arif (6 – 2008[c]) 5, 4*, 4 (1 ct); R.A.Jones (1 – 2007[c]) 2; M.S.Mason (6 – 2002[c]) 6, 25, 6 (2 ct).

BOWLING

	O	M	R	W	Avge	Best	5wI	10wM
S.P.Jones	211	39	757	42	18.02	5-30	4	–
Kabir Ali	311.3	53	1106	59	18.74	6-58	4	–
Imran Arif	158.5	30	575	22	26.13	5-50	1	–
M.S.Mason	125	40	294	10	29.40	2-26	–	–
S.J.Magoffin	202	45	755	23	32.82	4-49	–	–
G.M.Andrew	238.5	35	1018	27	37.70	5-58	1	–
G.J.Batty	349.3	87	950	25	38.00	5-33	1	–

Also bowled: C.D.Whelan 55.5 4 327 8 40.87 4-66 – –
M.M.Ali 28-6-93-0; C.R.D.Fernando 24.1-2-130-2; A.J.Harris 28-8-91-1; R.A.Jones 10-2-41-0; D.K.H.Mitchell 29-6-63-0; V.S.Solanki 7-3-11-0.

The First-Class Averages (pp 136–153) give the records of Worcestershire's players in all first-class county matches (Worcestershire's other opponents being Loughborough UCCE), with the exception of A.J.Harris, whose first-class figures for Worcestershire are as above.

†Worcestershire revised their capping policy in 2002 and now award players with their County Colours ([c]) when they make their Championship debut.

WORCESTERSHIRE RECORDS

FIRST-CLASS CRICKET

Highest Total	For 701-6d		v	Surrey	Worcester	2007
	V 701-4d		by	Leics	Worcester	1906
Lowest Total	For 24		v	Yorkshire	Huddersfield	1903
	V 30		by	Hampshire	Worcester	1903
Highest Innings	For 405*	G.A.Hick	v	Somerset	Taunton	1988
	V 331*	J.D.B.Robertson	for	Middlesex	Worcester	1949

Highest Partnership for each Wicket

1st	309	H.K.Foster/F.L.Bowley	v	Derbyshire	Derby	1901
2nd	316	S.C.Moore/V.S.Solanki	v	Glos	Cheltenham	2008
3rd	438*	G.A.Hick/T.M.Moody	v	Hampshire	Southampton	1997
4th	330	B.F.Smith/G.A.Hick	v	Somerset	Taunton	2006
5th	393	E.G.Arnold/W.B.Burns	v	Warwicks	Birmingham	1909
6th	265	G.A.Hick/S.J.Rhodes	v	Somerset	Taunton	1988
7th	256	D.A.Leatherdale/S.J.Rhodes	v	Notts	Nottingham	2002
8th	184	S.J.Rhodes/S.R.Lampitt	v	Derbyshire	Kidderminster	1991
9th	181	J.A.Cuffe/R.D.Burrows	v	Glos	Worcester	1907
10th	119	W.B.Burns/G.A.Wilson	v	Somerset	Worcester	1906

Best Bowling	For	9- 23	C.F.Root	v	Lancashire	Worcester	1931
(Innings)	V	10- 51	J.Mercer	for	Glamorgan	Worcester	1936
Best Bowling	For	15- 87	A.J.Conway	v	Glos	Moreton-in-M	1914
(Match)	V	17-212	J.C.Clay	for	Glamorgan	Swansea	1937

Most Runs – Season		2654	H.H.I.H.Gibbons	(av 52.03)	1934
Most Runs – Career		34490	D.Kenyon	(av 34.18)	1946-67
Most 100s – Season		10	G.M.Turner		1970
		10	G.A.Hick		1988
Most 100s – Career		106	G.A.Hick		1984-2008
Most Wkts – Season		207	C.F.Root	(av 17.52)	1925
Most Wkts – Career		2143	R.T.D.Perks	(av 23.73)	1930-55
Most Career W-K Dismissals		1095	S.J.Rhodes	(991 ct/104 st)	1985-2004
Most Career Catches in the Field		528	G.A.Hick		1984-2008

LIMITED-OVERS CRICKET

Highest Total	FPT	404-3		v	Devon	Worcester	1987
	P40	316-5		v	Glos	Worcester	2008
	T20	227-6		v	Northants	Kidderminster	2007
Lowest Total	FPT	98		v	Durham	Chester-le-St	1968
	P40	86		v	Yorkshire	Leeds	1969
	T20	86		v	Northants	Worcester	2006
Highest Innings	FPT	180*	T.M.Moody	v	Surrey	The Oval	1994
	P40	160	T.M.Moody	v	Kent	Worcester	1991
	T20	116*	G.A.Hick	v	Northants	Luton	2004
Best Bowling	FPT	7-19	N.V.Radford	v	Beds	Bedford	1991
	P40	6-16	Shoaib Akhtar	v	Glos	Worcester	2005
	T20	4-11	D.K.H.Mitchell	v	Glos	Bristol	2008

118

YORKSHIRE

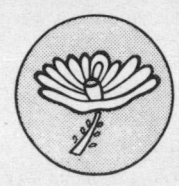

Formation of Present Club: 8 January 1863
Substantial Reorganisation: 10 December 1891
Inaugural First-Class Match: 1864
Colours: Dark Blue, Light Blue and Gold
Badge: White Rose
County Championships (since 1890): (30) 1893, 1896, 1898, 1900, 1901, 1902, 1905, 1908, 1912, 1919, 1922, 1923, 1924, 1925, 1931, 1932, 1933, 1935, 1937, 1938, 1939, 1946, 1959, 1960, 1962, 1963, 1966, 1967, 1968, 2001
Joint Champions: (1) 1949
Gillette/NatWest/C&G/FP Trophy Winners: (3) 1965, 1969, 2002
Benson and Hedges Cup Winners: (1) 1987
Pro 40/National League (Div 1) Winners: (0); best – 2nd 2000
Sunday League Winners: (1) 1983
Twenty20 Cup Winners: (0); best – Quarter-Finalist 2007

Chief Executive: Stewart M.Regan, Headingley Cricket Ground, Leeds, LS6 3BU • Tel: 0113 278 7394 • Fax: 0113 278 4099 • Email: cricket@yorkshireccc.org.uk • Web: www.yorkshireccc.org.uk

Director of Cricket: Martyn D.Moxon. **Captain:** A.McGrath. **Vice-Captain:** J.A.Rudolph. **Overseas Players:** Naved-ul-Hasan. **2009 Beneficiary:** A.McGrath. **Head Groundsman:** Andy Fogarty. **Scorer:** John T.Potter. ‡ New registration. NQ Not qualified for England.

‡**AZEEM RAFIQ,** b Karachi, Pakistan 27 Feb 1991. RHB, OB. Yorkshire 2nd XI 2007. England U19s 2008-09. Awaiting f-c debut. T20 HS – . T20 BB – .

BAIRSTOW, Jonathan Marc (St Peter's S, York) b Bradford 26 Sep 1989. Son of D.L.Bairstow (Yorkshire 1970-90; GW 1976-77 to 1977-78; England 1979 to 1980-81) and brother of A.D.Bairstow (Derbyshire 1995). RHB, WK. Inaugural winner of Young Wisden Schools Cricketer of the Year 2008. Yorkshire 2nd XI 2007-08. Awaiting f-c debut.

BALLANCE, Gary Simon (Peterhouse S, Marondera, Zimbabwe; Harrow S), b Harare, Zimbabwe 22 Nov 1989. Nephew of G.S.Ballance (Rhodesia B 1978-79) and D.L.Houghton (Rhodesia/Zimbabwe 1978-79 to 1997-98). 5'10". LHB, LB. Debut (Yorkshire) 2008. Derbyshire (List A) 2006-07. HS 5 v Kent (Canterbury) 2008 – on debut. LO HS 73 Dc v Hants (Southampton) 2006 (P40).

‡**BLAIN, John** Angus Rae (Penicuik HS; Jewel & Esk Valley C), b Edinburgh, Scotland 4 Jan 1979. 6'1". RHB, RMF. Northamptonshire 1997-2003. Scotland 1996 to 2007-08. **LOI** (Scot): 31 (1999 to 2008); HS 30* v Canada (Mombasa) 2006-07; BB 5-22 v Netherlands (Dublin) 2008. F-c Tour (Scot): Namibia (2007-08). HS 93 Scotland v Ireland (Belfast) 2007. CC HS 34 Nh v Surrey (Northampton) 2001. BB 6-42 Nh v Kent (Canterbury) 2001. LO HS 32 Scot v Warwks (Edinburgh) 2007. LO BB 5-22 (see LOI). IT20 HS 3*. IT20 BB 2-23.

BRESNAN, Timothy Thomas (Castleford HS and TC; Pontefract New C), b Pontefract 28 Feb 1985. 6'0". RHB, RMF. Debut (Yorkshire) 2003; cap 2006. MCC 2006. **LOI:** 5 (2006 to 2008); HS 20 v SL (Manchester) 2006; BB 2-34 v Scot (Edinburgh) 2008. F-c Tour (Eng A): B 2006-07. HS 126* Eng A v Indians (Chelmsford) 2007. Y HS 116 v Surrey (Oval) 2007, sharing in Yorkshire record 9th wicket partnership of 246 with J.N.Gillespie. BB 5-42 v Worcs (Worcester) 2005. LO HS 61 v Leics (Leeds) 2003 (NL). BB 4-25 v Somerset (Leeds) 2005 (NL). IT20 6*. IT20 BB – . T20 HS 42. T20 BB 3-21.

BROPHY, Gerard Louis (Christian Brothers C, Boksburg; Witwatersrand TC), b Welkom, Orange Free State, South Africa 26 Nov 1975. 5'11". British/EU passport. Qualified for England 2006. RHB, WK. Transvaal/Gauteng 1996-97 to 1998-99. Free State 1999-00 to 2000-01. Northamptonshire 2002-05. Yorkshire debut 2006. F-c Tour (SA Acad): Z 1998. HS 185 SA Academy v Zim President's XI (Harare) 1998-99. UK HS 181 Nh v Sussex (Hove) 2004. Y HS 100* v Hants (Southampton) 2007. LO HS 66 v Glamorgan (Cardiff) 2007 (P40). T20 HS 57.

GALE, Andrew William (Whitcliffe Mount S; Heckmondwike GS), b Dewsbury 28 Nov 1983. 6'2". LHB, LB. Debut (Yorkshire) 2004, 2006 to date; cap 2008. HS 150 v Surrey (Oval) 2008. BB 1-33 v LU (Leeds) 2007. LO HS 89 v Leics (Leeds) 2008. T20 HS 56.

GUY, Simon Mark (Wickersley CS), b Rotherham 17 Nov 1978. 5'7". RHB, WK. Debut (Yorkshire) 2000. No f-c appearances in 2008. HS 52* v Durham (Leeds) 2006. LO HS 40 v Leics (Leeds) 2005 (NL). T20 HS 7.

HANNON-DALBY, Oliver James b Halifax 20 Jun 1989. LHB, RMF. Debut (Yorkshire) 2008. Yorkshire 2nd XI debut 2006. HS 1 and BB 1-58 v Surrey (Oval) 2008 – on debut.

‡**HODGSON, Lee** John b Middlesbrough 29 Jun 1986. RHB, RFM. Surrey 2008 (1 match). HS 63 and BB-Sy v Notts (Oval) 2008 – on debut. LOI HS and BB – .

HOGGARD, Matthew James (Grangefield S, Pudsey), b Leeds 31 Dec 1976. 6'2". RHB, RFM. Debut (Yorkshire) 1996; cap 2000; benefit 2008. Free State 1998-99 to 1999-00. MCC 2004-07. MBE 2005. *Wisden* 2005. **Tests**: 67 (2000 to 2007-08); HS 38 v WI (Oval) 2004; BB 7-61 (12-205 match) v SA (Johannesburg) 2004-05; hat-trick v WI (Bridgetown) 2003-04. **LOI**: 26 (2001-02 to 2005-06); HS 7 v I (Cochin) 2005; BB 5-49 v Z (Harare) 2001-02. F-c Tours: A 2002-03, 2006-07; SA 2004-05; WI 2003-04; NZ 2001-02, 2007-08; I 2001-02, 2005-06; P 2000-01, 2005-06; SL 2000-01, 2003-04, 2007-08; B 2003-04. HS 89* v Glamorgan (Leeds) 2004. 50 wkts (2); most – 50 (2000, 2005). BB 7-49 v Somerset (Leeds) 2003. Hat-trick 2003-04. LO HS 7* (*twice*). LO BB 5-28 v Leics (Leicester) 2000 (NL). T20 HS 18. T20 BB 3-23.

^NQ**KRUIS, Gideon** ('**Deon**') Jacobus (St Albans C, Pretoria; Pretoria U), b Pretoria, South Africa 9 May 1974. 6'3". RHB, RFM. N Transvaal 1993-94 to 1996-97. Griqualand West 1997-98 to 2003-04. MCC 2000-01. Eagles 2004-05. Yorkshire debut 2005; cap 2006. Kolpak registration. HS 59 GW v B (Kimberley) 2000-01. Y HS 50* and BB 5-47 v Surrey (Leeds) 2008. 50 wkts (1): 64 (2005). BB 7-58 GW v Northerns (Pretoria) 1997-98. LO HS 31* v Surrey (Oval) 2006 (P40). LO BB 4-17 v Derbys (Leeds) 2007 (P40). T20 HS 5*. T20 BB 2-15.

LEE, James Edward (Immanuel Community C), b Sheffield 23 Dec 1988. 6'1". LHB, RMF. Debut (Yorkshire) 2006. HS 21* and BB-v Yorks (Manchester) 2006 – in only f-c match. No l-o appearances.

LYTH, Adam (Caedmon S, Whitby; Whitby Community C), b Whitby 25 Sep 1987. 5'8". LHB, RM. Debut (Yorkshire) 2007. HS 132 v Notts (Nottingham) 2008. BB 1-12 v LU (Leeds) 2007. CC BB 1-20 v Somerset (Scarborough) 2008. LO HS 38* v Glos (Bristol) 2008 (FPT).

McGRATH, Anthony (Yorkshire Martyrs Collegiate S), b Bradford 6 Oct 1975. 6'2". RHB, RM. Debut (Yorkshire) 1995; cap 1999; captain 2003, 2009; benefit 2009. MCC 1999-00. **Tests**: 4 (2003); HS 81 v Z (Chester-le-St) 2003; BB 3-16 v Z (Lord's) 2003 – on debut. **LOI**: 14 (2003 to 2004); HS 52 v SA (Manchester) 2003; BB 1-13 v WI (Nottingham) 2004. F-c Tours (Eng A): A 1996-97; P 1995-96; Z 1995-96 (Y); B 1999-00 (MCC). 1000 runs (2); most – 1425 (2005). HS 188* v Warwks (Birmingham) 2007. BB 5-39 v Derbys (Derby) 2004. LO HS 148 v Somerset (Taunton) 2006 (P40). LO BB 4-41 v Surrey (Leeds) 2003 (NL). T20 HS 72*. T20 BB 3-27.

NQNAVED-UL-HASAN, Rana (Government HS, Sheikhupura), b Sheikhupura, Pakistan 28 Feb 1978. 5'11". RHB, RMF. Debut Pakistan A v England A (Multan) 1995-96. Lahore 1999-00. Pakistan Customs 2000-01. Sheikhupura 2000-01 to 2001-02. Allied Bank 2001-02. WAPDA 2002-03 to date. Sialkot 2003-04 to 2005-06. Sussex 2005-07; cap 2005. Punjab 2006-07. Yorkshire debut 2008. Herefordshire 2002. **Tests** (P): 9 (2004-05 to 2006-07); HS 42* v E (Lahore) 2005-06; BB 3-30 v E (Faisalabad) 2005-06. **LOI** (P): 62 (2002-03 to 2006-07); HS 29 v A (Melbourne) 2004-05; BB 6-27 v I (Jamshedpur) 2004-05. F-c Tours (P): A 2004-05; SA 2006-07; WI 2004-05; I 2004-05. HS 139 Sx v Middlesex (Lord's) 2005. Y HS 22 v Hants (Southampton) 2008. 50 wkts (2+3); most – 91 (2000-01). BB 7-49 Sheikhupura v Sialkot (Muridke) 2001-02. CC BB 7-62 (11-148 match) Sx v Yorks (Leeds) 2006. Y BB 4-86 v Kent (Scarborough) 2008. LO HS 74 Y v Derbys (Derby) 2008. LO BB 6-27 (see LOI). IT20 HS 17*. IT20 BB 1-26. T20 HS 40*. T20 BB 3-9.

PATTERSON, Steven Andrew (Malet Lambert CS; St Mary's SFC, Hull; Leeds U), b Hull 3 Oct 1983. RHB, RMF. Debut (Yorkshire) 2005. Bradford/Leeds UCCE 2003 (not f-c). HS 46 v Lancs (Manchester) 2006. BB 3-19 v Somerset (Taunton) 2008. LO HS 25* v Worcs (Leeds) 2006 (P40). LO BB 3-11 Yorks CB v Northants CB (Northampton) 2002.

PYRAH, Richard Michael (Ossett S; Wakefield C), b Dewsbury 1 Nov 1982. 6'0". RHB, RM. Debut (Yorkshire) 2004. HS 106 and 1-3 v LU (Leeds) 2007. CC HS 78 v Worcs (Worcester) 2005. CC BB 1-9 v Worcs (Worcester) 2005. LO HS 42 v Durham (Scarborough) 2004 (NL). LO BB 5-50 Yorks CB v Somerset (Scarborough) 2002 (CGT). T20 HS 33*. T20 BB 4-20 v Durham (Leeds) 2008 – Yorkshire record.

RASHID, Adil Usman (Belle Vue S, Bradford), b Bradford 17 Feb 1988. 5'8". RHB, LBG. Debut (Yorkshire) 2006. MCC 2007-08. YC 2007. Eng A. F-c Tours: WI 2008-09; I 2008-09; B 2006-07 (Eng A). Match double (114, 48, 8-157 and 2-45) for Eng U-19 v Ind U-19 (Taunton) 2006. HS 111 v Sussex (Hove) 2008. BB 7-107 v Hants (Southampton) 2008. LO HS 41* v Derbys (Leeds) 2008 (FPT). BB 3-37 v Derbys (Derby) 2008 (P40). T20 HS 10. T20 BB 4-24.

NQRUDOLPH, Jacobus Andries ('**Jacques**') (Afrikaanse Hoer Seunskool), b Springs, Transvaal, South Africa 4 May 1981. Elder brother of G.J.Rudolph (Limpopo and Namibia 2006-07 to date). 5'11". LHB, LBG. Northerns 1999-00 to 2003-04. Titans 2004-05, 2008-09. Eagles 2005-06 to 2007-08. Yorkshire debut 2007 (Kolpak registration) scoring 122 v Surrey (Oval); cap 2007. **Tests** (SA): 35 (2003 to 2006); HS 222* v B (Chittagong) 2003 – on debut; BB 1-1 v E (Leeds) 2003. **LOI** (SA): 43 (2003 to 2005-06); HS 81 v B (Dhaka) 2003. F-c Tours (SA): E 2003; A 2001-02, 2005-06; WI 2004-05; NZ 2003-04; I 2004-05; SL 2004, 2005-06, 2006; B 2003. 1000 runs (2); most – 1292 (2008). HS 222* (see Tests). UK HS 220 v Warwks (Scarborough) 2007. BB 5-80 Eagles v Cape Cobras (Cape Town) 2007-08. UK BB 1-1 (see Tests). Y BB 1-13 v Somerset (Scarborough) 2008. LO HS 134* South Africa A v Kenya (Laudium) 2001-02. LO BB 4-40 South Africa A v New Zealand A (Colombo) 2005-06. IT20 HS 6*. T20 HS 71. T20 BB 3-16.

SAYERS, Joseph John (St Mary's RC CS, Menston; Worcester C, Oxford) b Leeds 5 Nov 1983. 6'0". LHB, OB. Oxford U 2002-04; blue 2002-03-04. Yorkshire debut 2004; cap 2007. HS 187 v Kent (Tunbridge Wells) 2007. BB – . LO HS 62 v Glos (Leeds) 2003 (NL). LO BB 1-31 v Warwks (Birmingham) 2005 (NL). T20 HS 12.

SHAHZAD, Ajmal (Woodhouse Grove S; Bradford U), b Huddersfield 27 Jul 1985. 6'0". RHB, RMF. Debut (Yorkshire) 2006 (first British-born Asian to play for Yorkshire). HS 35 v Hants (Leeds) 2008. BB 4-22 v Sussex (Leeds) 2007. LO HS 33 v Durham (Chester-le-St) 2008 (FPT). LO BB 5-51 v Sri Lanka A (Leeds) 2007. T20 HS 7*. T20 BB 2-22.

TAYLOR, Christopher Robert (Benton Park HS, Rawdon), b Leeds 21 Feb 1981. 6'4". RHB, RMF. Yorkshire 2001-05, 2008. Derbyshire 2006-07. HS 121 De v Glamorgan (Cardiff) 2006. Y HS 52* v Surrey (Leeds) 2002. LO HS 111* De v Durham (Derby) 2006 (CGT). T20 HS 28*.

VAUGHAN, Michael Paul (Silverdale CS, Sheffield), b Salford, Lancs 29 Oct 1974. 6'2". RHB, OB. Debut (Yorkshire) 1993; cap 1995; benefit 2005. *Wisden* 2002. PCA 2002. OBE 2005. **ECB central contract 2008-09. Tests:** 82 (1999-00 to 2008, 51 as captain); HS 197 and BB 2-71 v I (Nottingham) 2002. Scored Eng record 1,481 runs (avge 61.70) with six hundreds in 2002. **LOI:** 86 (2000-01 to 2006-07, 60 as captain); HS 90* v Z (Bulawayo) 2004-05; BB 4-22 v SL (Manchester) 2002. F-c Tours (C=captain): A 1996-97 (Eng A), 2002-03; SA 1998-99C (Eng A), 1999-00, 2004-05C; WI 2003-04C; NZ 2001-02, 2007-08C; I 1994-95 (Eng A), 2001-02; P 2000-01, 2005-06C; SL 2000-01, 2003-04C, 2007-08C; Z 1995-96 (Y), 1998-99C (Eng A); B 2003-04C. 1000 runs (4); most – 1244 (1995). HS 197 (*see Tests*). Y HS 183 v Glamorgan (Cardiff) 1996. BB 4-39 v OU (Oxford) 1994. CC BB 4-47 v Somerset (Leeds) 2001. LO HS 125* v Somerset (Taunton) 2001 (BHC). LO BB 4-22 (*see LOI*). IT20 HS 27. T20 HS 34. T20 BB 1-21.

WAINWRIGHT, David John (Hemsworth HS and SFC; Loughborough U); b Pontefract 21 Mar 1985. LHB, SLA. Debut (Yorkshire) 2004. Loughborough UCCE 2005-06. British U 2006. HS 104* (batting at No 10) and Y BB 3-9 v Sussex (Hove) 2008. BB 4-48 LU v Worcs (Worcester) 2005. LO HS 26 and BB 2-30 v Surrey (Scarborough) 2007 (P40). T20 HS 2. T20 BB 3-6.

WHITE, Craig (Flora Hill HS, Bendigo, Australia; Bendigo HS), b Morley 16 Dec 1969. Brother-in-law of D.S.Lehmann (S Australia, Victoria, Yorkshire and Australia 1987-88 to 2007-08). 6'0". RHB, RFM/OB. Debut (Yorkshire) 1990; cap 1993; benefit 2002; captain 2004-06. Victoria 1990-91 (2 matches). **Tests:** 30 (1994 to 2002-03); HS 121 v I (Ahmedabad) 2001-02; BB 5-32 v WI (Oval) 2000. **LOI:** 51 (1994-95 to 2002 03); HS 57* v A (Melbourne) 2002-03; BB 5-21 v Z (Bulawayo) 1999-00. F-c Tours: A 1994-95, 1996-97 (Eng A), 2002-03; SA 1991-92 (Y), 1992-93 (Y); NZ 1996-97, 2001-02; I 2001-02; P 1995-96 (Eng A), 2000-01; SL 2000-01; Z 1996-97 (*part*). HS 186 v Lancs (Manchester) 2001. BB 8-55 v Glos (Gloucester) 1998 – inc hat-trick. Hat-trick 1998. LO HS 148 v Leics (Leicester) 1997 (SL). LO BB 5-19 v Somerset (Scarborough) 2002 (NL). T20 HS 55. T20 BB 1-0.

RELEASED/RETIRED
(Having made a County First-Class or List A appearance in 2008)

GOUGH, Darren (Priory CS, Lundwood), b Monk Bretton, Barnsley 18 Sep 1970. 5'11". RHB, RFM. Yorkshire 1989-2003, 2007-08; cap 1993; benefit 2001; captain 2007-08. Essex 2004-06; cap 2004. *Wisden* 1998. **Tests:** 58 (1994 to 2003); HS 65 v NZ (Manchester) 1994 – on debut; BB 6-42 v SA (Leeds) 1998; hat-trick v A (Sydney) 1998-99 – first for E v A since 1899. **LOI:** 158 (1994 to 2006); HS 46* v A (Chester-le-St) 2005; BB 5-44 v Z (Sydney) 1994-95 and 5-44 v A (Lord's) 1997. Took wickets with his sixth balls in both Tests and LOI. F-c Tours: A 1994-95, 1998-99; SA 1991-92 (Y), 1992-93 (Y), 1993-94 (Eng A), 1995-96, 1999-00; NZ 1996-97; P 2000-01; SL 2000-01; Z 1996-97. HS 121 Y v Warwks (Leeds) 1996. 50 wkts (5); most – 67 (1996). BB 7-28 (10-80 match) v Lancs (Leeds) 1995 (not CC). CC BB 7-42 (10-96 match) v Somerset (Taunton) 1993. 2 hat-tricks (1995, 1998-99); took 4 wkts in 5 balls v Kent (Leeds) 1995. LO HS 72* v Leics (Leicester) 1991 (SL). LO BB 7-27 v Ireland (Leeds) 1997 (NWT). IT20 HS – . IT20 BB 3-16. T20 HS 37. T20 BB 3-16.

^{NQ}**MORKEL, Morne** (Hoerskool, Vereeniging), b Vereeniging, South Africa 6 Oct 1984. Younger brother of J.A.Morkel (*see DURHAM*). LHB, RFM. Easterns 2003-04 to 2006-07. Titans 2004-05 to date. Kent (T20 only) 2007. Yorkshire 2008 (1 match). **Tests:** 15 (2006-07 to 2008-09); HS 40 v A (Sydney) 2008-09; BB 5-50 v B (Dhaka) 2007-08. **LOI** (SA): 16 (2007 to 2008-09); HS 23* v Z (Harare) 2007; BB 4-36 v WI (Cape Town) 2007-08. HS 82* and BB 6-47 (11-56 match) Titans v Warriors (E London) 2006-07. Y HS 8 and BB 1-33 v Notts (Leeds) 2008 – on UK debut. LO HS 35 Easterns v Northerns (Pretoria) 2005-06. LO BB 4-36 (*see LOI*). IT20 HS 1*. IT20 BB 4-17. T20 HS 7*. T20 BB 4-17.

G.L.Wood left the staff, without making a County First-Class or List A appearance in 2008.

YORKSHIRE 2008

RESULTS SUMMARY

	Place	Won	Lost	Tied	Drew	No Result
County Championship (1st Division)	7th	2	5		9	
All First-Class Matches		2	5		9	
FP Trophy (North Division)	Semi-Finalist	5	3			2
Pro40 League (2nd Division)	2nd	5	1	1		1
Twenty/20 Cup (North Division)	3rd	5	3	1		1

LV COUNTY CHAMPIONSHIP AVERAGES

BATTING AND FIELDING

Cap		M	I	NO	HS	Runs	Avge	100	50	Ct/St
2007	J.A.Rudolph	16	24	1	155	1292	56.17	5	6	24
2008	A.W.Gale	15	23	–	150	899	39.08	3	3	9
1999	A.McGrath	14	21	–	144	728	34.66	2	3	11
2006	T.T.Bresnan	14	20	5	84*	506	33.73	–	2	9
	D.J.Wainwright	4	6	1	104*	165	33.00	1	–	2
	A.Lyth	14	21	–	132	645	30.71	1	5	11
2006	G.J.Kruis	10	14	8	50*	183	30.50	–	1	2
2008	G.L.Brophy	16	24	1	70	546	23.73	–	4	43/6
2008	A.U.Rashid	16	24	2	111	516	23.45	1	2	6
1995	M.P.Vaughan	6	9	–	72	210	23.33	–	1	3
	C.R.Taylor	4	6	–	48	123	20.50	–	–	1
	Naved-ul-Hasan	7	10	3	22	114	16.28	–	–	3
	R.M.Pyrah	5	6	–	51	96	16.00	–	1	5
1993	D.Gough	8	11	1	34	148	14.80	–	–	4
	S.A.Patterson	4	5	2	17	36	12.00	–	–	1
2000	M.J.Hoggard	13	17	6	28*	126	11.45	–	–	2
2007	J.J.Sayers	6	9	–	22	76	8.44	–	–	6

Also batted: G.S.Ballance (1 match) 1, 5; O.J.Hannon-Dalby (1) 1; M.Morkel (1) 0, 8; B.W.Sanderson (2) 0*, 6; A.Shazad (1) 35.

BOWLING

	O	M	R	W	Avge	Best	5wI	10wM
M.J.Hoggard	342.5	66	1037	42	24.69	6- 57	1	–
S.A.Patterson	97.1	22	279	11	25.36	3- 19	–	–
T.T.Bresnan	421	77	1278	45	28.40	5- 94	1	–
A.U.Rashid	590.1	64	1886	62	30.41	7-107	4	–
Naved-ul-Hasan	153.1	21	606	16	37.87	4- 86	–	–
G.J.Kruis	295.3	68	903	22	41.04	5- 47	1	–
Also bowled:								
D.J.Wainwright	85.1	18	246	8	30.75	3- 9	–	–
A.McGrath	100.1	16	282	9	31.33	2- 27	–	–
D.Gough	149	25	528	9	58.66	2- 34	–	–

A.W.Gale 1-0-3-0; O.J.Hannon-Dalby 29-5-114-1; A.Lyth 30.1-5-105-1; M.Morkel 15.2-4-33-1; R.M.Pyrah 56-11-201-1; J.A.Rudolph 21.2-2-74-1; B.W.Sanderson 37-7-140-1; A.Shazad 24-7-64-3; M.P.Vaughan 6-0-47-0.

Yorkshire played no first-class fixtures outside the County Championship in 2008. The First-Class Averages (pp 136–153) give the records of Yorkshire players in all first-class county matches, with the exception of M.J.Hoggard, M.Morkel, A.U.Rashid and M.P.Vaughan, whose first-class figures for Yorkshire are as above.

YORKSHIRE RECORDS

FIRST-CLASS CRICKET

Highest Total	For 887		v	Warwicks	Birmingham	1896
	V 681-7d		by	Leics	Bradford	1996
Lowest Total	For 23		v	Hampshire	Middlesbrough	1965
	V 13		by	Notts	Nottingham	1901
Highest Innings	For 341	G.H.Hirst	v	Leics	Leicester	1905
	V 318*	W.G.Grace	for	Glos	Cheltenham	1876

Highest Partnership for each Wicket

1st	555	P.Holmes/H.Sutcliffe	v	Essex	Leyton	1932
2nd	346	W.Barber/M.Leyland	v	Middlesex	Sheffield	1932
3rd	323*	H.Sutcliffe/M.Leyland	v	Glamorgan	Huddersfield	1928
4th	358	D.S.Lehmann/M.J.Lumb	v	Durham	Leeds	2006
5th	340	E.Wainwright/G.H Hirst	v	Surrey	The Oval	1899
6th	276	M.Leyland/E.Robinson	v	Glamorgan	Swansea	1926
7th	254	W.Rhodes/D.C.F.Burton	v	Hampshire	Dewsbury	1919
8th	292	R.Peel/Lord Hawke	v	Warwicks	Birmingham	1896
9th	246	T.T.Bresnan/J.N.Gillespie	v	Surrey	The Oval	2007
10th	149	G.Boycott/G.B.Stevenson	v	Warwicks	Birmingham	1982

Best Bowling	For 10-10	H.Verity	v	Notts	Leeds	1932
(Innings)	V 10-37	C.V.Grimmett	for	Australians	Sheffield	1930
Best Bowling	For 17-91	H.Verity	v	Essex	Leyton	1933
(Match)	V 17-91	H.Dean	for	Lancashire	Liverpool	1913

Most Runs – Season	2883	H.Sutcliffe	(av 80.08)	1932
Most Runs – Career	38558	H.Sutcliffe	(av 50.20)	1919-45
Most 100s – Season	12	H.Sutcliffe		1932
Most 100s – Career	112	H.Sutcliffe		1919-45
Most Wkts – Season	240	W.Rhodes	(av 12.72)	1900
Most Wkts – Career	3597	W.Rhodes	(av 16.02)	1898-1930
Most Career W-K Dismissals	1186	D.Hunter	(863 ct/323 st)	1888-1909
Most Career Catches in the Field	665	J.Tunnicliffe		1891-1907

LIMITED-OVERS CRICKET

Highest Total	FPT	411-6		v	Devon	Exmouth	2004
	P40	352-6		v	Notts	Scarborough	2001
	T20	211-6		v	Leics	Leeds	2004
Lowest Total	FPT	76		v	Surrey	Harrogate	1970
	P40	54		v	Essex	Leeds	2003
	T20	97		v	Lancashire	Manchester	2005
Highest Innings	FPT	160	M.J.Wood	v	Devon	Exmouth	2004
	P40	191	D.S.Lehmann	v	Notts	Scarborough	2001
	T20	109	I.J.Harvey	v	Derbyshire	Leeds	2005
Best Bowling	FPT	7-27	D.Gough	v	Ireland	Leeds	1997
	P40	7-15	R.A.Hutton	v	Worcs	Leeds	1969
	T20	4-20	R.M.Pyrah	v	Durham	Leeds	2008

FIRST-CLASS UMPIRES 2009

† New appointment. See page 12 for key to abbreviations.

BAILEY, Robert John (Biddulph HS), b Biddulph, Staffs 28 Oct 1963. RHB, OB. Northamptonshire 1982-99; cap 1985; benefit 1993, captain 1996-97. Derbyshire 2000-01; cap 2000. Staffordshire 1980. YC 1984. **Tests:** 4 (1988 to 1989-90); HS 43 v WI (Oval) 1988. **LOI:** 4 (1984-85 to 1989-90); HS 43* v SL (Oval) 1988. Tours: SA 1991-92 (Nh); WI 1989-90; Z 1994-95 (Nh). 1000 runs (13); most – 1987 (1990). HS 224* Nh v Glamorgan (Swansea) 1986. BB 5-54 Nh v Notts (Northampton) 1993. F-c career: 374 matches; 21844 runs @ 40.52, 47 hundreds; 121 wickets @ 42.51; 272 ct. Appointed 2006.

BAINTON, Neil Laurence, b Romford, Essex 2 October 1970. No f-c appearances. Appointed 2006.

BENSON, Mark Richard (Sutton Valence S), b Shoreham, Sussex 6 Jul 1958. LHB, OB. Kent 1980-95; cap 1981; captain 1991-96 (did not play in 1996); benefit 1991. **Tests:** 1 (1986); HS 30 v I (Birmingham) 1986. **LOI:** 1 (1986); HS 24 v NZ (Leeds) 1986. 1000 runs (11); most – 1725 (1987). HS 257 K v Hants (Southampton) 1991. BB 2-55 K v Surrey (Dartford) 1986. F-c career: 292 matches; 18387 runs @ 40.23, 48 hundreds; 5 wickets @ 98.60; 140 ct. Appointed 2000. Umpired 26 Tests (2004-05 to 2008-09) and 72 LOI (2004 to 2008-09). ICC International Panel 2004-06. **ICC Elite Panel 2006 to date**. Occasionally available for ECB matches.

†BODENHAM, Martin John Dale, b Brighton, Sussex 23 Apr 1950. No f-c appearances. Former football referee who officiated at the 1997 League Cup final. Appointed 2009.

†COOK, Nicholas Grant Billson (Lutterworth GS), b Leicester 17 Jun 1956. 6'0". RHB, SLA. Leicestershire 1978-85; cap 1982. Northamptonshire 1986-94; cap 1987; benefit 1995. **Tests:** 15 (1983 to 1989); HS 31 v A (Oval) 1989; BB 6-65 (11-83 match) v P (Karachi) 1983-84. **LOI:** 3 (1983-84 to 1989-90); HS – ; BB 2-18 v P (Peshawar) 1987-88. F-c Tours: NZ 1979-80 (DHR), 1983-84; P 1983-84, 1987-88; SL 1985-86 (Eng B); Z 1980-81 (Le), 1984-85 (EC). HS 75 Le v Somerset (Taunton) 1980. 50 wkts (8); most – 90 (1982). BB 7-34 (10-97 match) Nh v Essex (Chelmsford) 1992. F-c career: 356 matches; 3137 runs @ 11.66; 879 wickets @ 29.01; 197 ct. Appointed 2009.

COWLEY, Nigel Geoffrey (Dutchy Manor SS, Mere), b Shaftesbury, Dorset 1 Mar 1953. RHB, OB. Dorset 1972. Hampshire 1974-89; cap 1978; benefit 1988, Glamorgan 1990. 1000 runs (1): 1042 (1984). HS 109* H v Somerset (Taunton) 1977. BB 6-48 H v Leics (Southampton) 1982. F-c career: 271 matches; 7309 runs @ 23.35, 2 hundreds; 437 wickets @ 34.04. Appointed 2006.

DUDLESTON, Barry (Stockport S), b Bebington, Cheshire 16 Jul 1945. RHB, SLA. Leicestershire 1966-80; cap 1969; benefit 1980. Gloucestershire 1981-83. Rhodesia 1976-77 to 1979-80. 1000 runs (8); most – 1374 (1970). HS 202 Le v Derbys (Leicester) 1979. BB 4-6 Le v Surrey (Leicester) 1972. F-c career: 295 matches; 14747 runs @ 32.48, 32 hundreds; 47 wickets @ 29.04. Appointed 1984. Umpired 2 Tests (1991 to 1992) and 4 LOI (1992 to 2001).

EVANS, Jeffery Howard, b Llanelli, Carms 7 Aug 1954. No f-c appearances. Appointed 2001. Umpired in Indian Cricket League 2007-08.

GARRATT, Steven Arthur, b Nottingham 5 Jul 1953. No f-c appearances. Reserve List 2003-07 standing in 20 f-c matches. Appointed 2008.

†GOUGH, Michael Andrew (English Martyrs RCS; Hartlepool SFC), b Hartlepool, Co Durham 18 Dec 1979. Son of M.P.Gough (Durham 1974-77). 6'5". RHB, OB. Durham 1998-2003. F-c Tours (Eng A): NZ 1999-00; B 1999-00. HS Du v CU (Cambridge) 1998. CC HS 103 Du v Essex (Colchester) 2002. BB 5-56 Du v Middlesex (Chester-le-St) 2001. F-c career: 67 matches; 2952 runs @ 25.44, 2 hundreds; 30 wickets @ 45.00; 57 catches. Reserve List 2006-08. Appointed 2009.

GOULD, Ian James (Westgate SS, Slough), b Taplow, Bucks 19 Aug 1957. LHB, WK. Middlesex 1975 to 1980-81, 1996; cap 1977. Auckland 1979-80. Sussex 1981-90; cap 1981; captain 1987; benefit 1990. MCC YC. **LOI:** 18 (1982-83 to 1983); HS 42 v A (Sydney) 1982-83. Tours: A 1982-83; P 1980-81 (Int); Z 1980-81 (M). HS 128 M v Worcs (Worcester) 1978. BB 3-10 Sx v Surrey (Oval) 1989. Middlesex coach 1991-2000. Reappeared in one match (v OU) 1996. F-c career: 298 matches; 8756 runs @ 26.05, 4 hundreds; 7 wickets @ 52.14; 603 dismissals (536 ct, 67 st). Appointed 2002. Umpired 2 Tests (2008-09) and 31 LOI (2006 to 2008-09).

HARRIS, Michael John ('*Pasty*') (Gerrans S, nr Truro), b St Just-in-Roseland, Cornwall 25 May 1944. RHB, LB, WK. Middlesex 1964-68; cap 1967. Nottinghamshire 1969-82; cap 1970; benefit 1977. E Province 1971-72. Wellington 1975-76. 1000 runs (11); most – 2238 (1971). Equalled Notts record with 9 hundreds in 1971. HS 201* Nt v Glamorgan (Nottingham) 1973. BB 4-16 Nt v Warwks (Nottingham) 1969. F-c career: 344 matches; 19196 runs @ 36.70, 41 hundreds; 79 wickets @ 43.78; 302 dismissals (288 ct, 14 st). Appointed 1998.

HARTLEY, Peter John (Greenhead GS; Bradford C), b Keighley, Yorks 18 Apr 1960. RHB, RMF. Warwickshire 1982. Yorkshire 1985-97; cap 1987; benefit 1996. Hampshire 1998-2000; cap 1998. Tours (Y): SA 1991-92; WI 1986-87; Z 1995-96. HS 127* Y v Lancs (Manchester) 1988. 50 wkts (7); most – 81 (1995). BB 9-41 (inc hat-trick, 4 wkts in 5 balls and 5 in 9; 11-68 match) Y v Derbys (Chesterfield) 1995. Hat-trick 1995. F-c career: 232 matches; 4321 runs @ 19.91, 2 hundreds; 683 wickets @ 30.21. Appointed 2003. Umpired 4 LOI (2007 to 2008). **ICC International Panel 2006 to date.**

HOLDER, John Wakefield (Combermere S), b St George, Barbados 19 Mar 1945. RHB, RFM. Hampshire 1968-72. HS 33 H v Sussex (Hove) 1971. BB 7-79 H v Glos (Gloucester) 1972. Hat-trick 1972. F-c career: 47 matches; 374 runs @ 10.68; 139 wickets @ 24.56. Appointed 1983. Umpired 11 Tests (1988 to 2001) and 19 LOI (1988 to 2001).

HOLDER, Vanburn Alonza (Richmond SM), b Deans Village, St Michael, Barbados 8 Oct 1945. RHB, RFM. Barbados 1966-67 to 1977-78. Worcestershire 1968-80; cap 1970; benefit 1979. Shropshire 1981. Tests (WI): 40 (1969 to 1978-79); HS 42 v NZ (P-o-S) 1971-72; BB 6-28 v A (P-o-S) 1977-78. **LOI** (WI): 12 (1973 to 1977-78); HS 30 v A (Castries) 1977-78; BB 5-50 v E (Birmingham) 1976. Tours (WI): E 1969, 1973, 1976; A 1975-76; I 1974-75, 1978-79; P 1973-74 (RW), 1974-75; SL 1974-75, 1978-79. HS 122 Barbados v Trinidad (Bridgetown) 1973-74. BB 7-40 Wo v Glamorgan (Cardiff) 1974. F-c career: 311 matches; 3559 runs @ 13.03, 1 hundred; 947 wickets @ 24.48. Appointed 1992.

ILLINGWORTH, Richard Keith (Salts GS), b Bradford, Yorks 23 Aug 1963. RHB, SLA. Worcestershire 1982-2000; cap 1986; benefit 1997. Natal 1988-89. Derbyshire 2001. Wiltshire 2005. **Tests:** 9 (1991 to 1995-96); HS 28 v SA (Pt Elizabeth) 1995-96; BB 4-96 v WI (Nottingham) 1995. Took wicket of P.V.Simmons with his first ball in Tests – v WI (Nottingham) 1991. **LOI:** 25 (1991 to 1995-96); HS 14 v P (Melbourne) 1991-92; BB 3-33 v Z (Albury) 1991-92. Tours: SA 1995-96; NZ 1991-92; P 1990-91 (Eng A); SL 1990-91 (Eng A); Z 1989-90 (Eng A), 1990-91 (Wo), 1993-94 (Wo), 1996-97 (Wo). HS 120* Wo v Warwks (Worcester) 1987 – as night-watchman. Scored 106 for England A v Z (Harare) 1989-90 – also as night-watchman. 50 wkts (5); most – 75 (1990). BB 7-50 Wo v OU (Oxford) 1985. F-c career: 376 matches; 7027 runs @ 22.45, 4 hundreds; 831 wickets @ 31.54; 161 ct. Appointed 2006.

JESTY, Trevor Edward (Privet County SS, Gosport), b Gosport, Hants 2 Jun 1948. RHB, RM. Hampshire 1966-84; cap 1971; benefit 1982. Surrey 1985-87; cap 1985; captain 1985. Lancashire 1987-88 to 1991; cap 1989. Border 1973-74. GW 1974-75 to 1980-81. Canterbury 1979-80. *Wisden* 1982. **LOI:** 10 (1982-83); HS 52* v NZ (Adelaide) 1982-83; BB 1-23 v A (Sydney) 1982-83. Tours: WI 1987-88 (La), 1982-83 (Int); Z 1988-89 (La). 1000 runs (10); most – 1645 (1982). HS 248 H v CU (Cambridge) 1984. Scored 122* La v OU (Oxford) 1991 in his final f-c innings. 50 wkts (2); most – 52 (1981). BB 7-75 H v Worcs (Southampton) 1976. F-c career: 490 matches; 21916 runs @ 32.71, 35 hundreds; 585 wickets @ 27.47. Appointed 1994. Umpired in Indian Cricket League 2007-08.

KETTLEBOROUGH, Richard Allan (Worksop C), b Sheffield, Yorks 15 Mar 1973. LHB, RM. Yorkshire 1994-97. Middlesex 1998-99. Tour: Z 1995-96 (Y). HS 108 Y v Essex (Leeds) 1996. BB 2-26 Y v Notts (Scarborough) 1996. F-c career: 33 matches; 1258 runs @ 25.16, 1 hundred; 3 wickets @ 81.00; 20 ct. Appointed 2006. **ICC International Panel (Third Umpire) 2009.**

LLONG, Nigel James (Ashford North S), b Ashford, Kent 11 Feb 1969. LHB, OB. Kent 1990-98; cap 1993. Tour: Z 1992-93 (K). HS 130 K v Hants (Canterbury) 1996. BB 5-21 K v Middx (Canterbury) 1996. F-c career: 68 matches; 3024 runs @ 31.17, 6 hundreds; 35 wickets @ 35.97. Appointed 2002. Umpired 4 Tests (2007-08 to 2008-09) and 24 LOI (2006 to 2008-09). **ICC International Panel 2004 to date.**

LLOYDS, Jeremy William (Blundell's S), b Penang, Malaya 17 Nov 1954. LHB, OB. Somerset 1979-84; cap 1982. Gloucestershire 1985-91; cap 1985. Orange Free State 1983-84 to 1987-88, Tour (Glos): SL 1986-87. 1000 runs (3); most – 1295 (1986). HS 132* Sm v Northants (Northampton) 1982. BB 7-88 Sm v Essex (Chelmsford) 1982. F-c career: 267 matches; 10679 runs @ 31.04, 10 hundreds; 333 wickets @ 38.86; 229 ct. Appointed 1998. Umpired 5 Tests (2003-04 to 2004-05) and 18 LOI (2000 to 2005-06). **ICC International Panel 2003-06.**

MALLENDER, Neil Alan (Beverley GS), b Kirk Sandall, Yorks 13 Aug 1961. RHB, RFM. Northamptonshire 1980-86 and 1995-96; cap 1984. Somerset 1987-94; cap 1987; benefit 1994. Otago 1983-84 to 1992-93; captain 1990-91 to 1992-93. **Tests:** 2 (1992) HS 4 v P (Oval) 1992; BB 5-50 v P (Leeds) 1992 – on debut. Tour: Z 1994-95 (Nh). HS 100* Otago v CD (Palmerston N) 1991-92. UK HS 87* Sm v Sussex (Hove) 1990. 50 wkts (6); most – 56 (1983). BB 7-27 Otago v Auckland (Auckland) 1984-85. UK BB 7-41 Nh v Derbys (Northampton) 1982. F-c career: 345 matches; 4709 runs @ 17.18, 1 hundred; 937 wickets @ 26.31; 111 ct. Appointed 1999. Umpired 3 Tests (2003-04) and 22 LOI (2001 to 2003-04), including 2002-03 World Cup. **ICC Elite Panel 2004.**

†MILLNS, David James (Garibaldi CS; N Notts C; Nottingham Trent U), b Clipstone, Notts 27 Feb 1965. 6'3". LHB, RF. Nottinghamshire 1988-89, 2000-01; cap 2000. Leicestershire 1990-99; cap 1991; benefit 1999. Tasmania 1994-95. Boland 1996-97. F-c Tours: A 1992-93 (Eng A); SA 1996-97 (Le). HS Le v Northants (Northampton) 1997. 50 wkts (4); most – 76 (1994). BB 9-37 (12-91 match) Le v Derbys (Derby) 1991. F-c career: 171 matches; 3082 runs @ 22.01, 3 hundreds; 553 wickets @ 27.35; 76 catches. Reserve List 2007-08. Appointed 2009.

ROBINSON, Robert Timothy (Dunstable GS; High Pavement SFC; Sheffield U), b Sutton in Ashfield 21 Nov 1958. RHB, RM. Nottinghamshire 1978-99; cap 1983; captain 1988-95; benefit 1992. *Wisden* 1985. **Tests:** 29 (1984-85 to 1989); HS 175 v A (Leeds) 1985. **LOI:** 26 (1984-85 to 1988); HS 83 v P (Sharjah) 1986-87. Tours: A 1987 88; SA 1989-90 (Eng XI), 1996-97 (Nt); NZ 1987-88; WI 1985-86; I/SL 1984-85; P 1987-88. 1000 runs (14) inc 2000 (1): 2032 (1984). HS 220* v Yorks (Nottingham) 1990. BB 1-22. F-c career: 425 matches; 27571 runs @ 42.15, 63 hundreds; 4 wickets @ 72.25; 257 ct. Appointed 2007.

SHARP, George (Elwick Road SS, Hartlepool), b West Hartlepool, Co Durham 12 Mar 1950. RHB, WK, occ LM. Northamptonshire 1968-85; cap 1973; benefit 1982. HS 98 Nh v Yorks (Northampton) 1983. BB 1-47. F-c career: 306 matches; 6254 runs @ 19.85; 1 wicket @ 70.00; 655 dismissals (565 ct, 90 st). Appointed 1992. Umpired 15 Tests (1996 to 2001-02) and 31 LOI (1995-96 to 2001-02). **ICC International Panel 1996 to 2001-02.**

STEELE, John Frederick (Endon SS), b Brown Edge, Staffs 23 Jul 1946. RHB, SLA. Brother of D.S. Steele (Northants, Derbys and England 1963-84). Leicestershire 1970-83; cap 1971; benefit 1983. Glamorgan 1984-86; cap 1984. Natal 1973-74 to 1977-78. Staffordshire 1965-69. Tour: SA 1974-75 (DHR). 1000 runs (6); most – 1347 (1972). HS 195 Le v Derbys (Leicester) 1971. BB 7-29 Natal B v GW (Umzinto) 1973-74 and 7-29 Le v Glos (Leicester) 1980. F-c career: 379 matches; 15054 runs @ 28.95, 21 hundreds; 584 wickets @ 27.04; 413 ct. Appointed 1997.

WILLEY Peter (Seaham SS), b Sedgefield, Co Durham 6 Dec 1949. RHB, OB. Northamptonshire 1966-83; cap 1971; benefit 1981. Leicestershire 1984-91; cap 1984; captain 1987. E Province 1982-83 to 1984-85. Northumberland 1992. **Tests:** 26 (1976 to 1986); HS 102* v WI (St John's) 1980-81; BB 2-73 v WI (Lord's) 1980. **LOI:** 26 (1977 to 1985-86); HS 64 v A (Sydney) 1979-80; BB 3-33 v A (Melbourne) 1979-80. Tours: A 1979-80; SA 1972-73 (DHR), 1981-82 (SAB); WI 1980-81, 1985-86; I 1979-80; SL 1977-78 (DHR). 1000 runs (10); most – 1783 (1982). HS 227 Nh v Somerset (Northampton) 1976. 50 wkts (3); most – 52 (1979). BB 7-37 Nh v OU (Oxford) 1975. F-c career: 559 matches; 24361 runs @ 30.56, 44 hundreds; 756 wickets @ 30.95. Appointed 1993. Umpired 25 Tests (1995-96 to 2003-04) and 34 LOI (1996 to 2003), including 1999 and 2002-03 World Cups. **ICC International Panel 1996 to 2001-02 and 2003-04.**

RESERVE FIRST-CLASS LIST: Keith Coburn, Ismail Dawood, Mark A.Eggleston, Stephen C. Gale, Andrew Hicks, Graham D.Lloyd, Steven J.Malone, Steve J.O'Shaughnessy.

**Test Match statistics to 22 March 2009 (but excluding the NZ v I series);
LOI statistics to 14 March 2009.**

INTERNATIONAL UMPIRES AND REFEREES 2009

ELITE PANEL OF UMPIRES 2009

The Elite Panel of ICC Umpires and Referees was introduced in April 2002 to raise standards and guarantee impartial adjudication. Two umpires from this panel stand in Test matches while one officiates with a home umpire from the Supplementary International Panel in limited-overs internationals.

Full Names	Birthdate	Birthplace	Tests	Debut	LOI	Debut
ALIM Sarwar DAR	06.06.68	Jhang, Pakistan	55	2003-04	110	1999-00
ASAD RAUF	12.05.56	Lahore, Pakistan	24	2004-05	58	1999-00
BENSON, Mark Richard	06.07.58	Shoreham, England	26	2004-05	72	2004
BOWDEN, Brent Fraser	11.04.63	Auckland, New Zealand	54	1999-00	125	1994-95
DAVIS, Stephen James	09.04.52	London, England	17	1997-98	79	1992-93
DE SILVA, E.Asoka Ranjit	28.03.56	Kalutara, Sri Lanka	37	2000	82	1999-00
DOCTROVE, Billy Raymond	03.07.55	Marigot, Dominica	22	2000	80	1997-98
GOULD, Ian James	19.08.57	Taplow, England	2	2008-09	31	2006
HARPER, Daryl John	23.10.61	Adelaide, Australia	80	1998-99	158	1993-94
HILL, Anthony Lloyd	26.06.51	Auckland, New Zealand	9	2001-02	60	1997-98
KOERTZEN, Rudolf Eric ('Rudi')	26.03.49	Knysna, South Africa	98	1992-93	193	1992-93
TAUFEL, Simon James Arthur	21.01.71	Sydney, Australia	54	2000-01	138	1998-99

ELITE PANEL OF REFEREES 2009

Full Names	Birthdate	Birthplace	Tests	Debut	LOI	Debut
BROAD, Brian Christopher	29.09.57	Bristol, England	35	2003-04	137	2003-04
CROWE, Jeffrey John	14.09.58	Auckland, New Zealand	32	2004-05	102	2003-04
HURST, Alan George	15.07.50	Melbourne, Australia	27	2004-05	70	2004-05
MADUGALLE, Ranjan Senerath	22.04.59	Kandy, Sri Lanka	109	1993-94	226	1993-94
MAHANAMA, Roshan Siriwardena	31.05.66	Colombo, Sri Lanka	24	2004	111	2004
PYCROFT, Andrew John	06.06.56	Harare, Zimbabwe				
SRINATH, Javagal	31.08.69	Mysore, India	13	2006	51	2006-07

Nominated by their respective cricket boards, members from this panel officiate in home LOI and supplement the Elite panel for Test matches. Specialist third umpires have been selected to undertake adjudication involving television replays. The number of Test matches/LOI in which they have stood is shown in brackets.

			Third Umpire
Australia	B.N.J.Oxenford (-/5)	R.J.Tucker (-/3)	P.R.Reiffel (-/1)
Bangladesh	Nadir Shah (-/23)	Enamal Haque (-/14)	Aktaruddin Sahin (2/16)
England	P.J.Hartley (-/4)	N.J.Llong (4/24)	R.A.Kettleborough (-/-)
India	A.M.Saheba (2/26)	S.L.Shastri (2/19)	S.K.Tarapore (-/3)
New Zealand	G.A.Baxter (-/24)	E.A.Watkin (2/22)	
Pakistan	Zamir Haider (-/7)	Nadeem Ghauri (5/38)	Ahsan Raza (-/-)
South Africa	I.L.Howell (9/63)	B.G.Jerling (4/75)	K.H.Hurter (-/5), M.Erasmus (-/3)
Sri Lanka	M.G.Silva (3/19)	T.H.Wijewardene (4/48)	H.D.P.K.Dharmasena (-/-)
West Indies	C.R.Duncan (2/13)	N.Malcolm (-/2)	C.E.Mack (-/1), G.E.Greaves (-/-)
Zimbabwe	K.C.Barbour (4/44)	R.B.Tiffin (44/108)	

**Test Match statistics to 22 March 2009 (but excluding the NZ v I series);
LOI statistics to 14 March 2009.**

UNIVERSITY FIRST-CLASS REGISTER 2008

CAMBRIDGE († Blue 2008)

Full Names	Birthdate	Birthplace	College	Bat/Bowl	F-C Debut
†ANSARI, Akbar Shahzaman	03.07.88	Ascot, Berkshire	Trinity Hall	RHB/LB	2008
BAKER, Fergus Braan	18.05.87	Leicester	Downing	LHB/SLA	2007
BALLARD, Edward Christopher	15.08.89	Harlow, Essex	(Anglia RU)	RHB/LB	2008
BOTT, Mark Daniel	13.05.86	Nottingham	(Anglia RU)	RHB/LB	2006
FRIEDLANDER, Matthew James	01.08.79	Durban, S Africa	(Anglia RU)	RHB/RFM	2003-04
GRAY, Stephen Kevin	06.07.88	Barking, Essex	(Anglia RU)	RHB/WK	2008
†HEMINGWAY, Thomas Lewis	19.05.86	Stevenage, Herts	Trinity Hall	RHB/OB	2007
†HEYWOOD, James John Neville	24.09.82	Eastbourne	Homerton	RHB/WK	2003
†JACKLIN, Benjamin David	26.04.84	Leeds	Magdalene	RHB/RM	2005
†JAMES, Michael Insley	09.03.87	Burton-on-Trent	(Anglia RU)	RHB/RMF	2008
JOGIA, Kunal Ashokkumar	18.09.84	Leicester	(Anglia RU)	RHB/RSM	2006
†KEMP, Robin Andrew	29.09.84	Luton	St John's	RHB/RM	2005
LEE, Nicholas Trevor	16.10.83	Dartford	(Anglia RU)	RHB/LB	2004
†MacLENNAN, Scott Keith	30.11.87	Glasgow, Scotland	St John's	RHB/RM	2007
MOHAMMAD AMIN	19.10.84	Gujranwala, Pakistan	(Anglia RU)	RIIB/RMF	2005
†O'DRISCOLL, William John Finian	16.07.87	Gloucester	Gonville & Caius	RHB/RM	2007
†OWEN, Frederick Gerard	25.09.85	Chester	Corpus Christi	RHB	2006
RIST, William Henry	22.03.87	Guildford	(Anglia RU)	RHB/WK	2007
†TIMMS, Richard Thomas	09.09.84	Bristol	Clare	RHB/RFM	2005
†WHITTINGTON, Nicholas Matthew Hay	27.08.81	Wellington, NZ	Trinity Hall	RHB/RM	2008
WOODHOUSE, Adam	24.06.87	King's Lynn, Norfolk	(Anglia RU)	RHB/RM	2008

DURHAM

Full Names	Birthdate	Birthplace	College	Bat/Bowl	F-C Debut
BUTTLEMAN, Joseph Edward Lewis	23.08.87	Basildon, Essex	St Hild & St Bede	RHB/RFM	2007
CARLISLE, Lucas Jonathon	01.06.88	Nottingham	Collingwood	LHB	2008
DIXEY, Paul Garrod	02.11.87	Canterbury	Hatfield	RHB/WK	2005
FOSTER, Patrick John	20.03.87	Nairobi, Kenya	St Hild & St Bede	RHB/RFM	2007
GALE, Daniel James	15.06.89	Tadworth, Surrey	St Aidan's	RHB/SLA	2008
GLOVER, John Charles	29.08.89	Cardiff, Wales	St Aidan's	RHB/RMF	2008
JOHNSTON, Paul Robert Archibald	13.12.88	Hartlepool, Co. Durham	John Snow	LHB	2008
LEGGET, Charles William Stuart	21.01.88	Edinburgh, Scotland	Grey	RHB/RM	2008
MORGAN, Charles Felix Derrington	09.07.89	Leicester	St Aidan's	RHB/WK	2008
MUMTAZ HABIBULLAH	01.01.87	Kabul, Afghanistan	Trevelyan	RHB/RMF	2008
PAGET, Christopher David	02.11.87	Stafford	Van Mildert	RHB/OB	2004
PROWTING, Nicholas Roger	26.10.85	Chelmsford	Van Mildert	RHB/RM	2006
RAWLINSON, Hugh Christopher Luke	14.04.88	Lambeth, London	St Hild & St Bede	RHB, RM	2008
THOMPSON, Greg James	17.09.87	Lisburn, N.Ireland	St Mary's	RHB/LB	2004
WILLIAMS, Robert Edward Morgan	19.01.87	Pembury, Kent	St Mary's	RHB/RMF	2007

LOUGHBOROUGH

Full Names	Birthdate	Birthplace	Bat/Bowl	F-C Debut
BAER, Michael	31.03.87	St Asaph, N Wales	RHB/RM	
BORRINGTON, Paul Michael	24.05.88	Nottingham	RHB.OB	2005
BRATHWAITE, Ruel Marlon Ricardo	06.09.85	Bridgetown, Barbados	RHB/RFM	2006
COPE, Alan Charles	17.07.88	Guildford, Surrey	RHB/RMF	2008
FLOWERS, Thomas Oliver	26.01.88	Leicester	RHB.OB	2008
HUGHES, Jonathan Adam	12.09.85	Slough, Buckinghamshire	RHB/RMF	2007
JONES, Henry David	08.03.89	Kingston, Surrey	RHB/RFM	2008
KING, Richard Eric	03.01.84	Hitchin, Herts	RHB/LMF	2003
MALCOLM-HANSEN, Richard Johan Anders	22.04.86	Farnborough, Kent	RHB/OB	2007
MORRIS, Richard Kyle	26.09.87	Newbury, Berkshire	RHB/RMF	2006
PARSONS, Thomas William	02.05.87	Melbourne, Australia	RHB/RFM	2007
PRATT, Daniel Matthew	31.01.86	Croydon, Surrey	RHB/WK	
SPRIEGEL, Matthew Neil William	04.03.87	Epsom, Surrey	LHB/OB	2007
WILLIAMS, Daniel Mark	12.81	Newbury, Berkshire	RHB/RMF	2008

OXFORD († Blue 2008)

Full Names	Birthdate	Birthplace	College	Bat/Bowl	F-C Debut
ABEL, Edward	30.01.88	Salisbury, Wiltshire	Brookes U	LHB/SLA	2008
†BALL, Alexander Henry	03.10.86	Westminster, London	St Catherine's	RHB/OB	2007
BRADSHAW, Duncan Phillip	19.02.86	Harare, Zimbabwe	(Brookes U)	RHB/RFM	2006
†CRAWLEY, Spencer Henry	05.08.87	Westminster, London	Oxford U	RHB/OB	2008
†DINGLE, Lewis Allen	16.09.88	Blackpool	Christ Church	RHB/RMF	2007
DUFFELL, Charlie Basil Royson	20.10.86	Hanover, Germany	(Brookes U)	RHB/WK	
†FROGGETT, Thomas Joseph	05.05.88	Wakefield	St John's	RHB/WK	2007
†HILL, Charles Michael McLean	27.11.85	Wimbledon	Trinity	LHB/SLC	2007
HOOPER, John Harry Patrick	14.01.86	Tooting Bec	(Brookes U)	LHB/LM	2006
†HOWELL, Thomas Henry	14.09.87	Derby	New	RHB/LB	2007
KALAM, Tarique	20.03.87	Cape Town, SA	(Brookes U)	RHB/RMF	2006
†KRUGER, Neil	15.08.81	Cape Town, SA	Green	RHB/RM	2008
LETT, Robin Jonathan Hugh	23.12.86	Westminster	(Brookes U)	RHB/RM	2006
MACADAM, James Chalmers	29.06.88	Paddington, London	Keble	RHB/RMF	2007
†McKERCHER, Brendan Thomas	23.01.83	Edinburgh	Keble	RHB/RM	2008
McMAHON, Paul Joseph	12.03.83	Wigan	Wadham	RHB/OB	2002
†MORSE, Edward James	30.01.86	Stevenage	St Edmund H	RHB/RM	2005
RYAN, Luke Charles	05.08.88	Welwyn Garden City	(Brookes U)	RHB/SLA	2007
†SADLER, Oliver James	02.04.87	Newcastle-u-Lyme	Oriel	RHB/SLA	
†STRACHAN, Jonathan Peter	09.08.87	Cape Town, SA	Queen's	RHB/RMF	2008
WILSHAW, Peter James	15.07.87	Newcastle-u-Lyme	(Brookes U)	RHB/RM	2008
YOUNG, Peter James William	14.09.86	Hammersmith	(Brookes U)	LHB/RM	2006

2008 TOURING TEAMS FIRST-CLASS REGISTER

NEW ZEALAND

Full Names	Birthdate	Birthplace	Team	Type	F-C Debut
ELLIOTT, Grant David	21.03.79	Johannesburg, SA	Wellington	RHB/RFM	1996 97
FLYNN, Daniel Raymond	16.04.85	Rotorua	N Districts	LHB/SLA	2004-05
FULTON, Peter Gordon	01.02.79	Christchurch	Canterbury	RHB/RM	2000-01
HOPKINS, Gareth James	24.11.76	Lower Hutt	N Districts	RHB/WK	1997-98
HOW, Jamie Michael	19.05.81	New Plymouth	C Districts	RHB/RM	2000-01
McCULLUM, Brendon Barrie	27.09.81	Dunedin	Otago	RHB/WK	1999-00
MARSHALL, James Andrew Hamilton	15.02.79	Warkworth	N Districts	RHB/RM	1997-98
MARTIN, Christopher Stewart	10.12.74	Christchurch	Canterbury	RHB/RFM	1997-98
MASON, Michael James	27.08.74	Carterton	C Districts	RHB/RFM	1997-98
MILLS, Kyle David	15.03.79	Auckland	Auckland	RHB/RFM	1998-99
O'BRIEN, Iain Edward	10.07.76	Lower Hutt	Wellington	RHB/RM	2000-01
ORAM, Jacob David Philip	28.07.78	Palmerston North	C Districts	LHB/RM	1997-98
PATEL, Jeetan Shashi	07.11.80	Wellington	Wellington	RHB/OB	1999-00
REDMOND, Aaron James	23.09.79	Auckland	Otago	RHB/LB	1999-00
SOUTHEE, Timothy Grant	11.12.88	Whangarei	N Districts	RHB/RMF	2006-07
TAYLOR, Luteru Ross Poutoa Lote	08.03.84	Lower Hutt	C Districts	RHB/OB	2002-03
VETTORI, Daniel Luca	27.01.79	Auckland	N Districts	RHB/SLA	1996-97

SOUTH AFRICA

Full Names	Birthdate	Birthplace	Team	Type	F-C Debut
AMLA, Hasim Mahomed	31.03.83	Durban	Dolphins	RHB/RM	1999-00
BOUCHER, Mark Verdon	03.12.76	East London	Warriors	RHB/WK	1995-96
DE VILLIERS, Abraham Benjamin	17.02.84	Pretoria	Titans	RHB/WK	2003-04
DUMINY, Jean-Paul	14.04.84	Cape Town	Cape Cobras	LHB/OB	2001-02
HARRIS, Paul Lee	02.11.78	Salisbury, Rhodesia	Titans	LHB/SLA	1998-99
KALLIS, Jacques Henry	16.10.75	Cape Town	Cape Cobras	RHB/RFM	1993-94
McKENZIE, Neil Douglas	24.11.75	Johannesburg	Lions	RHB/RM	1994-95
MORKEL, Morne	06.10.84	Vereeniging	Titans	LHB/RFM	2003-04
NEL, Andre	15.07.77	Germiston	Titans	RHB/RFM	1996-97
NTINI, Makhaya	06.07.77	Mdingi	Warriors	RHB/RMF	1995-96
PETERSON, Robin John	04.08.79	Port Elizabeth	Warriors	LHB/SLA	1998-99
PRINCE, Ashwell Gavin	28.05.77	Port Elizabeth	Cape Cobras	LHB	1995-96
SMITH, Graeme Craig	01.02.81	Johannesburg	Cape Cobras	LHB/OB	1999-00
STEYN, Dale Willem	27.06.83	Phalaborwa	Titans	RHB/RF	2003-04
ZONDEKI, Monde	25.07.82	King William's T	Cape Cobras	RHB/RF	2000-01

BANGLADESH A

Full Names	Birthdate	Birthplace	Team	Type	F-C Debut
DHIMAN GHOSH	23.11.87	Dinajpur	Dhaka Warriors	RHB/WK	2003-04
DOLAR MAHMUD, Mohammad	30.12.88	Naraiil, Khulna	Khulna	RHB/RFM	2004-05
JUNAID SIDDIQUE, Mohammad	30.10.87	Rajshahi	Rajshahi	LHB/OB	2003-04
MOSHARRAF HOSSAIN, Khondaker	20.11.81	Dhaka	Dhaka	LHB/SLA	2001-02
MUSHFIQUR RAHIM, Mohammad	01.09.88	Bogra	Sylhet	RHB/WK	2004-05
NAIM ISLAM, Mohammad	31.12.86	Gaibandha	Rajshahi	RHB/OB	2003-04
NAZIMUDDIN, Mohammed	01.10.85	Chittagong	Chittagong	RHB/RM	2001-02
NAZMUL HOSSAIN, Mohammad	05.10.87	Hobigonj	Sylhet	RHB/RFM	2004-05
RAJIN SALEH, Khondokar	20.11.83	Sylhet	Sylhet	RHB/OB	2000-01
RAQIBUL HASAN, Mohammad	08.10.87	Jamalpur	Barisal	RHB/LB	2004-05
RUBEL HOSSAIN, Mohammad	01.01.90	Chittagong	Chittagong	RHB/RMF	2007-08
SAJIDUL ISLAM	18.01.88	Rangpur	Barisal	LHB/LM	2005-06
SHAKIB AL HASAN	24.03.87	Magura, Khulna	Khulna	LHB/SLA	2004-05
SYED RASEL	03.07.84	Jessore	Khulna	LHB/LMF	2001-02
TAMIM IQBAL Khan	20.03.89	Chittagong	Chittagong	LHB/SLA	2004-05

THE 2008 FIRST-CLASS SEASON STATISTICAL HIGHLIGHTS

FIRST TO INDIVIDUAL TARGETS

1000 RUNS	S.C.Moore	Worcestershire	31 July
2000 RUNS	–	Most 1451 – S.C.Moore (Worcestershire)	
100 WICKETS	–	Most 67 – J.A.Tomlinson (Hampshire)	

TEAM HIGHLIGHTS

HIGHEST INNINGS TOTALS (* Second innings)

672-7d	Worcestershire v Gloucestershire	Cheltenham
654-6d*	Somerset v Hampshire	Taunton

HIGHEST FOURTH INNINGS TOTALS

388-8	Warwickshire (set 383) v Northamptonshire	Northampton
367	Northamptonshire (set 461) v Middlesex	Northampton
353-7	Oxford U (set 378) v Cambridge U	Oxford
353-8	Gloucestershire (set 351) v Loughborough UCCE	Bristol

LOWEST INNINGS TOTALS

70	Durham UCCE v Derbyshire	Derby
76	Durham UCCE v Durham	Chester-le-St
78	Essex v Glamorgan	Southend
78	Kent v Durham	Chester-le-St
90	Durham v Lancashire	Manchester
92	Kent v Lancashire	Liverpool
96	Hampshire v Durham	Basingstoke

LARGE MARGINS OF VICTORY

Inns & 143 runs	Nottinghamshire (532) beat Surrey (267, 122)	The Oval
295 runs	Durham (406, 205-6d) beat Yorkshire (194, 122)	Chester-le-St

NARROW MARGINS OF VICTORY

4 runs	Hampshire (239, 256) beat Durham (202, 289)	Chester-le-St
1 wicket	Bangladesh A (190, 285-9) beat Derbyshire (298-6d, 176-8d)	Derby

MOST EXTRAS IN AN INNINGS

B	LB	W	NB		
56	12	16	7	21	Middlesex (583) v Essex	Lord's
55	16	14	13	12	Surrey (397) v Kent	The Oval

Under ECB regulations, Test matches excluded, two penalty extras were scored for each no-ball.

BATTING HIGHLIGHTS

100 HUNDREDS

On 2nd August, during his 112* for Surrey v Yorkshire at Leeds, M.R.Ramprakash became the 25th batsman to score 100 first-class hundreds.

DOUBLE HUNDREDS

I.R.Bell	215	Warwickshire v Gloucestershire	Birmingham
N.Boje	226*	Northamptonshire v Worcestershire	Northampton
M.A.Butcher	205	Surrey v Yorkshire	The Oval
T.Frost	242*	Warwickshire v Essex	Chelmsford
L.Klusener	202*	Northamptonshire v Glamorgan	Northampton
Mohd Yousuf Youhana	205*	Lancashire v Yorkshire	Leeds
C.J.L.Rogers	248*	Derbyshire v Warwickshire	Birmingham
M.R.Ramprakash	200*	Surrey v Somerset	Taunton
W.R.Smith	201*	Durham v Surrey	Guildford
V.S.Solanki	270	Worcestershire v Gloucestershire	Cheltenham

HUNDREDS IN THREE CONSECUTIVE INNINGS

M.R.Ramprakash (Surrey)	112*	v Yorkshire	Leeds
	200*	v Somerset	Taunton
	178	v Sussex	The Oval

Between dismissals he scored 490 runs off 875 balls in 19 hours 24 minutes with 56 fours and 4 sixes.

HUNDRED IN EACH INNINGS OF A MATCH

M.van Jaarsveld	114* 115*	Kent v Surrey	The Oval

FASTEST HUNDRED AGAINST GENUINE BOWLING

D.J.Pipe (133)	71 balls	Derbyshire v Worcestershire	Chesterfield

This innings would have been rewarded with the Walter Lawrence Trophy if the organisers had not decided to make it available for all forms of limited overs cricket, including the 20-over variety.

S.D.Peters (Northamptonshire) scored 100 off 59 balls in 55 minutes v Essex at Northampton against the 'bowling' of wicket-keeper J.S.Foster (12-0-122-1) and specialist batsman M.L.Pettini (12-0-129-0).

HUNDREDS BEFORE LUNCH

	Day		
S.D.Peters	0*-130* 4	Northamptonshire v Essex	Northampton

Against low calibre 'bowling' – see note to previous section.

HUNDRED ON FIRST-CLASS DEBUT

N.Kruger	172	Oxford U v Cambridge U	Oxford

HUNDRED ON FIRST-CLASS DEBUT IN BRITAIN

D.J.Malan	132*	Middlesex v Northamptonshire	Uxbridge

CARRYING BAT THROUGH COMPLETED INNINGS

S.C.Moore	109*	Worcestershire (249) v Warwickshire	Birmingham
C.J.L.Rogers	248*	Derbyshire (474) v Warwickshire	Birmingham

LONG INNINGS

Min	Balls		
598	466	T.Frost (242*)	Warwickshire v Essex	Chelmsford

FIRST-WICKET PARTNERSHIP OF 100 IN EACH INNINGS

| 109/102* | D.K.H.Mitchell/S.C.Moore | Worcestershire v Glamorgan | Worcester |
| 101*/135* | A.J.Strauss/B.A.Godleman | Middlesex v Northamptonshire | Northampton |

OTHER NOTABLE PARTNERSHIPS († *County record*)

Qualifications: 1st – 4th wkts: 250 runs; 5th – 6th: 225; 7th: 200; 8th: 175; 9th: 150; 10th: 100.

Second Wicket

316†	S.C.Moore/V.S.Solanki	Worcestershire v Gloucestershire	Cheltenham
299*	R.W.T.Key/J.C.Tredwell	Kent v New Zealanders	Canterbury
272	M.E.Trescothick/ J.L.Langer	Somerset v Hampshire	Taunton
259	S.A.Newman/M.R.Ramprakash	Surrey v Yorkshire	Leeds

Third Wicket

| 294 | J.E.R.Gallian/R.S.Bopara | Essex v Northamptonshire | Chelmsford |
| 258 | P.J.Horton/Mohd Yousuf Youhana | Lancashire v Yorkshire | Leeds |

Fourth Wicket

| 286 | K.P.Pietersen/I.R.Bell | England v South Africa (1st Test) | Lord's |

Sixth Wicket

| 270 | H.D.Ackerman/J.J.Cobb | Leicestershire v Middlesex | Lord's |
| 232 | M.A.Butcher/M.J.Nicholson | Surrey v Yorkshire | The Oval |

Seventh Wicket

| 203 | J.L.Clare/G.G.Wagg | Derbyshire v Northamptonshire | Northampton |

BOWLING HIGHLIGHTS

EIGHT OR MORE WICKETS IN AN INNINGS

| A.M.Davies | 8-24 | Durham v Hampshire | Basingstoke |
| J.A.Tomlinson | 8-46 | Hampshire v Somerset | Taunton |

TEN OR MORE WICKETS IN A MATCH

A.M.Davies	(2)	10- 45	Durham v Kent	Chester-le-St
		11- 75	Durham v Hampshire	Basingstoke
M.A.Ealham		10- 76	Nottinghamshire v Yorkshire	Nottingham
Imran Tahir		12-189	Hampshire v Lancashire	Manchester
T.J.Murtagh		10-127	Middlesex v Essex	Lord's
A.J.Shantry		10-129	Glamorgan v Warwickshire	Birmingham
J.A.Tomlinson		10-194	Hampshire v Somerset	Taunton
J.J.van der Wath		12-128	Northamptonshire v Middlesex	Uxbridge
G.G.Wagg		10-133	Derbyshire v Gloucestershire	Derby
C.R.Woakes		10-162	Warwickshire v Glamorgan	Birmingham

HAT-TRICK

| S.J.Harmison | | Durham v Sussex | Hove |

MATCH DOUBLES

100 RUNS AND 10 WICKETS

| G.G.Wagg | 29, 72; 6-56, 4-77 | Derbyshire v Gloucestershire | Derby |

HUNDRED IN EACH INNINGS AND FIVE WICKETS

| M.van Jaarsveld | 114*, 115*; 5-33 | Kent v Surrey | The Oval |

WICKET-KEEPING HIGHLIGHTS

SIX OR MORE WICKET-KEEPING DISMISSALS IN AN INNINGS

S.M.Davies		6 ct	Worcestershire v Northamptonshire	Northampton
G.O.Jones		6 ct	Kent v Durham	Chester-le-St
N.Pothas	(2)	6 ct	Hampshire v Durham	Chester-le-St
		6 ct	Hampshire v Lancashire	Southampton
C.M W.Read		6 ct	Nottinghamshire v Lancashire	Nottingham
B.J.M.Scott		5 ct, 1 st	Middlesex v Derbyshire	Lord's
L.D.Sutton		7 ct	Lancashire v Yorkshire	Leeds

NINE OR MORE WICKET-KEEPING DISMISSALS IN A MATCH

S.J.Adshead	9ct	Gloucestershire v Derbyshire	Bristol
M.V.Boucher	9ct	South Africa v England (2nd Test)	Leeds
G.O.Jones	9ct	Kent v Nottinghamshire	Nottingham
N.Pothas	10ct	Hampshire v Durham	Chester-le-St

COUNTY CAPS AWARDED IN 2008

Derbyshire	C. K. Langeveldt, C. J. L. Rogers
Essex	J.E.R.Gallian, D.D.Masters, A.Nel
Glamorgan	–
Gloucestershire	R.K.J.Dawson, M.T.Gitsham, A.J.Harris, O.J.Newby, W.T.S.Porterfield, I.D.Saxelby, D.H.Wigley, R.J.Woodman
Hampshire	M.J.Lumb, J.A.Tomlinson
Kent	Azhar Mahmood, J.L.Denly
Lancashire	–
Leicestershire	H.H.Dippenaar
Middlesex	†T.Henderson, E.J.G.Morgan, T.J.Murtagh, D.P.Nannes, S.D.Udal
Northamptonshire	N.Boje, R.A.White
Nottinghamshire	S.R.Patel, D.J.Pattinson, A.G.Prince, A.C.Voges
Somerset	Z.de Bruyn, A.C.Thomas
Surrey	–
Sussex	C.D.Hopkinson, Mohammad Sami, C.D.Nash
Warwickshire	I.D.K.Salisbury, I.J.Westwood
Worcestershire (colours)	G.M.Andrew, C.R.D.Fernando, A.J.Harris, Imran Arif, S.P.Jones, S.J.Magoffin, C.D.Whelan
Yorkshire	G.L.Brophy, A.W.Gale, A.U.Rashid

† No first-class appearances for Middlesex.

Durham abolished their capping system after 2005. Gloucestershire award caps on first-class debut. Worcestershire award club colours on Championship debut. Glamorgan's capping system is now based on a player's number of appearances and not on his performances.

2008 FIRST-CLASS AVERAGES

These averages involve the total of exactly 500 cricketers who appeared in the 172 first-class matches played (excluding three abandoned without play) by 30 teams in England and Wales during the 2008 season.

'Cap' denotes the season in which the player was awarded a 1st XI cap by the county he represented in 2008. If he played for more than one county in 2008, the county(ies) who awarded him his cap is underlined. Durham abolished both their capping and 'awards' systems after the 2005 season. Gloucestershire now cap players on first-class debut. For Worcestershire players, 2008[C] denotes the award of county colours in 2008.

Team abbreviations: BA – Bangladesh A; CU – Cambridge University/Cambridge UCCE; De – Derbyshire; Du – Durham; DU – Durham UCCE; E – England; EL – England Lions; Ex – Essex; Gm – Glamorgan; Gs – Gloucestershire; H – Hampshire; K – Kent; La – Lancashire; Le – Leicestershire; LU – Loughborough UCCE; M – Middlesex; MCC – Marylebone Cricket Club; Nh – Northamptonshire; Nt – Nottinghamshire; NZ – New Zealand(ers); OU – Oxford University/Oxford UCCE; SA – South Africa(ns); Sm – Somerset; Sy – Surrey; Sx – Sussex; Wa – Warwickshire; Wo – Worcestershire; Y – Yorkshire.

† Left-handed batsman. Cap: a dash (–) denotes a non county player. A blank denotes uncapped by his current county.

BATTING AND FIELDING

	Cap	M	I	NO	HS	Runs	Avge	100	50	Ct/St
Abdul Razzaq (Sy)		1	2	–	4	4	2.00	–	–	–
† E.Abel (OU)		3	4	1	27*	68	22.66	–	–	1
H.D.Ackerman (Le)	2005	16	26	3	199	1302	56.60	6	3	12
A.R.Adams (Nt)	2007	8	11	1	58	133	13.30	–	1	4
C.J.Adams (Sx)	1998	15	23	3	61	474	23.70	–	2	13
† J.H.K.Adams (H)	2006	7	12	–	50	206	17.16	–	1	10
S.J.Adshead (Gs)	2004	1	1	–	47	47	47.00	–	–	9
† U.Afzaal (Sy)		16	26	5	134*	975	46.42	2	7	7
R.G.Aga (Sx)		5	6	1	26	71	14.20	–	–	–
J.S.Ahmed (Ex)		1	1	1	16*	16	–	–	–	–
M.Ahmed (Wo)		1	–					–	–	2
Kabir Ali (Wo)	2002[c]	11	15	2	46	236	18.15	–	–	3
Kadeer Ali (Gs)	2005	12	22	–	161	791	35.95	3	2	7
† M.M.Ali (Wo)	2007[c]	6	9	2	92	210	30.00	–	1	1
J.Allenby (Le)		17	23	3	138*	586	29.30	1	3	17
T.R.Ambrose (E/Wa)	2007	14	19	3	156*	500	31.25	1	2	42
H.M.Amla (SA)	–	7	10	1	172	663	73.66	3	2	6
† J.M.Anderson (E/La)	2003	10	11	4	34	92	13.14	–	–	9
† G.M.Andrew (Wo)	2008[c]	12	15	3	38*	199	16.58	–	–	5
A.S.Ansari (CU)	–	4	7	2	193	308	61.60	1	1	2
† J.E.Anyon (Wa)		7	6	2	6	14	3.50	–	–	4
Azhar Mahmood (K)	2008	6	8	2	116	306	51.00	1	1	4
† M.Baer (LU)		1	1	–	8	8	8.00	–	–	–
S.P.Bailey (Nh)		1	2	–	15	18	9.00	–	–	1
† F.B.Baker (CU)	–	2	2	–	4	6	3.00	–	–	1
M.Balac (Wa)		1	1	–	11	11	11.00	–	–	1
D.J.Balcombe (H)		6	10	3	20*	85	12.14	–	–	1
A.H.Ball (OU)	–	2	3	1	38*	98	49.00	–	–	3
† G.S.Ballance (Y)		1	2	–	5	6	3.00	–	–	–
E.C.Ballard (CU)	–	2	4	–	1	1	0.25	–	–	1
† V.Banerjee (Gs)	2006	6	6	1	15	22	4.40	–	–	1
G.J.Batty (Wo)	2002[c]	15	20	6	66	422	30.14	–	3	6

F-C	Cap	M	I	NO	HS	Runs	Avge	100	50	Ct/St
J.N.Batty (Sy)	2001	16	25	4	136*	616	29.33	2	3	34/4
W.A.T.Beer (Sx)		2	2	1	6*	6	6.00	–	–	–
I.R.Bell (E/Wa)	2001	11	17	1	215	813	50.81	2	2	11
C.C.Benham (H)		8	13	–	89	374	28.76	–	3	9
D.M.Benkenstein (Du)	2005	15	23	4	110	817	43.00	1	7	5
J.G.E.Benning (Sy)		6	8	–	69	159	19.87	–	1	1
G.K.Berg (M)		3	5	–	35	118	23.60	–	–	1
† D.J.Birch (De)		12	20	1	77	652	34.31	–	3	6
† I.D.Blackwell (Sm)	2001	17	25	1	158	1115	46.45	4	7	8
† A.J.Blake (K)		1	–							–
† N.Boje (Nh)	2008	13	17	1	226*	644	40.25	2	1	9
S.E.Bond (H)		4	5	–	17	33	6.60	–	–	–
R.S.Bopara (Ex/MCC/EL)	2005	15	26	3	150	1256	54.60	4	7	11
P.M.Borrington (De/LU)		12	20	4	102*	537	33.56	1	3	10
† A.G.Botha (Wa)		13	16	3	62	283	21.76	–	3	16
M.D.Bott (CU)	–	2	3	–	27	27	9.00	–	–	4
M.V.Boucher (SA)	–	7	8	2	45*	169	28.16	–	–	22/1
† M.A.G.Boyce (Le)		17	26	1	106	674	26.96	1	4	2
D.P.Bradshaw (OU)	–	3	3	1	127*	141	70.50	1	–	2
R.M.R.Brathwaite (LU)	–	1	–							–
G.R.Breese (Du)		2	2	1	121*	184	184.00	1	1	1
T.T.Bresnan (Y)	2006	14	20	5	84*	506	33.73	–	2	9
† S.C.J.Broad (E/Nt)		10	11	1	76	357	35.70	–	4	3
G.L.Brophy (Y)	2008	16	24	1	70	546	23.73	–	4	43/6
A.D.Brown (Sy)	1994	7	9	2	76*	252	36.00	–	2	4
D.O.Brown (Gs)		9	15	4	83	385	35.00	–	3	5
J.F.Brown (Nh)	2000	10	7	2	13	39	7.80	–	–	2
† K.R.Brown (La)		3	4	1	40	55	18.33	–	–	1
M.J.Brown (H)	2007	14	26	3	104*	940	40.86	1	6	10
T.G.Burrows (H)		2	3	2	13*	30	30.00	–	–	8
D.A.Burton (M)		1	–							–
† M.A.Butcher (Sy)	1996	6	10	1	205	521	57.88	2	1	4
J.E.L.Buttleman (DU)	–	3	4	1	56*	73	24.33	–	1	2
A.R.Caddick (Sm)	1992	10	12	4	35*	140	17.50	–	–	2
† M.A.Carberry (H/MCC/EL)	2006	16	29	3	108	815	31.34	1	4	6
† L.J.Carlisle (DU)	–	2	4	2	18*	28	14.00	–	–	1
† N.M.Carter (Wa)	2005	13	14	–	84	430	30.71	–	4	3
M.A.Chambers (Ex)		3	5	3	7	9	4.50	–	–	1
† S.Chanderpaul (Du)		8	12	1	138	411	37.36	1	2	2
G.Chapple (La)	1994	11	13	2	52*	288	26.18	–	1	4
M.J.Chilton (La)	2002	7	12	1	102	303	27.54	1	1	1
V.Chopra (Ex)		11	18	1	155	497	29.23	1	2	12
J.L.Clare (De)		13	18	5	129*	555	42.69	1	5	5
R.Clarke (De/Wa)		13	20	–	81	518	25.90	–	3	26
† M.E.Claydon (Du)		1	2	–	40	44	22.00	–	–	–
S.J.Cliff (Le)		3	3	–	15	24	8.00	–	–	1
† R.S.Clinton (Sy)		1	–							–
J.J.Cobb (Le)		8	10	3	148*	419	59.85	1	2	5
† K.J.Coetzer (Du)		4	7	–	23	56	8.00	–	–	2
P.D.Collingwood (E/Du)	1998	8	13	3	135	317	31.70	1	1	15
P.T.Collins (Sy)		12	13	4	21	53	5.88	–	–	2
C.D.Collymore (Sx)		9	12	5	20	57	8.14	–	–	2

F-C	Cap	M	I	NO	HS	Runs	Avge	100	50	Ct/St
N.R.D.Compton (M)	2006	5	8	–	27	68	8.50	–	–	2
† A.N.Cook (E/Ex)	2005	11	19	–	95	732	38.52	–	7	6
S.J.Cook (K)	2007	1	–							–
A.C.Cope (LU)	–	1	2	–	51	51	25.50	–	1	–
D.G.Cork (La)	2004	9	11	1	43	162	16.20	–	–	5
D.A.Cosker (Gm)	2000	8	13	2	42	160	14.54	–	–	4
J.P.Crawley (H)	2002	9	16	1	104	416	27.73	1	2	3
S.H.Crawley (OU)	–	1	2	1	20*	24	24.00	–	–	–
R.D.B.Croft (Gm)	1992	15	20	4	89*	474	29.62	–	2	2
S.J.Croft (La)		13	19	1	122	585	32.50	1	3	6
A.R.Crook (Nh)		1	2	1	19*	24	24.00	–	–	–
S.P.Crook (Nh)		4	6	–	63	223	37.16	–	2	–
G.D.Cross (La)		1	2	–	38	38	19.00	–	–	1
R.A.G.Cummins (Le)		2	2	–	22	44	22.00	–	–	2
L.M.Daggett (Le/Wa)		5	5	1	17	32	8.00	–	–	–
J.W.M.Dalrymple (Gm)		16	25	1	106	723	30.12	1	6	8
Danish Kaneria (Ex)	2004	9	14	3	22	123	11.18	–	–	5
A.M.Davies (Du)	2005	12	15	6	19	68	7.55	–	–	1
† S.M.Davies (Wo)	2005ᶜ	16	24	6	99*	748	41.55	–	5	72
L.A.Dawson (H)		5	8	1	100*	193	27.57	1	–	4
R.K.J.Dawson (Gs)	2008	5	7	1	40	132	22.00	–	–	3
† K.J.Dean (De)	1998	4	5	2	25	46	15.33	–	–	–
Z.de Bruyn (Sm)	2008	16	25	3	120	997	45.31	3	5	8
J.L.Denly (K)	2008	17	30	–	149	905	30.16	2	4	6
J.W.Dernbach (Sy)		10	12	3	16*	78	8.66	–	–	–
A.B.de Villiers (SA)	–	7	10	2	174	588	73.50	2	1	7
N.J.Dexter (Ex/K)		10	13	1	105	350	29.16	1	2	6
Dhiman Ghosh (BA)	–	3	5	1	50*	94	23.50	–	1	6
L.A.Dingle (OU)	–	1	2	1	6*	7	7.00	–	–	–
H.H.Dippenaar (Le)	2008	12	19	2	84*	431	25.35	–	3	19
† M.J.Di Venuto (Du)	2000	16	28	4	184	1115	46.45	2	8	16
P.G.Dixey (DU)	–	3	4	–	31	46	11.50	–	–	4
Dolar Mahmud (BA)	–	2	3	–	24	37	12.33	–	–	–
N.D.Doshi (De)		9	9	4	17*	25	5.00	–	–	3
C.B.R.Duffell (OU)	–	3	2	1	38	75	75.00	–	–	1/1
† J.P.Duminy (SA)	–	2	4	–	166	246	61.50	1	1	2
F.du Plessis (La)		12	19	1	57	453	25.16	–	4	4
D.du Preez (Le)		10	13	3	22	122	12.20	–	–	1
W.J.Durston (Sm)		5	8	4	62*	229	57.25	–	2	1
J.du Toit (Le)		10	16	–	103	399	24.93	1	1	4
M.A.Ealham (Nt)	2004	14	17	1	130*	329	20.56	1	–	9
† N.J.Edwards (Sm)		8	15	–	99	341	22.73	–	2	8
G.D.Elliott (NZ)	–	1	–							–
† S.M.Ervine (H)	2005	13	22	1	94*	587	27.95	–	5	19
D.Evans (M)		10	13	3	12*	45	4.50	–	–	2
R.S.Ferley (Nt)		1	1	1	26*	26	–	–	–	1
C.R.D.Fernando (Wo)	2008ᶜ	1	2	–	11	11	5.50	–	–	–
S.T.Finn (M)		13	15	5	26*	87	8.70	–	–	5
† I.D.Fisher (Gs)	2004	1	1	–	4	4	4.00	–	–	–
L.J.Fletcher (Nt)		1	–							–
A.Flintoff (E/La)	1998	8	14	4	62*	245	24.50	–	1	8
G.W.Flower (Ex)	2005	5	7	–	39	87	12.42	–	–	3

F-C	Cap	M	I	NO	HS	Runs	Avge	100	50	Ct/St
T.O.Flowers (LU)	–	2	3	1	25*	51	25.50	–	–	1
† D.R.Flynn (NZ)	–	7	11	3	49	163	20.37	–	–	2
J.S.Foster (Ex/MCC)	2001	17	25	4	132*	926	44.09	3	4	59/1
P.J.Foster (DU)	–	3	3	–	2	3	1.00	–	–	–
† J.D.Francis (Sm)	–	2	3	–	59	70	23.33	–	1	–
† P.J.Franks (Nt)	1999	8	11	2	52	245	27.22	–	1	5
M.J.Friedlander (CU)	–	2	2	1	4*	4	4.00	–	–	–
T.J.Froggett (OU)	–	1	2	1	21*	25	25.00	–	–	2/1
T.Frost (Wa)	1999	13	18	6	242*	1003	83.58	2	4	26/2
P.G.Fulton (NZ)	–	2	2	–	57	73	36.50	–	1	–
† A.W.Gale (Y)	2008	15	23	–	150	899	39.08	3	3	9
D.J.Gale (DU)	–	2	2	1	0*	0	0.00	–	–	1
J.E.R.Gallian (Ex)	2008	17	31	–	171	848	27.35	1	5	26
C.M.Gazzard (Sm)	–	1	1	–	6	6	6.00	–	–	–
A.P.R.Gidman (Gs)	2004	13	23	3	73	481	24.05	–	2	2
J.N.Gillespie (Gm)	–	13	20	5	52	332	22.13	–	1	4
M.T.Gitsham (Gs)	2008	4	6	2	35*	58	14.50	–	–	1
J.C.Glover (DU)	–	3	3	1	9*	10	5.00	–	–	–
† B.A.Godleman (M)	–	15	25	–	106	736	29.44	1	3	5
M.W.Goodwin (Sx)	2001	16	25	2	184	1343	58.39	6	5	3
D.Gough (Y)	1993	8	11	1	34	148	14.80	–	–	4
R.N.Grant (Gm)	–	6	11	–	75	239	21.72	–	2	5
S.K.Gray (CU)	–	2	4	1	26*	31	10.33	–	–	2
C.G.Greenidge (Gs)	2005	1	1	–	1	1	1.00	–	–	–
† D.A.Griffiths (H)	–	1	1	–	4	4	4.00	–	–	–
T.D.Groenewald (Wa)	–	3	3	–	78	78	26.00	–	1	2
A.D.Hales (Nt)	–	1	–							
A.J.Hall (Nh)	–	10	9	1	58	257	32.12	–	2	19
R.J.Hamilton-Brown (Sx)	–	2	3	–	62	108	36.00	–	1	–
† O.J.Hannon-Dalby (Y)	–	1	1	–	1	1	1.00	–	–	4
M.A.Hardinges (Gs)	2004	6	9	2	82	268	38.28	–	2	4
† A.Harinath (MCC)	–	1	1	–	33	33	33.00	–	–	1
† B.W.Harmison (D)	–	12	18	1	39	281	16.52	–	–	10
S.J.Harmison (E/Du)	1999	14	15	6	49*	172	19.11	–	–	1
A.J.Harris (Gs/Nt/Wo)	2008/00/08c	4	4	2	11*	14	7.00	–	–	–
J.A.R.Harris (Gm)	–	5	9	2	46	167	23.85	–	–	–
P.L.Harris (SA)	–	7	7	2	50*	146	29.20	–	1	2
R.J.Harris (Sx)	–	1	1	–	19	19	19.00	–	–	1
D.S.Harrison (Gm)	–	14	18	2	64*	325	20.31	–	2	2
M.Hayward (H)	–	1	2	1	17*	24	24.00	–	–	–
T.L.Hemingway (CU)	–	4	5	2	34*	66	22.00	–	–	2
† D.L.Hemp (Gm)	1994	15	25	3	104	763	34.68	2	5	10
C.W.Henderson (Le)	–	16	21	4	66	349	20.52	–	4	2
J.J.N.Heywood (CU)	–	1	2	–	11	21	10.50	–	–	2
G.A.Hick (Wo)	1986	11	18	3	149	689	45.93	2	2	25
J.C.Hildreth (Sm)	2007	18	32	2	158	962	32.06	1	6	8
† C.M.M.Hill (OU)	–	1	2	–	29	42	21.00	–	–	–
† W.W.Hinds (De)	–	9	13	–	76	407	31.30	–	3	1
A.J.Hodd (Sx)	–	3	4	–	81	99	24.75	–	1	7
B.J.Hodge (La)	2006	2	2	1	43*	44	44.00	–	–	4
L.J.Hodgson (Sy)	–	1	2	–	63	66	33.00	–	1	2
G.P.Hodnett (Gs)	2005	3	5	–	57	75	15.00	–	1	5

139

F-C	Cap	M	I	NO	HS	Runs	Avge	100	50	Ct/St
† K.W.Hogg (La)		2	2	–	33	33	16.50	–	–	
M.J.Hoggard (Y/EL)	2000	14	18	6	28*	154	12.83	–	–	3
S.M.Hole (Wa)		1	–						–	
† J.H.P.Hooper (OU)	–	3	5	2	56	111	37.00	–	1	2
G.J.Hopkins (NZ)	–	3	4	–	63	100	25.00	–	1	7
C.D.Hopkinson (Sx)	2008	17	27	3	106	789	32.87	1	4	12
P.J.Horton (La)	2007	16	26	3	152	1087	47.26	3	7	10
D.M.Housego (M)		2	4	–	36	66	16.50	–	–	
J.M.How (NZ)	–	6	11	1	74	372	37.20	–	4	3
T.H.Howell (OU)	–	1	2	–	24	41	20.50	–	–	
† B.H.N.Howgego (Nh)		1	2	1	15	16	16.00	–	–	1
J.A.Hughes (LU)	–	3	3	–	19	44	14.66	–	–	
I.D.Hunter (De)		6	6	1	17	37	7.40	–	–	1
Imran Arif (Wo)	2008c	6	3	1	5	13	6.50	–	–	1
Imran Tahir (H)		7	8	4	24*	85	21.25	–	–	3
A.J.Ireland (Gs)	2007	9	13	6	16*	30	4.28	–	–	3
B.D.Jacklin (CU)	–	1	1	–	0	0	0.00	–	–	
M.I.James (CU)	–	1	1	–	0	0	0.00	–	–	
† N.A.James (Wa)		1	1	–	34	34	34.00	–	–	1
W.I.Jefferson (Nt)		13	21	1	98	442	22.10	–	2	19
T.M.Jewell (Sy)		1	–						–	
K.A.Jogia (CU)	–	3	5	1	104*	253	63.25	1	1	2
R.M.Johnson (Wa)		1	1	–	72	72	72.00	–	1	1
† P.R.A.Johnston (DU)	–	2	4	1	34	65	21.66	–	–	4
G.O.Jones (K)	2003	17	26	4	106	668	30.36	1	3	64/3
H.D.Jones (LU)	–	2	2	1	6*	6	6.00	–	–	
P.S.Jones (Sm)	2001	9	12	2	27*	199	19.90	–	–	1
R.A.Jones (Wo)	2007c	2	1	–	2	2	2.00	–	–	
† S.P.Jones (Wo)	2008c	9	11	4	25	97	13.85	–	–	
C.J.Jordan (Sy)		8	9	2	57	123	17.57	–	1	2
R.H.Joseph (M)		15	18	5	23*	118	9.07	–	–	1
† E.C.Joyce (MCC/M)	2002	17	28	1	101	966	35.77	1	7	12
† Junaid Siddique (BA)	–	4	7	–	50	141	20.14	–	1	3
T.Kalam (OU)	–	3	2	–	4	6	3.00	–	–	1
J.H.Kallis (SA)	–	7	11	3	160*	391	48.87	1	3	6
† M.Kartik (M)	2007	7	10	2	44	161	20.12	–	–	9
† G.Keedy (La)	2000	13	18	4	64	243	17.35	–	1	2
J.M.Kemp (K)		10	17	1	102	412	25.75	1	3	16
R.A.Kemp (CU)	–	1	1	–	4	4	4.00	–	–	1
A.N.Kervezee (Wo)		1	1	–	41	41	41.00	–	–	1
R.W.T.Key (K/EL)	2001	16	27	3	178*	918	38.25	2	4	5
A.Khan (K)		6	7	1	21*	46	7.66	–	–	1
C.Kieswetter (Sm)		17	26	4	67*	635	28.86	–	2	48/2
N.Killeen (Du)	1999	2	2	1	4*	5	5.00	–	–	1
R.E.King (LU)	–	3	4	1	31	91	30.33	–	–	1
S.P.Kirby (Gs/MCC)	2005	13	17	6	28	84	7.63	–	–	3
R.J.Kirtley (Sx)	1998	2	2	–	19	19	9.50	–	–	
R.K.Kleinveldt (H)		1	2	–	16	20	10.00	–	–	1
† F.A.Klokker (De)		6	8	1	103*	160	22.85	1	–	10
† L.Klusener (Nh)	2006	14	20	5	202*	1095	73.00	2	9	3
G.J-P.Kruger (Le)		10	12	1	7	39	3.54	–	–	1
N.Kruger (OU)	–	1	2	–	172	209	104.50	1	–	

140

F-C	Cap	M	I	NO	HS	Runs	Avge	100	50	Ct/St
G.J.Kruis (Y)	2006	10	14	8	50*	183	30.50	–	1	2
G.A.Lamb (H)		9	15	2	54*	272	20.92	–	1	7
† J.L.Langer (Sm)	2007	15	26	1	188	1083	43.32	3	7	15
C.K.Langeveldt (De)	2008	12	15	3	40	208	17.33	–	–	5
S.G.Law (La)	2002	13	21	2	158*	704	37.05	1	4	11
J.J.C.Lawson (Le)		2	2	–	35	35	17.50	–	–	1
M.A.K.Lawson (De/M)		2	2	1	5	8	8.00	–	–	–
N.T.Lee (CU)	–	3	5	1	48*	120	30.00	–	–	–
C.W.S.Legget (DU)		1	1	–	4	4	4.00	–	–	–
R.J.H.Lett (OU)		3	3	–	50	55	18.33	–	1	1
J.Lewis (Gs)	1998	14	20	5	51	253	16.86	–	1	1
† J.D.Lewry (Sx)	1996	15	18	3	27	101	6.73	–	–	7
C.J.Liddle (Sx)		2	3	1	4*	8	4.00	–	–	–
R J.Logan (Nh)		1	1	–	1	1	1.00	–	–	–
J.Louw (Nh)		7	8	3	82	281	56.20	–	2	1
M.B.Loye (La)	2003	10	16	1	61	203	13.53	–	1	6
D.S.Lucas (Nh)		16	16	4	35	112	9.33	–	–	3
† M.J.Lumb (H)	2008	16	27	2	107	818	32.72	1	6	17
† T.Lungley (De)	2007	4	4	1	50	108	36.00	–	1	2
† A.Lyth (Y)		14	21	–	132	645	30.71	1	5	11
J.C.Macadam (OU)	–	1	1	1	4*	4	–	–	–	–
B.B.McCullum (NZ)	–	6	12	1	97	426	38.72	–	3	15
A.McGrath (Y)	1999	14	21	–	144	728	34.66	2	3	11
N.D.McKenzie (SA/Du)		10	19	2	138	546	32.11	1	2	10
B.T.McKerchar (OU)	–	1	2	–	16	23	11.50	–	–	–
† R.McLaren (K)	2007	16	23	3	65*	464	23.20	–	2	6
S.K.MacLennan (CU)	–	1	2	–	43	51	25.50	–	–	–
C.S.MacLeod (Wa)		1	–							1
P.J.McMahon (OU)	–	3	2	–	21	31	15.50	–	–	2
D.L.Maddy (Wa)	2007	14	22	3	138	778	40.94	3	3	9
† S.J.Magoffin (Wo)	2008c	7	9	2	33	85	12.14	–	–	–
S.I.Mahmood (La)	2007	12	15	4	33	113	10.27	–	–	3
† D.J.Malan (M)		10	16	2	132*	556	39.71	1	4	3
R.J.A.Malcolm-Hansen (Le/LU)		5	7	1	93	248	41.33	–	2	2
M.N.Malik (Le)		15	20	5	41	178	11.86	–	–	2
H.J.H.Marshall (Gs)	2006	16	29	1	121	850	30.35	2	5	6
J.A.H.Marshall (NZ)	–	6	11	1	128	250	25.00	1	–	4
S.J.Marshall (La)		2	1	1	29*	29	–	–	–	1
C.S.Martin (NZ/Wa)		11	8	4	4*	4	1.00	–	–	2
R.S.C.Martin-Jenkins (Sx)	2000	17	23	5	73*	642	35.66	–	6	4
A.D.Mascarenhas (H)	1998	15	24	2	99	673	30.59	–	3	8
M.J.Mason (NZ)	–	2	3	–	30	44	14.66	–	–	–
M.S.Mason (Wo)	2002c	7	3	–	25	37	12.33	–	–	2
D.D.Masters (Ex)	2008	14	17	3	27	147	10.50	–	–	3
† J.K.Maunders (Ex)		3	5	–	105	217	43.40	1	1	–
T.L.Maynard (Gm)		5	7	–	26	82	11.71	–	–	5
S.C.Meaker (Sy)		2	2	–	16	22	11.00	–	–	–
J.C.Mickleburgh (Ex)		3	4	–	72	150	37.50	–	2	3
J.D.Middlebrook (Ex)	2003	14	19	3	75	414	25.87	–	1	8
A.S.Miller (Wa)		1	1	1	4*	4	–	–	–	–
K.D.Mills (NZ)	–	5	9	2	57	160	22.85	–	2	1
D.K.H.Mitchell (Wo)	2005c	16	29	6	102	922	40.08	1	4	9

F-C	Cap	M	I	NO	HS	Runs	Avge	100	50	Ct/St
Mohammad Amin (CU)	–	2	2	–	6	7	3.50	–	–	1
Mohammad Sami (Sx)	2008	3	4	1	28*	38	12.66	–	–	–
Mohd Yousuf Youhana (La)	–	2	3	1	205*	248	124.00	1	–	–
S.C.Moore (Wo)	2003ᶜ	16	30	4	156	1451	55.80	6	6	8
C.F.D.Morgan (DU)	–	1	1	–	0	0	0.00	–	–	1
† E.J.G.Morgan (M)	2008	17	29	7	137*	1085	49.31	3	5	19
† J.A.Morkel (Du)		1	1	–	37	37	37.00	–	–	2
† M.Morkel (SA/Y)		7	8	–	18	62	7.75	–	–	2
R.K.Morris (LU)	–	3	3	1	88	89	44.50	–	1	–
E.J.Morse (OU)	–	4	3	–	36	57	19.00	–	–	1
† Mosharraf Hossain (BA)	–	3	5	1	31	83	20.75	–	–	–
G.J.Muchall (Du)	2005	1	1	–	12	12	12.00	–	–	1
S.J.Mullaney (La)		2	3	–	33	48	16.00	–	–	1
Mumtaz Habibullah (DU)	–	1	1	1	8*	8	–	–	–	1
M.K.Munday (Sm)		5	5	1	21	35	8.75	–	–	1
C.P.Murtagh (Sy)		4	5	–	12	28	5.60	–	–	2
† T.J.Murtagh (M)	2008	17	25	3	49	402	18.27	–	–	4
Murtaza Hussain (Sy)		4	7	2	56	83	16.60	–	1	1
Mushfiqur Rahim (BA)	–	3	4	1	60*	146	48.66	–	2	6
Mushtaq Ahmed (Sx)	2003	6	10	1	20	65	7.22	–	–	1
† P.Mustard (Du)		16	24	1	92	483	21.00	–	4	56/2
Naim Islam (BA)	–	3	4	–	30	93	23.25	–	–	1
J.K.H.Naik (Le)		1	–							1
D.P.Nannes (M)	2008	5	4	–	5	8	2.00	–	–	2
G.R.Napier (Ex)	2003	7	8	–	76	164	20.50	–	1	–
C.D.Nash (Sx)	2008	17	30	4	108	980	37.69	2	5	2
D.C.Nash (M)	2000	4	7	3	100*	351	87.75	1	3	9
Naved-ul-Hasan (Y)		7	10	3	22	114	16.28	–	–	3
Nazimuddin (BA)	–	4	7	1	75	169	28.16	–	1	–
Nazmul Hossain (BA)	–	3	4	1	13	28	9.33	–	–	1
J.Needham (De)		8	14	6	36	168	21.00	–	–	5
A.Nel (SA/Ex)	2008	7	7	3	56	68	17.00	–	1	1
† M.A.G.Nelson (Nh)		2	3	–	42	51	17.00	–	–	–
† T.J.New (De/Le)		16	25	3	109	573	26.04	1	1	26/2
O.J.Newby (Gs/La)	2008	10	7	2	13	26	5.20	–	–	3
† S.A.Newman (Sy)	2005	15	25	–	129	1044	41.76	2	8	8
M.J.Nicholson (Sy)	2007	9	12	3	133	453	50.33	1	1	4
† P.A.Nixon (Le)	1994	16	24	6	106*	954	53.00	1	6	53/1
† M.J.North (Gs)	2007	12	20	2	104	900	50.00	1	8	13
M.Ntini (SA)	–	7	6	3	9	13	4.33	–	–	–
I.E.O'Brien (NZ)	–	5	7	1	31*	58	9.66	–	–	–
N.J.O'Brien (Nh)		14	21	1	168	917	45.85	2	5	44/3
W.J.F.O'Driscoll (CU)	–	4	6	1	42	160	32.00	–	–	1
G.Onions (Du/MCC/EL)		9	11	2	36	119	13.22	–	–	3
† J.D.P.Oram (NZ)	–	5	9	1	101	279	34.87	1	1	1
J.Ormond (Sy)	2003	7	7	1	64*	84	14.00	–	1	4
F.G.Owen (CU)	–	2	4	–	50	99	24.75	–	1	–
C.D.Paget (DU)	–	3	4	1	9	20	6.66	–	–	–
A.P.Palladino (Ex)		6	11	4	30*	99	14.14	–	–	7
† M.S.Panesar (E/Nh)	2006	14	16	5	30*	84	7.63	–	–	2
G.T.Park (Du)		1	2	–	19	21	10.50	–	–	1
L.C.Parker (Wa)		3	4	–	61	119	29.75	–	1	2

F-C	Cap	M	I	NO	HS	Runs	Avge	100	50	Ct/St
T.W.Parsons (LU)	–	3	2	1	12	14	14.00	–	–	–
J.S.Patel (NZ)	–	3	2	1	22*	24	24.00	–	–	2
S.R.Patel (Nt)	2008	14	22	3	135	977	51.42	2	7	7
S.A.Patterson (Y)		4	5	2	17	36	12.00	–	–	1
D.J.Pattinson (E/Nt)	2008	13	14	–	33	139	9.92	–	–	1
† C.T.Peploe (M)		1	1	1	6*	6	–	–	–	–
S.D.Peters (Nh)	2007	16	26	3	130*	949	41.26	3	5	14
† R.J.Peterson (SA)	–	1	1	1	103*	103	–	1	–	1
M.L.Pettini (Ex)	2006	18	28	5	153*	856	37.21	1	6	9
V.D.Philander (M)		3	6	1	30	77	15.40	–	–	1
B.J.Phillips (Sm)		10	13	4	53*	203	22.55	–	1	3
† T.J.Phillips (Ex)	2006	3	4	1	16	41	13.66	–	–	3
K.P.Pietersen (E/H)	2005	8	12	–	152	707	58.91	4	1	5
D.J.Pipe (De)	2007	9	15	3	133	504	42.00	1	3	23/1
L.E.Plunkett (Du)		7	9	2	68*	191	27.28	–	2	5
N.S.Poonia (Wa)		12	19	–	111	516	27.15	1	2	5
† W.T.S.Porterfield (Gs)	2008	13	24	–	93	763	31.79	–	7	7
N.Pothas (H)	2003	14	23	5	137*	963	53.50	3	3	45/1
M.J.Powell (Gm)	2000	16	26	3	120	725	31.52	1	3	15
M.J.Powell (Wa)	1999	11	16	1	68*	373	24.86	–	2	6
T.Poynton (De)		1	2	–	14	15	7.50	–	–	4/2
D.M.Pratt (LU)	–	3	2	–	47	52	26.00	–	–	2/1
† A.G.Prince (SA/Nt)	2008	10	14	2	149	649	54.08	3	2	4
M.J.Prior (Sx/EL)	2003	15	23	1	133*	1040	47.27	3	7	37/1
N.R.Prowting (DU)	–	3	6	1	45*	87	17.40	–	–	–
R.M.Pyrah (Y)		5	6	–	51	96	16.00	–	1	5
Rajin Saleh (BA)	–	1	2	1	29	50	50.00	–	–	1
M.R.Ramprakash (Sy)	2002	14	23	3	200*	1235	61.75	6	1	4
† W.B.Rankin (Wa)	–	5	6	3	12*	31	10.33	–	–	2
Raqibul Hasan (BA)	–	3	5	–	28	70	14.00	–	–	–
A.U.Rashid (MCC/Y/EL)	2008	18	27	2	111	587	23.48	1	2	6
H.C.L.Rawlinson (DU)	–	3	4	–	9	15	3.75	–	–	3
O.P.Rayner (Sx)		11	13	4	22	159	17.66	–	–	8
C.M.W.Read (Nt)	1999	16	21	5	142	726	45.37	1	5	53/2
† D.J.Redfern (De)		4	6	1	69*	159	31.80	–	1	1
A.J.Redmond (NZ)	–	7	13	–	146	473	36.38	2	1	1
† G.P.Rees (Gm)		16	28	1	140	1088	40.29	3	6	20
H Riazuddin (H)		1	1	–	4	4	4.00	–	–	–
A.Richardson (M)	2005	9	8	2	26	79	13.16	–	–	3
W.H.Rist (CU)	–	1	1	–	11	11	11.00	–	–	–
C.J.L.Rogers (De)	2008	16	27	3	248*	1372	57.16	4	8	15
D.T.Rowe (Le)		3	2	–	1	2	1.00	–	–	–
Rubel Hossain (BA)	–	4	5	1	9	11	2.75	–	–	–
W.D.Rudge (Gs)	2005	2	2	2	19*	26	–	–	–	–
† J.A.Rudolph (Y)	2007	16	24	1	155	1292	56.17	5	6	24
L.C.Ryan (OU)	–	2	1	–	18	18	18.00	–	–	1
† J.L.Sadler (De)		8	14	–	50	301	21.50	–	1	2
O.J.Sadler (OU)	–	2	4	1	77	141	47.00	–	1	–
M.J.Saggers (K)	2001	11	16	7	33	101	11.22	–	–	1
Sajidul Islam (BA)	–	3	4	2	25*	48	24.00	–	–	–
D.J.G.Sales (Nh)	1999	17	27	4	173	1137	49.43	3	4	14
I.D.K.Salisbury (Wa)	2008	13	14	2	81	393	32.75	–	3	7

143

F-C	Cap	M	I	NO	HS	Runs	Avge	100	50	Ct/St
B.W.Sanderson (Y)		2	2	1	6	6	6.00	–	–	–
Saqlain Mushtaq (Sy)	1998	14	16	4	50	206	17.16	–	1	2
I.D.Saxelby (Gs)	2008	3	3	1	11*	20	10.00	–	–	1
† J.J.Sayers (Y)	2007	6	9	–	22	76	8.44	–	–	6
† C.P.Schofield (Sy)		2	4	–	20	36	9.00	–	–	–
B.J.M.Scott (M)	2007	15	22	3	164*	754	39.68	1	7	50/3
B.M.Shafayat (Nt)		10	15	2	118	541	41.61	2	2	7
O.A.Shah (MCC/M/EL)	2000	14	25	1	144	1012	42.16	3	6	14
A.Shahzad (Y)		1	1	–	35	35	35.00	–	–	–
† Shakib Al Hasan (BA)	–	3	5	1	33	90	22.50	–	–	–
† A.J.Shantry (Gm)		7	9	4	16	32	6.40	–	–	3
Shoaib Akhtar (Sy)		2	4	1	32	69	23.00	–	–	2
C.E.Shreck (MCC/Nt)	2006	16	18	12	4*	13	2.16	–	–	8
† R.J.Sidebottom (E/Nt)	2004	7	9	3	22	65	10.83	–	–	2
C.E.W.Silverwood (M)	2006	3	3	2	33*	70	70.00	–	–	1
B.F.Smith (Wo)	2002^c	16	25	1	99	1075	44.79	–	11	12
E.T.Smith (M)	2005	6	10	–	88	397	39.70	–	4	3
† G.C.Smith (SA)	–	6	10	2	154*	491	61.37	2	1	10
G.M.Smith (De)		13	21	1	113	665	33.25	1	6	1
G.P.Smith (Le)		6	10	–	54	215	21.50	–	1	2
† T.C.Smith (La/Le)		10	12	3	63	295	32.77	–	1	7
W.R.Smith (Du)		12	20	2	201*	925	51.38	3	3	2
S.D.Snell (Gs)	2005	16	24	4	127	944	47.20	1	9	38/1
V.S.Solanki (Wo)	1998	15	25	1	270	1127	46.95	4	5	7
T.G.Southee (NZ)	–	4	3	–	21	28	9.33	–	–	–
C.M.Spearman (Gs)	2002	5	9	1	95	173	21.62	–	1	2
† M.N.W.Spriegel (LU/Sy)		12	19	1	51	418	23.22	–	1	2
D.I.Stevens (K)	2005	14	21	1	127	463	23.15	1	1	9
D.W.Steyn (SA)	–	3	2	1	19	29	29.00	–	–	–
† M.D.Stoneman (Du)		13	22	1	60*	429	20.42	–	3	4
J.P.Strachan (OU)		1	1	–	5	5	5.00	–	–	1
† A.J.Strauss (E/M)	2001	16	27	1	172	1223	47.03	3	6	18
† S.D.Stubbings (De)	2001	10	18	2	62*	506	31.62	–	2	5
A.V.Suppiah (Sm)		3	5	–	61	163	32.60	–	1	–
† I.J.Sutcliffe (La)	2003	7	11	–	50	164	14.90	–	1	3
L.D.Sutton (La)		15	21	4	55	461	27.11	–	1	54/2
G.P.Swann (Nt/EL)	2005	14	18	2	82	586	36.62	–	5	16
† Syed Rasel (BA)	–	1	2	–	4	8	4.00	–	–	–
N.Tahir (Wa)		6	6	2	37	69	17.25	–	–	1
† Tamim Iqbal (BA)	–	4	7	–	78	250	35.71	–	3	–
C.G.Taylor (Gs)	2001	17	30	4	137	1101	42.34	2	8	6
C.R.Taylor (Y)		4	6	–	48	123	20.50	–	–	1
J.W.A.Taylor (Le)		4	5	–	51	64	12.80	–	1	4
L.R.P.L.Taylor (NZ)	–	6	12	1	154*	429	39.00	2	–	11
F.D.Telo (De)		8	15	–	69	272	18.13	–	2	3
R.N.ten Doeschate (Ex)	2006	17	24	2	146	860	39.09	2	4	10
A.C.Thomas (Sm)	2008	11	15	3	43	231	19.25	–	–	4
G.J.Thompson (DU)	–	2	2	–	21	34	17.00	–	–	–
M.A.Thornely (Sx)		2	4	1	6*	13	4.33	–	–	2
C.D.Thorp (Du)		12	15	4	29*	145	13.18	–	–	6
R.T.Timms (CU)	–	4	7	–	55	137	19.57	–	1	5
† J.A.Tomlinson (H)	2008	16	20	10	35*	145	14.50	–	–	4

144

F-C	Cap	M	I	NO	HS	Runs	Avge	100	50	Ct/St
† J.C.Tredwell (K/MCC)	2007	18	29	3	123*	587	22.57	1	3	20
P.D.Trego (Sm)	2007	16	23	3	86	849	42.45	–	7	3
C.T.Tremlett (H/EL)	2004	13	19	2	60	299	17.58	–	3	6
† M.E.Trescothick (Sm)	1999	16	28	1	158	1258	46.59	3	8	19
I.J.L.Trott (Wa)	2005	16	25	5	181	1240	62.00	3	6	16
† J.O.Troughton (Wa)	2002	14	20	5	138*	747	49.80	1	6	13
A.J.Tudor (Ex/<u>Sy</u>)	1999	9	15	1	68	276	19.71	–	1	1
M.L.Turner (Sm)		2	3	–	4	7	2.33	–	–	1
S.D.Udal (M)	2008	14	20	6	91	556	39.71	–	4	1
J.J.van der Wath (Nh)		11	10	3	75*	148	21.14	–	1	–
M.van Jaarsveld (K)	2005	16	27	3	133	1150	47.91	4	7	28
M.P.Vaughan (E/Y)	1995	12	18	–	106	450	25.00	1	1	4
† D.L.Vettori (NZ)	–	4	7	1	48	83	13.83	–	–	–
L.Vincent (La)		6	12	1	83	272	24.72	–	2	6
A.C.Voges (Nt)	2008	12	20	3	77	627	36.88	–	4	11
G.G.Wagg (De)	2007	16	23	3	108	538	26.90	1	2	6
M.A.Wagh (Nt)	2007	15	24	2	141	1033	46.95	2	8	3
† D.J.Wainwright (Y)		4	6	1	104*	165	33.00	1	–	2
A.G.Wakely (Nh)		5	8	1	53	118	16.85	–	1	4
† M.J.Walker (K)	2000	6	10	1	23	94	10.44	–	–	–
† M.A.Wallace (Gm)	2003	16	24	–	72	668	27.83	–	4	31/5
S.J.Walters (Sy)		6	8	–	40	127	15.87	–	–	3
H.T.Waters (Gm)		1	1	1	10*	10	–	–	–	1
† R.E.Watkins (Gm)		6	9	2	33	94	13.42	–	–	3
M.H.Wessels (Nh)		13	19	1	95	576	32.00	–	6	13/2
T.Westley (Ex)		9	17	3	93*	307	21.92	–	2	5
† I.J.Westwood (Wa)	2008	11	17	–	176	506	29.76	1	2	5
A.G.Wharf (Gm)	2000	10	14	3	51*	237	21.54	–	1	3
A.J.Wheater (Ex)		2	1	–	22	22	22.00	–	–	3
C.D.Whelan (Wo)	2008[c]	6	5	2	58	82	27.33	–	1	1
G.G.White (Nh)		1	1	–	0	0	0.00	–	–	–
R.A.White (Nh)	2008	15	25	4	132*	1037	49.38	3	6	11
W.A.White (De)		4	6	1	18	40	8.00	–	–	2
R.A.Whiteley (De)		1	2	–	27	45	22.50	–	–	–
N.M.H.Whittington (CU)	–	1	1	–	83	83	83.00	–	1	1
D.H.Wigley (<u>Gs</u>/Nh)	2008	9	11	4	18*	60	8.57	–	–	2
D.M.Williams (LU)	–	2	3	–	11	25	8.33	–	–	–
R.E.M Williams (DU)	–	1	1	–	4	4	4.00	–	–	–
† C.M.Willoughby (Sm)	2007	17	17	11	18	70	11.66	–	–	1
P.J.Wilshaw (OU)	–	1	1	–	20	20	20.00	–	–	1
P.J.Wiseman (Du)		16	22	2	65	479	23.95	–	3	1
C.R.Woakes (Wa)		11	12	3	64*	247	27.44	–	1	7
M.J.Wood (Gm)		7	12	1	83*	212	19.27	–	1	5
M.J.Wood (Nt)		14	21	1	98	539	26.95	–	4	4
A.Woodhouse (CU)	–	1	2	–	2	2	1.00	–	–	–
† R.J.Woodman (Gs)	2008	1	2	–	13	15	7.50	–	–	–
C.J.C.Wright (Ex)		11	12	3	71*	181	20.11	–	1	4
L.J.Wright (Sx/EL)	2007	13	20	3	155*	621	36.52	2	1	8
† M.H.Yardy (Sx)	2005	16	27	1	93	954	36.69	–	7	8
Yasir Arafat (K)	2007	12	19	5	90*	395	28.21	–	2	1
† P.J.W.Young (OU)	–	3	3	–	31	53	17.66	–	–	2
M.Zondeki (Wa/SA)		5	5	3	9	21	10.50	–	–	–

BOWLING

See BATTING AND FIELDING section for details of matches, caps and teams.

	Cat	O	M	R	W	Avge	Best	5wI	10wM
Abdul Razzaq (Sy)	RFM	24.1	5	77	3	25.66	3- 46	–	–
A.R.Adams (Nt)	RMF	230.4	64	594	31	19.16	4- 39	–	–
C.J.Adams (Sx)	RM/OB	2	0	13	0				
J.H.K.Adams (H)	LM	12	1	42	0				
U.Afzaal (Sy)	SLA	104	15	395	4	98.75	2- 62	–	–
R.G.Aga (Sx)	RMF	61.5	16	232	9	25.77	4- 63	–	–
J.S.Ahmed (Ex)	RMF	34.4	5	127	5	25.40	3- 42	–	–
M.Ahmed (Wo)	RFM	16	5	70	2	35.00	1- 28	–	–
Kabir Ali (Wo)	RMF	311.3	53	1106	59	18.74	6- 58	4	–
M.M.Ali (Wo)	OB	37	6	133	0				
J.Allenby (Le)	RM	270.4	70	736	26	28.30	4- 40	–	–
H.M.Amla (SA)	LB	3	0	21	0				
J.M.Anderson (E/La)	RFM	347.4	75	1031	49	21.04	7- 43	2	–
G.M.Andrew (Wo)	RMF	238.5	35	1018	27	37.70	5- 58	1	–
A.S.Ansari (CU)	LB	74	4	311	9	34.55	4- 50	–	–
J.E.Anyon (Wa)	RFM	228.2	32	844	26	32.46	6- 82	1	–
Azhar Mahmood (K)	RFM	147	28	404	21	19.23	6- 55	2	–
M.Baer (LU)	SLA	22	0	110	0				
S.P.Bailey (Nh)	RFM	26	2	127	3	42.33	2-119	–	–
F.B.Baker (CU)	SLA	43	1	217	2	108.50	2- 75	–	–
D.J.Balcombe (H)	RFM	113.1	20	412	9	45.77	2- 1	–	–
V.Banerjee (Gs)	SLA	135.4	31	457	7	65.28	3- 31	–	–
G.J.Batty (Wo)	OB	387.3	102	1042	34	30.64	5- 33	2	–
W.A.T.Beer (Sx)	LB	16	0	81	1	81.00	1- 18	–	–
D.M.Benkenstein (Du)	RM/OB	25	7	60	1	60.00	1- 13	–	–
J.G.E.Benning (Sy)	RM	44	10	144	1	144.00	1- 41	–	–
G.K.Berg (M)	RMF	52	13	171	5	34.20	3- 38	–	–
I.D.Blackwell (Sm)	SLA	401	87	978	22	44.45	4- 74	–	–
A.J.Blake (K)	RMF	4	1	17	0				
N.Boje (Nh)	SLA	401.5	88	1194	33	36.18	4- 26	–	–
S.E.Bond (H)	RF	99.1	15	365	19	19.21	7- 66	2	–
R.S.Bopara (Ex/MCC/EL)	RM	269.5	47	959	28	34.25	4- 33	–	–
P.M.Borrington (De/LU)	OB	1	0	5	0				
A.G.Botha (Wa)	SLA	246	56	677	15	45.13	4- 77	–	–
M.A.G.Boyce (Le)	RM	6	0	61	0				
D.P.Bradshaw (OU)	RFM	23.3	6	91	1	91.00	1- 28	–	–
R.M.R.Brathwaite (LU)	RFM	4	0	18	0				
G.R.Breese (Du)	OB	7	1	22	1	22.00	1- 22	–	–
T.T.Bresnan (Y)	RMF	421	77	1278	45	28.40	5- 94	1	–
S.C.J.Broad (E/Nt)	RFM	320.4	67	1091	32	34.09	4- 39	–	–
A.D.Brown (Sy)	LB	6	3	5	0				
D.O.Brown (Gs)	RM	115.3	25	432	16	27.00	5- 38	1	–
J.F.Brown (Nh)	OB	281.4	61	825	10	82.50	2- 33	–	–
D.A.Burton (M)	RMF	23	1	97	1	97.00	1- 97	–	–
J.E.L.Buttleman (DU)	RFM	38.3	7	137	6	22.83	2- 32	–	–
A.R.Caddick (Sm)	RFM	282.2	55	1047	25	41.88	5-118	1	–
M.A.Carberry (H/MCC/EL)	OB	13	1	31	0				
N.M.Carter (Wa)	LFM	373.4	70	1278	41	31.17	6-100	2	–
M.A.Chambers (Ex)	RFM	66	11	251	8	31.37	3- 37	–	–

F-C	Cat	O	M	R	W	Avge	Best	5wI	10wM
S.Chanderpaul (Du)	LB	4	0	19	0				
G.Chapple (La)	RFM	332.5	93	861	42	20.50	6- 40	2	–
V.Chopra (Ex)	RM	1.4	0	14	0				
J.L.Clare (De)	RMF	257.4	47	871	31	28.09	7- 74	1	–
R.Clarke (De/Wa)	RFM	162.2	23	630	15	42.00	4- 87	–	–
M.E.Claydon (Du)	RMF	28	9	94	1	94.00	1- 64	–	–
S.J.Cliff (Le)	RM	74.2	20	241	10	24.10	4- 42	–	–
J.J.Cobb (Le)	LB	20	3	90	4	22.50	2- 11	–	–
P.D.Collingwood (E/Du)	RMF	42	10	136	5	27.20	3- 17	–	–
P.T.Collins (Sy)	LFM	309.2	59	1121	27	41.51	4-111	–	–
C.D.Collymore (Sx)	RFM	268.2	81	727	26	27.96	4- 47	–	–
A.N.Cook (E/Ex)	OB	1	0	1	0				
S.J.Cook (K)	RM	7	0	25	0				
D.G.Cork (La)	RFM	202	48	551	20	27.55	3- 33	–	–
D.A.Cosker (Gm)	SLA	186.2	25	656	19	34.52	5- 81	1	–
R.D.B.Croft (Gm)	OB	510.2	132	1262	45	28.04	6- 45	2	–
S.J.Croft (La)	RMF	161	25	586	16	36.62	4- 51	–	–
A.R.Crook (Nh)	OB	2.2	1	5	1	5.00	1- 5	–	–
S.P.Crook (Nh)	RFM	73.3	17	286	1	286.00	1- 9	–	–
R.A.G.Cummins (Le)	RM	84.2	16	268	7	38.28	3- 73	–	–
L.M.Daggett (Le/Wa)	RFM	169	34	593	19	31.21	4- 41	–	–
J.W.M.Dalrymple (Gm)	OB	114	14	406	7	58.00	2- 23	–	–
Danish Kaneria (Ex)	LBG	315.2	65	852	40	21.30	7-157	4	–
A.M.Davies (Du)	RMF	254.2	72	600	41	14.63	8- 24	4	2
L.A.Dawson (H)	SLA	57.1	12	213	6	35.50	2- 32	–	–
R.K.J.Dawson (Gs)	OB	87	13	346	1	346.00	1-113	–	–
K.J.Dean (De)	LMF	89.3	19	262	14	18.71	6- 46	1	–
Z.de Bruyn (Sm)	RM	108.3	16	366	7	52.28	2- 19	–	–
J.L.Denly (K)	LB	14	2	47	0				
J.W.Dernbach (Sy)	RMF	216	33	844	23	36.69	6- 72	1	–
N.J.Dexter (Ex/K)	RM	2	0	9	0				
Dhiman Ghosh (BA)	OB	3	0	11	1	11.00	1- 10	–	–
L.A.Dingle (OU)	RMF	18	2	83	0				
Dolar Mahmud (BA)	OB	38	9	146	2	73.00	1- 28	–	–
N.D.Doshi (De)	SLA	257	58	825	13	63.46	3- 84	–	–
J.P.Duminy (SA)	OB	8	1	14	0				
F.du Plessis (SA)	LB	118	14	355	8	44.37	3- 61	–	–
D.du Preez (Le)	RM	272.3	73	730	32	22.81	5- 48	1	–
W.J.Durston (Sm)	OB	40	2	120	0				
J.du Toit (Le)	RM	18	1	83	4	20.75	3- 31	–	–
M.A.Ealham (Nt)	RMF	362.4	102	887	30	29.56	7- 59	1	1
N.J.Edwards (Sm)	RM	1	0	1	0				
G.D.Elliott (NZ)	RMF	10	2	42	0				
S.M.Ervine (H)	RM	124	12	499	9	55.44	4- 42	–	–
D.Evans (M)	RFM	241	50	954	30	31.80	6- 35	2	–
R.S.Ferley (Nt)	SLA	55.1	9	136	2	68.00	1- 60	–	–
C.R.D.Fernando (Wo)	RFM	24.1	2	130	2	65.00	1- 27	–	–
S.T.Finn (M)	RFM	298.2	46	1086	28	38.78	4- 80	–	–
I.D.Fisher (Gs)	SLA	8	6	7	0				
L.J.Fletcher (Nt)	RMF	20	5	70	1	70.00	1- 70	–	–
A.Flintoff (E/La)	RF	263.1	72	664	22	30.18	4- 21	–	–
G.W.Flower (Ex)	SLA	21	1	69	2	34.50	1- 10	–	–

147

F-C	Cat	O	M	R	W	Avge	Best	5wI	10wM
D.R.Flynn (NZ)	SLA	1	0	3	0				
J.S.Foster (Ex/MCC)	(WK)	12	0	122	1	122.00	1-122	–	–
P.J.Foster (DU)	RFM	65	18	193	5	38.60	2- 44	–	–
P.J.Franks (Nt)	RMF	172	32	632	12	52.66	2- 25	–	–
M.J.Friedlander (CU)	RFM	24	6	74	2	37.00	2- 44	–	–
T.Frost (Wa)	(WK)	2	0	3	0				
A.W.Gale (Y)	LB	1	0	3	0				
D.J.Gale (DU)	SLA	6	0	35	0				
J.E.R.Gallian (Ex)	RM	4	0	12	0				
A.P.R.Gidman (Gs)	RM	70.1	7	226	9	25.11	3- 35	–	–
J.N.Gillespie (Gm)	RFM	348.5	107	902	24	37.58	4- 32	–	–
M.T.Gitsham (Gs)	LB	95.3	16	271	3	90.33	1- 12	–	–
J.C.Glover (DU)	RMF	49.4	7	188	6	31.33	3- 56	–	–
D.Gough (Y)	RFM	149	25	528	9	58.66	2- 34	–	–
R.N.Grant (Gm)	RM	17	4	44	1	44.00	1- 8	–	–
C.G.Greenidge (Gs)	RMF	21	5	62	5	12.40	5- 62	1	–
D.A.Griffiths (H)	RFM	42	8	178	2	89.00	1- 38	–	–
T.D.Groenewald (Wa)	RMF	92	20	303	11	27.54	5- 24	1	–
A.J.Hall (Nh)	RFM	173.4	40	535	24	22.29	5- 81	1	–
R.J.Hamilton-Brown (Sx)	OB	22.5	1	85	3	28.33	2- 54	–	–
O.J.Hannon-Dalby (Y)	RMF	29	5	114	1	114.00	1- 58	–	–
M.A.Hardinges (Gs)	RMF	99.3	22	366	10	36.60	2- 13	–	–
B.W.Harmison (Du)	RMF	113.3	21	437	16	27.31	4- 27	–	–
S.J.Harmison (E/Du)	RF	472.1	117	1486	65	22.86	6-122	2	–
A.J.Harris (Gs/Nt/Wo)	RM	56	14	192	1	192.00	1- 31	–	–
J.A.R.Harris (Gm)	RFM	109.2	25	362	11	32.90	3- 40	–	–
P.L.Harris (SA)	SLA	188.5	38	609	14	43.50	3-129	–	–
R.J.Harris (Sx)	RM	17	9	36	4	9.00	4- 36	–	–
D.S.Harrison (Gm)	RMF	364.4	72	1150	30	38.33	4- 49	–	–
M.Hayward (H)	RF	25.1	4	101	3	33.66	2- 87	–	–
T.L.Hemingway (CU)	OB	159.4	32	570	10	57.00	2- 32	–	–
C.W.Henderson (Le)	SLA	545.3	158	1294	41	31.56	5- 39	1	–
J.C.Hildreth (Sm)	RMF	8	0	38	0				
C.M.M.Hill (OU)	SLC	59	7	166	2	83.00	1- 77	–	–
W.W.Hinds (De)	RM	88	13	261	10	26.10	3- 22	–	–
B.J.Hodge (La)	OB	10	2	26	2	13.00	2- 24	–	–
L.J.Hodgson (Sy)	RFM	9	1	58	0				
G.P.Hodnett (Gs)	LB	19	0	132	2	66.00	2- 91	–	–
K.W.Hogg (La)	RFM	22	8	60	4	15.00	3- 26	–	–
M.J.Hoggard (Y/EL)	RFM	372.5	76	1096	45	24.35	6- 57	1	–
S.M.Hole (Wa)	RM	18	3	40	2	20.00	2- 29	–	–
C.D.Hopkinson (Sx)	RM	2	0	16	0				
J.M.How (NZ)	OB	1	0	4	0				
T.H.Howell (OU)	LB	18	3	80	5	16.00	3- 52	–	–
J.A.Hughes (LU)	RMF	15.5	1	84	1	84.00	1- 38	–	–
I.D.Hunter (De)	RMF	132.3	34	332	8	41.50	2- 12	–	–
Imran Arif (Wo)	RFM	158.5	30	575	22	26.13	5- 50	1	–
Imran Tahir (H)	LBG	258.2	58	734	44	16.68	7- 66	3	1
A.J.Ireland (Gs)	RMF	218.1	39	846	23	36.78	3- 33	–	–
B.D.Jacklin (CU)	RM	32.1	7	93	3	31.00	2- 42	–	–
M.I.James (CU)	RMF	6	1	25	0				
N.A.James (Wa)	SLA	3	1	6	1	6.00	1- 6	–	–

148

F-C	Cat	O	M	R	W	Avge	Best	5wI	10wM
T.M.Jewell (Sy)	RFM	7	2	16	1	16.00	1- 16	–	–
K.A.Jogia (CU)	RSM	16	0	79	0				
H.D.Jones (LU)	RFM	40	7	114	1	114.00	1- 26	–	–
P.S.Jones (Sm)	RMF	227.2	37	848	27	31.40	5- 53	2	–
R.A.Jones (Wo)	RMF	36.2	10	140	1	140.00	1- 20	–	–
S.P.Jones (Wo)	RF	211	39	757	42	18.02	5- 30	4	–
C.J.Jordan (Sy)	RFM	159	27	570	12	47.50	3- 32	–	–
R.H.Joseph (K)	RFM	419.1	87	1433	55	26.05	6- 32	2	–
Junaid Siddique (BA)	OB	25	0	97	1	97.00	1- 30	–	–
T.Kalam (OU)	RMF	61	11	244	2	122.00	1- 45	–	–
J.H.Kallis (SA)	RMF	109	23	335	11	30.45	3- 31	–	–
M.Kartik (M)	SLA	224	60	545	16	34.06	4-101	–	–
G.Keedy (La)	SLA	421.3	85	1157	28	41.32	5- 56	1	–
R.A.Kemp (CU)	RM	15	3	55	1	55.00	1- 27	–	–
R.W.T.Key (K/EL)	RM/OB	2	1	2	0				
A.Khan (K)	RFM	145.1	36	433	21	20.61	3- 10	–	–
N.Killeen (Du)	RMF	38	12	65	8	8.12	5- 15	1	–
R.E.King (LU)	LMF	27	4	122	3	40.66	3- 48	–	–
S.P.Kirby (Gs/MCC)	RFM	386.1	88	1149	40	28.72	5- 60	1	–
R.J.Kirtley (Sx)	RFM	42	7	130	2	65.00	2- 88	–	–
R.K.Kleinveldt (H)	RFM	9	1	42	1	42.00	1- 17	–	–
F.A.Klokker (De)	(WK)	10	0	99	0				
L.Klusener (Nh)	RM/OB	183.2	43	638	6	106.33	1- 21	–	–
G.J.P.Kruger (Le)	RMF	300.1	59	970	32	30.31	5- 47	2	–
G.J.Kruis (Y)	RFM	295.3	68	903	22	41.04	5- 47	1	–
G.A.Lamb (H)	RM/OB	140.4	21	571	8	71.37	2- 69	–	–
J.L.Langer (Sm)	RM	2	0	6	0				
C.K.Langeveldt (De)	RFM	418.1	105	1238	55	22.50	5- 40	3	–
J.J.C.Lawson (Le)	RFM	38	6	188	2	94.00	1- 41	–	–
M.A.K.Lawson (De/M)	LB	16	0	83	0				
N.T.Lee (CU)	LB	4.4	0	24	1	24.00	1- 24	–	–
C.W.S.Legget (DU)	RM	10	2	43	2	21.50	2- 43	–	–
J.Lewis (Gs)	RMF	392.5	123	1009	35	28.82	5- 64	1	–
J.D.Lewry (Sx)	LFM	387.5	66	1234	41	30.09	4- 56	–	–
C.J.Liddle (Sx)	LFM	32	8	74	1	74.00	1- 39	–	–
R.J.Logan (Nh)	RMF	19	1	117	1	117.00	1- 87	–	–
J.Louw (Nh)	RMF	178	40	545	15	36.33	3- 42	–	–
D.S.Lucas (Nh)	LMF	423.4	77	1533	36	42.58	5- 30	1	–
T.Lungley (De)	RM	85.1	13	326	9	36.22	4- 70	–	–
A.Lyth (Y)	RM	30.1	5	105	1	105.00	1- 20	–	–
J.C.Macadam (OU)	RMF	19	4	66	1	66.00	1- 41	–	–
A.McGrath (Y)	RM	100.1	16	282	9	31.33	2- 27	–	–
N.D.McKenzie (SA/Du)	RM	5	0	19	0				
R.McLaren (K)	RMF	400	83	1179	50	23.58	6- 75	2	–
C.S.MacLeod (Wa)	RMF	18.1	3	56	4	14.00	3- 36	–	–
P.J.McMahon (OU)	OB	119	18	361	8	45.12	3- 78	–	–
D.L.Maddy (Wa)	RM/OB	154	38	442	17	26.00	4- 25	–	–
S.J.Magoffin (Wo)	RFM	202	45	755	23	32.82	4- 49	–	–
S.I.Mahmood (La)	RF	322.5	66	1147	35	32.77	5- 76	1	–
D.J.Malan (M)	LB	58.2	6	204	4	51.00	2- 26	–	–
R.J.A.Malcolm-Hansen (Le/LU)	OB	36	9	100	1	100.00	1- 40	–	–
M.N.Malik (Le)	RFM	466.5	86	1475	42	35.11	6- 46	3	–

F-C	Cat	O	M	R	W	Avge	Best	5wI	10wM
H.J.H.Marshall (Gs)	RM	62	12	204	1	204.00	1- 31	–	–
J.A.H.Marshall (NZ)	RM	6	0	19	0				
S.J.Marshall (La)	LB	45	10	171	2	85.50	1- 47	–	–
C.S.Martin (NZ/Wa)	RFM	293.1	62	1002	26	38.53	5- 84	1	–
R.S.C.Martin-Jenkins (Sx)	RFM	387.3	111	1052	32	32.87	3- 36	–	–
A.D.Mascarenhas (H)	RMF	394.4	132	977	41	23.82	6- 67	2	–
M.J.Mason (NZ)	RFM	53	17	176	8	22.00	4- 65	–	–
M.S.Mason (Wo)	RFM	143.4	45	329	11	29.90	2- 26	–	–
D.D.Masters (Ex)	RMF	442.3	154	980	42	23.33	6- 24	2	–
S.C.Meaker (Sy)	RMF	35.1	3	139	4	34.75	3- 86	–	–
J.C.Mickleburgh (Ex)	RMF	4	0	11	0				
J.D.Middlebrook (Ex)	OB	344.2	55	1086	31	35.03	5- 69	1	–
A.S.Miller (Wa)	RFM	20	5	45	3	15.00	2- 35	–	–
K.D.Mills (NZ)	RFM	127.1	26	345	13	26.53	3- 41	–	–
D.K.H.Mitchell (Wo)	RM	31	7	65	0				
Mohammad Amin (CU)	RMF	46	4	242	0				
Mohammad Samı (Sx)	RFM	81	21	265	9	29.44	5- 95	1	–
M.Morkel (SA/Y)	RFM	182.4	29	664	21	31.61	4- 52	–	–
R.K.Morris (LU)	RMF	29	4	108	2	54.00	1- 38	–	–
E.J.Morse (OU)	RM	99.5	17	315	13	24.23	6-102	1	–
Mosharraf Hossain (BA)	SLA	84	9	278	4	69.50	3- 69	–	–
S.J.Mullaney (La)	RM	9.5	2	35	1	35.00	1- 3	–	–
Mumtaz Habibullah (DU)	RMF	12	2	47	0				
M.K.Munday (Sm)	LB	101.2	11	410	10	41.00	3- 18	–	–
T.J.Murtagh (M)	RFM	505.5	87	1734	64	27.09	7- 95	3	1
Murtaza Hussain (Sy)	OB	123.1	23	365	7	52.14	3- 82	–	–
Mushtaq Ahmed (Sx)	LBG	226.1	32	777	19	40.89	5- 83	1	–
Naim Islam (BA)	OB	16	0	67	0				
J.K.H.Naik (Le)	OB	25	4	70	3	23.33	3- 70	–	–
D.P.Nannes (M)	LFM	107.4	20	393	20	19.65	6- 32	1	–
G.R.Napier (Ex)	RM	172.5	35	567	22	25.77	6-103	1	–
C.D.Nash (Sx)	OB	23.3	1	63	3	21.00	3- 7	–	–
Naved-ul-Hasan (Y)	RMF	153.1	21	606	16	37.87	4- 86	–	–
Nazimuddin (BA)	RM	10.2	0	38	0				
Nazmul Hossain (BA)	RMF	68	7	262	6	43.66	5- 90	1	–
J.Needham (De)	OB	162.1	28	503	19	26.47	6- 49	1	–
A.Nel (SA/Ex)	RFM	221.2	49	624	19	32.84	3- 25	–	–
M.A.G.Nelson (Nh)	RFM	8	0	62	0				
T.J.New (De/Le)	RM	2	0	7	1	7.00	1- 7	–	–
O.J.Newby (Gs/La)	RMF	193.5	30	793	25	31.72	5- 69	1	–
M.J.Nicholson (Sy)	RFM	188	37	625	11	56.81	3- 44	–	–
P.A.Nixon (Le)	RM	5	0	41	0				
M.J.North (Gs)	OB	191	29	585	13	45.00	3- 57	–	–
M.Ntini (SA)	RF	184	35	681	20	34.05	5- 94	1	–
I.E.O'Brien (NZ)	RMF	140.1	34	402	15	26.80	4- 74	–	–
W.J.F.O'Driscoll (CU)	RM	118.3	19	500	7	71.42	2- 67	–	–
G.Onions (Du/MCC/EL)	RMF	196.1	53	671	25	26.84	5- 75	1	–
J.D.P.Oram (M)	RM	114	37	248	8	31.00	3- 34	–	–
J.Ormond (Sy)	RFM	158.2	27	561	13	43.15	4- 90	–	–
C.D.Paget (DU)	OBF	28	3	112	2	56.00	1- 24	–	–
A.P.Palladino (Ex)	RMF	158.5	56	412	18	22.88	4- 29	–	–
M.S.Panesar (E/Nh)	SLA	530.5	98	1525	40	38.12	6- 37	2	–

F-C	Cat	O	M	R	W	Avge	Best	5wI	10wM
G.T.Park (Du)	RM	8	3	20	2	10.00	2- 20	–	–
T.W.Parsons (LU)	RFM	58.5	16	196	4	49.00	2- 28	–	–
J.S.Patel (NZ)	OB	80.3	12	320	2	160.00	2-135	–	–
S.R.Patel (Nt)	SLA	171.3	39	455	12	37.91	2- 26	–	–
S.A.Patterson (Y)	RMF	97.1	22	279	11	25.36	3- 19	–	–
D.J.Pattinson (E/Nt)	RFM	386.2	82	1255	49	25.61	6- 30	4	–
C.T.Peploe (M)	SLA	8.5	3	15	2	7.50	2- 15	–	–
R.J.Peterson (SA)	SLA	6	3	28	2	14.00	2- 25	–	–
M.L.Pettini (Ex)	RM	12	0	129	0			–	–
V.D.Philander (M)	RMF	108.5	27	277	10	27.70	3- 45	–	–
B.J.Phillips (Sm)	RFM	216.1	49	665	21	31.66	3- 34	–	–
T.J.Phillips (Ex)	SLA	14	2	50	1	50.00	1- 18	–	–
K.P.Pietersen (E/H)	OB	25.3	1	89	1	89.00	1- 0	–	–
L.E.Plunkett (Du)	RFM	129.1	16	520	16	32.50	3- 49	–	–
W.T.S.Porterfield (Gs)	OB	6	0	57	1	57.00	1- 57	–	–
M.J.Powell (Wa)	RM	16	0	1	0			–	–
A.G.Prince (SA/Nt)	SLA	11	0	49	2	24.50	2- 11	–	–
R.M.Pyrah (Y)	RM	56	11	201	1	201.00	1- 14	–	–
Rajin Saleh (BA)	OB	2	0	13	0			–	–
W.B.Rankin (Wa)	RFM	86.3	9	362	12	30.16	4- 80	–	–
A.U.Rashid (MCC/Y/EL)	LB	638.1	69	2069	65	31.83	7-107	4	–
O.P.Rayner (Sx)	OB	347.3	53	1042	31	33.61	5- 49	2	–
C.M.W.Read (Nt)	(WK)	4	0	20	0			–	–
D.J.Redfern (De)	OB	18	3	54	1	54.00	1- 7	–	–
A.J.Redmond (NZ)	LB	29	4	125	2	62.50	2- 35	–	–
H.Riazuddin (H)	RFM	29	5	99	1	99.00	1- 21	–	–
A.Richardson (M)	RMF	264.5	73	644	28	23.00	5- 34	1	–
C.J.L.Rogers (De)	LBG	3.4	0	13	0			–	–
D.T.Rowe (Le)	RM	58	13	235	4	58.75	2- 75	–	–
Rubel Hossain (BA)	RMF	107.5	8	430	8	53.75	3- 86	–	–
W.D.Rudge (Gs)	RM	52	9	190	4	47.50	3- 76	–	–
J.A.Rudolph (Y)	LBG	21.2	2	74	1	74.00	1- 13	–	–
L.C.Ryan (OU)	SLA	40.1	1	201	3	67.00	2-114	–	–
J.L.Sadler (De)	LBG	10	0	57	1	57.00	1- 57	–	–
O.J.Sadler (OU)	SLA	30	6	61	0			–	–
M.J.Saggers (K)	RMF	276.5	69	873	24	36.37	4- 26	–	–
Sajidul Islam (BA)	LMF	69	3	280	1	280.00	1- 75	–	–
I.D.K.Salisbury (Wa)	LBG	268.4	39	865	31	27.90	6-100	5	–
B.W.Sanderson (Y)	RMF	37	7	140	1	140.00	1- 87	–	–
Saqlain Mushtaq (Sy)	OB	396.4	57	1288	40	32.20	6- 50	3	–
I.D.Saxelby (Gs)	RMF	47	8	218	2	109.00	1- 64	–	–
C.P.Schofield (Sy)	LBG	39.4	5	143	1	143.00	1- 69	–	–
B.J.M.Scott (M)	(WK)	0.3	0	1	0			–	–
B.M.Shafayat (Nt)	RMF	17	1	59	0			–	–
O.A.Shah (MCC/M/EL)	OB	20.4	4	89	1	89.00	1- 7	–	–
A.Shahzad (Y)	RMF	24	7	64	3	21.33	2- 43	–	–
Shakib Al Hasan (BA)	SLA	56	13	168	5	33.60	3- 49	–	–
A.J.Shantry (Gm)	LFM	183.2	50	545	30	18.16	5- 52	2	1
Shoaib Akhtar (Sy)	RF	33	4	117	1	117.00	1- 54	–	–
C.E.Shreck (MCC/Nt)	RFM	614.3	156	1817	61	29.78	5- 40	2	–
R.J.Sidebottom (E/Nt)	LFM	301	86	750	33	22.72	6- 67	2	–
C.E.W.Silverwood (M)	RFM	60.4	12	160	6	26.66	2- 11	–	–

F-C	Cat	O	M	R	W	Avge	Best	5wI	10wM
G.M.Smith (De)	OB/RM	142.3	19	502	11	45.63	2-53	–	–
G.P.Smith (Le)	LB	5	0	64	1	64.00	1-64	–	–
T.C.Smith (La/Le)	RMF	266.2	67	747	24	31.12	3-28	–	–
S.D.Snell (Gs)	(WK)	3	0	15	0				
V.S.Solanki (Wo)	OB	7	3	11	0				
T.G.Southee (NZ)	RFM	94.3	21	329	12	27.41	5-42	1	–
M.N.W.Spriegel (LU/Sy)	OB	66	4	249	7	35.57	2-28	–	–
D.I.Stevens (K)	RM	123	26	322	10	32.20	4-70	–	–
D.W.Steyn (SA)	RF	98.3	20	341	8	42.62	4-76	–	–
J.P.Strachan (OU)	RMF	31	7	98	1	98.00	1-63	–	–
A.J.Strauss (E/M)	LM	1	0	5	0				
S.D.Stubbings (De)	OB	6	0	42	0				
A.V.Suppiah (Sm)	SLA	46	5	165	2	82.50	2-54	–	–
G.P.Swann (Nt/EL)	OB	360.5	73	959	32	29.96	4-25	–	–
Syed Rasel (BA)	LFM	24	4	96	1	96.00	1-96	–	–
N.Tahir (Wa)	RFM	175.5	39	561	8	70.12	3-49	–	–
Tamim Iqbal (BA)	OB	14	0	52	0				
C.G.Taylor (Gs)	OB	48	3	175	2	87.50	1-14	–	–
F.D.Telo (De)	RM	5	0	36	1	36.00	1-36	–	–
R.N.ten Doeschate (Ex)	RMF	281	43	992	43	23.06	6-57	2	–
A.C.Thomas (Sm)	RFM	253.2	52	817	30	27.23	5-46	2	–
G.J.Thompson (DU)	LB	4	2	30	1	30.00	1-30	–	–
M.A.Thornely (Sx)	RM	4	0	25	0				
C.D.Thorp (Du)	RMF	321.2	76	981	50	19.62	7-88	3	–
J.A.Tomlinson (H)	LFM	464.2	90	1659	67	24.76	8-46	4	1
J.C.Tredwell (K/MCC)	OB	396.2	65	1327	27	49.14	3-19	–	–
P.D.Trego (Sm)	RMF	193.2	44	694	28	24.78	4-52	–	–
C.T.Tremlett (H/EL)	RMF	383.2	94	1071	31	34.54	5-67	1	–
I.J.L.Trott (Wa)	RM	152.5	42	463	10	46.30	3-44	–	–
J.O.Troughton (Wa)	SLA	6	1	25	0				
A.J.Tudor (Ex/Sy)	RFM	201	38	736	14	52.57	3-46	–	–
M.L.Turner (Sm)	RMF	41	7	178	3	59.33	3-53	–	–
S.D.Udal (M)	OB	368.2	73	1122	34	33.00	5-36	1	–
J.J.van der Wath (Nh)	RFM	274.4	62	869	43	20.20	7-60	3	1
M.van Jaarsveld (K)	OB	77	12	220	11	20.00	5-33	1	–
M.P.Vaughan (E/Y)	OB	6	0	47	0				
D.L.Vettori (NZ)	SLA	128.2	24	346	13	26.61	5-66	1	–
A.C.Voges (Nt)	SLA	15	4	37	3	12.33	3-21	–	–
G.G.Wagg (De)	LM	456	89	1590	59	26.94	6-56	2	1
M.A.Wagh (Nt)	OB	9	4	11	0				
D.J.Wainwright (Y)	SLA	85.1	18	246	8	30.75	3- 9	–	–
A.G.Wakely (Nh)	OB	1	0	4	0				
M.J.Walker (K)	RM	9	1	40	1	40.00	1-34	–	–
S.J.Walters (Sy)	RM	15	2	52	0				
H.T.Waters (Gm)	RMF	9	4	26	1	26.00	1- 9	–	–
R.E.Watkins (Gm)	RM	121.2	20	469	7	67.00	3-76	–	–
M.H.Wessels (Nh)	(WK)	2	0	13	0				
T.Westley (Ex)	OB	15	1	58	1	58.00	1-19	–	–
I.J.Westwood (Wa)	OB	2	0	2	0				
A.G.Wharf (Gm)	RMF	192.2	17	896	21	42.66	3-10	–	–
C.D.Whelan (Wo)	RMF	80.5	10	401	10	40.10	4-66	–	–
G.G.White (Nh)	SLA	19	4	63	0				

F-C	Cat	O	M	R	W	Avge	Best	5wI	10wM
W.A.White (De)	RMF	98	13	374	8	46.75	2- 33	–	–
R.A.Whiteley (De)	(WK)	11	1	38	0				
D.H.Wigley (Gs/Nh)	RFM	208	38	844	24	35.16	5- 78	1	–
R.E.M.Williams (DU)	RMF	13	4	39	4	9.75	4- 39	–	–
C.M.Willoughby (Sm)	LMF	511	137	1399	54	25.90	4- 65	–	–
P.J.Wiseman (Du)	OB	197	43	614	17	36.11	4- 87	–	–
C.R.Woakes (Wa)	RM	308	84	922	45	20.48	6- 68	3	1
M.J.Wood (Gm)	OB	1	1	0	0				
A.Woodhouse (CU)	RM	6.2	0	53	0				
R.J.Woodman (Gs)	LMF	11.3	0	65	4	16.25	4- 65	–	–
C.J.C.Wright (Ex)	RM	239.5	56	792	29	27.31	6- 22	1	–
L.J.Wright (Sx/EL)	RM	190.3	32	740	12	61.66	2- 46	–	–
M.H.Yardy (Sx)	LM/SLA	112.4	10	367	2	183.50	1- 32	–	–
Yasir Arafat (K)	RM	317.4	62	1105	38	29.07	6- 86	1	–
P.J.W.Young (OU)	RM	34	6	120	2	60.00	1- 26	–	–
M.Zondeki (Wa/SA)	RF	110.2	23	416	10	41.60	4-125	–	–

SCORING OF EXTRAS 2009

The variable penalties involved in scoring no-balls and wides in our international and county cricket remain unchanged from last season:

COMPETITION	NO-BALL PENALTY	WIDE PENALTY
npower Test Matches NatWest Series L-O Internationals }	1 + other runs scored	1 + other runs scored
LV County Championship Second XI Championship }	2 + other runs scored	1 + other runs scored
Tourist Matches (First-Class) Tourist Matches (Limited-Overs) }	1 + other runs scored	1 + other runs scored
NatWest International Twenty20	1 + other runs scored + a free hit for a foot fault	1 + other runs scored
Friends Provident Trophy (50 overs) NatWest Pro 40 League (40 overs) Twenty20 Cup (20 overs) Second XI Trophy }	2 + other runs scored + a free hit for a foot fault	1 + other runs scored

COUNTY CHAMPIONSHIP 2008
LV FINAL TABLES

DIVISION 1

	P	W	L	D	A	Bonus Points Bat	Bonus Points Bowl	Deduct Points	Total Points
1 **DURHAM** (2)	16	6	3	6	1	37	41	–	190
2 Nottinghamshire (-)	16	5	3	7	1	37	43	–	182
3 Hampshire (5)	16	5	4	7	–	33	47	–	178
4 Somerset (-)	16	3	2	11	–	44	44	–	174
5 Lancashire (3)	16	5	2	8	1	24	40	–	170
6 Sussex (1)	16	2	2	12	–	45	38	–	159
7 Yorkshire (6)	16	2	5	9	–	50	45	–	159
8 Kent (7)	16	4	6	6	–	30	44	–	154
9 Surrey (4)	16	–	5	10	1	45	36	1	124

DIVISION 2

	P	W	L	D	A	Bonus Points Bat	Bonus Points Bowl	Deduct Points	Total Points
1 **WARWICKSHIRE** (-)	16	5	–	11	–	53	46	–	213
2 Worcestershire (-)	16	6	2	7	1	40	45	5	196
3 Middlesex (3)	16	4	5	7	–	46	45	–	175
4 Northamptonshire (5)	16	3	3	10	–	52	35	–	169
5 Essex (4)	16	5	6	5	–	36	45	3	168
6 Derbyshire (6)	16	4	3	9	–	33	46	4	167
7 Leicestershire (8)	16	3	4	9	–	29	43	–	150
8 Glamorgan (9)	16	3	5	7	1	26	36	–	136
9 Gloucestershire (7)	16	–	5	11	–	42	38	2	122

SCORING OF CHAMPIONSHIP POINTS 2008

(a) For a win, 14 points, plus any points scored in the first innings.

(b) In a tie, each side to score seven points, plus any points scored in the first innings.

(c) In a drawn match, each side to score four points, plus any points scored in the first innings (see also paragraph (f) below).

(d) If the scores are equal in a drawn match, the side batting in the fourth innings to score seven points plus any points scored in the first innings, and the opposing side to score four points plus any points scored in the first innings.

(e) First Innings Points (awarded only for performances **in the first 130 overs** of each first innings and retained whatever the result of the match).
  • A maximum of five batting points to be available as under:-
    200 to 249 runs – 1 point; 250 to 299 runs – 2 points; 300 to 349 runs – 3 points; 350 to 399 runs – 4 points; 400 runs or over – 5 points.
  • A maximum of three bowling points to be available as under:-
    3 to 5 wickets taken – 1 point; 6 to 8 wickets taken – 2 points; 9 to 10 wickets taken – 3 points.

(f) If play starts when fewer than eight hours' playing time remains (in which event a one innings match shall be played as provided for in First-Class Playing Condition 18), no first innings points shall be scored. The side winning on the one innings to score 14 points. In a tie, each side to score seven points. In a drawn match, each side to score four points. If the scores are equal in a drawn match, the side batting in the second innings to score seven points and the opposing side to score four points.

(g) If a match is abandoned without a ball being bowled, each side to score four points.

(h) The side which has the highest aggregate of points gained at the end of the season shall be the Champion County of their respective Division. Should any sides in the Championship table be equal on points, the following tie-breakers will be applied in the order stated: most wins, fewest losses, team achieving most points in contests between teams level on points, most wickets taken, most runs scored. At the end of the season, the top two teams from the Second Division will be promoted and the bottom two teams from the First Division will be relegated.

COUNTY CHAMPIONS

The English County Championship was not officially constituted until December 1889. Prior to that date there was no generally accepted method of awarding the title; although the 'least matches lost' method existed, it was not consistently applied. Rules governing playing qualifications were agreed in 1873 and the first unofficial points system 15 years later.

Research has produced a list of champions dating back to 1826, but at least seven different versions exist for the period from 1864 to 1889 (see *The Wisden Book of Cricket Records*). Only from 1890 can any authorised list of county champions commence.

That first official Championship was contested between eight counties: Gloucestershire, Kent, Lancashire, Middlesex, Nottinghamshire, Surrey, Sussex and Yorkshire. The remaining counties were admitted in the following seasons: 1891 – Somerset, 1895 – Derbyshire, Essex, Hampshire, Leicestershire and Warwickshire, 1899 – Worcestershire, 1905 – Northamptonshire, 1921 – Glamorgan, and 1992 – Durham.

The Championship pennant was introduced by the 1951 champions, Warwickshire, and the Lord's Taverners' Trophy was first presented in 1973. The first sponsors, Schweppes (1977 to 1983), were succeeded by Britannic Assurance (1984 to 1998), PPP Healthcare (1999-2000), CricInfo (2001), Frizzell (2002 to 2005) and Liverpool Victoria (2006 to 2008). Based on their previous season's positions, the 18 counties were separated into two divisions in 2000. From 2000 to 2005 the bottom three Division 1 teams were relegated and the top three Division 2 sides promoted. This was reduced to two teams from the end of the 2006 season.

1890	Surrey
1891	Surrey
1892	Surrey
1893	Yorkshire
1894	Surrey
1895	Surrey
1896	Yorkshire
1897	Lancashire
1898	Yorkshire
1899	Surrey
1900	Yorkshire
1901	Yorkshire
1902	Yorkshire
1903	Middlesex
1904	Lancashire
1905	Yorkshire
1906	Kent
1907	Nottinghamshire
1908	Yorkshire
1909	Kent
1910	Kent
1911	Warwickshire
1912	Yorkshire
1913	Kent
1914	Surrey
1919	Yorkshire
1920	Middlesex
1921	Middlesex
1922	Yorkshire
1923	Yorkshire
1924	Yorkshire
1925	Yorkshire
1926	Lancashire
1927	Lancashire
1928	Lancashire
1929	Nottinghamshire
1930	Lancashire
1931	Yorkshire

1932	Yorkshire
1933	Yorkshire
1934	Lancashire
1935	Yorkshire
1936	Derbyshire
1937	Yorkshire
1938	Yorkshire
1939	Yorkshire
1946	Yorkshire
1947	Middlesex
1948	Glamorgan
1949	Middlesex / Yorkshire
1950	Lancashire / Surrey
1951	Warwickshire
1952	Surrey
1953	Surrey
1954	Surrey
1955	Surrey
1956	Surrey
1957	Surrey
1958	Surrey
1959	Yorkshire
1960	Yorkshire
1961	Hampshire
1962	Yorkshire
1963	Yorkshire
1964	Worcestershire
1965	Worcestershire
1966	Yorkshire
1967	Yorkshire
1968	Yorkshire
1969	Glamorgan
1970	Kent
1971	Surrey
1972	Warwickshire
1973	Hampshire

1974	Worcestershire
1975	Leicestershire
1976	Middlesex
1977	Kent / Middlesex
1978	Kent
1979	Essex
1980	Middlesex
1981	Nottinghamshire
1982	Middlesex
1983	Essex
1984	Essex
1985	Middlesex
1986	Essex
1987	Nottinghamshire
1988	Worcestershire
1989	Worcestershire
1990	Middlesex
1991	Essex
1992	Essex
1993	Middlesex
1994	Warwickshire
1995	Warwickshire
1996	Leicestershire
1997	Glamorgan
1998	Leicestershire
1999	Surrey
2000	Surrey
2001	Yorkshire
2002	Surrey
2003	Sussex
2004	Warwickshire
2005	Nottinghamshire
2006	Sussex
2007	Sussex
2008	Durham

COUNTY CHAMPIONSHIP RESULTS 2008

DIVISION 1

	DURHAM	HANTS	KENT	LANCS	NOTTS	SOM'T	SURREY	SUSSEX	YORKS
DURHAM	–	C-le-St H 4	C-le-St Du 43	C-le-St Drawn	C-le-St Aban'd	C-le-St Drawn	C-le-St Drawn	C-le-St Drawn	C-le-St Du 295
HANTS	Basing H 2w	–	So'ton Drawn	So'ton La 6w	So'ton Nt 6w	So'ton Drawn	So'ton Drawn	So'ton Drawn	So'ton H 10w
KENT	Cant Du 1/71	Cant Drawn	–	Cant K 211	Cant Nt 10w	Tun W Sm 20	Cant Drawn	Cant Drawn	Cant K 3w
LANCS	Man La 232	Man Drawn	L'pool La 70	–	Man Drawn	Man Drawn	B'pool Aban'd	Man Drawn	Man Drawn
NOTTS	N'ham Drawn	N'ham H 203	N'ham K 3w	N'ham Nt 7w	–	N'ham Drawn	N'ham Drawn	N'ham Sx 73	N'ham Nt 112
SOM'T	Taunton Drawn	Taunton Drawn	Taunton Sm 246	Taunton La 8w	Taunton Drawn	–	Taunton Drawn	Taunton Drawn	Taunton Y 40
SURREY	Guildford Du 10w	Oval H 1/122	Oval K 4w	Oval Drawn	Oval Nt 1/143	Croydon Sm 8w	–	Oval Drawn	Oval Drawn
SUSSEX	Hove Du 7w	Arundel Sx 10w	Hove Drawn	Hove La 8w	Hove Drawn	Horsham Drawn	Hove Drawn	–	Hove Drawn
YORKS	Leeds Du 8w	Leeds Y 1/27	Scar Drawn	Leeds Drawn	Leeds Drawn	Scar Drawn	Leeds Drawn	Scar Drawn	–

DIVISION 2

	DERBYS	ESSEX	GLAM	GLOS	LEICS	MIDDX	N'HANTS	WARWKS	WORCS
DERBYS	–	Derby De 4w	Derby Drawn	Derby De 117	Derby Drawn	Derby De 7w	Ch'field Drawn	Derby Drawn	Ch'field De 1/95
ESSEX	Chelms Ex 145	–	Southend Gm 202	Chelms Ex 8w	Chelms Drawn	Chelms Ex 2w	Chelms Drawn	Chelms Wa 6w	Colchester Wo 6w
GLAM	Cardiff Drawn	Cardiff Drawn	–	Cardiff Drawn	Cardiff Gm 10w	Colwyn B Drawn	Swansea Nh 1/99	Cardiff Wa 5w	Cardiff Aban'd
GLOS	Bristol Drawn	Bristol Drawn	Bristol Gm 114	–	Chelt'm Drawn	Bristol Drawn	Bristol Drawn	Glos Drawn	Chelt'm Wo 1/142
LEICS	Leics Le 8w	Leics Ex 1/74	Leics Le 1/16	Leics Drawn	–	Leics Le 6w	Leics Drawn	Leics Drawn	Leics Wo 10w
MIDDX	Lord's M 6w	Lord's M 1/38	Lord's Drawn	Lord's Drawn	Lord's Drawn	–	Uxbridge Drawn	Uxbridge Wa 1/56	Lord's Wo 10w
N'HANTS	No'ton Drawn	No'ton Drawn	No'ton Drawn	No'ton Nh 6w	No'ton Nh 8w	No'ton M 63	–	No'ton Wa 2w	No'ton Drawn
WARWKS	B'ham Drawn	B'ham Drawn	B'ham Wa 179	B'ham Drawn	B'ham Drawn	B'ham Drawn	B'ham Drawn	–	B'ham Drawn
WORCS	Worcs Drawn	Worcs Wo 75	Worcs Wo 10w	Worcs Drawn	Worcs Drawn	Kidd'ster M 8w	Worcs Drawn	Worcs Drawn	–

COUNTY CHAMPIONSHIP RESULTS 2009

KEEP YOUR OWN RECORD (see page 156)

DIVISION 1

	DURHAM	HANTS	LANCS	NOTTS	SOM'T	SUSSEX	WARWKS	WORCS	YORKS
DURHAM	–	C-le-St	C-le-St	C-le-St	C-le-St	C-le-St	C-le-St	C-le-St	C-le-St
HANTS	So'ton	–	So'ton	So'ton	So'ton	So'ton	So'ton	So'ton	B'stoke
LANCS	Man	L'pool	–	Man	Man	Man	Man	Man	Man
NOTTS	N'ham	N'ham	N'ham	–	N'ham	N'ham	N'ham	N'ham	N'ham
SOM'T	Taunton	Taunton	Taunton	Taunton	–	Taunton	Taunton	Taunton	Taunton
SUSSEX	Hove	Arundel	Hove	Horsham	Hove	–	Hove	Hove	Hove
WARWKS	B'ham	B'ham	B'ham	B'ham	B'ham	B'ham	–	B'ham	B'ham
WORCS	Worcs	Worcs	Worcs	Worcs	Worcs	Worcs	Worcs	–	Worcs
YORKS	Leeds	Leeds	Leeds	Scar	Leeds	Leeds	Scar	Leeds	–

DIVISION 2

	DERBYS	ESSEX	GLAM	GLOS	KENT	LEICS	MIDDX	N'HANTS	SURREY
DERBYS		Derby	Derby	Ch'field	Derby	Derby	Derby	Ch'field	Derby
ESSEX	Chelms	–	Chelms	Southend	Chelms	Chelms	Chelms	Chelms	Colchester
GLAM	Cardiff	Cardiff	–	Cardiff	Cardiff	Colwyn B	Swansea	Cardiff	Cardiff
GLOS	Chelt'm	Bristol	Bristol	–	Bristol	Bristol	Bristol	Chelt'm	Bristol
KENT	Cant	Tun W	Cant	Beckenham	–	Cant	Cant	Cant	Cant
LEICS	Leics	Leics	Leics	Leics	Leics	–	Leics	Leics	Leics
MIDDX	Uxbridge	Lord's	Lord's	Lord's	Uxbridge	Southgate	–	Lord's	Lord's
N'HANTS	No'ton	No'ton	No'ton	No'ton	No'ton	No'ton	No'ton	–	No'ton
SURREY	Croydon	Guildford	Oval	Oval	Oval	Oval	Oval	Oval	–

NATWEST LIMITED-OVERS INTERNATIONALS 2008

ENGLAND v NEW ZEALAND

TWENTY20 INTERNATIONAL

Old Trafford, Manchester, 13 June. Toss: England. **ENGLAND** won by nine wickets. New Zealand 123-9 (20). England 127-1 (17.3; I.R.Bell 60*, K.P.Pietersen 42*). Award: I.R.Bell.

LIMITED-OVERS INTERNATIONALS

Riverside, Chester-le-Street, 15 June. Toss: New Zealand. **ENGLAND** won by 114 runs. England 307-5 (50; K.P.Pietersen 110*, P.D.Collingwood 64). New Zealand 193 (42.5; P.D.Collingwood 4-15). Award: K.P.Pietersen.

Edgbaston, Birmingham, 18 June. Toss: New Zealand. **NO RESULT.** England 162 (24/24; L.J.Wright 52; G.D.Elliott 3-23). New Zealand (set 160 from 23 overs) 127-2 (19/23; B.B.McCullum 60*). No award.

County Ground, Bristol, 21 June. Toss: England. **NEW ZEALAND** won by 22 runs. New Zealand 182 (50; G.D.Elliott 56; J.M.Anderson 3-61). England 160 (46.2; T.G.Southee 4-38). Award: K.D.Mills (47, 2-42).

Kennington Oval, London, 25 June. Toss: New Zealand. **NEW ZEALAND** won by one wicket. England 245 (49.4; R.S.Bopara 58, O.A.Shah 63; T.G.Southee 3-47). New Zealand 246-9 (50; S.B.Styris 69). Award: S.B.Styris.

Lord's, London, 28 June. Toss: England. **NEW ZEALAND** won by 51 runs. New Zealand 266-5 (50; S.B.Styris 87*, J.D.P.Oram 52). England 215 (47.5; O.A.Shah 69; T.G.Southee 3-49, D.L.Vettori 3-32). Match award: S.B.Styris. Series award: T.G.Southee.

ENGLAND v SOUTH AFRICA

TWENTY20 INTERNATIONAL

Riverside, Chester-le-Street, 20 August. MATCH ABANDONED without a ball bowled. No toss.

LIMITED-OVERS INTERNATIONALS

Headingley, Leeds, 22 August (floodlit). Toss: England. **ENGLAND** won by 20 runs. England 275-4 (50; K.P.Pietersen 90*, A.Flintoff 78). South Africa 255 (49.4; J.H.Kallis 52). Award: K.P.Pietersen.

Trent Bridge, Nottingham, 26 August (floodlit). Toss: South Africa. **ENGLAND** won by ten wickets. South Africa 83 (23; S.C.J.Broad 5-23, A.Flintoff 3-29). England 85-0 (14.1). Award: S.C.J.Broad.

Kennington Oval, London, 29 August. Toss: South Africa. **ENGLAND** won by 126 runs. England 296-7 (50; I.R.Bell 73, A.Flintoff 78*). South Africa 170 (42.4; S.R.Patel 5-41). Award: S.R.Patel.

Lord's, London, 31 August. Toss: England. **ENGLAND** won by seven wickets (D/L Method). South Africa 183-6 (32.1/32.1; H.H.Gibbs 74; A.Flintoff 3-21). England (set 137 from 20 overs) 137-3 (17.4/20). Award: A.Flintoff.

Sophia Gardens, Cardiff, 3 September (floodlit). Toss: England. **NO RESULT.** South Africa 6-1 (3/43). No match award. Series award: A.Flintoff.

DUCKWORTH/LEWIS – A BRIEF EXPLANATION

The Duckworth/Lewis (D/L) method has been around now for 12 years and it is generally accepted as being a very fair method for resetting targets in interrupted one-day matches. However, ask a typical cricket fan as to how the calculations are done and the fallback excuse of not being good at maths at school is frequently trotted out. But if you can work out how much tax you have to pay on your net income then D/L calculations are well within your grasp.

You may well have heard that the D/L method is based on the idea of resources – these are the combination of wickets and overs that a team has for its innings. However, it's not just the numbers of these that matter; it is also their relative value – wickets and overs have different relative importance as an innings progresses. For example, having lots of wickets in hand without overs left in which to use them is of little value, just as if lots of overs remain they have little value if there are no wickets left with which to use them. In conducting their innings, teams need to manage these twin resources in order to maximise the total they set or maximise their chances of winning the match. Through some neat behind-the-scenes mathematics and statistical analysis of hundreds of matches, Duckworth and Lewis have produced a table that represents the average percentages remaining of their twin resources of a 50-over innings. In the extract of the table supplied you will see that teams start with all 50 overs and 10 wickets – and therefore 100% of their resources. As an innings progresses a team receives its overs, loses its wickets and thereby consumes its resources. The table works always in overs left – in that way it can be used for matches that are shorter than 50 overs – and tells us what percentage of their combined resources remains.

Wickets lost:	0	2	4	6	9
Overs remaining:-					
50	100.0	85.1	62.7	34.9	4.7
40	89.3	77.8	59.5	34.6	4.7
30	75.1	67.3	54.1	33.6	4.7
25	66.5	60.5	50.0	32.6	4.7
20	56.6	52.4	44.6	30.8	4.7
10	32.1	30.8	28.3	22.8	4.7
5	17.2	16.8	16.1	14.3	4.6

Suppose that a team has batted for 45 overs and has lost 6 wickets. With 5 overs left, for 6 wickets lost the table shows it has 14.3% of its resources remaining. If its innings is now terminated, these resources are lost and it had available for its innings 100 – 14.3 = 85.7% resources compared with the 100% for a complete 50-over innings.

These figures came into play in a crucial Group match of the 2003 World Cup in South Africa. Against the host nation, Sri Lanka scored 268 in their 100% resources of 50 overs. Rain began to fall and abandonment looked likely at the end of the 45th over of South Africa's innings. Charts of the D/L method were consulted and the relevant figure was obtained through the comparative resources of the two teams. The calculation was 268 × 85.7/100 = 229.676. This meant that in order to win SA needed to reach 230 by the end of the 45th over if the match were abandoned. A score of 229 would be the score to tie.

How would South Africa know this? You will have seen the D/L par-score displayed on scoreboards. These numbers come from the par-score sheet that is distributed during the interval to team camps, match officials and the media. The par-score is given for the end of every one of the combinations of overs left and wickets lost (and even on a ball-by-ball basis). This sheet is clearly labelled as the score to tie. In the World Cup match the SA camp told the batsmen, Boucher and Klusener, that they needed to get to 229 by the end of the over. Thanks to a six from Boucher off the penultimate ball of the over, they achieved this – and to avoid losing his wicket, which would have raised the par-score, Boucher blocked the last ball. Play was duly abandoned at the end of the over but the dismay in the SA camp was palpable when it was finally realised that the 229 the batsmen had been told to score was in fact the score to tie and not to win the match. So a tie it was and the misreading of the clear information available led to the elimination of the host nation from the tournament.

Whenever a stoppage occurs within an innings, the table provides the information by which to calculate the resources lost. Suppose that there are 20 overs left with only 4 wickets down and a stoppage reduces the innings by 10 overs so there are now only 10 overs left on the resumption. You will see from the table that the team went off with 44.6% resources left and came back with 28.3% left. The stoppage would have cost 44.6 – 28.3 = 16.3% of its resources so that it would have available 100 – 16.3 = 83.7% resources for its innings if there are no more stoppages (but if there are, the resources available are further reduced in the same way) and, in most cases, the target comes from reducing the first innings score in proportion to the resources available as in the World Cup example.

Sometimes teams start with fewer than 50 overs either due to a shorter match competition, such as the Pro40 or Twenty20, or due to a delayed start. For a 25-over innings, for instance, teams start with 66.5% resources compared with a 50-over innings. Although they have half the overs they still have all 10 wickets and therefore more than half their resources – the table says about two-thirds compared with a 50-over innings. Any loss of overs would reduce this further in the same way and using the same figures as in the table.

So you see that it really is simple to calculate targets following interruptions during the second innings. The method is simply to adjust the first innings score in proportion to the resources available to the two teams – rounding up to win and one fewer to tie.

A distinctive feature of the D/L method compared with previous methods of adjusting targets is that it compensates the team batting first for stoppages within its innings – its batting strategy has been based on the full 50 overs and so to have it curtailed is usually a disadvantage. The D/L method usually sets an enhanced target, that is, a target which is quite a few runs more than the team batting first scored. This has the effect of compensating it for the unexpected shortening of the first innings and the advantage that the team batting second has from knowing in advance of its shorter innings.

How this is achieved, together with further detailed descriptions of the Duckworth/Lewis method and some frequently asked questions, can be found at the Cricinfo website: www.cricinfo.com/db/ABOUT_CRICKET/RAIN_RULES/ and a booklet is available from Acumen Books at www.acumenbooks.co.uk/ducklew.htm.

One of these FAQs concerns the effect that powerplays have on D/L calculations. Data on powerplays are not yet sufficient to do a thorough analysis, but the logic is similar to the old 15-over rule on which there are plenty of data. These show that the greater runs scored in these overs are consistent with what is expected from the D/L method for the overs and the *wickets* used up in those periods of more attacking fields. Consequently it is unlikely that the powerplays have any significant effect on D/L target calculations. But the situation will be kept under review.

Although rain is usually the cause of stoppages and D/L adjusted targets, interruptions have occurred for several other causes including sandstorms, snow, floodlight failures, crowd disturbances and, on a few occasions, due to the sun!

Cases at the higher levels of the game usually run to 80-100 per year and the total usage is approaching 1000 since the method's first use on 1st January 1997 in which England lost to Zimbabwe when they would have won by the old, unfair average run-rate method.

There have been some advances in the methodology since January 1997. With higher totals being more prevalent, and the introduction of Twenty20 matches which fit well into the D/L system, teams need to score a bigger percentage of their runs in the earlier stages of their innings than those suggested by the standard tables. Consequently, higher scores lead to the need for the table to be adjusted and this needs the computer to do the calculations. Whereas what is now known as the Standard Edition, using a single table of resources as described here, is used at lower levels of the game where computers aren't necessary or available, the higher levels of the game now use the more advanced computerised version called the Professional Edition. In this edition, the computer in effect produces a different table of resources for every match, but thereafter the calculations are the same as described here.

FRIENDS PROVIDENT TROPHY 2008

After following virtually the same knock-out format since its inauguration as the Gillette Cup in 1963, this competition was drastically revamped for the 2006 season. The Minor Counties were omitted and the 18 first-class counties, joined by Ireland and Scotland, were divided into two leagues or conferences. The winner of each league contested the final at Lord's. A semi-final stage was added for the 2007 competition when Friends Provident took over the sponsorship. Quarter-finals were restored in 2008 when the 20 teams were divided into four divisions.

MIDLANDS

		P	W	L	NR	A	Pts	Net RR
1	LEICESTERSHIRE	8	5	2	–	1	11	0.69
2	NOTTINGHAMSHIRE	8	4	2	–	2	10	0.01
3	Northamptonshire	8	4	2	–	2	10	0.56
4	Warwickshire	8	2	4	–	2	6	–0.14
5	Ireland	8	1	6	–	1	3	–0.86

NORTH

		P	W	L	NR	A	Pts	Net RR
1	DURHAM	8	5	3	–	–	10	0.43
2	YORKSHIRE	8	4	2	2	–	10	0.54
3	Derbyshire	8	3	2	1	2	9	–0.14
4	Lancashire	8	3	3	1	1	8	0.24
5	Scotland	8	1	6	–	1	3	–1.09

SOUTH/EAST

		P	W	L	NR	A	Pts	Net RR
1	KENT	8	5	2	–	1	11	0.67
2	ESSEX	8	4	3	–	1	9	–0.03
3	Middlesex	8	3	3	–	2	8	0.06
4	Surrey	8	3	4	1	1	7	–0.62
5	Sussex	8	1	4	1	2	5	–0.53

SOUTH/WEST

		P	W	L	NR	A	Pts	Net RR
1	GLOUCESTERSHIRE	8	4	1	1	2	11	0.70
2	SOMERSET	8	3	2	1	2	9	0.30
3	Worcestershire	8	3	3	1	1	8	–0.12
4	Hampshire	8	3	4	–	1	7	–0.43
5	Glamorgan	8	1	4	1	2	5	–0.21

Points: Win 2; Lost 0; No Result (play started) 1; Abandoned (no play) 1.

QUARTER-FINALS

At Riverside, Chester-le-Street, on 4 June. Toss: Nottinghamshire. DURHAM beat Nottinghamshire by one wicket. Nottinghamshire 188 (47.2; S.R.Patel 114). Durham 189-9 (49; M.J.Di Venuto 70; S.R.Patel 3-27). Award: S.R.Patel.

At County Ground, Bristol, on 4 June. Toss: Yorkshire. YORKSHIRE beat Gloucestershire by six wickets. Gloucestershire 201 (45.2; C.G.Taylor 54; S.J.Adshead 71; T.T.Bresnan 4-31, M.J.Hoggard 3-26). Yorkshire 205-4 (44.1; C.White 55, J.A.Rudolph 53*). Award: T.T.Bresnan.

At County Ground, Beckenham on 4 (*no play*), 5 June. Toss: Kent. KENT beat Somerset by 37 runs. Kent 259-5 (50 overs; R.W.T.Key 73, N.J.Dexter 101*). Somerset 222 (45.5 overs; C.Kieswetter 90; Yasir Arafat 3-23). Award: N.J.Dexter.

At Grace Road, Leicester, on 4 June. Toss: Essex. ESSEX beat Leicestershire by 118 runs. Essex 350-5 (50; R.S.Bopara 201*, J.S.Foster 61). Leicestershire 232 (41; M.A.G.Boyce 57, P.A.Nixon 62). Award: R.S.Bopara.

SEMI-FINALS

At Riverside, Chester-le-Street, on 4 July. Toss: Durham. KENT beat Durham by 83 runs. Kent 301-4 (50; J.L.Denly 102, M.van Jaarsveld 122*; S.J.Harmison 4-47). Durham 218 (43.1; W.R.Smith 56, D.M.Benkenstein 80*; J.C.Tredwell 3-37). Award: M.van Jaarsveld.

At County Ground, Chelmsford, on 5 July. Toss: Essex. ESSEX beat Yorkshire by 87 runs. Essex 285-8 (50; A.N.Cook 95, G.R.Napier 61 – 34 balls, 6 sixes). Yorkshire 198 (42.5; A.W.Gale 64, A.McGrath 53; Danish Kaneria 3-32, R.N.ten Doeschate 3-30); Award: G.R.Napier.

WHAT IS A KOLPAK REGISTRATION?

The Kolpak ruling was made by the European Court of Justice on 8 May 2003 in favour of Maros Kolpak, a Slovak handball player. The Court's decision was based upon the dictum that no resident of the European Union should be prevented from working in another part of the EU.

Specifically the case meant that, in professional sports, if a sporting club chose a player who resided in the EU, then there could be no law preventing this. For example, a German basketball team could not be prevented from hiring a Greek player since both nations are members of the EU. Moreover, since Kolpak was not from the EU at the time the case was decided, but from a country that had an associate trading relationship, the decision meant that any player from any nation which had such a relationship with the EU, provided that they held a valid UK work permit, must be treated for the purposes of employment as if they were a citizen of an EU country.

Counties could already employ any number of EU residents under the Bosman ruling. However, there are no other strong cricketing countries within the EU, and so Kolpak, not Bosman, has had the significant impact on county cricket. The largest group of countries with an associate agreement with the EU is the ACP countries, which include South Africa, Zimbabwe, and many of the islands which supply the West Indies cricket team.

There is no residential requirement. The ECB had originally stated that a player must not have represented their own country for over twelve months in order to qualify for Kolpak status but after Jacques Rudolph signed for Yorkshire, they admitted that they were powerless to enforce this rule.

In an effort to combat the influx of Kolpak players, the ECB has linked the central payments made to counties, to the amount of English qualified players who represent the county.

Kolpak players are not qualified for England; the main requirement for that qualification is that the player must be a British or an Irish citizen and, if born outside England or Wales, he must complete a four-year residence period.

2008 FRIENDS PROVIDENT TROPHY FINAL

ESSEX v KENT

At Lord's, London on 16 August.
Result: **ESSEX** won by five wickets.
Toss: Kent. Award: G.W.Flower.

KENT		Runs	Balls	4/6	Fall
J.L.Denly	b Napier	11	19	2	2- 19
* R.W.T.Key	c Foster b Masters	7	13	1	1- 15
M.van Jaarsveld	c Cook b Wright	58	75	4	7-138
J.M.Kemp	b Masters	16	31	2	3- 58
D.I.Stevens	c Foster b Wright	0	6	–	4- 59
† G.O.Jones	lbw b Kaneria	19	39	3	5- 94
Azhar Mahmood	c Flower b Kaneria	2	8	–	6-100
R.McLaren	b Bopara	63	71	4	10-214
Yasir Arafat	b Bopara	27	34	2	8-204
J.C.Tredwell	run out (Cook)	0	–	–	9-209
R.H.Joseph	not out	2	5	–	
Extras	(LB 7, NB 2)	9			
Total	(50 overs; 197 minutes)	**214**			

HAMPSHIRE		Runs	Balls	4/6	Fall
* M.L.Pettini	lbw b Mahmood	10	18	1	1- 32
J.E.R.Gallian	b Mahmood	28	45	3	2- 60
A.N.Cook	c Stevens b Joseph	33	51	4	4- 93
R.S.Bopara	lbw b Joseph	7	20	–	3- 88
G.W.Flower	not out	70	97	6	
† J.S.Foster	c Jones b Joseph	18	35	1	5-161
R.N.ten Doeschate	not out	30	29	2	
G.R.Napier					
C.J.C.Wright					
D.D.Masters					
Danish Kaneria					
Extras	(LB 7, W 11, NB 4)	22			
Total	(48.5 overs; 5 wickets; 205 minutes)	**218**			

ESSEX	O	M	R	W	KENT	O	M	R	W
Masters	10	2	34	2	Azhar Mahmood	9.5	0	53	2
Napier	8	1	23	1	Yasir Arafat	9	1	40	0
Wright	8	0	36	2	Joseph	10	1	40	3
Bopara	8	0	46	2	McLaren	10	0	34	0
Danish Kaneria	10	0	42	2	Stevens	8	0	35	0
Ten Doeschate	6	0	26	0	Tredwell	2	0	9	0

Umpires: N.J.Llong and G.Sharp.

FRIENDS PROVIDENT TROPHY

PRINCIPAL RECORDS 1963-2008
(Including Gillette Cup, NatWest Trophy and C&G Trophy Matches)

Highest Total	496-4		Surrey v Glos	The Oval	2007
Highest Total in a Final	322-5		Warwicks v Sussex	Lord's	1993
Highest Total Batting Second	429		Glamorgan v Surrey	The Oval	2002
Highest Total to Win Batting Second	359-8		Hampshire v Surrey	The Oval	2005
Lowest Total	39		Ireland v Sussex	Hove	1985
Lowest Total in a Final	57		Essex v Lancashire	Lord's	1996
Lowest Total to Win Batting First	98		Worcs v Durham	Chester-le-St	1968

Highest Score	268	A.D.Brown	Surrey v Glamorgan	The Oval	2002
Fastest Hundred	36 balls	G.D.Rose	Somerset v Devon	Torquay	1990
Most Hundreds	8	R.A.Smith	Hampshire		1985-03
	8	N.V.Knight	Essex/Warwickshire		1992-06
	8	G.A.Hick	Worcestershire		1986-08
Most Runs	3040	(av 51.52)	G.A.Hick	Worcestershire	1986-08

Highest Partnership for each Wicket

1st	311	A.J.Wright/N.J.Trainor	Glos v Scotland	Bristol	1997
2nd	286	I.S.Anderson/A.Hill	Derbys v Cornwall	Derby	1986
3rd	309*	T.S.Curtis/T.M.Moody	Worcs v Surrey	The Oval	1994
4th	234*	D.Lloyd/C.H.Lloyd	Lancashire v Glos	Manchester	1978
5th	202*	I.J.L.Trott/T.R.Ambrose	Warwicks v Northants	Birmingham	2007
6th	226	N.J.Llong/M.V.Fleming	Kent v Cheshire	Bowdon	1999
7th	170	D.R.Brown/A.F.Giles	Warwicks v Essex	Birmingham	2003
8th	174	R.W.T.Key/J.C.Tredwell	Kent v Surrey	The Oval	2007
9th	155	C.M.W.Read/A.J.Harris	Notts v Durham	Nottingham	2006
10th	81	S.Turner/R.E.East	Essex v Yorkshire	Leeds	1982

Best Bowling	8-21	M.A.Holding	Derbys v Sussex	Hove	1988
Most Wickets	88	(av 14.35)	A.A.Donald	Warwks/Worcs	1987-02

Most Wicket-Keeping Dismissals in an Innings

8 (8ct)		D.J.Pipe	Worcs v Herts	Hertford	2001

Most Match Wins: 104 – Lancashire.　　　　**Most Cup/Trophy Wins:** 7 – Lancashire.

GILLETTE CUP WINNERS

1963	Sussex	1970	Lancashire	1977	Middlesex
1964	Sussex	1971	Lancashire	1978	Sussex
1965	Yorkshire	1972	Lancashire	1979	Somerset
1966	Warwickshire	1973	Gloucestershire	1980	Middlesex
1967	Kent	1974	Kent		
1968	Warwickshire	1975	Lancashire		
1969	Yorkshire	1976	Northamptonshire		

NATWEST TROPHY WINNERS

1981	Derbyshire	1988	Middlesex	1995	Warwickshire
1982	Surrey	1989	Warwickshire	1996	Lancashire
1983	Somerset	1990	Lancashire	1997	Essex
1984	Middlesex	1991	Hampshire	1998	Lancashire
1985	Essex	1992	Northamptonshire	1999	Gloucestershire
1986	Sussex	1993	Warwickshire	2000	Gloucestershire
1987	Nottinghamshire	1994	Worcestershire		

CHELTENHAM & GLOUCESTER TROPHY WINNERS

2001	Somerset	2003	Gloucestershire	2005	Hampshire
2002	Yorkshire	2004	Gloucestershire	2006	Sussex

FRIENDS PROVIDENT TROPHY WINNERS

2007	Durham	2008	Essex

NATWEST PRO40 LEAGUE 2008

This competition, scheduled to be scrapped after the 2009 season, was drastically revamped in 2006, with each county playing its divisional opponents once instead of twice and with Scotland omitted. The bottom two First Division teams were relegated and replaced by the top two from the Second Division. A play-off for a First Division place was introduced between the team finishing third in the Second Division (given a home tie) and the one finishing seventh in the First Division.

FIRST DIVISION	P	W	L	T	NR	Pts	Net RR
1 SUSSEX (5)	8	5	1	–	2	12	–0.10
2 Hampshire (4)	8	4	2	–	2	10	0.63
3 Durham (–)	8	4	3	–	1	9	0.36
4 Nottinghamshire (2)	8	4	4	–	–	8	0.25
5 Gloucestershire (6)	8	3	3	–	2	8	–0.46
6 Somerset (–)	8	3	4	1	–	7	–0.15
7 Worcestershire (1)	8	2	3	1	2	7	0.11
8 Lancashire (3)	8	1	3	–	4	6	–0.81
9 Middlesex (–)	8	2	5	–	1	5	–0.13

SECOND DIVISION	P	W	L	T	NR	Pts	Net RR
1 ESSEX (–)	8	6	–	1	1	14	1.47
2 Yorkshire (6)	8	5	1	1	1	12	0.25
3 Glamorgan (9)	8	5	3	–	–	10	0.11
4 Kent (5)	8	4	2	–	2	10	1.62
5 Surrey (4)	8	4	4	–	–	8	–0.44
6 Warwickshire (–)	8	3	3	–	2	8	–0.24
7 Leicestershire (7)	8	1	4	1	2	5	–0.46
8 Derbyshire (8)	8	1	6	1	–	3	–0.89
9 Northamptonshire (–)	8	–	6	–	2	2	–0.99

Horizontal rules segregate the counties relegated and promoted for the 2009 competition. 2007 final positions for that division are shown in brackets. Win = 2 points. Tie (T)/No Result (NR) = 1 point.

Positions of counties finishing equal on points are decided by most wins or, if equal, the side with higher net run-rate will take precedence (overall run-rate in all matches, i.e. total runs scored times 100 divided by balls received, minus the run-rate of its opponents in those same matches). If still equal, the team with the higher number of wickets taken per balls bowled in matches in which results were achieved will take precedence. If still equal, lots will be drawn.

PLAY-OFF MATCH

At Sophia Gardens, Cardiff, on 21 September. Toss: Worcestershire. WORCESTERSHIRE beat Glamorgan by 103 runs. Worcestershire 186-6 (40; V.S.Solanki 53, M.M.Ali 51). Glamorgan 83 (23.5; C.R.D.Fernando 3-21, A.J.Harris 3-7, G.J.Batty 4-14). Award: G.J.Batty.

HIGHEST BATTING AGGREGATE	– Div 1	556	(av 69.50)	M.E.Trescothick	Somerset
	– Div 2	349	(av 49.85)	J.A.Rudolph	Yorkshire
HIGHEST BOWLING AGGREGATE	– Div 1	14	(av 14.00)	G.P.Swann	Nottinghamshire
	– Div 2	24	(av 13.08)	J.W.Dernbach	Surrey

PRO40/NATIONAL/SUNDAY LEAGUE CHAMPIONS

1969	Lancashire	1983	Yorkshire	1997	Warwickshire
1970	Lancashire	1984	Essex	1998	Lancashire
1971	Worcestershire	1985	Essex	1999	Lancashire
1972	Kent	1986	Hampshire	2000	Gloucestershire
1973	Kent	1987	Worcestershire	2001	Kent
1974	Leicestershire	1988	Worcestershire	2002	Glamorgan
1975	Hampshire	1989	Lancashire	2003	Surrey
1976	Kent	1990	Derbyshire	2004	Glamorgan
1977	Leicestershire	1991	Nottinghamshire	2005	Essex
1978	Hampshire	1992	Middlesex	2006	Essex
1979	Somerset	1993	Glamorgan	2007	Worcestershire
1980	Warwickshire	1994	Warwickshire	2008	Sussex
1981	Essex	1995	Kent		
1982	Sussex	1996	Surrey		

PRINCIPAL PRO40 RECORDS 1969-2008

Highest Total		377-9	Somerset v Sussex	Hove	2003
Highest Total Batting Second		323-5	Sussex v Leics	Horsham	2004
Lowest Total		23	Middlesex v Yorks	Leeds	1974
Largest Victory (Runs)		220	Somerset v Glamorgan	Neath	1990
Highest Scores	203	A.D.Brown	Surrey v Hampshire	Guildford	1997
	191	D.S.Lehmann	Yorks v Notts	Scarborough	2001
	184	M.E.Trescothick	Somerset v Glos	Taunton	2008
	176	G.A.Gooch	Essex v Glamorgan	Southend	1983
	175*	I.T.Botham	Somerset v Northants	Wellingborough	1986
Fastest Hundred	44 balls	M.A.Ealham	Kent v Derbyshire	Maidstone	1995
Most Sixes (Inns)	13	I.T.Botham	Somerset v Northants	Wellingborough	1986
Highest Partnership for each Wicket					
1st	239	G.A.Gooch/B.R.Hardie	Essex v Notts	Nottingham	1985
2nd	302	M.E.Trescothick/C.Kieswetter	Somerset v Glos	Taunton	2008
3rd	228*	M.W.Goodwin/C.J.Adams	Sussex v Middlesex	Hove	2003
4th	219	C.G.Greenidge/C.L.Smith	Hampshire v Surrey	Southampton	1987
5th	221*	R.R.Sarwan/M.A.Hardinges	Glos v Lancashire	Manchester	2005
6th	167	C.L.Cairns/C.M.W.Read	Notts v Sussex	Nottingham	2003
7th	164	J.N.Snape/M.A.Hardinges	Glos v Notts	Nottingham	2001
8th	116*	N.D.Burns/P.A.J.DeFreitas	Leics v Northants	Leicester	2001
9th	105	D.G.Moir/R.W.Taylor	Derbyshire v Kent	Derby	1984
10th	82	G.Chapple/P.J.Martin	Lancashire v Worcs	Manchester	1996
Best Bowling	8-26	K.D.Boyce	Essex v Lancashire	Manchester	1971
	7-15	R.A.Hutton	Yorkshire v Worcs	Leeds	1969
	7-16	S.D.Thomas	Glamorgan v Surrey	Swansea	1998
	7-30	M.P.Bicknell	Surrey v Lancashire	The Oval	1999
	7-39	A.Hodgson	Northants v Somerset	Northampton	1976
	7-41	A.N.Jones	Sussex v Notts	Nottingham	1986
Four Wkts in Four Balls		A.Ward	Derbyshire v Sussex	Derby	1970
		V.C.Drakes	Notts v Derbys	Nottingham	1999
Most Economical Analysis					
8-8-0-0		B.A.Langford	Somerset v Essex	Yeovil	1969
Most Expensive Analysis					
9-0-99-1		M.R.Strong	Northants v Glos	Cheltenham	2001
Most Wicket-Keeping Dismissals in an Innings					
7 (6ct, 1st)		R.W.Taylor	Derbyshire v Lancs	Manchester	1975
Most Catches in an Innings by a Fielder					
5		J.M.Rice	Hampshire v Warwicks	Southampton	1978
5		D.J.G.Sales	Northants v Essex	Northampton	2007

BENSON AND HEDGES CUP

PRINCIPAL RECORDS 1972-2002

Highest Total		388-7	Essex v Scotland	Chelmsford	1992
Highest Total Batting Second		318-5	Lancashire v Leics	Manchester	1995
Lowest Total		50	Hampshire v Yorks	Leeds	1991
Largest Victory (Runs)		172	Essex v Scotland	Chelmsford	1992
Highest Score	198*	G.A.Gooch	Essex v Sussex	Hove	1982
Fastest Hundred	62 min	M.A.Nash	Glamorgan v Hants	Swansea	1976

Highest Partnership for each Wicket

1st	252	V.P.Terry/C.L.Smith	Hants v Combined U	Southampton	1990
2nd	285*	C.G.Greenidge/D.R.Turner	Hants v Minor C (S)	Amersham	1973
3rd	271	C.J.Adams/M.G.Bevan	Sussex v Essex	Chelmsford	2000
4th	207	R.C.Russell/A.J.Wright	Glos v British U	Bristol	1998
5th	160	A.J.Lamb/D.J.Capel	Northants v Leics	Northampton	1986
6th	167*	M.G.Bevan/R.J.Blakey	Yorkshire v Lancs	Manchester	1996
7th	149*	J.D.Love/C.M.Old	Yorks v Scotland	Bradford	1981
8th	112	D.C.Nash/A.A.Noffke	Middlesex v Sussex	Lord's	2002
9th	83	P.G.Newman/M.A.Holding	Derbyshire v Notts	Nottingham	1985
10th	80*	D.L.Bairstow/M.Johnson	Yorkshire v Derbys	Derby	1981

Best Bowling	7-12	W.W.Daniel	Middx v Minor C (E)	Ipswich	1978
	7-22	J.R.Thomson	Middx v Hampshire	Lord's	1981
	7-24	Mushtaq Ahmed	Somerset v Ireland	Taunton	1997
	7-32	R.G.D.Willis	Warwicks v Yorks	Birmingham	1981
Four Wickets in Four Balls		S.M.Pollock	Warwicks v Leics	Birmingham	1996

Most Wicket-Keeping Dismissals in an Innings

8 (8ct)		D.J.S.Taylor	Somerset v Combined U	Taunton	1982

Most Catches in an Innings

5		V.J.Marks	Combined U v Kent	Oxford	1976

BENSON AND HEDGES CUP WINNERS

1972	Leicestershire	1983	Middlesex	1994	Warwickshire
1973	Kent	1984	Lancashire	1995	Lancashire
1974	Surrey	1985	Leicestershire	1996	Lancashire
1975	Leicestershire	1986	Middlesex	1997	Surrey
1976	Kent	1987	Yorkshire	1998	Essex
1977	Gloucestershire	1988	Hampshire	1999	Gloucestershire
1978	Kent	1989	Nottinghamshire	2000	Gloucestershire
1979	Essex	1990	Lancashire	2001	Surrey
1980	Northamptonshire	1991	Worcestershire	2002	Warwickshire
1981	Somerset	1992	Hampshire		
1982	Somerset	1993	Derbyshire		

TWENTY20 CUP 2008

GROUP TABLES

MIDLANDS/WALES/WEST	P	W	L	T	NR	Pts	Net RR
1 WARWICKSHIRE (1)	10	6	1	1	2	15	0.69
2 NORTHAMPTONSHIRE (4)	10	6	3	–	1	13	0.43
3 GLAMORGAN (6)	10	3	3	–	4	10	–0.17
4 Somerset (5)	10	3	4	–	3	9	0.31
5 Worcestershire (3)	10	3	6	–	1	7	–0.48
6 Gloucestershire (2)	10	1	5	1	3	6	–0.93

NORTH	P	W	L	T	NR	Pts	Net RR
1 DURHAM (5)	10	6	1	1	2	15	0.98
2 LANCASHIRE (2)	10	6	3	–	1	13	0.92
3 *Yorkshire (3)	10	5	3	1	1	10	–0.31
4 Nottinghamshire (1)	10	4	5	–	1	9	0.10
5 Derbyshire (6)	10	3	7	–	–	6	–0.42
6 Leicestershire (4)	10	2	7	–	1	5	–0.08

SOUTH	P	W	L	T	NR	Pts	Net RR
1 MIDDLESEX (5)	10	8	2	–	–	16	0.73
2 ESSEX (4)	10	6	3	1	–	13	0.93
3 KENT (2)	10	6	4	–	–	12	0.64
4 Hampshire (6)	10	5	4	1	–	11	–0.50
5 Sussex (1)	10	2	8	–	–	4	–0.87
6 Surrey (3)	10	2	8	–	–	4	–0.90

QUARTER-FINALS: ESSEX beat Northamptonshire by 59 runs at Chelmsford.
MIDDLESEX beat Lancashire by 12 runs at the Oval.
KENT beat Warwickshire by 42 runs at Birmingham.
DURHAM beat Glamorgan by 44 runs at Chester-le-Street.
Yorkshire's quarter-final v Durham was cancelled pending investigations into them fielding an ineligible player. They were subsequently disqualified from the competition and replaced by Glamorgan in the quarter-finals.

SEMI-FINALS: KENT beat Essex by 14 runs at Southampton.
MIDDLESEX beat Durham by eight wickets at Southampton.

LEADING AGGREGATES 2008

BATTING (325 runs)		M	I	NO	HS	Runs	Avge	100	50	R/100b	Sixes
J.L.Denly	Kent	13	13	–	91	451	34.69	–	5	118.9	16
A.McGrath	Yorkshire	9	9	2	72*	392	56.00	–	4	132.4	11
M.W.Goodwin	Sussex	10	10	2	79*	345	43.12	–	3	126.3	3
R.W.T.Key	Kent	13	13	–	52	345	26.53	–	1	133.7	5
M.A.Carberry	Hampshire	10	10	1	58	334	37.11	–	4	124.6	6
G.R.Napier	Essex	12	11	1	152*	326	32.60	1	–	195.2	28

BOWLING (20 wickets)		O	M	R	W	Avge	BB	4w	R/Over
Yasir Arafat	Kent	44	–	341	23	14.82	4-17	2	7.75
T.Henderson	Middlesex	47	–	349	21	16.61	4-29	1	7.42
A.J.Hall	Northamptonshire	34.1	–	271	20	13.55	6-21	2	7.93
Danish Kaneria	Essex	45.1	–	276	20	13.80	4-22	1	6.11
T.J.Murtagh	Middlesex	50	–	400	20	20.00	3-15	–	8.00

TWENTY20 CUP FINAL 2008

KENT v MIDDLESEX

At Rose Bowl, Southampton, on 26 July.
Result: **MIDDLESEX** won by three runs
Toss: Middlesex. Award: O.A.Shah.

MIDDLESEX		Runs	Balls	4/6	Fall
B.A.Godleman	b Arafat	1	6	–	1- 19
* E.C.Joyce	c Jones b Cook	23	12	5	2- 47
T.Henderson	c Key b McLaren	43	33	4/2	3- 83
O.A.Shah	b McLaren	75	35	6/5	4-162
E.J.G.Morgan	c Tredwell b Mahmood	23	18	2	5-173
D.J.Malan	not out	6	8	–	
S.D.Udal	b Arafat	1	3	–	6-179
† B.J.M.Scott	not out	6	5	1	
T.J.Murtagh					
M.Kartik					
D.P.Nannes					
Extras	(B 5, LB 1, W 3)	9			
Total	(20 overs; 6 wickets)	**187**			

KENT		Runs	Balls	4/6	Fall
J.L.Denly	c Godleman b Udal	31	25	5	2- 91
* R.W.T.Key	c Scott b Kartik	52	30	9/1	1- 89
J.M.Kemp	run out (Henderson)	49	38	3/3	5-184
Yasir Arafat	run out (Joyce)	1	1	–	3- 96
D.I.Stevens	c Joyce b Nannes	33	23	1/2	4-166
Azhar Mahmood	not out	6	4	1	
M.van Jaarsveld					
R.McLaren					
† G.O.Jones					
J.C.Tredwell					
S.J.Cook					
Extras	(LB 6, W 4, NB 2)	12			
Total	(20 overs; 5 wickets)	**184**			

KENT	O	M	R	W	MIDDLESEX	O	M	R	W
Yasir Arafat	4	0	20	2	Murtagh	4	0	32	0
Azhar Mahmood	4	0	33	1	Nannes	4	0	37	1
McLaren	4	0	36	2	Henderson	4	0	58	0
Cook	4	0	35	1	Kartik	4	0	30	1
Tredwell	2	0	27	0	Udal	4	0	21	1
Stevens	2	0	30	0					

Umpires: J.W.Lloyds and N.A.Mallender.

TWENTY20 CUP WINNERS

2003	Surrey	2005	Somerset	2007	Kent
2004	Leicestershire	2006	Leicestershire	2008	Middlesex

TWENTY20 CUP RECORDS 2003-08

Highest Total	250-3		Somerset v Glos	Taunton	2006
Lowest Total	67		Sussex v Hampshire	Hove	2004
Highest Scores	152*	G.R.Napier	Essex v Sussex	Chelmsford	2008
	116*	G.A.Hick	Worcs v Northants	Luton	2004
	116*	I.J.Thomas	Glamorgan v Somerset	Taunton	2004
	116*	C.L.White	Somerset v Glos	Taunton	2006
	112	A.Symonds	Kent v Middlesex	Maidstone	2004
	111*	L.Klusener	Northants v Worcs	Kidderminster	2007
	111	D.L.Maddy	Leics v Yorks	Leeds	2004
	110	G.A.Hick	Worcs v Northants	Kidderminster	2007
Most Sixes (Innings)	16	G.R.Napier	Essex v Sussex	Chelmsford	2008

Highest Partnership for each Wicket

1st	175	V.S.Solanki/G.A.Hick	Worcs v Northants	Kidderminster	2007
2nd	186	J.L.Langer/C.L.White	Somerset v Glos	Taunton	2006
3rd	121	S.R.Patel/D.J.Hussey	Notts v Northants	Nottingham	2006
	121	H.D.Ackerman/P.A.Nixon	Leics v Derbys	Derby	2007
	121	J.A.Rudolph/A.McGrath	Yorkshire v Leics	Leicester	2008
4th	139	M.R.Ramprakash/R.Clarke	Surrey v Glos	Bristol	2006
5th	117	M.van Jaarsveld/M.J.Walker	Kent v Leics	Leicester	2004
6th	98*	R.W.T.Key/M.J.Walker	Kent v Middlesex	Beckenham	2006
7th	67	O.A.C.Banks/B.J.Phillips	Somerset v Northants	Northampton	2008
8th	68	M.W.Alleyne/J.Lewis	Glos v Glamorgan	Cardiff	2005
9th	59*	G.Chapple/P.J.Martin	Lancs v Leics	Leicester	2003
10th	59	H.H.Streak/J.E.Anyon	Warwicks v Worcs	Birmingham	2005

Best Analyses

	6-21	A.J.Hall	Northants v Worcs	Northampton	2008
	6-24	T.J.Murtagh	Surrey v Middlesex	Lord's	2005
	5-11	Mushtaq Ahmed	Sussex v Essex	Hove	2005
	5-13	M.Kartik	Middlesex v Essex	Lord's	2007
	5-14	A.D.Mascarenhas	Hampshire v Sussex	Hove	2004
	5-19	N.M.Carter	Warwicks v Worcs	Birmingham	2005

Hat-Tricks

A.D.Mascarenhas	Hampshire v Sussex	Hove	2004
D.G.Cork	Lancs v Notts	Manchester	2004
J.E.Anyon	Warwicks v Somerset	Birmingham	2005
J.N.Snape	Leics v Yorkshire	Leicester	2007
R.McLaren	Kent v Glos	Birmingham	2007
N.D.Doshi	Derbys v Durham	Chester-le-St	2008
J.Allenby	Leics v Lancs	Manchester	2008
D.P.Nannes	Middlesex v Essex	Chelmsford	2008

Most Economical Innings Analyses (Qualification: 4 overs)

4-1-6-2	J.Louw	Northants v Warwicks	Birmingham	2004
4-0-6-1	M.W.Alleyne	Glos v Worcs	Worcester	2004
4-1-7-1	R.S.C.Martin-Jenkins	Sussex v Hampshire	Hove	2004
4-1-7-4	N.Killeen	Durham v Leics	Leicester	2004
4-0-7-0	R.J.Sidebottom	Notts v Surrey	Nottingham	2006

Most Maiden Overs in an Innings

4-2-9-1	M.Morkel	Kent v Surrey	Beckenham	2007

Most Expensive Innings Analyses

4-0-67-1	R.J.Kirtley	Sussex v Essex	Chelmsford	2008
4-0-65-2	M.J.Hoggard	Yorkshire v Lancs	Leeds	2005

INDIAN PREMIER LEAGUE 2008

This inaugural BCCI/ICC approved domestic Twenty20 tournament was played during April/June 2008.

		P	W	L	T	NR	Pts	Net RR
1	RAJASTHAN Royals	14	11	3	–	–	22	0.63
2	Punjab Kings XI	14	10	4	–	–	20	0.51
3	Chennai (Madras) Super Kings	14	8	6	–	–	16	–0.19
4	Delhi Daredevils	14	7	6	–	1	15	0.34
5	Mumbai (Bombay) Indians	14	7	7	–	–	14	0.57
6	Kolkata (Calcutta) Knight Riders	14	6	7	–	1	13	–0.14
7	Bangalore Royal Challengers	14	4	10	–	–	8	–1.16
8	Deccan Chargers	14	2	12	–	–	8	–0.46

FINAL: At Dr D.Y.Patil Sports Academy, Bombay, on 1 June 2008 (floodlit). Toss: Rajasthan. **RAJASTHAN ROYALS** beat CHENNAI SUPER KINGS by three wickets. Chennai 163-5 (20; S.K.Raina 43; Y.K.Pathan 3-22). Rajasthan 164-7 (20; Y.K.Pathan 56). Award: Y.K.Pathan.

TOURNAMENT AWARDS

PLAYER: S.R.Watson (Rajasthan). **BATSMAN:** S.E.Marsh (Punjab). **BOWLER:** Sohail Tanvir (Rajasthan).

HIGHEST TOTAL:	240-5 (20)	Chennai v Punjab	Mohali	2008
LOWEST TOTAL:	67 (15.2)	Kolkata v Mumbai	Mumbai	2008

500 RUNS IN A SEASON

Runs			M	I	NO	HS	Avge	100	50	6s	4s	R/100B
616	S.E.Marsh	Punjab	11	11	2	115	68.44	1	5	26	59	139.7
534	G.Gambhir	Delhi	14	14	1	86	41.07	–	5	8	68	140.9
514	S.T.Jayasuriya	Mumbai	14	14	2	114*	42.83	1	2	31	57	166.3

HUNDREDS

Score	Balls				
158*	73	B.B.McCullum	Kolkata v Bangalore	Bangalore	2008
117*	53	A.Symonds	Deccan v Rajasthan	Hyderabad	2008
116*	54	M.E.K.Hussey	Chennai v Punjab	Mohali	2008
115	69	S.E.Marsh	Punjab v Rajasthan	Mohali	2008
114*	48	S.T.Jayasuriya	Mumbai v Chennai	Mumbai	2008
109*	47	A.C.Gilchrist	Deccan v Mumbai	Mumbai	2008

MOST WICKETS IN A SEASON

Wkts			Matches	Overs	Mdns	Runs	Avge	Best	4w	R/Over
22	Sohail Tanvir	Rajasthan	11	41.1	–	266	12.09	6-14	2	6.46
19	S.K.Warne	Rajasthan	15	52	1	404	21.26	3-19	–	7.76
19	S.Sreesanth	Punjab	15	51.1	–	442	23.26	3-29	–	8.63

MOST WICKETS IN AN INNINGS

6-14	Sohail Tanvir	Rajasthan v Chennai	Jaipur	2008
5-17	A.Mishra	Delhi v Deccan	Delhi	2008
5-24	L.Balaji	Chennai v Punjab	Chennai	2008

INDIAN CRICKET LEAGUE

Six Twenty20 tournaments, unsanctioned by either the BCCI or the ICC, have been staged in India during November/December 2007, March/April 2008 and September/November 2008.

RESULTS 2007-08/2008-09	P	W	L	T	NR
Ahmedabad *Rockets*	15	4	11	–	–
Bengal *Royal Tigers*	25	12	13	–	–
Chandigarh *Lions*	22	9	12	1	–
Chennai (Madras) *Superstars*	25	15	10	–	–
Delhi *Giants/Jets*	22	10	11	1	–
Dhaka *Warriors*	8	4	4	–	–
Hyderabad *Heroes*	28	18	9	1	–
Lahore *Badshahs*	22	16	5	1	–
Mumbai (Bombay) *Champs*	21	4	17	–	–
Bangladesh XI	2	1	1	–	–
India XI	7	5	2	–	–
Pakistan XI	6	2	4	–	–
World XI	7	3	4	–	–

HIGHEST TOTAL:	219-4 (20)	Chandigarh v Mumbai	Panchkula	2007-08
LOWEST TOTAL:	74	Bengal v Chennai	Panchkula	2007-08

700 RUNS IN A CAREER

Runs			M	I	NO	HS	Avge	100	50	R/100B
849	Abdul Razzaq	Hyderabad/Pakistan	34	33	7	78*	32.65	–	6	132.0
826	Imran Nazir	Lahore/Pakistan	27	27	6	111*	39.33	1	5	147.5
775	Imran Farhat	Chandigarh/Lahore/Pak	34	34	2	94	24.21	–	4	127.3
767	R.Sathish	Chennai/India	32	31	9	86*	34.86	–	5	158.8
753	I.J.Harvey	Chennai/World	28	27	3	63*	31.37	–	5	130.7

HUNDREDS

Score	Balls				
111*	44	Imran Nazir	Lahore v Hyderabad	Ahmedabad	2008-09
100	60	Alok Kapali	Dhaka v Hyderabad	Hyderabad	2008-09

40 WICKETS IN A CAREER

Wkts			Matches	Overs	Mdns	Runs	Avge	Best	4w	R/Over
40	A.G.Murtaza	Delhi/India	29	114.3	1	677	16.67	4-7	1	5.82
40	Naved-ul-Hasan	Lahore/Pakistan	26	99.3	–	710	17.75	5-22	2	7.13
40	Abdul Razzaq	Hyderabad/Pakistan	34	124.1	2	897	22.42	4-23	1	7.22

MOST WICKETS IN AN INNINGS

7-15	A.Absolem	Hyderabad v Ahmedabad	Hyderabad	2007-08
6-21	T.Kumaran	Chennai v Mumbai	Panchkula	2007-08
5-13	Azhar Mahmood	Lahore v Hyderabad	Panchkula	2007-08
5-22	Naved-ul-Hasan	Lahore v Hyderabad	Hyderabad	2007-08

MINOR COUNTIES CHAMPIONSHIP
FINAL TABLES 2008
EASTERN DIVISION

	P	W	L	D	Bonus Points Bat	Points Bowl	Total Points	Net Runs/Wkt
1 LINCOLNSHIRE (10)	6	3	–	3	17	24	101	17.95
2 Staffordshire (3)	6	3	1	2*	16	16	92	6.42
3 Suffolk (5)	6	2	–	4†	17	20	87	19.92
4 Cambridgeshire (4)	6	2	1	3	14	23	81	0.74
5 Bedfordshire (8)	6	2	1	3†	11	14	71	–4.17
6 Cumberland (7)	6	1	3	2†	7	20	53	–1.58
7 Northumberland (1)	6	–	–	6*†	11	8	49	–9.17
8 Buckinghamshire (9)	6	1	3	2	6	20	48‡	–10.40
9 Norfolk (2)	6	–	2	4†	8	18	44	–4.80
10 Hertfordshire (6)	6	–	3	3†	5	13	32	–19.07

WESTERN DIVISION

	P	W	L	D	Bonus Points Bat	Points Bowl	Total Points	Net Runs/Wkt
1 BERKSHIRE (3)	6	3	1	2	19	15	90	7.99
2 Cheshire (1)	6	2	–	4	24	17	89	12.05
3 Oxfordshire (5)	6	2	–	4†	10	18	76‡	5.10
4 Cornwall (7)	6	2	2*	2	13	18	75	–3.02
5 Dorset (8)	6	2	1	3	13	17	74	1.90
6 Shropshire (2)	6	2	2	2*	13	16	73	5.32
7 Wales Minor Counties (4)	6	1	2	3	9	15	52	–5.84
8 Devon (6)	6	–	1	5†	10	17	49	–0.54
9 Herefordshire (10)	6	1*	3	2	4	19	43	–15.28
10 Wiltshire (9)	6	–	3	3*	11	15	42	–9.93

Win = 16 points. Draw/Tie = 4 points. 2007 final positions are shown in brackets.
* Includes a match reduced to a single innings (points: win 12; draw 8; loss 4).
† Includes a match abandoned without a ball bowled (6 points).
‡ Two points deducted for slow over rate.

2008 CHAMPIONSHIP FINAL
At Falkland CC Ground, Newbury, on 7, 8, 9, 10 September. Toss: Berkshire. **BERKSHIRE** beat LINCOLNSHIRE by eight wickets. Berkshire 358-6 closed (90; D.J.F.Shilvock 82, B.H.D.Mordt 100*; B.W.Houston 3-92) and 60-2 (8.2). Lincolnshire 105 (32.1; C.D.Crowe 6-42) and, following on, 311 (74.1; M.P.Dowman 68, V Atri 61, P.G.Cook 62; C.D.Crowe 6 107, T.L.Lambert 4-59). Award: C.D.Crowe.

2008 MCCA TROPHY FINAL
At Lord's, London, on 6 August. Toss: Berkshire. **DEVON** beat BERKSHIRE by 40 runs. Devon 290-4 (50; C.M.Mole 67, R.I.Dawson 96, N.D.Hancock 53*). Berkshire 250 (48; B.H.D.Mordt 79; I.E.Bishop 4-40, N.D.Hancock 3-63). Award: ???????

MINOR COUNTIES RECORDS

Highest Total	621		Surrey v Devon	The Oval	1928
Lowest Total	14		Cheshire v Staffs	Stoke	1909
Highest Score	282	E.Garnett	Berkshire v Wiltshire	Reading	1908
Most Runs – Season	1212	A.F.Brazier	Surrey II		1949
Record Partnership:					
2nd wkt	388*	T.H.Clark/A.F.Brazier	Surrey II v Sussex II	The Oval	1949
Best Bowling – Innings	10- 11	S.Turner	Cambs v Cumberland	Penrith	1987
– Match	18-100	N.W.Harding	Kent II v Wiltshire	Swindon	1937
Most Wickets – Season	119	S.F.Barnes	Staffordshire		1906

MINOR COUNTIES CHAMPIONS

1895	Norfolk	1933	*Undecided*	1977	Suffolk
	Durham	1934	Lancashire II	1978	Devon
	Worcestershire	1935	Middlesex II	1979	Suffolk
1896	Worcestershire	1936	Hertfordshire	1980	Durham
1897	Worcestershire	1937	Lancashire II	1981	Durham
1898	Worcestershire	1938	Buckinghamshire	1982	Oxfordshire
1899	Northamptonshire	1939	Surrey II	1983	Hertfordshire
	Buckinghamshire	1946	Suffolk	1984	Durham
1900	Glamorgan	1947	Yorkshire II	1985	Cheshire
	Durham	1948	Lancashire II	1986	Cumberland
	Northamptonshire	1949	Lancashire II	1987	Buckinghamshire
1901	Durham	1950	Surrey II	1988	Cheshire
1902	Wiltshire	1951	Kent II	1989	Oxfordshire
1903	Northamptonshire	1952	Buckinghamshire	1990	Hertfordshire
1904	Northamptonshire	1953	Berkshire	1991	Staffordshire
1905	Norfolk	1954	Surrey II	1992	Staffordshire
1906	Staffordshire	1955	Surrey II	1993	Staffordshire
1907	Lancashire II	1956	Kent II	1994	Devon
1908	Staffordshire	1957	Yorkshire II	1995	Devon
1909	Wiltshire	1958	Yorkshire II	1996	Devon
1910	Norfolk	1959	Warwickshire II	1997	Devon
1911	Staffordshire	1960	Lancashire II	1998	Staffordshire
1912	*In abeyance*	1961	Somerset II	1999	Cumberland
1913	Norfolk	1962	Warwickshire II	2000	Dorset
1920	Staffordshire	1963	Cambridgeshire	2001	Cheshire
1921	Staffordshire	1964	Lancashire II		Lincolnshire
1922	Buckinghamshire	1965	Somerset II	2002	Herefordshire
1923	Buckinghamshire	1966	Lincolnshire		Norfolk
1924	Berkshire	1967	Cheshire	2003	Lincolnshire
1925	Buckinghamshire	1968	Yorkshire II	2004	Bedfordshire
1926	Durham	1969	Buckinghamshire		Devon
1927	Staffordshire	1970	Bedfordshire	2005	Cheshire
1928	Berkshire	1971	Yorkshire II		Suffolk
1929	Oxfordshire	1972	Bedfordshire	2006	Devon
1930	Durham	1973	Shropshire	2007	Cheshire
1931	Leicestershire II	1974	Oxfordshire	2008	Berkshire
1932	Buckinghamshire	1975	Hertfordshire		
		1976	Durham		

LEADING CHAMPIONSHIP AGGREGATES 2008

BATTING

		M	I	NO	HS	Runs	Avge	100	50
B.L.Spendlove	(Cheshire)	6	11	1	145	628	62.80	2	4
Atiq-ur-Rehman	(Shropshire)	5	8	1	175	563	80.42	2	3
N.R.C.Dumelow	(Cheshire)	6	11	2	150	530	58.88	2	2
P.N.G.Morgan	(Lincolnshire)	7	12	3	128	471	52.33	1	2
R.W.Cook	(Lincolnshire)	7	10	1	154	471	52.33	1	2
S.P.Naylor	(Berkshire)	6	9	3	125	462	77.00	2	1
P.J.Wilshaw	(Staffordshire)	6	10	1	138	450	50.00	1	2
D.N.Leech	(Cheshire)	4	8	–	154	449	56.12	2	2
D.E.Barnes	(Berkshire)	7	12	3	123*	419	46.55	2	1
J.Hibberd	(Wiltshire)	6	10	5	82	418	83.60	–	4
M.J.Symington	(Northumberland)	5	9	2	116	417	59.57	1	2
J.A.Duffy	(Cheshire)	6	11	–	87	415	37.72	–	6
M.P.Dowman	(Lincolnshire)	7	10	–	88	404	40.40	–	4
J.M.Hudson	(Devon)	5	8	2	113	404	67.33	1	2
T.R.Ward	(Norfolk)	5	7	–	149	398	56.85	1	3
T.C.Hicks	(Dorset)	6	7	1	91	390	65.00	–	4

		M	I	NO	HS	Runs	Avge	100	50
T.B.Huggins	(Suffolk)	5	8	–	160	389	48.62	1	2
P.G.Cook	(Lincolnshire)	7	9	–	114	363	40.33	1	2
T.G.Sharp	(Cornwall)	6	9	–	85	357	39.66	–	4
P.B.Muchall	(Northumberland)	5	9	1	130	356	44.50	2	–
D.C.Shirazi	(Wiltshire)	5	8	–	107	353	44.12	2	1
S.A.Kellett	(Cambridgeshire)	6	10	3	105*	351	50.14	1	1
B.J.France	(Suffolk)	5	8	–	91	348	43.50	–	4
M.A.Sheikh	(Staffordshire)	5	7	1	94	342	57.00	–	4
V.Atri	(Lincolnshire)	5	9	1	88	336	42.00	–	2
J.T.Ralph	(Shropshire)	6	9	–	74	333	37.00	–	3
A.Worthy	(Northumberland)	5	9	–	121	325	36.11	1	–
A.J.Hall	(Cheshire)	4	8	–	90	320	40.00	–	4
C.S.Knightley	(Oxfordshire)	4	5	1	103	318	79.50	1	3
M.H.Adnan	(Suffolk)	5	7	3	105*	310	77.50	1	2
M.A.Jones	(Buckinghamshire)	6	12	1	56	301	27.36	–	2

BOWLING

		O	M	R	W	Avge	BB	5wI	10wM
A.K.D.Gray	(Shropshire)	222.4	56	482	36	13.38	9-56	2	1
B.W.Houston	(Lincolnshire)	172.1	50	471	28	16.82	6-37	2	–
T.L.Lambert	(Berkshire)	158.2	28	548	26	21.07	6-87	1	–
G.D.Morris	(Staffordshire)	201.2	33	671	26	25.80	4-54	–	–
M.A.Sheikh	(Staffordshire)	163.1	43	425	25	17.00	6-18	1	–
R.J.Harrison	(Cornwall)	179	47	567	25	22.68	6-65	1	–
C.D.Crowe	(Berkshire)	181.5	34	589	24	24.54	6-42	3	1
A.J.Syddall	(Cheshire)	154.1	31	539	23	23.43	6-67	2	–
G.W.Walker	(Norfolk)	218	51	650	23	28.26	5-35	2	–
Ajaz Akhtar	(Cambridgeshire)	181	55	471	22	21.40	5-99	1	–
N.R.C.Dumelow	(Cheshire)	206.4	51	671	21	31.95	4-54	–	–
R.W.Banham	(Dorset)	118	27	381	20	19.05	6-74	1	–
J.A.Brooks	(Oxfordshire)	114	22	484	19	25.47	5-62	1	–
S.A.Roberts	(Herefordshire)	163.2	39	512	19	26.94	5-56	1	–
S.F.Stanway	(Buckinghamshire)	294	90	690	19	36.31	4-83	–	–
A.Onyon	(Lincolnshire)	119.5	35	297	18	16.50	5-43	1	–
T.S.Anning	(Devon)	129	34	373	18	20.72	5-68	1	–
G.M.Harper	(Buckinghamshire)	123	20	432	18	24.00	6-27	2	1
J.S.Smith	(Cambridgeshire)	126	25	455	18	25.27	5-95	1	–
J.E.Bishop	(Suffolk)	130.5	22	477	18	26.50	4-72	–	–
S.A.Taylor	(Shropshire)	97.1	22	303	17	17.82	6-54	2	–
J.D.Williams	(Cambridgeshire)	129.2	24	481	17	28.29	5-58	1	–
G.R.Willott	(Staffordshire)	161	35	503	17	29.58	4-45	–	–
S.A.Wedge	(Herefordshire)	122	14	522	17	30.70	6-61	2	–
M.A.Sharp	(Cumberland)	121.4	42	291	16	18.18	5-52	1	–
T.G.Sharp	(Cornwall)	130.5	38	357	16	22.31	4-32	–	–
A.C.McGarry	(Suffolk)	123.5	23	387	16	24.18	4-80	–	–
J.D.Shantry	(Shropshire)	140	40	317	15	21.13	5-77	2	1
T.C.Hicks	(Dorset)	117	23	382	15	25.46	5-51	1	–
C.Brown	(Norfolk)	172	44	418	15	27.86	4-24	–	–
R.L.Johnson	(Berkshire)	133.3	28	421	15	28.06	4-37	–	–

SECOND XI CHAMPIONSHIP 2008
FINAL TABLE

	P	W	L	D	Deduct	Bonus Points Bat	Bonus Points Bowl	Total Points	Avge
1 DURHAM (5)	15	8	–	7	–	42	38	220	14.67
2 Middlesex (6)	13	5	2	6	–	35	40	169	13.00
3 Somerset (2)	11	3	1	7	1	31	35	135	12.27
4 Worcestershire (18)	12	4	3	5	1.5	20	34	128.5	10.71
5 Yorkshire (10)	14	4	4	6	–	29	38	147	10.50
6 Surrey (11)	15	4	1	10	1	32	29	156	10.40
7 Sussex (1)	13	3	1	9	–	26	29	133	10.23
8 Kent (20)	7	1	1	5	0.5	15	18	69.5	9.93
9 Nottinghamshire (12)	11	2	3	6	–	20	37	109	9.91
10 Warwickshire (8)	13	3	3	7	–	22	36	128	9.85
11 Essex (17)	10	3	3	4	7.5	17	30	97.5	9.75
12 Gloucestershire (16)	11	3	4	4	–	17	30	105	9.55
13 Northamptonshire (13)	11	2	3	6	0.5	20	33	104.5	9.50
14 Lancashire (4)	15	3	5	7	–	31	36	136	9.07
15 Hampshire (3)	11	2	–	9	6	19	18	95	8.64
16 Derbyshire (9)	14	2	4	8	–	21	38	119	8.50
17 Glamorgan (19)	11	1	5	5	–	23	27	84	7.64
18 Leicestershire (7)	12	1	5	6	2	15	30	81	6.75
19 Scotland A (15)	6	–	3	3	–	5	22	39	6.50
20 MCC Young Cricketers (14)	15	1	4	10	–	18	25	97	6.47

Win = 14 points, plus any first-innings points. Draw = 4 points, plus any first-innings points. Abandoned without a ball bowled = 4 points.

Tie-breakers for teams finishing with equal average points are (i) highest season ratio of runs scored per wickets lost and (ii) the lowest season ratio of runs conceded per wickets taken.

2007 final positions are shown in brackets.

SECOND XI CHAMPIONS

1959	Gloucestershire	1976	Kent	1993	Middlesex
1960	Northamptonshire	1977	Yorkshire	1994	Somerset
1961	Kent	1978	Sussex	1995	Hampshire
1962	Worcestershire	1979	Warwickshire	1996	Warwickshire
1963	Worcestershire	1980	Glamorgan	1997	Lancashire
1964	Lancashire	1981	Hampshire	1998	Northamptonshire
1965	Glamorgan	1982	Worcestershire	1999	Middlesex
1966	Surrey	1983	Leicestershire	2000	Middlesex
1967	Hampshire	1984	Yorkshire	2001	Hampshire
1968	Surrey	1985	Nottinghamshire	2002	Kent
1969	Kent	1986	Lancashire	2003	Yorkshire
1970	Kent	1987	Kent/Yorkshire	2004	Somerset
1971	Hampshire	1988	Surrey	2005	Kent
1972	Nottinghamshire	1989	Middlesex	2006	Kent
1973	Essex	1990	Sussex	2007	Sussex
1974	Middlesex	1991	Yorkshire	2008	Durham
1975	Surrey	1992	Surrey		

SECOND XI TROPHY 2008

Final: HAMPSHIRE 220 for 7 (50 overs; J.M.Vince 58, K.J.Latouf 44) beat ESSEX 213 (46.4 overs; A.J. Wheater 52*) by 7 runs at Chelmsford.

YOUNG CRICKETER OF THE YEAR

This annual award, made by The Cricket Writers' Club, which celebrated its 60th anniversary in 2006, is currently restricted to players qualified for England, Andrew Symonds meeting that requirement at the time of his award, and under the age of 23 on 1st May. In 1986 their ballot resulted in a dead heat. Up to 22 March 2009 their selections have gained a tally of 2,026 international Test match caps (shown in brackets).

1950	R.Tattersall (16)	1980	G.R.Dilley (41)
1951	P.B.H.May (66)	1981	M.W.Gatting (79)
1952	F.S.Trueman (67)	1982	N.G.Cowans (19)
1953	M.C.Cowdrey (114)	1983	N.A.Foster (29)
1954	P.J.Loader (13)	1984	R.J.Bailey (4)
1955	K.F.Barrington (82)	1985	D.V.Lawrence (5)
1956	B.Taylor	1986 {	A.A.Metcalfe
1957	M.J.Stewart (8)		J.J.Whitaker (1)
1958	A.C.D.Ingleby-Mackenzie	1987	R.J.Blakey (2)
1959	G.Pullar (28)	1988	M.P.Maynard (4)
1960	D.A.Allen (39)	1989	N.Hussain (96)
1961	P.H.Parfitt (37)	1990	M.A.Atherton (115)
1962	P.J.Sharpe (12)	1991	M.R.Ramprakash (52)
1963	G.Boycott (108)	1992	I.D.K.Salisbury (15)
1964	J.M.Brearley (39)	1993	M.N.Lathwell (2)
1965	A.P.E.Knott (95)	1994	J.P.Crawley (37)
1966	D.L.Underwood (86)	1995	A.Symonds (26–Australia)
1967	A.W.Greig (58)	1996	C.E.W.Silverwood (6)
1968	R.M.H.Cottam (4)	1997	B.C.Hollioake (2)
1969	A.Ward (5)	1998	A.Flintoff (74)
1970	C.M.Old (46)	1999	A.J.Tudor (10)
1971	J.Whitehouse	2000	P.J.Franks
1972	D.R.Owen-Thomas	2001	O.A.Shah (6)
1973	M.Hendrick (30)	2002	R.Clarke (2)
1974	P.H.Edmonds (51)	2003	J.M.Anderson (35)
1975	A.Kennedy	2004	I.R.Bell (46)
1976	G.Miller (34)	2005	A.N.Cook (41)
1977	I.T.Botham (102)	2006	S.C.J.Broad (15)
1978	D.I.Gower (117)	2007	A.U.Rashid
1979	P.W.G.Parker (1)	2008	R.S.Bopara (4)

THE PROFESSIONAL CRICKETERS' ASSOCIATION
PLAYER OF THE YEAR

Founded in 1967, the Professional Cricketers' Association introduced this award, decided by their membership, in 1970. Since 1998 it has been presented at their Annual Awards Dinner at the Royal Albert Hall. Only John Lever and Andrew Flintoff have won the award in successive years.

1970 {	M.J.Procter	1983	K.S.McEwan	1997	S.P.James
	J.D.Bond	1984	R.J.Hadlee	1998	M.B.Loye
1971	L.R.Gibbs	1985	N.V.Radford	1999	S.G.Law
1972	A.M.E.Roberts	1986	C.A.Walsh	2000	M.E.Trescothick
1973	P.G.Lee	1987	R.J.Hadlee	2001	D.P.Fulton
1974	B.Stead	1988	G.A.Hick	2002	M.P.Vaughan
1975	Zaheer Abbas	1989	S.J.Cook	2003	Mushtaq Ahmed
1976	P.G.Lee	1990	G.A.Gooch	2004	A.Flintoff
1977	M.J.Procter	1991	Waqar Younis	2005	A.Flintoff
1978	J.K.Lever	1992	C.A.Walsh	2006	M.R.Ramprakash
1979	J.K.Lever	1993	S.L.Watkin	2007	O.D.Gibson
1980	R.D.Jackman	1994	B.C.Lara	2008	M.Van Jaarsveld
1981	R.J.Hadlee	1995	D.G.Cork		
1982	M.D.Marshall	1996	P.V.Simmons		

FIRST-CLASS CAREER RECORDS

Compiled by **Philip Bailey**

The following career records are for all players who appeared in first-class cricket during the 2008 season, and are complete to the end of that season. Some players who did not appear in 2008 but may do so in 2009 are included.

BATTING AND FIELDING

'1000' denotes instances of scoring 1000 runs in a season. Where these have been achieved outside the British Isles they are shown after a plus sign.

	M	I	NO	HS	Runs	Avge	100	50	1000	Ct/St
Abdul Razzaq	111	174	27	203*	4965	33.77	8	25	–	30
Abel, E.	3	4	1	27*	68	22.66	–	–	–	3
Ackerman, H.D.	204	342	32	309*	13563	43.75	38	69	3+1	170
Adams, A.R.	90	120	10	124	2618	23.80	3	11	–	55
Adams, C.J.	336	546	41	239	19535	38.68	48	93	9	404
Adams, J.H.K.	71	127	11	262*	3722	32.08	4	18	1	57
Adshead, S.J.	66	108	17	148*	2812	30.90	1	17	–	170/14
Afzaal, U.	206	356	39	168*	12104	38.18	28	63	6	97
Aga, R.G.	13	22	3	43	209	11.00	–	–	–	6
Ahmed, J.S.	6	5	4	16*	44	44.00	–	–	–	3
Ahmed, M.	1	–	–	–	–	–	–	–	–	2
Ali, Kabir	108	148	21	84*	2238	17.62	–	7	–	27
Ali, Kadeer	77	140	5	161	3832	28.38	6	20	–	39
Ali, M.M.	16	24	2	92	624	28.36	–	6	–	5
Allenby, J.	35	53	9	138*	1580	35.90	2	9	–	34
Ambrose, T.R.	90	140	12	251*	4376	34.18	6	25	–	202/14
Amjad Khan	63	72	24	78	870	18.12	–	3	–	10
Amla, H.M.	101	168	15	249	7074	46.23	21	34	0+2	81
Anderson, J.M.	81	95	43	37*	491	9.44	–	–	–	35
Andrew, G.M.	23	29	4	44	362	14.48	–	–	–	10
Ansari, A.S.	4	7	2	193	308	61.60	1	1	–	2
Anyon, J.E.	43	54	21	37*	325	9.84	–	–	–	15
Azhar Mahmood	151	234	29	204*	6557	31.98	9	33	–	126
Baer, M.	1	1	–	8	8	8.00	–	–	–	–
Bailey, S.P.	1	2	–	15	18	9.00	–	–	–	1
Baker, F.B.	4	5	–	18	41	8.20	–	–	–	1
Balac, M.	1	1	–	11	11	11.00	–	–	–	6
Balcombe, D.J.	18	27	6	73	356	16.95	–	1	–	6
Ball, A.H.	3	5	2	44*	148	49.33	–	–	–	3
Ballance, G.S.	1	2	–	5	6	3.00	–	–	–	–
Ballard, E.C.	2	4	–	1	1	0.25	–	–	–	1
Banerjee, V.	26	36	14	29	207	9.40	–	–	–	6
Banks, O.A.C.	59	91	14	100	1832	23.79	1	10	–	33
Batty, G.J.	122	186	36	133	4061	27.07	2	21	–	81
Batty, J.N.	175	268	34	168*	7851	33.55	18	37	1	454/60
Beer, W.A.T.	2	2	1	6*	6	6.00	–	–	–	–
Bell, I.R.	134	230	21	262*	9157	43.81	23	49	2	92
Benham, C.C.	35	58	1	95	1509	26.47	–	9	–	33
Benkenstein, D.M.	191	291	37	259	11733	46.19	28	63	3	129
Benning, J.G.E.	34	53	4	128	1601	32.67	4	7	–	14
Berg, G.K.	3	5	–	35	118	23.60	–	–	–	1
Birch, D.J.	16	27	1	130	888	34.15	1	4	–	7
Blackwell, I.D.	147	221	16	247*	8154	39.77	21	41	3	55

F-C	M	I	NO	HS	Runs	Avge	100	50	1000	Ct/St
Blain, J.A.R.	42	47	16	93	495	15.96	–	2	–	12
Blake, A.J.	1	–	–	–	–	–	–	–	–	–
Boje, N.	188	278	49	226*	7703	33.63	8	43	–	113
Bond, S.E.	58	67	20	100	774	16.46	1	2	–	22
Bopara, R.S.	79	130	18	229	4572	40.82	10	19	1	53
Borrington, P.M.	16	26	4	102*	689	31.31	1	4	–	12
Botha, A.G.	113	176	25	156*	3619	23.96	4	17	–	90
Bott, M.D.	6	10	1	27	74	8.22	–	–	–	7
Boucher, M.V.	178	259	38	134	7395	33.46	8	45	–	600/34
Boyce, M.A.G.	19	29	1	106	689	24.60	1	4	–	2
Bradshaw, D.P.	7	11	3	127*	349	43.62	1	1	–	2
Brathwaite, R.M.R.	8	10	3	76*	140	20.00	–	1	–	–
Breese, G.R.	112	180	20	165*	4270	26.68	4	27	–	92
Bresnan, T.T.	73	99	19	126*	2177	27.21	3	10	–	31
Broad, S.C.J.	46	56	13	91*	1092	25.39	–	8	–	14
Brophy, G.L.	92	145	16	185	3898	30.21	6	19	–	229/19
Brown, A.D.	247	388	43	295*	14957	43.35	44	62	8	246/1
Brown, B.C.	1	1	–	46	46	46.00	–	–	–	–
Brown, D.O.	23	39	4	83	975	27.85	–	7	–	12
Brown, J.F.	129	147	59	38	655	7.44	–	–	–	26
Brown, K.R.	5	8	1	40	116	16.57	–	–	–	2
Brown, M.J.	76	136	15	133	4139	34.20	7	24	1	64
Burrows, T.G.	6	9	2	42	169	24.14	–	–	–	22
Burton, D.A.	2	2	1	52*	53	53.00	–	1	–	–
Butcher, M.A.	275	470	37	259	17619	40.69	38	93	8	253
Buttleman, J.E.L.	4	6	1	56*	89	17.80	–	1	–	2
Caddick, A.R.	270	353	69	92	4244	14.94	–	9	–	87
Cairns, C.L.	217	341	38	158	10702	35.32	13	71	1	78
Carberry, M.A.	83	147	14	192*	5132	38.58	13	24	1	34
Carlisle, L.J.	2	4	2	18*	28	14.00	–	–	–	1
Carter, N.M.	87	115	21	103	1937	20.60	1	7	–	24
Chambers, M.A.	4	6	4	7	11	5.50	–	–	–	1
Chanderpaul, S.	228	372	64	303*	16363	53.12	46	83	1+1	135
Chapple, G.	227	310	57	155	6311	24.94	6	28	–	76
Cheetham, S.P.	1	–	–	–	–	–	–	–	–	1
Chilton, M.J.	150	245	17	131	7268	31.87	18	26	1	111
Chopra, V.	36	60	5	155	1715	31.18	2	11	–	34
Clare, J.L.	15	21	5	129*	597	37.31	1	5	–	5
Clark, S.R.	93	120	32	62	1189	13.51	–	1	–	26
Clarke, R.	89	142	13	214	4719	36.58	10	20	1	113
Claydon, M.E.	6	5	1	40	96	24.00	–	–	–	–
Cliff, S.J.	5	6	2	15	45	11.25	–	–	–	1
Clinton, R.S.	43	70	5	108*	1837	28.26	4	9	–	24
Clough, G.D.	12	17	2	55	156	10.40	–	1	–	4
Cobb, J.J.	9	12	3	148*	442	49.11	1	2	–	5
Coetzer, K.J.	27	48	6	153*	1392	33.14	3	4	–	16
Collingwood, P.D.	161	284	23	206	9301	35.63	20	45	2	178
Collins, P.T.	115	143	37	25	677	6.38	–	–	–	28
Collymore, C.D.	97	141	65	20	594	7.81	–	–	–	34
Compton, N.R.D.	40	69	7	190	2128	34.32	6	9	1	20
Cook, A.N.	88	158	11	195	6625	45.06	18	36	3	89
Cook, S.J.	104	133	18	93*	1887	16.40	–	5	–	31
Cope, A.C.	1	2	–	51	51	25.50	–	1	–	–
Cork, D.G.	287	418	55	200*	9127	25.14	8	50	–	205
Cosker, D.A.	153	195	58	52	1784	13.02	–	1	–	98
Crawley, J.P.	343	570	57	311*	24053	46.88	54	131	10	214/1

F-C	M	I	NO	HS	Runs	Avge	100	50	1000	Ct/St
Crawley, S.H.	1	2	1	20*	24	24.00	–	–	–	–
Croft, R.D.B.	365	541	96	143	11791	26.49	7	51	–	171
Croft, S.J.	26	40	3	122	936	25.29	1	5	–	19
Crook, A.R.	11	18	2	88	493	30.81	–	3	–	8
Crook, S.P.	33	44	7	97	1177	31.81	–	8	–	10
Cross, G.D.	8	13	1	72	309	25.75	–	3	–	27/8
Cummins, R.A.G.	22	27	11	34*	221	13.81	–	–	–	7
Daggett, L.M.	22	29	13	33	132	8.25	–	–	–	1
Dalrymple, J.W.M.	91	147	13	244	4450	33.20	6	25	–	46
Danish Kaneria	142	178	71	65	1090	10.18	–	1	–	48
Davies, A.M.	66	93	34	62	658	11.15	–	1	–	15
Davies, S.M.	62	102	12	192	3258	36.20	4	14	1	197/12
Dawson, L.A.	6	8	1	100*	193	27.57	1	–	–	–
Dawson, R.K.J.	96	143	17	87	2673	21.21	–	11	–	51
Dean, K.J.	119	158	52	54*	1222	11.52	–	2	–	22
De Bruyn, Z.	119	201	23	266*	7565	42.50	19	36	0+1	78
Denly, J.L.	40	69	4	149	2359	36.29	6	12	1	16
Dernbach, J.W.	20	23	8	16*	112	7.46	–	–	–	2
De Villiers, A.B.	66	117	11	217*	4667	44.02	9	26	0+1	103/2
Dexter, N.J.	29	41	8	131*	1339	40.57	3	8	–	19
Dhiman Ghosh	40	70	7	115	1820	28.88	2	8	–	98/11
Dingle, L.A.	2	3	1	6*	7	3.50	–	–	–	–
Dippenaar, H.H.	148	245	21	250*	9330	41.65	28	37	0+1	146
Di Venuto, M.J.	281	501	32	230	21097	44.98	47	128	8	326
Dixey, P.G.	9	15	1	31	170	12.14	–	–	–	19/1
Dolar Mahmud	15	28	4	63	312	13.00	–	1	–	6
Doshi, N.D.	62	77	20	37	530	9.29	–	–	–	11
Drew, B.G.	19	26	7	28	223	11.73	–	–	–	10
Duffell, C.B.R.	6	7	2	38	90	18.00	–	–	–	6/1
Duminy, J.P.	45	75	14	169	3236	53.04	9	18	–	31
Du Plessis, F.	39	67	5	156	2195	35.40	3	15	–	30
Du Preez, D.	41	56	6	122	910	18.20	1	3	–	9
Durston, W.J.	33	55	11	146*	1672	38.00	1	12	–	34
Du Toit, J.	13	20	1	103	558	29.36	1	3	–	7
Ealham, M.A.	267	402	60	153*	10856	31.74	13	65	1	152
Edwards, N.J.	49	82	–	212	2898	35.34	3	15	1	35
Elliott, G.D.	42	66	3	196*	1907	30.26	5	9	–	29
Ervine, S.M.	83	132	13	126	3662	30.77	5	22	–	82
Evans, D.	14	18	4	12*	52	3.71	–	–	–	3
Ferley, R.S.	30	38	10	78*	613	21.89	–	2	–	9
Fernando, C.R.D.	88	95	27	42	491	7.22	–	–	–	35
Finn, S.T.	17	20	7	26*	91	7.00	–	–	–	5
Fisher, I.D.	79	119	19	103*	2201	22.01	1	7	–	27
Fletcher, L.J.	1	–	–	–	–	–	–	–	–	–
Flintoff, A.	171	271	22	167	8588	34.48	15	50	–	176
Flower, G.W.	184	312	23	243*	10766	37.25	23	58	–	171
Flowers, T.O.	2	3	1	25*	51	25.50	–	–	–	1
Flynn, D.R.	30	51	7	110	1379	31.34	4	4	–	10
Foster, J.S.	140	207	27	212	6362	35.34	12	31	1	374/34
Foster, P.J.	6	8	–	19	49	6.12	–	–	–	1
Francis, J.D.	57	101	8	125*	2748	29.54	6	15	1	32
Franklin, J.E.C.	89	131	19	208	3106	27.73	3	14	–	31
Franks, P.J.	154	221	43	123*	4677	26.27	3	22	–	54
Friedlander, M.J.	14	19	1	81	260	14.44	–	1	–	5
Froggett, T.J.	2	3	2	21*	46	46.00	–	–	–	3/1
Frost, T.	105	152	27	242*	4181	33.44	5	20	1	251/18

180

F-C	M	I	NO	HS	Runs	Avge	100	50	1000	Ct/St
Frylinck, R.	16	23	2	100*	539	25.66	1	4	–	4
Fulton, P.G.	65	106	11	301*	4275	45.00	7	23	–	47
Gale, A.W.	30	47	–	150	1419	30.19	4	5	–	18
Gale, D.J.	2	2	1	0*	0	0.00	–	–	–	1
Gallian, J.E.R.	252	430	35	312	15021	38.02	37	72	6	226
Gazzard, C.M.	28	43	6	74	738	19.94	–	1	–	58/1
Gibbs, H.H.	185	319	13	228	13076	42.73	31	58	–	164
Gidman, A.P.R.	98	173	20	142	5595	36.56	11	33	3	54
Gidman, W.R.S.	1	2	–	8	8	4.00	–	–	–	–
Gillespie, J.N.	189	256	65	201*	3742	19.59	3	10	–	68
Gitsham, M.T.	4	6	2	35*	58	14.50	–	–	–	1
Glover, J.C.	3	3	1	9*	10	5.00	–	–	–	–
Goddard, L.J.	10	14	4	91	324	32.40	–	2	–	22
Godleman, B.A.	31	50	3	113*	1647	35.04	2	10	–	27
Goodwin, M.W.	234	408	32	335*	18380	48.88	58	77	7+1	133
Gough, D.	248	326	60	121	4607	17.31	1	20	–	51
Grant, R.N.	25	42	1	79	888	21.65	–	4	–	10
Gray, S.K.	2	4	1	26*	31	10.33	–	–	–	2
Greenidge, C.G.	50	61	8	46	444	8.37	–	–	–	18
Griffiths, D.A.	7	10	4	31*	62	10.33	–	–	–	1
Groenewald, T.D.	17	21	4	78	368	21.64	–	2	–	11
Guy, S.M.	36	50	6	52*	727	16.52	–	1	–	97/12
Hales, A.D.	1	–	–	–	–	–	–	–	–	–
Hall, A.J.	136	193	26	163	5610	33.59	5	38	–	110
Hamilton-Brown, R.J.	3	5	–	62	122	24.40	–	1	–	1
Hannon-Dalby, O.J.	1	1	1	1	1	1.00	–	–	–	–
Hardinges, M.A.	50	76	9	172	1778	26.53	4	6	–	26
Harinath, A.	4	6	–	69	161	26.83	–	2	–	4
Harmison, B.W.	30	51	5	110	1202	26.13	3	5	–	22
Harmison, S.J.	168	225	62	49*	1675	10.27	–	–	–	25
Harris, A.J.	127	171	43	41*	1083	8.46	–	–	–	36
Harris, J.A.R.	14	23	4	87*	363	19.10	–	1	–	4
Harris, P.L.	77	94	15	55	1123	14.21	–	2	–	31
Harris, R.J.	27	47	5	74	759	18.07	–	3	–	12
Harrison, D.S.	82	116	16	88	1666	16.66	–	6	–	26
Harvey, I.J.	165	272	29	209*	8409	34.60	15	46	–	114
Hayward, M.	128	145	53	55*	1060	11.52	–	1	–	35
Hemingway, T.L.	5	6	2	34*	70	17.50	–	–	–	3
Hemp, D.L.	268	456	43	247*	15250	36.92	30	83	6	181
Henderson, C.W.	204	277	62	81	4082	18.98	–	14	–	72
Henderson, T.	86	137	17	81	1897	15.80	–	6	–	31
Heywood, J.J.N.	10	15	2	27	86	6.61	–	–	–	16
Hick, G.A.	526	871	84	405*	41112	52.23	136	158	19+1	709
Hildreth, J.C.	79	133	11	227*	4736	38.81	10	26	1	61
Hill, C.M.M.	2	3	–	29	42	14.00	–	–	–	1
Hinds, W.W.	137	233	9	213	7778	34.72	18	39	–	65
Hodd, A.J.	22	31	7	123	868	36.16	2	5	–	39/7
Hodge, B.J.	211	370	37	302*	16005	48.06	48	59	2+3	123
Hodgson, L.J.	1	2	–	63	66	33.00	–	1	–	2
Hodnett, G.P.	19	32	1	168	1020	32.90	2	7	–	14
Hogg, K.W.	41	50	5	71	1015	22.55	–	7	–	11
Hoggard, M.J.	179	229	67	89*	1458	9.00	–	3	–	50
Hole, S.M.	2	2	1	24	24	24.00	–	–	–	–
Hooper, J.H.P.	7	12	3	79	265	29.44	–	2	–	3
Hopkins, G.J.	102	162	24	175*	4319	31.29	7	19	–	267/18
Hopkinson, C.D.	55	90	4	106	2262	26.30	1	15	–	37

F-C	M	I	NO	HS	Runs	Avge	100	50	1000	Ct/St
Horton, P.J.	42	69	8	152	2804	45.96	6	16	2	33/1
Housego, D.M.	2	4	–	36	66	16.50	–	–	–	–
How, J.M.	70	120	9	169	3777	34.02	8	22	–	71
Howell, T.H.	2	4	–	82	123	30.75	–	1	–	–
Howgego, B.H.N.	1	2	1	15	16	16.00	–	–	–	–
Hughes, J.A.	6	8	1	45	149	21.28	–	–	–	–
Hughes, P.J.	7	12	3	116	559	62.11	1	6	–	7
Hunter, I.D.	56	74	18	65	935	16.69	–	2	–	16
Imran Arif	6	3	1	5	13	6.50	–	–	–	1
Imran Tahir	73	89	18	48	770	10.84	–	–	–	37
Ireland, A.J.	21	34	12	16*	93	4.22	–	–	–	6
Jacklin, B.D.	4	6	2	19*	34	8.50	–	–	–	1
James, M.I.	1	1	–	0	0	0.00	–	–	–	–
James, N.A.	1	1	–	34	34	34.00	–	–	–	1
Jefferson, W.I.	87	153	12	222	5111	36.24	11	20	1	81
Jewell, T.M.	1									
Jogia, K.A.	8	13	2	104*	438	39.81	1	2	–	8
Johnson, R.M.	1	1	–	72	72	72.00	–	1	–	1
Johnston, P.R.A.	2	4	1	34	65	21.66	–	–	–	4
Jones, G.O.	109	161	20	108*	4351	30.85	7	24	–	341/22
Jones, H.D.	2	2	1	6*	6	6.00	–	–	–	–
Jones, P.S.	122	144	36	114	2003	18.54	2	5	–	24
Jones, R.A.	5	6	1	24	40	8.00	–	–	–	1
Jones, S.P.	88	108	35	46	899	12.31	–	–	–	17
Jordan, C.J.	13	15	4	57	220	20.00	–	1	–	3
Joseph, R.H.	37	48	18	36*	330	11.00	–	–	–	8
Joyce, E.C.	127	210	17	211	8661	44.87	19	50	5	97
Junaid Siddique	22	41	1	114*	1038	25.95	1	6	–	19
Kalam, T.	9	10	2	64	131	16.37	–	1	–	4
Kallis, J.H.	212	347	50	200	16084	54.15	47	86	1	191
Kartik, M.	125	150	21	96	2420	18.75	–	11	–	86
Keedy, G.	170	194	97	64	1138	11.73	–	2	–	46
Kemp, J.M.	109	177	21	188	5445	34.90	12	27	–	140
Kemp, R.A.	5	7	1	7	18	3.00	–	–	–	2
Kervezee, A.N.	11	16	2	98	424	30.28	–	2	–	4
Key, R.W.T.	191	330	21	221	12818	41.48	37	50	5	109
Kieswetter, C.	31	42	7	93	1012	28.91	–	5	–	94/2
Killeen, N.	102	145	31	48	1302	11.42	–	–	–	26
King, R.E.	13	18	1	31	207	12.17	–	–	–	1
Kirby, S.P.	102	139	44	57	775	8.15	–	1	–	20
Kirtley, R.J.	167	228	75	59	1995	13.03	–	4	–	58
Kleinveldt, R.K.	40	62	7	115*	1097	19.94	1	5	–	22
Klokker, F.A.	7	12	2	103*	371	37.10	2	–	–	16
Klusener, L.	197	283	60	202*	9521	42.69	21	48	3	99
Kruger, G.J.P.	90	112	30	58	896	10.92	–	2	–	20
Kruger, N.	1	2	–	172	209	104.50	1	–	–	–
Kruis, G.J.	121	171	56	59	1718	14.93	–	3	–	44
Lamb, G.A.	38	59	7	100*	1175	22.59	1	6	–	31
Langer, J.L.	345	601	55	342	27551	50.45	84	106	5+6	307
Langeveldt, C.K.	87	109	38	56	1039	14.63	–	1	–	25
Latouf, K.J.	1	1	–	29	29	29.00	–	–	–	–
Law, S.G.	365	597	65	263	27041	50.82	79	128	9+2	406
Lawson, J.J.C.	54	75	22	35	434	8.18	–	–	–	15
Lawson, M.A.K.	17	23	6	44	205	12.05	–	–	–	7
Laxman, V.V.S.	209	340	38	353	15450	51.15	44	71	0+4	222/1
Lee, N.T.	7	12	1	48*	210	19.09	–	–	–	1

F-C	M	I	NO	HS	Runs	Avge	100	50	1000	Ct/St
Legget, C.W.S.	1	1	–	4	4	4.00	–	–	–	–
Lett, R.J.H.	9	13	1	57	263	21.91	–	4	–	3
Lewis, C.C.	189	275	34	247	7406	30.73	9	34	–	154
Lewis, J.	180	250	53	62	2857	14.50	–	6	–	41
Lewry, J.D.	181	237	62	72	1783	10.18	–	2	–	52
Liddle, C.J.	14	14	5	53	113	12.55	–	1	–	5
Logan, R.J.	54	73	16	37*	527	9.24	–	–	–	16
Louw, J.	102	149	22	124	2689	21.17	1	14	–	32
Loye, M.B.	232	370	33	322*	13520	40.11	39	54	6	115
Lucas, D.S.	48	57	16	49	763	18.60	–	–	–	8
Lumb, M.J.	113	193	14	144	5879	32.84	9	39	1	78
Lungley, T.	42	61	13	50	701	14.60	–	1	–	15
Lyth, A.	15	22	–	132	676	30.72	1	5	–	11
Macadam, J.C.	2	2	1	7	11	11.00	–	–	–	–
McCullum, B.B.	74	126	7	160	3974	33.39	6	22	–	200/13
McGrath, A.	198	333	25	188*	11475	37.25	27	55	2	144
McKenzie, N.D.	170	287	32	226	11139	43.68	28	56	–	137
McKerchar, B.T.	1	2	–	16	23	11.50	–	–	–	–
McLaren, R.	71	104	17	140	2450	28.16	2	13	–	37
MacLennan, S.K.	2	4	1	43	60	20.00	–	–	–	–
MacLeod, C.S.	2	–	–	–	–	–	–	–	–	1
McMahon, P.J.	21	23	3	99	371	18.55	–	2	–	13
Maddy, D.L.	242	392	27	229*	12247	33.55	26	58	4	251
Magoffin, S.J.	47	63	18	45	611	13.57	–	–	–	14
Mahmood, S.I.	66	86	14	94	975	13.54	–	2	–	13
Malan, D.J.	14	23	2	132*	714	34.00	1	5	–	5
Malcolm-Hansen, R.J.A.	6	9	1	93	283	35.37	–	2	–	2
Malik, M.N.	66	87	30	41	558	9.78	–	–	–	10
Marshall, H.J.H.	113	192	13	168	6346	35.45	15	30	1	55
Marshall, J.A.H.	102	175	8	235	4996	29.91	9	26	–	103
Marshall, S.J.	21	31	7	126*	809	33.70	1	3	–	6
Martin, C.S.	130	160	76	25	345	4.10	–	–	–	25
Martin-Jenkins, R.S.C.	162	246	36	205*	6520	31.04	3	35	1	46
Mascarenhas, A.D.	171	260	28	131	5931	25.56	7	22	–	68
Mason, M.J.	67	91	26	64*	1089	16.75	–	1	–	18
Mason, M.S.	76	92	23	63	976	14.14	–	3	–	15
Masters, D.D.	103	127	25	119	1342	13.15	1	2	–	30
Maunders, J.K.	72	129	3	180	3761	29.84	6	19	–	38
Maynard, T.L.	7	10	–	26	117	11.70	–	–	–	5
Meaker, S.C.	2	2	–	16	22	11.00	–	–	–	–
Mickleburgh, J.C.	3	4	–	72	150	37.50	–	2	–	3
Middlebrook, J.D.	135	191	25	127	4209	25.35	4	16	–	70
Miller, A.S.	1	1	–	4*	4	–	–	–	–	–
Mills, K.D.	57	83	22	117*	1718	28.16	1	11	–	20
Mitchell, D.K.H.	31	55	12	134*	1660	38.60	3	9	–	25
Mohammad Amin	9	9	2	25*	50	7.14	–	–	–	2
Mohammad Sami	94	127	37	49	1326	14.73	–	–	–	36
Mohammad Yousuf	122	202	20	223	9354	51.39	28	44	3	77
Moore, S.C.	84	151	15	246	5793	42.59	13	28	3	41
Morgan, C.F.D.	1	1	–	0	0	0.00	–	–	–	1
Morgan, E.J.G.	36	60	9	209*	2095	41.07	5	10	1	29/1
Morkel, J.A.	55	78	14	204*	2718	42.46	4	17	–	22
Morkel, M.	32	40	6	57	524	15.41	–	1	–	15
Morris, R.K.	5	5	1	88	97	24.25	–	1	–	1
Morse, E.J.	12	11	3	36	69	8.62	–	–	–	4
Mosharraf Hossain	33	53	6	85	911	19.38	–	4	–	15

F-C	M	I	NO	HS	Runs	Avge	100	50	1000	Ct/St
Muchall, G.J.	92	166	7	219	4541	28.55	7	23	–	60
Mullaney, S.J.	4	5	1	165*	257	64.25	1	–	–	3
Mumtaz Habibullah	3	4	1	10	20	6.66	–	–	–	1
Munday, M.K.	27	24	10	21	106	7.57	–	–	–	11
Murtagh, C.P.	12	18	2	107	287	17.93	1	–	–	7
Murtagh, T.J.	69	94	26	74*	1602	23.55	–	6	–	23
Murtaza Hussain	138	198	39	117	3432	21.58	1	12	–	67
Mushfiqur Rahim	27	47	6	115*	1111	27.09	2	7	–	47/4
Mushtaq Ahmed	309	389	57	90*	5124	15.43	–	20	–	119
Mustard, P.	83	134	7	130	3329	26.21	2	17	–	277/12
Naeem Islam	43	73	8	126	2343	36.04	4	16	–	33/1
Naik, J.K.H.	7	7	3	15	60	15.00	–	–	–	5
Nannes, D.P.	14	16	2	31*	77	5.50	–	–	–	4
Napier, G.R.	85	116	21	125	2910	30.63	3	18	–	34
Nash, C.D.	47	79	6	108	2362	32.35	2	17	–	17
Nash, D.C.	135	195	43	114	5532	36.39	11	27	–	281/23
Naved-ul-Hasan	108	153	18	139	3058	22.65	3	9	–	54
Nazimuddin	57	101	8	204	3358	36.10	7	20	–	25
Nazmul Hossain	24	39	10	49	347	11.96	–	–	–	11
Needham, J.	14	24	9	48	329	21.93	–	–	–	7
Nel, A.	107	120	37	56	1127	13.57	–	1	–	39
Nelson, M.A.G.	3	4	–	42	64	16.00	–	–	–	1
New, T.J.	50	84	10	125	2367	31.98	2	17	–	66/5
Newby, O.J.	30	26	7	38*	174	9.15	–	–	–	6
Newman, S.A.	88	151	3	219	6305	42.60	13	38	4	70
Nicholson, M.J.	124	171	34	133	3258	23.78	4	6	–	70
Nixon, P.A.	326	482	108	144*	12955	34.63	19	63	1	875/67
North, M.J.	116	204	19	239*	8129	43.94	20	46	0+1	86
Ntini, M.	159	181	60	34*	1128	9.32	–	–	–	37
O'Brien, I.E.	59	68	19	44	401	8.18	–	–	–	8
O'Brien, N.J.	69	101	14	176	3184	36.59	8	13	–	191/24
O'Driscoll, W.J.F.	6	7	1	42	188	31.33	–	–	–	2
Onions, G.	55	74	21	41	695	13.11	–	–	–	12
Oram, J.D.P.	76	122	16	155	3679	34.70	8	17	–	34
Ormond, J.	137	165	39	64*	1911	15.16	–	3	–	31
Owen, F.G.	4	7	–	50	141	20.14	–	1	–	–
Paget, C.D.	9	12	3	46	93	10.33	–	–	–	3
Palladino, A.P.	36	43	16	41	328	12.14	–	–	–	18
Panesar, M.S.	89	115	41	39*	585	7.90	–	–	–	22
Park, G.T.	18	30	6	100*	845	35.20	1	4	–	21
Parker, L.C.	28	43	3	140	1103	27.57	1	5	–	15
Parsons, T.W.	5	5	1	12	24	6.00	–	–	–	–
Patel, J.S.	66	80	31	58*	863	17.61	–	2	–	21
Patel, S.R.	41	61	6	176	2678	48.69	8	15	–	19
Patterson, S.A.	11	12	3	46	121	13.44	–	–	–	3
Pattinson, D.J.	18	22	2	33	154	7.70	–	–	–	2
Peploe, C.T.	30	41	7	46	530	15.58	–	–	–	11
Peters, S.D.	164	279	24	178	8315	32.60	18	41	2	125
Peterson, R.J.	85	133	17	130	3048	26.27	5	10	–	37
Pettini, M.L.	63	103	11	208*	3194	34.71	4	20	1	50
Philander, V.D.	35	55	5	168	1305	26.10	1	6	–	12
Phillips, B.J.	90	127	21	100*	2212	20.86	1	12	–	22
Phillips, T.J.	47	64	8	89	1074	19.17	–	3	–	30
Pietersen, K.P.	127	213	15	254*	10172	51.37	36	39	3	109
Pipe, D.J.	68	103	17	133*	2377	27.63	4	9	–	190/19
Plunkett, L.E.	68	102	21	74*	1591	19.64	–	6	–	37

F-C	M	I	NO	HS	Runs	Avge	100	50	1000	Ct/St
Pollock, S.M.	186	267	55	150*	7021	33.11	6	35	–	132
Poonia, N.S.	13	20	–	111	551	27.55	1	2	–	5
Porterfield, W.T.S.	24	40	1	166	1271	32.58	1	8	–	21
Pothas, N.	190	295	55	165	9788	40.78	23	48	–	535/45
Powell, M.J. (Wa)	149	246	12	236	7395	31.60	12	40	1	105
Powell, M.J. (Gm)	176	298	28	299	10577	39.17	23	51	5	113
Poynton, T.	3	5	–	14	17	3.40	–	–	–	7/2
Pratt, D.M.	3	2	–	47	52	26.00	–	–	–	2/1
Prince, A.G.	148	232	30	184	8498	42.06	21	40	–	90
Prior, M.J.	134	212	20	201*	7563	39.39	18	41	3	312/22
Prowting, N.R.	9	17	1	78	314	19.62	–	1	–	3
Pyrah, R.M.	12	17	1	106	438	27.37	1	2	–	6
Rajin Saleh	69	124	11	131*	4052	35.85	8	20	–	52
Ramprakash, M.R.	415	684	87	301*	31894	53.42	103	135	18	239
Rankin, W.B.	12	13	6	12*	46	6.57	–	–	–	7
Raqibul Hasan	22	39	1	313*	1418	37.31	2	8	–	15
Rashid, A.U.	43	61	9	111	1660	31.92	2	10	–	17
Rawlinson, H.C.L.	3	4	–	9	15	3.75	–	–	–	3
Rayner, O.P.	20	24	6	101	353	19.61	1	–	–	17
Read, C.M.W.	206	306	50	240	8552	33.40	12	46	1	601/32
Redfern, D.J.	9	13	2	69*	339	30.81	–	2	–	6
Redmond, A.J.	73	124	9	146	3652	31.75	6	20	–	46
Rees, G.P.	29	51	2	140	1601	32.67	5	9	1	29
Riazuddin, H.	1	1	–	4	4	4.00	–	–	–	–
Richardson, A.	102	102	38	91	721	11.26	–	1	–	28
Rist, W.H.	3	3	–	11	24	8.00	–	–	–	2
Rogers, C.J.L.	125	223	13	319	10209	48.61	28	52	2+1	120
Rowe, D.T.	9	9	1	85	139	17.37	–	1	–	1
Rubel Hossain	6	8	1	9	15	2.14	–	–	–	1
Rudge, W.D.	12	14	5	19*	73	8.11	–	–	–	4
Rudolph, J.A.	139	238	16	222*	9710	43.73	28	44	2	128
Ryan, L.C.	3	3	–	18	23	7.66	–	–	–	1
Sadler, J.L.	60	103	12	145	2931	32.20	3	16	1	40
Sadler, O.J.	4	8	3	77	250	50.00	–	2	–	1
Saggers, M.J.	115	143	41	64	1160	11.37	–	2	–	27
Sajidul Islam	27	41	18	64*	356	15.47	–	1	–	10
Saker, N.C.	18	23	4	58*	272	14.31	–	1	–	5
Sales, D.J.G.	188	299	28	303*	11458	42.28	23	57	6	167
Salisbury, I.D.K.	324	414	81	103	7012	21.05	3	26	–	206
Sanderson, B.W.	2	2	1	6	6	6.00	–	–	–	–
Saqlain Mushtaq	194	263	59	101*	3407	16.70	1	14	–	67
Saxelby, I.D.	3	3	1	11*	20	10.00	–	–	–	1
Sayers, J.J.	59	96	8	187	2815	31.98	8	12	–	32
Schofield, C.P.	78	109	15	99	2659	28.28	–	21	–	45
Scott, B.J.M.	60	90	18	164*	2148	29.83	3	13	–	159/19
Shafayat, B.M.	90	153	6	161	4732	32.19	8	27	1	78/6
Shah, O.A.	196	333	31	203	12984	42.99	35	66	8	154
Shahzad, A.	8	9	3	35	102	17.00	–	–	–	–
Shakib Al Hasan	28	51	6	108	1445	32.11	2	7	–	17
Shankar, A.	12	20	–	143	384	19.20	1	–	–	5
Shantry, A.J.	15	19	9	38*	108	10.80	–	–	–	6
Shoaib Akhtar	130	182	50	59*	1619	12.26	–	1	–	40
Shreck, C.E.	69	78	46	19	116	3.62	–	–	–	26
Sidebottom, R.J.	126	163	48	54	1361	11.83	–	1	–	45
Silverwood, C.E.W.	178	234	47	80	2962	15.83	–	9	–	41
Smith, B.F.	312	488	53	204	17869	41.07	40	94	8	196

F-C	M	I	NO	HS	Runs	Avge	100	50	1000	Ct/St
Smith, D.R.	60	99	6	114	2562	27.54	5	8	–	62
Smith, E.T.	191	325	19	213	12789	41.79	34	54	8	85
Smith, G.C.	107	186	12	311	8712	50.06	24	32	–	147
Smith, G.M.	39	68	5	113	1610	25.55	1	12	–	10
Smith, G.P.	6	10	–	54	215	21.50	–	1	–	2
Smith, T.C.	33	38	10	63	660	23.57	–	1	–	29
Smith, T.M.J.	1	1	–	2	2	2.00	–	–	–	–
Smith, W.R.	53	87	5	201*	2599	31.69	6	6	–	27
Snape, J.N.	121	180	31	131	4194	28.14	3	23	–	74
Snell, S.D.	22	36	5	127	1142	36.83	1	10	–	50/1
Solanki, V.S.	235	387	24	270	13306	36.65	25	71	4	244
Southee, T.G.	17	19	3	77*	278	17.37	–	2	–	1
Spearman, C.M.	195	351	16	341	12815	38.25	30	55	3	188
Spriegel, M.N.W.	15	25	2	51	518	22.52	–	1	–	6
Stayt, T.P.	3	3	1	6	9	4.50	–	–	–	2
Stevens, D.I.	138	226	14	208	6807	32.10	13	38	1	111
Steyn, D.W.	65	74	19	82	712	12.94	–	2	–	12
Stoneman, M.D.	21	37	1	101	798	22.16	1	4	–	9
Strachan, J.P.	1	1	–	5	5	5.00	–	–	–	1
Strauss, A.J.	162	288	13	177	11283	41.02	28	50	4	135
Stubbings, S.D.	132	240	13	151	7261	31.98	12	37	3	60
Suppiah, A.V.	28	47	1	123	1324	28.78	1	8	–	11
Sutcliffe, I.J.	191	305	28	203	9464	34.16	16	51	3	110
Sutton, L.D.	130	210	30	151*	5812	32.28	9	18	–	315/14
Swann, G.P.	171	240	17	183	6034	27.05	4	31	–	125
Syed Rasel	42	65	22	33	445	10.34	–	–	–	7
Tahir, N.	37	39	12	49	437	16.18	–	–	–	3
Tamim Iqbal	23	40	1	118	1510	38.71	2	13	–	7
Taylor, B.V.	53	68	26	40	431	10.26	–	–	–	6
Taylor, C.G.	114	201	15	196	6436	34.60	16	26	2	74
Taylor, C.R.	39	65	3	121	1615	26.04	3	8	–	23
Taylor, J.W.A.	4	5	–	51	64	12.80	–	1	–	4
Taylor, L.R.P.L.	50	83	3	217	3060	38.25	7	16	–	49
Telo, F.D.	25	45	3	134*	1401	33.35	3	6	–	8
Ten Doeschate, R.N.	55	75	8	259*	3309	49.38	13	10	–	30
Thomas, A.C.	83	123	26	119*	2492	25.69	2	8	–	29
Thompson, G.J.	12	10	3	38	132	18.85	–	–	–	7
Thompson, J.G.	1	2	–	21	32	16.00	–	–	–	–
Thornely, M.A.	4	7	1	11	28	4.66	–	–	–	6
Thorp, C.D.	37	54	7	75	626	13.31	–	2	–	15
Timms, R.T.	7	13	–	57	242	18.61	–	2	–	5
Tomlinson, J.A.	38	50	23	35*	240	8.88	–	–	–	10
Tredwell, J.C.	71	103	12	123*	1994	21.91	2	8	–	72
Trego, P.D.	67	97	13	140	3049	36.29	6	17	–	20
Tremlett, C.T.	85	114	31	64	1563	18.83	–	6	–	25
Trescothick, M.E.	239	412	21	284	14828	37.92	31	76	2	293
Trott, I.J.L.	116	196	21	210	7102	40.58	14	37	4	116
Troughton, J.O.	93	143	14	162	5085	39.41	14	27	1	43
Tudor, A.J.	125	163	32	144	2877	21.96	2	9	–	35
Turner, M.L.	8	8	2	57	89	14.83	–	1	–	2
Udal, S.D.	274	387	74	117*	7317	23.37	1	32	–	117
Van der Wath, J.J.	81	120	22	113*	2376	24.24	2	14	–	25
Van Jaarsveld, M.	201	340	31	262*	13904	44.99	41	67	4+1	284
Vaughan, M.P.	262	460	27	197	16136	37.26	42	68	4	117
Vettori, D.L.	132	186	27	137*	4388	27.59	4	25	–	62
Vincent, L.	92	151	11	224	4922	35.15	10	29	–	108

F-C	M	I	NO	HS	Runs	Avge	100	50	1000	Ct/St
Voges, A.C.	52	88	13	180	2966	39.54	7	12	–	62
Wagg, G.G.	50	73	10	108	1669	26.49	1	9	–	18
Wagh, M.A.	172	284	24	315	10420	40.07	25	53	6	76
Wainwright, D.J.	14	18	4	104*	439	31.35	1	1	–	9
Wakely, A.G.	9	16	1	66	287	19.13	–	3	–	5
Walker, M.J.	183	301	32	275*	9768	36.31	25	40	3	121
Wallace, M.A.	134	219	16	128	5577	27.47	6	28	–	344/27
Walters, S.J.	17	26	1	70	521	20.84	–	2	–	15
Waters, H.T.	23	37	18	34	145	7.63	–	–	–	6
Watkins, R.E.	33	56	4	87	951	18.28	–	2	–	18
Wessels, M.H.	51	83	7	107	2150	28.28	3	13	–	100/10
Westley, T.	15	26	5	93*	530	25.23	–	3	–	8
Westwood, I.J.	51	87	9	178	2811	36.03	6	14	–	24
Wharf, A.G.	121	184	29	128*	3570	23.03	6	14	–	63
Wheater, A.J.	2	1	–	22	22	22.00	–	–	–	3
Whelan, C.D.	9	8	3	58	92	18.40	–	1	–	1
White, C.	276	438	57	186	12395	32.53	21	62	–	167
White, G.G.	6	6	–	65	108	18.00	–	1	–	1
White, R.A.	70	119	11	277	3690	34.16	6	17	1	44
White, W.A.	11	16	3	19*	146	11.23	–	–	–	5
Whiteley, R.A.	1	2	–	27	45	22.50	–	–	–	–
Whittington, N.M.H.	1	1	–	83	83	83.00	–	1	–	1
Wigley, D.H.	38	47	14	70	458	13.87	–	2	–	17
Williams, D.M.	2	3	–	11	25	8.33	–	–	–	–
Williams, R.E.M.	6	9	4	15	34	6.80	–	–	–	2
Willoughby, C.M.	177	202	92	47	676	6.14	–	–	–	37
Wilshaw, P.J.	7	12	–	63	361	30.08	–	3	–	5
Wilson, G.C.	5	6	1	27	51	10.20	–	–	–	9
Wiseman, P.J.	186	254	51	130	4254	20.95	2	16	–	79
Woakes, C.R.	13	15	4	64*	274	24.90	–	1	–	11
Wood, M.J. (Gm)	136	236	21	207	7032	32.70	16	31	4	118
Wood, M.J. (Nt)	90	153	7	297	4914	33.65	9	31	1	30
Woodhouse, A.	1	2	–	2	2	1.00	–	–	–	–
Woodman, R.J.	4	6	1	46*	69	13.80	–	–	–	–
Wright, B.J.	12	19	2	108	401	23.58	1	2	–	15
Wright, C.J.C.	29	37	6	76	625	20.16	–	3	–	9
Wright, J.	45	63	12	155*	1536	30.11	3	7	–	24
Yardy, M.H.	103	175	16	257	6165	38.77	12	31	1	74
Yasir Arafat	142	217	33	122	5095	27.69	4	28	–	44
Young, P.J.W.	9	13	1	54	280	23.33	–	1	–	4
Zondeki, M.	71	98	31	59	626	9.34	–	1	–	22

BOWLING

'50wS' denotes instances of taking 50 or more wickets in a season. Where these have been achieved outside the British Isles they are shown after a plus sign.

	Runs	Wkts	Avge	Best	5wI	10wM	50wS
Abdul Razzaq	10316	316	32.64	7- 51	10	2	–
Ackerman, H.D.	57	0					
Adams, A.R.	8358	352	23.74	6- 25	13	2	–
Adams, C.J.	1935	41	47.19	4- 28	–	–	–
Adams, J.H.K.	569	10	56.90	2- 16	–	–	–
Afzaal, U.	4513	83	54.37	4-101	–	–	–
Aga, R.G.	668	22	30.36	4- 63	–	–	–
Ahmed, J.S.	487	11	44.27	3- 42	–	–	–

F-C	Runs	Wkts	Avge	Best	5wI	10wM	50wS
Ahmed, M.	70	2	35.00	1- 28	–	–	–
Ali, Kabir	11035	418	26.39	8- 50	20	4	5
Ali, Kadeer	289	3	96.33	1- 4	–	–	–
Ali, M.M.	572	3	190.66	2- 50	–	–	–
Allenby, J.	1421	41	34.65	5-125	1	–	–
Ambrose, T.R.	1	0					
Amjad Khan	6625	211	31.39	6- 52	6	–	2
Amla, H.M.	221	1	221.00	1- 10	–	–	–
Anderson, J.M.	8376	291	28.78	7- 43	13	1	2
Andrew, G.M.	2007	55	36.49	5- 58	1	–	–
Ansari, A.S.	311	9	34.55	4- 50	–	–	–
Anyon, J.E.	4198	108	38.87	6- 82	2	–	–
Azhar Mahmood	13048	515	25.33	8- 61	21	3	0+1
Baer, M.	110	0					
Bailey, S.P.	127	3	42.33	2-119	–	–	–
Baker, F.B.	345	4	86.25	2- 75	–	–	–
Balcombe, D.J.	1732	36	48.11	5-112	1	–	–
Banerjee, V.	2724	49	55.59	4- 38	–	–	–
Banks, O.A.C.	6072	165	36.80	7- 70	6	1	–
Batty, G.J.	11452	352	32.53	7- 52	15	1	2
Batty, J.N.	61	1	61.00	1- 21	–	–	–
Beer, W.A.T.	81	1	81.00	1- 18	–	–	–
Bell, I.R.	1490	47	31.70	4- 4	–	–	–
Benham, C.C.	37	0					
Benkenstein, D.M.	3059	85	35.98	4- 16	–	–	–
Benning, J.G.E.	938	12	78.16	3- 57	–	–	–
Berg, G.K.	171	5	34.20	3- 38	–	–	–
Blackwell, I.D.	10076	239	42.15	7- 90	7	–	–
Blain, J.A.R.	4266	120	35.55	6- 42	4	–	–
Blake, A.J.	17	0					
Boje, N.	17069	532	32.08	8- 93	22	2	–
Bond, S.E.	5177	211	24.53	7- 66	11	1	–
Bopara, R.S.	3946	90	43.84	5- 75	1	–	–
Borrington, P.M.	5	0					
Botha, A.G.	9380	275	34.10	8- 53	8	1	1
Boucher, M.V.	26	1	26.00	1- 6	–	–	–
Boyce, M.A.G.	61	0					
Bradshaw, D.P.	176	1	176.00	1- 28	–	–	–
Brathwaite, R.M.R.	748	13	57.53	3- 61	–	–	–
Breese, G.R.	8288	274	30.24	7- 60	12	3	–
Bresnan, T.T.	6008	190	31.62	5- 42	3	–	–
Broad, S.C.J.	4617	153	30.17	5- 67	6	–	–
Brophy, G.L.	1	0					
Brown, A.D.	635	5	127.00	3- 25	–	–	–
Brown, D.O.	1251	28	44.67	5- 38	1	–	–
Brown, J.F.	14035	414	33.90	7- 69	22	5	3
Brown, K.R.	7	0					
Burton, D.A.	226	1	226.00	1- 97	–	–	–
Butcher, M.A.	4237	125	33.89	5- 86	1	–	–
Buttleman, J.E.L.	167	6	27.83	2- 32	–	–	–
Caddick, A.R.	30862	1170	26.37	9- 32	78	17	12
Cairns, C.L.	18322	647	28.31	8- 47	30	6	3
Carberry, M.A.	521	7	74.42	2- 85	–	–	–
Carter, N.M.	8425	230	36.63	6- 63	8	–	–

F-C	Runs	Wkts	Avge	Best	5wI	10wM	50wS
Chambers, M.A.	335	9	37.22	3- 37	–	–	–
Chanderpaul, S.	2453	56	43.80	4- 48	–	–	–
Chapple, G.	19213	693	27.72	7- 53	27	2	4
Cheetham, S.P.	127	1	127.00	1- 44	–	–	–
Chilton, M.J.	664	10	66.40	1- 1	–	–	–
Chopra, V.	39	0					
Clare, J.L.	1074	41	26.19	7- 74	2	–	–
Clark, S.R.	9318	344	27.08	8- 58	13	1	–
Clarke, R.	5215	125	41.72	4- 21	–	–	–
Claydon, M.E.	576	10	57.60	3- 26	–	–	–
Cliff, S.J.	367	11	33.36	4- 42	–	–	–
Clinton, R.S.	207	2	103.50	2- 30	–	–	–
Clough, G.D.	766	16	47.87	3- 69	–	–	–
Cobb, J.J.	134	4	33.50	2- 11	–	–	–
Coetzer, K.J.	22	0					
Collingwood, P.D.	4584	119	38.52	5- 52	1	–	–
Collins, P.T.	10136	380	26.67	6- 24	9	–	0+1
Collymore, C.D.	7851	290	27.07	7- 57	10	2	–
Compton, N.R.D.	123	1	123.00	1- 94	–	–	–
Cook, A.N.	118	3	39.33	3- 13	–	–	–
Cook, S.J.	8347	259	32.22	8- 63	9	–	–
Cork, D.G.	23828	895	26.62	9- 43	32	5	7
Cosker, D.A.	13897	366	37.96	6-140	4	–	–
Crawley, J.P.	283	2	141.50	1- 7	–	–	–
Croft, R.D.B.	37463	1049	35.71	8- 66	48	9	9
Croft, S.J.	921	22	41.86	4- 51	–	–	–
Crook, A.R.	574	8	71.75	3- 71	–	–	–
Crook, S.P.	2649	53	49.98	4- 56	–	–	–
Cummins, R.A.G.	2184	49	44.57	5- 60	1	–	–
Daggett, L.M.	1959	53	36.96	8- 94	2	–	–
Dalrymple, J.W.M.	5776	127	45.48	5- 49	1	–	–
Danish Kaneria	18144	680	26.68	7- 39	47	6	2+1
Davies, A.M.	4722	223	21.17	8- 24	12	2	1
Dawson, L.A.	213	6	35.50	2- 32	–	–	–
Dawson, R.K.J.	8160	187	43.63	6- 82	5	–	–
Dean, K.J.	10470	401	26.10	8- 52	17	4	2
De Bruyn, Z.	5609	143	39.22	7- 67	3	–	–
Denly, J.L.	354	10	35.40	2- 13	–	–	–
Dernbach, J.W.	1679	41	40.95	6- 72	1	–	–
De Villiers, A.B.	99	2	49.50	2- 49	–	–	–
Dexter, N.J.	523	9	58.11	2- 40	–	–	–
Dhiman Ghosh	178	9	19.77	3- 7	–	–	–
Dingle, L.A.	98	0					
Dippenaar, H.H.	17	0					
Di Venuto, M.J.	484	5	96.80	1- 0	–	–	–
Dolar Mahmud	1147	43	26.67	7- 52	2	–	–
Doshi, N.D.	5851	149	39.26	7-110	6	3	1
Drew, B.G.	2114	52	40.65	6- 94	2	–	–
Duminy, J.P.	739	16	46.18	4- 89	–	–	–
Du Plessis, F.	719	23	31.26	4- 39	–	–	–
Du Preez, D.	3323	144	23.07	7-108	5	1	0+1
Durston, W.J.	1407	24	58.62	3- 23	–	–	–
Du Toit, J.	246	5	49.20	3- 31	–	–	–
Ealham, M.A.	16979	615	27.60	8- 36	23	2	1

F-C	Runs	Wkts	Avge	Best	5wI	10wM	50wS
Edwards, N.J.	194	2	97.00	1- 16	–	–	–
Elliott, G.D.	2148	60	35.80	4- 56	–	–	–
Ervine, S.M.	5770	144	40.06	6- 82	5	–	–
Evans, D.	1123	35	32.08	6- 35	2	–	–
Ferley, R.S.	2687	57	47.14	6-136	1	–	–
Fernando, C.R.D.	7237	254	28.49	6- 29	6	–	–
Finn, S.T.	1378	41	33.60	4- 51	–	–	–
Fisher, I.D.	6713	157	42.75	5- 30	7	1	–
Fletcher, L.J.	70	1	70.00	1- 70	–	–	–
Flintoff, A.	10116	319	31.71	5- 24	3	–	–
Flower, G.W.	5573	165	33.77	7- 31	3	–	–
Flynn, D.R.	87	0					
Foster, J.S.	128	1	128.00	1-122	–	–	–
Foster, P.J.	505	16	31.56	4- 26	–	–	–
Francis, J.D.	164	4	41.00	1- 1	–	–	–
Franklin, J.E.C.	7690	310	24.81	7- 30	11	1	–
Franks, P.J	13128	407	32.25	7- 56	11	–	2
Friedlander, M.J.	1070	26	41.15	6- 78	1	–	–
Frost, T.	18	0					
Frylinck, R.	1195	48	24.89	6- 94	1	–	–
Fulton, P.G.	399	11	36.27	4- 49	–	–	–
Gale, A.W.	36	1	36.00	1- 33	–	–	–
Gale, D.J.	35	0					
Gallian, J.E.R.	4164	96	43.37	6-115	1	–	–
Gibbs, H.H.	78	3	26.00	2- 14	–	–	–
Gidman, A.P.R.	3832	83	46.16	4- 47	–	–	–
Gidman, W.R.S.	86	4	21.50	3- 37	–	–	–
Gillespie, J.N.	16540	613	26.98	8- 50	22	2	0+1
Gitsham, M.T.	271	3	90.33	1- 12	–	–	–
Glover, J.C.	188	6	31.33	3- 56	–	–	–
Godleman, B.A.	35	0					
Goodwin, M.W.	363	7	51.85	2- 23	–	–	–
Gough, D.	23217	855	27.15	7- 28	33	3	5
Grant, R.N.	268	6	44.66	1- 7	–	–	–
Greenidge, C.G.	5034	145	34.71	6- 40	6	–	1
Griffiths, D.A.	618	14	44.14	4- 46	–	–	–
Groenewald, T.D.	1129	26	43.42	5- 24	1	–	–
Guy, S.M.	8	0					
Hall, A.J.	10528	406	25.93	6- 77	14	1	–
Hamilton-Brown, R.J.	85	3	28.33	2- 54	–	–	–
Hannon-Dalby, O.J.	114	1	114.00	1- 58	–	–	–
Hardinges, M.A.	3851	95	40.53	5- 51	1	–	–
Harmison, B.W.	723	19	38.05	4- 27	–	–	–
Harmison, S.J.	17189	607	28.31	7- 12	22	1	5
Harris, A.J.	12909	407	31.71	7- 54	16	3	2
Harris, J.A.R.	1173	44	26.65	7- 66	2	1	–
Harris, P.L.	7609	252	30.19	6- 54	12	–	0+1
Harris, R.J.	2515	71	35.42	7-108	2	–	–
Harrison, D.S.	7350	200	36.75	5- 48	6	–	1
Harvey, I.J.	11693	425	27.51	8-101	15	2	–
Hayward, M.	12263	431	28.45	6- 31	9	2	1
Hemingway, T.L.	673	14	48.07	4- 58	–	–	–
Hemp, D.L.	821	17	48.29	3- 23	–	–	–
Henderson, C.W.	21131	673	31.39	7- 57	23	1	–

F-C	Runs	Wkts	Avge	Best	5wI	10wM	50wS
Henderson, T.	7024	262	26.80	7- 67	10	1	–
Hick, G.A.	10308	232	44.43	5- 18	5	1	–
Hildreth, J.C.	316	4	79.00	2- 39	–	–	–
Hill, C.M.M.	198	2	99.00	1- 77	–	–	–
Hinds, W.W.	1388	39	35.58	3- 9	–	–	–
Hodge, B.J.	2881	72	40.01	4- 17	–	–	–
Hodgson, L.J.	58	0					
Hodnett, G.P.	142	2	71.00	2- 91	–	–	–
Hogg, K.W.	2756	70	39.37	5- 48	1	–	–
Hoggard, M.J.	16802	622	27.01	7- 49	20	1	2
Hole, S.M.	105	2	52.50	2- 29	–	–	–
Hopkins, G.J.	13	0					
Hopkinson, C.D.	262	2	131.00	1- 20	–	–	–
How, J.M.	1018	19	53.57	3- 57	–	–	–
Howell, T.H.	80	5	16.00	3- 52	–	–	–
Hughes, J.A.	239	7	34.14	3- 33	–	–	–
Hunter, I.D.	5242	129	40.63	5- 63	1	–	–
Imran Arif	575	22	26.13	5- 50	1	–	–
Imran Tahir	7045	284	24.80	8- 76	17	4	0+1
Ireland, A.J.	1823	56	32.55	7- 36	1	1	–
Jacklin, B.D.	362	5	72.40	2- 42	–	–	–
James, M.I.	25	0					
James, N.A.	6	1	6.00	1- 6	–	–	–
Jefferson, W.I.	60	1	60.00	1- 16	–	–	–
Jewell, T.M.	16	1	16.00	1- 16	–	–	–
Jogia, K.A.	79	0					
Jones, G.O.	18	0					
Jones, H.D.	114	1	114.00	1- 26	–	–	–
Jones, P.S.	11953	319	37.47	6- 25	9	1	2
Jones, R.A.	435	8	54.37	3- 37	–	–	–
Jones, S.P.	7947	260	30.56	6- 45	15	1	–
Jordan, C.J.	1060	32	33.12	3- 32	–	–	–
Joseph, R.H.	3446	111	31.04	6- 32	4	–	1
Joyce, E.C.	1016	10	101.60	2- 34	–	–	–
Junaid Siddique	99	1	99.00	1- 30	–	–	–
Kalam, T.	720	10	72.00	3- 54	–	–	–
Kallis, J.H.	11429	375	30.47	6- 54	8	–	–
Kartik, M.	11053	424	26.06	9- 70	23	3	1
Keedy, G.J.	16270	509	31.96	7- 93	24	5	3
Kemp, J.M.	4996	186	26.86	6- 56	5	–	–
Kemp, R.A.	339	10	33.90	3- 23	–	–	–
Kervezee, A.N.	59	2	29.50	1- 14	–	–	–
Key, R.W.T.	94	0					
Killeen, N.	8215	262	31.35	7- 70	9	–	1
King, R.E.	941	17	55.35	4- 34	–	–	–
Kirby, S.P.	10618	364	29.17	8- 80	14	4	1
Kirtley, R.J.	16422	608	27.00	7- 21	29	4	7
Kleinveldt, R.K.	3337	107	31.18	8- 47	4	1	–
Klokker, F.A.	99	0					
Klusener, L.	15447	508	30.40	8- 34	20	4	–
Kruger, G.J.P.	8817	300	29.39	8-112	13	2	–
Kruis, G.J.	11988	384	31.21	7- 58	19	1	1
Lamb, G.A.	1425	39	36.53	7- 73	1	–	–
Langer, J.L.	210	5	42.00	2- 17	–	–	–

191

F-C	Runs	Wkts	Avge	Best	5wI	10wM	50wS
Langeveldt, C.K.	8064	283	28.49	6- 48	9	1	1
Law, S.G.	4236	83	51.03	5- 39	1	–	–
Lawson, J.J.C.	5100	174	29.31	7- 78	6	–	–
Lawson, M.A.K.	1782	42	42.42	6- 88	4	–	–
Laxman, V.V.S.	728	21	34.66	3- 11	–	–	–
Lee, N.T.	24	1	24.00	1- 24	–	–	–
Legget, C.W.S.	43	2	21.50	2- 43	–	–	–
Lewis, C.C.	16225	543	29.88	6- 22	20	3	2
Lewis, J.	16681	621	26.86	8- 95	32	5	6
Lewry, J.D.	16299	611	26.67	8-106	31	4	5
Liddle, C.J.	962	17	56.58	3- 42	–	–	–
Logan, R.J.	5246	133	39.44	6- 93	4	–	–
Louw, J.	9399	289	32.52	6- 39	11	1	1
Loye, M.B.	61	1	61.00	1- 8	–	–	–
Lucas, D.S.	4277	115	37.19	5- 30	4	–	–
Lumb, M.J.	242	6	40.33	2- 10	–	–	–
Lungley, T.	3623	117	30.96	5- 20	3	–	1
Lyth, A.	117	2	58.50	1- 12	–	–	–
Macadam, J.C.	101	1	101.00	1- 41	–	–	–
McGrath, A.	3728	109	34.20	5- 39	1	–	–
McKenzie, N.D.	364	7	52.00	2- 13	–	–	–
McLaren, R.	5593	230	24.31	8- 38	10	1	1+1
MacLeod, C.S.	86	4	21.50	3- 36	–	–	–
McMahon, P.J.	1948	52	37.46	5- 30	1	–	–
Maddy, D.L.	6585	205	32.12	5- 37	5	–	–
Magoffin, S.J.	4460	153	29.15	8- 47	4	–	–
Mahmood, S.I.	5902	185	31.90	5- 37	4	–	–
Malan, D.J.	356	7	50.85	2- 26	–	–	–
Malcolm-Hansen, R.J.A.	128	1	128.00	1- 40	–	–	–
Malik, M.N.	6467	179	36.12	6- 46	7	–	–
Marshall, H.J.H.	697	11	63.36	1- 6	–	–	–
Marshall, J.A.H.	299	4	74.75	1- 5	–	–	–
Marshall, S.J.	2147	32	67.09	6-128	1	–	–
Martin, C.S.	12575	407	30.89	6- 54	18	1	0+1
Martin-Jenkins, R.S.C.	10867	331	32.83	7- 51	6	–	–
Mascarenhas, A.D.	11200	405	27.65	6- 25	16	–	1
Mason, M.J.	5384	220	24.47	6- 56	8	1	–
Mason, M.S.	6375	237	26.89	8- 45	8	1	3
Masters, D.D.	8457	278	30.42	6- 24	10	–	–
Maunders, J.K.	928	24	38.66	4- 15	–	–	–
Maynard, T.L.	18	0					
Meaker, S.C.	139	4	34.75	3- 86	–	–	–
Mickleburgh, J.C.	11	0					
Middlebrook, J.D.	11861	305	38.88	6- 82	8	1	1
Miller, A.S.	45	3	15.00	2- 35	–	–	–
Mills, K.D.	4409	169	26.08	5- 33	3	1	–
Mitchell, D.K.H.	280	7	40.00	3- 50	–	–	–
Mohammad Amin	1043	11	94.81	3- 66	–	–	–
Mohammad Sami	10070	318	31.66	8- 39	17	2	–
Mohammad Yousuf	24	0					
Moore, S.C.	321	5	64.20	1- 13	–	–	–
Morgan, E.J.G.	46	2	23.00	2- 24	–	–	–
Morkel, J.A.	4388	144	30.47	6- 36	3	–	–
Morkel, M.	3099	103	30.08	6- 66	4	–	–

F-C	Runs	Wkts	Avge	Best	5wI	10wM	50wS
Morris, R.K.	274	5	54.80	2- 58	–	–	–
Morse, E.J.	1055	29	36.37	6-102	2	–	–
Mosharraf Hossain	3437	122	28.17	9-105	5	1	–
Muchall, G.J.	615	15	41.00	3- 26	–	–	–
Mullaney, S.J.	84	1	84.00	1- 3	–	–	–
Mumtaz Habibullah	233	4	58.25	3- 92	–	–	–
Munday, M.K.	2182	76	28.71	8- 55	4	2	–
Murtagh, C.P.	8	0					
Murtagh, T.J.	5596	182	30.74	7- 95	7	1	1
Murtaza Hussain	13137	544	24.14	9- 54	36	7	0+5
Mushtaq Ahmed	36127	1407	25.67	9- 48	104	32	9+2
Naeem Islam	751	17	44.17	3- 7	–	–	–
Naik, J.K.H.	514	7	73.42	3- 70	–	–	–
Nannes, D.P.	1407	51	27.58	6- 32	1	–	–
Napier, G.R.	6555	164	39.96	6-103	3	–	–
Nash, C.D.	647	12	53.91	3- 7	–	–	–
Nash, D.C.	105	2	52.50	1- 8	–	–	–
Naved-ul-Hasan	11357	470	24.16	7- 49	26	4	2+3
Nazimuddin	95	2	47.50	1- 9	–	–	–
Nazmul Hossain	1577	53	29.75	5- 30	2	–	–
Needham, J.	915	28	32.67	6- 49	1	–	–
Nel, A.	9928	368	26.97	6- 25	12	1	–
Nelson, M.A.G.	124	2	62.00	2- 62	–	–	–
New, T.J.	175	5	35.00	2- 18	–	–	–
Newby, O.J.	2398	74	32.40	5- 69	1	–	–
Newman, S.A.	22	0					
Nicholson, M.J.	12147	406	29.91	7- 62	11	–	–
Nixon, P.A.	141	0					
North, M.J.	3673	81	45.34	4- 16	–	–	–
Ntini, M.	16132	555	29.06	7- 37	23	4	–
O'Brien, I.E.	5113	209	24.46	8- 55	9	1	–
O'Brien, N.J.	4	1	4.00	1- 4	–	–	–
O'Driscoll, W.J.F.	555	7	79.28	2- 67	–	–	–
Onions, G.	5180	153	33.85	8-101	4	–	1
Oram, J.D.P.	3640	143	25.45	6- 45	3	–	–
Ormond, J.	13479	448	30.08	7- 63	20	1	4
Paget, C.D.	449	6	74.83	3- 63	–	–	–
Palladino, A.P.	2754	70	39.34	6- 41	2	–	–
Panesar, M.S.	9872	319	30.94	7-181	19	3	3
Park, G.T.	320	2	160.00	2- 20	–	–	–
Parker, L.C.	274	6	45.66	2- 37	–	–	–
Parsons, T.W.	312	8	39.00	3- 70	–	–	–
Patel, J.S.	5240	126	41.58	6- 32	3	–	–
Patel, S.R.	1170	34	34.41	4- 68	–	–	–
Patterson, S.A.	574	15	38.26	3- 19	–	–	–
Pattinson, D.J.	1702	60	28.36	6- 30	4	–	–
Peploe, C.T.	2839	56	50.69	4- 31	–	–	–
Peters, S.D.	31	1	31.00	1- 19	–	–	–
Peterson, R.J.	7854	227	34.59	6- 67	10	1	–
Pettini, M.L.	129	0					
Philander, V.D.	2539	114	22.27	7- 64	3	–	–
Phillips, B.J.	6004	197	30.47	6- 29	4	–	–
Phillips, T.J.	3937	82	48.01	5- 41	1	–	–
Pietersen, K.P.	3104	60	51.73	4- 31	–	–	–

F-C	Runs	Wkts	Avge	Best	5wI	10wM	50wS
Plunkett, L.E.	6423	202	31.79	6- 74	5	–	2
Pollock, S.M.	15508	667	23.25	7- 33	22	2	0+1
Porterfield, W.T.S.	57	1	57.00	1- 57	–	–	–
Pothas, N.	63	1	63.00	1- 16	–	–	–
Powell, M.J. (Wa)	745	11	67.72	2- 16	–	–	–
Powell, M.J. (Gm)	132	2	66.00	2- 39	–	–	–
Prince, A.G.	166	4	41.50	2- 11	–	–	–
Prowting, N.R.	39	0					
Pyrah, R.M.	278	5	55.60	1- 3	–	–	–
Rajin Saleh	722	5	144.40	2- 44	–	–	–
Ramprakash, M.R.	2196	34	64.58	3- 32	–	–	–
Rankin, W.B.	994	42	23.66	5- 39	1	–	–
Raqibul Hasan	202	4	50.50	1- 4	–	–	–
Rashid, A.U.	4691	140	33.50	7-107	8	–	1
Rayner, O.P.	1804	51	35.37	5- 49	3	–	–
Read, C.M.W.	88	0					
Redfern, D.J.	124	3	41.33	1- 7	–	–	–
Redmond, A.J.	4033	87	46.35	4- 35	–	–	–
Riazuddin, H.	99	1	99.00	1- 21	–	–	–
Richardson, A.	8739	303	28.84	8- 46	9	1	1
Rogers, C.J.L.	119	1	119.00	1- 16	–	–	–
Rowe, D.T.	684	18	38.00	5- 61	1	–	–
Rubel Hossain	657	11	59.72	3- 86	–	–	–
Rudge, W.D.	1046	20	52.30	3- 46	–	–	–
Rudolph, J.A.	2324	58	40.06	5- 80	3	–	–
Ryan, L.C.	283	4	70.75	2-114	–	–	–
Sadler, J.L.	250	3	83.33	1- 5	–	–	–
Sadler, O.J.	102	3	34.00	3- 41	–	–	–
Saggers, M.J.	10249	405	25.30	7- 79	18	–	4
Sajidul Islam	2402	80	30.02	5- 61	1	–	–
Saker, N.C.	1578	31	50.90	5- 76	1	–	–
Sales, D.J.G.	174	9	19.33	4- 25	–	–	–
Salisbury, I.D.K.	28865	884	32.65	8- 60	40	6	7
Sanderson, B.W.	140	1	140.00	1- 87	–	–	–
Saqlain Mushtaq	19630	833	23.56	8- 65	60	15	5+1
Saxelby, I.D.	218	2	109.00	1- 64	–	–	–
Sayers, J.J.	54	0					
Schofield, C.P.	6436	196	32.83	6-120	5	–	–
Scott, B.J.M.	1	0					
Shafayat, B.M.	498	4	124.50	2- 25	–	–	–
Shah, O.A.	1324	22	60.18	3- 33	–	–	–
Shahzad, A.	452	12	37.66	4- 22	–	–	–
Shakib Al Hasan	1846	52	35.50	6- 79	2	–	–
Shantry, A.J.	984	51	19.29	5- 49	3	1	–
Shoaib Akhtar	12041	451	26.69	6- 11	28	2	0+1
Shreck, C.E.	7532	268	28.10	8- 31	18	2	2
Sidebottom, R.J.	10371	410	25.29	7- 47	17	2	2
Silverwood, C.E.W.	15394	570	27.00	7- 93	25	1	3
Smith, B.F.	488	4	122.00	1- 5	–	–	–
Smith, D.R.	2479	87	28.49	4- 22	–	–	–
Smith, E.T.	119	1	119.00	1- 60	–	–	–
Smith, G.C.	1048	11	95.27	2-145	–	–	–
Smith, G.M.	1624	39	41.64	3- 31	–	–	–
Smith, G.P.	64	1	64.00	1- 64	–	–	–

F-C	Runs	Wkts	Avge	Best	5wI	10wM	50wS
Smith, T.C.	2256	69	32.69	4- 57	–	–	–
Smith, T.M.J.	79	1	79.00	1- 52	–	–	–
Smith, W.R.	494	8	61.75	3- 34	–	–	–
Snape, J.N.	5583	113	49.40	5- 65	1	–	–
Snell, S.D	15	0					
Solanki, V.S.	3956	84	47.09	5- 40	4	1	–
Southee, T.G.	1628	61	26.68	6- 68	3	–	–
Spearman, C.M.	55	1	55.00	1- 37	–	–	–
Spriegel, M.N.W.	355	10	35.50	2- 28	–	–	–
Stayt, T.P.	218	4	54.50	3- 51	–	–	–
Stevens, D.I.	2385	64	37.23	4- 36	–	–	–
Steyn, D.W.	6790	278	24.42	8- 41	16	4	0+2
Strachan, J.P.	98	1	98.00	1- 63	–	–	–
Strauss, A.J.	79	2	39.50	1- 16	–	–	–
Stubbings, S.D.	121	0					
Suppiah, A.V.	950	14	67.85	3- 46	–	–	–
Sutcliffe, I.J.	330	9	36.66	2- 21	–	–	–
Swann, G.P.	14213	432	32.90	7- 33	15	3	1
Syed Rasel	3463	119	29.10	8- 67	3	2	–
Tahir, N.	2734	85	32.16	7-107	1	–	–
Tamim Iqbal	67	0					
Taylor, B.V.	4483	135	33.20	6- 32	4	–	–
Taylor, C.G.	1038	18	57.66	4- 52	–	–	–
Taylor, L.R.P.L.	326	4	81.50	2- 34	–	–	–
Telo, F.D.	48	1	48.00	1- 36	–	–	–
Ten Doeschate, R.N.	3398	102	33.31	6- 20	4	–	–
Thomas, A.C.	7136	269	26.52	7- 54	13	1	–
Thompson, G.J.	605	17	35.58	3- 76	–	–	–
Thornely, M.A.	25	0					
Thorp, C.D.	2870	109	26.33	7- 88	5	1	1
Timms, R.T.	75	0					
Tomlinson, J.A.	3918	114	34.36	8- 46	6	1	1
Tredwell, J.C.	6364	154	41.32	6- 47	3	1	–
Trego, P.D.	4638	125	37.10	6- 59	1	–	–
Tremlett, C.T.	7719	275	28.06	6- 44	7	–	–
Trescothick, M.E.	1541	36	42.80	4- 36	–	–	–
Trott, I.J.L.	1904	44	43.27	7- 39	1	–	–
Troughton, J.O.	1416	22	64.36	3- 1	–	–	–
Tudor, A.J.	10606	347	30.56	7- 48	14	–	–
Turner, M.L.	742	15	49.46	4- 30	–	–	–
Udal, S.D.	24771	758	32.67	8- 50	34	4	7
Van der Wath, J.J.	6700	260	25.76	7- 60	14	1	–
Van Jaarsveld, M.	1178	37	31.83	5- 33	1	–	–
Vaughan, M.P.	5245	114	46.00	4- 39	–	–	–
Vettori, D.L.	13488	420	32.11	7- 87	25	3	–
Vincent, L.	527	10	52.70	2- 37	–	–	–
Voges, A.C.	865	22	39.31	4- 92	–	–	–
Wagg, G.G.	5005	159	31.47	6- 38	5	1	2
Wagh, M.A.	4611	100	46.11	7-222	2	–	–
Wainwright, D.J.	1012	30	33.73	4- 48	–	–	–
Wakely, A.G.	131	3	43.66	2- 62	–	–	–
Walker, M.J.	1121	22	50.95	2- 21	–	–	–
Walters, S.J.	149	3	49.66	1- 4	–	–	–
Waters, H.T.	1479	39	37.92	5- 86	1	–	–

195

F-C	Runs	Wkts	Avge	Best	5wI	10wM	50wS
Watkins, R.E.	1927	39	49.41	4- 40	–	–	–
Wessels, M.H.	13	0					
Westley, T.	82	2	41.00	1- 19	–	–	–
Westwood, I.J.	173	4	43.25	2- 46	–	–	–
Wharf, A.G.	10941	293	37.34	6- 59	5	1	1
Whelan, C.D.	614	21	29.23	4- 66	–	–	–
White, C.	11260	395	28.50	8- 55	11	–	–
White, G.G.	284	3	94.66	2- 35	–	–	–
White, R.A.	800	14	57.14	2- 30	–	–	–
White, W.A.	1200	31	38.70	5- 87	1	–	–
Whiteley, R.A.	38	0					
Wigley, D.H.	3702	104	35.59	5- 77	2	–	–
Williams, R.E.M.	563	17	33.11	5- 70	2	–	–
Willoughby, C.M.	16443	662	24.83	7- 44	27	3	3+2
Wilshaw, P.J.	68	2	34.00	1- 20	–	–	–
Wiseman, P.J.	15727	466	33.74	9- 13	18	4	–
Woakes, C.R.	1114	49	22.73	6- 68	3	1	–
Wood, M.J. (Gm)	43	2	21.50	1- 4	–	–	–
Wood, M.J. (Nt)	68	0					
Woodhouse, A.	53	0					
Woodman, R.J.	333	6	55.50	4- 65	–	–	–
Wright, B.J.	89	2	44.50	1- 14	–	–	–
Wright, C.J.C.	2416	52	46.46	6- 22	1	–	–
Wright, L.J.	2469	55	44.89	3- 33	–	–	–
Yardy, M.H.	1683	22	76.50	5- 83	1	–	–
Yasir Arafat	13497	573	23.55	7-102	32	3	0+4
Young, P.J.W.	454	4	113.50	1- 26	–	–	–
Zondeki, M.	6372	221	28.83	6- 39	9	1	0+1

LIMITED-OVERS INTERNATIONALS CAREER RECORDS

Compiled by **Philip Bailey**

These records, complete to 14 March 2009 (the conclusion of the New Zealand v India series), include all players registered for county cricket for the 2009 season at the time of going to press, plus those who have appeared in LOI matches for ICC full member countries since 1 September 2007. They exclude all matches involving multinational teams, as well as any abandoned without a ball bowled, regardless of the toss having been made.

ENGLAND – BATTING AND FIELDING

	M	I	NO	HS	Runs	Avge	100	50	Ct/St
K.Ali	14	9	3	39	93	15.50	–	–	1
T.R.Ambrose	5	5	1	6	10	2.50	–	–	3
J.M.Anderson	101	42	20	15	126	5.72	–	–	28
G.J.Batty	7	5	1	3	6	1.50	–	–	4
I.R.Bell	79	76	6	126*	2483	35.47	1	15	23
I.D.Blackwell	34	29	2	82	403	14.92	–	1	8
R.S.Bopara	33	29	8	60	601	28.61	–	4	11
T.T.Bresnan	5	4	1	20	51	17.00	–	–	1
S.C.J.Broad	42	27	13	45*	284	20.28	–	–	12
A.D.Brown	16	16	–	118	354	22.12	1	1	6
G.Chapple	1	1	–	14	14	14.00	–	–	–
R.Clarke	20	13	–	39	144	11.07	–	–	11
P.D.Collingwood	154	139	29	120*	3773	34.30	4	20	88
A.N.Cook	23	23	–	102	702	30.52	1	3	7
D.G.Cork	32	21	3	31*	180	10.00	–	–	6
J.P.Crawley	13	12	1	73	235	21.36	–	2	1/1
R.D.B.Croft	50	36	12	32	345	14.37	–	–	11
J.W.M.Dalrymple	27	26	1	67	487	19.48	–	2	12
M.A.Ealham	64	45	4	45	716	17.46	–	–	9
A.Flintoff	135	117	16	123	3290	32.57	3	18	42
J.S.Foster	11	6	3	13	41	13.66	–	–	13/7
P.J.Franks	1	1	–	4	4	4.00	–	–	1
S.J.Harmison	54	24	13	13*	73	6.63	–	–	8
M.J.Hoggard	26	6	2	7	17	4.25	–	–	5
G.O.Jones	49	41	8	80	815	24.69	–	4	68/4
S.P.Jones	8	1	–	1	1	1.00	–	–	–
E.C.Joyce	17	17	–	107	471	27.70	1	3	6
R.W.T.Key	5	5	–	19	54	10.80	–	–	1
R.J.Kirtley	11	2	–	1	2	1.00	–	–	5
M.B.Loye	7	7	–	45	142	20.28	–	–	–
A.McGrath	14	12	2	52	166	16.60	–	1	4
D.L.Maddy	8	6	–	53	113	18.83	–	1	1
S.I.Mahmood	25	15	4	22*	85	7.72	–	–	1
A.D.Mascarenhas	11	7	2	52	150	30.00	–	1	3
P.Mustard	10	10	–	83	233	23.30	–	1	9/2
P.A.Nixon	19	18	4	49	297	21.21	–	–	20/3
M.S.Panesar	26	8	3	13	26	5.20	–	–	3
S.R.Patel	11	5	–	31	116	23.20	–	–	4
K.P.Pietersen	85	76	15	116	3029	49.65	7	20	30
L.E.Plunkett	27	24	10	56	295	21.07	–	1	7
M.J.Prior	33	31	3	52	637	22.75	–	1	39/3
C.M.W.Read	36	24	7	30*	300	17.64	–	–	41/2
I.D.K.Salisbury	4	2	1	5	7	7.00	–	–	1
O.A.Shah	52	48	6	107*	1288	30.66	1	9	15

	M	I	NO	HS	Runs	Avge	100	50	Ct/St
R.J.Sidebottom	16	10	5	15	51	10.20	–	–	3
C.E.W.Silverwood	7	4	–	12	17	4.25	–	–	–
V.S.Solanki	51	46	5	106	1097	26.75	2	5	16
A.J.Strauss	78	77	7	152	2239	31.98	2	14	28
G.P.Swann	15	11	1	34	146	14.60	–	–	7
C.T.Tremlett	9	6	2	19*	38	9.50	–	–	2
M.E.Trescothick	123	122	6	137	4335	37.37	12	21	49
J.O.Troughton	6	5	1	20	36	9.00	–	–	1
A.J.Tudor	3	2	1	6	9	9.00	–	–	1
S.D.Udal	11	7	4	11*	35	11.66	–	–	1
M.P.Vaughan	86	83	10	90*	1982	27.15	–	16	25
A.G.Wharf	13	5	3	9	19	9.50	–	–	1
C.White	51	41	5	57*	568	15.77	–	1	12
L.J.Wright	16	11	1	52	229	22.90	–	2	6
M.H.Yardy	6	5	1	19	49	12.25	–	–	1

ENGLAND – BOWLING

	O	M	R	W	Avge	Best	4wI	R/Over
K.Ali	112.1	4	682	20	34.10	4-45	1	6.08
J.M.Anderson	812.3	71	4017	127	31.62	4-23	7	4.94
G.J.Batty	60.2	1	294	4	73.50	2-40	–	4.87
I.R.Bell	14.4	0	88	6	14.66	3-9	–	6.00
I.D.Blackwell	205	8	877	24	36.54	3-26	–	4.27
R.S.Bopara	45.1	2	240	5	48.00	2-43	–	5.31
T.T.Bresnan	33	3	203	4	50.75	2-34	–	6.15
S.C.J.Broad	345.5	26	1710	62	27.58	5-23	3	4.94
A.D.Brown	1	0	5	0	–	–	–	5.00
G.Chapple	4	0	14	0	–	–	–	3.50
R.Clarke	78.1	3	415	11	37.72	2-28	–	5.30
P.D.Collingwood	651.2	11	3272	84	38.95	6-31	4	5.02
D.G.Cork	295.2	18	1368	41	33.36	3-27	–	4.63
R.D.B.Croft	411	25	1743	45	38.73	3-51	–	4.24
J.W.M.Dalrymple	140	2	666	14	47.57	2-5	–	4.75
M.A.Ealham	537.5	34	2197	67	32.79	5-15	3	4.08
A.Flintoff	897	66	3872	162	23.90	5-56	7	4.31
P.J.Franks	9	0	48	0	–	–	–	5.33
S.J.Harmison	458.1	29	2342	76	30.81	5-33	3	5.11
M.J.Hoggard	217.4	13	1152	32	36.00	5-49	1	5.29
S.P.Jones	58	9	275	7	39.28	2-43	–	4.74
R.J.Kirtley	91.3	4	481	9	53.44	2-33	–	5.25
A.McGrath	38	2	175	4	43.75	1-13	–	4.60
S.I.Mahmood	192.3	7	1128	29	38.89	4-50	1	5.85
A.D.Mascarenhas	71	5	317	6	52.83	3-23	–	4.46
M.S.Panesar	218	10	980	24	40.83	3-25	–	4.49
S.R.Patel	56.4	2	319	11	29.00	5-41	1	5.62
K.P.Pietersen	34.5	0	201	5	40.20	2-22	–	5.77
L.E.Plunkett	215.1	7	1260	37	34.05	3-24	–	5.85
I.D.K.Salisbury	31	1	177	5	35.40	3-41	–	5.70
O.A.Shah	19	0	126	3	42.00	1-8	–	6.63
R.J.Sidebottom	144.1	11	661	24	27.54	3-19	–	4.58
C.E.W.Silverwood	51	0	244	6	40.66	3-43	–	4.78
V.S.Solanki	18.3	0	105	1	105.00	1-17	–	5.67
A.J.Strauss	1	0	3	0	–	–	–	3.00
G.P.Swann	108	7	511	18	28.38	4-34	1	4.73
C.T.Tremlett	79.5	2	419	9	46.55	4-32	1	5.24

ENGLAND – BOWLING (continued)

	O	M	R	W	Avge	Best	4wI	R/Over
M.E.Trescothick	38.4	0	219	4	54.75	2-7	–	5.66
A.J.Tudor	21.1	1	136	4	34.00	2-30	–	6.42
S.D.Udal	102	4	400	9	44.44	2-37	–	3.92
M.P.Vaughan	132.4	2	649	16	40.56	4-22	1	4.89
A.G.Wharf	97.2	10	428	18	23.77	4-24	1	4.39
C.White	394	25	1726	65	26.55	5-21	2	4.38
L.J.Wright	31	0	157	3	52.33	2-34	–	5.06
M.H.Yardy	42	3	135	4	33.75	3-24	–	3.21

AUSTRALIA – BATTING AND FIELDING

	M	I	NO	HS	Runs	Avge	100	50	Ct/St
N.W.Bracken	98	30	15	21*	188	12.53	–	–	20
S.R.Clark	35	11	7	16*	67	16.75	–	–	10
M.J.Clarke	143	127	27	130	4258	42.58	3	32	55
C.J.Ferguson	4	4	3	55*	102	102.00	–	1	2
B.Geeves	1	1	1	0*	0	–	–	–	1
A.C.Gilchrist	283	275	11	172	9415	35.66	15	55	414/54
B.J.Haddin	43	39	3	109	1171	32.52	1	6	45/4
R.J.Harris	1	1	–	7	7	7.00	–	–	–
N.M.Hauritz	9	5	3	20*	42	21.00	–	–	2
M.L.Hayden	160	154	15	181*	6131	44.10	10	36	68
B.W.Hilfenhaus	9	4	3	5	7	7.00	–	–	2
B.J.Hodge	25	21	2	123	575	30.26	1	3	16
G.B.Hogg	123	65	26	71*	790	20.25	–	2	36
J.R.Hopes	46	32	2	63	626	20.86	–	1	14
D.J.Hussey	15	14	–	79	415	29.64	–	4	7
M.E.K.Hussey	100	79	28	109*	2761	54.13	2	19	62
M.G.Johnson	50	23	8	24*	128	8.53	–	–	9
J.L.Langer	8	7	2	36	160	32.00	–	–	2/1
B.Lee	170	84	35	57	829	16.91	–	2	41
S.E.Marsh	14	14	1	81	566	43.53	–	5	1
A.A.Noffke	1	–	–	–	–	–	–	–	–
R.T.Ponting	306	297	35	164	11093	42.33	25	64	132
L.Ronchi	4	2	–	64	76	38.00	–	1	5/2
P.M.Siddle	1	–	–	–	–	–	–	–	–
A.Symonds	190	154	32	156	4938	40.47	6	29	77
S.W.Tait	22	4	2	11	24	12.00	–	–	2
D.A.Warner	6	6	–	69	106	17.66	–	1	1
S.R.Watson	69	52	17	126	1189	33.97	1	6	17
C.L.White	25	19	6	45	315	24.23	–	–	11

AUSTRALIA – BOWLING

	O	M	R	W	Avge	Best	4wI	R/Over
N.W.Bracken	805.5	83	3526	155	22.74	5-47	7	4.37
S.R.Clark	274.4	16	1336	48	27.83	4-54	2	4.86
M.J.Clarke	331.2	4	1677	48	34.93	5-35	2	5.06
B.Geeves	5	0	11	2	5.50	2-11	–	2.20
R.J.Harris	10	0	54	1	54.00	1-54	–	5.40
N.M.Hauritz	69	1	368	11	33.45	4-39	1	5.33
M.L.Hayden	1	0	18	0	–	–	–	18.00
B.W.Hilfenhaus	76.2	6	419	12	34.91	2-43	–	5.48
B.J.Hodge	11	0	51	1	51.00	1-17	–	4.63
G.B.Hogg	927.1	37	4188	156	26.84	5-32	5	4.51
J.R.Hopes	298	23	1257	39	32.23	3-30	–	4.21
D.J.Hussey	35.5	0	195	2	97.50	1-9	–	5.44

	O	M	R	W	Avge	Best	4wI	R/Over
M.E.K.Hussey	32	1	167	2	83.50	1-22	–	5.21
M.G.Johnson	395	26	1919	74	25.93	5-26	4	4.85
B.Lee	1451	108	6847	296	23.13	5-22	18	4.71
A.A.Noffke	9	0	46	1	46.00	1-46	–	5.11
R.T.Ponting	25	0	104	3	34.66	1-12	–	4.16
P.M.Siddle	3	0	13	1	13.00	1-13	–	4.33
A.Symonds	954.1	29	4774	127	37.59	5-18	3	5.00
S.W.Tait	180	4	961	38	25.28	4-39	1	5.33
S.R.Watson	440.2	14	2109	62	34.01	4-43	1	4.78
C.L.White	50.4	2	323	11	29.36	3-5	–	6.37

SOUTH AFRICA – BATTING AND FIELDING

	M	I	NO	HS	Runs	Avge	100	50	Ct/St
H.M.Amla	15	14	3	140	567	51.54	1	3	6
D.M.Benkenstein	23	20	3	69	305	17.94	–	1	3
G.H.Bodi	2	2	–	51	83	41.50	–	1	1
L.L.Bosman	11	9	–	88	202	22.44	–	1	3
J.Botha	39	21	9	46	236	19.66	–	–	18
M.V.Boucher	270	198	52	147*	4234	29.00	1	25	373/18
A.B.de Villiers	75	71	9	146	2371	38.24	3	15	44
H.H.Dippenaar	101	89	14	125*	3300	44.00	4	25	33
J.P.Duminy	42	35	9	90	993	38.19	–	6	11
H.H.Gibbs	239	232	16	175	7785	36.04	20	36	104
A.J.Hall	88	56	13	81	905	21.04	–	3	29
P.L.Harris	3	–	–	–	–	–	–	–	2
C.W.Henderson	4	–	–	–	–	–	–	–	–
J.H.Kallis	282	268	51	139	10028	46.21	16	71	105
J.M.Kemp	79	60	18	100*	1371	32.64	1	9	31
G.J.P.Kruger	3	2	1	0	0	0.00	–	–	1
C.K.Langeveldt	59	14	5	12	41	4.55	–	–	9
J.Louw	3	1	–	23	23	23.00	–	–	–
N.D.McKenzie	64	55	10	131*	1688	37.51	2	10	21
J.A.Morkel	33	21	5	97	410	25.62	–	1	7
M.Morkel	16	4	2	23*	35	17.50	–	–	4
A.Nel	79	22	12	30*	127	12.70	–	–	21
M.Ntini	170	44	21	42*	188	8.17	–	–	30
J.L.Ontong	25	14	1	32	167	12.84	–	–	12
W.D.Parnell	1	–	–	–	–	–	–	–	–
A.N.Petersen	5	3	–	80	124	41.33	–	1	–
V.D.Philander	7	5	2	23	73	24.33	–	–	2
S.M.Pollock	294	196	70	90	3193	25.34	–	13	104
A.G.Prince	49	38	11	89*	940	34.81	–	2	26
J.A.Rudolph	43	37	6	81	1157	37.32	–	7	11
G.C.Smith	135	133	9	134*	5111	41.21	7	37	72
D.W.Steyn	22	4	3	6	15	15.00	–	–	2
T.Tshabalala	4	1	1	2*	2	–	–	–	–
L.L.Tsotsobe	1	–	–	–	–	–	–	–	2
J.J.van der Wath	10	8	2	37*	89	14.83	–	–	3
M.van Jaarsveld	11	7	1	45	124	20.66	–	–	4
V.B.van Jaarsveld	2	2	–	5	9	4.50	–	–	1
M.N.van Wyk	6	6	–	82	195	32.50	–	2	1
C.M.Willoughby	3	2	–	0	0	0.00	–	–	–
M.Zondeki	11	2	2	3*	4	–	–	–	3

LOI   SOUTH AFRICA – BOWLING

	O	M	R	W	Avge	Best	4wI	R/Over
D.M.Benkenstein	10.5	1	44	4	11.00	3-5	–	4.06
G.H.Bodi	1	0	8	0	–	–	–	8.00
J.Botha	296	5	1301	38	34.23	4-19	1	4.39
J.P.Duminy	78.1	2	378	9	42.00	3-31	–	4.83
A.J.Hall	556.5	30	2515	95	26.47	5-18	4	4.51
P.L.Harris	30	4	83	3	27.66	2-30	–	2.76
C.W.Henderson	36.1	2	132	7	18.85	4-17	1	3.64
J.H.Kallis	1599	71	7693	242	31.78	5-30	4	4.81
J.M.Kemp	195.1	10	915	29	31.55	3-20	–	4.68
G.J.P.Kruger	23	1	139	2	69.50	1-43	–	6.04
C.K.Langeveldt	468.3	25	2334	82	28.46	5-39	3	4.98
J.Louw	26	1	148	2	74.00	1-45	–	5.69
N.D.McKenzie	7.4	0	27	0	–	–	–	3.52
J.A.Morkel	223.4	10	1139	38	29.97	4-29	2	5.09
M.Morkel	137.2	4	667	21	31.76	4-36	1	4.85
A.Nel	633.3	58	2935	106	27.68	5-45	4	4.63
M.Ntini	1425.5	122	6386	264	24.18	6-22	12	4.47
J.L.Ontong	89.4	3	396	9	44.00	3-30	–	4.41
W.D.Parnell	10	0	52	1	52.00	1-52	–	5.20
A.N.Petersen	1	0	7	0	–	–	–	7.00
V.D.Philander	45.5	5	209	6	34.83	4-12	1	4.56
S.M.Pollock	2571.4	308	9409	387	24.31	6-35	17	3.65
A.G.Prince	2	0	3	0	–	–	–	1.50
J.A.Rudolph	4	0	26	0	–	–	–	6.50
G.C.Smith	171	0	951	18	52.83	3-30	–	5.56
D.W.Steyn	171.1	14	921	31	29.70	4-16	1	5.38
T.Tshabalala	25	2	151	3	50.33	1-30	–	6.04
L.L.Tsotsobe	9	1	50	4	12.50	4-50	1	5.55
J.J.van der Wath	87.4	2	551	13	42.38	2-21	–	6.28
M.van Jaarsveld	5.1	0	18	2	9.00	1-0	–	3.48
C.M.Willoughby	28	2	148	2	74.00	2-39	–	5.28
M.Zondeki	84	7	440	11	40.00	2-40	–	5.23

WEST INDIES – BATTING AND FIELDING

	M	I	NO	HS	Runs	Avge	100	50	Ct/St
L.S.Baker	6	2	–	2	2	1.00	–	–	1
O.A.C.Banks	5	5	–	33	83	16.60	–	–	–
C.S.Baugh	30	22	7	29	223	14.86	–	–	19/4
S.J.Benn	4	4	1	23*	31	10.33	–	–	–
D.J.Bravo	88	71	16	112*	1291	23.47	1	2	37
P.A.Browne	5	5	1	49*	134	33.50	–	–	2
S.Chanderpaul	241	226	35	150	7858	41.14	9	53	68
S.Chattergoon	18	17	2	54*	370	24.66	–	2	6
P.T.Collins	30	12	5	10*	30	4.28	–	–	8
C.D.Collymore	84	35	17	13*	104	5.77	–	–	12
N.Deonarine	5	5	–	41	99	19.80	–	–	2
F.H.Edwards	44	18	11	13	64	9.14	–	–	3
S.E.Findlay	9	8	1	59*	146	20.85	–	1	5
A.D.S.Fletcher	4	4	–	26	58	14.50	–	–	1
C.H.Gayle	191	186	14	153*	7056	41.02	19	36	85
W.W.Hinds	114	107	9	127*	2835	28.92	5	14	28
L.R.Johnson	3	3	–	51	79	26.33	–	1	–
R.N.Lewis	26	19	5	49	248	17.71	–	–	6
X.M.Marshall	24	24	3	157*	375	17.85	1	–	9
N.O.Miller	11	5	3	25*	50	25.00	–	–	3

201

	M	I	NO	HS	Runs	Avge	100	50	Ct/St
D.Mohammed	7	1	1	0*	0	–	–	–	1
R.S.Morton	49	44	4	110*	1330	33.25	2	9	17
B.P.Nash	9	7	3	39*	104	26.00	–	–	1
B.A.Parchment	7	7	–	48	122	17.42	–	–	–
K.A.Pollard	8	7	–	19	47	6.71	–	–	3
D.B.L.Powell	54	25	3	48*	118	5.36	–	–	12
D.Ramdin	56	43	13	74*	594	19.80	–	2	78/4
R.Rampaul	30	9	2	26*	88	12.57	–	–	3
K.A.J.Roach	2	–	–	–	–	–	–	–	–
D.J.G.Sammy	17	11	2	51	154	17.11	–	1	6
M.N.Samuels	107	99	16	108*	2513	30.27	2	18	29
R.R.Sarwan	141	131	27	115*	4594	44.17	3	30	38
D.R.Smith	71	56	3	68	791	14.92	–	2	24
D.S.Smith	26	24	2	91	512	23.27	–	2	10
J.E.Taylor	56	23	7	43*	157	9.81	–	–	16

WEST INDIES – BOWLING

	O	M	R	W	Avge	Best	4wI	R/Over
L.S.Baker	45	1	217	8	27.12	3-47	–	4.82
O.A.C.Banks	45	1	189	7	27.00	2-24	–	4.20
S.J.Benn	39	1	199	2	99.50	1-39	–	5.10
D.J.Bravo	569.1	24	3013	98	30.74	4-32	2	5.29
S.Chanderpaul	123.2	0	636	14	45.42	3-18	–	5.15
S.Chatergoon	13.2	0	48	1	48.00	1-1	–	3.60
P.T.Collins	262.5	18	1212	39	31.07	5-43	1	4.61
C.D.Collymore	679	45	2924	83	35.22	5-51	2	4.30
N.Deonarine	24	0	158	5	31.60	2-18	–	6.58
F.H.Edwards	325.5	22	1646	56	29.39	6-22	2	5.05
C.H.Gayle	1057	36	4976	151	32.95	5-46	4	4.70
W.W.Hinds	157.3	3	837	28	29.89	3-24	–	5.31
R.N.Lewis	173.4	2	895	20	44.75	3-43	–	5.15
X.M.Marshall	1.3	0	6	0	–	–	–	4.00
N.O.Miller	85	7	382	12	31.83	3-19	–	4.49
D.Mohammed	58.5	5	235	10	23.50	3-37	–	3.99
R.S.Morton	1	0	2	0	–	–	–	2.00
B.P.Nash	49	3	224	5	44.80	3-56	–	4.57
K.A.Pollard	17	0	97	1	97.00	1-40	–	5.70
D.B.L.Powell	470	35	2212	70	31.60	4-27	2	4.70
R.Rampaul	184.5	13	919	25	36.76	4-41	1	4.97
K.A.J.Roach	18	1	78	3	26.00	2-29	–	4.33
D.J.G.Sammy	98.2	3	488	10	48.80	2-2	–	4.96
M.N.Samuels	513.1	11	2465	57	43.24	3-25	–	4.80
R.R.Sarwan	96.5	3	586	16	36.62	3-31	–	6.05
D.R.Smith	377.2	18	1813	49	37.00	5-45	4	4.80
J.E.Taylor	471.3	27	2206	84	26.26	5-48	4	4.67

NEW ZEALAND – BATTING AND FIELDING

	M	I	NO	HS	Runs	Avge	100	50	Ct/St
N.T.Broom	8	8	2	29	107	17.83	–	–	–
I.G.Butler	18	8	4	24	30	7.50	–	–	6
C.D.Cumming	13	13	1	45*	161	13.41	–	–	6
B.J.Diamanti	1	1	1	26*	26	–	–	–	1
G.D.Elliott	21	13	5	115	421	52.62	1	2	4
D.R.Flynn	16	13	2	35	167	15.18	–	–	4
P.G.Fulton	49	46	5	112	1334	32.53	1	8	18

	M	I	NO	HS	Runs	Avge	100	50	Ct/St
M.R.Gillespie	32	14	8	28	93	15.50	–	–	6
M.J.Guptill	12	11	3	122*	448	56.00	1	3	3
P.A.Hitchcock	14	7	3	11*	41	10.25	–	–	4
G.J.Hopkins	12	5	–	25	41	8.20	–	–	16
J.M.How	31	28	1	139	930	34.44	1	7	13
B.B.McCullum	153	127	22	166	2987	28.44	1	15	165/13
P.D.McGlashan	4	2	1	56*	63	63.00	–	1	7
H.J.H.Marshall	66	62	9	101*	1454	27.43	1	12	18
J.A.H.Marshall	10	10	–	161	250	25.00	1	1	–
C.S.Martin	20	7	2	3	8	1.60	–	–	7
M.J.Mason	25	6	3	13*	22	7.33	–	–	4
K.D.Mills	102	56	23	54	545	16.51	–	1	27
I.E.O'Brien	10	2	2	3*	3	–	–	–	1
J.D.P.Oram	130	94	12	101*	2022	24.65	1	11	39
J.S.Patel	38	12	6	34	72	12.00	–	–	11
J.D.Ryder	17	15	1	105	555	39.64	1	2	5
M.S.Sinclair	54	50	4	118*	1304	28.34	2	8	17
T.G.Southee	21	10	3	32	96	13.71	–	–	1
C.M.Spearman	51	50	–	86	936	18.72	–	5	15
S.B.Styris	157	135	21	141	3715	32.58	4	23	61
L.R.P.L.Taylor	63	57	11	128*	1770	38.47	3	10	36
E.P.Thompson	1	–	–	–	–	–	–	–	–
D.L.Vettori	235	140	44	83	1445	15.05	–	3	63
L.Vincent	102	99	10	172	2413	27.11	3	11	41

NEW ZEALAND – BOWLING

	O	M	R	W	Avge	Best	4wI	R/Over
I.G.Butler	118.5	2	675	17	39.70	3-41	–	5.68
C.D.Cumming	3	0	17	0	–	–	–	5.66
B.J.Diamanti	2	0	25	0	–	–	–	12.50
G.D.Elliott	62.2	5	318	13	24.46	3-14	–	5.10
D.R.Flynn	1	0	6	0	–	–	–	6.00
M.R.Gillespie	253.3	30	1369	37	37.00	4-58	1	5.40
P.A.Hitchcock	93	5	468	12	39.00	3-30	–	5.03
C.S.Martin	158	14	804	18	44.66	3-62	–	5.08
M.J.Mason	186.3	15	956	30	31.86	4-24	1	5.12
K.D.Mills	840.2	77	3936	149	26.41	5-25	7	4.68
I.E.O'Brien	75.3	3	488	14	34.85	3-68	–	6.46
J.D.P.Oram	917.4	78	4050	131	30.91	5 26	4	4.41
J.S.Patel	294.2	9	1469	42	34.97	3-11	–	4.99
J.D.Ryder	40.4	0	267	8	33.37	3-29	–	6.56
T.G.Southee	171	7	923	26	35.50	4-38	1	5.39
C.M.Spearman	0.3	0	6	0	–	–	–	12.00
S.B.Styris	885.3	38	4208	122	34.49	6-25	5	4.75
L.R.P.L.Taylor	5	0	32	0	–	–	–	6.40
E.P.Thompson	4	0	42	0	–	–	–	10.50
D.L.Vettori	1832.2	76	7640	233	32.78	5-7	8	4.16
L.Vincent	3.2	1	25	1	25.00	1-0	–	7.50

INDIA – BATTING AND FIELDING

	M	I	NO	HS	Runs	Avge	100	50	Ct/St
A.B.Agarkar	191	113	26	95	1269	14.58	–	3	53
S.Badrinath	3	3	1	27*	39	19.50	–	–	2
L.Balaji	30	16	6	21*	120	12.00	–	–	11
P.P.Chawla	21	10	5	13*	28	5.60	–	–	9

INDIA – BATTING AND FIELDING (continued)

	M	I	NO	HS	Runs	Avge	100	50	Ct/St
M.S.Dhoni	132	119	32	183*	4211	48.40	3	30	129/38
R.S.Dravid	329	304	39	153	10464	39.48	12	80	193/14
G.Gambhir	74	73	7	150	2537	38.43	6	15	23
S.C.Ganguly	308	297	23	183	11221	40.95	22	71	99
M.S.Gony	2	–	–	–	–	–	–	–	–
Harbhajan Singh	183	95	26	46	888	12.86	–	–	50
R.A.Jadeja	1	1	1	60*	60	–	–	1	–
K.D.Karthik	26	20	5	63	330	22.00	–	2	23/2
M.Kartik	37	14	5	32*	126	14.00	–	–	10
Z.Khan	156	83	31	34*	662	12.73	–	–	35
V.Kohli	5	5	–	54	159	31.80	–	1	3
P.Kumar	23	10	3	15	62	8.85	–	–	6
V.V.S.Laxman	86	83	7	131	2338	30.76	6	10	39
P.P.Ojha	9	4	3	16*	27	27.00	–	–	5
M.M.Patel	41	15	8	15	52	7.42	–	–	6
I.K.Pathan	107	78	18	83	1368	22.80	–	5	18
Y.K.Pathan	22	14	6	59*	200	25.00	–	2	6
R.R.Powar	31	19	5	54	163	11.64	–	1	3
S.K.Raina	65	55	11	116*	1558	35.40	2	10	29
V.Sehwag	195	190	8	130	6314	34.69	11	34	76
I.Sharma	27	8	4	8	20	5.00	–	–	7
R.G.Sharma	37	35	10	70*	680	27.20	–	4	16
R.P.Singh	47	17	9	12*	60	7.50	–	–	11
S.Sreesanth	41	16	8	10*	34	4.25	–	–	6
S.R.Tendulkar	425	415	39	186*	16684	44.37	43	91	129
M.K.Tiwary	1	1	–	2	2	2.00	–	–	–
R.V.Uthappa	38	34	5	86	786	27.10	–	5	15
Yuvraj Singh	229	210	29	139	6758	37.33	11	40	69

INDIA – BOWLING

	O	M	R	W	Avge	Best	4wI	R/Over
A.B.Agarkar	1580.4	100	8021	288	27.85	6-42	12	5.07
L.Balaji	241.1	11	1344	34	39.52	4-48	1	5.57
P.P.Chawla	183.4	6	911	28	32.53	4-23	2	4.96
R.S.Dravid	31	1	170	4	42.50	2-43	–	5.48
G.Gambhir	1	0	13	0	–	–	–	13.00
S.C.Ganguly	757.1	30	3835	100	38.35	5-16	3	5.06
M.S.Gony	13	1	76	2	38.00	2-65	–	5.84
Harbhajan Singh	1592	72	6707	203	33.03	5-31	4	4.21
R.A.Jadeja	6	0	40	0	–	–	–	6.66
M.Kartik	317.5	19	1612	37	43.56	6-27	1	5.07
Z.Khan	1302.3	95	6367	212	30.03	5-42	8	4.88
P.Kumar	182	15	904	30	30.13	4-31	3	4.96
V.V.S.Laxman	7	0	40	0	–	–	–	5.71
P.P.Ojha	80	5	336	12	28.00	4-38	1	4.20
M.M.Patel	304.1	27	1464	46	31.82	4-49	1	4.81
I.K.Pathan	865.4	48	4546	152	29.90	5-27	5	5.25
Y.K.Pathan	75.2	0	399	10	39.90	1-1	–	5.29
R.R.Powar	256	6	1191	34	35.02	3-24	–	4.65
S.K.Raina	22.2	0	118	1	118.00	1-23	–	5.28
V.Sehwag	652.1	12	3415	85	40.17	3-25	–	5.23
I.Sharma	214.3	7	1214	40	30.35	4-38	3	5.65
R.G.Sharma	21.5	2	98	0	–	–	–	4.48
R.P.Singh	360.3	28	1935	60	32.25	4-35	2	5.36
S.Sreesanth	320.5	14	1856	59	31.45	6-55	2	5.78

INDIA – BOWLING (continued)

	O	M	R	W	Avge	Best	4wI	R/Over
S.R.Tendulkar	1335.5	24	6806	154	44.19	5-32	6	5.09
Yuvraj Singh	541.2	13	2782	71	39.18	4-6	2	5.13

PAKISTAN – BATTING AND FIELDING

	M	I	NO	HS	Runs	Avge	100	50	Ct/St
Abdur Rauf	4	–	–	–	–	–	–	–	2
Abdur Rehman	11	8	1	31	59	8.42	–	–	2
Azhar Mahmood	143	110	26	67	1521	18.10	–	3	37
Bazid Khan	5	5	–	66	131	26.20	–	2	1
Danish Kaneria	18	10	8	6*	12	6.00	–	–	2
Fawad Alam	11	9	7	63*	156	78.00	–	1	3
Iftikhar Anjum	56	30	18	32	212	17.66	–	–	10
Imran Nazir	74	74	2	160	1784	24.77	2	9	24
Kamran Akmal	94	79	11	124	1726	25.38	4	2	98/14
Kamran Hussain	2	1	1	28*	28	–	–	–	–
Khalid Latif	1	1	–	19	19	19.00	–	–	–
Khurram Manzoor	7	7	–	83	236	33.71	–	3	3
Mansoor Amjad	1	1	–	5	5	5.00	–	–	–
Misbah-ul-Haq	46	40	8	79*	1224	38.25	–	7	23
Mohammad Asif	28	11	5	6	33	5.50	–	–	2
Mohammad Hafeez	48	48	1	92	874	18.59	–	4	20
Moh'd Yousuf Youhana	262	248	40	141*	9076	43.63	15	60	50
Nasir Jamshed	9	9	2	74	343	49.00	–	4	3
Naumanullah	1	1	–	5	5	5.00	–	–	–
Rizwan Ahmed	1	–	–	–	–	–	–	–	1
Saeed Ajmal	5	2	2	4*	6	–	–	–	1
Salman Butt	63	63	4	136	2347	39.77	8	10	19
Samiullah Khan	2	–	–	–	–	–	–	–	–
Sarfraz Ahmed	8	2	–	19	26	13.00	–	–	6/3
Shahid Afridi	266	249	16	109	5494	23.57	4	29	93
Shoaib Akhtar	135	64	31	43	313	9.48	–	–	17
Shoaib Malik	173	154	21	143	4749	35.70	6	31	63
Sohail Khan	4	1	–	4	4	4.00	–	–	–
Sohail Tanvir	29	16	5	59	162	14.72	–	1	7
Umar Gul	54	19	7	27	113	9.41	–	–	6
Wahab Riaz	5	4	1	3	4	1.33	–	–	1
Yasir Arafat	8	6	2	27	48	12.00	–	–	1
Yasir Hamid	56	56	1	127*	2028	36.87	3	12	14
Younus Khan	181	175	19	144	5306	34.01	6	35	96

PAKISTAN – BOWLING

	O	M	R	W	Avge	Best	4wI	R/Over
Abdur Rauf	35.4	1	212	8	26.50	3-24	–	5.94
Abdur Rehman	99	6	437	12	36.41	2-20	–	4.41
Azhar Mahmood	1040.2	58	4813	123	39.13	6-18	5	4.62
Bazid Khan	2	0	11	0	–	–	–	5.50
Danish Kaneria	142.2	11	682	15	45.46	3-31	–	4.79
Fawad Alam	60.2	0	332	4	83.00	1-8	–	5.50
Iftikhar Anjum	447.5	39	2219	71	31.25	4-42	2	4.95
Imran Nazir	8.1	0	48	1	48.00	1-3	–	5.87
Kamran Hussain	17	0	67	3	22.33	2-32	–	3.94
Mansoor Amjad	8	1	44	1	44.00	1-44	–	5.50
Misbah-ul-Haq	4	0	30	0	–	–	–	7.50
Mohammad Asif	226.4	26	997	31	32.16	3-28	–	4.39
Mohammad Hafeez	286.5	9	1278	38	33.63	3-17	–	4.45

	O	M	R	W	Avge	Best	4wI	R/Over
Moh'd Yousuf Youhana	0.2	0	1	1	1.00	1-0	–	3.00
Rizwan Ahmed	4	0	26	0	–	–	–	6.50
Saeed Ajmal	46.2	0	190	4	47.50	2-19	–	4.10
Salman Butt	11.3	0	90	0	–	–	–	7.82
Samiullah Khan	20	0	115	0	–	–	–	5.75
Shahid Afridi	1848.5	49	8572	241	35.56	5-11	4	4.63
Shoaib Akhtar	1063.3	83	4952	214	23.14	6-16	10	4.65
Shoaib Malik	988.3	29	4509	126	35.78	4-19	1	4.56
Sohail Khan	33.1	1	163	5	32.60	3-30	–	4.91
Sohail Tanvir	244	13	1203	44	27.34	5-48	3	4.93
Umar Gul	425	33	2095	83	25.24	5-17	3	4.92
Wahab Riaz	40.1	5	202	10	20.20	3-22	–	5.02
Yasir Arafat	49	0	274	4	68.50	1-28	–	5.59
Yasir Hamd	3	0	26	0	–	–	–	8.66
Younus Khan	35.2	1	211	2	105.50	1-3	–	5.97

SRI LANKA – BATTING AND FIELDING

	M	I	NO	HS	Runs	Avge	100	50	Ct/St
M.K.D.I.Amerasinghe	8	4	4	5*	6	–	–	–	1
T.M.Dilshan	160	137	27	137*	3423	31.11	2	16	69/1
C.R.D.Fernando	131	53	30	20	231	10.04	–	–	25
S.T.Jayasuriya	428	416	18	189	13085	32.87	28	67	121
D.P.M.D.Jayawardena	294	275	28	128	7773	31.46	9	47	153
S.H.T.Kandamby	12	12	1	93*	310	28.18	–	2	2
C.K.Kapugedera	59	51	2	95	1044	21.30	–	5	18
K.M.D.N.Kulasekara	52	34	16	39*	272	15.11	–	–	14
K.S.Lokuarachchi	21	18	3	69	210	14.00	–	1	5
M.F.Maharoof	91	62	15	69*	973	20.70	–	2	19
S.L.Malinga	53	25	11	15	92	6.57	–	–	11
A.D.Mathews	5	5	1	52*	91	22.75	–	1	1
B.A.W.Mendis	28	13	7	15*	66	11.00	–	–	4
M.T.T.Mirando	24	20	4	54*	317	19.81	–	1	2
J.Mubarak	38	36	6	72	696	23.20	–	4	12
M.Muralitharan	322	153	59	33*	610	6.48	–	–	125
M.D.K.Perera	4	4	–	30	44	11.00	–	–	–
K.T.G.D.Prasad	4	2	–	8	16	8.00	–	–	–
K.C.Sangakkara	239	222	24	138*	7149	36.10	10	45	222/60
L.P.C.Silva	55	48	4	107*	1324	30.09	1	11	17
W.U.Tharanga	76	72	1	120	2168	30.53	6	9	13
M.L.Udawatte	9	9	–	73	257	28.55	–	2	–
W.P.U.C.J.Vaas	321	219	72	50*	2018	13.72	–	1	59
B.S.M.Warnapura	3	3	–	30	35	11.66	–	–	3
K.Weeraratne	15	9	1	41	160	20.00	–	–	3

SRI LANKA – BOWLING

	O	M	R	W	Avge	Best	4wI	R/Over
M.K.D.I.Amerasinghe	71	6	363	9	40.33	3-44	–	5.11
T.M.Dilshan	435.1	8	2050	47	43.61	4-29	2	4.71
C.R.D.Fernando	945	47	4916	162	30.34	6-27	3	5.20
S.T.Jayasuriya	2393	45	11370	310	36.67	6-29	12	4.75
D.P.M.D.Jayawardena	94.4	1	539	7	77.00	2-56	–	5.69
S.H.T.Kandamby	1	0	3	0	–	–	–	3.00
C.K.Kapugedera	38	0	192	2	96.00	1-24	–	5.05
K.M.D.N.Kulasekara	388.4	40	1715	64	26.79	4-40	1	4.41
K.S.Lokuarachchi	168.3	7	725	31	23.38	4-44	1	4.30

SRI LANKA – BOWLING (continued)

	O	M	R	W	Avge	Best	4wI	R/Over
M.F.Maharoof	631.2	45	2997	116	25.83	6-14	5	4.74
S.L.Malinga	420.5	33	2021	79	25.58	4-44	4	4.80
A.D.Mathews	20	1	92	1	92.00	1-19	–	4.60
B.A.W.Mendis	213.1	14	841	64	13.14	6-13	6	3.94
M.T.T.Mirando	163.3	11	756	29	26.06	5-47	1	4.62
J.Mubarak	18.3	0	76	2	38.00	1-10	–	4.10
M.Muralitharan	2889.1	192	11225	494	22.72	7-30	24	3.88
M.D.K.Perera	7	0	28	1	28.00	1-17	–	4.00
K.T.G.D.Prasad	27	2	156	4	39.00	2-29	–	5.77
L.P.C.Silva	4	1	21	1	21.00	1-21	–	5.25
W.P.U.C.J.Vaas	2620.1	278	10955	399	27.45	8-19	13	4.18
K.Weeraratne	80	6	385	6	64.16	3-46	–	4.81

ZIMBABWE – BATTING AND FIELDING

	M	I	NO	HS	Runs	Avge	100	50	Ct/St
G.B.Brent	70	54	20	59*	408	12.00	–	1	20
R.W.Chakabva	1	1	–	41	41	41.00	–	–	2
C.J.Chibhabha	41	41	–	73	928	22.63	–	7	18
E.Chigumbura	85	78	7	79	1716	24.16	–	10	28
A.G.Cremer	5	1	–	4	4	4.00	–	–	2
K.M.Dabengwa	32	29	7	45	433	19.68	–	–	10
S.M.Ervine	42	34	7	100	698	25.85	1	2	5
G.W.Flower	219	212	18	142*	6536	33.69	6	40	86
M.W.Goodwin	71	70	3	112*	1818	27.13	2	8	20
T.Maruma	5	4	–	32	41	10.25	–	–	1
H.Masakadza	68	68	3	87	1551	23.86	–	12	27
S.Matsikenyeri	89	87	5	90	1718	20.95	–	10	31
C.B.Mpofu	33	20	10	4	22	2.20	–	–	3
T.Mupariwa	33	27	9	33	165	9.16	–	–	8
F.Mutizwa	5	4	1	61	124	41.33	–	1	4/2
R.W.Price	52	29	10	23*	183	9.63	–	–	11
E.C.Rainsford	34	19	10	9*	39	4.33	–	–	8
V.Sibanda	75	74	2	116	1595	22.15	1	11	24
T.Taibu	107	94	17	107*	2035	26.42	1	10	95/14
B.R.M.Taylor	75	74	6	98	1929	28.36	–	12	43/12
P.Utseya	88	72	25	68*	650	13.82	–	2	28
M.N.Waller	5	5	–	63	93	18.60	–	1	–
S.C.Williams	34	34	6	71	851	30.39	–	9	12
C.Zhuwawo	1	1	–	16	16	16.00	–	–	–

ZIMBABWE – BOWLING

	O	M	R	W	Avge	Best	4wI	R/Over
G.B.Brent	565	40	2776	75	37.01	4-22	3	4.91
C.J.Chibhabha	83	1	618	12	51.50	2-36	–	7.44
E.Chigumbura	336.1	19	1948	54	36.07	4-28	1	5.79
A.G.Cremer	45.5	5	172	15	11.46	4-31	2	3.75
K.M.Dabengwa	156.5	2	790	21	37.61	3-15	–	5.03
S.M.Ervine	274.5	10	1561	41	38.07	3-29	–	5.67
G.W.Flower	903.2	11	4187	104	40.25	4-32	2	4.63
M.W.Goodwin	41.2	1	210	4	52.50	1-12	–	5.08
T.Maruma	24.5	1	150	2	75.00	2-50	–	6.04
H.Masakadza	108.1	3	589	17	34.64	3-39	–	5.44
S.Matsikenyeri	137.2	2	696	14	49.71	2-33	–	5.06
C.B.Mpofu	256.5	19	1297	36	36.02	6-52	2	5.04
T.Mupariwa	279.2	22	1349	52	25.94	4-39	3	4.82

	O	M	R	W	Avge	Best	4wI	R/Over
R.W.Price	449.3	37	1710	43	39.76	4-22	1	3.80
E.C.Rainsford	274.5	26	1181	35	33.74	3-16	–	4.29
V.Sibanda	15	0	87	2	43.50	1-12	–	5.80
T.Taibu	14	1	61	2	30.50	2-42	–	4.35
B.R.M.Taylor	35	0	224	8	28.00	3-54	–	6.40
P.Utseya	739.4	43	2959	59	50.15	3-35	–	4.00
S.C.Williams	101.4	1	530	9	58.88	3-23	–	5.21
C.Zhuwawo	3	0	15	0	–	–	–	5.00

BANGLADESH – BATTING AND FIELDING

	M	I	NO	HS	Runs	Avge	100	50	Ct/St
Abdur Razzak	81	53	22	33	467	15.06	–	–	20
Aftab Ahmed	80	80	6	92	1874	25.32	–	14	27
Alok Kapali	65	62	3	115	1170	19.83	1	5	25
Dhiman Ghosh	14	12	3	30	126	14.00	–	–	9/4
Dolar Mahmud	4	3	–	20	20	6.66	–	–	–
Farhad Reza	32	29	6	50	390	16.95	–	1	12
Imrul Kayes	3	3	–	14	27	9.00	–	–	1
Junaid Siddique	17	17	–	85	233	13.70	–	1	6
Mahbubul Alam	2	1	–	22	22	22.00	–	–	1
Mahmudullah	24	19	5	58*	355	25.35	–	1	3
Mashrafe Mortaza	101	79	14	51*	1032	15.87	–	1	32
Mehrab Hossain	16	15	–	54	251	16.73	–	1	6
Mohammad Ashraful	137	131	12	109	2761	23.20	2	16	27
Mosharraf Hossain	3	3	–	8	15	5.00	–	–	–
Mushfiqur Rahim	46	40	8	57	595	18.59	–	2	28/7
Naeem Islam	11	8	3	46*	156	31.20	–	–	6
Nazimuddin	7	7	–	47	90	12.85	–	–	–
Nazmul Hossain	24	16	8	6*	33	4.12	–	–	4
Raqibul Hasan	23	22	2	89	579	28.95	–	5	6
Rubel Hossain	5	2	1	0*	0	0.00	–	–	2
Shahadat Hossain	43	22	14	12*	58	7.25	–	–	5
Shahriar Nafis	60	60	5	123*	1857	33.76	4	10	11
Shakib Al Hasan	62	60	12	134*	1599	33.31	2	10	11
Syed Rasel	39	21	7	15	64	4.57	–	–	8
Tamim Iqbal	53	53	–	129	1370	25.84	1	8	17
Tushar Imran	41	40	–	65	574	14.35	–	2	6

BANGLADESH – BOWLING

	O	M	R	W	Avge	Best	4wI	R/Over
Abdur Razzak	704.5	36	3098	111	27.90	5-33	3	4.39
Aftab Ahmed	123.1	0	656	12	54.66	5-31	1	5.32
Alok Kapali	228	8	1194	24	49.75	3-49	–	5.23
Dolar Mahmud	17.1	0	165	3	55.00	1-27	–	9.61
Farhad Reza	187.5	11	1015	22	46.13	5-42	1	5.40
Junaid Siddique	2	0	13	0	–	–	–	6.50
Mahbubul Alam	14	1	91	1	91.00	1-25	–	6.50
Mahmudullah	135	3	683	11	62.09	2-19	–	5.05
Mashrafe Mortaza	864.1	78	3917	134	29.23	6-26	6	4.53
Mehrab Hossain	25.1	0	115	3	38.33	2-30	–	4.56
Mohammad Ashraful	69	2	421	11	38.27	3-26	–	6.10
Mosharraf Hossain	22	0	100	1	100.00	1-26	–	4.54
Naeem Islam	88.1	3	391	11	35.54	3-32	–	4.43
Nazmul Hossain	175.5	14	928	25	37.12	4-40	1	5.27
Rubel Hossain	33.3	5	151	8	18.87	4-33	1	4.50

BANGLADESH – BOWLING (continued)

	O	M	R	W	Avge	Best	4wI	R/Over
Shahadat Hossain	299.3	16	1691	41	41.24	3-34	–	5.64
Shakib Al Hasan	507.5	33	2044	68	30.05	3-11	–	4.02
Syed Rasel	337.3	39	1448	50	28.96	4-22	1	4.29
Tamim Iqbal	0.1	0	6	0	–	–	–	36.00
Tushar Imran	21	0	103	1	103.00	1-24	–	4.90

ASSOCIATES – BATTING AND FIELDING

	M	I	NO	HS	Runs	Avge	100	50	Ct/St
R.G.Aga (Kenya)	2	2	–	1	1	0.50	–	–	–
J.A.R.Blain (Scotland)	31	23	6	30*	241	14.17	–	–	6
K.J.Coetzer (Scotland)	1	1	–	0	0	0.00	–	–	–
A.N.Kervezee (Netherlands)	18	15	2	62	341	26.23	–	1	6
E.J.G.Morgan (Ireland)	21	21	1	115	600	30.00	1	3	8
N.J.O'Brien (Ireland)	29	29	1	72	708	25.28	–	7	22/5
N.S.Poonia (Scotland)	16	16	–	67	199	12.43	–	1	4
W.T.S.Porterfield (Ireland)	29	29	2	112*	736	27.25	2	2	15
A.D.Poynter (Ireland)	4	3	1	22*	30	15.00	–	–	–
W.B.Rankin (Ireland)	14	6	4	7*	16	8.00	–	–	3
R.N.ten Doeschate (Netherlands)	19	18	5	109*	662	50.92	1	4	7
G.C.Wilson (Ireland)	9	9	–	51	153	17.00	–	1	5/1

ASSOCIATES – BOWLING

	O	M	R	W	Avge	Best	4wI	R/Over
R.G.Aga	13	0	87	2	43.50	2-17	–	6.69
J.A.R.Blain	202.3	11	1062	38	27.94	5-22	2	5.24
A.N.Kervezee	1	0	8	0	–	–	–	8.00
W.B.Rankin	82.2	5	458	16	28.62	3-32	–	5.56
R.N.ten Doeschate	145.3	8	713	35	20.37	4-31	2	4.90

TEST MATCH CAREER RECORDS

Compiled by **Philip Bailey**

These records, complete to 22 March 2009 (the end of the South Africa v Australia series, but excluding the 1st New Zealand v India Test), contain all players registered for county cricket in 2009 at the time of going to press, plus those who have played Test cricket since 1 September 2007 (Test No. 1841). They do not include matches, erroneously entitled Tests, that involve multi-national teams.

ENGLAND – BATTING AND FIELDING

	M	I	NO	HS	Runs	Avge	100	50	Ct/St
U.Afzaal	3	6	1	54	83	16.60	–	1	–
K.Ali	1	2	–	9	10	5.00	–	–	–
T.R.Ambrose	11	16	1	102	447	29.80	1	3	31
Amjad Khan	1	–	–	–	–	–	–	–	–
J.M.Anderson	35	46	25	34	298	14.19	–	–	14
G.J.Batty	7	8	1	38	144	20.57	–	–	3
I.R.Bell	46	83	9	199	3004	40.59	8	19	44
I.D.Blackwell	1	1	–	4	4	4.00	–	–	1
R.S.Bopara	4	6	–	104	146	24.33	1	–	1
S.C.J.Broad	15	20	4	76	467	29.18	–	3	4
M.A.Butcher	71	131	7	173*	4288	34.58	8	23	61
A.R.Caddick	62	95	12	49*	861	10.37	–	–	21
R.Clarke	2	3	–	55	96	32.00	–	1	1
P.D.Collingwood	46	82	8	206	3247	43.87	9	12	60
A.N.Cook	41	75	4	139*	3078	43.35	8	19	35
D.G.Cork	37	56	8	59	864	18.00	–	3	18
J.P.Crawley	37	61	9	156*	1800	34.61	4	9	29
R.D.B.Croft	21	34	8	37*	421	16.19	–	–	10
R.K.J.Dawson	7	13	3	19*	114	11.40	–	–	3
M.A.Ealham	8	13	3	53*	210	21.00	–	–	4
A.Flintoff	74	121	8	167	3595	31.81	5	25	51
J.S.Foster	7	12	3	48	226	25.11	–	–	17/1
J.E.R.Gallian	3	6	–	28	74	12.33	–	–	1
S.J.Harmison	60	81	21	49*	711	11.85	–	–	7
M.J.Hoggard	67	92	27	38	473	7.27	–	–	24
G.O.Jones	34	53	4	100	1172	23.91	1	6	128/5
S.P.Jones	18	18	5	44	205	15.76	–	–	4
R.W.T.Key	15	26	1	221	775	31.00	1	3	11
R.J.Kirtley	4	7	1	12	32	5.33	–	–	3
J.Lewis	1	2	–	20	27	13.50	–	–	–
A.McGrath	4	5	–	81	201	40.20	–	2	3
D.L.Maddy	3	4	–	24	46	11.50	–	–	4
S.I.Mahmood	8	11	1	34	81	8.10	–	–	–
J.Ormond	2	4	1	18	38	12.66	–	–	–
M.S.Panesar	38	49	16	26	176	5.33	–	–	9
D.J.Pattinson	1	2	–	13	21	10.50	–	–	–
K.P.Pietersen	50	91	4	226	4445	51.09	16	14	31
L.E.Plunkett	9	13	2	44*	126	11.45	–	–	3
M.J.Prior	16	26	6	131*	960	48.00	2	7	37/1
M.R.Ramprakash	52	92	6	154	2350	27.32	2	12	39
C.M.W.Read	15	23	4	55	360	18.94	–	1	48/6
M.J.Saggers	3	3	1	1	1	0.33	–	–	1
I.D.K.Salisbury	15	25	3	50	368	16.72	–	1	5
C.P.Schofield	2	3	–	57	67	22.33	–	1	–
O.A.Shah	6	10	–	88	269	26.90	–	2	2
R.J.Sidebottom	21	29	11	31	298	16.55	–	–	5
C.E.W.Silverwood	6	7	3	10	29	7.25	–	–	2
A.J.Strauss	60	111	4	177	4736	44.26	17	14	67
G.P.Swann	5	5	2	20*	42	14.00	–	–	3
C.T.Tremlett	3	5	1	25*	50	12.50	–	–	1
M.E.Trescothick	76	143	10	219	5825	43.79	14	29	95
A.J.Tudor	10	16	4	99*	229	19.08	–	1	3
S.D.Udal	4	7	1	33*	109	18.16	–	–	1
M.P.Vaughan	82	147	9	197	5719	41.44	18	18	44
C.White	30	50	7	121	1052	24.46	1	5	14

TEST
ENGLAND – BOWLING

	O	M	R	W	Avge	Best	5wI	10wM
U.Afzaal	9	0	49	1	49.00	1- 49	–	–
K.Ali	36	5	136	5	27.20	3- 80	–	–
Amjad Khan	29	1	122	1	122.00	1-111	–	–
J.M.Anderson	1186.2	246	4146	117	35.43	7- 43	5	–
G.J.Batty	232.2	34	733	11	66.63	3- 55	–	–
I.R.Bell	18	3	76	1	76.00	1- 33	–	–
I.D.Blackwell	19	2	71	0	–	–	–	–
R.S.Bopara	39	6	147	1	147.00	1- 39	–	–
S.C.J.Broad	492.2	104	1543	38	40.60	5- 85	1	–
M.A.Butcher	150.1	27	541	15	36.06	4- 42	–	–
A.R.Caddick	2259.4	501	6999	234	29.91	7- 46	13	1
R.Clarke	29	11	60	4	15.00	2- 7	–	–
P.D.Collingwood	236.3	39	770	14	55.00	3- 23	–	–
A.N.Cook	1	0	1	0	–	–	–	–
D.G.Cork	1279.4	264	3906	131	29.81	7- 43	5	–
R.D.B.Croft	769.5	195	1825	49	37.24	5- 95	1	–
R.K.J.Dawson	186	20	677	11	61.54	4-134	–	–
M.A.Ealham	176.4	43	488	17	28.70	4- 21	–	–
A.Flintoff	2329	484	6886	211	32.63	5- 58	2	–
J.E.R.Gallian	14	1	62	0	–	–	–	–
S.J.Harmison	2155.4	416	6924	217	31.90	7- 12	8	1
M.J.Hoggard	2318.1	493	7564	248	30.50	7- 61	7	1
S.P.Jones	470.1	78	1666	59	28.23	6- 53	3	–
R.J.Kirtley	179.5	50	561	19	29.52	6- 34	1	–
J.Lewis	41	9	122	3	40.66	3- 68	–	–
A.McGrath	17	1	56	4	14.00	3- 16	–	–
D.L.Maddy	14	1	40	0	–	–	–	–
S.I.Mahmood	188.2	25	762	20	38.10	4- 22	–	–
J.Ormond	62	12	185	2	92.50	1- 70	–	–
M.S.Panesar	1472	304	4216	125	33.72	6- 37	8	1
D.J.Pattinson	30.1	2	96	2	48.00	2- 95	–	–
K.P.Pietersen	122.3	9	518	4	129.50	1- 0	–	–
L.E.Plunkett	256.2	39	916	23	39.82	3- 17	–	–
M.R.Ramprakash	149.1	16	477	4	119.25	1- 2	–	–
M.J.Saggers	82.1	20	247	7	35.28	2- 29	–	–
I.D.K.Salisbury	415.2	50	1539	20	76.95	4-163	–	–
C.P.Schofield	18	2	73	0	–	–	–	–
O.A.Shah	5	0	31	0	–	–	–	–
R.J.Sidebottom	771	182	2133	77	27.70	7- 47	5	1
C.E.W.Silverwood	138	27	444	11	40.36	5- 91	1	–
G.P.Swann	280.5	68	773	27	28.62	5- 57	2	–
C.T.Tremlett	143.1	36	386	13	29.69	3- 12	–	–
M.E.Trescothick	50	6	155	1	155.00	1- 34	–	–
A.J.Tudor	252	51	963	28	34.39	5- 44	1	–
S.D.Udal	99.2	13	344	8	43.00	4- 14	–	–
M.P.Vaughan	163	21	561	6	93.50	2- 71	–	–
C.White	659.5	119	2220	59	37.62	5- 32	3	–

TEST

AUSTRALIA – BATTING AND FIELDING

	M	I	NO	HS	Runs	Avge	100	50	Ct/St
D.E.Bollinger	1	1	1	0*	0	–	–	–	–
B.Casson	1	1	–	10	10	10.00	–	–	2
S.R.Clark	22	23	7	39	210	13.12	–	–	4
M.J.Clarke	46	74	9	151	3160	48.61	10	13	38
A.C.Gilchrist	95	135	20	204*	5475	47.60	17	25	374/35
B.J.Haddin	15	26	2	169	901	37.54	1	2	55/1
N.M.Hauritz	4	6	–	41	72	12.00	–	–	1
M.L.Hayden	102	182	14	380	8437	50.22	29	28	125
B.W.Hilfenhaus	3	5	1	16	28	7.00	–	–	1
B.J.Hodge	6	11	2	203*	503	55.88	1	2	9
G.B.Hogg	7	10	3	79	186	26.57	–	1	1
P.J.Hughes	3	6	–	160	415	69.16	2	1	2
M.E.K.Hussey	37	64	9	182	3041	55.29	9	14	31
P.A.Jaques	11	19	–	150	902	47.47	3	6	7
M.G.Johnson	21	28	8	123*	694	34.70	1	3	6
S.M.Katich	37	64	5	157	2647	44.86	7	15	25
J.J.Krejza	2	4	1	32	71	23.66	–	–	4
J.L.Langer	104	180	12	250	7674	45.67	23	30	72
B.Lee	75	88	18	64	1447	20.67	–	5	22
A.B.McDonald	4	6	1	68	107	21.40	–	1	2
B.E.McGain	1	2	–	2	2	1.00	–	–	–
S.C.G.MacGill	43	45	9	43	349	9.69	–	–	16
M.J.North	2	4	–	117	160	40.00	1	–	2
R.T.Ponting	130	219	26	257	10860	56.26	37	45	147
C.J.L.Rogers	1	2	–	15	19	9.50	–	–	1
P.M.Siddle	7	12	3	23	106	11.77	–	–	4
A.Symonds	26	41	5	162*	1462	40.61	2	10	22
S.W.Tait	3	5	2	8	20	6.66	–	–	1
S.R.Watson	7	11	–	78	223	20.27	–	1	–
C.L.White	4	7	2	46	146	29.20	–	–	1

AUSTRALIA – BOWLING

	O	M	R	W	Avge	Best	5wI	10wM
D.E.Bollinger	44	9	131	2	65.50	2- 53	–	–
B.Casson	32	4	129	3	43.00	3- 86	–	–
S.R.Clark	810.4	201	2067	90	22.96	5- 32	2	–
M.J.Clarke	237.4	41	680	18	37.77	6- 9	1	–
N.M.Hauritz	168	44	452	14	32.28	3- 16	–	–
M.L.Hayden	9	0	40	0	–	–	–	–
B.W.Hilfenhaus	125	26	366	7	52.28	2- 68	–	–
B.J.Hodge	2	0	8	0	–	–	–	–
G.B.Hogg	254	40	933	17	54.88	2- 40	–	–
M.E.K.Hussey	28	4	100	1	100.00	1- 22	–	–
M.G.Johnson	885.2	173	2633	94	28.01	8- 61	2	1
S.M.Katich	143.1	15	533	18	29.61	6- 65	1	–
J.J.Krejza	123.5	8	562	13	43.23	8-215	1	1
J.L.Langer	1	0	3	0	–	–	–	–
B.Lee	2737.1	544	9458	308	30.70	5- 30	10	–
A.B.McDonald	122	40	300	9	33.33	3- 25	–	–
B.E.McGain	18	2	149	0	–	–	–	–
S.C.G.MacGill	1848.4	362	5956	199	29.92	8-108	11	2
M.J.North	38	9	98	2	49.00	1- 29	–	–
R.T.Ponting	89.5	23	242	5	48.40	1- 0	–	–
P.M.Siddle	311.1	92	802	29	27.65	5- 59	1	–
A.Symonds	349	81	896	24	37.33	3- 50	–	–
S.W.Tait	69	6	302	5	60.40	3- 97	–	–
S.R.Watson	155.4	28	460	14	32.85	4- 42	–	–
C.L.White	93	8	342	5	68.40	2- 71	–	–

TEST

SOUTH AFRICA – BATTING AND FIELDING

	M	I	NO	HS	Runs	Avge	100	50	Ct/St
H.D.Ackerman	4	8	–	57	161	20.12	–	1	1
H.M.Amla	37	65	4	176*	2460	40.32	6	14	34
N.Boje	43	62	10	85	1312	25.23	–	4	18
J.Botha	2	2	1	25	45	45.00	–	–	1
M.V.Boucher	125	176	21	125	4671	30.13	5	29	451/22
A.B.de Villiers	52	89	8	217*	3558	43.92	9	17	75/1
H.H.Dippenaar	38	62	5	177*	1718	30.14	3	7	27
J.P.Duminy	6	10	2	166	389	48.62	1	2	9
H.H.Gibbs	90	154	7	228	6167	41.95	14	26	94
A.J.Hall	21	33	4	163	760	26.20	1	3	16
P.L.Harris	24	33	4	46	304	10.48	–	–	12
C.W.Henderson	7	7	–	30	65	9.28	–	–	2
J.H.Kallis	130	219	32	189*	10194	54.51	31	51	143
J.M.Kemp	4	6	–	55	80	13.33	–	1	3
I.Khan	1	1	–	20	20	20.00	–	–	1
C.K.Langeveldt	6	4	2	10	16	8.00	–	–	2
N.D.McKenzie	58	94	7	226	3253	37.39	5	16	54
J.A.Morkel	1	1	–	58	58	58.00	–	1	–
M.Morkel	17	22	1	40	263	12.52	–	–	3
A.Nel	36	42	8	34	337	9.91	–	–	16
M.Ntini	99	113	42	32*	688	9.69	–	–	25
R.J.Peterson	6	7	1	61	163	27.16	–	1	5
S.M.Pollock	108	156	39	111	3781	32.31	2	16	72
A.G.Prince	48	77	12	162*	3074	47.29	11	8	29
J.A.Rudolph	35	63	7	222*	2028	36.21	5	8	22
G.C.Smith	76	133	9	6330	6330	51.04	18	25	101
D.W.Steyn	33	41	8	76	393	11.90	–	1	9
M.van Jaarsveld	9	15	2	73	397	30.53	–	3	11
C.M.Willoughby	2	–	–	–	–	–	–	–	–
M.Zondeki	6	5	–	59	82	16.40	–	1	1

SOUTH AFRICA – BOWLING

	O	M	R	W	Avge	Best	5wI	10wM
H.M.Amla	7	0	28	0	–	–	–	–
N.Boje	1436.4	292	4265	100	42.65	5- 62	3	–
J.Botha	37.3	2	178	4	44.50	2- 57	–	–
M.V.Boucher	1.2	0	6	1	6.00	1- 6	–	–
A.B.de Villiers	33	6	99	2	49.50	2- 49	–	–
H.H.Dippenaar	2	1	1	0	–	–	–	–
J.P.Duminy	35	5	125	2	62.50	1- 14	–	–
H.H.Gibbs	1	0	4	0	–	–	–	–
A.J.Hall	500.1	95	1617	45	35.93	3- 1	–	–
P.L.Harris	846.5	171	2315	71	32.60	6-127	2	–
C.W.Henderson	327	79	928	22	42.18	4-116	–	–
J.H.Kallis	2830	722	7983	257	31.06	6- 54	5	–
J.M.Kemp	79.5	20	222	9	24.66	3- 33	–	–
C.K.Langeveldt	166.3	27	593	16	37.06	5- 46	1	–
N.D.McKenzie	15	0	68	0	–	–	–	–
J.A.Morkel	32	4	132	1	132.00	1- 44	–	–
M.Morkel	516.5	65	1920	55	34.90	5- 50	1	–
A.Nel	1271.4	280	3919	123	31.86	6- 32	3	1
M.Ntini	3402.2	744	11009	388	28.37	7- 37	18	4
R.J.Peterson	159.5	41	497	14	35.50	5- 33	1	–
S.M.Pollock	4058.5	1222	9733	421	23.11	7- 87	16	1
A.G.Prince	16	1	47	1	47.00	1- 2	–	–
J.A.Rudolph	110.4	13	432	4	108.00	1- 1	–	–
G.C.Smith	219.5	28	801	8	100.12	2-145	–	–
D.W.Steyn	1112.4	200	4029	170	23.70	6- 49	11	3
M.van Jaarsveld	7	0	28	0	–	–	–	–
C.M.Willoughby	50	18	125	1	125.00	1- 47	–	–
M.Zondeki	130	25	480	19	25.26	6- 39	1	–

TEST

WEST INDIES – BATTING AND FIELDING

	M	I	NO	HS	Runs	Avge	100	50	Ct/St
L.S.Baker	2	2	1	0*	0	0.00	–	–	1
O.A.C.Banks	10	16	4	50*	318	26.50	–	1	6
S.J.Benn	7	10	1	28	113	12.55	–	–	3
D.J.Bravo	31	57	1	113	1833	32.73	2	11	30
S.Chanderpaul	119	202	32	203*	8502	50.01	21	52	50
S.Chattergoon	4	7	–	46	127	18.14	–	–	4
P.T.Collins	32	47	7	24	235	5.87	–	–	7
C.D.Collymore	30	52	27	16*	197	7.88	–	–	6
F.H.Edwards	41	65	20	21	221	4.91	–	–	7
D.Ganga	48	86	2	135	2160	25.71	3	9	30
C.H.Gayle	80	140	5	317	5401	40.00	10	30	78
R.O.Hinds	14	23	1	84	501	22.77	–	2	7
W.W.Hinds	45	80	1	213	2608	33.01	5	14	32
A.S.Jaggernauth	1	2	1	0*	0	0.00	–	–	–
R.N.Lewis	5	10	–	40	89	8.90	–	–	–
X.M.Marshall	7	12	–	85	243	20.25	–	2	7
R.S.Morton	15	27	1	70*	573	22.03	–	4	20
B.P.Nash	7	9	–	109	401	44.55	1	3	2
B.A.Parchment	2	4	–	20	55	13.75	–	–	1
D.B.L.Powell	37	57	5	36*	407	7.82	–	–	8
D.Ramdin	34	58	7	166	1202	23.56	1	5	99/2
D.J.G.Sammy	5	9	–	38	147	16.33	–	–	3
M.N.Samuels	29	53	4	105	1408	28.73	2	9	13
R.R.Sarwan	79	138	8	291	5535	42.57	14	31	47
L.M.P.Simmons	1	2	–	24	32	16.00	–	–	1
D.R.Smith	10	14	1	105*	320	24.61	1	–	9
D.S.Smith	29	51	2	108	1210	24.69	1	4	26
J.E.Taylor	26	40	6	106	591	17.38	1	1	4

WEST INDIES – BOWLING

	O	M	R	W	Avge	Best	5wI	10wM
L.S.Baker	56	8	201	4	50.25	2-39	–	–
O.A.C.Banks	400.1	62	1367	28	48.82	4-87	–	–
S.J.Benn	309.4	49	948	20	47.40	4-31	–	–
D.J.Bravo	856.3	161	2771	70	39.58	6-55	2	–
S.Chanderpaul	280	50	845	8	105.62	1- 2	–	–
P.T.Collins	1160.4	221	3671	106	34.63	6-53	3	–
C.D.Collymore	1056.1	245	3004	93	32.30	7-57	4	1
F.H.Edwards	1155.1	136	4594	115	39.94	7-87	7	–
D.Ganga	31	2	106	1	106.00	1-20	–	–
C.H.Gayle	1100.5	219	2887	70	41.24	5-34	2	–
R.O.Hinds	278.3	52	832	12	69.33	2-45	–	–
W.W.Hinds	187.1	41	590	16	36.87	3-79	–	–
A.S.Jaggernauth	23	0	96	1	96.00	1-74	–	–
R.N.Lewis	147.1	27	456	4	114.00	2-42	–	–
X.M.Marshall	2	2	0	0	–	–	–	–
R.S.Morton	11	0	50	0	–	–	–	–
B.P.Nash	53	8	176	1	176.00	1-34	–	–
D.B.L.Powell	1179.3	219	4068	85	47.85	5-25	1	–
D.J.G.Sammy	140.3	25	441	13	33.92	7-66	1	–
M.N.Samuels	266	36	889	7	127.00	2-49	–	–
R.R.Sarwan	336	33	1156	23	50.26	4-37	–	–
L.M.P.Simmons	11	0	55	0	–	–	–	–
D.R.Smith	108.3	20	344	7	49.14	3-71	–	–
D.S.Smith	1	0	3	0	–	–	–	–
J.E.Taylor	766.3	144	2709	79	34.29	5-11	3	–

TEST   **NEW ZEALAND – BATTING AND FIELDING**

	M	I	NO	HS	Runs	Avge	100	50	Ct/St
M.D.Bell	18	32	2	107	729	24.30	2	3	19
S.E.Bond	17	18	7	41*	139	12.63	–	–	6
C.D.Cumming	11	19	2	74	441	25.94	–	1	3
G.D.Elliott	3	5	1	9	27	6.75	–	–	2
S.P.Fleming	111	189	10	274*	7172	40.06	9	46	171
D.R.Flynn	9	16	5	95	471	42.81	–	2	4
J.E.C.Franklin	23	31	6	122*	514	20.56	1	1	10
P.G.Fulton	8	12	1	75	272	24.72	–	1	8
M.R.Gillespie	3	5	1	16*	25	6.25	–	–	–
G.J.Hopkins	1	2	–	15	27	13.50	–	–	3
J.M.How	18	34	1	92	771	23.36	–	4	17
B.B.McCullum	41	67	4	143	1990	31.58	2	12	121/9
T.G.McIntosh	2	4	1	107	197	65.66	1	–	–
H.J.H.Marshall	13	19	2	160	652	38.35	2	2	1
J.A.H.Marshall	7	11	–	52	218	19.81	–	1	5
C.S.Martin	45	65	30	12*	76	2.17	–	–	9
K.D.Mills	18	28	5	57	287	12.47	–	1	4
I.E.O'Brien	14	20	2	14*	61	3.38	–	–	2
J.D.P.Oram	31	55	10	133	1667	37.04	5	5	14
M.H.W.Papps	8	16	1	86	246	16.40	–	2	11
J.S.Patel	6	7	2	27*	69	13.80	–	–	2
A.J.Redmond	7	14	1	83	299	23.00	–	2	5
J.D.Ryder	6	11	2	91	444	49.33	–	4	6
M.S.Sinclair	32	54	5	214	1595	32.55	3	4	31
T.G.Southee	4	7	2	77*	108	21.60	–	1	–
C.M.Spearman	19	37	2	112	922	26.34	1	3	21
S.B.Styris	29	48	4	170	1586	36.04	5	6	23
L.R.P.L.Taylor	14	26	1	154*	862	34.48	2	4	21
D.L.Vettori	88	130	21	137*	2992	27.44	2	18	44
L.Vincent	23	40	1	224	1332	34.15	3	9	19

NEW ZEALAND – BOWLING

	O	M	R	W	Avge	Best	5wI	10wM
S.E.Bond	513.1	105	1769	79	22.39	6- 51	4	1
G.D.Elliott	40	8	129	2	64.50	1- 15	–	–
J.E.C.Franklin	644.1	118	2322	79	29.39	6-119	3	–
M.R.Gillespie	86	15	380	11	34.54	5-136	1	–
J.M.How	1	0	4	0	–	–	–	–
H.J.H.Marshall	1	0	4	0	–	–	–	–
C.S.Martin	1433.4	308	4899	146	33.55	6- 54	8	1
K.D.Mills	459.2	114	1334	43	31.02	4- 16	–	–
I.E.O'Brien	396.4	97	1209	43	28.11	6- 75	1	–
J.D.P.Oram	794.2	232	1871	60	31.18	4- 41	–	–
J.S.Patel	272	79	720	22	32.72	5-110	1	–
A.J.Redmond	12.3	2	62	3	20.66	2- 47	–	–
J.D.Ryder	19	3	67	2	33.50	2- 7	–	–
M.S.Sinclair	4	0	13	0	–	–	–	–
T.G.Southee	124.3	24	423	10	42.30	5- 55	1	–
S.B.Styris	326.4	77	1015	20	50.75	3- 28	–	–
L.R.P.L.Taylor	3.2	0	10	0	–	–	–	–
D.L.Vettori	3569.2	891	9354	285	32.82	7- 87	18	3
L.Vincent	1	0	2	0	–	–	–	–

TEST

INDIA – BATTING AND FIELDING

	M	I	NO	HS	Runs	Avge	100	50	Ct/St
P.P.Chawla	2	2	–	4	5	2.50	–	–	–
M.S.Dhoni	35	56	6	148	1807	36.14	1	14	81/17
R.S.Dravid	130	225	26	270	10486	52.69	26	53	179
G.Gambhir	22	39	2	206	1826	49.35	4	9	22
S.C.Ganguly	113	188	17	239	7212	42.17	16	35	71
Harbhajan Singh	74	104	20	66	1402	16.69	–	6	38
W.Jaffer	31	58	1	212	1944	34.10	5	11	27
K.D.Karthik	21	34	1	129	967	29.30	1	7	46/5
M.Kartik	8	10	1	43	88	9.77	–	–	2
Z.Khan	62	82	20	75	774	12.48	–	2	17
A.Kumble	132	173	32	110*	2506	17.77	1	5	60
V.V.S.Laxman	102	169	24	281	6446	44.45	13	37	107
A.Mishra	5	5	1	23	42	10.50	–	–	2
M.M.Patel	9	10	3	13	32	4.57	–	–	5
P.A.Patel	20	30	7	69	683	29.69	–	4	41/8
I.K.Pathan	29	40	5	102	1105	31.57	1	6	8
V.Sehwag	65	112	4	319	5534	51.24	15	17	49
I.Sharma	15	21	12	23	118	13.11	–	–	5
R.P.Singh	13	17	3	30	91	6.50	–	–	6
S.Sreesanth	14	21	7	35	217	15.50	–	–	2
S.R.Tendulkar	156	256	27	248*	12429	54.27	41	51	100
M.Vijay Krishna	1	2	–	41	74	37.00	–	–	1
Yuvraj Singh	25	40	5	169	1262	36.05	3	5	25

INDIA – BOWLING

	O	M	R	W	Avge	Best	5wI	10wM
P.P.Chawla	34.1	6	137	3	45.66	2- 66	–	–
M.S.Dhoni	2	0	14	0	–	–	–	–
R.S.Dravid	20	4	39	1	39.00	1- 18	–	–
S.C.Ganguly	519.3	108	1681	32	52.53	3- 28	–	–
Harbhajan Singh	3430.5	654	9698	314	30.88	8- 84	22	5
W.Jaffer	11	3	18	2	9.00	2- 18	–	–
M.Kartik	322	74	.820	24	34.16	4- 44	–	–
Z.Khan	2044.5	415	6707	197	34.04	5- 29	6	–
A.Kumble	6808.2	1576	18355	619	29.65	10- 74	35	8
V.V.S.Laxman	54	12	126	2	63.00	1- 2	–	–
A.Mishra	205	37	593	20	29.65	5- 71	1	–
M.M.Patel	315	68	940	28	33.57	4- 25	–	–
I.K.Pathan	980.4	212	3226	100	32.26	7- 59	7	2
V.Sehwag	387.1	58	1149	29	39.62	5-104	1	–
I.Sharma	444.4	82	1390	44	31.59	5-118	1	–
R.P.Singh	388.2	52	1564	40	39.10	5- 59	1	–
S.Sreesanth	478.5	113	1573	50	31.46	5- 40	1	–
S.R.Tendulkar	646.4	80	2227	42	53.02	3- 10	–	–
Yuvraj Singh	71	8	232	6	38.66	2- 9	–	–

TEST   **PAKISTAN – BATTING AND FIELDING**

	M	I	NO	HS	Runs	Avge	100	50	Ct/St
Abdur Rehman	2	3	1	25*	34	17.00	–	–	1
Azhar Mahmood	21	34	4	136	900	30.00	3	1	14
Danish Kaneria	53	69	31	29	260	6.84	–	–	16
Faisal Iqbal	23	38	2	139	954	26.50	1	7	17
Inzamam-ul-Haq	119	198	22	329	8829	50.16	25	46	81
Kamran Akmal	40	66	5	158*	2102	34.45	6	8	129/19
Khurram Manzoor	2	2	1	59*	86	86.00	–	1	–
Misbah-ul-Haq	12	19	2	161*	713	41.94	2	1	12
Mohammad Asif	11	16	6	12*	60	6.00	–	–	2
Mohammad Hafeez	11	21	1	104	677	33.85	2	3	4
Mohammad Sami	33	51	13	49	458	12.05	–	–	7
Mohammad Talha	1	–	–	–	–	–	–	–	–
Moh'd Yousuf Youhana	79	134	12	223	6770	55.49	23	28	59
Naved-ul-Hasan	9	15	3	42*	239	19.91	–	–	3
Salman Butt	21	38	–	122	1118	29.42	2	6	8
Shoaib Akhtar	46	67	13	47	544	10.07	–	–	12
Shoaib Malik	23	36	5	148*	1132	36.51	1	7	10
Sohail Khan	1	–	–	–	–	–	–	–	–
Sohail Tanvir	2	3	–	13	17	5.66	–	–	2
Umar Gul	18	20	2	26	136	7.55	–	–	4
Yasir Arafat	3	3	1	50*	94	47.00	–	1	–
Yasir Hamid	23	45	3	170	1450	34.52	2	8	16
Younus Khan	60	106	7	313	5129	51.80	16	20	66

PAKISTAN – BOWLING

	O	M	R	W	Avge	Best	5wI	10wM
Abdur Rehman	125	21	352	11	32.00	4-105	–	–
Azhar Mahmood	502.3	111	1402	39	35.94	4- 50	–	–
Danish Kaneria	2601.2	475	7846	225	34.87	7- 77	12	2
Faisal Iqbal	1	0	7	0	–	–	–	–
Inzamam-ul-Haq	1.3	0	8	0	–	–	–	–
Mohammad Asif	389	91	1180	51	23.13	6- 44	4	1
Mohammad Hafeez	125	23	319	4	79.75	1- 11	–	–
Mohammad Sami	1164	183	4161	81	51.37	5- 36	2	–
Mohammad Talha	17	0	88	1	88.00	1- 88	–	–
Moh'd Yousuf Youhana	1	0	3	0	–	–	–	–
Naved-ul-Hasan	260.5	36	1044	18	58.00	3- 30	–	–
Salman Butt	22.5	1	106	1	106.00	1- 36	–	–
Shoaib Akhtar	1357.1	237	4574	178	25.69	6- 11	12	2
Shoaib Malik	316.1	43	1094	15	72.93	4- 42	–	–
Sohail Khan	27	2	164	0	–	–	–	–
Sohail Tanvir	84	15	316	5	63.20	3- 83	–	–
Umar Gul	672	105	2382	76	31.34	6-135	4	–
Yasir Arafat	104.3	12	438	9	48.66	5-161	1	–
Yasir Hamid	12	0	72	0	–	–	–	–
Younus Khan	53	7	218	2	109.00	1- 24	–	–

TEST

SRI LANKA – BATTING AND FIELDING

	M	I	NO	HS	Runs	Avge	100	50	Ct/St
M.K.D.I.Amerasinghe	1	2	2	0*	0	–	–	–	–
M.S.Atapattu	90	156	15	249	5502	39.02	16	17	58
T.M.Dilshan	52	82	9	168	3052	41.80	8	12	55
C.R.D.Fernando	33	40	13	36*	198	7.33	–	–	10
H.M.R.K.B.Herath	14	18	3	33*	137	9.13	–	–	2
S.T.Jayasuriya	110	188	14	340	6973	40.07	14	31	78
D.P.M.D.Jayawardena	102	167	12	374	8251	53.23	25	32	142
H.A.P.W.Jayawardena	25	32	4	120*	693	24.75	1	2	50/18
C.K.Kapugedera	7	13	2	96	376	34.18	–	4	3
K.M.D.N.Kulasekara	6	9	1	64	121	15.12	–	1	2
M.F.Maharoof	20	31	4	72	538	19.92	–	3	6
S.L.Malinga	28	34	13	42*	192	9.14	–	–	7
B.A.W.Mendis	6	5	1	17	25	6.25	–	–	1
M.T.T.Mirando	4	7	–	14	59	8.42	–	–	1
J.Mubarak	10	17	1	48	254	15.87	–	–	13
M.Muralitharan	126	155	53	67	1176	11.52	–	1	67
N.T.Paranavitana	2	3	–	21	30	10.00	–	–	–
K.T.G.D.Prasad	2	2	–	36	39	19.50	–	–	–
T.T.Samaraweera	49	75	11	231	3269	51.07	9	18	33
K.C.Sangakkara	80	132	9	287	6764	54.99	18	30	153/20
L.P.C.Silva	11	17	1	152*	537	33.56	1	2	7
W.U.Tharanga	15	26	1	165	713	28.52	1	3	11
W.P.U.C.J.Vaas	110	161	35	100*	3085	24.48	1	13	30
M.G.Vandort	20	33	2	140	1144	36.90	4	4	6
B.S.M.Warnapura	11	18	1	120	723	42.52	2	6	13
U.W.M.B.C.A.Welagedara	1	–	–	–	–	–	–	–	1

SRI LANKA – BOWLING

	O	M	R	W	Avge	Best	5wI	10wM
M.K.D.I.Amerasinghe	25	1	105	1	105.00	1- 62	–	–
M.S.Atapattu	8	0	24	1	24.00	1- 9	–	–
T.M.Dilshan	137.2	31	406	11	36.90	4- 10	–	–
C.R.D.Fernando	854.2	129	3072	88	34.90	5- 42	3	–
H.M.R.K.B.Herath	484.1	98	1418	36	39.38	4- 38	–	–
S.T.Jayasuriya	1364.4	323	3366	98	34.34	5- 34	2	–
D.P.M.D.Jayawardena	85.1	17	273	5	54.60	2- 32	–	–
K.M.D.N.Kulasekara	135	26	440	5	88.00	2- 45	–	–
M.F.Maharoof	438	99	1458	24	60.75	4- 52	–	–
S.L.Malinga	796.1	106	3076	91	33.80	5- 68	2	–
B.A.W.Mendis	273.1	49	784	34	23.05	6-117	2	1
M.T.T.Mirando	84.5	9	355	8	44.37	3- 59	–	–
J.Mubarak	14	2	50	0	–	–	–	–
M.Muralitharan	6949.2	1746	16924	765	22.12	9- 51	66	22
N.T.Paranavitana	5	0	33	0	–	–	–	–
K.T.G.D.Prasad	66.2	5	308	9	34.22	3- 82	–	–
T.T.Samaraweera	215.1	36	679	14	48.50	4- 49	–	–
K.C.Sangakkara	11	0	38	0	–	–	–	–
L.P.C.Silva	17	2	65	1	65.00	1- 57	–	–
W.P.U.C.J.Vaas	3867.2	882	10411	354	29.40	7- 71	12	2
B.S.M.Warnapura	9	0	40	0	–	–	–	–
U.W.M.B.C.A.Welagedara	22	2	76	4	19.00	2- 17	–	–

TEST

ZIMBABWE – BATTING AND FIELDING

	M	I	NO	HS	Runs	Avge	100	50	Ct/St
S.M.Ervine	5	8	–	86	261	32.62	–	3	7
G.W.Flower	67	123	6	201*	3457	29.54	6	15	43
M.W.Goodwin	19	37	4	166*	1414	42.84	3	8	10

ZIMBABWE – BOWLING

	O	M	R	W	Avge	Best	5wI	10wM
S.M.Ervine	95	18	388	9	43.11	4-116	–	–
G.W.Flower	563	122	1537	25	61.48	4- 41	–	–
M.W.Goodwin	19.5	3	69	0	–	–	–	–

BANGLADESH – BATTING AND FIELDING

	M	I	NO	HS	Runs	Avge	100	50	Ct/St
Abdur Razzak	5	9	3	33	129	21.50	–	–	2
Aftab Ahmed	14	27	3	82*	514	21.41	–	1	6
Enamul Haque	13	23	15	9	40	5.00	–	–	3
Habibul Bashar	50	99	1	113	3026	30.87	3	24	22
Imrul Kayes	4	8	–	33	82	10.25	–	–	2
Junaid Siddique	10	19	–	74	409	21.52	–	3	6
Mahbubul Alam	4	7	3	2	5	1.25	–	–	–
Mashrafe Mortaza	35	65	5	79	758	12.63	–	3	9
Mehrab Hossain	7	13	1	83	243	20.25	–	1	2
Mohammad Ashraful	48	93	4	158*	2125	23.87	5	7	19
Mohammad Rafique	33	63	6	111	1059	18.57	1	4	7
Mushfiqur Rahim	14	27	2	80	546	21.84	–	4	17/1
Naeem Islam	2	4	–	19	44	11.00	–	–	1
Rajin Saleh	24	46	2	89	1141	25.93	–	7	15
Raqibul Hasan	3	6	–	28	88	14.66	–	–	2
Sajidul Islam	2	4	–	6	14	3.50	–	–	–
Shahadat Hossain	21	40	12	31	198	7.07	–	–	3
Shahriar Nafis	15	30	–	138	810	27.00	1	4	11
Shakib Al Hasan	12	22	1	96	556	26.47	–	2	6
Tamim Iqbal	10	18	–	84	411	22.83	–	2	2

BANGLADESH – BOWLING

	O	M	R	W	Avge	Best	5wI	10wM
Abdur Razzak	188	27	561	7	80.14	3-93	–	–
Aftab Ahmed	52.2	8	225	5	45.00	2-31	–	–
Enamul Haque	490.3	89	1499	35	42.82	7-95	3	1
Habibul Bashar	47	1	217	0	–	–	–	–
Imrul Kayes	1	0	7	0	–	–	–	–
Junaid Siddique	2	0	2	0	–	–	–	–
Mahbubul Alam	97.5	19	314	5	62.80	2-62	–	–
Mashrafe Mortaza	991.5	202	3213	78	41.19	4-60	–	–
Mehrab Hossain	67.5	3	281	4	70.25	2-29	–	–
Mohammad Ashraful	234.1	9	1081	17	63.58	2-42	–	–
Mohammad Rafique	1457.2	301	4076	100	40.76	6-77	7	–
Naeem Islam	20	2	46	1	46.00	1-11	–	–
Rajin Saleh	73	5	268	2	134.00	1- 9	–	–
Raqibul Hasan	2	0	5	0	–	–	–	–
Sajidul Islam	36	4	175	3	58.33	2-71	–	–
Shahadat Hossain	519.2	52	2188	50	43.76	6-27	2	–
Shakib Al Hasan	389.2	79	1113	35	31.80	7-36	4	–
Tamim Iqbal	2	0	4	0	–	–	–	–

LEADING CURRENT FIRST-CLASS PLAYERS

These are the leading career batting/bowling averages and wicket-keeping/fielding aggregates among players currently registered for first-class county cricket at the time of going to press. All figures are to the end of the 2008 English season.

BATTING (Qualification: 100 innings)

	Runs	Avge		Runs	Avge
M.R.Ramprakash	31894	53.42	O.A.Shah	12984	42.99
S.Chanderpaul	16363	53.12	H.H.Gibbs	13076	42.73
K.P.Pietersen	10172	51.37	S.A.Newman	6305	42.60
V.V.S.Laxman	15450	51.15	S.C.Moore	5793	42.59
J.L.Langer	27551	50.45	Z.De Bruyn	7565	42.50
M.W.Goodwin	18380	48.88	D.J.G.Sales	11458	42.28
C.J.L.Rogers	10209	48.61	A.G.Prince	8498	42.06
J.P.Crawley	24053	46.88	H.H.Dippenaar	9330	41.65
D.M.Benkenstein	11733	46.19	R.W.T.Key	12818	41.48
A.N.Cook	6625	45.06	B.F.Smith	17869	41.07
M.Van Jaarsveld	13904	44.99	A.J.Strauss	11283	41.02
M.J.Di Venuto	21097	44.98	R.S.Bopara	4572	40.82
E.C.Joyce	8661	44.87	N.Pothas	9788	40.78
M.J.North	8129	43.94	M.A.Butcher	17619	40.69
I.R.Bell	9157	43.81	I.J.L.Trott	7102	40.58
H.D.Ackerman	13563	43.75	M.B.Loye	13520	40.11
J.A.Rudolph	9710	43.73	M.A.Wagh	10420	40.07
A.D.Brown	14957	43.35	I.D.Blackwell	8154	39.77

WICKET-KEEPING (Qualification: 300 dismissals)

	Total	Ct	St		Total	Ct	St
P.A.Nixon	942	875	67	M.A.Wallace	371	344	27
C.M.Read	633	601	32	G.O.Jones	363	341	22
N.Pothas	580	535	45	M.J.Prior	334	312	22
J.N.Batty	514	454	60	L.D.Sutton	319	315	14
J.S.Foster	408	374	34	D.C.Nash	304	281	23

BOWLING (Qualification: 100 wickets)

	Wkts	Ave		Wkts	Ave
A.M.Davies	223	21.17	M.Kartik	424	26.06
Yasir Arafat	573	23.55	C.D.Thorp	109	26.33
A.R.Adams	352	23.74	A.R.Caddick	1170	26.37
Murtaza Hussain	544	24.14	Kabir Ali	418	26.39
Naved-ul-Hasan	470	24.16	A.C.Thomas	269	26.52
R.McLaren	230	24.31	D.G.Cork	895	26.62
I.E.O'Brien	209	24.46	J.D.Lewry	611	26.67
Imran Tahir	284	24.80	P.T.Collins	380	26.67
C.M.Willoughby	662	24.83	Danish Kaneria	680	26.68
R.J.Sidebottom	410	25.29	T.Henderson	262	26.80
M.J.Saggers	405	25.30	J.Lewis	621	26.86
Azhar Mahmood	515	25.33	J.M.Kemp	186	26.86
J.J.Van Der Wath	260	25.76	M.S.Mason	237	26.89
A.J.Hall	406	25.93	A.Nel	368	26.97

FIELDING (Qualification: 250 catches)

M.J.Di Venuto	326	M Van Jaarsveld	284
J.L.Langer	307	M.A.Butcher	253
M.E.Trescothick	293	D.L.Maddy	251

LIMITED-OVERS 'LIST A' CAREER RECORDS

Compiled by **Philip Bailey**

The following career records, to the end of the 2008 season, include all players currently registered with first-class counties. These records are restricted to performances in limited overs matches of 'List A' status as defined by the Association of Cricket Statisticians and Historians now incorporated by ICC into their Classification of Cricket. The following matches qualify for List A status and are included in the figures that follow: Limited-Overs Internationals; Other International matches (e.g. Commonwealth Games, 'A' team internationals); Premier domestic limited-overs tournaments in Test status countries; Official tourist matches against the main first-class teams.

The following matches do NOT qualify for inclusion: World Cup warm-up games; Tourist matches against first-class teams outside the major domestic competitions (e.g. Universities, Minor Counties etc.); Festival, pre-season friendly games and Twenty20 Cup matches.

Specialist wicket-keepers' *Ct/St* are shown in the bowlers' *Econ* column.

	M	Runs	Avge	HS	100	50	Wkts	Avge	Best	Econ
Abdul Razzaq	285	5626	30.24	112	2	30	330	30.08	6-35	4.79
Ackerman, H.D.	210	5916	32.86	139	3	40	0	–	–	6.50
Adams, A.R.	136	1343	18.14	90*	–	1	173	28.80	5- 7	4.72
Adams, C.J.	369	11481	39.72	163	21	69	32	38.03	5-16	5.24
Adams, J.H.K.	23	483	25.42	90	–	2	1	88.00	1-34	7.23
Adshead, S.J.	81	1199	22.20	77	–	5	–	–	–	87/27
Afzaal, U.	171	5026	36.68	132	6	32	53	26.96	4-49	5.91
Aga, R.G.	12	72	7.20	16	–	–	14	30.00	4-14	6.36
Ahmed, J.S.	6	1	–	1*	–	–	10	20.20	4-32	5.05
Ahmed, M.	1	–	–	–	–	–	1	34.00	1-34	11.33
Ali, Kabir	155	1080	15.21	92	–	3	226	25.17	5-36	5.14
Ali, Kadeer	48	1509	32.10	114	2	10	1	59.00	1- 4	5.61
Ali, M.M.	35	730	22.81	100	1	5	7	45.71	2-45	5.74
Allenby, J.	42	831	25.96	91*	–	4	40	26.75	5-43	5.03
Ambrose, T.R.	88	2041	29.57	135	3	8	–	–	–	93/12
Amjad Khan	54	269	11.69	65*	–	1	60	31.65	4-26	5.17
Anderson, J.M.	145	215	8.95	15	–	–	196	28.02	4-23	4.75
Andrew, G.M.	59	317	12.19	33	–	–	60	33.51	4-48	6.24
Anyon, J.E.	36	22	4.40	12	–	–	38	31.50	3- 6	5.51
Azhar Mahmood	268	3599	21.17	101*	2	14	289	31.36	6-18	4.57
Balcombe, D.J.	5	2	1.00	2	–	–	4	32.25	2-39	4.60
Ballance, G.S.	4	129	32.25	73	–	1	–	–	–	–
Banks, O.A.C.	55	1009	30.57	77*	–	7	66	26.86	4-23	4.30
Batty, G.J.	166	1818	17.65	83*	–	5	143	33.97	4-14	4.52
Batty, J.N.	178	2726	22.90	158*	1	13	–	–	–	185/33
Bell, I.R.	168	5154	35.30	137	3	38	33	34.48	5-41	5.29
Benham, C.C.	37	1144	35.75	158	3	6	–	–	–	–
Benkenstein, D.M.	256	6141	35.29	107*	1	36	83	29.69	4-16	4.99
Benning, J.G.E.	76	2458	34.13	189*	3	15	31	35.06	4-43	6.73
Berg, G.K.	6	92	23.00	65	–	1	7	29.57	4-50	6.67
Birch, D.J.	16	369	24.60	76	–	2	–	–	–	–
Blackwell, I.D.	216	4951	27.65	134*	3	30	162	36.49	5-26	4.79
Blain, J.A.R.	95	542	15.05	32	–	–	126	26.47	5-22	5.01
Blake, A.J.	3	15	–	11*	–	–	1	61.00	1-25	5.08
Boje, N.	258	3526	25.92	129	2	14	247	31.81	5-21	4.29
Bopara, R.S.	116	2849	35.61	201*	4	16	77	28.40	4-52	5.48
Botha, A.G.	122	1467	21.89	60*	–	4	119	29.90	5-43	4.87
Boyce, M.A.G.	13	275	34.37	59	–	2	–	–	–	–
Breese, G.R.	122	1334	19.33	68*	–	3	130	27.65	5-41	4.57

L-O	M	Runs	Avge	HS	100	50	Wkts	Avge	Best	Econ
Bresnan, T.T.	126	1105	18.41	61	–	2	121	35.04	4-25	4.96
Broad, S.C.J.	53	271	18.06	45*	–	–	78	26.94	5-23	4.90
Brophy, G.L.	95	1476	23.80	66	–	8	–	–	–	90/18
Brown, A.D.	376	10838	31.78	268	19	49	14	40.07	3-39	6.47
Brown, B.C.	2	4	2.00	4	–	–	–	–	–	–/–
Brown, D.O.	20	309	25.75	63*	–	1	11	39.00	3-29	5.87
Brown, J.F.	153	136	6.18	16	–	–	137	38.39	5-19	4.36
Brown, K.R.	5	72	14.40	41	–	–	–	–	–	–
Brown, M.J.	15	365	30.41	96*	–	2	–	–	–	–
Burrows, T.G.	3	18	9.00	16	–	–	–	–	–	3/2
Butcher, M.A.	191	4460	31.85	139	2	28	49	45.10	3-23	5.24
Caddick, A.R.	262	810	10.65	39	–	–	341	26.64	6-30	4.24
Carberry, M.A.	93	2124	26.22	88	–	19	1	41.00	1-21	5.85
Carter, N.M.	136	1950	19.11	135	1	6	189	25.05	5-31	4.78
Chambers, M.A.	2	1	–	1*	–	–	2	27.00	1-26	6.00
Chanderpaul, S.	341	10843	41.22	150	9	79	56	24.78	4-22	4.95
Chapple, G.	259	1951	17.89	81*	–	9	286	29.00	6-18	4.50
Cheetham, S.P.	4	3	–	3*	–	–	7	18.00	3-25	4.50
Chilton, M.J.	159	3885	29.65	115	4	19	41	24.19	5-26	5.50
Chopra, V.	20	488	25.68	102	1	3	–	–	–	–
Clare, J.L.	15	87	7.90	18	–	–	14	40.00	3-39	5.77
Clark, S.R.	131	194	8.43	26*	–	–	179	26.71	6-27	4.30
Clarke, R.	124	2404	25.30	98*	–	12	76	37.78	4-49	5.66
Claydon, M.E.	9	17	5.66	9	–	–	12	28.58	3-31	4.51
Cliff, S.J.	4	0	–	0*	–	–	5	30.20	4-26	5.39
Clinton, R.S.	19	191	14.69	56	–	1	2	29.00	2-16	7.25
Cobb, J.J.	3	31	15.50	28	–	–	–	–	–	–
Coetzer, K.J.	34	610	21.03	76	–	4	0	–	–	4.70
Collingwood, P.D.	317	8063	33.18	120*	6	48	196	34.43	6-31	4.84
Collins, P.T.	78	145	6.59	55*	–	1	123	23.24	7-11	4.29
Collymore, C.D.	125	146	6.08	13*	–	–	134	31.51	5-27	4.30
Compton, N.R.D.	43	831	28.65	110*	1	4	0	–	–	5.00
Cook, A.N.	55	1657	33.14	125	2	8	0	–	–	3.33
Cook, S.J.	164	1193	17.04	67*	–	2	205	28.01	6-37	4.72
Cork, D.G.	282	3995	21.36	93	–	19	343	27.55	6-21	4.24
Cosker, D.A.	176	490	9.80	39*	–	–	179	33.15	5-54	4.73
Crawley, J.P.	304	8512	31.88	114	7	55	0	–	–	94/4
Croft, R.D.B.	394	6369	23.41	143	4	31	403	32.30	6-20	4.32
Croft, S.J.	36	753	30.12	70	–	4	25	28.12	4-24	4.88
Crook, A.R.	21	444	27.75	162*	1	–	12	34.33	3-32	5.84
Crook, S.P.	27	153	10.20	23	–	–	20	48.30	4-20	6.03
Cross, G.D.	28	404	17.56	76	–	1	2	13.00	2-26	18/6
Cummins, R.A.G.	22	23	7.66	10	–	–	29	24.34	3-21	4.94
Dalrymple, J.W.M.	142	2833	26.72	107	2	16	104	35.47	4-14	5.06
Danish Kaneria	118	225	7.75	33*	–	–	184	21.66	5-21	4.12
Davies, A.M.	72	166	7.54	31*	–	–	68	29.94	4-13	4.16
Davies, S.M.	68	1552	31.67	119	2	8	–	–	–	61/17
Dawson, L.A.	10	198	24.75	45	–	–	11	22.00	4-45	5.62
Dawson, R.K.J.	110	523	9.86	41	–	–	111	31.07	4-13	4.87
Dean, K.J.	145	261	8.70	16*	–	–	161	30.51	5-32	4.58
De Bruyn, Z.	131	3190	32.88	113*	2	18	88	31.96	5-44	5.32
Denly, J.L.	44	1037	28.02	102*	2	4	0	–	–	6.00
Dernbach, J.W.	39	89	7.41	21	–	–	73	22.24	5-31	6.13
Dexter, N.J.	27	602	31.68	135*	2	1	14	27.57	3-17	5.21

222

L-O	M	Runs	Avge	HS	100	50	Wkts	Avge	Best	Econ
Dippenaar, H.H.	210	6500	39.63	125*	8	44	0	–	–	2.00
Di Venuto, M.J.	290	8832	33.20	173*	15	45	5	36.20	1-10	5.43
Drew, B.G.	18	117	16.71	33*	–	–	26	31.84	5-36	5.64
Du Plessis, F.	51	1424	36.51	114	1	11	27	29.00	4-47	5.14
Du Preez, D.	49	685	36.05	107*	1	2	53	35.01	4-22	4.78
Durston, W.J.	53	952	30.70	62*	–	6	19	43.52	3-44	6.17
Du Toit, J.	16	324	27.00	144	1	–	2	33.00	2-30	6.00
Ealham, M.A.	409	6211	23.88	112	1	26	470	26.46	6-53	4.09
Edwards, N.J.	5	113	22.60	65	–	1	–	–	–	–
Ervine, S.M.	141	3162	30.69	134*	5	14	138	33.66	5-50	5.54
Evans, D.	2	–	–	–	–	–	3	30.66	3-36	4.60
Ferley, R.S.	42	256	17.06	42	–	–	54	28.11	4-33	4.84
Finn, S.T.	14	7	3.50	4	–	–	15	34.13	3-23	5.22
Fisher, I.D.	70	291	10.39	37*	–	–	69	31.15	3-18	4.78
Fletcher, L.J.	4	2	2.00	2*	–	–	3	36.33	2-41	3.11
Flintoff, A.	274	6524	30.20	143	6	34	279	22.32	5-56	4.13
Flower, G.W.	337	9885	34.08	148*	11	67	177	35.22	4-32	4.45
Foster, J.S.	134	1845	23.65	69*	–	6	–	–	–	164/37
Francis, J.D.	70	1827	33.83	103*	1	12	–	–	–	–
Franks, P.J.	145	1604	21.10	84*	–	4	163	27.87	6-27	4.89
Frost, T.	85	605	19.51	56	–	2	–	–	–	78/19
Frylinck, R.	23	430	39.09	82*	–	3	28	22.78	5-39	5.10
Gale, A.W.	60	1336	29.68	89	–	8	–	–	–	–
Gallian, J.E.R.	228	6684	32.44	134	11	40	55	32.87	5-15	5.29
Gazzard, C.M.	53	954	23.85	157	1	4	–	–	–	51/7
Gibbs, H.H.	350	10724	34.81	175	24	57	2	28.50	1-16	5.18
Gidman, A.P.R.	126	2677	25.74	105	2	15	51	40.17	5-42	5.20
Gidman, W.R.S.	3	33	11.00	21	–	–	4	15.25	2-21	4.35
Gitsham, M.T.	2	15	15.00	15	–	–	–	–	–	–
Goddard, L.J.	8	100	25.00	36	–	–	–	–	–	13/–
Godleman, B.A.	8	184	26.28	48	–	–	–	–	–	–
Goodwin, M.W.	311	9309	35.39	167	12	59	7	43.71	1- 9	5.23
Grant, R.N.	41	679	18.86	45	–	–	7	45.00	2-21	7.65
Griffiths, D.A.	3	3	–	3*	–	–	1	142.00	1-53	6.76
Groenewald, T.D.	27	217	13.56	36	–	–	19	40.57	3-25	6.13
Guy, S.M.	26	260	16.25	40	–	–	–	–	–	23/7
Hales, A.D.	1	–	–	–	–	–	–	–	–	–
Hall, A.J.	250	4779	29.86	129*	5	26	288	26.80	5-18	4.54
Hamilton-Brown, R.J.	18	161	13.41	35	–	–	13	27.46	3-28	5.31
Harmison, B.W.	28	381	18.14	57	–	1	11	30.45	3-43	5.22
Harmison, S.J.	128	230	7.66	25*	–	–	174	28.89	5-33	4.86
Harris, A.J.	145	217	7.00	34	–	–	190	28.53	5-35	5.04
Harris, J.A.R.	9	43	7.16	15	–	–	16	18.06	4-48	4.98
Harrison, D.S.	69	377	13.46	37*	–	–	78	29.01	5-26	4.69
Hayward, M.	149	206	9.36	19*	–	–	201	27.01	5-37	4.99
Henderson, C.W.	213	1043	16.82	45	–	–	263	25.79	6-29	4.25
Henderson, T.	106	1500	21.12	126*	1	8	124	27.34	5- 5	4.33
Hildreth, J.C.	92	2148	28.64	122	2	7	6	30.83	2-26	7.40
Hinds, W.W.	194	4769	28.21	127*	6	26	49	27.32	4-35	5.39
Hodd, A.J.	17	228	19.00	42	–	–	–	–	–	9/–
Hodge, B.J.	214	7322	40.90	164	19	35	38	34.42	5-28	5.29
Hodgson, L.J.	2	–	–	–	–	–	0	–	–	6.50
Hodnett, G.P.	4	114	28.50	50	–	1	–	–	–	–
Hogg, K.W.	98	761	16.91	66*	–	1	96	29.34	4-20	4.72

223

L-O	M	Runs	Avge	HS	100	50	Wkts	Avge	Best	Econ
Hoggard, M.J.	127	67	3.72	7*	–	–	177	25.15	5-28	4.45
Hopkinson, C.D.	91	1390	23.16	123*	1	6	15	37.33	3-19	5.93
Horton, P.J.	26	424	18.43	56	–	1	–	–	–	–
Hughes, P.J.	3	115	38.33	68	–	1	–	–	–	–
Hunter, I.D.	82	310	8.37	39	–	–	91	31.96	4-29	4.92
Imran Arif	5	17	–	16*	–	–	5	39.60	1-17	6.52
Imran Tahir	48	155	14.09	41*	–	–	74	21.74	5-27	4.33
Ireland, A.J.	49	77	7.00	17	–	–	67	28.74	4-16	5.17
Jefferson, W.I.	85	2767	35.02	132	4	15	2	4.50	2- 9	2.25
Johnson, R.M.	2	26	13.00	20	–	–	–	–	–	–
Jones, G.O.	137	2227	23.44	86	–	8	–	–	–	162/26
Jones, P.S.	176	628	12.56	42	–	–	237	29.56	6-56	5.26
Jones, R.A.	2	6	6.00	6	–	–	1	–	–	7.16
Jones, S.P.	34	76	15.20	26	–	–	31	39.96	5-32	5.11
Jordan, C.J.	14	61	7.62	38	–	–	22	25.50	3-28	5.38
Joseph, R.H.	26	26	13.00	15	–	–	34	24.41	5-13	4.77
Joyce, E.C.	165	4757	34.22	115*	4	33	6	51.50	2-10	7.02
Kartik, M.	158	534	10.89	37*	–	–	194	30.21	6-27	4.34
Keedy, G.	51	121	12.10	33	–	–	54	28.57	5-30	4.65
Kemp, J.M.	243	5365	35.76	107*	3	39	179	29.07	6-20	4.77
Kervezee, A.N.	20	392	26.13	62	–	1	0	–	–	9.40
Key, R.W.T.	173	4927	31.99	120*	5	32	–	–	–	–
Kieswetter, C.	29	866	34.64	121	1	5	–	–	–	34/5
Killeen, N.	221	683	9.48	32	–	–	295	24.32	6-31	4.13
Kirby, S.P.	56	72	4.80	15	–	–	67	33.26	5-36	5.64
Kirtley, R.J.	231	419	9.74	30*	–	–	344	23.02	5-27	4.66
Kleinveldt, R.K.	45	491	18.18	54*	–	1	55	27.01	4-29	4.52
Klokker, F.A.	21	568	37.86	138*	1	4	–	–	–	22/5
Kruger, G.J.P.	114	115	6.76	20*	–	–	158	25.51	6-23	4.79
Kruis, G.J.	119	407	12.33	31*	–	–	144	29.40	4-17	4.62
Langer, J.L.	225	7603	38.79	146	14	51	7	30.71	3-51	6.68
Langeveldt, C.K.	170	311	7.23	33*	–	–	259	23.39	5- 7	4.54
Lawson, M.A.K.	4	30	7.50	20	–	–	3	47.00	2-50	7.16
Laxman, V.V.S.	167	4944	34.57	131	9	27	8	68.50	2-42	4.71
Lewis, J.	183	657	10.26	40	–	–	239	26.92	5-19	4.49
Lewry, J.D.	79	217	7.48	16*	–	–	100	27.68	4-29	4.64
Liddle, C.J.	14	13	4.33	11	–	–	10	53.20	3-60	6.33
Louw, J.	111	1173	18.91	72	–	3	166	23.96	5-27	4.75
Loye, M.B.	287	8586	34.34	127	10	56	–	–	–	–
Lucas, D.S.	51	150	10.00	32	–	–	59	32.10	4-27	5.72
Lumb, M.J.	139	3801	30.65	108	1	28	0	–	–	14.00
Lungley, T.	73	371	11.96	45	–	–	82	29.09	4-28	5.12
Lyth, A.	18	196	17.81	38*	–	–	0	–	–	3.00
McGrath, A.	262	6760	32.65	148	7	38	75	32.38	4-41	5.03
McLaren, R.	77	1309	37.40	82*	–	8	77	29.45	5-46	4.87
MacLeod, C.S.	5	18	9.00	10*	–	–	1	100.00	1-44	5.26
Maddy, D.L.	322	8263	30.83	167*	11	50	188	29.09	4-16	5.07
Mahmood, S.I.	103	355	8.45	29	–	–	146	26.23	5-16	5.17
Mahomed, U.	1	3	3.00	3	–	–	–	–	–	–
Malan, D.J.	13	196	16.33	42	–	–	1	50.00	1-24	6.25
Malcolm-Hansen, R.J.A.	14	157	14.27	71	–	1	8	47.62	3-38	5.41
Malik, M.N.	69	97	9.70	11	–	–	66	35.92	4-42	5.24
Marshall, H.J.H.	194	4620	28.34	122	5	30	2	70.00	1-14	6.94
Martin-Jenkins, R.S.C.	208	1865	15.04	68*	–	3	219	29.49	4-22	4.25

L-O	M	Runs	Avge	HS	100	50	Wkts	Avge	Best	Econ
Mascarenhas, A.D.	215	3622	24.47	79	–	24	252	25.40	5-27	4.26
Mason, M.S.	72	158	7.90	25	–	–	85	28.09	4-34	4.32
Masters, D.D.	107	437	12.48	39	–	–	98	33.21	5-17	4.53
Maunders, J.K.	31	640	22.85	109*	1	1	4	25.75	2-16	4.44
Maynard, T.L.	17	393	23.11	71	–	3	–	–	–	–
Mcakeı, S.C.	2	–	–	–	–	–	1	57.00	1-57	7.12
Middlebrook, J.D.	139	1235	18.71	47	–	–	109	34.31	4-27	4.62
Mitchell, D.K.H.	26	453	26.64	92	–	4	13	43.00	4-42	6.35
Moore, S.C.	77	1857	27.30	105*	2	10	1	42.00	1- 1	7.20
Morgan, E.J.G.	76	2104	33.39	115	3	11	0	–	–	8.80
Muchall, G.J.	77	1649	29.44	101*	1	8	1	137.00	1-15	5.07
Mullaney, S.J.	6	26	13.00	12	–	–	6	16.16	3-13	5.01
Munday, M.K.	1	–	–	–	–	–	1	39.00	1-39	7.80
Murtagh, C.P.	4	108	108.00	74	–	1	–	–	–	–
Murtagh, T.J.	95	550	13.09	35*	–	–	139	26.94	4-14	5.15
Murtaza Hussain	106	774	14.60	85	–	1	131	25.73	5-18	4.20
Mustard, P.	102	2156	26.29	108	1	12	–	–	–	108/21
Naik, J.K.H.	6	15	7.50	13	–	–	7	29.57	3-24	4.77
Napier, G.R.	158	1701	16.67	79	–	8	158	24.81	6-29	5.04
Nash, C.D.	29	618	22.88	82	–	3	6	33.66	3- 8	5.48
Nash, D.C.	120	1480	20.84	67	–	6	–	–	–	91/18
Naved-ul-Hasan	141	1551	20.40	74	–	7	221	25.61	6-27	5.17
Needham, J.	28	203	18.45	42	–	–	12	60.41	2-36	5.47
Nelson, M.A.G.	9	113	22.60	26	–	–	2	50.00	1-26	6.38
New, T.J.	34	751	25.89	68	–	3	–	–	–	7/2
Newby, O.J.	15	24	4.80	7*	–	–	10	54.60	2-37	5.85
Newman, S.A.	74	1817	25.95	106	1	11	–	–	–	–
Nixon, P.A.	390	6938	26.08	101	1	32	0	–	–	413/98
North, M.J.	115	3235	33.69	134*	5	23	55	30.10	4-26	5.20
O'Brien, N.J.	83	1326	23.26	95	–	9	–	–	–	64/24
Onions, G.	47	102	7.28	19	–	–	53	31.15	3-39	5.20
Ormond, J.	119	359	8.97	32	–	–	146	27.30	4-12	4.45
Palladino, A.P.	21	43	4.77	16	–	–	22	30.63	3-32	5.18
Panesar, M.S.	44	98	10.88	17*	–	–	43	35.30	5-20	4.36
Park, G.T.	16	198	18.00	42*	–	–	0	–	–	3.75
Patel, S.R.	78	1670	32.74	114	1	9	63	23.31	5-41	4.88
Patterson, S.A.	18	69	69.00	25*	–	–	16	43.00	3-11	5.10
Pattinson, D.J.	24	47	6.71	13*	–	–	34	24.29	4-29	4.97
Peters, S.D.	143	2684	21.82	107	2	15	–	–	–	–
Pettini, M.L.	84	1888	26.59	144	3	13	–	–	–	–
Phillips, B.J.	97	833	18.51	44*	–	–	108	30.04	4-25	4.82
Phillips, T.J.	34	196	16.33	24*	–	–	34	22.17	5-34	4.73
Pietersen, K.P.	190	6257	44.37	147	11	40	38	48.76	3-14	5.28
Pipe, D.J.	64	730	18.25	83	–	3	–	–	–	58/17
Plunkett, L.E.	77	715	23.83	72	–	2	99	30.91	4-15	5.26
Poonia, N.S.	31	578	19.26	75	–	3	–	–	–	–
Pope, J.I.	1	9	9.00	9	–	–	–	–	–	2/1
Porterfield, W.T.S.	47	1261	28.65	112*	2	7	–	–	–	–
Pothas, N.	218	4236	35.89	114*	3	23	–	–	–	199/49
Powell, M.J. (Gm)	195	4550	27.74	114*	1	25	1	26.00	1-26	6.50
Poynton, T.	1	–	–	–	–	–	–	–	–	–
Prince, A.G.	186	3942	31.04	89*	–	21	0	–	–	5.67
Prior, M.J.	164	3862	27.19	144	4	21	–	–	–	144/25
Pyrah, R.M.	54	509	16.96	42	–	–	58	24.77	5-50	5.51

225

L-O	M	Runs	Avge	HS	100	50	Wkts	Avge	Best	Econ
Ramprakash, M.R.	390	12550	39.58	147*	14	83	46	29.43	5-38	4.68
Rankin, W.B.	19	25	6.25	7*	–	–	19	33.10	3-32	5.67
Rashid, A.U.	23	151	15.10	41*	–	–	17	37.58	3-37	5.21
Rayner, O.P.	15	151	21.57	61	–	1	10	50.60	2-31	6.24
Read, C.M.W.	236	3951	28.00	135	2	12	–	–	–	240/53
Redfern, D.J.	11	185	23.12	57*	–	1	0	–	–	5.33
Rees, G.P.	6	163	27.16	63	–	1	–	–	–	–
Riazuddin, H.	3	–	–	–	–	–	2	43.50	1-15	3.62
Richardson, A.	61	104	10.40	21*	–	–	57	36.87	5-35	4.70
Roberts, A.	1	1	1.00	1	–	–	1	22.00	1-22	5.50
Robson, S.D.	1	21	21.00	21	–	–	–	–	–	–
Rogers, C.J.L.	90	2580	32.25	117*	2	18	2	13.00	2-22	6.50
Rowe, D.T.	7	22	11.00	17	–	–	2	106.50	1-26	7.60
Roy, J.J.	2	6	3.00	6	–	–	0	–	–	12.00
Rudolph, J.A.	154	5237	43.64	134*	7	33	10	34.10	4-40	5.42
Sadler, J.L.	83	1716	26.40	113*	1	6	1	33.00	1-33	4.12
Saggers, M.J.	123	302	9.15	34*	–	–	166	25.28	5-22	4.50
Saker, N.C.	23	74	10.57	22	–	–	18	52.33	4-43	6.05
Sales, D.J.G.	229	6353	33.97	161	4	44	0	–	–	4.78
Salisbury, I.D.K.	255	1582	13.29	59*	–	1	257	32.37	5-30	4.60
Sayers, J.J.	13	249	22.63	62	–	2	1	71.00	1-31	7.88
Schofield, C.P.	113	1391	22.43	75*	–	6	108	27.34	5-31	5.21
Scott, B.J.M.	78	604	18.30	73*	–	4	–	–	–	65/26
Shafayat, B.M.	100	1981	23.03	104	1	7	24	30.41	4-33	5.54
Shah, O.A.	277	7643	33.52	134	11	47	18	41.94	2- 2	6.01
Shahzad, A.	9	60	12.00	33	–	–	12	27.83	5-51	4.91
Shankar, A.	1	27	27.00	27	–	–	–	–	–	–
Shantry, A.J.	9	26	8.66	15	–	–	11	20.72	5-37	4.65
Shreck, C.E.	48	44	7.33	9*	–	–	62	30.48	5-19	5.11
Sidebottom, R.J.	154	404	10.91	32	–	–	162	30.16	6-40	4.28
Silverwood, C.E.W.	192	1002	13.72	61	–	4	250	24.58	5-28	4.27
Smith, B.F.	379	9581	30.61	115	3	59	2	60.50	1- 2	5.71
Smith, D.R.	108	1610	19.16	96	–	7	64	38.03	5-45	4.83
Smith, G.M.	38	821	22.80	88	–	4	21	37.00	3-19	5.96
Smith, G.P.	2	71	35.50	58	–	1	–	–	–	–
Smith, T.C.	26	178	17.80	52	–	1	29	25.06	3- 8	4.56
Smith, T.M.J.	8	22	11.00	15	–	–	5	62.40	2-45	6.00
Smith, W.R.	49	1101	26.85	103	1	8	1	6.00	1- 6	7.20
Snell, S.D.	12	42	4.66	17	–	–	–	–	–	–
Solanki, V.S.	334	8953	31.74	164*	13	51	26	35.57	4-14	5.32
Spearman, C.M.	276	7719	29.23	153	8	48	0	–	–	7.81
Spriegel, M.N.W.	10	189	63.00	54	–	1	5	53.20	1-17	4.66
Stayt, T.P.	1	–	–	–	–	–	0	–	–	7.03
Stevens, D.I.	192	4717	28.93	133	4	30	44	33.45	5-32	4.82
Stoneman, M.D.	1	21	21.00	21	–	–	–	–	–	–
Strauss, A.J.	199	5461	30.50	163	6	34	0	–	–	3.00
Stubbings, S.D.	114	2624	26.24	110	1	15	–	–	–	–
Suppiah, A.V.	42	940	24.73	79	–	5	29	33.37	4-39	5.61
Sutton, L.D.	139	1796	18.70	83	–	6	–	–	–	155/19
Swann, G.P.	196	2786	19.75	83	–	14	205	27.25	5-17	4.39
Tahir, N.	13	19	9.50	13*	–	–	5	67.60	2-47	4.56
Taylor, B.V.	132	186	6.41	21*	–	–	164	26.12	5-28	4.42
Taylor, C.G.	139	2521	23.34	93	–	15	8	32.25	2- 5	5.56
Taylor, C.R.	22	738	46.12	111*	2	2	–	–	–	–

226

L-O	M	Runs	Avge	HS	100	50	Wkts	Avge	Best	Econ
Taylor, J.W.A.	4	80	80.00	43*	–	–	–	–	–	–
Telo, F.D.	22	476	26.44	90	–	4	–	–	–	–
Ten Doeschate, R.N.	89	2085	40.88	109*	1	12	90	21.25	5-50	5.37
Thomas, A.C.	92	425	14.65	27*	–	–	107	31.18	4-31	4.82
Thompson, J.G.	2	8	4.00	7	–	–	–	–	–	–
Thornely, M.A.	1						–	–	–	–
Thorp, C.D.	35	261	17.40	52	–	1	45	26.13	6-17	4.32
Tomlinson, J.A.	22	18	2.25	6	–	–	20	35.75	4-47	4.83
Tredwell, J.C.	122	1108	19.43	88	–	4	116	32.50	4-16	4.72
Trego, P.D.	70	758	15.79	78	–	2	69	31.85	5-44	5.72
Tremlett, C.T.	104	389	8.84	38*	–	–	147	25.46	4-25	4.65
Trescothick, M.E.	303	9976	37.36	184	26	46	57	28.70	4-50	4.89
Trott, I.J.L.	131	4019	41.86	125*	8	24	42	25.33	4-55	5.68
Troughton, J.O.	107	2411	27.71	115*	2	11	25	25.76	4-23	5.25
Tudor, A.J.	79	464	12.54	56	–	1	109	24.43	4-26	4.78
Turner, M.L.	9	23	11.50	11*	–	–	11	32.63	3-39	5.74
Udal, S.D.	384	2702	15.89	78	–	8	432	30.15	5-43	4.42
Van der Wath, J.J.	125	1909	27.66	91	–	11	158	27.77	4-31	4.83
Van Jaarsveld, M.	235	7433	40.39	124	12	48	24	40.33	3-43	5.28
Vaughan, M.P.	276	6958	28.75	125*	3	43	78	32.53	4-22	4.61
Vincent, L.	194	5036	28.77	172	7	27	4	54.25	2-25	6.11
Voges, A.C.	52	1895	47.37	100*	1	17	13	54.69	3-33	5.26
Wagg, G.G.	62	623	14.15	45	–	–	69	31.02	4-35	5.63
Wagh, M.A.	98	2343	27.24	102*	1	17	25	34.48	4-35	4.71
Wainwright, D.J.	19	62	20.66	26	–	–	12	38.25	2-30	5.04
Wakely, A.G.	4	18	4.50	14	–	–	2	7.00	2-14	4.66
Walker, M.J.	257	5665	28.32	117	3	34	30	24.66	4-24	5.01
Wallace, M.A.	128	1516	19.43	85	–	2	–	–	–	128/29
Walters, S.J.	25	383	20.15	91	–	1	2	71.50	1-12	6.08
Waters, H.T.	12	22	5.50	8	–	–	8	66.25	3-47	6.16
Watkins, R.E.	20	215	16.53	39	–	–	16	40.62	2-25	6.39
Wessels, M.H.	57	1299	27.63	100	1	7	–	–	–	44/–
Westley, T.	3	37	18.50	36	–	–				
Westwood, I.J.	34	637	24.50	65	–	3	2	75.00	1-28	4.68
Wharf, A.G.	154	1411	16.21	72	–	1	192	28.91	6- 5	5.12
Whelan, C.D.	11	15	2.50	6	–	–	9	40.11	4-78	6.94
White, C.	362	7317	26.51	148	5	30	337	25.10	5-19	4.38
White, G.G.	6	16	5.33	14	–	–	4	43.50	2-44	4.97
White, R.A.	64	1197	20.28	111	2	5	2	27.50	2-18	6.11
Whiteley, R.A.	1	24	24.00	24	–	–	0	–	–	6.00
Wigley, D.H.	23	32	2.90	10	–	–	15	55.46	4-37	6.30
Willoughby, C.M.	193	132	5.28	12*	–	–	240	27.07	6-16	4.13
Wilson, G.C.	25	476	21.63	58	–	5	–	–	–	20/4
Wiseman, P.J.	120	967	15.34	65*	–	2	84	40.64	4-45	4.27
Woakes, C.R.	10	68	17.00	31*	–	–	3	77.33	1-21	5.52
Wood, M.J. (Gm)	152	3464	27.49	160	5	16	3	32.66	3-45	6.46
Wood, M.J. (Nt)	83	2072	27.62	129	2	14	–	–	–	–
Woodman, R.J.	5	14	14.00	14	–	–	1	163.00	1-38	6.52
Wright, B.J.	28	547	21.88	61	–	3	0	–	–	5.75
Wright, C.J.C.	33	102	9.27	23	–	–	24	45.37	3- 3	5.26
Wright, L.J.	95	1153	20.22	125	1	3	70	36.44	4-12	5.23
Yardy, M.H.	128	2041	20.61	98*	–	11	77	35.62	6-27	4.83
Yasir Arafat	175	1979	21.05	87	–	7	289	23.29	6-24	4.77

FIRST-CLASS CRICKET RECORDS

To the end of the 2008 season

TEAM RECORDS

HIGHEST INNINGS TOTALS

1107	Victoria v New South Wales	Melbourne	1926-27
1059	Victoria v Tasmania	Melbourne	1922-23
952-6d	Sri Lanka v India	Colombo	1997-98
951-7d	Sind v Baluchistan	Karachi	1973-74
944-6d	Hyderabad v Andhra	Secunderabad	1993-94
918	New South Wales v South Australia	Sydney	1900-01
912-8d	Holkar v Mysore	Indore	1945-46
910-6d	Railways v Dera Ismail Khan	Lahore	1964-65
903-7d	England v Australia	The Oval	1938
900-6d	Queensland v Victoria	Brisbane	2005-06
887	Yorkshire v Warwickshire	Birmingham	1896
863	Lancashire v Surrey	The Oval	1990
860-6d	Tamil Nadu v Goa	Panjim	1988-89
850-7d	Somerset v Middlesex	Taunton	2007

Excluding penalty runs in India, there have been 32 innings totals of 800 runs or more in first-class cricket. Tamil Nadu's total of 860-6d was boosted by 52 penalty runs.

HIGHEST SECOND INNINGS TOTAL

770	New South Wales v South Australia	Adelaide	1920-21

HIGHEST FOURTH INNINGS TOTAL

654-5	England (set 696 to win) v South Africa	Durban	1938-39

HIGHEST MATCH AGGREGATE

2376-37	Maharashtra v Bombay	Poona	1948-49

RECORD MARGIN OF VICTORY

Innings and 851 runs: Railways v Dera Ismail Khan   Lahore   1964-65

MOST RUNS IN A DAY

721	Australians v Essex	Southend	1948

MOST HUNDREDS IN AN INNINGS

6	Holkar v Mysore	Indore	1945-46

LOWEST INNINGS TOTALS

12	†Oxford University v MCC and Ground	Oxford	1877
12	Northamptonshire v Gloucestershire	Gloucester	1907
13	Auckland v Canterbury	Auckland	1877-78
13	Nottinghamshire v Yorkshire	Nottingham	1901
14	Surrey v Essex	Chelmsford	1983
15	MCC v Surrey	Lord's	1839
15	†Victoria v MCC	Melbourne	1903-04
15	†Northamptonshire v Yorkshire	Northampton	1908
15	Hampshire v Warwickshire	Birmingham	1922

† *Batted one man short*

There have been 27 instances of a team being dismissed for under 20.

LOWEST MATCH AGGREGATE BY ONE TEAM
34 (16 and 18)   Border v Natal   East London   1959-60

LOWEST COMPLETED MATCH AGGREGATE BY BOTH TEAMS
105   MCC v Australians   Lord's   1878

FEWEST RUNS IN AN UNINTERRUPTED DAY'S PLAY
95   Australia (80) v Pakistan (15-2)   Karachi   1956-57

TIED MATCHES
Before 1949 a match was considered to be tied if the scores were level after the fourth innings, even if the side batting last had wickets in hand when play ended. Law 22 was amended in 1948 and since then a match has been tied only when the scores are level after the fourth innings has been completed. There have been 56 tied first-class matches, five of which would not have qualified under the current law. The most recent are:

Warwickshire (446-7d & forfeit) v Essex (66-0d & 380)   Birmingham   2003
Worcestershire (262 & 247) v Zimbabweans (334 & 175)   Worcester   2003

BATTING RECORDS
HIGHEST INDIVIDUAL INNINGS

501*	B.C.Lara	Warwickshire v Durham	Birmingham	1994
499	Hanif Mohammed	Karachi v Bahawalpur	Karachi	1958-59
452*	D.G.Bradman	New South Wales v Queensland	Sydney	1929-30
443*	B.B.Nimbalkar	Maharashtra v Kathiawar	Poona	1948-49
437	W.H.Ponsford	Victoria v Queensland	Melbourne	1927-28
429	W.H.Ponsford	Victoria v Tasmania	Melbourne	1922-23
428	Aftab Baloch	Sind v Baluchistan	Karachi	1973-74
424	A.C.MacLaren	Lancashire v Somerset	Taunton	1895
405*	G.A.Hick	Worcestershire v Somerset	Taunton	1988
400*	B.C.Lara	West Indies v England	St John's	2003-04
394	Naved Latif	Sargodha v Gujranwala	Gujranwala	2000-01
385	B.Sutcliffe	Otago v Canterbury	Christchurch	1952-53
383	C.W.Gregory	New South Wales v Queensland	Brisbane	1906-07
380	M.L.Hayden	Australia v Zimbabwe	Perth	2003-04
377	S.V.Manjrekar	Bombay v Hyderabad	Bombay	1990-91
375	B.C.Lara	West Indies v England	St John's	1993-94
374	D.P.M.D.Jayawardena	Sri Lanka v South Africa	Colombo	2006
369	D.G.Bradman	South Australia v Tasmania	Adelaide	1935-36
366	N.H.Fairbrother	Lancashire v Surrey	The Oval	1990
366	M.V.Sridhar	Hyderabad v Andhra	Secunderabad	1993-94
365*	C.Hill	South Australia v NSW	Adelaide	1900-01
365*	G.St A.Sobers	West Indies v Pakistan	Kingston	1957-58
364	L.Hutton	England v Australia	The Oval	1938
359*	V.M.Merchant	Bombay v Maharashtra	Bombay	1943-44
359	R.B.Simpson	New South Wales v Queensland	Brisbane	1963-64
357*	R.Abel	Surrey v Somerset	The Oval	1899
357	D.G.Bradman	South Australia v Victoria	Melbourne	1935-36
356	B.A.Richards	South Australia v W Australia	Perth	1970-71
355*	G.R.Marsh	W Australia v S Australia	Perth	1989-90
355	B.Sutcliffe	Otago v Auckland	Dunedin	1949-50
353	V.V.S.Laxman	Hyderabad v Karnataka	Bangalore	1999-00
352	W.H.Ponsford	Victoria v New South Wales	Melbourne	1926-27
350	Rashid Israr	Habib Bank v National Bank	Lahore	1976-77

There have been 166 triple hundreds in first-class cricket, W.V.Raman (313) and Arjan Kripal Singh (302*) for Tamil Nadu v Goa at Panjim in 1988-89 providing the only instance of two batsmen scoring 300 in the same innings.

MOST HUNDREDS IN SUCCESSIVE INNINGS

6	C.B.Fry	Sussex and Rest of England		1901
6	D.G.Bradman	South Australia and D.G.Bradman's XI		1938-39
6	M.J.Procter	Rhodesia		1970-71

TWO DOUBLE HUNDREDS IN A MATCH

244	202*	A.E.Fagg	Kent v Essex	Colchester	1938

TRIPLE HUNDRED AND HUNDRED IN A MATCH

333	123	G.A.Gooch	England v India	Lord's	1990

DOUBLE HUNDRED AND HUNDRED IN A MATCH MOST TIMES

4	Zaheer Abbas	Gloucestershire	1976-81

TWO HUNDREDS IN A MATCH MOST TIMES

8	Zaheer Abbas	Gloucestershire and PIA	1976-82
8	R.T.Ponting	Tasmania, Australia and Australians	1992-2006
7	W.R.Hammond	Gloucestershire, England and MCC	1927-45

MOST HUNDREDS IN A SEASON

18	D.C.S.Compton	1947	16	J.B.Hobbs	1925

100 HUNDREDS IN A CAREER

	Total		100th Hundred	
	Hundreds	Inns	Season	Inns
J.B.Hobbs	197	1315	1923	821
E.H.Hendren	170	1300	1928-29	740
W.R.Hammond	167	1005	1935	679
C.P.Mead	153	1340	1927	892
G.Boycott	151	1014	1977	645
H.Sutcliffe	149	1088	1932	700
F.E.Woolley	145	1532	1929	1031
G.A.Hick	136	871	1998	574
L.Hutton	129	814	1951	619
G.A.Gooch	128	990	1992-93	820
W.G.Grace	126	1493	1895	1113
D.C.S.Compton	123	839	1952	552
T.W.Graveney	122	1223	1964	940
D.G.Bradman	117	338	1947-48	295
I.V.A.Richards	114	796	1988-89	658
Zaheer Abbas	108	768	1982-83	658
A.Sandham	107	1000	1935	871
M.C.Cowdrey	107	1130	1973	1035
T W Hayward	104	1138	1913	1076
M.R.Ramprakash	103	684	2008	676
G.M.Turner	103	792	1982	779
J.H.Edrich	103	979	1977	945
L.E.G.Ames	102	951	1950	915
G.E.Tyldesley	102	961	1934	919
D.L.Amiss	102	1139	1986	1081

MOST 400s: 2 – B.C.Lara, W.H.Ponsford
MOST 300s or more: 6 – D.G.Bradman; 4 – W.R.Hammond, W.H.Ponsford
MOST 200s or more: 37 – D.G.Bradman; 36 – W.R.Hammond; 22 – E.H.Hendren

MOST RUNS IN A MONTH

1294 (avge 92.42)   L.Hutton   Yorkshire   June 1949

MOST RUNS IN A SEASON

Runs			I	NO	HS	Avge	100	Season
3816	D.C.S.Compton	Middlesex	50	8	246	90.85	18	1947
3539	W.J.Edrich	Middlesex	52	8	267*	80.43	12	1947
3518	T.W.Hayward	Surrey	61	8	219	66.37	13	1906

The feat of scoring 3000 runs in a season has been achieved 28 times, the most recent instance being by W.E.Alley (3019) in 1961. The highest aggregate in a season since 1969 is 2755 by S.J.Cook in 1991.

1000 RUNS IN A SEASON MOST TIMES

28   W.G.Grace (Gloucestershire), F.E.Woolley (Kent)

HIGHEST BATTING AVERAGE IN A SEASON

(Qualification: 12 innings)

Avge			I	NO	HS	Runs	100	Season
115.66	D.G.Bradman	Australians	26	5	278	2429	13	1938
104.66	D.R.Martyn	Australians	14	5	176*	942	5	2001
103.54	M.R.Ramprakash	Surrey	24	2	301*	2278	8	2006
102.53	G.Boycott	Yorkshire	20	5	175*	1538	6	1979
102.00	W.A.Johnston	Australians	17	16	28*	102	–	1953
101.70	G.A.Gooch	Essex	30	3	333	2746	12	1990
101.30	M.R.Ramprakash	Surrey	25	5	266*	2026	10	2007
100.12	G.Boycott	Yorkshire	30	5	233	2503	13	1971

FASTEST HUNDRED AGAINST AUTHENTIC BOWLING

35 min   P.G.H.Fender   Surrey v Northamptonshire   Northampton   1920

FASTEST DOUBLE HUNDRED

113 min R.J.Shastri   Bombay v Baroda   Bombay   1984-85

FASTEST TRIPLE HUNDRED

181 min D.C.S.Compton   MCC v NE Transvaal   Benoni   1948-49

MOST SIXES IN AN INNINGS

16   A.Symonds   Gloucestershire v Glamorgan   Abergavenny   1995

MOST SIXES IN A MATCH

20   A.Symonds   Gloucestershire v Glamorgan   Abergavenny   1995

MOST SIXES IN A SEASON

80   I.T.Botham   Somerset and England   1985

MOST FOURS IN AN INNINGS

72   B.C.Lara   Warwickshire v Durham   Birmingham   1994

MOST RUNS OFF ONE OVER

36	G.St A.Sobers	Nottinghamshire v Glamorgan	Swansea	1968
36	R.J.Shastri	Bombay v Baroda	Bombay	1984-85

Both batsmen hit for six all six balls of overs bowled by M.A.Nash and Tilak Raj respectively.

MOST RUNS IN A DAY

390*   B.C.Lara   Warwickshire v Durham   Birmingham   1994

There have been 19 instances of a batsman scoring 300 or more runs in a day.

LONGEST INNINGS

1015 min R.Nayyar (271)   Himachal Pradesh v Jammu & Kashmir Chamba   1999-00

HIGHEST PARTNERSHIPS FOR EACH WICKET

First Wicket

561	Waheed Mirza/Mansoor Akhtar	Karachi W v Quetta	Karachi	1976-77
555	P.Holmes/H.Sutcliffe	Yorkshire v Essex	Leyton	1932
554	J.T.Brown/J.Tunnicliffe	Yorkshire v Derbys	Chesterfield	1898

Second Wicket

576	S.T.Jayasuriya/R.S.Mahanama	Sri Lanka v India	Colombo (RPS)	1997-98
475	Zahir Alam/L.S.Rajput	Assam v Tripura	Gauhati	1991-92
465*	J.A.Jameson/R.B.Kanhai	Warwickshire v Glos	Birmingham	1974

Third Wicket

624	K.C.Sangakkara/D.P.M.D.Jayawardena	Sri Lanka v South Africa	Colombo	2006
467	A.H.Jones/M.D.Crowe	N Zealand v Sri Lanka	Wellington	1990-91
459	C.J.L.Rogers/M.J.North	W Australia v Victoria	Perth	2006-07
456	Khalid Irtiza/Aslam Ali	United Bank v Multan	Karachi	1975-76
451	Mudassar Nazar/Javed Miandad	Pakistan v India	Hyderabad	1982-83
445	P.E.Whitelaw/W.N.Carson	Auckland v Otago	Dunedin	1936-37
438*	G.A.Hick/T.M.Moody	Worcestershire v Hants	Southampton	1997

Fourth Wicket

577	V.S.Hazare/Gul Mahomed	Baroda v Holkar	Baroda	1946-47
574*	C.L.Walcott/F.M.M.Worrell	Barbados v Trinidad	Port-of-Spain	1945-46
502*	F.M.M.Worrell/J.D.C.Goddard	Barbados v Trinidad	Bridgetown	1943-44
470	A.I.Kallicharran/G.W.Humpage	Warwickshire v Lancs	Southport	1982

Fifth Wicket

464*	M.E.Waugh/S.R.Waugh	NSW v W Australia	Perth	1990-91
420	Mohd. Ashraful/Marshall Ayub	Dhaka v Chittagong	Chittagong	2006-07
410*	A.S.Chopra/S.Badrinath	India A v South Africa A	Delhi	2007-08
405	S.G.Barnes/D.G.Bradman	Australia v England	Sydney	1946-47
401	M.B.Loye/D.Ripley	Northants v Glamorgan	Northampton	1998

Sixth Wicket

487*	G.A.Headley/C.C.Passailaigue	Jamaica v Tennyson's	Kingston	1931-32
428	W.W.Armstrong/M.A.Noble	Australians v Sussex	Hove	1902
411	R.M.Poore/E.G.Wynyard	Hampshire v Somerset	Taunton	1899

Seventh Wicket

460	Bhupinder Singh jr/P.Dharmani	Punjab v Delhi	Delhi	1994-95
347	D.St E.Atkinson/C.C.Depeiza	W Indies v Australia	Bridgetown	1954-55
344	K.S.Ranjitsinhji/W.Newham	Sussex v Essex	Leyton	1902

Eighth Wicket

433	V.T.Trumper/A.Sims	Australians v C'bury	Christchurch	1913-14
313	Wasim Akram/Saqlain Mushtaq	Pakistan v Zimbabwe	Sheikhupura	1996-97
292	R.Peel/Lord Hawke	Yorkshire v Warwicks	Birmingham	1896

Ninth Wicket

283	J.Chapman/A.Warren	Derbys v Warwicks	Blackwell	1910
268	J.B.Commins/N.Boje	SA 'A' v Mashonaland	Harare	1994-95
251	J.W.H.T.Douglas/S.N.Hare	Essex v Derbyshire	Leyton	1921

Tenth Wicket

307	A.F.Kippax/J.E.H.Hooker	NSW v Victoria	Melbourne	1928-29
249	C.T.Sarwate/S.N.Banerjee	Indians v Surrey	The Oval	1946
239	Aqil Arshad/Ali Raza	Lahore Whites v Hyderabad	Lahore	2004-05
235	F.E.Woolley/A.Fielder	Kent v Worcs	Stourbridge	1909

35,000 RUNS IN A CAREER

	Career	I	NO	HS	Runs	Avge	100
J.B.Hobbs	1905-34	1315	106	316*	61237	50.65	197
F.E.Woolley	1906-38	1532	85	305*	58969	40.75	145
E.H.Hendren	1907-38	1300	166	301*	57611	50.80	170
C.P.Mead	1905-36	1340	185	280*	55061	47.67	153
W.G.Grace	1865-1908	1493	105	344	54896	39.55	126
W.R.Hammond	1920-51	1005	104	336*	50551	56.10	167
H.Sutcliffe	1919-45	1088	123	313	50138	51.95	149
G.Boycott	1962-86	1014	162	261*	48426	56.83	151
T.W.Graveney	1948-71/72	1223	159	258	47793	44.91	122
G.A.Gooch	1973-2000	990	75	333	44846	49.01	128
T.W.Hayward	1893-1914	1138	96	315*	43551	41.79	104
D.L.Amiss	1960-87	1139	126	262*	43423	42.86	102
M.C.Cowdrey	1950-76	1130	134	307	42719	42.89	107
A.Sandham	1911-37/38	1000	79	325	41284	44.82	107
G.A.Hick	1983/84-2008	871	84	405*	41112	52.23	136
I.Hutton	1934-60	814	91	364	40140	55.51	129
M.J.K.Smith	1951-75	1091	139	204	39832	41.84	69
W.Rhodes	1898-1930	1528	237	267*	39802	30.83	58
J.H.Edrich	1956-78	979	104	310*	39790	45.47	103
R.E.S.Wyatt	1923-57	1141	157	232	39405	40.04	85
D.C.S.Compton	1936-64	839	88	300	38942	51.85	123
G.E.Tyldesley	1909-36	961	106	256*	38874	45.46	102
J.T.Tyldesley	1895-1923	994	62	295*	37887	40.60	86
K.W.R.Fletcher	1962-88	1167	170	228*	37665	37.77	63
C.G.Greenidge	1970-92	889	75	273*	37354	45.88	92
J.W.Hearne	1909-36	1025	116	285*	37252	40.98	96
L.E.G.Ames	1926-51	951	95	295	37248	43.51	102
D.Kenyon	1946-67	1159	59	259	37002	33.63	74
W.J.Edrich	1934-58	964	92	267*	36965	42.39	86
J.M.Parks	1949-76	1227	172	205*	36673	34.76	51
M.W.Gatting	1975-98	861	123	258	36549	49.52	94
D.Denton	1894-1920	1163	70	221	36479	33.37	69
G.H.Hirst	1891-1929	1215	151	341	36323	34.13	60
I.V.A.Richards	1971/72-93	796	63	322	36212	49.40	114
A.Jones	1957-83	1168	72	204*	36049	32.89	56
W.G.Quaife	1894-1928	1203	185	255*	36012	35.37	72
R.E.Marshall	1945/46-72	1053	59	228*	35725	35.94	68
G.Gunn	1902-32	1061	82	220	35208	35.96	62

BOWLING RECORDS

ALL TEN WICKETS IN AN INNINGS

This feat has been achieved 80 times in first-class matches (excluding 12-a-side fixtures).
Three Times: A.P.Freeman (1929, 1930, 1931)
Twice: V.E.Walker (1859, 1865); H.Verity (1931, 1932); J.C.Laker (1956)

Instances since 1945:

W.E.Hollies	Warwickshire v Notts	Birmingham	1946
J.M.Sims	East v West	Kingston on Thames	1948
J.K.R.Graveney	Gloucestershire v Derbyshire	Chesterfield	1949
T.E.Bailey	Essex v Lancashire	Clacton	1949
R.Berry	Lancashire v Worcestershire	Blackpool	1953
S.P.Gupte	President's XI v Combined XI	Bombay	1954-55
J.C.Laker	Surrey v Australians	The Oval	1956

K.Smales	Nottinghamshire v Glos	Stroud	1956
G.A.R.Lock	Surrey v Kent	Blackheath	1956
J.C.Laker	England v Australia	Manchester	1956
P.M.Chatterjee	Bengal v Assam	Jorhat	1956-57
J.D.Bannister	Warwicks v Combined Services	Birmingham (M & B)	1959
A.J.G.Pearson	Cambridge U v Leicestershire	Loughborough	1961
N.I.Thomson	Sussex v Warwickshire	Worthing	1964
P.J.Allan	Queensland v Victoria	Melbourne	1965-66
I.J.Brayshaw	Western Australia v Victoria	Perth	1967-68
Shahid Mahmood	Karachi Whites v Khairpur	Karachi	1969-70
E.E.Hemmings	International XI v W Indians	Kingston	1982-83
P.Sunderam	Rajasthan v Vidarbha	Jodhpur	1985-86
S.T.Jefferies	Western Province v OFS	Cape Town	1987-88
Imran Adil	Bahawalpur v Faisalabad	Faisalabad	1989-90
G.P.Wickremasinghe	Sinhalese v Kalutara	Colombo	1991-92
R.L.Johnson	Middlesex v Derbyshire	Derby	1994
Naeem Akhtar	Rawalpindi B v Peshawar	Peshawar	1995-96
A.Kumble	India v Pakistan	Delhi	1998-99
D.S.Mohanty	East Zone v South Zone	Agartala	2000-01
O.D.Gibson	Durham v Hampshire	Chester-le-Street	2007
M.W.Olivier	Warriors v Eagles	Bloemfontein	2007-08

MOST WICKETS IN A MATCH

| 19 | J.C.Laker | England v Australia | Manchester | 1956 |

MOST WICKETS IN A SEASON

Wkts		Season	Matches	Overs	Mdns	Runs	Avge
304	A.P.Freeman	1928	37	1976.1	423	5489	18.05
298	A.P.Freeman	1933	33	2039	651	4549	15.26

The feat of taking 250 wickets in a season has been achieved on 12 occasions, the last instance being by A.P.Freeman in 1933. 200 or more wickets in a season have been taken on 59 occasions, the last being by G.A.R.Lock (212 wickets, average 12.02) in 1957.

The highest aggregates of wickets taken in a season since the reduction of County Championship matches in 1969 are as follows:

Wkts		Season	Matches	Overs	Mdns	Runs	Avge
134	M.D.Marshall	1982	22	822	225	2108	15.73
131	L.R.Gibbs	1971	23	1024.1	295	2475	18.89
125	F.D.Stephenson	1988	22	819.1	196	2289	18.31
121	R.D.Jackman	1980	23	746.2	220	1864	15.40

Since 1969 there have been 50 instances of bowlers taking 100 wickets in a season.

MOST HAT-TRICKS IN A CAREER

7	D.V.P.Wright
6	T.W.J.Goddard, C.W.L.Parker
5	S.Haigh, V.W.C.Jupp, A.E.G.Rhodes, F.A.Tarrant

2000 WICKETS IN A CAREER

	Career	Runs	Wkts	Avge	100w
W.Rhodes	1898-1930	69993	**4187**	16.71	23
A.P.Freeman	1914-36	69577	**3776**	18.42	17
C.W.L.Parker	1903-35	63817	**3278**	19.46	16
J.T.Hearne	1888-1923	54352	**3061**	17.75	15
T.W.J.Goddard	1922-52	59116	**2979**	19.84	16
W.G.Grace	1865-1908	51545	**2876**	17.92	10
A.S.Kennedy	1907-36	61034	**2874**	21.23	15
D.Shackleton	1948-69	53303	**2857**	18.65	20
G.A.R.Lock	1946-70/71	54709	**2844**	19.23	14

	Career	Runs	Wkts	Avge	100w
F.J.Titmus	1949-82	63313	**2830**	22.37	16
M.W.Tate	1912-37	50571	**2784**	18.16	13+1
G.H.Hirst	1891-1929	51282	**2739**	18.72	15
C.Blythe	1899-1914	42136	**2506**	16.81	14
D.L.Underwood	1963-87	49993	**2465**	20.28	10
W.E.Astill	1906-39	57783	**2431**	23.76	9
J.C.White	1909-37	43759	**2356**	18.57	14
W.E.Hollies	1932-57	48656	**2323**	20.94	14
F.S.Trueman	1949-69	42154	**2304**	18.29	12
J.B.Statham	1950-68	36999	**2260**	16.37	13
R.T.D.Perks	1930-55	53771	**2233**	24.07	16
J.Briggs	1879-1900	35431	**2221**	15.95	12
D.J.Shepherd	1950-72	47302	**2218**	21.32	12
F.G.Dennett	1903-26	42571	**2147**	19.82	12
T.Richardson	1892-1905	38794	**2104**	18.43	10
T.E.Bailey	1945-67	48170	**2082**	23.13	9
R.Illingworth	1951-83	42023	**2072**	20.28	10
F.E.Woolley	1906-38	41066	**2068**	19.85	8
N.Gifford	1960-88	48731	**2068**	23.56	4
G.Geary	1912-38	41339	**2063**	20.03	11
D.V.P.Wright	1932-57	49307	**2056**	23.98	10
J.A.Newman	1906-30	51111	**2032**	25.15	9
A.Shaw	1864-97	24580	**2026+1**	12.12	9
S.Haigh	1895-1913	32091	**2012**	15.94	11

ALL-ROUND RECORDS
THE 'DOUBLE'

3000 runs and 100 wickets: J.H.Parks (1937)

2000 runs and 200 wickets: G.H.Hirst (1906)

2000 runs and 100 wickets: F.E.Woolley (4), J.W.Hearne (3), W.G.Grace (2), G.H.Hirst (2), W.Rhodes (2), T.E.Bailey, D.E.Davies, G.L.Jessop, V.W.C.Jupp, J.Langridge, F.A.Tarrant, C.L.Townsend, L.F.Townsend

1000 runs and 200 wickets: M.W.Tate (3), A.E.Trott (2), A.S.Kennedy

Most Doubles: 16 – W.Rhodes; 14 – G.H.Hirst; 10 – V.W.C.Jupp

Double in Debut Season: D.B.Close (1949) – aged 18, the youngest to achieve this feat.

The feat of scoring 1000 runs and taking 100 wickets in a season has been achieved on 305 occasions, R.J.Hadlee (1984) and F.D.Stephenson (1988) being the only players to complete the 'double' since the reduction of County Championship matches in 1969.

WICKET-KEEPING RECORDS
EIGHT DISMISSALS IN AN INNINGS

9	(8ct, 1st)	Tahir Rashid	Habib Bank v PACO	Gujranwala	1992-93
9	(7ct, 2st)	W.R.James	Matabeleland v Mashonaland CD	Bulawayo	1995-96
8	(8ct)	A.T.W.Grout	Queensland v W Australia	Brisbane	1959-60
8	(8ct)	D.E.East	Essex v Somerset	Taunton	1985
8	(8ct)	S.A.Marsh	Kent v Middlesex	Lord's	1991
8	(6ct, 2st)	T.J.Zoehrer	Australians v Surrey	The Oval	1993
8	(7ct, 1st)	D.S.Berry	Victoria v South Australia	Melbourne	1996-97
8	(7ct, 1st)	Y.S.S.Mendis	Bloomfield v Kurunegala Youth	Colombo	2000-01
8	(7ct, 1st)	S.Nath	Assam v Tripura (*on debut*)	Gauhati	2001-02
8	(8ct)	J.N.Batty	Surrey v Kent	The Oval	2004
8	(8ct)	Golam Mabud	Sylhet v Dhaka	Dhaka	2005-06

TWELVE DISMISSALS IN A MATCH

13	(11ct, 2st)	W.R.James	Matabeleland v Mashonaland CD	Bulawayo	1995-96
12	(8ct, 4st)	E.Pooley	Surrey v Sussex	The Oval	1868
12	(9ct, 3st)	D.Tallon	Queensland v NSW	Sydney	1938-39
12	(9ct, 3st)	H.B.Taber	NSW v South Australia	Adelaide	1968-69

MOST DISMISSALS IN A SEASON

128	(79ct, 49st)	L.E.G.Ames		1929

1000 DISMISSALS IN A CAREER

	Career	Dismissals	Ct	St
R.W.Taylor	1960-88	**1649**	1473	176
J.T.Murray	1952-75	**1527**	1270	257
H.Strudwick	1902-27	**1497**	1242	255
A.P.E.Knott	1964-85	**1344**	1211	133
R.C.Russell	1981-2004	**1320**	1192	128
F.H.Huish	1895-1914	**1310**	933	377
B.Taylor	1949-73	**1294**	1083	211
S.J.Rhodes	1981-2004	**1263**	1139	124
D.Hunter	1889-1909	**1253**	906	347
H.R.Butt	1890-1912	**1228**	953	275
J.H.Board	1891-1914/15	**1207**	852	355
H.Elliott	1920-47	**1206**	904	302
J.M.Parks	1949-76	**1181**	1088	93
R.Booth	1951-70	**1126**	948	178
L.E.G.Ames	1926-51	**1121**	703	418
D.L.Bairstow	1970-90	**1099**	961	138
G.Duckworth	1923-47	**1096**	753	343
H.W.Stephenson	1948-64	**1082**	748	334
J.G.Binks	1955-75	**1071**	895	176
T.G.Evans	1939-69	**1066**	816	250
A.Long	1960-80	**1046**	922	124
G.O.Dawkes	1937-61	**1043**	895	148
R.W.Tolchard	1965-83	**1037**	912	125
W.L.Cornford	1921-47	**1017**	675	342

FIELDING RECORDS

MOST CATCHES IN AN INNINGS

7	M.J.Stewart	Surrey v Northamptonshire	Northampton	1957
7	A.S.Brown	Gloucestershire v Nottinghamshire	Nottingham	1966

MOST CATCHES IN A MATCH

10	W.R.Hammond	Gloucestershire v Surrey	Cheltenham	1928

MOST CATCHES IN A SEASON

78	W.R.Hammond	1928	77	M.J.Stewart	1957

750 CATCHES IN A CAREER

1018	F.E.Woolley	1906-38	784	J.G.Langridge	1928-55
887	W.G.Grace	1865-1908	764	W.Rhodes	1898-1930
830	G.A.R.Lock	1946-70/71	758	C.A.Milton	1948-74
819	W.R.Hammond	1920-51	754	E.H.Hendren	1907-38
813	D.B.Close	1949-86			

UNIVERSITY MATCH RESULTS

Played: 163. Wins: Cambridge 56; Oxford 53. Drawn: 54. Abandoned: 1

In 2001, for the very first time, Cambridge hosted the University Match, cricket's oldest surviving first-class fixture, after the ECB's re-organisation of university cricket around six centres of excellence had removed it from Lord's. Dating from 1827 it has, wartime interruptions apart, been played annually since 1838. With the exception of five matches played in the area of Oxford (1829, 1843, 1846, 1848 and 1850), all the previous fixtures had been staged at Lord's. Since 2001 it has been played over four days rather than three.

In 2003, Oxford (with Brookes), Cambridge (with Anglia) and Durham were joined by Loughborough in playing three first-class matches against counties. The other two centres – Cardiff (with UWIC and Glamorgan), and Leeds (with Bradford and Leeds Metropolitan) – also play three counties apiece but without first-class status. That status is under severe threat beyond the 2009 season.

1827	Drawn	1876	Cambridge	1921	Cambridge	1968	Drawn
1829	Oxford	1877	Oxford	1922	Cambridge	1969	Drawn
1836	Oxford	1878	Cambridge	1923	Oxford	1970	Drawn
1838	Oxford	1879	Cambridge	1924	Cambridge	1971	Drawn
1839	Cambridge	1880	Cambridge	1925	Drawn	1972	Cambridge
1840	Cambridge	1881	Oxford	1926	Cambridge	1973	Drawn
1841	Cambridge	1882	Cambridge	1927	Cambridge	1974	Drawn
1842	Cambridge	1883	Cambridge	1928	Drawn	1975	Drawn
1843	Cambridge	1884	Oxford	1929	Drawn	1976	Oxford
1844	Drawn	1885	Cambridge	1930	Cambridge	1977	Drawn
1845	Cambridge	1886	Oxford	1931	Oxford	1978	Drawn
1846	Oxford	1887	Oxford	1932	Drawn	1979	Cambridge
1847	Cambridge	1888	Drawn	1933	Drawn	1980	Drawn
1848	Oxford	1889	Cambridge	1934	Drawn	1981	Drawn
1849	Cambridge	1890	Cambridge	1935	Cambridge	1982	Cambridge
1850	Oxford	1891	Cambridge	1936	Cambridge	1983	Drawn
1851	Cambridge	1892	Oxford	1937	Oxford	1984	Oxford
1852	Oxford	1893	Cambridge	1938	Drawn	1985	Drawn
1853	Oxford	1894	Oxford	1939	Oxford	1986	Cambridge
1854	Oxford	1895	Cambridge	1946	Oxford	1987	Drawn
1855	Oxford	1896	Oxford	1947	Drawn	1988	Abandoned
1856	Cambridge	1897	Cambridge	1948	Oxford	1989	Drawn
1857	Oxford	1898	Oxford	1949	Cambridge	1990	Drawn
1858	Oxford	1899	Drawn	1950	Drawn	1991	Drawn
1859	Cambridge	1900	Drawn	1951	Oxford	1992	Cambridge
1860	Cambridge	1901	Drawn	1952	Drawn	1993	Oxford
1861	Cambridge	1902	Cambridge	1953	Cambridge	1994	Drawn
1862	Cambridge	1903	Oxford	1954	Drawn	1995	Oxford
1863	Oxford	1904	Drawn	1955	Drawn	1996	Drawn
1864	Oxford	1905	Cambridge	1956	Drawn	1997	Drawn
1865	Oxford	1906	Cambridge	1957	Cambridge	1998	Cambridge
1866	Oxford	1907	Cambridge	1958	Cambridge	1999	Drawn
1867	Cambridge	1908	Oxford	1959	Oxford	2000	Drawn
1868	Cambridge	1909	Drawn	1960	Drawn	2001	Oxford
1869	Cambridge	1910	Oxford	1961	Drawn	2002	Drawn
1870	Cambridge	1911	Oxford	1962	Drawn	2003	Oxford
1871	Oxford	1912	Cambridge	1963	Drawn	2004	Oxford
1872	Cambridge	1913	Cambridge	1964	Drawn	2005	Oxford
1873	Oxford	1914	Oxford	1965	Drawn	2006	Oxford
1874	Oxford	1919	Oxford	1966	Oxford	2007	Drawn
1875	Oxford	1920	Drawn	1967	Drawn	2008	Drawn

CAMBRIDGE UNIVERSITY RECORDS
ALL FIRST-CLASS MATCHES

Highest Total	For 703-9d		v	Sussex	Hove	1890
	V 730-3		by	W Indians	Cambridge	1950
Lowest Total	For 30		v	Yorkshire	Cambridge	1928
	V 32		by	Oxford U	Lord's	1878
Highest Innings	For 254*	K.S.Duleepsinhji	v	Middlesex	Cambridge	1927
	V 304*	E.de C.Weekes	for	W Indians	Cambridge	1950
Highest Partnership						
(2nd wicket)	429*	J.G.Dewes/G.H.G.Doggart	v	Essex	Cambridge	1949
Best Innings Bowling	10-69	S.M.J.Woods	v	Thornton's XI	Cambridge	1890
Best Match Bowling	15-88	S.M.J.Woods	v	Thornton's XI	Cambridge	1890
Most Runs – Season	1581			D.S.Sheppard	(av 79.05)	1952
Most Runs – Career	4310			J.M.Brearley	(av 38.48)	1961-68
Most 100s – Season	7			D.S.Sheppard		1952
Most 100s – Career	14			D.S.Sheppard		1950-52
Most Wkts – Season	80			O.S.Wheatley	(av 17.63)	1958
Most Wkts – Career	208			G.Goonesena	(av 21.82)	1954-57

UNIVERSITY MATCH RECORDS

Highest Total	604		Oxford	2002
Lowest Total	39		Lord's	1858
Highest Innings	211	G.Goonesena	Lord's	1957
Best Innings Bowling	8-44	G.E.Jeffery	Lord's	1873
Best Match Bowling	13-73	A.G.Steel	Lord's	1878

Hat Tricks: F.C.Cobden (1870), A.G.Steel (1879), P.H.Morton (1880), J.F.Ireland (1911), R.G.H.Lowe (1926).

OXFORD UNIVERSITY RECORDS
ALL FIRST-CLASS MATCHES

Highest Total	For 651		v	Sussex	Hove	1895
	V 679-7d		by	Australians	Oxford	1938
Lowest Total	For 12		v	MCC	Oxford	1877
	V 24		by	MCC	Oxford	1846
Highest Innings	For 281	K.J.Key	v	Middlesex	Chiswick Park	1887
	V 338	W.W.Read	for	Surrey	The Oval	1888
Highest Partnership						
(3rd wicket)	408	S.Oberoi/D.R.Fox	v	Cambridge U	Cambridge	2005
Best Innings Bowling	10-38	S.E.Butler	v	Cambridge U	Lord's	1871
Best Match Bowling	15-65	B.J.T.Bosanquet	v	Sussex	Oxford	1900
Most Runs – Season	1307			Nawab of Pataudi sr	(av 93.35)	1931
Most Runs – Career	3319			N.S.Mitchell-Innes	(av 47.41)	1934-37
Most 100s – Season	6			Nawab of Pataudi sr		1931
	6			M.P.Donnelly		1946
Most 100s – Career	9			A.M.Crawley		1927-30
	9			Nawab of Pataudi sr		1928-31
	9			N S Mitchell-Innes		1934-37
	9			M.P.Donnelly		1946-47
Most Wkts – Season	70			I.A.R.Peebles	(av 18.15)	1930
Most Wkts – Career	182			R.H.B.Bettington	(av 19.38)	1920-23

UNIVERSITY MATCH RECORDS

Highest Total	610-5d		Cambridge	2005
Lowest Total	32		Lord's	1878
Highest Innings	247	S.Oberoi	Cambridge	2005
Best Innings Bowling	10-38	S.E.Butler	Lord's	1871
Best Match Bowling	15-95	S.E.Butler	Lord's	1871

Match Doubles: P.R.le Couteur (160 and 11-66 in 1910); G.J.Toogood (149 and 10-93 in 1985)

238

LIMITED-OVERS INTERNATIONALS RESULTS

1970-71 to 14 March 2009

These records exclude all matches involving multinational teams, as well as any abandoned without a ball bowled, regardless of the toss having been made.

	Opponents	Matches	E	A	SA	WI	NZ	I	P	SL	Z	B	Ass	Tied	NR
England	Australia	93	37	52	–	–	–	–	–	–	–	–	–	2	2
	South Africa	40	15	–	22	–	–	–	–	–	–	–	–	1	2
	West Indies	75	32	–	–	39	–	–	–	–	–	–	–	–	4
	New Zealand	69	29	–	–	–	34	–	–	–	–	–	–	2	4
	India	70	30	–	–	–	–	38	–	–	–	–	–	–	2
	Pakistan	63	35	–	–	–	–	–	26	–	–	–	–	–	2
	Sri Lanka	43	22	–	–	–	–	–	–	21	–	–	–	–	–
	Zimbabwe	30	21	–	–	–	–	–	–	–	8	–	–	–	1
	Bangladesh	8	8	–	–	–	–	–	–	–	–	0	–	–	–
	Associates	12	11	–	–	–	–	–	–	–	–	–	0	–	1
Australia	South Africa	72	–	37	32	–	–	–	–	–	–	–	–	3	–
	West Indies	119	–	58	–	57	–	–	–	–	–	–	–	2	2
	New Zealand	117	–	80	–	–	32	–	–	–	–	–	–	–	5
	India	96	–	57	–	–	–	32	–	–	–	–	–	–	7
	Pakistan	74	–	43	–	–	–	–	27	–	–	–	–	1	3
	Sri Lanka	68	–	46	–	–	–	–	–	20	–	–	–	–	2
	Zimbabwe	27	–	25	–	–	–	–	–	–	1	–	–	–	1
	Bangladesh	16	–	15	–	–	–	–	–	–	–	1	–	–	–
	Associates	12	–	12	–	–	–	–	–	–	–	–	0	–	–
S Africa	West Indies	45	–	–	32	12	–	–	–	–	–	–	–	–	1
	N Zealand	50	–	–	29	–	17	–	–	–	–	–	–	–	4
	India	57	–	–	35	–	–	20	–	–	–	–	–	–	2
	Pakistan	52	–	–	35	–	–	–	16	–	–	–	–	–	1
	Sri Lanka	45	–	–	22	–	–	–	–	21	–	–	–	1	1
	Zimbabwe	27	–	–	24	–	–	–	–	–	2	–	–	–	1
	Bangladesh	13	–	–	12	–	–	–	–	–	–	1	–	–	–
	Associates	17	–	–	17	–	–	–	–	–	–	–	0	–	–
W Indies	New Zealand	50	–	–	–	24	20	–	–	–	–	–	–	–	6
	India	90	–	–	–	53	–	35	–	–	–	–	–	1	1
	Pakistan	113	–	–	–	64	–	–	47	–	–	–	–	2	–
	Sri Lanka	46	–	–	–	26	–	–	–	18	–	–	–	–	2
	Zimbabwe	36	–	–	–	27	–	–	–	–	8	–	–	–	1
	Bangladesh	13	–	–	–	11	–	–	–	–	–	0	–	–	2
	Associates	15	–	–	–	13	–	–	–	–	–	–	1	–	1
N Zealand	India	80	–	–	–	–	36	39	–	–	–	–	–	–	5
	Pakistan	78	–	–	–	–	29	–	47	–	–	–	–	1	1
	Sri Lanka	67	–	–	–	–	34	–	–	30	–	–	–	1	2
	Zimbabwe	28	–	–	–	–	19	–	–	–	7	–	–	1	1
	Bangladesh	14	–	–	–	–	13	–	–	–	–	1	–	–	–
	Associates	11	–	–	–	–	11	–	–	–	–	–	0	–	–
India	Pakistan	117	–	–	–	–	–	45	68	–	–	–	–	–	4
	Sri Lanka	111	–	–	–	–	–	59	–	42	–	–	–	–	10
	Zimbabwe	49	–	–	–	–	–	39	–	–	8	–	–	2	–
	Bangladesh	19	–	–	–	–	–	17	–	–	–	2	–	–	–
	Associates	22	–	–	–	–	–	20	–	–	–	–	2	–	–
Pakistan	Sri Lanka	114	–	–	–	–	–	–	68	42	–	–	–	1	3
	Zimbabwe	40	–	–	–	–	–	–	36	–	2	–	–	1	1
	Bangladesh	25	–	–	–	–	–	–	24	–	–	1	–	–	–
	Associates	17	–	–	–	–	–	–	16	–	–	–	1	–	–
Sri Lanka	Zimbabwe	43	–	–	–	–	–	–	–	36	6	–	–	–	1
	Bangladesh	26	–	–	–	–	–	–	–	24	–	2	–	–	–
	Associates	13	–	–	–	–	–	–	–	12	–	–	1	–	–
Zimbabwe	Bangladesh	37	–	–	–	–	–	–	–	–	20	17	–	–	–
	Associates	33	–	–	–	–	–	–	–	–	26	–	4	1	2
Bangladesh	Associates	27	–	–	–	–	–	–	–	–	–	19	8	–	–
Associates	Associates	69	–	–	–	–	–	–	–	–	–	–	65	–	4
		2812	**240**	**425**	**260**	**326**	**245**	**344**	**375**	**266**	**88**	**44**	**82**	**23**	**95**

239

MERIT TABLE OF ALL L–O INTERNATIONALS
1970-71 to 14 March 2009

	Matches	Won	Lost	Tied	No Result	% Won (exc NR)
South Africa	418	260	140	5	12	64.04
Australia	694	425	239	8	22	63.24
West Indies	602	326	251	5	20	56.01
Pakistan	693	375	297	6	15	55.31
India	711	344	333	3	31	50.59
England	503	240	240	5	18	49.48
Sri Lanka	576	266	286	3	21	47.93
New Zealand	564	245	286	5	28	45.71
Zimbabwe	350	88	248	5	9	25.80
Bangladesh	198	44	152	–	2	22.45
Associate Members (v Full*)	231	17	207	1	6	7.59

* Results of games between two Associate Members are excluded from this list; Associate Members have participated in 300 LOIs, 69 LOIs being between Associate Members.

TEAM RECORDS
HIGHEST TOTALS

443-9	(50 overs)	Sri Lanka v Holland	Amstelveen	2006
438-9	(49.5 overs)	South Africa v Australia	Johannesburg	2005-06
434-4	(50 overs)	Australia v South Africa	Johannesburg	2005-06
418-5	(50 overs)	South Africa v Zimbabwe	Potchefstroom	2006-07
413-5	(50 overs)	India v Bermuda	Port-of-Spain	2006-07
402-2	(50 overs)	New Zealand v Ireland	Aberdeen	2008
398-5	(50 overs)	Sri Lanka v Kenya	Kandy	1995-96
397-5	(44 overs)	New Zealand v Zimbabwe	Bulawayo	2005
392-4	(50 overs)	India v New Zealand	Christchurch	2008-09
392-6	(50 overs)	South Africa v Pakistan	Pretoria	2006-07
391-4	(50 overs)	England v Bangladesh	Nottingham	2005
387-5	(50 overs)	India v England	Rajkot	2008-09
377-6	(50 overs)	Australia v South Africa	Basseterre	2006-07
376-2	(50 overs)	India v New Zealand	Hyderabad, India	1999-00
374-4	(50 overs)	India v Hong Kong	Karachi	2008
373-6	(50 overs)	India v Sri Lanka	Taunton	1999
371-9	(50 overs)	Pakistan v Sri Lanka	Nairobi	1996-97
368-5	(50 overs)	Australia v Sri Lanka	Sydney	2005-06
363-3	(50 overs)	South Africa v Zimbabwe	Bulawayo	2001-02
363-5	(50 overs)	New Zealand v Canada	Gros Islet	2006-07
363-5	(50 overs)	India v Sri Lanka	Colombo (RPS)	2008-09
363-7	(55 overs)	England v Pakistan	Nottingham	1992
360-4	(50 overs)	West Indies v Sri Lanka	Karachi	1987-88
359-2	(50 overs)	Australia v India	Johannesburg	2002-03
359-5	(50 overs)	Australia v India	Sydney	2003-04
358-4	(50 overs)	South Africa v Bangladesh	Benoni	2008-09
357-9	(50 overs)	Sri Lanka v Bangladesh	Lahore	2008
358-5	(50 overs)	Australia v Holland	Basseterre	2006-07
356-4	(50 overs)	South Africa v West Indies	St George's	2006-07
356-9	(50 overs)	India v Pakistan	Vishakhapatnam	2004-05
354-3	(50 overs)	South Africa v Kenya	Cape Town	2001-02
353-3	(40 overs)	South Africa v Holland	Basseterre	2006-07
353-5	(50 overs)	India v New Zealand	Hyderabad, India	2003-04
353-6	(50 overs)	Pakistan v England	Karachi	2005-06
351-3	(50 overs)	India v Kenya	Paarl	2001-02
351-4	(50 overs)	Pakistan v South Africa	Durban	2006-07
351-7	(50 overs)	Zimbabwe v Kenya	Mombasa	2008-09
350-6	(50 overs)	India v Sri Lanka	Nagpur	2005-06
350-9	(49.3 overs)	New Zealand v Australia	Hamilton	2006-07

The highest for Bangladesh is 301-7 (v Kenya, Bogra, 2005-06).

HIGHEST TOTALS BATTING SECOND

WINNING:	438-9	(49.5 overs)	South Africa v Australia	Johannesburg	2005-06
LOSING:	344-8	(50.0 overs)	Pakistan v India	Karachi	2003-04

HIGHEST MATCH AGGREGATES

872-13	(99.5 overs)	South Africa v Australia	Johannesburg	2005-06
726-14	(95.1 overs)	New Zealand v India	Christchurch	2008-09

LARGEST RUNS MARGINS OF VICTORY

290 runs	New Zealand beat Ireland	Aberdeen	2008
257 runs	India beat Bermuda	Port-of-Spain	2006-07
256 runs	Australia beat Namibia	Potschefstroom	2002-03
256 runs	India beat Hong Kong	Karachi	2008
245 runs	Sri Lanka beat India	Sharjah	2000-01
243 runs	Sri Lanka beat Bermuda	Port-of-Spain	2006-07
234 runs	Sri Lanka beat Pakistan	Lahore	2008-09
233 runs	Pakistan beat Bangladesh	Dhaka	1999-00
232 runs	Australia beat Sri Lanka	Adelaide	1984-85
229 runs	Australia beat Holland	Basseterre	2006-07
224 runs	Australia beat Pakistan	Nairobi	2002
221 runs	South Africa beat Holland	Basseterre	2006-07
217 runs	Pakistan beat Sri Lanka	Sharjah	2001-02
215 runs	Australia beat New Zealand	St George's	2006-07
210 runs	New Zealand beat USA	The Oval	2004
209 runs	South Africa beat West Indies	Cape Town	2003-04
208 runs	South Africa beat Kenya	Cape Town	2001-02
208 runs	Australia beat India	Sydney	2003-04
206 runs	New Zealand beat Australia	Adelaide	1985-86
206 runs	Sri Lanka beat Holland	Colombo (RPS)	2002-03
203 runs	Australia beat Scotland	Basseterre	2006-07
202 runs	England beat India	Lord's	1975
202 runs	South Africa beat Kenya	Nairobi	1996-97
202 runs	Zimbabwe beat Kenya	Dhaka	1998-99
200 runs	India beat Bangladesh	Dhaka	2002-03

LOWEST TOTALS (Excluding reduced innings)

35	18.0 overs)	Zimbabwe v Sri Lanka	Harare	2003-04
36	(18.4 overs)	Canada v Sri Lanka	Paarl	2002-03
38	(15.4 overs)	Zimbabwe v Sri Lanka	Colombo (SSC)	2001-02
43	(19.5 overs)	Pakistan v West Indies	Cape Town	1992-93
45	(40.3 overs)	Canada v England	Manchester	1979
45	(14.0 overs)	Namibia v Australia	Potschefstroom	2002-03
54	(26.3 overs)	India v Sri Lanka	Sharjah	2000-01
54	(23.2 overs)	West Indies v South Africa	Cape Town	2003-04
55	(28.3 overs)	Sri Lanka v West Indies	Sharjah	1986-87
63	(25.5 overs)	India v Australia	Sydney	1980-81
64	(35.5 overs)	New Zealand v Pakistan	Sharjah	1985-86
65	(24.0 overs)	USA v Australia	Southampton	2004
65	(24.3 overs)	Zimbabwe v India	Harare	2005
67	(31.0 overs)	Zimbabwe v Sri Lanka	Harare	2008-09
68	(31.3 overs)	Scotland v West Indies	Leicester	1999
69	(28.0 overs)	South Africa v Australia	Sydney	1993-94
69	(22.5 overs)	Zimbabwe v Kenya	Harare	2005-06
70	(25.2 overs)	Australia v England	Birmingham	1977
70	(26.3 overs)	Australia v New Zealand	Adelaide	1985-86

The lowest for England is 86 (v A, Manchester, 2001), and for Bangladesh 74 (v A, Darwin, 2008).

241

LOWEST MATCH AGGREGATES

73-11	(23.2 overs)	Canada (36) v Sri Lanka (37-1)	Paarl	2002-03
75-11	(27.2 overs)	Zimbabwe (35) v Sri Lanka (40-1)	Harare	2003-04
78-11	(20.0 overs)	Zimbabwe (38) v Sri Lanka (40-1)	Colombo (SSC)	2001-02

BATTING RECORDS

HIGHEST INDIVIDUAL INNINGS

194	Saeed Anwar	Pakistan v India	Madras	1996-97
189*	I.V.A.Richards	West Indies v England	Manchester	1984
189	S.T.Jayasuriya	Sri Lanka v India	Sharjah	2000-01
188*	G.Kirsten	South Africa v UAE	Rawalpindi	1995-96
186*	S.R.Tendulkar	India v New Zealand	Hyderabad	1999-00
183*	M.S.Dhoni	India v Sri Lanka	Jaipur	2005-06
183	S.C.Ganguly	India v Sri Lanka	Taunton	1999
181*	M.L.Hayden	Australia v New Zealand	Hamilton	2006-07
181	I.V.A.Richards	West Indies v Sri Lanka	Karachi	1987-88
175*	Kapil Dev	India v Zimbabwe	Tunbridge Wells	1983
175	H.H.Gibbs	South Africa v Australia	Johannesburg	2005-06
173	M.E.Waugh	Australia v West Indies	Melbourne	2000-01
172*	C.B.Wishart	Zimbabwe v Namibia	Harare	2002-03
172	A.C.Gilchrist	Australia v Zimbabwe	Hobart	2003-04
172	L.Vincent	New Zealand v Zimbabwe	Bulawayo	2005
171*	G.M.Turner	New Zealand v East Africa	Birmingham	1975
169*	D.J.Callaghan	South Africa v New Zealand	Pretoria	1994-95
169	B.C.Lara	West Indies v Sri Lanka	Sharjah	1995-96
167*	R.A.Smith	England v Australia	Birmingham	1993
166	B.B.McCullum	New Zealand v Ireland	Aberdeen	2008
164*	R.T.Ponting	Australia v South Africa	Johannesburg	2005-06
163*	S.R.Tendulkar	India v New Zealand	Christchurch	2008-09
161	A.C.Hudson	South Africa v Holland	Rawalpindi	1995-96
161	J.A.H.Marshall	New Zealand v Ireland	Aberdeen	2008
160	Imran Nazir	Pakistan v Zimbabwe	Kingston	2006-07
159*	D.Mongia	India v Zimbabwe	Gauhati	2001-02
158	D.I.Gower	England v New Zealand	Brisbane	1982-83
158	M.L.Hayden	Australia v West Indies	North Sound	2006-07
157*	X.M.Marshall	West Indies v Canada	King City (NW)	2008
157	S.T.Jayasuriya	Sri Lanka v Holland	Amstelveen	2006
156	B.C.Lara	West Indies v Pakistan	Adelaide	2004-05
156	A.Symonds	Australia v New Zealand	Wellington	2005-06
154	A.C.Gilchrist	Australia v Sri Lanka	Melbourne	1998-99
153*	I.V.A.Richards	West Indies v Australia	Melbourne	1979-80
153*	M.Azharuddin	India v Zimbabwe	Cuttack	1997-98
153*	S.C.Ganguly	India v New Zealand	Gwalior	1999-00
153*	C.H.Gayle	West Indies v Zimbabwe	Bulawayo	2003-04
153	B.C.Lara	West Indies v Pakistan	Sharjah	1993-94
153	R.Dravid	India v New Zealand	Hyderabad	1999-00
153	H.H.Gibbs	South Africa v Bangladesh	Potchefstroom	2002-03
152*	D.L.Haynes	West Indies v India	Georgetown	1988-89
152*	C.H.Gayle	West Indies v South Africa	Johannesburg	2003-04
152	C.H.Gayle	West Indies v Kenya	Nairobi	2001-02
152	S.R.Tendulkar	India v Namibia	Pietermaritzburg	2002-03
152	A.J.Strauss	England v Bangladesh	Nottingham	2005
152	S.T.Jayasuriya	Sri Lanka v England	Leeds	2006
151*	S.T.Jayasuriya	Sri Lanka v India	Bombay	1996-97
151	A.Symonds	Australia v Sri Lanka	Sydney	2005-06
150	S.Chanderpaul	West Indies v South Africa	East London	1998-99
150	G.Gambhir	India v Sri Lanka	Colombo (RPS)	2008-09

The highest for Bangladesh is 134* by Shakib Al Hasan (v Canada, St John's, 2006-07).

HUNDRED ON DEBUT

D.L.Amiss	103	England v Australia	Manchester	1972
D.L.Haynes	148	West Indies v Australia	St John's	1977-78
A.Flower	115*	Zimbabwe v Sri Lanka	New Plymouth	1991-92
Salim Elahi	102*	Pakistan v Sri Lanka	Gujranwala	1995-96
M.J.Guptill	122*	New Zealand v West Indies	Auckland	2008-09

Shahid Afridi scored 102 for P v SL, Nairobi, 1996-97, in his second match having not batted in his first.

| **Fastest 100** | 37 balls | Shahid Afridi (102) | P v SL | Nairobi | 1996-97 |
| **Fastest 50** | 17 balls | S.T.Jayasuriya (76) | SL v P | Singapore | 1995-96 |

CARRYING BAT THROUGH INNINGS (SIDE ALL OUT)

G.W.Flower	84*	Zimbabwe (205) v England	Sydney	1994-95
Saeed Anwar	103*	Pakistan (219) v Zimbabwe	Harare	1994-95
N.V.Knight	125*	England (246) v Pakistan	Nottingham	1996
R.D.Jacobs	49*	West Indies (110) v Australia	Manchester	1999
D.R.Martyn	116*	Australia (191) v New Zealand	Auckland	1999-00
H.H.Gibbs	59*	South Africa (101†) v Pakistan	Sharjah	1999-00
A.J.Stewart	100*	England (192) v West Indies	Nottingham	2000
Javed Omar	33*	Bangladesh (103) v Zimbabwe	Harare	2000-01

† One batsman retired hurt.

5000 RUNS IN A CAREER

		LOI	I	NO	HS	Runs	Avge	100	50
S.R.Tendulkar	I	425	415	39	186*	**16684**	44.37	43	91
S.T.Jayasuriya	SL	428	416	18	189	**13085**	32.87	28	67
Inzamam-ul-Haq	P	375	348	52	137*	**11701**	39.53	10	83
S.C.Ganguly	I	308	297	23	183	**11221**	40.95	22	71
R.T.Ponting	A	306	297	35	164	**11093**	42.33	25	64
R.Dravid	I	329	304	39	153	**10464**	39.48	12	80
B.C.Lara	WI	294	285	32	169	**10348**	40.90	19	62
J.H.Kallis	SA	282	268	51	139	**10028**	46.21	16	71
A.C.Gilchrist	A	283	275	11	172	**9415**	35.66	15	55
M.Azharuddin	I	334	308	54	153*	**9378**	36.92	7	58
P.A.de Silva	SL	308	296	30	145	**9284**	34.90	11	64
M.Yousuf Youhana	P	262	248	40	141*	**9076**	43.63	15	60
Saeed Anwar	P	247	244	19	194	**8823**	39.21	20	43
D.L.Haynes	WI	238	237	28	152*	**8648**	41.37	17	57
M.S.Atapattu	SL	267	259	32	132*	**8529**	37.57	11	59
M.E.Waugh	A	244	236	20	173	**8500**	39.35	18	50
S.P.Fleming	NZ	277	268	21	134*	**8007**	32.41	8	49
S.Chanderpaul	WI	241	226	35	150	**7858**	41.14	9	53
H.H.Gibbs	SA	239	232	16	175	**7785**	36.04	20	36
D.P.M.D.Jayawardena	SL	294	275	28	128	**7773**	31.46	9	47
S.R.Waugh	A	325	288	58	120*	**7569**	32.90	3	45
A.Ranatunga	SL	269	255	47	131*	**7454**	35.83	4	49
Javed Miandad	P	233	218	41	119*	**7381**	41.70	8	50
Salim Malik	P	283	256	38	102	**7171**	32.89	5	47
K.C.Sangakkara	SL	239	222	24	138*	**7149**	36.10	10	45
N.J.Astle	NZ	221	217	14	145*	**7090**	34.92	16	41
C.H.Gayle	WI	191	186	14	153*	**7056**	41.02	19	36
M.G.Bevan	A	232	196	67	108*	**6912**	53.58	6	46
G.Kirsten	SA	185	185	19	188*	**6798**	40.95	13	45
A.Flower	Z	213	208	16	145	**6786**	35.34	4	55
Yuvraj Singh	I	229	210	29	139	**6758**	37.33	11	40
I.V.A.Richards	WI	187	167	24	189*	**6721**	47.00	11	45
Ijaz Ahmed	P	250	232	29	139*	**6564**	32.33	10	37
G.W.Flower	Z	219	212	18	142*	**6536**	33.69	6	40
A.R.Border	A	273	252	39	127*	**6524**	30.62	3	39
V.Sehwag	I	195	190	8	130	**6314**	34.69	11	34

		LOI	I	NO	HS	Runs	Avge	100	50
R.B.Richardson	WI	224	217	30	122	**6248**	33.41	5	44
M.L.Hayden	A	160	154	15	181*	**6131**	44.10	10	36
D.M.Jones	A	164	161	25	145	**6068**	44.61	7	46
D.C.Boon	A	181	177	16	122	**5964**	37.04	5	37
J.N.Rhodes	SA	245	220	51	121	**5935**	35.11	2	33
Ramiz Raja	P	198	197	15	119*	**5841**	32.09	9	31
C.L.Hooper	WI	227	206	43	113*	**5761**	35.34	7	29
W.J.Cronje	SA	188	175	31	112	**5565**	38.64	2	39
Shahid Afridi	P	266	249	16	109	**5494**	23.57	4	29
A.Jadeja	I	196	179	36	119	**5359**	37.47	6	30
Younus Khan	P	181	175	19	144	**5306**	34.01	6	35
D.R.Martyn	A	205	179	51	144*	**5259**	41.08	5	36
A.D.R.Campbell	Z	188	184	14	131*	**5185**	30.50	7	30
R.S.Mahanama	SL	213	198	23	119*	**5162**	29.49	4	35
C.G.Greenidge	WI	128	127	13	133*	**5134**	45.03	11	31
G.C.Smith	SA	135	133	9	133*	**5111**	41.21	7	37

The most for England is 4677 in 162 innings by A.J.Stewart, and for Bangladesh 2761 (131) by Mohammad Ashraful.

15 HUNDREDS

		Inns	100	E	A	SA	WI	NZ	I	P	SL	Z	B	Ass
S.R.Tendulkar	I	415	**43**	1	8	3	4	5	–	5	7	5	–	5
S.T.Jayasuriya	SL	416	**28**	4	2	–	1	5	7	3	–	1	4	1
R.T.Ponting	A	297	**25**	3	–	2	1	6	5	1	4	1	1	1
S.C.Ganguly	I	297	**22**	1	1	3	–	3	–	2	4	3	1	4
H.H.Gibbs	SA	232	**20**	2	2	–	5	2	2	2	1	2	1	1
Saeed Anwar	P	244	**20**	–	1	–	2	4	4	–	7	2	–	–
C.H.Gayle	WI	186	**19**	2	–	3	–	1	4	3	–	2	1	3
B.C.Lara	WI	285	**19**	1	3	3	–	2	–	5	2	1	1	1
M.E.Waugh	A	236	**18**	1	–	2	3	3	3	1	1	3	–	1
D.L.Haynes	WI	237	**17**	2	6	–	–	2	2	4	1	–		–
N.J.Astle	NZ	217	**16**	2	1	1	1	–	5	2	–	3	–	1
J.H.Kallis	SA	268	**16**	1	1	–	4	3	1	1	3	1	–	1
A.C.Gilchrist	A	275	**15**	2	–	2	–	2	1	1	6	1	–	
M.Yousuf Youhana	P	248	**15**	–	1	2	2	1	1	–	2	3	3	–

The most for England is 12 by M.E.Trescothick (in 122 innings), for Zimbabwe 7 by A.D.R.Campbell (184), and for Bangladesh 4 by Shahriar Nafis (60).

HIGHEST PARTNERSHIP FOR EACH WICKET

1st	286	W.U.Tharanga/S.T.Jayasuriya	Sri Lanka v England	Leeds	2006
2nd	331	S.R.Tendulkar/R.Dravid	India v New Zealand	Hyderabad (Ind)	1999-00
3rd	237*	R.Dravid/S.R.Tendulkar	India v Kenya	Bristol	1999
4th	275*	M.Azharuddin/A.Jadeja	India v Zimbabwe	Cuttack	1997-98
5th	223	M.Azharuddin/A.Jadeja	India v Sri Lanka	Colombo (RPS)	1997-98
6th	165	M.E.K.Hussey/B.J.Haddin	Australia v West Indies	Kuala Lumpur	2006-07
	165	C.D.McMillan/B.B.McCullum	New Zealand v Australia	Hamilton	2006-07
7th	130	A.Flower/H.H.Streak	Zimbabwe v England	Harare	2001-02
8th	138*	J.M.Kemp/A.J.Hall	South Africa v India	Cape Town	2006-07
9th	126*	Kapil Dev/S.M.H.Kirmani	India v Zimbabwe	Tunbridge Wells	1983
10th	106*	I.V.A.Richards/M.A.Holding	West Indies v England	Manchester	1984

BOWLING RECORDS
SIX WICKETS IN AN INNINGS

8-19	W.P.U.C.J Vaas	Sri Lanka v Zimbabwe	Colombo (SSC)	2001-02
7-15	G.D.McGrath	Australia v Namibia	Potchefstroom	2002-03
7-20	A.J.Bichel	Australia v England	Port Elizabeth	2002-03
7-30	M.Muralitharan	Sri Lanka v India	Sharjah	2000-01
7-36	Waqar Younis	Pakistan v England	Leeds	2001
7-37	Aqib Javed	Pakistan v India	Sharjah	1991-92

7-51	W.W.Davis	West Indies v Australia	Leeds	1983
6-12	A.Kumble	India v West Indies	Calcutta	1993-94
6-13	B.A.W.Mendis	Sri Lanka v India	Karachi	2008
6-14	G.J.Gilmour	Australia v England	Leeds	1975
6-14	Imran Khan	Pakistan v India	Sharjah	1984-85
6-14	M.F.Maharoof	Sri Lanka v West Indies	Bombay	2006-07
6-15	C.E.H.Croft	West Indies v England	Kingstown	1980-81
6-16	Shoaib Akhtar	Pakistan v New Zealand	Karachi	2001-02
6-18	Azhar Mahmood	Pakistan v West Indies	Sharjah	1999-00
6-19	H.K.Olonga	Zimbabwe v England	Cape Town	1999-00
6-19	S.E.Bond	New Zealand v Zimbabwe	Harare	2005
6-20	B.C.Strang	Zimbabwe v Bangladesh	Nairobi	1997-98
6-22	F.H.Edwards	West Indies v Zimbabwe	Harare	2003-04
6-22	M.Ntini	South Africa v Australia	Cape Town	2005-06
6-23	A.A.Donald	South Africa v Kenya	Nairobi	1996-97
6-23	A.Nehra	India v England	Durban	2002-03
6-23	S.E.Bond	New Zealand v Australia	Port Elizabeth	2002-03
6-25	S.B.Styris	New Zealand v West Indies	Port-of-Spain	2002
6-25	W.P.U.C.J.Vaas	Sri Lanka v Bangladesh	Pietermaritzburg	2002-03
6-26	Waqar Younis	Pakistan v Sri Lanka	Sharjah	1989-90
6-26	Mashrafe Mortaza	Bangladesh v Kenya	Nairobi	2006
6-27	Naved-ul-Hasan	Pakistan v India	Jamshedpur	2004-05
6-27	M.Kartik	India v Australia	Bombay	2007-08
6-27	C.R.D.Fernando	Sri Lanka v England	Colombo (RPS)	2007-08
6-28	H.K.Olonga	Zimbabwe v Kenya	Nagpur	1987-88
6-29	B.P.Patterson	West Indies v India	Moratuwa	1992-93
6-29	S.T.Jayasuriya	Sri Lanka v England	Moratuwa	1992-93
6-29	B.A.W.Mendis	Sri Lanka v Zimbabwe	Harare	2008-09
6-30	Waqar Younis	Pakistan v New Zealand	Auckland	1993-94
6-31	P.D.Collingwood	England v Bangladesh	Nottingham	2005
6-35	S.M.Pollock	South Africa v West Indies	East London	1998-99
6-35	Abdul Razzaq	Pakistan v Bangladesh	Dhaka	2001-02
6-39	K.H.MacLeay	Australia v India	Nottingham	1983
6-41	I.V.A.Richards	West Indies v India	Delhi	1989-90
6-42	A.B.Agarkar	India v Australia	Melbourne	2003-04
6-44	Waqar Younis	Pakistan v New Zealand	Sharjah	1996-97
6-49	L.Klusener	South Africa v Sri Lanka	Lahore	1997-98
6-50	A.H.Gray	West Indies v Australia	Port-of-Spain	1990-91
6-52	C.B.Mpofu	Zimbabwe v Kenya	Nairobi (Gym)	2008-09
6-55	S.Sreesanth	India v England	Indore	2005-06
6-59	Waqar Younis	Pakistan v Australia	Nottingham	2001
6-59	A.Nehra	India v Sri Lanka	Colombo (RPS)	2005

150 WICKETS IN A CAREER

		LOI	Balls	R	W	Avge	Best	5w	R/Over
Wasim Akram	P	356	18186	11812	502	23.52	5-15	6	3.89
M.Muralitharan	SL	322	17335	11225	494	22.72	7-30	10	3.88
Waqar Younis	P	262	12698	9919	416	23.84	7-36	13	4.68
W.P.U.C.J.Vaas	SL	321	15721	10955	399	27.45	8-19	4	4.17
S.M.Pollock	SA	294	15430	9410	387	24.31	6-35	5	3.65
G.D.McGrath	A	247	12850	8315	377	22.05	7-15	7	3.88
A.Kumble	I	269	14376	10300	334	30.83	6-12	2	4.29
J.Srinath	I	229	11935	8847	315	28.08	5-23	3	4.44
S.T.Jayasuriya	SL	428	14258	11370	310	36.67	6-29	4	4.75
B.Lee	A	170	8706	6847	296	23.13	5-22	7	4.71
S.K.Warne	A	193	10600	7514	291	25.82	5-33	1	4.25
Saqlain Mushtaq	P	169	8770	6275	288	21.78	5-20	6	4.29
A.B.Agarkar	I	191	9484	8021	288	27.85	6-42	2	5.07
A.A.Donald	SA	164	8561	5926	272	21.78	6-23	2	4.15
M.Ntini	SA	170	8555	6386	264	24.18	6-22	4	4.47
Kapil Dev	I	225	11202	6945	253	27.45	5-43	1	3.72
Abdul Razzaq	P	227	9707	7546	245	30.80	6-35	3	4.66
J.H.Kallis	SA	282	9594	7693	242	31.78	5-30	2	4.81
Shahid Afridi	P	266	11093	8572	241	35.56	5-11	2	4.63

		LOI	Balls	R	W	Avge	Best	5w	R/Over
H.H.Streak	Z	187	9414	7065	237	29.81	5-32	1	4.50
D.Gough	E	158	8421	6154	234	26.29	5-44	2	4.38
D.L.Vettori	NZ	235	10994	7640	234	32.78	5- 7	2	4.16
C.A.Walsh	WI	205	10822	6915	227	30.46	5- 1	1	3.83
C.E.L.Ambrose	WI	176	9353	5430	225	24.13	5-17	4	3.48
Shoaib Akhtar	P	135	6381	4952	214	23.14	6-16	4	4.65
Z.Khan	I	156	7815	6367	212	30.03	5-42	1	4.88
Harbhajan Singh	I	183	9552	6707	203	33.03	5-31	2	4.21
C.Z.Harris	NZ	248	10667	7613	203	37.50	5-42	1	4.28
C.J.McDermott	A	138	7460	5018	203	24.71	5-44	1	4.03
C.L.Cairns	NZ	214	8132	6557	200	32.78	5-42	1	4.83
B.K.V.Prasad	I	161	8129	6332	196	32.30	5-27	1	4.67
S.R.Waugh	A	325	8883	6764	195	34.68	4-33	–	4.56
C.L.Hooper	WI	227	9573	6957	193	36.04	4-34	–	4.36
L.Klusener	SA	171	7336	5751	192	29.95	6-49	6	4.70
Aqib Javed	P	163	8012	5721	182	31.43	7-37	4	4.28
Imran Khan	P	175	7462	4845	182	26.62	6-14	1	3.90
C.R.D.Fernando	SL	131	5670	4916	162	30.34	6-271	–	5.20
A.Flintoff	E	135	5382	3872	162	23.90	5-56	1	4.31
Mushtaq Ahmed	P	144	7543	5361	161	33.29	5-36	1	4.26
R.J.Hadlee	NZ	115	6182	3407	158	21.56	5-25	5	3.31
M.Prabhakar	I	130	6360	4534	157	28.87	5-33	2	4.27
M.D.Marshall	WI	136	7175	4233	157	26.96	4-18	–	3.54
G.B.Hogg	A	123	5563	4188	156	26.84	5-32	2	4.51
N.W.Bracken	A	98	4835	3526	155	22.74	5-47	2	4.40
S.R.Tendulkar	I	425	8015	6806	154	44.19	5-32	2	5.09
I.K.Pathan	I	107	5194	4546	152	29.90	5-27	1	5.25
U.D.U.Chandana	SL	147	6136	4809	151	31.84	5-61	1	4.70
C.H.Gayle	WI	191	6342	4976	151	32.95	5-46	1	4.70

The most for Bangladesh is 134 by Mashrafe Mortaza (101 LOI).

HAT-TRICKS

Jalaluddin	Pakistan v Australia	Hyderabad	1982-83
B.A.Reid	Australia v New Zealand	Sydney	1985-86
C.Sharma	India v New Zealand	Nagpur	1987-88
Wasim Akram	Pakistan v West Indies	Sharjah	1989-90
Wasim Akram	Pakistan v Australia	Sharjah	1989-90
Kapil Dev	India v Sri Lanka	Calcutta	1990-91
Aqib Javed	Pakistan v India	Sharjah	1991-92
D.K.Morrison	New Zealand v India	Napier	1993-94
Waqar Younis	Pakistan v New Zealand	East London	1994-95
Saqlain Mushtaq	Pakistan v Zimbabwe	Peshawar	1996-97
E.A.Brandes	Zimbabwe v England	Harare	1996-97
A.M.Stuart	Australia v Pakistan	Melbourne	1996-97
Saqlain Mushtaq	Pakistan v Zimbabwe	The Oval	1999
W.P.U.C.J Vaas	Sri Lanka v Zimbabwe	Colombo (SSC)	2001-02
Mohammad Sami	Pakistan v West Indies	Sharjah	2001-02
W.P.U.C.J Vaas[1]	Sri Lanka v Bangladesh	Pietermaritzburg	2002-03
B.Lee	Australia v Kenya	Durban	2002-03
J.M.Anderson	England v Pakistan	The Oval	2003
S.J.Harmison	England v India	Nottingham	2004
C.K.Langeveldt	South Africa v West Indies	Bridgetown	2004-05
Shahadat Hossain	Bangladesh v Zimbabwe	Harare	2006
J.E.Taylor	West Indies v Australia	Bombay	2006-07
S.E.Bond	New Zealand v Australia	Hobart	2006-07
S.L.Malinga	Sri Lanka v South Africa	Providence	2006-07

[1] The first three balls of the match. Took four wickets in opening over (W W W 4 wide W 0).

WICKET-KEEPING RECORDS

SIX DISMISSALS IN AN INNINGS

6	(6ct)	A.C.Gilchrist	Australia v South Africa	Cape Town	1999-00
6	(6ct)	A.J.Stewart	England v Zimbabwe	Manchester	2000
6	(5ct/1st)	R.D.Jacobs	West Indies v Sri Lanka	Colombo (RPS)	2001-02
6	(5ct/1st)	A.C.Gilchrist	Australia v England	Sydney	2002-03
6	(6ct)	A.C.Gilchrist	Australia v Namibia	Potchefstroom	2002-03
6	(6ct)	A.C.Gilchrist	Australia v Sri Lanka	Colombo (RPS)	2003-04
6	(6ct)	M.V.Boucher	South Africa v Pakistan	Cape Town	2006-07
6	(5ct/1st)	M.S.Dhoni	India v England	Leeds	2007
6	(6ct)	A.C.Gilchrist	Australia v India	Baroda	2007-08
6	(5ct/1st)	A.C.Gilchrist	Australia v India	Sydney	2007-08
6	(6ct)	M.J.Prior	England v South Africa	Nottingham	2008

100 DISMISSALS IN A CAREER

Total			LOI	Ct	St
468‡	A.C.Gilchrist	Australia	274	414	83
391	M.V.Boucher	South Africa	270	373	18
287‡	Moin Khan	Pakistan	211	214	73
263†‡	K.C.Sangakkara	Sri Lanka	197	202	61
233	I.A.Healy	Australia	168	194	39
220‡	Rashid Latif	Pakistan	164	182	38
207‡	R.S.Kaluwitharana	Sri Lanka	187	132	75
204‡	P.J.L.Dujon	West Indies	167	183	21
187	R.D.Jacobs	West Indies	146	159	28
172†‡	B.B.McCullum	New Zealand	146	159	13
167	M.S.Dhoni	India	132	129	38
165	D.J.Richardson	South Africa	122	148	17
165†‡	A.Flower	Zimbabwe	185	133	32
163†‡	A.J.Stewart	England	138	148	15
154‡	N.R.Mongia	India	139	110	44
136†‡	A.C.Parore	New Zealand	148	111	25
126	Khaled Masud	Bangladesh	125	91	35
124	R.W.Marsh	Australia	92	120	4
112	Kamran Akmal	Pakistan	94	98	14
109	T.Taibu	Zimbabwe	107	95	14
103	Salim Yousuf	Pakistan	86	81	22

† Excluding catches taken in the field. ‡ Excluding matches when not wicket-keeper.

FIELDING RECORDS

FIVE CATCHES IN AN INNINGS

5	J.N.Rhodes	South Africa v West Indies	Bombay	1993-94

100 CATCHES IN A CAREER

Total			LOI
156	M.Azharuddin	India	334
153	D.P.M.D.Jayawardena	Sri Lanka	294
132	S.P.Fleming	New Zealand	277
132	R.T.Ponting	Australia	306
129	S.R.Tendulkar	India	425
127	A.R.Border	Australia	273
125	M.Muralitharan	Sri Lanka	322
122	R.Dravid	India	329
121	S.T.Jayasuriya	Sri Lanka	428
120	C.L.Hooper	West Indies	227
117	B.C.Lara	West Indies	294

Total			LOI
113	Inzamam-ul-Haq	Pakistan	375
111	S.R.Waugh	Australia	325
109	R.S.Mahanama	Sri Lanka	213
108	M.E.Waugh	Australia	244
105	J.H.Kallis	South Africa	282
105	J.N.Rhodes	South Africa	245
104	H.H.Gibbs	South Africa	239
104	S.M.Pollock	South Africa	294
101	I.V.A.Richards	West Indies	187
100	S.C.Ganguly	India	308

The most for England is 88 by P.D.Collingwood (154), for Zimbabwe 86 by G.W.Flower (219), and for Bangladesh 32 by Mashrafe Mortaza (101).

ALL-ROUND RECORDS
50 RUNS AND 5 WICKETS IN A MATCH

I.V.A.Richards	119	5-41	West Indies v New Zealand	Dunedin	1986-87
K.Srikkanth	70	5-27	India v New Zealand	Vishakhapatnam	1988-89
M.E.Waugh	57	5-24	Australia v West Indies	Melbourne	1992-93
L.Klusener	54	6-49	South Africa v Sri Lanka	Lahore	1997-98
Abdul Razzaq	70*	5-48	Pakistan v India	Hobart	1999-00
G.A.Hick	80	5-33	England v Zimbabwe	Harare	1999-00
Shahid Afridi	61	5-40	Pakistan v England	Lahore	2000-01
S.C.Ganguly	71*	5-34	India v Zimbabwe	Kanpur	2000-01
S.B.Styris	63*	6-25	New Zealand v West Indies	Port-of-Spain	2002
R.C.Irani	53	5-26	England v India	The Oval	2002
C.H.Gayle	60	5-46	West Indies v Australia	St George's	2002-03
P.D.Collingwood	112*	6-31	England v Bangladesh	Nottingham	2005
S.Dhaniram	79	5-32	Canada v Bermuda	King City (NW)	2008

1000 RUNS AND 100 WICKETS

England	I.T.Botham (2113/145), A.Flintoff (3290/162).
Australia	S.P.O'Donnell (1242/108), A.Symonds (4938/127); S.K.Warne (1016/291); S.R.Waugh (7569/195).
South Africa	W.J.Cronje (5565/114); J.H.Kallis (10028/242); L.Klusener (3576/192); S.M.Pollock (3193/387).
West Indies	C.H.Gayle (7056/151); C.L.Hooper (5761/193); I.V.A.Richards (6721/118).
New Zealand	C.L.Cairns (4881/200); R.J.Hadlee (1751/158); C.Z.Harris (4379/203); J.D.P.Oram (2022/131); S.B.Styris (3715/122); D.L.Vettori (1445/233).
India	A.B.Agarkar (1269/288); S.C.Ganguly (11221/100); Kapil Dev (3782/253); I.K.Pathan (1368/152); M Prabhakar (1858/157); R.J.Shastri (3108/129); S.R.Tendulkar (16684/154)
Pakistan	Abdul Razzaq (4417/245); Azhar Mahmood (1521/123); Imran Khan (3709/182); Mudassar Nazar (2654/111); Shahid Afridi (5494/241); Shoaib Malik (4749/126); Wasim Akram (3717/502).
Sri Lanka	U.D.U.Chandana (1627/151); P.A.de Silva (9284/106); H.D.P.K.Dharmasena (1222/138); S.T.Jayasuriya (13085/310); W.P.U.C.J.Vaas (2018/399)
Zimbabwe	G.W.Flower (6536/104); H.H.Streak (2901/237)
Bangladesh	Mashrafe Mortaza (1032/134) Mohammad Rafique (1190/119)
Kenya	T.M.Odoyo (1972/106)

APPEARANCE RECORDS – 250 MATCHES

428	S.T.Jayasuriya	Sri Lanka		294	S.M.Pollock	South Africa
425	S.R.Tendulkar	India		283	A.C.Gilchrist	Australia
375	Inzamam-ul-Haq	Pakistan		283	Salim Malik	Pakistan
356	Wasim Akram	Pakistan		282	J.H.Kallis	South Africa
334	M.Azharuddin	India		277	S.P.Fleming	New Zealand
329	R.Dravid	India		273	A.R.Border	Australia
325	S.R.Waugh	Australia		270	M.V.Boucher	South Africa
322	M.Muralitharan	Sri Lanka		269	A.Kumble	India
321	W.P.U.C.J.Vaas	Sri Lanka		269	A.Ranatunga	Sri Lanka
308	P.A.de Silva	Sri Lanka		268	M.S.Atapattu	Sri Lanka
308	S.C.Ganguly	India		266	Shahid Afridi	Pakistan
306	R.T.Ponting	Australia		262	Waqar Younis	Pakistan
294	D.P.M.D.Jayawardena	Sri Lanka		262	M.Yousuf Youhana	Pakistan
294	B.C.Lara	West Indies		250	Ijaz Ahmed	Pakistan

The most for England is 170 by A.J.Stewart, for Zimbabwe 219 by G.W.Flower, and for Bangladesh 137 by Mohammad Ashraful.

The most consecutive appearances is 172 by A.Flower for Zimbabwe (Feb 1992-Apr 2001).

100 MATCHES AS CAPTAIN

LOI			W	L	T	NR	% Won (exc NR)
216	S.P.Fleming	New Zealand	98	106	1	13	48.27
193	A.Ranatunga	Sri Lanka	89	95	1	8	48.10
178	A.R.Border	Australia	107	67	1	3	61.14
175	R.T.Ponting	Australia	128	36	2	9	77.11
174	M.Azharuddin	India	90	76	2	6	53.57
146	S.C.Ganguly	India	76	65	–	5	53.90
139	Imran Khan	Pakistan	75	59	1	4	55.55
138	W.J.Cronje	South Africa	99	35	1	3	73.33
124	B.C.Lara	West Indies	59	59	–	7	50.42
118	S.T.Jayasuriya	Sri Lanka	66	47	2	3	57.39
113	G.C.Smith	South Africa	67	40	1	5	62.04
109	Wasim Akram	Pakistan	66	41	2	–	60.55
108	I.V.A.Richards	West Indies	68	36	–	4	65.38
106	S.R.Waugh	Australia	67	35	3	1	63.80

The most for England is 60 by M.P.Vaughan, for Zimbabwe 86 by A.D.R.Campbell, and for Bangladesh 69 by Habibul Bashar.

100 LOI UMPIRING APPEARANCES

193	R.E.Koertzen	South Africa	09.12.1992	to	14.03.2009
179	S.A.Bucknor	Jamaica	18.03.1989	to	13.02.2009
171	D.R.Shepherd	England	09.06.1983	to	12.07.2005
158	D.J.Harper	Australia	14.01.1994	to	26.01.2009
138	S.J.A.Taufel	Australia	13.01.1999	to	08.02.2009
137	D.B.Hair	Australia	14.12.1991	to	24.08.2008
125	B.F.Bowden	New Zealand	23.03.1995	to	31.07.2008
110	Alim Dar	Pakistan	16.02.2000	to	28.11.2008
108	R.B.Tiffin	Zimbabwe	25.10.1992	to	30.11.2008
107	D.L.Orchard	South Africa	02.12.1994	to	07.12.2003
100	R.S.Dunne	New Zealand	06.02.1989	to	26.02.2002

INTERNATIONAL TWENTY20 RECORDS

These records exclude matches abandoned without a ball bowled, regardless of the toss having been made.

MATCH RESULTS

Matches completed by 16 March 2009

Team	Opponents	Matches	Won	Lost	Tied
Australia	Bangladesh	1	1	–	–
	England	3	2	1	–
	India	3	1	2	–
	New Zealand	3	3	–	–
	Pakistan	1	–	1	–
	South Africa	4	3	1	–
	Sri Lanka	1	1	–	–
	West Indies	1	–	1	–
	Zimbabwe	1	–	1	–
Bangladesh	Australia	1	–	1	–
	Kenya	1	1	–	–
	Pakistan	3	–	3	–
	South Africa	2	–	2	–
	Sri Lanka	1	–	1	–
	West Indies	1	1	–	–
	Zimbabwe	1	1	–	–
England	Australia	3	1	2	–
	India	1	–	1	–
	New Zealand	4	3	1	–
	Pakistan	1	–	1	–
	South Africa	1	–	1	–
	Sri Lanka	1	–	1	–
	West Indies	3	1	2	–
	Zimbabwe	1	1	–	–
India	Australia	3	2	1	–
	England	1	1	–	–
	New Zealand	3	–	3	–
	Pakistan	2	1	–	1
	South Africa	2	2	–	–
	Sri Lanka	1	1	–	–
Kenya	Bangladesh	1	–	1	–
	New Zealand	1	–	1	–
	Pakistan	1	–	1	–
	Sri Lanka	1	–	1	–
	Netherlands	1	–	1	–
	Canada	1	1	–	–
	Ireland	1	–	1	–
	Scotland	1	–	1	–
New Zealand	Australia	3	–	3	–
	England	4	1	3	–
	India	3	3	–	–
	Kenya	1	1	–	–
	Pakistan	1	–	1	–
	South Africa	3	1	2	–
	Sri Lanka	3	1	2	–
	West Indies	3	1	–	2
Pakistan	Australia	1	1	–	–
	Bangladesh	3	3	–	–
	England	1	1	–	–
	India	2	–	1	1
	Kenya	1	1	–	–
	New Zealand	1	1	–	–
	Scotland	1	1	–	–
	South Africa	1	–	1	–
	Sri Lanka	3	2	1	–
	Canada	1	1	–	–
	Zimbabwe	1	1	–	–
Scotland	Pakistan	1	–	1	–
	Ireland	1	–	1	–
	Bermuda	1	1	–	–
	Netherlands	1	1	–	–
	Kenya	1	1	–	–
South Africa	Australia	4	1	3	–
	Bangladesh	2	2	–	–
	England	1	1	–	–
	India	2	–	2	–
	New Zealand	3	2	1	–
	Pakistan	1	1	–	–
	West Indies	3	2	1	–
Sri Lanka	Australia	1	–	1	–
	Bangladesh	1	1	–	–
	England	1	1	–	–
	Kenya	1	1	–	–
	New Zealand	3	2	1	–
	Pakistan	3	1	2	–
	Zimbabwe	1	1	–	–
	Canada	1	1	–	–
	India	1	–	1	–
West Indies	Bangladesh	1	1	–	–
	England	3	2	1	–
	New Zealand	3	–	1	2
	South Africa	3	1	2	–
	Australia	1	1	–	–
Zimbabwe	Australia	1	1	–	–
	Bangladesh	1	–	1	–
	England	1	–	1	–
	Sri Lanka	1	–	1	–
	Canada	2	1	–	1

Opponents	Matches	Won	Lost	Tied		Opponents	Matches	Won	Lost	Tied
	Pakistan	1	–	1	–		Kenya	1	–	1	–
Netherlands	Kenya	1	1	–	–		Bermuda	1	1	–	–
	Canada	1	–	1	–		Pakistan	1	–	1	–
	Scotland	1	1	–	–		Zimbabwe	2	–	1	1
Ireland	Scotland	1	1	–	–		Sri Lanka	1	–	1	–
	Bermuda	1	1	–	–	Bermuda	Scotland	1	–	1	–
	Kenya	1	1	–	–		Ireland	1	–	1	–
Canada	Netherlands	1	1	–	–		Canada	1	–	1	–

MATCH RESULTS SUMMARY

	Matches	Won	Lost	Tied			Matches	Won	Lost	Tied
Australia	18	11	7	0		South Africa	16	9	7	0
Bangladesh	10	3	7	0		Sri Lanka	13	8	5	0
England	15	6	9	0		West Indies	11	4	5	2
India	12	7	4	1		Zimbabwe	7	2	4	1
Kenya	8	1	7	0		Netherlands	3	2	1	0
New Zealand	21	8	11	2		Ireland	3	3	0	0
Pakistan	16	12	3	1		Canada	7	2	4	1
Scotland	5	2	3	0		Bermuda	3	0	3	0

INTERNATIONAL TWENTY20 RECORDS

(To 16 March 2009)

TEAM RECORDS

HIGHEST INNINGS TOTALS

† Batting Second

260-6	Sri Lanka v Kenya	Johannesburg	2007-08
221-5	Australia v England	Sydney	2006-07
218-4	India v England	Durban	2007-08
214-5	Australia v New Zealand	Auckland	2004-05
209-3	Australia v South Africa	Brisbane	2005-06
208-2†	South Africa v West Indies	Johannesburg	2007-08
208-8	West Indies v England	The Oval	2007
205-6	West Indies v South Africa	Johannesburg	2007-08
203-5	Pakistan v Bangladesh	Karachi	2007-08
201-4	South Africa v Australia	Johannesburg	2005-06
200-6†	England v India	Durban	2007-08

LOWEST COMPLETED INNINGS TOTALS

† Batting Second

67	(17.2)	Kenya v Ireland	Belfast	2008
70		Bermuda v Canada	Belfast	2008
73	(16.5)	Kenya v New Zealand	Durban	2007-08
74	(17.3)	India v Australia	Melbourne	2007-08
75†	(19.2)	Canada v Zimbabwe	King City (NW)	2008-09
79†	(14.3)	Australia v England	Southampton	2005
83†	(15.5)	Bangladesh v Sri Lanka	Johannesburg	2007-08
88†	(19.3)	Kenya v Sri Lanka	Johannesburg	2007-08
91	(19.4)	Canada v Kenya	Belfast	2008
92	(19.4)	Kenya v Pakistan	Nairobi	2007-08
97	(18.4)	Netherlands v Canada	Belfast	2008
99-7		Bermuda v Scotland	Belfast	2008

BATTING RECORDS
MOST RUNS IN A CAREER

Runs			M	I	NO	HS	Avge	50	R/100B
582	B.B.McCullum	NZ	21	21	4	69*	34.23	4	125.4
398	Misbah-ul-Haq	P	14	13	6	87*	56.85	3	127.6
383	Shoaib Malik	P	16	15	3	57	31.91	2	124.8
375	K.P.Pietersen	E	15	15	1	79	26.78	1	144.2
374	R.T.Ponting	A	13	12	2	98*	37.40	2	134.5
364	G.C.Smith	SA	12	12	2	89*	36.40	3	127.3
344	P.D.Collingwood	E	15	14	-	79	24.57	2	139.8
341	S.T.Jayasuriya	SL	11	11	1	88	34.10	3	154.3
337	A.Symonds	A	12	10	4	85*	56.16	2	170.2
328	G.Gambhir	I	12	11	-	75	29.81	4	128.3
323	L.R.P.L.Taylor	NZ	17	16	1	63	21.53	2	127.7
308	M.L.Hayden	A	9	9	3	73*	51.33	4	143.9

HIGHEST INDIVIDUAL INNINGS

Score	Balls				
117	57	C.H.Gayle	WI v SA	Johannesburg	2007-08
98*	55	R.T.Ponting	A v NZ	Auckland	2004-05
96	56	D.R.Martyn	A v SA	Brisbane	2005-06
90*	55	H.H.Gibbs	SA v WI	Johannesburg	2007-08
89*	58	G.C.Smith	SA v A	Johannesburg	2005-06
89*	56	J.M.Kemp	SA v NZ	Durban	2007-08
89	43	D.A.Warner	A v SA	Melbourne	2008-09
88	44	S.T.Jayasuriya	SL v K	Johannesburg	2007-08
87*	53	Misbah-ul-Haq	P v B	Karachi	2007-08
85*	46	A.Symonds	A v NZ	Perth	2007-08
81	50	Nazimuddin	B v P	Nairobi	2007-08

HIGHEST PARTNERSHIP FOR EACH WICKET

1st	145	C.H.Gayle/D.S.Smith	WI v SA	Johannesburg	2007-08
2nd	111	G.C.Smith/H.H.Gibbs	SA v A	Johannesburg	2005-06
3rd	120*	H.H.Gibbs/J.M.Kemp	SA v WI	Johannesburg	2007-08
4th	101	Younus Khan/Shoaib Malik	P v SL	Johannesburg	2007-08
5th	119*	Shoaib Malik/Misbah-ul-Haq	P v A	Johannesburg	2007-08
6th	77*	R.T.Ponting/M.E.K.Hussey	A v NZ	Auckland	2004-05
7th	91	P.D.Collingwood/M.H.Yardy	E v WI	The Oval	2007
8th	61	S.K.Raina/Harbhajan Singh	I v NZ	Christchurch	2008-09
9th	44	S.L.Malinga/C.R.D.Fernando	SL v NZ	Auckland	2006-07
10th	28	J.D.P.Oram/J.S.Patel	NZ v A	Perth	2007-08

BOWLING RECORDS
MOST WICKETS IN A CAREER

Wkts			Matches	Overs	Mdns	Runs	Avge	Best	R/Over
21	D.L.Vettori	NZ	14	56	0	300	14.28	4-20	5.35
20	Umar Gul	P	13	47.4	1	244	12.20	4-13	5.11
19	Shahid Afridi	P	15	57.3	2	351	18.47	4-19	6.10
18	Abdur Razzak	B	10	38	1	240	13.33	4-16	6.31
18	N.W.Bracken	A	15	49.5	2	316	17.55	3-11	6.34
16	J.S.Patel	NZ	11	33.1	1	269	16.81	3-20	8.11
15	P.M.Pollock	SA	12	40.3	1	290	20.60	3-28	7.62
15	C.R.D.Fernando	SL	13	46.0	3	337	22.46	3-19	7.32
15	I.K.Pathan	I	13	44	1	344	22.93	3-16	7.81

MOST WICKETS IN AN INNINGS

4- 7	M.R.Gillespie	NZ v K	Durban	2007-08
4- 9	D.W.Steyn	SA v WI	Port Elizabeth	2007-08
4-13	R.P.Singh	I v SA	Durban	2007-08
4-13	Umar Gul	P v SL	King City (NW)	2008-09
4-15	B.A.W.Mendis	SL v Z	King City (NW)	2008-09
4-16	Abdur Razzak	B v SA	Johannesburg	2008-09
4-17	M.Morkel	SA v NZ	Durban	2007-08
4-17	B.A.W.Mendis	SL v Ca	King City (NW)	2008-09
4-18	Mohammad Asif	P v I	Durban	2007-08
4-19	Shahid Afridi	P v Sc	Durban	2007-08
4-19	H.S.Baidwan	Ca v Ne	Belfast	2008
4-19	K.Weeraratne	SL v P	King City (NW)	2008-09
4-20	D.L.Vettori	NZ v I	Johannesburg	2007-08
4-20	S.R.Clark	A v SL	Cape Town	2007-08
4-21	A.R.Cusack	Ire v Sc	Belfast	2008
4-22	P.D.Collingwood	E v SL	Southampton	2006
4-24	J.Lewis	E v A	Southampton	2005
4-25	Umar Gul	P v Sc	Durban	2007-08
4-29	M.S.Kasprowicz	A v NZ	Auckland	2004-05
4-31	E.Chigumbura	Z v E	Cape Town	2007-08
4-34	Shakib Al Hasan	B v WI	Johannesburg	2007-08

HAT-TRICK

B.Lee	Australia v Bangladesh	Melbourne	2007-08

WICKET-KEEPING RECORDS

MOST DISMISSALS IN A CAREER

Dis			Matches	Ct	St
17	A.C.Gilchrist	Australia	13	17	0
17	Kamran Akmal	Pakistan	16	8	9
16	B.B.McCullum	New Zealand	21	13	3
12	Mushfiqur Rahim	Bangladesh	9	5	7

MOST DISMISSALS IN AN INNINGS

4 (4 ct)	A.C.Gilchrist	Australia v Zimbabwe	Cape Town	2007-08
4 (4 ct)	M.J.Prior	England v South Africa	Cape Town	2007-08
4 (4 ct)	A.C.Gilchrist	Australia v New Zealand	Perth	2007-08

MOST STUMPINGS IN AN INNINGS

3	Kamran Akmal	Pakistan v Kenya	Nairobi	2007-08
3	T.Taibu	Zimbabwe v Canada	King City (NW)	2008-09

FIELDING RECORDS

MOST CATCHES IN A CAREER

Total			Matches
13	L.R.P.L.Taylor	New Zealand	17
10	A.B.de Villiers	South Africa	13
10	M.E.K.Hussey	Australia	15

MOST CATCHES IN AN INNINGS

3	K.P.Pietersen	England v Australia	Southampton	2005
3	B.Lee	Australia v Sri Lanka	Cape Town	2007-08
3	L.R.P.L.Taylor	New Zealand v Australia	Perth	2007-08

WOMEN'S LIMITED-OVERS RECORDS

1973 to 22 March 2009

RESULTS SUMMARY

	LOI	Won	Lost	Tied	No Result
Australia	227	177	45	1	4
Denmark	33	6	27	–	–
England	230	126	95	2	7
India	173	90	78	1	4
International XI	18	3	14	–	1
Ireland	102	37	62	–	3
Jamaica	5	1	4	–	–
Japan	5	–	5	–	–
Netherlands	86	18	68	–	–
New Zealand	232	124	101	2	5
Pakistan	70	12	57	–	1
Scotland	8	1	7	–	–
South Africa	74	31	39	–	4
Sri Lanka	74	37	36	–	1
Trinidad & Tobago	6	2	4	–	–
West Indies	65	27	36	–	2
Young England	6	1	5	–	–

TEAM RECORDS

HIGHEST INNINGS TOTALS

455-5 (50)	New Zealand v Pakistan	Christchurch	1996-97
412-3 (50)	Australia v Denmark	Bombay	1997-98

LOWEST INNINGS TOTALS

22 (23.4)	Netherlands v West Indies	Deventer	2008
23 (24.1)	Pakistan v Australia	Melbourne	1996-97
24 (21.3)	Scotland v England	Reading	2001

BATTING RECORDS

2000 RUNS IN LOI

Runs		Career	M	I	NO	HS	Avge	100	50
4844	B.J.Clark (A)	1991-2005	118	114	12	229*	47.49	5	30
4715	K.L.Rolton (A)	1995-2008	137	128	32	154*	49.11	8	32
4064	D.A.Hockley (NZ)	1982-2000	118	115	18	117	41.89	4	34
3657	C.M.Edwards (E)	1997-2009	124	116	16	173*	36.57	4	24
3611	S.C.Taylor (E)	1998-2009	109	104	15	156*	40.57	8	19
3550	M.Raj (I)	1999-2009	115	103	28	114*	47.33	2	28
2919	H.M.Tiffen (NZ)	1999-2009	117	111	16	100	30.72	1	18
2844	E.C.Drumm (NZ)	1992-2006	101	94	13	116	35.11	2	19
2706	A.Chopra (I)	1995-2009	116	101	20	100	33.40	1	17
2630	L.M.Keightley (A)	1995-2005	82	78	12	156*	39.84	4	21
2237	L.C.Sthalekar (A)	2001-2009	88	81	18	104*	35.50	2	15
2201	R.J.Rolls (NZ)	1997-2007	104	91	3	114	25.01	2	12
2121	J.A.Brittin (E)	1979-1998	63	59	9	138*	42.42	5	8
2091	J.Sharma (I)	2002-2008	77	75	7	138*	30.75	2	14

HIGHEST INDIVIDUAL INNINGS

229*	B.J.Clark	Australia v Denmark	Bombay	1997-98
173*	C.M.Edwards	England v Ireland	Poona	1997-98
168	S.W.Bates	New Zealand v Pakistan	Sydney	2008-09
156*	L.M.Keightley	Australia v Pakistan	Melbourne	1996-97
156*	S.C.Taylor	England v India	Lord's	2006
154*	K.L.Rolton	Australia v Sri Lanka	Christchurch	2000-01
153*	J.Logtenberg	South Africa v Netherlands	Deventer	2007
151	K.L.Rolton	Australia v Ireland	Dublin	2005

HIGHEST PARTNERSHIP FOR EACH WICKET

1st	268	S.J.Taylor/C.M.G.Atkins	E v SA	Lord's	2008
2nd	262	H.M.Tiffen/S.W.Bates	NZ v P	Sydney	2008-09
3rd	244	K.L.Rolton/L.C.Sthalekar	A v Ire	Dublin	2005
4th	224*	J.Logtenberg//M.du Preez	SA v Ne	Deventer	2007
5th	188*	S.C.Taylor/J.Cassar	E v SL	Lincoln, NZ	2001-02
6th	139*	S.J.McGlashan/N.J.Browne	NZ v SA	Bowral	2008-09
7th	104*	S.J.Tsukigawa/N.J.Browne	NZ v E	Madras	2006-07
8th	85*	S.I.Clarke/N.J.Shaw	E v Sc	Reading	2001
9th	73	L.R.F.Askew/I.T.Guha	E v NZ	Madras	2006-07
10th	43	A.Sharma/G.Sultana	I v E	Sydney	2008-09

BOWLING RECORDS

100 WICKETS IN LOI

Wkts		Career	M	Overs	Runs	Avge	Best	4wI
180	C.L.Fitzpatrick (A)	1993-2007	109	1002.5	3023	16.79	5-14	11
141	N.David (I)	1995-2008	97	815.2	2305	16.34	5-20	6
109	J.Goswami (I)	2002-2009	100	789.1	2471	22.66	5-16	4
102	C.E.Taylor (E)	1988-2005	105	856.4	2443	23.95	4-13	2

MOST WICKETS IN AN INNINGS

7-4	Sajjida Shah	Pakistan v Japan	Amsterdam	2003
7-8	J.M.Chamberlain	England v Denmark	Haarlem	1991
7-24	S.Nitschke	Australia v England	Kidderminster	2005
6-10	J.Lord	New Zealand v India	Auckland	1981-82
6-10	M.Maben	India v Sri Lanka	Kandy	2003-04
6-20	G.L.Page	New Zealand v Trinidad & T	St Albans	1973
6-32	B.McNeill	New Zealand v England	Lincoln, NZ	2007-08

WICKET-KEEPING AND FIELDING RECORDS

100 DISMISSALS IN LOI

Total			Career	LOI	Ct	St
133	R.J.Rolls	New Zealand	1997-2007	104	89	44
114	J.Smit	England	1993-2007	109	69	45

SIX DISMISSALS IN AN INNINGS

6 (4ct, 2st)	S.L.Illingworth	New Zealand v Australia	Beckenham	1993
6 (1ct, 5st)	V.Kalpana	India v Denmark	Slough	1993
6 (2ct, 4st)	Batool Fatima	Pakistan v West Indies	Karachi	2003-04

Total			LOI	Career
45	B.J.Clark	Australia	118	1991-2005
41	D.A.Hockley	New Zealand	118	1982-2000

FOUR CATCHES IN AN INNINGS IN THE FIELD

4	Z.J.Goss	Australia v New Zealand	Adelaide	1995-96

APPEARANCE RECORDS
120 APPEARANCES

137	K.L.Rolton	Australia	1995-2009
124	C.M.Edwards	England	1997-2009

100 MATCHES AS CAPTAIN

			Won	Lost	No Result	
101	B.J.Clark	Australia	83	17	1	1994-2005

ICC WOMEN'S WORLD CUP FINAL

North Sydney Oval, 22 March 2009. Toss: New Zealand. **ENGLAND** won by four wickets. New Zealand 166 (47.2; L.R.Doolan 48, H.M.Tiffen 30; N.J.Shaw 4-34). England 167-6 (46.1; C.M.G.Atkins 40, S.J.Taylor 39; L.R.Doolan 3-23). Award: N.J.Shaw.

WORLD CUP FINALS

Year	Venue	Winner	Finalist
1973	England	England	Australia
1978	India	Australia	England
1982	New Zealand	Australia	England
1988	Australia	Australia	England
1993	England	England	New Zealand
1997	India	Australia	New Zealand
2000	New Zealand	New Zealand	Australia
2005	South Africa	Australia	India

WOMEN'S TEST CRICKET RECORDS

1934-35 to 1 March 2009
RESULTS SUMMARY

| | Opponents | Tests | Won by | | | | | | | | | | | Drawn |
			E	A	NZ	SA	WI	I	P	SL	Ire	H	
England	Australia	43	8	10	–	–	–	–	–	–	–	–	25
	New Zealand	23	6	–	0	–	–	–	–	–	–	–	17
	South Africa	6	2	–	–	0	–	–	–	–	–	–	4
	West Indies	3	2	–	–	–	0	–	–	–	–	–	1
	India	12	1	–	–	–	–	1	–	–	–	–	10
Australia	New Zealand	13	–	4	1	–	–	–	–	–	–	–	8
	West Indies	2	–	0	–	–	0	–	–	–	–	–	2
	India	9	–	4	–	–	–	0	–	–	–	–	5
New Zealand	South Africa	3	–	–	1	0	–	–	–	–	–	–	2
	India	6	–	–	0	–	–	0	–	–	–	–	6
South Africa	India	1	–	–	–	0	–	1	–	–	–	–	–
	Holland	1	–	–	–	1	–	–	–	–	–	0	–
West Indies	India	6	–	–	–	–	1	1	–	–	–	–	4
	Pakistan	1	–	–	–	–	0	–	0	–	–	–	1
Pakistan	Sri Lanka	1	–	–	–	–	–	–	0	1	–	–	–
	Ireland	1	–	–	–	–	–	–	0	–	1	–	–
		131	19	18	2	1	1	3	0	1	1	0	85

	Tests	Won	Lost	Drawn	Toss Won
England	87	19	11	57	52
Australia	67	18	9	40	22
New Zealand	45	2	10	33	21
South Africa	11	1	4	6	6
West Indies	12	1	3	8	6†
India	34	3	6	25	16†
Pakistan	3	–	2	1	1
Sri Lanka	1	1	–	–	1
Ireland	1	1	–	–	–
Holland	1	–	1	–	–

† Results of tosses in five of the six India v West Indies Tests in 1976-77 are not known

TEAM RECORDS
HIGHEST INNINGS TOTALS

569-6d	Australia v England	Guildford	1998
525	Australia v India	Ahmedabad	1983-84
517-8	New Zealand v England	Scarborough	1996
503-5d	England v New Zealand	Christchurch	1934-35
497	England v South Africa	Shenley	2003
467	India v England	Taunton	2002
455	England v South Africa	Taunton	2003
440	West Indies v Pakistan	Karachi	2003-04
427-4d	Australia v England	Worcester	1998
426-7d	Pakistan v West Indies	Karachi	2003-04
426-9d	India v England	Blackpool	1986
414	England v New Zealand	Scarborough	1996

414	England v Australia	Guildford	1998
404-9d	India v South Africa	Paarl	2001-02
403-8d	New Zealand v India	Nelson	1994-95

The highest totals for countries not included above are:

316	South Africa v England	Shenley	2003
193-3d	Ireland v Pakistan	Dublin	2000
108	Holland v South Africa	Rotterdam	2007

LOWEST INNINGS TOTALS

35	England v Australia	Melbourne	1957-58
38	Australia v England	Melbourne	1957-58
44	New Zealand v England	Christchurch	1934-35
47	Australia v England	Brisbane	1934-35
50	Holland v South Africa	Rotterdam	2007
53	Pakistan v Ireland	Dublin	2000

The lowest innings totals for countries not included above are:

65	India v West Indies	Jammu	1976-77
67	West Indies v England	Canterbury	1979
89	South Africa v New Zealand	Durban	1971-72

BATTING RECORDS
1000 RUNS IN TESTS

		Career	M	I	NO	HS	Avge	100	50
1935	J.A.Brittin (E)	1979-98	27	44	5	167	49.61	5	11
1594	R.Heyhoe-Flint (E)	1960-79	22	38	3	179	45.54	3	10
1317	C.M.Edwards (E)	1996-2008	17	31	2	117	45.41	3	7
1301	D.A.Hockley (NZ)	1979-96	19	29	4	126*	52.04	4	7
1164	C.A.Hodges (E)	1984-92	18	31	2	158*	40.13	2	6
1110	S.Agarwal (I)	1984-95	13	23	1	190	50.45	4	4
1078	E.Bakewell (E)	1968-79	12	22	4	124	59.88	4	7
1008	S.C.Taylor (E)	1999-2008	14	25	2	177	43.82	4	2
1007	M.E.Maclagan (E)	1934-51	14	25	1	119	41.95	2	6

HIGHEST INDIVIDUAL INNINGS ‡ *On debut*

242	Kiran Baluch	P v WI	Karachi	2003-04
214	M.Raj	I v E	Taunton	2002
209*	K.L.Rolton	A v E	Leeds	2001
204	K.E.Flavell	NZ v E	Scarborough	1996
204‡	M.A.J.Goszko	A v E	Shenley	2001
200	J.Broadbent	A v E	Guildford	1998
193	D.A.Annetts	A v E	Collingham	1987
190	S.Agarwal	I v E	Worcester	1986
189	E.A.Snowball	E v NZ	Christchurch	1934-35
179	R.Heyhoe-Flint	E v A	The Oval	1976
177	S.C.Taylor	E v SA	Shenley	2003
176*	K.L.Rolton	A v E	Worcester	1998
167	J.A.Brittin	E v A	Harrogate	1998
161*	E.C.Drumm	E v A	Christchurch	1994-95
160	B.A.Daniels	E v NZ	Scarborough	1996
158*	C.A.Hodges	E v NZ	Canterbury	1984

| 155* | P.F.McKelvey | NZ v E | Wellington | 1968-69 |

FIVE HUNDREDS

		_M_	_I_	_E_	_A_	_NZ_	Opponents _SA_	_WI_	_IND_	_P_	_SL_	_IRE_
5	J.A.Brittin (E)	27	44	–	3	1	–	1	–	–	–	–

HIGHEST PARTNERSHIP FOR EACH WICKET

1st	241	Kiran Baluch/Sajjida Shah	P v WI	Karachi	2003-04
2nd	235	E.A.Snowball/M.E.Hide	E v NZ	Christchurch	1934-35
3rd	309	L.A.Reeler/D.A.Annetts	A v E	Collingham	1987
4th	253	K.L.Rolton/L.C.Broadfoot	A v E	Leeds	2001
5th	138	J.Logtenberg/C.van der Westhuizen	SA v E	Shenley	2003
6th	132	B.A.Daniels/K.M.Leng	E v NZ	Scarborough	1996
7th	157	M.Raj/J.Goswami	I v E	Taunton	2002
8th	181	S.J.Griffiths/D.L.Wilson	A v NZ	Auckland	1989-90
9th	107	B.Botha/M.Payne	SA v NZ	Cape Town	1971-72
10th	119	S.Nitschke/C.R.Smith	A v E	Hove	2005

BOWLING RECORDS

50 WICKETS IN TESTS

Wkts		Career	M	Balls	Runs	Avge	Best	5wI	10wM
77	M.B.Duggan (E)	1949-63	17	3734	1039	13.49	7- 6	5	–
68	E.R.Wilson (A)	1948-58	11	2885	803	11.80	7- 7	4	2
63	D.F.Edulji (I)	1976-91	20	5098†	1624	25.77	6- 64	1	–
60	M.E.Maclagan (E)	1934-51	14	3432	935	15.58	7- 10	3	–
60	C.L.Fitzpatrick (A)	1991-2006	13	3603	1147	19.11	5-292	–	–
60	S.Kulkarni (I)	1976-91	19	3320†	1647	27.45	6- 99	5	–
57	R.H.Thompson (A)	1972-85	16	4304	1040	18.24	5- 33	1	–
55	J.Lord (NZ)	1966-79	15	3108	1049	19.07	6-119	4	1
50	E.Bakewell (E)	1968-79	12	2697	831	16.62	7- 61	3	1

† _Excludes balls bowled in Sixth Test v West Indies 1976-77_

TEN WICKETS IN A TEST

13-226	Shaiza Khan	P v WI	Karachi	2003-04
11- 16	E.R.Wilson	A v E	Melbourne	1957-58
11- 63	J.M.Greenwood	E v WI	Canterbury	1979
11-107	L.C.Pearson	E v A	Sydney	2002-03
10- 65	E.R.Wilson	A v NZ	Wellington	1947-48
10- 75	E.Bakewell	E v WI	Birmingham	1979
10- 78	J.Goswami	I v E	Taunton	2006
10-107	K.Price	A v I	Lucknow	1983-84
10-118	D.A.Gordon	A v E	Melbourne	1968-69
10-137	J.Lord	NZ v A	Melbourne	1978-79

SEVEN WICKETS IN AN INNINGS

8-53	N.David	I v E	Jamshedpur	1995-96
7- 6	M.B.Duggan	E v A	Melbourne	1957-58
7- 7	E.R.Wilson	A v E	Melbourne	1957-58
7-10	M.E.Maclagan	E v A	Brisbane	1934-35
7-18	A.Palmer	A v E	Brisbane	1934-35
7-24	L.Johnston	A v NZ	Melbourne	1971-72
7-34	G.E.McConway	E v I	Worcester	1986
7-41	J.A.Burley	NZ v E	The Oval	1966
7-51	L.C.Pearson	E v A	Sydney	2002-03

| 7-59 | Shaiza Khan | P v WI | Karachi | 2003-04 |
| 7-61 | E.Bakewell | E v WI | Birmingham | 1979 |

HAT-TRICKS

| E.R.Wilson | Australia v England | Melbourne | 1957-58 |
| Shaiza Khan | Pakistan v West Indies | Karachi | 2003-04 |

WICKET-KEEPING, FIELDING AND APPEARANCE RECORDS
25 DISMISSALS IN TESTS

Total			Tests	Ct	St	
58	C.Matthews	Australia	20	46	12	1984-95
43	J.Smit	England	21	39	4	1992-2006
36	S.A.Hodges	England	11	19	17	1969-79
28	B.A.Brentnall	New Zealand	10	16	12	1966-72

EIGHT DISMISSALS IN A TEST

| 9 (8ct, 1st) | C.Matthews | A v I | Adelaide | 1990-91 |
| 8 (6ct, 2st) | L.Nye | E v NZ | New Plymouth | 1991-92 |

SIX DISMISSALS IN AN INNINGS

| 8 (6ct, 2st) | L.Nye | E v NZ | New Plymouth | 1991-92 |
| 6 (2ct, 4st) | B.A.Brentnall | NZ v SA | Johannesburg | 1971-72 |

20 CATCHES IN THE FIELD IN TESTS

Total			Tests	
25	C.A.Hodges	England	18	1984-92
21	S.Shah	India	20	1976-91
20	L.A.Fullston	Australia	12	1984-87

25 TEST MATCH APPEARANCES

| 27 | J.A.Brittin | England | 1979-98 |

12 MATCHES AS CAPTAIN

			Won	Lost	Drawn	
14	P.F.McKelvey	New Zealand	2	3	9	1966–79
12	R.Heyhoe-Flint	England	2	–	10	1966–76
12	S.Rangaswamy	India	1	2	9	1976–84

INTERNATIONAL TEST MATCH RESULTS

Matches completed by 22 March 2009, but excluding the 1st New Zealand v India Test.

	Opponents	Tests	Won by										Tied	Drawn
			E	A	SA	WI	NZ	I	P	SL	Z	B		
England	Australia	316	97	131	–	–	–	–	–	–	–	–	–	88
	South Africa	134	55	–	28	–	–	–	–	–	–	–	–	51
	West Indies	143	41	–	–	53	–	–	–	–	–	–	–	49
	New Zealand	94	45	–	–	–	8	–	–	–	–	–	–	41
	India	99	34	–	–	–	–	19	–	–	–	–	–	46
	Pakistan	67	19	–	–	–	–	–	12	–	–	–	–	36
	Sri Lanka	21	8	–	–	–	–	–	–	6	–	–	–	7
	Zimbabwe	6	3	–	–	–	–	–	–	–	0	–	–	3
	Bangladesh	4	4	–	–	–	–	–	–	–	–	0	–	–
Australia	South Africa	83	–	47	18	–	–	–	–	–	–	–	–	18
	West Indies	105	–	50	–	32	–	–	–	–	–	–	1	22
	New Zealand	48	–	24	–	–	7	–	–	–	–	–	–	17
	India	76	–	34	–	–	–	18	–	–	–	–	1	23
	Pakistan	52	–	24	–	–	–	–	11	–	–	–	–	17
	Sri Lanka	20	–	13	–	–	–	–	–	1	–	–	–	6
	Zimbabwe	3	–	3	–	–	–	–	–	–	0	–	–	–
	Bangladesh	4	–	4	–	–	–	–	–	–	–	0	–	–
South Africa	West Indies	22	–	–	14	3	–	–	–	–	–	–	–	5
	New Zealand	35	–	–	20	–	4	–	–	–	–	–	–	11
	India	22	–	–	10	–	–	5	–	–	–	–	–	7
	Pakistan	16	–	–	8	–	–	–	3	–	–	–	–	5
	Sri Lanka	17	–	–	8	–	–	–	–	4	–	–	–	5
	Zimbabwe	7	–	–	6	–	–	–	–	–	0	–	–	1
	Bangladesh	8	–	–	8	–	–	–	–	–	–	0	–	–
West Indies	New Zealand	37	–	–	–	10	9	–	–	–	–	–	–	18
	India	82	–	–	–	30	–	11	–	–	–	–	–	41
	Pakistan	44	–	–	–	14	–	–	15	–	–	–	–	15
	Sri Lanka	12	–	–	–	3	–	–	–	6	–	–	–	3
	Zimbabwe	6	–	–	–	4	–	–	–	–	–	–	–	2
	Bangladesh	4	–	–	–	3	–	–	–	–	–	0	–	1
New Zealand	India	44	–	–	–	–	9	14	–	–	–	–	–	21
	Pakistan	45	–	–	–	–	6	–	21	–	–	–	–	18
	Sri Lanka	24	–	–	–	–	9	–	–	5	–	–	–	10
	Zimbabwe	13	–	–	–	–	7	–	–	–	0	–	–	6
	Bangladesh	8	–	–	–	–	7	–	–	–	–	0	–	1
India	Pakistan	59	–	–	–	–	–	9	12	–	–	–	–	38
	Sri Lanka	29	–	–	–	–	–	11	–	5	–	–	–	13
	Zimbabwe	11	–	–	–	–	–	7	–	–	2	–	–	2
	Bangladesh	5	–	–	–	–	–	4	–	–	–	0	–	1
Pakistan	Sri Lanka	34	–	–	–	–	–	–	15	7	–	–	–	12
	Zimbabwe	14	–	–	–	–	–	–	8	–	2	–	–	4
	Bangladesh	6	–	–	–	–	–	–	6	–	–	0	–	–
Sri Lanka	Zimbabwe	15	–	–	–	–	–	–	–	10	0	–	–	5
	Bangladesh	12	–	–	–	–	–	–	–	12	–	0	–	–
Zimbabwe	Bangladesh	8	–	–	–	–	–	–	–	–	4	1	–	3
		1914	306	330	120	152	66	98	103	56	8	1	2	672

	Tests	Won	Lost	Drawn	Tied	Toss Won
England	884	306	257	321	–	425
Australia	707	330	184	191	2	355
South Africa	344	120	121	103	–	164
West Indies	455	152	146	156	1	240
New Zealand	348	66	139	143	–	177
India	427	98	136	192	1	221
Pakistan	337	103	89	145	–	159
Sri Lanka	184	56	67	61	–	94
Zimbabwe	83	8	49	26	–	49
Bangladesh	59	1	52	6	–	28

INTERNATIONAL TEST CRICKET RECORDS

(Matches completed by 22 March 2009, but excluding the 1st New Zealand v India test)

TEAM RECORDS

HIGHEST INNINGS TOTALS

952-6d	Sri Lanka v India	Colombo (RPS)	1997-98
903-7d	England v Australia	The Oval	1938
849	England v West Indies	Kingston	1929-30
790-3d	West Indies v Pakistan	Kingston	1957-58
765-6d	Pakistan v Sri Lanka	Karachi	2008-09
758-8d	Australia v West Indies	Kingston	1954-55
756-5d	Sri Lanka v South Africa	Colombo (SSC)	2006
751-5d	West Indies v England	St John's	2003-04
749-9d	West Indies v England	Bridgetown	2008-09
747	West Indies v South Africa	St John's	2004-05
735-6d	Australia v Zimbabwe	Perth	2003-04
729-6d	Australia v England	Lord's	1930
713-3d	Sri Lanka v Zimbabwe	Bulawayo	2003-04
708	Pakistan v England	The Oval	1987
705-7d	India v Australia	Sydney	2003-04
701	Australia v England	The Oval	1934
699-5	Pakistan v India	Lahore	1989-90
695	Australia v England	The Oval	1930
692-8d	West Indies v England	The Oval	1995
687-8d	West Indies v England	The Oval	1976
682-6d	South Africa v England	Lord's	2003
681-8d	West Indies v England	Port-of-Spain	1953-54
679-7d	Pakistan v India	Lahore	2005-06
676-7	India v Sri Lanka	Kanpur	1986-87
675-5d	India v Pakistan	Multan	2003-04
674-6	Pakistan v India	Faisalabad	1984-85
674	Australia v India	Adelaide	1947-48
671-4	New Zealand v Sri Lanka	Wellington	1990-91
668	Australia v West Indies	Bridgetown	1954-55
664	India v England	The Oval	2007
660-5d	West Indies v New Zealand	Wellington	1994-95
659-8d	Australia v England	Sydney	1946-47
658-8d	England v Australia	Nottingham	1938
658-9d	South Africa v West Indies	Durban	2003-04
657-7d	India v Australia	Calcutta	2000-01
657-8d	Pakistan v West Indies	Bridgetown	1957-58

656-8d	Australia v England	Manchester	1964
654-5	England v South Africa	Durban	1938-39
653-4d	England v India	Lord's	1990
653-4d	Australia v England	Leeds	1993
652-7d	England v India	Madras	1984-85
652-7d	Australia v South Africa	Johannesburg	2001-02
652-8d	West Indies v England	Lord's	1973
652	Pakistan v India	Faisalabad	1982-83
651	South Africa v Australia	Capetown	2008-09
650-6d	Australia v West Indies	Bridgetown	1964-65

The highest for Zimbabwe is 563-9d (v WI, Harare, 2001), and for Bangladesh 488 (v Z, Chittagong, 2004-05).

LOWEST INNINGS TOTALS

† One batsman absent

26	New Zealand v England	Auckland	1954-55
30	South Africa v England	Port Elizabeth	1895-96
30	South Africa v England	Birmingham	1924
35	South Africa v England	Cape Town	1898-99
36	Australia v England	Birmingham	1902
36	South Africa v Australia	Melbourne	1931-32
42	Australia v England	Sydney	1887-88
42	New Zealand v Australia	Wellington	1945-46
42†	India v England	Lord's	1974
43	South Africa v England	Cape Town	1888-89
44	Australia v England	The Oval	1896
45	England v Australia	Sydney	1886-87
45	South Africa v Australia	Melbourne	1931-32
46	England v West Indies	Port-of-Spain	1993-94
47	South Africa v England	Cape Town	1888-89
47	New Zealand v England	Lord's	1958
47	West Indies v England	Kingston	2003-04

The lowest for Pakistan is 53† (v A, Sharjah, 2002-03), for Sri Lanka 71 (v P, Kandy, 1994-95), for Zimbabwe 54 (v SA, Cape Town, 2004-05), and for Bangladesh 62 (v SL, Colombo PPS, 2006-07).

BATTING RECORDS

5000 RUNS IN A TEST CAREER

Runs			M	I	NO	HS	Avge	100	50
12429	S.R.Tendulkar	I	156	256	27	248*	54.27	41	51
11912	B.C.Lara	WI	130	230	6	400*	53.17	34	48
11174	A.R.Border	A	156	265	44	205	50.56	27	63
10927	S.R.Waugh	A	168	260	46	200	51.06	32	50
10860	R.T.Ponting	A	130	219	26	257	56.26	37	45
10486	R.Dravid	I	130	225	26	270	52.69	26	53
10194	J.H.Kallis	SA	130	219	32	189*	54.51	31	51
10122	S.M.Gavaskar	I	125	214	16	236*	51.12	34	45
8900	G.A.Gooch	E	118	215	6	333	42.58	20	46
8832	Javed Miandad	P	124	189	21	280*	52.57	23	43
8829	Inzamam-ul-Haq	P	119	198	22	329	50.16	25	46
8540	I.V.A.Richards	WI	121	182	12	291	50.23	24	45
8502	S.Chanderpaul	WI	119	202	32	203*	50.01	21	52

Runs			M	I	NO	HS	Avge	100	50
8463	A.J.Stewart	E	133	235	21	190	39.54	15	45
8437	M.L.Hayden	A	102	182	14	380	50.22	29	28
8251	D.P.M.D.Jayawardena	SL	102	167	12	374	53.23	25	32
8231	D.I.Gower	E	117	204	18	215	44.25	18	39
8114	G.Boycott	E	108	193	23	246*	47.72	22	42
8032	G.St A.Sobers	WI	93	160	21	365*	57.78	26	30
8029	M.E.Waugh	A	128	209	17	153*	41.81	20	47
7728	M.A.Atherton	E	115	212	7	185*	37.70	16	46
7674	J.L.Langer	A	104	180	12	250	45.67	23	30
7624	M.C.Cowdrey	E	114	188	15	182	44.06	22	38
7558	C.G.Greenidge	WI	108	185	16	226	44.72	19	34
7525	M.A.Taylor	A	104	186	13	334*	43.49	19	40
7515	C.H.Lloyd	WI	110	175	14	242*	46.67	19	39
7487	D.L.Haynes	WI	116	202	25	184	42.29	18	39
7422	D.C.Boon	A	107	190	20	200	43.65	21	32
7289	G.Kirsten	SA	101	176	15	275	45.27	21	34
7249	W.R.Hammond	E	85	140	16	336*	58.45	22	24
7212	S.C.Ganguly	I	113	188	17	239	42.17	16	35
7172	S.P.Fleming	NZ	111	189	10	274*	40.06	9	46
7110	G.S.Chappell	A	87	151	19	247*	53.86	24	31
6996	D.G.Bradman	A	52	80	10	334	99.94	29	13
6973	S.T.Jayasuriya	SL	110	188	14	340	40.07	14	31
6971	L.Hutton	E	79	138	15	364	56.67	19	33
6868	D.B.Vengsarkar	I	116	185	22	166	42.13	17	35
6806	K.F.Barrington	E	82	131	15	256	58.67	20	35
6770	M. Yousuf Youhana	P	79	134	12	223	55.49	23	28
6764	K.C.Sangakkara	SL	80	132	9	287	54.99	18	30
6744	G.P.Thorpe	E	100	179	28	200*	44.66	16	39
6446	V.V.S.Laxman	I	102	169	24	281	44.45	13	37
6361	P.A.de Silva	SL	93	159	11	267	42.97	20	22
6330	G.C.Smith	SA	76	133	9	277	51.04	18	25
6227	R.B.Kanhai	WI	79	137	6	256	47.53	15	28
6215	M.Azharuddin	I	99	147	9	199	45.03	22	21
6167	H.H.Gibbs	SA	90	154	7	228	41.95	14	26
6149	R.N.Harvey	A	79	137	10	205	48.41	21	24
6080	G.R.Viswanath	I	91	155	10	222	41.93	14	35
5949	R.B.Richardson	WI	86	146	12	194	44.39	16	27
5825	M.E.Trescothick	E	76	143	10	219	43.79	14	29
5807	D.C.S.Compton	E	78	131	15	278	50.06	17	28
5768	Salim Malik	P	103	154	22	237	43.69	15	29
5764	N.Hussain	E	96	171	16	207	37.19	14	33
5762	C.L.Hooper	WI	102	173	15	233	36.46	13	27
5719	M.P.Vaughan	E	82	147	9	197	41.44	18	18
5535	R.R.Sarwan	WI	79	138	8	291	42.57	14	31
5534	V.Sehwag	I	65	112	4	319	51.24	15	17
5502	M.S.Atapattu	SL	90	156	15	249	39.02	16	17
5475	A.C.Gilchrist	A	95	135	20	204*	47.60	17	25
5444	M.D.Crowe	NZ	77	131	11	299	45.36	17	18
5410	J.B.Hobbs	E	61	102	7	211	56.94	15	28
5401	C.H.Gayle	WI	80	140	5	317	40.00	10	30
5357	K.D.Walters	A	74	125	14	250	48.26	15	33
5345	I.M.Chappell	A	75	136	10	196	42.42	14	26
5334	J.G.Wright	NZ	82	148	7	185	37.82	12	23
5312	M.J.Slater	A	74	131	7	219	42.84	14	21
5248	Kapil Dev	I	131	184	15	163	31.05	8	27
5234	W.M.Lawry	A	67	123	12	210	47.15	13	27

Runs			M	I	NO	HS	Avge	100	50
5200	I.T.Botham	E	102	161	6	208	33.54	14	22
5138	J.H.Edrich	E	77	127	9	310*	43.54	12	24
5129	Younus Khan	P	60	106	7	313	51.80	16	20
5105	A.Ranatunga	SL	93	155	12	135*	35.69	4	38
5062	Zaheer Abbas	P	78	124	11	274	44.79	12	20

The most for Zimbabwe is 4794 (63 innings) by A.Flower, and for Bangladesh 3026 by Habibul Bashar (99 innings).

750 RUNS IN A SERIES

Runs			Series	M	I	NO	HS	Avge	100	50
974	D.G.Bradman	A v E	1930	5	7	–	334	139.14	4	–
905	W.R.Hammond	E v A	1928-29	5	9	1	251	113.12	4	–
839	M.A.Taylor	A v E	1989	6	11	1	219	83.90	2	5
834	R.N.Harvey	A v SA	1952-53	5	9	–	205	92.66	4	3
829	I.V.A.Richards	WI v E	1976	4	7	–	291	118.42	3	2
827	C.L.Walcott	WI v A	1954-55	5	10	–	155	82.70	5	2
824	G.St A.Sobers	WI v P	1957-58	5	8	2	365*	137.33	3	3
810	D.G.Bradman	A v E	1936-37	5	9	–	270	90.00	3	1
806	D.G.Bradman	A v SA	1931-32	5	5	1	299*	201.50	4	–
798	B.C.Lara	WI v E	1993-94	5	8	–	375	99.75	2	2
779	E.de C.Weekes	WI v I	1948-49	5	7	–	194	111.28	4	2
774	S.M.Gavaskar	I v WI	1970-71	4	8	3	220	154.80	4	3
765	B.C.Lara	WI v E	1995	6	10	1	179	85.00	3	3
761	Mudassar Nazar	P v I	1982-83	6	8	2	231	126.83	4	1
758	D.G.Bradman	A v E	1934	5	8	–	304	94.75	2	1
753	D.C.S.Compton	E v SA	1947	5	8	–	208	94.12	4	2
752	G.A.Gooch	E v I	1990	3	6	–	333	125.33	3	2

HIGHEST INDIVIDUAL INNINGS

400*	B.C.Lara	WI v E	St John's	2003-04
380	M.L.Hayden	A v Z	Perth	2003-04
375	B.C.Lara	WI v E	St John's	1993-94
374	D.P.M.D.Jayawardena	SL v SA	Colombo (SSC)	2006
365*	G.St A.Sobers	WI v P	Kingston	1957-58
364	L.Hutton	E v A	The Oval	1938
340	S.T.Jayasuriya	SL v I	Colombo (RPS)	1997-98
337	Hanif Mohammed	P v WI	Bridgetown	1957-58
336*	W.R.Hammond	E v NZ	Auckland	1932-33
334*	M.A.Taylor	A v P	Peshawar	1998-99
334	D.G.Bradman	A v E	Leeds	1930
333	G.A.Gooch	E v I	Lord's	1990
329	Inzamam-ul-Haq	P v NZ	Lahore	2001-02
325	A.Sandham	E v WI	Kingston	1929-30
319	V.Sehwag	I v SA	Chennai	2007-08
317	C.H.Gayle	WI v SA	St John's	2004-05
313	Younus Khan	P v SL	Karachi	2008-09
311	R.B.Simpson	A v E	Manchester	1964
310*	J.H.Edrich	E v NZ	Leeds	1965
309	V.Sehwag	I v P	Multan	2003-04
307	R.M.Cowper	A v E	Melbourne	1965-66
304	D.G.Bradman	A v E	Leeds	1934
302	L.G.Rowe	WI v E	Bridgetown	1973-74

299*	D.G.Bradman	A v SA	Adelaide	1931-32
299	M.D.Crowe	NZ v SL	Wellington	1990-91
291	I.V.A.Richards	WI v E	The Oval	1976
291	R.R.Sarwan	WI v E	Bridgetown	2008-09
287	R.E.Foster	E v A	Sydney	1903-04
287	K.C.Sangakkara	SL v SA	Colombo (SSC)	2006
285*	P.B.H.May	E v WI	Birmingham	1957
281	V.V.S.Laxman	I v A	Calcutta	2000-01
280*	Javed Miandad	P v I	Hyderabad	1982-83
278	D.C.S.Compton	E v P	Nottingham	1954
277	B.C.Lara	WI v A	Sydney	1992-93
277	G.C.Smith	SA v E	Birmingham	2003
275*	D.J.Cullinan	SA v NZ	Auckland	1998-99
275	G.Kirsten	SA v E	Durban	1999-00
274*	S.P.Fleming	NZ v SL	Colombo (SSC)	2002-03
274	R.G.Pollock	SA v A	Durban	1969-70
274	Zaheer Abbas	P v E	Birmingham	1971
271	Javed Miandad	P v NZ	Auckland	1988-89
270*	G.A.Headley	WI v E	Kingston	1934-35
270	D.G.Bradman	A v E	Melbourne	1936-37
270	R.Dravid	I v P	Rawalpindi	2003-04
270	K.C.Sangakkara	SL v Z	Bulawayo	2003-04
268	G.N.Yallop	A v P	Melbourne	1983-84
267*	B.A.Young	NZ v SL	Dunedin	1996-97
267	P.A.de Silva	SL v NZ	Wellington	1990-91
267	Younis Khan	P v I	Bangalore	2004-05
266	W.H.Ponsford	A v E	The Oval	1934
266	D.L.Houghton	Z v SL	Bulawayo	1994-95
262*	D.L.Amiss	E v WI	Kingston	1973-74
262	S.P.Fleming	NZ v SA	Cape Town	2005-06
261*	R.R.Sarwan	WI v B	Kingston	2004
261	F.M.M.Worrell	WI v E	Nottingham	1950
260	C.C.Hunte	WI v P	Kingston	1957-58
260	Javed Miandad	P v E	The Oval	1987
259	G.M.Turner	NZ v WI	Georgetown	1971-72
259	G.C.Smith	SA v E	Lord's	2003
258	T.W.Graveney	E v WI	Nottingham	1957
258	S.M.Nurse	WI v NZ	Christchurch	1968-69
257*	Wasim Akram	P v Z	Sheikhupura	1996-97
257	R.T.Ponting	A v I	Melbourne	2003-04
256	R.B.Kanhai	WI v I	Calcutta	1958-59
256	K.F.Barrington	E v A	Manchester	1964
255*	D.J.McGlew	SA v NZ	Wellington	1952-53
254	D.G.Bradman	A v E	Lord's	1930
254	V.Sehwag	I v P	Lahore	2005-06
253	S.T.Jayasuriya	SL v P	Faisalabad	2004-05
251	W.R.Hammond	E v A	Sydney	1928-29
250	K.D.Walters	A v NZ	Christchurch	1976-77
250	S.F.A.F.Bacchus	WI v I	Kanpur	1978-79
250	J.L.Langer	A v E	Melbourne	2002-03

The highest for Bangladesh is 158* by Mohammad Ashraful (v I, Chittagong, 2004-05).

20 HUNDREDS

			200	Inn	E	A	SA	WI	NZ	I	P	SL	Z	B
41	S.R.Tendulkar	I	4	256	7	10	3	3	–	2	7	3	3	
37	R.T.Ponting	A	4	213	7	–	8	7	2	6	4	1	1	1
34	S.M.Gavaskar	I	4	214	4	8	–	13	2	–	5	2	–	–
34	B.C.Lara	WI	8	230	7	9	4	–	1	2	4	5	1	1
32	S.R.Waugh	A	1	260	10	–	2	7	2	2	3	3	1	2
31	J.H.Kallis	SA	–	219	5	4	–	7	5	2	4	–	3	1
29	D.G.Bradman	A	12	80	19	–	4	2	–	4	–	–	–	–
29	M.L.Hayden	A	2	182	5	–	6	5	1	6	1	3	2	–
27	A.R.Border	A	2	265	8	–	3	5	4	6	1	–	–	
26	G.St A.Sobers	WI	2	160	10	4	–	1	8	3	–	–		
26	R.Dravid	I	5	225	4	3	1	3	4	–	5	1	3	2
26	Inzamam-ul-Haq	P	2	198	5	1	–	4	3	3	–	5	2	2
25	D.P.M.D.Jayawardena	SL	5	151	6	1	5	1	2	4	1	–	1	4
25	G.S.Chappell	A	4	151	9	–	5	3	1	6	–	–		
24	I.V.A.Richards	WI	3	182	8	5	–	1	8	2	–	–		
23	M.Younis Youhana	P	4	134	6	1	–	7	1	4	–	2	2	
23	J.L.Langer	A	3	180	5	–	2	3	4	3	4	2	–	
23	Javed Miandad	P	6	189	2	6	–	2	7	5	–	1	–	
22	W.R.Hammond	E	7	140	–	9	6	1	4	2	–			
22	M.Azharuddin	I	–	147	6	2	4	–	2	–	3	5	–	
22	M.C.Cowdrey	E	–	188	–	5	3	6	2	3	3	–		
22	G.Boycott	E	1	193	–	7	1	5	2	4	3	–		
21	R.N.Harvey	A	2	137	6	–	8	3	–	4	–			
21	G.Kirsten	SA	3	176	5	–	3	2	3	2	1	1	2	
21	D.C.Boon	A	1	190	7	–	3	3	6	1	1	–		
21	S.Chanderpaul	WI	1	202	5	4	–	1	5	1	–	–	1	
20	K.F.Barrington	E	1	131	–	5	2	3	3	4	–	–		
20	P.A.de Silva	SL	2	159	2	1	–	2	5	8	–	1	1	
20	M.E.Waugh	A	–	209	6	–	4	4	1	3	1	–		
20	G.A.Gooch	E	2	215	–	4	–	5	4	5	1	1	–	

The most for New Zealand is 17 by M.D.Crowe (131 innings), for Zimbabwe 12 by A.Flower (112), and for Bangladesh 5 by Mohammad Ashraful (93 innings).

The most double hundreds by batsmen not included above are 6 by M.S.Atapattu (16 hundreds for Sri Lanka), 6 by K.C.Sangakkara (18 hundreds for Sri Lanka), 5 by V.Sehwag (15 hundreds for India), 4 by L.Hutton (19 for England), 4 by C.G.Greenidge (19 for West Indies), 4 by Zaheer Abbas (12 for Pakistan) and 4 by G.C.Smith (18 hundreds for South Africa).

HIGHEST PARTNERSHIP FOR EACH WICKET

1st	415	N.D.McKenzie/G.C.Smith	SA v B	Chittagong	2007-08
2nd	576	S.T.Jayasuriya/R.S.Mahanama	SL v I	Colombo (RPS)	1997-98
3rd	624	K.C.Sangakkara/D.P.M.D.Jayawardena	SL v SA	Colombo (SSC)	2006
4th	437	D.P.M.D.Jayawardena/T.T.Samaraweera	SL v P	Karachi	2008-09
5th	405	S.G.Barnes/D.G.Bradman	A v E	Sydney	1946-47
6th	346	J.H.W.Fingleton/D.G.Bradman	A v E	Melbourne	1936-37
7th	347	D.St E.Atkinson/C.C.Depeiza	WI v A	Bridgetown	1954-55
8th	313	Wasim Akram/Saqlain Mushtaq	P v Z	Sheikhupura	1996-97
9th	195	M.V.Boucher/P.L.Symcox	SA v P	Johannesburg	1997-98
10th	151	B.F.Hastings/R.O.Collinge	NZ v P	Auckland	1972-73
	151	Azhar Mahmood/Mushtaq Ahmed	P v SA	Rawalpindi	1997-98

BOWLING RECORDS
200 WICKETS IN TESTS

Wkts			M	Balls	Runs	Avge	5 wI	10 wM
765	M.Muralitharan	SL	126	41696	16924	22.12	66	22
702	S.K.Warne	A	144	40518	17924	25.53	37	10
619	A.Kumble	I	132	40850	18355	29.65	35	8
560	G.D.McGrath	A	123	29140	12144	21.68	29	3
519	C.A.Walsh	WI	132	30019	12688	24.44	22	3
434	Kapil Dev	I	131	27740	12867	29.64	23	2
431	R.J.Hadlee	NZ	86	21918	9612	22.30	36	9
421	S.M.Pollock	SA	108	24453	9733	23.11	16	1
414	Wasim Akram	P	104	22627	9779	23.62	25	5
405	C.E.L.Ambrose	WI	98	22104	8500	20.98	22	3
388	M.Ntini	SA	99	20414	11009	28.37	18	4
383	I.T.Botham	E	102	21815	10878	28.40	27	4
376	M.D.Marshall	WI	81	17584	7876	20.94	22	4
373	Waqar Younis	P	87	16224	8788	23.56	22	5
362	Imran Khan	P	88	19458	8258	22.81	23	6
355	D.K.Lillee	A	70	18467	8493	23.92	23	7
354	W.P.U.C.J.Vaas	SL	110	23204	10411	29.40	12	2
330	A.A.Donald	SA	72	15519	7344	22.25	20	3
325	R.G.D.Willis	E	90	17357	8190	25.20	16	–
314	Harbhajan Singh	I	74	20585	9698	30.88	22	5
309	L.R.Gibbs	WI	79	27115	8989	29.09	18	2
308	B.Lee	A	75	16423	9458	30.71	10	–
307	F.S.Trueman	E	67	15178	6625	21.57	17	3
297	D.L.Underwood	E	86	21862	7674	25.83	17	6
291	C.J.McDermott	A	71	16586	8332	28.63	14	2
285	D.L.Vettori	NZ	88	21416	9354	32.82	18	3
266	B.S.Bedi	I	67	21364	7637	28.71	14	1
259	J.Garner	WI	58	13169	5433	20.97	7	–
259	J.N.Gillespie	A	71	14234	6770	26.13	8	–
257	J.H.Kallis	SA	130	16980	7983	31.06	5	–
252	J.B.Statham	E	70	16056	6261	24.84	9	1
249	M.A.Holding	WI	60	12680	5898	23.68	13	2
248	R.Benaud	A	63	19108	6704	27.03	16	1
248	M.J.Hoggard	E	67	13909	7564	30.50	7	1
246	G.D.McKenzie	A	60	17681	7328	29.78	16	3
242	B.S.Chandrasekhar	I	58	15963	7199	29.74	16	2
236	A.V.Bedser	E	51	15918	5876	24.89	15	5
236	Abdul Qadir	P	67	17126	7742	32.80	15	5
236	J.Srinath	I	67	15104	7196	30.49	10	1
235	G.St A.Sobers	WI	93	21599	7999	34.03	6	–
234	A.R.Caddick	E	62	13558	6999	29.91	13	1
229	D.Gough	E	58	11821	6503	28.39	9	–
228	R.R.Lindwall	A	61	13650	5251	23.03	12	–
225	Danish Kaneria	P	53	15608	7846	34.87	12	2
218	C.L.Cairns	NZ	62	11698	6410	29.40	13	1
217	S.J.Harmison	E	60	12934	6924	31.90	8	1
216	C.V.Grimmett	A	37	14513	5231	24.21	21	7
216	H.H.Streak	Z	65	13559	6079	28.14	7	–
212	M.G.Hughes	A	53	12285	6017	28.38	7	1
211	A.Flintoff	E	74	13974	6886	32.63	2	–
208	Saqlain Mushtaq	P	49	14070	6206	29.83	13	3
202	A.M.E.Roberts	WI	47	11136	5174	25.61	11	2
202	J.A.Snow	E	49	12021	5387	26.66	8	1
200	J.R.Thomson	A	51	10535	5601	28.00	8	–

The most for Bangladesh is 100 in 33 Tests by Mohammad Rafique.

35 WICKETS IN A SERIES

Wkts			Series	M	Balls	Runs	Avge	5 wI	10 wM
49	S.F.Barnes	E v SA	1913-14	4	1356	536	10.93	7	3
46	J.C.Laker	E v A	1956	5	1703	442	9.60	4	2
44	C.V.Grimmett	A v SA	1935-36	5	2077	642	14.59	5	3
42	T.M.Alderman	A v E	1981	6	1950	893	21.26	4	–
41	R.M.Hogg	A v E	1978-79	6	1740	527	12.85	5	2
41	T.M.Alderman	A v E	1989	6	1616	712	17.36	6	1
40	Imran Khan	P v I	1982-83	6	1339	558	13.95	4	2
40	S.K.Warne	A v E	2005	5	1517	797	19.92	3	2
39	A.V.Bedser	E v A	1953	5	1591	682	17.48	5	1
39	D.K.Lillee	A v E	1981	6	1870	870	22.30	2	1
38	M.W.Tate	E v A	1924-25	5	2528	881	23.18	5	1
37	W.J.Whitty	A v SA	1910-11	5	1395	632	17.08	2	–
37	H.J.Tayfield	SA v E	1956-57	5	2280	636	17.18	4	1
36	A.E.E.Vogler	SA v E	1909-10	5	1349	783	21.75	4	1
36	A.A.Mailey	A v E	1920-21	5	1465	946	26.27	4	2
36	G.D.McGrath	A v E	1997	6	1499	701	19.47	2	–
35	G.A.Lohmann	E v SA	1895-96	3	520	203	5.80	4	2
35	B.S.Chandrasekhar	I v E	1972-73	5	1747	662	18.91	4	–
35	M.D.Marshall	WI v E	1988	5	1219	443	12.65	3	1

The most for New Zealand is 33 by R.J.Hadlee (3 Tests v A, 1985-86), for Sri Lanka 30 by M.Muralitharan (3 Tests v Z, 2001-02), for Zimbabwe 22 by H.H.Streak (3 Tests v P, 1994-95), and for Bangladesh 18 by Enamul Haque II (2 Tests v Z, 2004-05).

15 WICKETS IN A TEST († On debut)

19- 90	J.C.Laker	E v A	Manchester	1956
17-159	S.F.Barnes	E v SA	Johannesburg	1913-14
16-136†	N.D.Hirwani	I v WI	Madras	1987-88
16-137†	R.A.L.Massie	A v E	Lord's	1972
16-220	M.Muralitharan	SL v E	The Oval	1998
15- 28	J.Briggs	E v SA	Cape Town	1888-89
15- 45	G.A.Lohmann	E v SA	Port Elizabeth	1895-96
15- 99	C.Blythe	E v SA	Leeds	1907
15-104	H.Verity	E v A	Lord's	1934
15-123	R.J.Hadlee	NZ v A	Brisbane	1985-86
15-124	W.Rhodes	E v A	Melbourne	1903-04
15-217	Harbhajan Singh	I v A	Madras	2000-01

The best analysis for South Africa is 13-132 by M.Ntini (v WI, Port-of-Spain, 2004-05), for West Indies 14-149 by M.A.Holding (v E, The Oval, 1976), for Pakistan 14-116 by Imran Khan (v SL, Lahore, 1981-82), for Zimbabwe 11-257 by A.G.Huckle (v NZ, Bulawayo, 1997-98), and for Bangladesh 12-200 by Enamul Haque II (v Z, Dhaka, 2004-05).

NINE WICKETS IN AN INNINGS

10-53	J.C.Laker	E v A	Manchester	1956
10-74	A.Kumble	I v P	Delhi	1998-99
9-28	G.A.Lohmann	E v SA	Johannesburg	1895-96
9-37	J.C.Laker	E v A	Manchester	1956
9-51	M.Muralitharan	SL v Z	Kandy	2001-02
9-52	R.J.Hadlee	NZ v A	Brisbane	1985-86
9-56	Abdul Qadir	P v E	Lahore	1987-88
9-57	D.E.Malcolm	E v SA	The Oval	1994
9-65	M.Muralitharan	SL v E	The Oval	1998
9-69	J.M.Patel	I v A	Kanpur	1959-60

9- 83	Kapil Dev	I v WI	Ahmedabad	1983-84
9- 86	Sarfraz Nawaz	P v A	Melbourne	1978-79
9- 95	J.M.Noreiga	WI v I	Port-of-Spain	1970-71
9-102	S.P.Gupte	I v WI	Kanpur	1958-59
9-103	S.F.Barnes	E v SA	Johannesburg	1913-14
9-113	H.J.Tayfield	SA v E	Johannesburg	1956-57
9-121	A.A.Mailey	A v E	Melbourne	1920-21

The best analysis for Zimbabwe is 8-109 by P.A.Strang (v NZ, Bulawayo, 2000-01), and for Bangladesh 7-95 by Enamul Haque II (v Z, Dhaka, 2004-05).

HAT-TRICKS

F.R.Spofforth	Australia v England	Melbourne	1878-79
W.Bates	England v Australia	Melbourne	1882-83
J.Briggs[7]	England v Australia	Sydney	1891-92
G.A.Lohmann	England v South Africa	Port Elizabeth	1895-96
J.T.Hearne	England v Australia	Leeds	1899
H.Trumble	Australia v England	Melbourne	1901-02
H.Trumble	Australia v England	Melbourne	1903-04
T.J.Matthews (2)[2]	Australia v South Africa	Manchester	1912
M.J.C.Allom[1]	England v New Zealand	Christchurch	1929-30
T.W.J.Goddard	England v South Africa	Johannesburg	1938-39
P.J.Loader	England v West Indies	Leeds	1957
L.F.Kline	Australia v South Africa	Cape Town	1957-58
W.W.Hall	West Indies v Pakistan	Lahore	1958-59
G.M.Griffin[7]	South Africa v England	Lord's	1960
L.R.Gibbs	West Indies v Australia	Adelaide	1960-61
P.J.Petherick[1/7]	New Zealand v Pakistan	Lahore	1976-77
C.A.Walsh[3]	West Indies v Australia	Brisbane	1988-89
M.G.Hughes[3/7]	Australia v West Indies	Perth	1988-89
D.W.Fleming[1]	Australia v Pakistan	Rawalpindi	1994-95
S.K.Warne	Australia v England	Melbourne	1994-95
D.G.Cork	England v West Indies	Manchester	1995
D.Gough[7]	England v Australia	Sydney	1998-99
Wasim Akram[4]	Pakistan v Sri Lanka	Lahore	1998-99
Wasim Akram[4]	Pakistan v Sri Lanka	Dhaka	1998-99
D.N.T.Zoysa[3]	Sri Lanka v Zimbabwe	Harare	1999-00
Abdul Razzaq	Pakistan v Sri Lanka	Galle	2000-01
G.D.McGrath	Australia v West Indies	Perth	2000-01
Harbhajan Singh	India v Australia	Calcutta	2000-01
Mohammad Sami[7]	Pakistan v Sri Lanka	Lahore	2001-02
J.J.C.Lawson[7]	West Indies v Australia	Bridgetown	2002-03
Alok Kapali[7]	Bangladesh v Pakistan	Peshawar	2003
A.M.Blignaut	Zimbabwe v Bangladesh	Harare	2003-04
M.J.Hoggard	England v West Indies	Bridgetown	2003-04
J.E.C.Franklin	New Zealand v Bangladesh	Dhaka	2004-05
I.K.Pathan[6/7]	India v Pakistan	Karachi	2005-06
R.J.Sidebottom[7]	England v New Zealand	Hamilton	2007-08

[1] On debut. [2] Hat-trick in each innings. [3] Involving both innings. [4] In successive Tests. [5] His first 3 balls (second over of the match). [6] The fourth, fifth and sixth balls of the match. [7] On losing side.

WICKET-KEEPING RECORDS
100 DISMISSALS IN TESTS†

Total			Tests	Ct	St
473	M.V.Boucher	South Africa	125	451	22
409	A.C.Gilchrist	Australia	95	374	35
395	I.A.Healy	Australia	119	366	29
355	R.W.Marsh	Australia	96	343	12
270†	P.J.L.Dujon	West Indies	79	265	5
269	A.P.E.Knott	England	95	250	19
241†	A.J.Stewart	England	82	227	14
228	Wasim Bari	Pakistan	81	201	27
219	R.D.Jacobs	West Indies	65	207	12
219	T.G.Evans	England	91	173	46
201†	A.C.Parore	New Zealand	67	194	7
198	S.M.H.Kirmani	India	88	160	38
189	D.L.Murray	West Indies	62	181	8
187	A.T.W.Grout	Australia	51	163	24
176	I.D.S.Smith	New Zealand	63	168	8
174	R.W.Taylor	England	57	167	7
165	R.C.Russell	England	54	153	12
152	D.J.Richardson	South Africa	42	150	2
151†	A.Flower	Zimbabwe	55	142	9
148	Kamran Akmal	Pakistan	40	129	19
147†	Moin Khan	Pakistan	66	127	20
146†	K.C.Sangakkara	Sri Lanka	50	126	20
141	J.H.B.Waite	South Africa	49	124	17
133	G.O.Jones	England	34	128	5
130	Rashid Latif	Pakistan	37	119	11
130	K.S.More	India	49	110	20
130	W.A.S.Oldfield	Australia	54	78	52
129	B.B.McCullum	New Zealand	41	120	9
119	R.S.Kaluwitharana	Sri Lanka	49	93	26
112†	J.M.Parks	England	43	101	11
107	N.R.Mongia	India	44	99	8
104	Salim Yousuf	Pakistan	32	91	13
101†	J.R.Murray	West Indies	31	98	3
101	D.Ramdin	West Indies	34	99	2

The most for Bangladesh is 87 (78 ct, 9 st) by Khaled Masud in 44 Tests.

† Excluding catches taken in the field

25 DISMISSALS IN A SERIES

28	R.W.Marsh	Australia v England	1982-83
27 (inc 2st)	R.C.Russell	England v South Africa	1995-96
27 (inc 2st)	I.A.Healy	Australia v England (6 Tests)	1997
26 (inc 3st)	J.H.B.Waite	South Africa v New Zealand	1961-62
26	R.W.Marsh	Australia v West Indies (6 Tests)	1975-76
26 (inc 5st)	I.A.Healy	Australia v England (6 Tests)	1993
26 (inc 1st)	M.V.Boucher	South Africa v England	1998
26 (inc 2st)	A.C.Gilchrist	Australia v England	2001
26 (inc 2st)	A.C.Gilchrist	Australia v England	2006-07
25 (inc 2st)	I.A.Healy	Australia v England	1994-95
25 (inc 2st)	A.C.Gilchrist	Australia v England	2002-03
25	A.C.Gilchrist	Australia v India	2007-08

TEN DISMISSALS IN A TEST

11	R.C.Russell	England v South Africa	Johannesburg	1995-96
10	R.W.Taylor	England v India	Bombay	1979-80
10	A.C.Gilchrist	Australia v New Zealand	Hamilton	1999-00

SEVEN DISMISSALS IN AN INNINGS

7	Wasim Bari	Pakistan v New Zealand	Auckland	1978-79
7	R.W.Taylor	England v India	Bombay	1979-80
7	I.D.S.Smith	New Zealand v Sri Lanka	Hamilton	1990-91
7	R.D.Jacobs	West Indies v Australia	Melbourne	2000-01

FIVE STUMPINGS IN AN INNINGS

5	K.S.More	India v West Indies	Madras	1987-88

FIELDING RECORDS
100 CATCHES IN TESTS

Total			Tests	Total			Tests
181	M.E.Waugh	Australia	128	120	M.C.Cowdrey	England	114
179	R.Dravid	India	130	115	C.L.Hooper	West Indies	102
171	S.P.Fleming	New Zealand	111	112	S.R.Waugh	Australia	168
164	B.C.Lara	West Indies	130	110	R.B.Simpson	Australia	62
157	M.A.Taylor	Australia	104	110	W.R.Hammond	England	85
156	A.R.Border	Australia	156	109	G.St A.Sobers	West Indies	93
147	R.T.Ponting	Australia	130	108	S.M.Gavaskar	India	125
143	J.H.Kallis	South Africa	130	107	V.V.S.Laxman	India	102
142	D.P.M.D.Jayawardena	Sri Lanka	102	105	I.M.Chappell	Australia	75
125	S.K.Warne	Australia	144	105	M.Azharuddin	India	99
125	M.L.Hayden	Australia	102	105	G.P.Thorpe	England	100
122	G.S.Chappell	Australia	87	103	G.A.Gooch	England	118
122	I.V.A.Richards	West Indies	121	101	G.C.Smith	South Africa	76
120	I.T.Botham	England	102				

The most for Pakistan is 93 by Javed Miandad (124), for Zimbabwe 60 by A.D.R.Campbell (60) and for Bangladesh 22 by Habibul Bashar (50).

15 CATCHES IN A SERIES

15	J.M.Gregory	Australia v England	1920-21

SEVEN CATCHES IN A TEST

7	G.S.Chappell	Australia v England	Perth	1974-75
7	Yajurvindra Singh	India v England	Bangalore	1976-77
7	H.P.Tillekeratne	Sri Lanka v New Zealand	Colombo (SSC)	1992-93
7	S.P.Fleming	New Zealand v Zimbabwe	Harare	1997-98
7	M.L.Hayden	Australia v Sri Lanka	Galle	2003-04

FIVE CATCHES IN AN INNINGS

5	V.Y.Richardson	Australia v South Africa	Durban	1935-36
5	Yajurvindra Singh	India v England	Bangalore	1976-77
5	M.Azharuddin	India v Pakistan	Karachi	1989-90
5	K.Srikkanth	India v Australia	Perth	1991-92
5	S.P.Fleming	New Zealand v Zimbabwe	Harare	1997-98

100 TEST MATCH APPEARANCES

		Opponents									
		E	A	SA	WI	NZ	I	P	SL	Z	B
168 S.R.Waugh	Australia	46	–	16	32	23	18	20	8	3	2
156 A.R.Border	Australia	47	–	6	31	23	20	22	7	–	–
156 S.R.Tendulkar	India	24	29	20	16	16	–	18	19	9	5
144 S.K.Warne	Australia	36	–	24	19	20	14	15	13	1	2
133 A.J.Stewart	England	–	33	23	24	16	9	13	9	6	–
132 C.A.Walsh	West Indies	36	38	10	–	10	15	18	3	2	–
132 A.Kumble	India	19	20	21	17	11	–	15	18	7	4
131 Kapil Dev	India	27	20	4	25	10	–	29	14	2	–
130 B.C.Lara	West Indies	30	30	18	–	11	17	12	8	2	2
130 R.Dravid	India	17	26	18	17	9	–	15	14	9	5
130 J.H.Kallis	South Africa	24	23	–	21	14	11	13	12	6	6
130 R.T.Ponting	Australia	26	–	21	18	13	23	10	12	3	4
128 M.E.Waugh	Australia	29	–	18	28	14	14	15	9	1	–
126 M.Muralitharan	Sri Lanka	16	12	15	12	12	18	16	–	14	11
125 S.M.Gavaskar	India	38	20	–	27	9	–	24	7	–	–
125 M.V.Boucher	South Africa	21	18	–	21	14	10	13	14	6	8
124 Javed Miandad	Pakistan	22	24	–	17	18	28	–	12	3	–
123 G.D.McGrath	Australia	30	–	17	23	14	11	17	8	1	2
121 I.V.A.Richards	West Indies	36	34	–	–	7	28	16	–	–	–
119 I.A.Healy	Australia	33	–	12	28	11	9	14	11	1	–
119 Inzamam-ul-Haq	Pakistan	19	13	13	15	12	10	–	20	11	6
119 S.Chanderpaul	West Indies	28	15	18	–	13	18	13	4	6	4
118 G.A.Gooch	England	–	42	3	26	15	19	10	3	–	–
117 D.I.Gower	England	–	42	–	19	13	24	17	2	–	–
116 D.L.Haynes	West Indies	36	33	1	–	10	19	16	1	–	–
116 D.B.Vengsarkar	India	26	24	–	25	11	–	22	8	–	–
115 M.A.Atherton	England	–	33	18	27	11	7	11	4	4	–
114 M.C.Cowdrey	England	–	43	14	21	18	8	10	–	–	–
113 S.C.Ganguly	India	12	24	17	12	8	–	12	14	9	5
111 S.P.Fleming	New Zealand	19	14	15	11	–	13	9	13	11	6
110 S.T.Jayasuriya	Sri Lanka	14	13	15	10	13	10	17	–	13	5
110 C.H.Lloyd	West Indies	34	29	–	–	8	28	11	–	–	–
110 W.P.U.C.J.Vaas	Sri Lanka	15	12	11	9	10	14	17	–	15	7
108 G.Boycott	England	–	38	7	29	15	13	6	–	–	–
108 C.G.Greenidge	West Indies	29	32	–	–	10	23	14	–	–	–
108 S.M.Pollock	South Africa	23	13	–	16	11	12	12	13	5	3
107 D.C.Boon	Australia	31	–	6	22	17	11	11	9	–	–
104 M.A.Taylor	Australia	33	–	11	20	11	9	12	8	–	–
104 J.L.Langer	Australia	21	–	11	18	14	14	13	8	3	2
104 Wasim Akram	Pakistan	18	13	4	17	9	12	–	19	10	2
103 Salim Malik	Pakistan	19	15	1	7	18	22	–	15	6	–
102 I.T.Botham	England	–	36	–	20	15	14	14	3	–	–
102 C.L.Hooper	West Indies	24	25	10	–	2	19	14	6	2	–
102 M.L.Hayden	Australia	20	–	19	15	11	18	6	7	2	4
102 V.V.S.Laxman	India	13	24	15	16	4	–	15	7	6	2
102 D.P.M.D.Jayawardena	Sri Lanka	16	10	12	9	9	12	15	–	8	11
101 G.Kirsten	South Africa	22	18	–	13	13	10	11	9	3	2
100 G.P.Thorpe	England	–	16	16	27	13	5	8	9	2	4

The most for Zimbabwe is 67 by G.W.Flower, and for Bangladesh 50 by Habibul Bashar.

100 CONSECUTIVE TEST APPEARANCES

153	A.R.Border	Australia	March 1979 to March 1994
107	M.E.Waugh	Australia	June 1993 to October 2002
106	S.M.Gavaskar	India	January 1975 to February 1987

50 TESTS AS CAPTAIN

			Won	Lost	Drawn	Tied
93	A.R.Border	Australia	32	22	38	1
80	S.P.Fleming	New Zealand	28	27	25	–
74	C.H.Lloyd	West Indies	36	12	26	–
68	G.C.Smith	South Africa	33	20	15	–
57	S.R.Waugh	Australia	41	9	7	–
56	A.Ranatunga	Sri Lanka	12	19	25	–
55	R.T.Ponting	Australia	37	9	9	–
54	M.A.Atherton	England	13	21	20	–
53	W.J.Cronje	South Africa	27	11	15	–
51	M.P.Vaughan	England	26	11	14	–
50	I.V.A.Richards	West Indies	27	8	15	–
50	M.A.Taylor	Australia	26	13	11	–

The most for India is 49 by S.C.Ganguly, for Pakistan 48 by Imran Khan, for Zimbabwe 21 by A.D.R.Campbell and H.H.Streak, and for Bangladesh 18 by Habibul Bashar.

50 TEST UMPIRING APPEARANCES

128	S.A.Bucknor	(West Indies)	28.04.1989 to 22.03.2009
98	R.E.Koertzen	(South Africa)	26.12.1992 to 19.02.2009
92	D.R.Shepherd	(England)	01.08.1985 to 07.06.2005
80	D.J.Harper	(Australia)	28.11.1998 to 10.03.2009
78	D.B.Hair	(Australia)	25.01.1992 to 08.06.2008
73	S.Venkataraghavan	(India)	29.01.1993 to 20.01.2004
66	H.D.Bird	(England)	05.07.1973 to 24.06.1996
55	Alim Dar	(Pakistan)	21.10.2003 to 02.03.2009
54	S.J.A.Taufel	(Australia)	26.12.2000 to 05.03.2009
54	B.F.Bowden	(New Zealand)	11.03.2000 to 10.03.2009

TEST MATCH SCORES
AUSTRALIA v INDIA (1st Test)

At Melbourne Cricket Ground on 26, 27, 28, 29 December 2007.
Toss: Australia. Result: **AUSTRALIA** won by 337 runs.
Debuts: None.

AUSTRALIA

P.A.Jaques	st Dhoni b Kumble	66	c and b Kumble		51
M.L.Hayden	c Dravid b Khan	124	c Ganguly b Harbhajan		47
*R.T.Ponting	b Khan	4	c Dravid b Harbhajan		3
M.E.K.Hussey	lbw b Kumble	2	c Tendulkar b Singh		36
M.J.Clarke	c Laxman b Singh	20	st Dhoni b Kumble		73
A.Symonds	c sub (K.D.Karthik) b Kumble	35	lbw b Khan		44
†A.C.Gilchrist	c Tendulkar b Kumble	23	c Singh b Harbhajan		35
G.B.Hogg	c Dravid b Khan	17	not out		35
B.Lee	lbw b Kumble	0	not out		11
M.G.Johnson	not out	15			
S.R.Clark	c Harbhajan b Khan	21			
Extras	(LB 5, W 2, NB 9)	16	(LB 3, NB 13)		16
Total	(92.4 overs; 397 min)	343	(7 wkts dec; 88 overs; 377 min)		351

INDIA

W.Jaffer	c Gilchrist b Lee	4	(2) c Gilchrist b Lee		15
R.Dravid	lbw b Clark	5	(1) lbw b Symonds		16
V.V.S.Laxman	c Ponting b Lee	26	c Clarke b Clark		42
S.R.Tendulkar	b Clark	62	c Gilchrist b Lee		15
S.C.Ganguly	b Hogg	43	c Ponting b Hogg		40
Yuvraj Singh	c Gilchrist b Clark	0	lbw b Hogg		5
†M.S.Dhoni	lbw b Clark	4	c Gilchrist b Johnson		11
*A.Kumble	c Gilchrist b Lee	27	c Gilchrist b Johnson		8
Harbhajan Singh	c Clarke b Hogg	2	run out		0
Z.Khan	c Gilchrist b Lee	11	not out		0
R.P.Singh	not out	2	b Johnson		2
Extras	(B 4, LB 3, NB 7)	14	(B 1, NB 6)		7
Total	(71.5 overs; 327 min)	196	(74 overs; 335 min)		161

INDIA	O	M	R	W		O	M	R	W	FALL OF WICKETS			
											A	I	A	I
Khan	23.4	1	94	4		20	2	93	1					
Singh	20	3	82	1		16	1	50	1	Wkt	1st	1st	2nd	2nd
Harbhajan Singh	20	3	61	0	(4)	26	0	101	3	1st	135	4	83	26
Ganguly	3	1	15	0						2nd	162	31	89	54
Kumble	25	4	84	5	(3)	25	2	102	2	3rd	165	55	139	77
Tendulkar	1	0	2	0	(5)	1	0	2	0	4th	225	120	161	118
										5th	241	122	243	125
AUSTRALIA										6th	281	122	288	144
Lee	19.5	6	46	4		14	3	43	2	7th	288	166	316	157
Johnson	13	5	25	0		15	6	21	3	8th	294	173	–	157
Symonds	3	1	8	0	(5)	13	5	25	1	9th	312	193	–	157
Clark	15	4	28	4	(3)	15	9	20	1	10th	343	196	–	161
Hogg	21	3	82	2	(4)	17	3	51	2					

Umpires: M.R.Benson (*England*) (20) and B.F.Bowden (*New Zealand*) (42).
Referee: M.J.Procter (*South Africa*) (44).   **Test No. 1854/69 (A689/I412)**

275

AUSTRALIA v INDIA (2nd Test)

At Sydney Cricket Ground on 2, 3, 4, 5, 6 January 2008.
Toss: Australia. Result: **AUSTRALIA** won by 122 runs.
Debuts: None.

AUSTRALIA

P.A.Jaques	c Dhoni b Singh	0	c Yuvraj b Kumble		42
M.L.Hayden	c Tendulkar b Singh	13	c Jaffer b Kumble		123
*R.T.Ponting	lbw b Harbhajan	55	c Laxman b Harbhajan		1
M.E.K.Hussey	c Tendulkar b Singh	41	not out		145
M.J.Clarke	lbw b Harbhajan	1	c Dravid b Kumble		0
A.Symonds	not out	162	c Dhoni b Singh		61
†A.C.Gilchrist	c Tendulkar b Singh	7	c Yuvraj b Kumble		1
G.B.Hogg	c Dravid b Kumble	79	c Dravid b Harbhajan		1
B.Lee	lbw b Kumble	59	not out		4
M.G.Johnson	c Ganguly b Kumble	28			
S.R.Clark	lbw b Kumble	0			
Extras	(B 2, LB 9, W 4, NB 3)	18	(B 3, LB 8, W 3, NB 9)		23
Total	(112.3 overs; 489 min)	463	(7 wkts dec; 107 overs; 474 min)		401

INDIA

W.Jaffer	b Lee	3	(2) c Clarke b Lee		0
R.Dravid	c Hayden b Johnson	53	(1) c Gilchrist b Symonds		38
V.V.S.Laxman	c Hussey b Hogg	109	lbw b Clark		20
S.R.Tendulkar	not out	154	b Clark		12
S.C.Ganguly	c Hussey b Hogg	67	c Clarke b Lee		51
Yuvraj Singh	lbw b Lee	12	c Gilchrist b Symonds		0
†M.S.Dhoni	c Gilchrist b Lee	2	lbw b Symonds		35
*A.Kumble	c Gilchrist b Lee	2	not out		45
Harbhajan Singh	c Hussey b Johnson	63	c Hussey b Clarke		7
R.P.Singh	c Gilchrist b Clark	13	lbw b Clarke		0
I.Sharma	c and b Lee	23	c Hussey b Clarke		0
Extras	(B 4, LB 13, W 6, NB 8)	31	(NB 2)		2
Total	(138.2 overs; 645 min)	532	(70.5 overs; 308 min)		210

INDIA	O	M	R	W		O	M	R	W
Singh	26	3	124	4		16	2	74	1
Sharma	23	3	87	0		14	2	59	0
Ganguly	6	1	13	0					
Harbhajan	27	3	108	2	(3) 33	6	92	2
Kumble	15.3	0	106	4	(4) 40	3	148	4
Tendulkar	5	0	14	0	(5) 2	0	6	0
Yuvraj Singh					(6) 2	0	11	0

AUSTRALIA	O	M	R	W		O	M	R	W
Lee	35.2	5	119	5		13	3	34	2
Johnson	37	2	148	2		11	4	33	0
Clark	25	3	80	1		12	4	32	2
Symonds	7	1	19	0	(5) 19	5	51	3
Hogg	30	2	121	2	(4) 14	2	55	0
Clarke	7	1	28	0	1.5	0	5	3

FALL OF WICKETS

	A	I	A	I
Wkt	1st	1st	2nd	2nd
1st	0	8	85	3
2nd	27	183	90	34
3rd	119	185	250	54
4th	119	293	250	115
5th	121	321	378	115
6th	134	330	393	137
7th	307	345	395	185
8th	421	474	–	210
9th	461	501	–	210
10th	463	532	–	210

Umpires: M.R.Benson (*England*) (21) and S.A.Bucknor (*West Indies*) (120).
Referee: M.J.Procter (*South Africa*) (45).   **Test No. 1855/70 (A690/1413)**

AUSTRALIA v INDIA (3rd Test)

At WACA Ground, Perth, on 16, 17, 18, 19 January 2008.
Toss: India. Result: **INDIA** won by 72 runs.
Debuts: Australia – C.J.L.Rogers.

INDIA

W.Jaffer	c Gilchrist b Lee	16		c Hussey b Clark	11
V.Sehwag	c Gilchrist b Johnson	29		b Clark	43
R.Dravid	c Ponting b Symonds	93	(4)	c Gilchrist b Lee	3
S.R.Tendulkar	lbw b Lee	71	(5)	lbw b Lee	13
S.C.Ganguly	c Hussey b Johnson	9	(6)	c Clarke b Johnson	0
V.V.S.Laxman	c Tait b Lee	27	(7)	c Gilchrist b Lee	79
†M.S.Dhoni	lbw b Clark	19	(8)	c Gilchrist b Symonds	38
I.K.Pathan	lbw b Johnson	28	(3)	c Ponting b Clark	46
*A.Kumble	c Rogers b Clark	1		c Clarke b Symonds	0
R.P.Singh	c Hussey b Johnson	0		c Gilchrist b Clark	30
I.Sharma	not out	0		not out	4
Extras	(LB 19, W 9, NB 9)	37		(LB 14, W 5, NB 8)	27
Total	**(98.2 overs; 463 min)**	**330**		**(80.4 overs; 368 min)**	**294**

AUSTRALIA

P.A.Jaques	c Laxman b Pathan	8	(2)	c Jaffer b Pathan	16
C.J.L.Rogers	lbw b Pathan	4	(1)	c Dhoni b Pathan	15
*R.T.Ponting	c Dravid b Sharma	20		c Dravid b Sharma	45
M.E.K.Hussey	c Dhoni b Singh	0		lbw b Singh	46
M.J.Clarke	c Dhoni b Sharma	23		st Dhoni b Kumble	81
A.Symonds	c Dravid b Kumble	66		lbw b Kumble	12
†A.C.Gilchrist	c Dhoni b Singh	55		b Sehwag	15
B.Lee	c Dhoni b Singh	11		c Laxman b Sehwag	0
M.G.Johnson	not out	6		not out	50
S.R.Clark	c Dhoni b Singh	0		c Dhoni b Pathan	32
S.W.Tait	c and b Kumble	8		b Singh	4
Extras	(B 4, LB 1, W 4, NB 2)	11		(LB 6, W 8, NB 10)	24
Total	**(50 overs; 241 min)**	**212**		**(86.5 overs; 399 min)**	**340**

AUSTRALIA	O	M	R	W	O	M	R	W
Lee	24	5	71	3	20.4	4	54	3
Johnson	28.2	7	86	4	10	0	58	1
Clark	17	4	45	2	19	4	61	4
Tait	13	1	59	0	8	0	33	0
Symonds	10	1	36	1	(6) 10	2	36	2
Clarke	6	1	14	0	(5) 13	2	38	0
INDIA								
Singh	14	2	68	4	21.5	4	95	2
Pathan	17	2	63	2	16	2	54	3
Sharma	7	0	34	2	17	0	63	1
Kumble	12	1	42	2	24	2	98	2
Sehwag					8	1	24	2

FALL OF WICKETS

	I	A	I	A
Wkt	1st	1st	2nd	2nd
1st	57	12	45	21
2nd	59	13	79	43
3rd	198	14	82	117
4th	214	43	116	159
5th	278	61	125	177
6th	284	163	160	227
7th	328	192	235	229
8th	330	195	235	253
9th	330	195	286	326
10th	330	212	294	340

Umpires: Asad Rauf (*Pakistan*) (16) and B.F.Bowden (*New Zealand*) (43).
Referee: M.J.Procter (*South Africa*) (46).   **Test No. 1856/71 (A691/I414)**

AUSTRALIA v INDIA (4th Test)

At Adelaide Oval on 24, 25, 26, 27, 28 January 2008.
Toss: India. Result: **MATCH DRAWN**.
Debuts: None.

INDIA

V.Sehwag	c Hayden b Lee	63	c Gilchrist b Symonds		151
I.K.Pathan	c Gilchrist b Johnson	9	lbw b Johnson		0
R.Dravid	c Ponting b Johnson	18	retired hurt		11
S.R.Tendulkar	c Hogg b Lee	153	run out		13
S.C.Ganguly	lbw b Hogg	7	c Hussey b Johnson		18
V.V.S.Laxman	c Gilchrist b Lee	51	c Gilchrist b Lee		12
†M.S.Dhoni	c Symonds b Johnson	16	c Hayden b Lee		20
*A.Kumble	c Gilchrist b Johnson	87	not out		9
Harbhajan Singh	c Gilchrist b Symonds	63	c Ponting b Hogg		7
R.P.Singh	c Johnson b Clarke	0			
I.Sharma	not out	14	(10) not out		2
Extras	(B 8, LB 21, W 3, NB 13)	45	(B 9, LB 9, W 3, NB 5)		26
Total	**(152.5 overs; 668 min)**	**526**	**(7 wkts dec; 90 overs; 394 min)**		**269**

AUSTRALIA

P.A.Jaques	b Kumble	60
M.L.Hayden	b Sharma	103
*R.T.Ponting	b Sehwag	140
M.E.K.Hussey	b Pathan	22
M.J.Clarke	c Laxman b Sharma	118
A.Symonds	b Sharma	30
†A.C.Gilchrist	c Sehwag b Pathan	14
G.B.Hogg	not out	16
B.Lee	c Dhoni b Pathan	1
M.G.Johnson	c Sharma b Harbhajan	13
S.R.Clark	b Sehwag	3
Extras	(B 10, LB 12, W 10, NB 11)	43
Total	**(181 overs; 778 min)**	**563**

AUSTRALIA	O	M	R	W		O	M	R	W	FALL OF WICKETS			
Lee	36	4	101	3		27	3	74	2		I	A	I
Johnson	37.5	6	126	4		16	1	33	2	*Wkt*	*1st*	*1st*	*2nd*
Clark	31	6	92	0	(4)	12	3	37	0	1st	34	159	2
Hogg	31	2	119	1	(5)	12	3	53	1	2nd	82	186	128
Clarke	10	0	39	1	(6)	1	0	2	0	3rd	122	241	162
Symonds	7	0	20	1	(3)	22	4	52	1	4th	156	451	186
										5th	282	490	237
INDIA										6th	336	506	253
Singh	4	0	14	0						7th	359	527	264
Pathan	36	2	112	3						8th	466	528	–
Sharma	40	6	115	3						9th	468	557	–
Harbhajan	48	5	128	1						10th	526	563	–
Kumble	30	4	109	1									
Sehwag	19	2	51	2									
Tendulkar	1	0	6	0									
Ganguly	3	1	6	0									

Umpires: Asad Rauf (*Pakistan*) (17) and B.F.Bowden (*New Zealand*) (44).
Referee: M.J.Procter (*South Africa*) (47).
In the second innings Dravid (11*) retired at 45.

Test No. 1857/72 (A692/I415)

SOUTH AFRICA v WEST INDIES (1st Test)

At St George's Park, Port Elizabeth, on 26, 27, 28, 29 December 2007.
Toss: South Africa. Result: **WEST INDIES** won by 128 runs.
Debuts: None.

WEST INDIES

*C.H.Gayle	c Kallis b Harris	66	c Boucher b Ntini	29
D.Ganga	c Boucher b Nel	33	run out	45
R.S.Morton	c Prince b Ntini	33	lbw b Kallis	5
M.N.Samuels	c Kallis b Steyn	94	b Steyn	40
S.Chanderpaul	b Nel	104	c Kallis b Steyn	8
D.J.Bravo	c and b Ntini	12	c Gibbs b Harris	10
†D.Ramdin	c Boucher b Ntini	1	c Gibbs b Steyn	0
D.J.G.Sammy	run out	38	lbw b Harris	3
J.E.Taylor	b Steyn	9	c Nel b Harris	22
D.B.L.Powell	not out	1	b Harris	6
F.H.Edwards	c Prince b Nel	0	not out	0
Extras	(B 2, LB 8, W 3, NB 4)	17	(B 1, W 1, NB 5)	7
Total	**(133.4 overs; 591 min)**	**408**	**(57.4 overs; 272 min)**	**175**

SOUTH AFRICA

*G.C.Smith	lbw b Taylor	28	(2) c Ganga b Edwards	11
H.H.Gibbs	c Ramdin b Powell	0	(1) lbw b Powell	0
H.M.Amla	b Powell	29	c Ramdin b Edwards	8
J.H.Kallis	c Bravo b Taylor	0	c Ramdin b Edwards	85
A.G.Prince	c Morton b Powell	20	c Gayle b Taylor	10
A.B.de Villiers	b Bravo	59	c Samuels b Taylor	60
†M.V.Boucher	c Powell b Taylor	20	b Taylor	13
P.L.Harris	c Taylor b Bravo	9	b Bravo	0
A.Nel	c Ganga b Bravo	16	c Ramdin b Sammy	34
D.W.Steyn	c Powell b Bravo	7	not out	33
M.Ntini	not out	0	c Powell b Samuels	1
Extras	(B 4, LB 1, W 1, NB 1)	7	(LB 4, W 1)	5
Total	**(62.1 overs; 295 min)**	**195**	**(74.5 overs; 339 min)**	**260**

SOUTH AFRICA	O	M	R	W	O	M	R	W
Steyn	31	4	121	2	17	3	67	3
Ntini	30	6	100	3	11	3	35	1
Nel	25.4	7	85	3	7	1	21	0
Harris	30	9	69	1	(5) 15.4	5	35	4
Kallis	17	8	23	0	(4) 7	1	16	1

WEST INDIES	O	M	R	W	O	M	R	W
Powell	17	4	58	3	14	2	47	1
Edwards	15	3	56	0	13	3	37	3
Taylor	13	4	46	3	18	1	66	3
Bravo	13.1	3	24	4	16	2	63	1
Sammy	4	2	6	0	7	0	29	1
Samuels					6.5	1	14	1

FALL OF WICKETS

	WI	SA	WI	SA
Wkt	1st	1st	2nd	2nd
1st	98	1	32	4
2nd	102	45	57	17
3rd	166	53	122	20
4th	277	63	123	45
5th	296	96	141	157
6th	304	129	141	183
7th	361	172	144	190
8th	385	181	144	192
9th	407	194	160	259
10th	408	195	175	260

Umpires: Alim Dar (*Pakistan*) (43) and R.B.Tiffin (*Zimbabwe*) (39).
Referee: R.S.Mahanama (*Sri Lanka*) (16). **Test No. 1858/20 (SA325/WI441)**

SOUTH AFRICA v WEST INDIES (2nd Test)

At Newlands, Cape Town, on 2, 3, 4, 5 January 2008.
Toss: West Indies. Result: **SOUTH AFRICA** won by seven wickets.
Debuts: None.

WEST INDIES

*C.H.Gayle	c McKenzie b Nel	46	(6) c Harris b Steyn	38
D.Ganga	c Boucher b Steyn	3	(1) b Ntini	22
R.S.Morton	c Ntini b Kallis	23	c Boucher b Steyn	1
M.N.Samuels	c Boucher b Ntini	51	lbw b Nel	18
S.Chanderpaul	not out	65	not out	70
D.J.Bravo	c Kallis b Ntini	0	(7) c Smith b Nel	12
†D.Ramdin	lbw b Steyn	21	(2) c Boucher b Kallis	32
R.N.Lewis	b Steyn	0	c Amla b Harris	1
J.E.Taylor	c and b Steyn	8	c Kallis b Steyn	21
D.B.L.Powell	c Kallis b Nel	0	c Smith b Steyn	1
F.H.Edwards	c De Villiers b Nel	2	c Harris b Nel	21
Extras	(B 5, LB 10, W 1, NB 8)	24	(B 4, LB 20, W 1)	25
Total	(92 overs; 419 min)	243	(101.5 overs; 467 min)	262

SOUTH AFRICA

*G.C.Smith	c Ramdin b Taylor	28	c Gayle b Lewis	85
N.D.McKenzie	c Gayle b Taylor	23		
H.M.Amla	lbw b Bravo	32	c Gayle b Lewis	37
J.H.Kallis	c Ramdin b Bravo	36	not out	22
A.G.Prince	run out	98	not out	12
A.B.de Villiers	c Ramdin b Bravo	2	(2) c sub (D.J.G.Sammy) b Bravo	23
†M.V.Boucher	b Bravo	59		
P.L.Harris	c Morton b Powell	4		
A.Nel	c Ramdin b Powell	5		
D.W.Steyn	c Morton b Lewis	19		
M.Ntini	not out	3		
Extras	(B 4, LB 5, W 3)	12	(LB 5, W 1, NB 1)	7
Total	(118.2 overs; 516 min)	321	(3 wkts; 35.2 overs; 157 min)	186

SOUTH AFRICA	O	M	R	W		O	M	R	W
Steyn	20	5	60	4	(3)	19.5	7	44	4
Ntini	22	7	63	2		26	8	62	1
Nel	22	5	61	3	(1)	27	12	62	3
Kallis	9	1	11	1		19	6	34	1
Harris	19	5	33	0		10	0	36	1
WEST INDIES									
Powell	35	4	123	2		11	0	57	0
Edwards	4.5	1	12	0					
Samuels	8.1	3	18	0	(4)	3	0	17	0
Taylor	21	6	51	2	(2)	6	0	31	0
Bravo	37	9	82	4	(3)	7	0	34	1
Lewis	12.2	3	26	1	(5)	8.2	0	42	2

FALL OF WICKETS				
	WI	SA	WI	SA
Wkt	1st	1st	2nd	2nd
1st	12	46	59	57
2nd	71	61	60	140
3rd	77	120	81	152
4th	183	123	93	–
5th	185	131	126	–
6th	220	260	133	–
7th	220	265	163	–
8th	237	284	167	–
9th	241	301	192	–
10th	243	321	262	–

Umpires: S.J.A.Taufel (*Australia*) (47) and R.B.Tiffin (*Zimbabwe*) (40).
Referee: R.S.Mahanama (*Sri Lanka*) (17).
In the second innings Gayle (1*) retired at 97 and resumed at 192.

Test No. 1859/21 (SA326/WI442)

SOUTH AFRICA v WEST INDIES (3rd Test)

At Kingsmead, Durban, on 10, 11, 12 January 2008.
Toss: South Africa. Result: **SOUTH AFRICA** won by an innings and 100 runs.
Debuts: West Indies – B.A.Parchment.

WEST INDIES

D.Ganga	c Smith b Steyn	3		c Kallis b Ntini	11
B.A.Parchment	c Gibbs b Pollock	11		lbw b Steyn	20
R.S.Morton	lbw b Pollock	1		lbw b Pollock	37
M.N.Samuels	c Boucher b Ntini	6		b Steyn	105
S.Chanderpaul	c Kallis b Ntini	0	(11)	absent ill	–
*D.J.Bravo	c Gibbs b Pollock	13	(5)	lbw b Steyn	75
†D.Ramdin	c Gibbs b Nel	30	(6)	c Boucher b Nel	25
D.J.G.Sammy	c Smith b Nel	28	(7)	c and b Steyn	17
J.E.Taylor	c Steyn b Pollock	25	(8)	not out	17
D.B.L.Powell	not out	15	(9)	b Steyn	0
F.H.Edwards	c Boucher b Nel	0	(10)	b Steyn	0
Extras	(B 1, LB 6)	7		(LB 8, W 1, NB 1)	10
Total	**(34.3 overs; 159 min)**	**139**		**(86.5 overs; 390 min)**	**317**

SOUTH AFRICA

*G.C.Smith	c Ramdin b Taylor	147
H.H.Gibbs	b Powell	27
H.M.Amla	c Bravo b Sammy	69
J.H.Kallis	c Morton b Samuels	74
A.G.Prince	not out	123
A.B.de Villiers	not out	103
†M.V.Boucher		
S.M.Pollock		
A.Nel		
D.W.Steyn		
M.Ntini		
Extras	(B 6, LB 7)	13
Total	**(4 wkts dec; 120 overs; 519 min)**	**556**

SOUTH AFRICA	O	M	R	W	O	M	R	W
Steyn	8	2	18	1	21.5	6	72	6
Ntini	7	1	30	2	20	4	95	1
Pollock	11	2	35	4	17	4	50	1
Nel	6.3	0	45	3	17	2	67	1
Kallis	2	1	4	0	8	2	14	0
Amla					3	0	11	0

WEST INDIES	O	M	R	W
Powell	26	1	128	1
Edwards	23	0	129	0
Taylor	25	3	92	1
Sammy	25	4	104	1
Samuels	21	0	90	1

FALL OF WICKETS

	WI	SA	WI
Wkt	1st	1st	2nd
1st	10	53	33
2nd	11	252	49
3rd	22	252	88
4th	26	374	232
5th	33	–	273
6th	57	–	292
7th	74	–	305
8th	116	–	305
9th	139	–	317
10th	139	–	–

Umpires: Alim Dar (*Pakistan*) (44) and S.J.A.Taufel (*Australia*) (48).
Referee: R.S.Mahanama (*Sri Lanka*) (18).   **Test No. 1860/22 (SA327/WI443)**

NEW ZEALAND v BANGLADESH (1st Test)

At University Oval, Dunedin, on 4, 5, 6 January 2008.
Toss: New Zealand. Result: **NEW ZEALAND** won by nine wickets.
Debuts: Bangladesh – Junaid Siddique, Sajidul Islam, Tamim Iqbal.

BANGLADESH

Batsman	1st innings		2nd innings	
Tamim Iqbal	c Fulton b Martin	53	b Mills	84
Junaid Siddique	c Fleming b Martin	1	c Fleming b Martin	74
Habibul Bashar	c McCullum b Martin	23	c Sinclair b Oram	11
*Mohammad Ashraful	lbw b Martin	0	c Cumming b O'Brien	23
Shahriar Nafis	b Vettori	16	lbw b Vettori	28
Aftab Ahmed	b Oram	0	c Bell b O'Brien	0
†Mushfiqur Rahim	c Bell b Mills	7	lbw b Vettori	6
Mashrafe Mortaza	b Oram	22	c McCullum b Vettori	10
Shahadat Hossain	c McCullum b Oram	0	(10) lbw b Vettori	0
Enamul Haque II	not out	2	(9) not out	6
Sajidul Islam	c McCullum b Mills	4	c McCullum b Martin	1
Extras	(B 1, LB 2, W 3, NB 3)	9	(LB 4, NB 7)	11
Total	(46.1 overs; 204 min)	137	(83.1 overs; 335 min)	254

NEW ZEALAND

Batsman	1st innings		2nd innings	
C.D.Cumming	lbw b Sajidul	1	(2) lbw b Mortaza	4
M.D.Bell	lbw b Ashraful	107	(1) not out	20
P.G.Fulton	b Hossain	14	not out	15
S.P.Fleming	c Rahim b Sajidul	14		
M.S.Sinclair	lbw b Mortaza	29		
J.D.P.Oram	b Mortaza	117		
†B.B.McCullum	c Siddique b Ashraful	7		
*D.L.Vettori	c Haque b Hossain	32		
K.D.Mills	c Rahim b Mortaza	0		
I.E.O'Brien	c Rahim b Mortaza	5		
C.S.Martin	not out	12		
Extras	(B 4, LB 10, W 2, NB 3)	19		
Total	(91 overs; 377 min)	357	(1 wkt; 8.1 overs; 36 min)	39

NEW ZEALAND	O	M	R	W		O	M	R	W
Martin	13	1	64	4		20.1	6	56	2
Mills	7.1	1	29	2		12	1	54	1
Oram	13	4	23	3	(5) 12	5	21	1
O'Brien	7	2	10	0	(3) 15	2	49	2
Vettori	6	2	8	1	(4) 24	6	70	4

BANGLADESH	O	M	R	W		O	M	R	W
Shahadat Hossain	18	0	95	2	(3) 1	0	6	0
Sajidul Islam	19	2	71	2		3	1	13	0
Mashrafe Mortaza	23	3	74	4	(1) 4	0	14	1
Enamul Haque	22	4	57	0					
Mohammad Ashraful	9	0	46	2	(4) 0.1	0	6	0

FALL OF WICKETS

	B	NZ	B	NZ
Wkt	1st	1st	2nd	2nd
1st	5	5	161	13
2nd	43	31	167	–
3rd	47	58	179	–
4th	82	121	205	–
5th	98	260	205	–
6th	100	270	222	–
7th	129	320	232	–
8th	129	320	252	–
9th	133	340	252	–
10th	137	357	254	–

Umpires: N.J.Llong (*England*) (1) and P.D.Parker (*Australia*) (9).
Referee: B.C.Broad (*England*) (24). **Test No. 1861/5 (NZ335/B50)**

NEW ZEALAND v BANGLADESH (2nd Test)

At Basin Reserve, Wellington, on 12, 13, 14 January 2008.
Toss: New Zealand. Result: **NEW ZEALAND** won by an innings and 137 runs.
Debuts: None.

BANGLADESH

Tamim Iqbal	c Sinclair b Mills	15	(11)	absent ill	–
Junaid Siddique	c Bell b Martin	13		c McCullum b Mills	2
Habibul Bashar	c McCullum b Martin	1		lbw b Martin	25
*Mohammad Ashraful	c McCullum b O'Brien	35		c Fleming b Mills	1
Shahriar Nafis	c Fulton b O'Brien	6	(1)	c Bell b Martin	12
Aftab Ahmed	not out	25	(5)	c Fleming b O'Brien	5
†Mushfiqur Rahim	lbw b Martin	8	(6)	c Bell b Oram	0
Shakib Al Hasan	c Fulton b Martin	5	(7)	not out	41
Shahadat Hossain	c McCullum b O'Brien	1	(8)	c McCullum b O'Brien	5
Sajidul Islam	c Fleming b Martin	6	(9)	run out	3
Mashrafe Mortaza	c Bell b Vettori	15	(10)	c Mills b Oram	6
Extras	(B 2, LB 11)	13		(LB 2, W 5, NB 6)	13
Total	**(45.3 overs; 198 min)**	**143**		**(47 overs; 202 min)**	**113**

NEW ZEALAND

C.D.Cumming	lbw b Shakib	42
M.D.Bell	c Rahim b Sajidul	1
P.G.Fulton	lbw b Mortaza	22
S.P.Fleming	c Aftab b Shakib	87
M.S.Sinclair	c Rahim b Hossain	47
J.D.P.Oram	c Rahim b Hossain	1
†B.B.McCullum	c Shakib b Hossain	40
*D.L.Vettori	c and b Aftab	94
K.D.Mills	b Mortaza	4
C.S.Martin	b Aftab	4
I.E.O'Brien	not out	0
Extras	(B 5, LB 23, W 10, NB 13)	51
Total	**(103.2 overs; 464 min)**	**393**

NEW ZEALAND	O	M	R	W		O	M	R	W
Martin	16	3	65	5		13	1	35	2
Mills	9	3	19	1		11	4	29	2
O'Brien	15	7	34	3	(4)	11	2	23	2
Oram	3	2	2	0	(3)	11	3	21	2
Vettori	2.3	0	10	1		1	0	3	0

BANGLADESH	O	M	R	W
Mashrafe Mortaza	29	5	100	2
Sajidul Islam	14	1	91	1
Shahadat Hossain	27	4	83	3
Aftab Ahmed	12.2	4	31	2
Shakib Al Hasan	19	7	44	2
Mohammad Ashraful	2	0	16	0

FALL OF WICKETS			
	B	NZ	B
Wkt	1st	1st	2nd
1st	17	2	10
2nd	18	35	14
3rd	49	118	30
4th	68	214	44
5th	71	216	45
6th	86	242	56
7th	110	323	79
8th	111	362	83
9th	122	390	113
10th	143	393	–

Umpires: N.J.Llong (*England*) (2) and P.D.Parker (*Australia*) (10).
Referee: B.C.Broad (*England*) (25).   **Test No. 1862/6 (NZ336/B51)**

BANGLADESH v SOUTH AFRICA (1st Test)

At Shere Bangla National Stadium, Mirpur, on 22, 23, 24, 25 February 2008.
Toss: Bangladesh. Result: **SOUTH AFRICA** won by five wickets.
Debuts: None.

BANGLADESH

Tamim Iqbal	c and b Steyn	0	b Steyn	2
Junaid Siddique	c Boucher b Steyn	1	c Boucher b Kallis	74
Shahriar Nafis	c Smith b Morkel	25	lbw b Steyn	16
Habibul Bashar	c McKenzie b Morkel	11	lbw b Steyn	2
*Mohammad Ashraful	c and b Botha	34	c Boucher b Ntini	24
Aftab Ahmed	c Ntini b Botha	44	lbw b Steyn	24
Shakib Al Hasan	c De Villiers b Morkel	30	c Boucher b Kallis	3
†Mushfiqur Rahim	b Morkel	7	c Boucher b Kallis	2
Mohammad Rafique	lbw b Morkel	0	b Kallis	14
Mashrafe Mortaza	b Steyn	29	c Smith b Kallis	11
Shahadat Hossain	not out	0	not out	1
Extras	(B 2, LB 4, W 2, NB 3)	11	(LB 4, W 1, NB 4)	9
Total	(54.4 overs; 262 min)	192	(73 overs; 342 min)	182

SOUTH AFRICA

N.D.McKenzie	lbw b Hossain	5	c Bashar b Hossain	26
*G.C.Smith	b Hossain	10	lbw b Rafique	62
H.M.Amla	lbw b Rafique	25	c Siddique b Rafique	46
J.H.Kallis	b Rafique	17	c Mortaza b Hossain	7
A.G.Prince	run out	10	lbw b Hossain	38
J.Botha	lbw b Hossain	25		
A.B.de Villiers	c and b Ashraful	46	(6) not out	19
†M.V.Boucher	lbw b Hossain	11	(7) not out	2
M.Morkel	c Rahim b Hossain	1		
D.W.Steyn	b Hossain	7		
M.Ntini	not out	3		
Extras	(B 1, LB 5, W 1, NB 3)	10	(B 2, LB 2, W 1)	5
Total	(60.3 overs; 259 min)	170	(5 wkts; 67.5 overs; 299 min)	205

SOUTH AFRICA	O	M	R	W	O	M	R	W	FALL OF WICKETS				
										B	SA	B	SA
Steyn	11.4	2	27	3	18	2	48	4					
Ntini	13	2	47	0	16	4	35	1	Wkt	1st	1st	2nd	2nd
Morkel	13	2	50	5	17	3	43	0	1st	0	12	3	52
Kallis	5	2	5	0	14	4	30	5	2nd	3	19	25	125
Botha	12	0	57	2	6	0	18	0	3rd	32	54	29	144
McKenzie					2	0	4	0	4th	60	69	85	144
									5th	82	77	148	193
BANGLADESH									6th	152	145	148	–
Mashrafe Mortaza	9	1	43	0	12	0	47	0	7th	152	156	151	–
Shahadat Hossain	15.3	8	27	6	19	0	70	3	8th	152	158	169	–
Mohammad Rafique	25	6	55	2	27.5	6	54	2	9th	192	163	181	–
Shakib Al Hasan	10	6	30	0	7	0	24	0	10th	192	170	182	–
Mohammad Ashraful	1	0	9	1	2	0	6	0					

Umpires: Alim Dar (*Pakistan*) (45) and S.A.Bucknor (*West Indies*) (121).
Referee: R.S.Madugalle (*Sri Lanka*) (100).   Test No. 1863/5 (B52/SA328)

BANGLADESH v SOUTH AFRICA (2nd Test)

At Chittagong Divisional Stadium on 29 February, 1, 2, 3 March 2008.
Toss: South Africa. Result: **SOUTH AFRICA** won by an innings and 205 runs.
Debuts: None.

SOUTH AFRICA

N.D.McKenzie	b Hossain	226
*G.C.Smith	b Razzak	232
H.M.Amla	lbw b Hossain	38
J.H.Kallis	not out	39
A.G.Prince	b Hossain	2
A.B.de Villiers	b Shakib	1
†M.V.Boucher	c Shakib b Rafique	21
R.J.Peterson	c Siddique b Rafique	4
D.W.Steyn		
M.Morkel		
M.Ntini		
Extras	(B 10, LB 7, W 1, NB 2)	20
Total	(7 wkts dec; 161.1 overs; 662 min)	**583**

BANGLADESH

Tamim Iqbal	c De Villiers b Steyn	14		c Steyn b Peterson	9
Junaid Siddique	c Boucher b Steyn	18		c Boucher b Steyn	0
Shahriar Nafis	c Smith b Steyn	69		c Kallis b Peterson	31
*Mohammad Ashraful	c Boucher b Steyn	0		c Boucher b Steyn	4
Abdur Razzaq	c Prince b Peterson	33	(7)	not out	32
Aftab Ahmed	retired hurt	21		absent hurt	–
Shakib Al Hasan	c Boucher b Ntini	40	(5)	c McKenzie b Steyn	2
†Mushfiqur Rahim	c Boucher b Ntini	15	(6)	c Kallis b Peterson	4
Mohammad Rafique	c Smith b Ntini	10	(8)	c and b Peterson	0
Mashrafe Mortaza	c Boucher b Ntini	1	(10)	c McKenzie b Morkel	4
Shahadat Hossain	not out	13	(9)	c Prince b Peterson	24
Extras	(LB 11, W 1, NB 13)	25		(B 6, LB 1, NB 2)	9
Total	(70.4 overs)	**259**		(39.5 overs)	**119**

BANGLADESH	O	M	R	W		O	M	R	W
Mashrafe Mortaza	28	6	92	0					
Shahadat Hossain	25	1	107	3					
Mohammad Rafique	44.1	5	132	2					
Abdur Razzak	31	1	129	1					
Shakib Al Hasan	25	4	68	1					
Mohammad Ashraful	3	0	20	0					
Aftab Ahmed	5	0	18	0					

SOUTH AFRICA	O	M	R	W		O	M	R	W
Steyn	22	7	66	4	(2)	11	2	35	3
Ntini	13.4	3	35	4	(1)	5	3	10	0
Morkel	13	0	71	0		4.5	1	21	1
Peterson	16	2	61	1	(5)	13	2	33	5
Kallis	6	1	15	0	(4)	6	3	13	0

FALL OF WICKETS

	SA	B	B
Wkt	1st	1st	2nd
1st	415	39	0
2nd	514	49	44
3rd	515	49	45
4th	519	118	49
5th	524	176	54
6th	579	232	58
7th	583	241	58
8th	–	246	114
9th	–	259	119
10th	–	–	–

Umpires: Alim Dar (*Pakistan*) (46) and S.A.Bucknor (*West Indies*) (122).
Referee: R.S.Madugalle (*Sri Lanka*) (101).　　　　**Test No. 1864/6 (B53/SA329)**
In the first innings Aftab retired hurt at 176.

NEW ZEALAND v ENGLAND (1st Test)

At Seddon Park, Hamilton, on 5, 6, 7, 8, 9 March 2008.
Toss: New Zealand. Result: **NEW ZEALAND** won by 189 runs.
Debuts: England – T.R.Ambrose.

NEW ZEALAND

J.M.How	c Collingwood b Panesar	92	c Hoggard b Sidebottom	39
M.D.Bell	c Cook b Harmison	19	c Ambrose b Sidebottom	0
S.P.Fleming	c Cook b Sidebottom	41	c Cook b Sidebottom	66
M.S.Sinclair	c and b Collingwood	8	c Cook b Sidebottom	2
L.R.P.L.Taylor	c and b Pietersen	120	(6) c and b Panesar	6
J.D.P.Oram	c Cook b Hoggard	10	(7) lbw b Sidebottom	0
†B.B.McCullum	c Ambrose b Sidebottom	51	(5) c Strauss b Panesar	0
*D.L.Vettori	c Strauss b Collingwood	88	c Cook b Sidebottom	35
K.D.Mills	not out	25	lbw b Panesar	11
J.S.Patel	c Strauss b Sidebottom	5	not out	13
C.S.Martin	b Sidebottom	0	not out	0
Extras	(B 1, LB 6, W 1, NB 3)	11	(LB 5)	5
Total	(138.3 overs; 575 min)	470	(9 wkts dec; 55 overs; 240 min)	177

ENGLAND

A.N.Cook	c sub (N.K.W.Horsley) b Martin	38	c McCullum b Mills	13
*M.P.Vaughan	c McCullum b Patel	63	lbw b Mills	9
M.J.Hoggard	c Fleming b Martin	2	(9) c McCullum b Martin	4
A.J.Strauss	b Vettori	43	(3) c McCullum b Mills	2
K.P.Pietersen	c and b Vettori	42	(4) lbw b Mills	6
I.R.Bell	b Mills	25	(5) not out	54
P.D.Collingwood	lbw b Oram	66	(6) b Vettori	2
†T.R.Ambrose	c Fleming b Patel	55	(7) b Martin	0
R.J.Sidebottom	not out	3	(8) c McCullum b Martin	0
S.J.Harmison	c Fleming b Patel	0	c Fleming b Patel	1
M.S.Panesar	lbw b Mills	0	c McCullum b Oram	8
Extras	(B 4, LB 1, NB 6)	11	(B 4, NB 7)	11
Total	(173.1 overs; 666 min)	348	(55 overs; 225 min)	110

ENGLAND	O	M	R	W		O	M	R	W	
Sidebottom	34.3	8	90	4		17	4	49	6‡	
Hoggard	26	2	122	1		12	3	29	0	
Harmison	23	3	97	1	(4)	4	0	24	0	
Panesar	37	10	101	1	(5)	16	2	50	3	
Collingwood	15	2	42	2	(3)	6	1	20	0	
Pietersen	3	1	11	1						

NEW ZEALAND	O	M	R	W		O	M	R	W	
Martin	32	15	60	2		13	4	33	3	
Mills	21.1	6	61	2		13	4	16	4	
Patel	43	14	107	3	(5)	11	2	39	1	
Oram	21	9	27	1	(3)	4	2	2	1	
Vettori	56	17	88	2	(4)	14	6	16	1	

FALL OF WICKETS

	NZ	E	NZ	E
Wkt	1st	1st	2nd	2nd
1st	44	84	1	19
2nd	108	86	99	24
3rd	129	130	109	25
4th	176	159	110	30
5th	191	203	115	59
6th	277	245	115	60
7th	425	335	119	60
8th	451	347	141	67
9th	470	347	173	77
10th	470	348	–	110

Umpires: S.J.Davis (*Australia*) (10) and D.J.Harper (*Australia*) (70).
Referee: J.Srinath (*India*) (7). **Test No. 1865/89 (NZ337/E868)**
‡ Including hat-trick.

NEW ZEALAND v ENGLAND (2nd Test)

At Basin Reserve, Wellington, on 13, 14, 15, 16, 17 March 2008.
Toss: New Zealand. Result: **ENGLAND** won by 126 runs.
Debuts: None.

ENGLAND

A.N.Cook	c McCullum b Oram	44	c Fleming b Mills	60
*M.P.Vaughan	b Oram	32	b McCullum b Mills	13
A.J.Strauss	c Sinclair b Mills	8	lbw b Oram	44
K.P.Pietersen	b Gillespie	31	run out	17
I.R.Bell	c McCullum b Martin	11	c Sinclair b Oram	41
P.D.Collingwood	lbw b Gillespie	65	lbw b Gillespie	59
†T.R.Ambrose	c Taylor b Mills	102	b Oram	5
S.C.J.Broad	b Oram	1	c McCullum b Martin	16
R.J.Sidebottom	c Bell b Gillespie	14	c How b Gillespie	0
M.S.Panesar	c McCullum b Gillespie	6	c Taylor b Martin	10
J.M.Anderson	not out	0	not out	12
Extras	(B 5, LB 15, NB 8)	28	(B 6, LB 5, NB 5)	16
Total	**(107 overs; 466 min)**	**342**	**(97.4 overs; 415 min)**	**293**

NEW ZEALAND

J.M.How	c Strauss b Anderson	7	c Bell b Sidebottom	8
M.D.Bell	b Anderson	0	c Ambrose b Broad	29
S.P.Fleming	c Pietersen b Anderson	34	b Broad	31
M.S.Sinclair	c Ambrose b Anderson	9	c Bell b Anderson	39
L.R.P.L.Taylor	c Ambrose b Anderson	53	lbw b Sidebottom	55
J.D.P.Oram	lbw b Sidebottom	8	c Pietersen b Sidebottom	30
†B.B.McCullum	c Strauss b Broad	25	c Sidebottom b Pancsar	85
*D.L.Vettori	not out	50	c Cook b Sidebottom	0
K.D.Mills	c Bell b Collingwood	1	lbw b Sidebottom	13
M.R.Gillespie	b Collingwood	0	c Ambrose b Anderson	9
C.S.Martin	b Collingwood	1	not out	0
Extras	(LB 8, W 1, NB 1)	10	(B 1, LB 10, W 1)	12
Total	**(57.5 overs; 273 min)**	**198**	**(100.3 overs; 430 min)**	**311**

NEW ZEALAND	O	M	R	W	O	M	R	W
Martin	20	1	80	1	24.4	4	77	2
Mills	30	4	86	2	23	5	59	2
Gillespie	20	2	79	4	(4) 15	1	63	2
Oram	29	11	46	3	(3) 20	9	44	3
Vettori	8	0	31	0	15	2	39	0
ENGLAND								
Sidebottom	17	3	36	1	31	10	105	5
Anderson	20	4	73	5	15	2	57	2
Broad	12	0	56	1	23	6	62	2
Collingwood	7.5	1	23	3	9	2	20	0
Panesar	1	0	2	0	21.3	1	53	1
Pietersen					1	0	3	0

FALL OF WICKETS				
	E	NZ	E	NZ
Wkt	1st	1st	2nd	2nd
1st	79	4	21	18
2nd	82	9	127	69
3rd	94	31	129	70
4th	126	102	160	151
5th	136	113	219	173
6th	300	133	231	242
7th	305	165	259	246
8th	335	176	260	270
9th	342	180	277	311
10th	342	198	293	311

Umpires: S.J.Davis (*Australia*) (11) and R.E.Koertzen (*South Africa*) (88).
Referee: J.Srinath (*India*) (8).   **Test No. 1866/90 (NZ338/E869)**

NEW ZEALAND v ENGLAND (3rd Test)

At McLean Park, Napier, on 22, 23, 24, 25, 26 March 2008.
Toss: England. Result: **ENGLAND** won by 121 runs.
Debuts: New Zealand – G.D.Elliott, T.G.Southee.

ENGLAND

A.N.Cook	b Martin	2	c McCullum b Patel	37
*M.P.Vaughan	lbw b Southee	2	c McCullum b Martin	4
A.J.Strauss	c How b Southee	0	c Bell b Patel	177
K.P.Pietersen	c How b Southee	129	c Taylor b Vettori	34
I.R.Bell	c and b Elliott	9	c Sinclair b Vettori	110
P.D.Collingwood	c Elliott b Patel	30	c and b Vettori	22
†T.R.Ambrose	c Taylor b Patel	11	c and b Vettori	31
S.C.J.Broad	c McCullum b Southee	42	not out	31
R.J.Sidebottom	c Bell b Southee	14	not out	12
M.S.Panesar	b Martin	0		
J.M.Anderson	not out	0		
Extras	(LB 9, W 3, NB 1)	13	(LB 3, W 1, NB 5)	9
Total	**(96.1 overs; 379 min)**	**253**	**(7 wkts dec; 131.5 overs; 513 min)**	**467**

NEW ZEALAND

J.M.How	c Strauss b Sidebottom	44	lbw b Panesar	11
M.D.Bell	lbw b Sidebottom	0	c Broad b Panesar	69
S.P.Fleming	c Collingwood b Sidebottom	59	c Ambrose b Panesar	66
M.S.Sinclair	c Broad b Sidebottom	7	c Ambrose b Broad	6
L.R.P.L.Taylor	c Ambrose b Broad	2	c Collingwood b Panesar	74
G.D.Elliott	c Ambrose b Sidebottom	6	c Bell b Broad	4
†B.B.McCullum	b Sidebottom	9	b Panesar	42
*D.L.Vettori	c Cook b Sidebottom	14	c Ambrose b Anderson	43
T.G.Southee	c Pietersen b Broad	5	(10) not out	77
J.S.Patel	c Panesar b Broad	4	(9) c Broad b Panesar	18
C.S.Martin	not out	4	b Sidebottom	5
Extras	(LB 13, W 1)	14	(B 6, LB 5, W 4, NB 1)	16
Total	**(48.4 overs; 229 min)**	**168**	**(118.5 overs; 465 min)**	**431**

NEW ZEALAND	O	M	R	W		O	M	R	W
Martin	26	6	74	2		18	2	60	1
Southee	23.1	8	55	5		24	5	84	0
Elliott	10	2	27	1		14	1	58	0
Vettori	19	6	51	0	(5)	45	6	158	4
Patel	18	3	37	2	(4)	30.5	4	104	2
ENGLAND									
Sidebottom	21.4	6	47	7		19.5	3	83	1
Anderson	7	1	54	0		17	2	99	1
Broad	17	3	54	3		32	10	78	2
Panesar	1	1	0	0		46	17	126	6
Collingwood	2	2	0	0		2	0	20	0
Pietersen						2	0	14	0

FALL OF WICKETS

	E	NZ	E	NZ
Wkt	1st	1st	2nd	2nd
1st	4	1	5	48
2nd	4	103	77	147
3rd	4	116	140	156
4th	36	119	327	160
5th	125	119	361	172
6th	147	137	424	276
7th	208	138	425	281
8th	240	152	–	329
9th	253	164	–	347
10th	253	168	–	431

Umpires: D.J.Harper (*Australia*) (71) and R.E.Koertzen (*South Africa*) (89).
Referee: J.Srinath (*India*) (9).　　　　Test No. 1867/91 (NZ339/E870)

WEST INDIES v SRI LANKA (1st Test)

At Providence Stadium, Antigua, on 22, 23, 24, 25, 26 March 2008.
Toss: Sri Lanka. Result: **SRI LANKA** won by 121 runs.
Debuts: West Indies – S.J.Benn.

SRI LANKA

M.G.Vandort	lbw b Taylor	52	c Ramdin b Gayle	24
B.S.M.Warnapura	c Ramdin b Bravo	120	c Ramdin b Bravo	62
K.C.Sangakkara	c Smith b Taylor	50	c sub (F.H.Edwards) b Bravo	21
*D.P.M.D.Jayawardena	lbw b Gayle	136	c Chanderpaul b Benn	33
T.T.Samaraweera	c sub (T.M.Dowlin) b Taylor	0	not out	56
T.M.Dilshan	lbw b Taylor	20	lbw b Taylor	4
†H.A.P.W.Jayawardena	b Powell	21	(9) not out	5
W.P.U.C.J.Vaas	not out	54	(7) c Ramdin b Benn	13
M.T.T.Mirando	c sub (T.M.Dowlin) b Gayle	0	(8) c Taylor b Benn	14
M.R.K.B.Herath	not out	13		
M.Muralitharan				
Extras	(LB 7, W 1, NB 2)	10	(B 2, LB 1, NB 5)	8
Total	**(8 wkts dec; 162 overs; 647 min)**	**476**	**(7 wkts dec; 57 overs; 246 min)**	**240**

WEST INDIES

*C.H.Gayle	lbw b Vaas	0	(6) not out	51
D.S.Smith	c HAPW Jayawardena b Mirando	14	(1) c Mirando b Vaas	10
R.R.Sarwan	c HAPW Jayawardena b Vaas	80	lbw b Mirando	72
M.N.Samuels	c HAPW Jayawardena b Mirando	5	c Sangakkara b Vaas	10
S.Chanderpaul	c Warnapura b Muralitharan	23	b Vaas	3
D.J.Bravo	lbw b Muralitharan	8	(2) c and b Muralitharan	83
R.O.Hinds	c HAPW Jayawardena b Muralitharan	37	c Sangakkara b Muralitharan	10
†D.Ramdin	c Sangakkara b Vaas	38	c DPMD Jayawardena b Mirando	1
S.J.Benn	run out	28	lbw b Muralitharan	7
J.E.Taylor	not out	27	c Dilshan b Vaas	12
D.B.L.Powell	c DPMD Jayawardena b Mirando	12	c Muralitharan b Vaas	14
Extras	(LB 4, NB 4)	8	(B 25, LB 3, NB 14)	42
Total	**(111.5 overs; 446 min)**	**280**	**(106.2 overs; 448 min)**	**315**

WEST INDIES	O	M	R	W	O	M	R	W
Powell	29	3	89	1	9	0	33	0
Taylor	33	8	110	4	8	0	37	1
Gayle	27	4	66	2	(5) 13	1	54	1
Bravo	30	3	74	1	(3) 14	0	54	2
Benn	40	6	120	0	(4) 13	0	59	3
Hinds	3	0	10	0				

SRI LANKA	O	M	R	W	O	M	R	W
Vaas	25	7	48	3	22.2	7	61	5
Mirando	20.5	3	59	3	17	2	70	2
Dilshan	1	0	2	0				
Muralitharan	40	6	112	3	(4) 45	6	112	3
Herath	25	6	55	0	(3) 22	7	44	0

FALL OF WICKETS

Wkt	1st SL	1st WI	2nd SL	2nd WI
1st	130	4	43	22
2nd	205	46	94	156
3rd	243	58	133	171
4th	243	99	159	178
5th	277	109	171	212
6th	331	162	192	229
7th	457	193	224	231
8th	459	236	–	244
9th	–	252	–	291
10th	–	280	–	315

Umpires: B.F.Bowden (*New Zealand*) (45) and S.J.A.Taufel (*Australia*) (49).
Referee: B.C.Broad (*England*) (26). Test No. 1868/11 (WI444/SL176)

WEST INDIES v SRI LANKA (2nd Test)

At Queen's Park Oval, Port-of-Spain, Trinidad, on 3, 4, 5, 6 April 2008.
Toss: West Indies. Result: **WEST INDIES** won by six wickets.
Debuts: West Indies – S.Chattergoon; Sri Lanka – M.K.D.I.Amersinghe.

SRI LANKA

Batsman	1st innings		2nd innings	
M.G.Vandort	c Ramdin b Edwards	30	run out	1
B.S.M.Warnapura	c Chattergoon b Edwards	35	c Chattergoon b Taylor	0
†K.C.Sangakkara	c Ramdin b Edwards	10	c Samuels b Powell	14
*D.P.M.D.Jayawardena	b Taylor	26	b Edwards	12
T.T.Samaraweera	c Gayle b Taylor	6	run out	125
T.M.Dilshan	c Ramdin b Edwards	62	b Taylor	25
L.P.C.Silva	c Powell b Bravo	76	c Samuels b Taylor	13
W.P.U.C.J.Vaas	c Ramdin b Powell	1	c Ramdin b Gayle	45
M.T.T.Mirando	run out	1	c Ramdin b Bravo	10
M Muralitharan	c Bravo b Powell	8	c Powell b Taylor	4
M.K.D.I.Amersinghe	not out	0	not out	0
Extras	(LB 8, W 5, NB 10)	23	(B 1, LB 10, W 6, NB 2)	19
Total	**(64.5 overs)**	**278**	**(75.1 overs)**	**268**

WEST INDIES

Batsman	1st innings		2nd innings	
*C.H.Gayle	c Vandort b Mirando	45	c Dilshan b Mirando	10
S.Chattergoon	b Vaas	46	lbw b Vaas	11
R.R.Sarwan	c Warnapura b Muralitharan	57	c Dilshan b Muralitharan	102
M.N.Samuels	lbw b Muralitharan	3	c Warnapura b Vaas	11
S.Chanderpaul	lbw b Mirando	18	not out	86
D.S.Smith	b Muralitharan	47	not out	14
D.J.Bravo	lbw b Amersinghe	26		
†D.Ramdin	c Jayawardena b Muralitharan	13		
J.E.Taylor	lbw b Vaas	13		
D.B.L.Powell	lbw b Muralitharan	3		
F.H.Edwards	not out	1		
Extras	(LB 5, W 2, NB 15)	22	(B 11, LB 2, W 2, NB 5)	20
Total	**(76.2 overs)**	**294**	**(4 wkts; 68.3 overs)**	**254**

WEST INDIES	O	M	R	W	O	M	R	W
Powell	17	7	59	2	13	4	49	1
Taylor	17.2	7	74	2	15.1	1	52	4
Edwards	18	4	84	4	14	1	62	1
Gayle	2	2	0	0	(5) 14	0	30	1
Bravo	10.3	2	53	1	(4) 19	5	64	1

SRI LANKA	O	M	R	W	O	M	R	W
Vaas	23	1	76	2	17	2	52	2
Amersinghe	12	1	62	1	(3) 13	0	43	0
Mirando	12	0	72	2	(2) 12	3	49	1
Muralitharan	29.2	4	79	4	24.3	4	92	1
Silva					2	0	5	0

FALL OF WICKETS				
	SL	WI	SL	WI
Wkt	*1st*	*1st*	*2nd*	*2nd*
1st	62	58	2	23
2nd	72	137	4	24
3rd	93	141	32	73
4th	112	177	32	230
5th	117	199	73	–
6th	222	246	99	–
7th	224	266	237	–
8th	248	289	252	–
9th	255	291	268	–
10th	278	294	268	–

Umpires: B.F.Bowden (*New Zealand*) (46) and S.J.A.Taufel (*Australia*) (50).
Referee: B.C.Broad (*England*) (27). **Test No. 1869/12 (WI445/SL177)**

INDIA v SOUTH AFRICA (1st Test)

At M.A.Chidambaram Stadium, Madras, on 26, 27, 28, 29, 30 March 2008.
Toss: South Africa. Result: **MATCH DRAWN.**
Debuts: None.

SOUTH AFRICA

*G.C.Smith	c Laxman b Kumble	73	(2) lbw b Harbhajan		35
N.D.McKenzie	c Dravid b Harbhajan	94	(1) not out		155
H.M.Amla	run out	159	c Dravid b Kumble		81
J.H.Kallis	c Jaffer b Harbhajan	13	c Singh b Harbhajan		19
A.G.Prince	c and b Kumble	23	c Jaffer b Harbhajan		5
A.B.de Villiers	c Dhoni b Sreesanth	44	c Ganguly b Sehwag		11
†M.V.Boucher	c Dravid b Sehwag	70	not out		11
M.Morkel	c and b Harbhajan	35			
P.L.Harris	c Dhoni b Harbhajan	5			
D.W.Steyn	c Singh b Harbhajan	15			
M.Ntini	not out	1			
Extras	(B 1, LB 5, W 1, NB 1)	8	(B 8, LB 5, NB 1)		14
Total	**(152.5 overs; 679 min)**	**540**	**(5 wkts dec; 109 overs; 445 min)**		**331**

INDIA

W.Jaffer	c Kallis b Harris	73
V.Sehwag	c McKenzie b Ntini	319
R.Dravid	c Kallis b Ntini	111
S.R.Tendulkar	c Kallis b Ntini	0
S.C.Ganguly	c Boucher b Harris	24
V.V.S.Laxman	c and b Harris	39
†M.S.Dhoni	c Boucher b Steyn	16
*A.Kumble	b Steyn	3
Harbhajan Singh	b Steyn	0
R.P.Singh	b Steyn	0
S.Sreesanth	not out	4
Extras	(B 20, LB 10, W 4, NB 4)	38
Total	**(155.1 overs; 760 min)**	**627**

INDIA	O	M	R	W		O	M	R	W
Singh	23	1	111	0	(2)	9	1	43	0
Sreesanth	26	5	104	1	(1)	12	0	42	0
Kumble	45	11	106	2	(5)	20	2	57	1
Harbhajan Singh	44.5	4	164	5	(3)	34	1	101	3
Sehwag	11	1	37	1	(6)	22	2	55	1
Ganguly	3	0	12	0	(4)	2	1	1	0
Laxman						10	2	19	0

SOUTH AFRICA	O	M	R	W
Steyn	32	3	103	4
Ntini	28	3	128	3
Morkel	25	4	76	0
Harris	53.1	6	203	3
Kallis	14	0	71	0
Prince	3	0	16	0

FALL OF WICKETS			
	SA	I	SA
Wkt	*1st*	*1st*	*2nd*
1st	132	213	53
2nd	196	481	210
3rd	244	481	264
4th	291	526	272
5th	357	573	306
6th	456	598	–
7th	510	610	–
8th	520	610	–
9th	529	612	–
10th	540	627	–

Umpires: Asad Rauf (*Pakistan*) (18) and A.L.Hill (*New Zealand*) (6).
Referee: R.S.Mahanama (*Sri Lanka*) (19).   **Test No. 1870/20 (I416/SA330)**

INDIA v SOUTH AFRICA (2nd Test)

At Sardar Patel Stadium, Motera, Ahmedabad, on 3, 4, 5 April 2008.
Toss: India. Result: **SOUTH AFRICA** won by an innings and 90 runs.
Debuts: None.

INDIA

W.Jaffer	c Smith b Ntini	9	(2) c De Villiers b Kallis		19
V.Sehwag	b Steyn	6	(1) lbw b Ntini		17
R.Dravid	b Steyn	3	c De Villiers b Morkel		17
V.V.S.Laxman	b Ntini	3	c Boucher b Morkel		35
S.C.Ganguly	b Ntini	0	c Boucher b Steyn		87
†M.S.Dhoni	c Boucher b Morkel	14	c Smith b Ntini		52
I.K.Pathan	not out	21	not out		43
*A.Kumble	b Morkel	0	b Harris		5
Harbhajan Singh	lbw b Steyn	1	lbw b Steyn		4
R.P.Singh	c Smith b Steyn	0	c Kallis b Steyn		8
S.Sreesanth	b Steyn	0	b Ntini		17
Extras	(B 4, LB 11, W 2, NB 2)	19	(B 5, LB 7, W 7, NB 5)		24
Total	(20 overs; 109 min)	76	(94.2 overs; 448 min)		328

SOUTH AFRICA

*G.C.Smith	lbw b Sreesanth	34
N.D.McKenzie	c Dravid b Harbhajan	42
H.M.Amla	c Jaffer b Harbhajan	16
J.H.Kallis	b Sreesanth	132
A.G.Prince	lbw b Harbhajan	2
A.B.de Villiers	not out	217
†M.V.Boucher	lbw b Kumble	21
M.Morkel	lbw b Harbhajan	1
P.L.Harris	not out	9
D.W.Steyn		
M.Ntini		
Extras	(B 2, LB 14, W 4)	20
Total	(7 wkts dec; 141.2 overs; 625 min)	494

SOUTH AFRICA	O	M	R	W	O	M	R	W	FALL OF WICKETS
Steyn	8	2	25	5	23	1	91	3	
Ntini	6	1	18	3	16.2	3	44	3	
Morkel	6	1	20	2	20	0	87	2	
Kallis					10	3	26	1	
Harris					25	4	68	1	

INDIA	O	M	R	W
Sreesanth	23	4	87	2
Singh	21	2	81	0
Pathan	21.2	3	85	0
Harbhajan Singh	40	5	135	4
Kumble	33	2	78	1
Ganguly	3	0	12	0

	I	SA	I
Wkt	1st	1st	2nd
1st	16	78	31
2nd	24	100	64
3rd	30	101	70
4th	30	117	125
5th	53	373	235
6th	55	439	268
7th	55	452	273
8th	56	–	292
9th	76	–	306
10th	76	–	328

Umpires: B.R.Doctrove (*West Indies*) (16) and A.L.Hill (*New Zealand*) (7).
Referee: R.S.Mahanama (*Sri Lanka*) (20).   **Test No. 1871/21 (I417/SA331)**

INDIA v SOUTH AFRICA (3rd Test)

At Modi Stadium, Green Park, Kanpur, on 11, 12, 13 April 2008.
Toss: South Africa. Result: **INDIA** won by eight wickets.
Debuts: None.

SOUTH AFRICA

N.D.McKenzie	st Dhoni b Chawla	36	lbw b Sreesanth	14
*G.C.Smith	c Jaffer b Yuvraj	69	b Sehwag	35
H.M.Amla	b Sharma	51	c Jaffer b Harbhajan	0
J.H.Kallis	b Harbhajan	1	c Jaffer b Sehwag	15
A.G.Prince	lbw b Sehwag	16	not out	22
A.B.de Villiers	c Ganguly b Chawla	25	c Laxman b Harbhajan	7
†M.V.Boucher	b Sharma	29	c Dhoni b Sharma	5
M.Morkel	c Dravid b Harbhajan	17	b Sharma	0
P.L.Harris	b Sharma	12	c Dravid b Harbhajan	0
D.W.Steyn	c sub (M.Kaif) b Harbhajan	0	b Harbhajan	7
M.Ntini	not out	0	c Ganguly b Sehwag	0
Extras	(LB 3, W 2, NB 4)	9	(B 12, LB 1, W 1, NB 2)	16
Total	**(87.3 overs; 379 min)**	**265**	**(55.5 overs; 259 min)**	**121**

INDIA

W.Jaffer	lbw b Morkel	15	lbw b Morkel	10
V.Sehwag	lbw b Steyn	8	c Prince b Harris	22
R.Dravid	c De Villiers b Morkel	29	(4) not out	18
V.V.S.Laxman	b Morkel	50		
S.C.Ganguly	c Amla b Steyn	87	(3) not out	13
Yuvraj Singh	c De Villiers b Harris	32		
*†M.S.Dhoni	st Boucher b Harris	32		
Harbhajan Singh	lbw b Steyn	6		
P.P.Chawla	c Smith b Ntini	4		
S.Sreesanth	c Prince b Harris	29		
I.Sharma	not out	0		
Extras	(B 8, LB 6, W 1, NB 4)	19	(NB 1)	1
Total	**(99.4 overs; 456 min)**	**325**	**(2 wkts; 13.1 overs; 57 min)**	**64**

INDIA	O	M	R	W		O	M	R	W
Sreesanth	11	0	32	0	(3)	9	4	9	1
Sharma	12.3	1	55	3		10	2	18	2
Harbhajan Singh	31	9	52	3	(1)	23	7	44	4
Chawla	16	3	66	2		4	0	18	0
Yuvraj Singh	11	1	39	1	(6)	1	0	7	0
Sehwag	6	2	18	1	(5)	8.5	2	12	3

SOUTH AFRICA	O	M	R	W		O	M	R	W
Steyn	20	1	71	3		2	0	15	0
Ntini	21	7	47	1		1	0	5	0
Morkel	15	2	63	3	(4)	5	1	8	1
Harris	32.4	8	101	3	(3)	5.1	0	36	1
Kallis	9	1	23	0					
Amla	2	0	6	0					

FALL OF WICKETS				
	SA	I	SA	I
Wkt	1st	1st	2nd	2nd
1st	61	18	26	32
2nd	152	35	27	32
3rd	160	113	65	–
4th	161	123	72	–
5th	199	188	90	–
6th	215	248	101	–
7th	241	268	101	–
8th	264	279	102	–
9th	265	279	114	–
10th	265	325	121	–

Umpires: Asad Rauf (*Pakistan*) (19) and B.R.Doctrove (*West Indies*) (17).
Referee: R.S.Mahanama (*Sri Lanka*) (21).   **Test No. 1872/22 (I418/SA332)**

ENGLAND v NEW ZEALAND (1st Test)

At Lord's, London, on 15, 16, 17, 18, 19 May 2008.
Toss: England. Result: **MATCH DRAWN**.
Debuts: New Zealand – D.R.Flynn, A.J.Redmond.

NEW ZEALAND

J.M.How	c Ambrose b Anderson	7	c Cook b Broad	68
A.J.Redmond	c Cook b Anderson	0	c Strauss b Anderson	17
J.A.H.Marshall	c Strauss b Broad	24	lbw b Sidebottom	0
L.R.P.L.Taylor	c Collingwood b Broad	19	lbw b Panesar	20
†B.B.McCullum	b Panesar	97	c Ambrose b Anderson	24
D.R.Flynn	b Anderson	9	not out	29
J.D.P.Oram	c Strauss b Sidebottom	28	b Sidebottom	101
*D.L.Vettori	b Sidebottom	48	not out	0
K.D.Mills	b Sidebottom	10		
T.G.Southee	b Sidebottom	1		
C.S.Martin	not out	0		
Extras	(B 16, LB 14, W 1, NB 3)	34	(B 4, LB 5, NB 1)	10
Total	**(86.2 overs; 386 min)**	**277**	**(6 wkts; 86.2 overs; 365 min)**	**269**

ENGLAND

A.J.Strauss	lbw b Oram	63
A.N.Cook	c McCullum b Martin	61
*M.P.Vaughan	c Marshall b Vettori	106
K.P.Pietersen	lbw b Vettori	3
I.R.Bell	c McCullum b Martin	16
P.D.Collingwood	c Taylor b Vettori	6
†T.R.Ambrose	lbw b Vettori	0
S.C.J.Broad	b Oram	25
R.J.Sidebottom	c Taylor b Mills	16
M.S.Panesar	c Flynn b Vettori	0
J.M.Anderson	not out	0
Extras	(B 3, LB 7, W 1, NB 12)	23
Total	**(111.3 overs; 488 min)**	**319**

ENGLAND	O	M	R	W	O	M	R	W	FALL OF WICKETS			
										NZ	E	NZ
Sidebottom	28.2	12	55	4	21.2	4	65	2	*Wkt*	*1st*	*1st*	*2nd*
Anderson	20	5	66	3	19	5	64	2	1st	2	121	47
Broad	24	4	85	2	17	4	54	1	2nd	18	148	52
Collingwood	3	1	11	0					3rd	41	152	99
Panesar	11	2	30	1	(4) 24	8	56	1	4th	76	180	115
Pietersen					(5) 5	0	21	0	5th	104	208	252
									6th	203	208	269
NEW ZEALAND									7th	222	269	–
Martin	32	8	76	2					8th	258	317	–
Mills	22	3	60	1					9th	260	318	–
Southee	16	2	59	0					10th	277	319	–
Oram	19	5	45	2								
Vettori	22.3	4	69	5								

Umpires: S.A.Bucknor (*West Indies*) (123) and S.J.A.Taufel (*Australia*) (51).
Referee: R.S.Madugalle (*Sri Lanka*) (102). Test No. 1873/92 (E871/NZ340)

ENGLAND v NEW ZEALAND (2nd Test)

At Old Trafford, Manchester, on 23, 24, 25, 26 May 2008.
Toss: New Zealand. Result: **ENGLAND** won by six wickets.
Debuts: None.

NEW ZEALAND

J.M.How	c Ambrose b Anderson	64		lbw b Panesar	29
A.J.Redmond	b Sidebottom	28		c Collingwood b Anderson	6
J.A.H.Marshall	lbw b Sidebottom	0		lbw b Panesar	28
L.R.P.L.Taylor	not out	154		lbw b Panesar	15
†B.B.McCullum	c Collingwood b Panesar	11		lbw b Panesar	0
D.R.Flynn	retired hurt	4		absent hurt	–
J.D.P.Oram	run out	38	(8)	c Ambrose b Sidebottom	7
*D.L.Vettori	run out	1	(6)	c Broad b Panesar	4
K.D.Mills	b Anderson	57	(7)	c Ambrose b Panesar	8
I.E.O'Brien	c Bell b Anderson	5	(9)	c Anderson b Sidebottom	6
C.S.Martin	b Anderson	0	(10)	not out	0
Extras	(B 4, LB 11, W 3, NB 1)	19		(LB 11)	11
Total	**(90.3 overs; 401 min)**	**381**		**(41.2 overs; 166 min)**	**114**

ENGLAND

A.J.Strauss	c McCullum b O'Brien	60		c Taylor b O'Brien	106
A.N.Cook	lbw b O'Brien	19		c Marshall b Vettori	28
*M.P.Vaughan	lbw b Vettori	30		c McCullum b Martin	48
K.P.Pietersen	c Taylor b Vettori	26		run out	42
R.J.Sidebottom	c How b Vettori	4			
I.R.Bell	c Taylor b O'Brien	8	(5)	not out	21
P.D.Collingwood	lbw b Vettori	2	(6)	not out	24
†T.R.Ambrose	c Taylor b Vettori	3			
S.C.J.Broad	c sub (J.S.Patel) b Mills	30			
M.S.Panesar	c McCullum b Mills	1			
J.M.Anderson	not out	3			
Extras	(B 2, LB 7, NB 7)	16		(B 9, LB 10, NB 6)	25
Total	**(83.3 overs; 329 min)**	**202**		**(4 wkts; 88 overs; 347 min)**	**294**

ENGLAND	O	M	R	W	O	M	R	W
Sidebottom	27	6	86	2	12.2	5	26	2
Anderson	20.3	0	118	4	8	1	21	1
Panesar	22	1	101	1	17	5	37	6
Broad	20	3	60	0	4	0	19	0
Collingwood	1	0	1	0				

NEW ZEALAND	O	M	R	W	O	M	R	W
Martin	10	3	31	0	13	1	45	1
Mills	9.3	1	38	2	6	0	17	0
O'Brien	23	9	49	5	(4) 20	2	62	1
Vettori	31	5	66	5	(3) 35	7	111	1
Oram	8	3	5	0	(6) 13	1	36	0
Redmond	2	1	4	0				
How					(5) 1	0	4	0

FALL OF WICKETS

	NZ	E	NZ	E
Wkt	1st	1st	2nd	2nd
1st	80	33	28	60
2nd	86	111	50	150
3rd	102	141	85	235
4th	123	145	85	248
5th	249	160	91	–
6th	250	164	91	–
7th	339	164	106	–
8th	368	179	114	–
9th	381	180	114	–
10th	–	202	–	–

Umpires: D.B.Hair (*Australia*) (77) and S.J.A.Taufel (*Australia*) (52).
Referee: R.S.Madugalle (*Sri Lanka*) (103).   **Test No. 1874/93 (E872/NZ341)**
In the first innings Flynn retired hurt at 136.

ENGLAND v NEW ZEALAND (3rd Test)

At Trent Bridge, Nottingham, on 5, 6, 7, 8 June 2008.
Toss: New Zealand. Result: **ENGLAND** won by an innings and 9 runs.
Debuts: New Zealand – G.J.Hopkins.

ENGLAND

A.J.Strauss	c Taylor b Mills	37
A.N.Cook	b Mills	6
*M.P.Vaughan	b O'Brien	16
K.P.Pietersen	c Hopkins b O'Brien	115
I.R.Bell	lbw b O'Brien	0
P.D.Collingwood	c Taylor b Mills	0
†T.R.Ambrose	c Hopkins b O'Brien	67
S.C.J.Broad	b Martin	64
J.M.Anderson	c Hopkins b Oram	28
R.J.Sidebottom	not out	7
M.S.Panesar	c McCullum b Vettori	0
Extras	(B 10, LB 9, W 1, NB 4)	24
Total	**(126.5 overs; 519 min)**	**364**

NEW ZEALAND

J.M.How	c Ambrose b Anderson	40	c Cook b Sidebottom	19
A.J.Redmond	b Anderson	1	c Ambrose b Broad	2
B.B.McCullum	b Anderson	9	b Anderson	71
L.R.P.L.Taylor	c Pietersen b Anderson	21	lbw b Broad	14
D.R.Flynn	lbw b Anderson	0	c Ambrose b Sidebottom	49
†G.J.Hopkins	lbw b Anderson	15	c Ambrose b Sidebottom	12
J.D.P.Oram	c Ambrose b Anderson	7	not out	50
*D.L.Vettori	c Strauss b Sidebottom	7	c Pietersen b Sidebottom	1
K.D.Mills	c Pietersen b Broad	1	c Strauss b Sidebottom	2
I.E.O'Brien	b Broad	0	c Collingwood b Sidebottom	4
C.S.Martin	not out	0	c Collingwood b Anderson	0
Extras	(B 8, LB 8, W 6)	22	(B 3, LB 4, W 1)	8
Total	**(46.3 overs; 214 min)**	**123**	**(72.3 overs; 327 min)**	**232**

NEW ZEALAND	O	M	R	W	O	M	R	W
Martin	22	5	83	1				
Mills	31	8	76	3				
O'Brien	23	4	74	4				
Oram	22	7	35	1				
Vettori	28.5	4	77	1				

ENGLAND	O	M	R	W	O	M	R	W
Sidebottom	17	4	49	1	24	7	67	6
Anderson	21.3	8	43	7	14.3	3	55	2
Collingwood	2	0	5	0	(5) 2	1	5	0
Broad	6	3	10	2	(3) 21	4	77	2
Panesar					(4) 11	4	21	0

FALL OF WICKETS

	E	NZ	NZ
Wkt	1st	1st	2nd
1st	14	2	21
2nd	44	14	33
3rd	84	62	58
4th	85	62	152
5th	86	77	169
6th	247	93	197
7th	262	108	205
8th	338	123	211
9th	361	123	225
10th	364	123	232

Umpires: S.A.Bucknor (*West Indies*) (124) and D.B.Hair (*Australia*) (78).
Referee: R.S.Madugalle (*Sri Lanka*) (104). **Test No. 1875/94 (E873/NZ342)**

WEST INDIES v AUSTRALIA (1st Test)

At Sabina Park, Kingston, Jamaica, on 22, 23, 24, 25, 26 May 2008.
Toss: Australia. Result: **AUSTRALIA** won by 95 runs.
Debuts: West Indies – A.S.Jaggernauth; Australia – B.J.Haddin.

AUSTRALIA

P.A.Jaques	lbw b Edwards	9	c Ramdin b Edwards		4
S.M.Katich	c Sammy b Edwards	12	lbw b Edwards		1
*R.T.Ponting	c Parchment b Bravo	158	c Bravo b Powell		5
M.E.K.Hussey	c Bravo b Jaggernauth	56	b Powell		1
B.J.Hodge	c Ramdin b Edwards	67	(6) c Ramdin b Bravo		27
M.G.Johnson	c Powell b Sammy	22	(5) c Ramdin b Powell		4
A.Symonds	not out	70	c Sammy b Morton		79
†B.J.Haddin	c Ramdin b Sammy	11	c Morton b Bravo		23
B.Lee	lbw b Edwards	4	c Ramdin b Edwards		9
S.R.Clark	c Bravo b Powell	3	not out		1
S.C.G.MacGill	b Edwards	2	c Morton b Bravo		0
Extras	(B 2, LB 13, NB 2)	17	(B 2, LB 10, NB 1)		13
Total	**(126.5 overs)**	**431**	**(56.5 overs)**		**167**

WEST INDIES

D.S.Smith	b Clark	32	lbw b Clark		28
B.A.Parchment	c Haddin b Clark	9	c Haddin b Clark		15
*R.R.Sarwan	c Haddin b Clark	7	c Symonds b Clark		12
R.S.Morton	c Clark b MacGill	67	lbw b Lee		9
S.Chanderpaul	c Hussey b MacGill	118	c and b Lee		11
D.J.Bravo	c Katich b Lee	46	c Johnson b Clark		0
†D.Ramdin	c Haddin b Lee	0	run out		36
D.J.G.Sammy	c Jaques b Johnson	0	lbw b Clark		35
D.B.L.Powell	b Lee	3	c Haddin b MacGill		27
F.H.Edwards	c Haddin b Johnson	1	not out		9
A.S.Jaggernauth	not out	0	c Jaques b MacGill		0
Extras	(B 2, LB 10, W 3, NB 14)	29	(B 4, LB 2, NB 3)		9
Total	**(106 overs)**	**312**	**(67 overs)**		**191**

WEST INDIES	O	M	R	W		O	M	R	W	FALL OF WICKETS				
Powell	29	4	99	1		15	5	36	3		A	WI	A	WI
Edwards	26.5	4	104	5		16	3	40	3	Wkt	1st	1st	2nd	2nd
Sammy	29	7	78	2	(5)	4	0	10	0	1st	18	47	5	22
Bravo	22	6	61	1	(3)	18.5	3	47	4	2nd	37	62	10	55
Jaggernauth	20	0	74	1	(4)	3	0	22	0	3rd	174	68	12	74
										4th	293	196	12	74
AUSTRALIA										5th	326	260	18	80
Lee	28	7	63	3		22	6	81	2	6th	350	262	70	82
Johnson	26	6	63	2	(3)	11	3	29	0	7th	368	263	144	149
Clark	19	2	59	3	(2)	20	8	32	5	8th	383	268	162	172
MacGill	22	2	100	2		14	2	43	2	9th	399	298	166	191
Symonds	11	4	15	0						10th	431	312	167	191

Umpires: Alim Dar (*Pakistan*) (47) and R.B.Tiffin (*Zimbabwe*) (41).
Referee: R.S.Mahanama (*Sri Lanka*) (22).   **Test No. 1876/103 (WI446/A693)**

WEST INDIES v AUSTRALIA (2nd Test)

At Sir Vivian Richards Stadium, North Sound, Antigua, on 30, 31 May, 1, 2, 3 June 2008.
Toss: Australia. Result: **MATCH DRAWN**.
Debuts: None.

AUSTRALIA

P.A.Jaques	lbw b Bravo	17	c Ramdin b Taylor		76
S.M.Katich	c Ramdin b Taylor	113			
*R.T.Ponting	c Marshall b Taylor	65	lbw b Taylor		38
M.E.K.Hussey	c Chanderpaul b Sammy	10	(2) c Ramdin b Bravo		40
M.J.Clarke	c Marshall b Powell	110	(4) run out		10
A.Symonds	c Ramdin b Edwards	18	(5) not out		43
†B.J.Haddin	c Morton b Taylor	33	(6) lbw b Edwards		7
B.Lee	not out	63	(7) c Ramdin b Edwards		4
M.G.Johnson	not out	29			
S.R.Clark					
S.C.G.MacGill					
Extras	(LB 7, W 5, NB 9)	21	(B8, LB 6, W 3, NB 9)		26
Total	**(7 wkts dec; 136 overs)**	**479**	**(6 wkts dec; 61.5 overs)**		**244**

WEST INDIES

D.S.Smith	c Symonds b Johnson	16	c Hussey b Lee		0
X.M.Marshall	lbw b Clarke	53	c Haddin b Clark		5
*R.R.Sarwan	c Clarke b MacGill	65	c Hussey b Johnson		128
R.S.Morton	c Katich b Clarke	2	lbw b Lee		14
S.Chanderpaul	not out	107	not out		77
D.J.Bravo	c Haddin b Lee	45	c sub (B.J.Hodge) b Lee		1
†D.Ramdin	lbw b Lee	0	not out		21
D.J.G.Sammy	lbw b Lee	0			
J.E.Taylor	b Lee	20			
D.B.L.Powell	lbw b Lee	0			
F.H.Edwards	c Haddin b Johnson	0			
Extras	(B 17, LB 13, W 2, NB 12)	44	(LB 8, NB 12)		20
Total	**(107 overs)**	**352**	**(5 wkts; 93 overs)**		**266**

WEST INDIES	O	M	R	W		O	M	R	W
Powell	29	3	101	1		13	3	47	0
Edwards	28	6	98	1		7.5	1	28	2
Taylor	27	5	95	3		12	0	33	2
Bravo	24	4	80	1	(5)	14	1	59	1
Sammy	21	2	71	1	(4)	12	1	45	0
Sarwan	7	0	27	0		3	0	18	0

AUSTRALIA	O	M	R	W		O	M	R	W
Lee	21	7	59	5		21	5	51	3
Johnson	24	5	72	2	(4)	20	3	70	1
Clark	14	0	39	0	(2)	18	8	22	1
MacGill	21	1	107	1	(5)	19	2	75	0
Clarke	15	7	20	2	(3)	6	3	16	0
Symonds	12	3	25	0	(7)	3	0	10	0
Hussey					(6)	6	2	14	0

FALL OF WICKETS

	A	WI	A	WI
Wkt	1st	1st	2nd	2nd
1st	36	55	74	4
2nd	172	103	163	19
3rd	199	105	178	84
4th	271	182	186	227
5th	296	314	222	236
6th	360	314	244	–
7th	414	318	–	–
8th	–	341	–	–
9th	–	341	–	–
10th	–	352	–	–

Umpires: M.R.Benson (*England*) (22) and R.B.Tiffin (*Zimbabwe*) (42).
Referee: R.S.Mahanama (*Sri Lanka*) (23).   Test No. 1877/104 (WI447/A694)

WEST INDIES v AUSTRALIA (3rd Test)

At Kensington Oval, Bridgetown, Barbados, on 12, 13, 14, 15, 16 June 2008.
Toss: West Indies. Result: **AUSTRALIA** won by 87 runs.
Debuts: Australia – B.Casson.

AUSTRALIA

P.A.Jaques	c Ramdin b Taylor	31	c Ramdin b Edwards	108
S.M.Katich	c Gayle b Edwards	36	c sub (D.J.G.Sammy) b Benn	157
*R.T.Ponting	lbw b Taylor	18	c sub (R.S.Morton) b Powell	39
M.E.K.Hussey	c Powell b Bravo	12	c Bravo b Benn	18
M.J.Clarke	c Ramdin b Bravo	0	not out	48
A.Symonds	c Chattergoon b Bravo	52	c Chanderpaul b Benn	2
†B.J.Haddin	lbw b Benn	32	not out	45
B.Casson	lbw b Edwards	10		
B.Lee	not out	23		
M.G.Johnson	c Benn b Taylor	0		
S.R.Clark	b Edwards	1		
Extras	(LB 7, W 21, NB 8)	36	(B 5, LB 2, W 5, NB 5, Pen 5)	22
Total	**(67.1 overs; 318 min)**	**251**	**(5 wkts dec; 145 overs; 605 min)**	**439**

WEST INDIES

*C.H.Gayle	c Casson b Lee	14	c Lee b Clark	26
S.Chattergoon	c Haddin b Lee	6	(8) c Haddin b Lee	13
R.R.Sarwan	c Hussey b Clark	20	lbw b Clarke	43
X.M.Marshall	c Casson b Symonds	39	(2) c Jaques b Casson	85
S.Chanderpaul	not out	79	(4) lbw b Clark	50
D.J.Bravo	c Haddin b Johnson	29	(5) c Jaques b Casson	69
†D.Ramdin	c Katich b Clarke	1	(6) lbw b Clark	8
J.E.Taylor	c Katich b Clarke	0	(7) c Haddin b Johnson	31
S.J.Benn	c Haddin b Johnson	3	c Hussey b Casson	13
D.B.L.Powell	c Haddin b Lee	9	c Haddin b Lee	6
F.H.Edwards	c Ponting b Johnson	1	not out	5
Extras	(LB 7, NB 8)	15	(B 10, LB 8, W 8, NB 12)	38
Total	**(58.5 overs; 287 min)**	**216**	**(105.4 overs; 477 min)**	**387**

WEST INDIES	O	M	R	W		O	M	R	W
Powell	11	5	43	0		16	6	40	1
Edwards	16.1	3	55	3		14	3	52	1
Taylor	12	2	46	3		22	3	64	0
Gayle	7	2	6	0		16	3	45	0
Bravo	15	5	61	3	(6)	23	4	63	0
Benn	6	0	33	1	(5)	47	7	154	3
Marshall						2	2	0	0
Sarwan						5	0	9	0

AUSTRALIA	O	M	R	W		O	M	R	W
Lee	15	2	64	3		25.4	3	109	2
Clark	15	4	41	1		24	8	58	3
Johnson	11.5	3	41	4		12	0	72	1
Symonds	8	4	17	1	(6)	2	0	6	0
Casson	7	1	43	0	(4)	25	3	86	3
Clarke	2	0	3	1	(5)	17	1	38	1

FALL OF WICKETS

	A	WI	A	WI
Wkt	1st	1st	2nd	2nd
1st	46	11	223	64
2nd	75	26	299	159
3rd	96	64	330	181
4th	96	108	358	303
5th	111	168	360	303
6th	198	188	–	345
7th	213	189	–	351
8th	244	195	–	375
9th	245	204	–	375
10th	251	216	–	387

Umpires: Alim Dar (*Pakistan*) (48) and M.R.Benson (*England*) (23).
Referee: R.S.Mahanama (*Sri Lanka*) (24).   Test No. 1878/105 (WI448/A695)

ENGLAND v SOUTH AFRICA (1st Test)

At Lord's, London, on 10, 11, 12, 13, 14 July 2008.
Toss: South Africa. Result: **MATCH DRAWN**.
Debuts: None.

ENGLAND

A.J.Strauss	lbw b Morkel	44			
A.N.Cook	c De Villiers b Morkel	60			
*M.P.Vaughan	b Steyn	2			
K.P.Pietersen	c Boucher b Morkel	152			
I.R.Bell	c and b Harris	199			
P.D.Collingwood	c Amla b Harris	7			
†T.R.Ambrose	c Smith b Morkel	4			
S.C.J.Broad	b Harris	76			
R.J.Sidebottom	not out	1			
M.S.Panesar					
J.M.Anderson					
Extras	(B 14, LB 12, W 7, NB 15)	48			
Total	**(8 wkts dec; 156.2 overs; 688 min)**	**593**			

SOUTH AFRICA

*G.C.Smith	c Bell b Anderson	8	c Pietersen b Anderson	107
N.D.McKenzie	b Panesar	40	c Ambrose b Anderson	138
H.M.Amla	c Ambrose b Broad	6	not out	104
J.H.Kallis	c Strauss b Sidebottom	7	b Sidebottom	13
A.G.Prince	c Ambrose b Sidebottom	101	not out	9
A.B.de Villiers	c Anderson b Panesar	42		
†M.V.Boucher	b Broad	4		
M.Morkel	b Panesar	6		
P.L.Harris	c Anderson b Panesar	6		
D.W.Steyn	c Sidebottom b Pietersen	19		
M.Ntini	not out	0		
Extras	(B 1, LB 4, W 3)	8	(B 8, LB 8, W 5, NB 1)	22
Total	**(93.3 overs; 412 min)**	**247**	**(3 wkts dec; 167 overs; 687 min)**	**393**

SOUTH AFRICA	O	M	R	W		O	M	R	W
Steyn	35	8	117	1					
Ntini	29	2	130	0					
Morkel	34	3	121	4					
Kallis	20	3	70	0					
Harris	38.2	8	129	3					

ENGLAND	O	M	R	W		O	M	R	W
Sidebottom	19	3	41	2	(3)	30	9	46	1
Anderson	21	7	36	1	(4)	32	7	78	2
Broad	23	3	88	2	(5)	26	7	78	0
Panesar	26	4	74	4	(1)	60	15	116	0
Collingwood	4	1	3	0	(6)	11	4	37	0
Pietersen	0.3	0	0	1	(2)	7	1	21	0
Cook						1	0	1	0

FALL OF WICKETS

	E	SA	SA
Wkt	1st	1st	2nd
1st	114	13	204
2nd	117	28	329
3rd	117	47	357
4th	403	83	–
5th	413	161	–
6th	422	166	–
7th	574	191	–
8th	593	203	–
9th	–	245	–
10th	–	247	–

Umpires: B.F.Bowden (*New Zealand*) (47) and D.J.Harper (*Australia*) (72).
Referee: J.J.Crowe (*New Zealand*) (25).   **Test No. 1879/131 (E874/SA333)**

ENGLAND v SOUTH AFRICA (2nd Test)

At Headingley, Leeds, on 18, 19, 20, 21 July 2008.
Toss: South Africa. Result: **SOUTH AFRICA** won by ten wickets.
Debuts: England – D.J.Pattinson.

ENGLAND

A.J.Strauss	c Boucher b Morkel	27		c Boucher b Ntini	0
A.N.Cook	c Boucher b Morkel	18		c Amla b Kallis	60
*M.P.Vaughan	c Smith b Steyn	0		c Boucher b Ntini	21
K.P.Pietersen	c Smith b Steyn	45	(5)	c Boucher b Kallis	13
I.R.Bell	b Kallis	31	(6)	c De Villiers b Morkel	4
†T.R.Ambrose	c Boucher b Ntini	12	(7)	c Boucher b Steyn	36
A.Flintoff	c Boucher b Steyn	17	(8)	c Kallis b Morkel	38
S.C.J.Broad	c De Villiers b Morkel	17	(9)	not out	67
J.M.Anderson	not out	11	(4)	lbw b Steyn	34
M.S.Panesar	c De Villiers b Morkel	0		b Steyn	10
D.J.Pattinson	c Boucher b Steyn	8		b Morkel	13
Extras	(LB 6, W 6, NB 5)	17		(B 4, LB 11, W 2, NB 14)	31
Total	**(52.3 overs; 251 min)**	**203**		**(107 overs; 486 min)**	**327**

SOUTH AFRICA

N.D.McKenzie	c Flintoff b Anderson	15	(2)	not out	6
*G.C.Smith	c Strauss b Flintoff	44	(1)	not out	3
H.M.Amla	lbw b Pattinson	38			
J.H.Kallis	b Anderson	4			
A.G.Prince	c Ambrose b Pattinson	149			
A.B.de Villiers	c Flintoff b Broad	174			
†M.V.Boucher	b Anderson	34			
M.Morkel	b Panesar	0			
P.L.Harris	c Anderson b Panesar	24			
D.W.Steyn	not out	10			
M.Ntini	c Pietersen b Panesar	1			
Extras	(B 2, LB 19, W 1, NB 7)	29			
Total	**(176.2 overs; 743 min)**	**522**		**(0 wkts; 1.1 overs; 5 min)**	**9**

SOUTH AFRICA	O	M	R	W	O	M	R	W
Steyn	18.3	2	76	4	28	7	97	3
Ntini	11	0	45	1	25	7	69	2
Morkel	15	4	52	4	22	4	61	3
Kallis	8	2	24	1	17	3	50	2
Harris					15	5	35	0

ENGLAND	O	M	R	W	O	M	R	W
Anderson	44	9	136	3				
Pattinson	30	2	95	2	0.1	0	1	0
Flintoff	40	12	77	1				
Broad	29	2	114	1	(1) 1	0	8	0
Panesar	29.2	6	65	3				
Pietersen	4	0	14	0				

FALL OF WICKETS				
	E	SA	E	SA
Wkt	1st	1st	2nd	2nd
1st	26	51	3	–
2nd	27	69	50	–
3rd	62	76	109	–
4th	106	143	123	–
5th	123	355	140	–
6th	150	422	152	–
7th	177	427	220	–
8th	181	511	238	–
9th	186	511	266	–
10th	203	522	327	–

Umpires: B.F.Bowden (*New Zealand*) (48) and D.J.Harper (*Australia*) (73).
Referee: J.J.Crowe (*New Zealand*) (26).   **Test No. 1880/132 (E875/SA334)**

ENGLAND v SOUTH AFRICA (3rd Test)

At Edgbaston, Birmingham, on 30, 31 July, 1, 2 August 2008.
Toss: England. Result: **SOUTH AFRICA** won by five wickets.
Debuts: None.

ENGLAND

A.J.Strauss	hit wicket b Nel	20	c Kallis b Morkel		25
A.N.Cook	c Kallis b Nel	76	c Boucher b Ntini		9
*M.P.Vaughan	c Boucher b Nel	0	c Amla b Nel		17
K.P.Pietersen	c Prince b Kallis	4	c De Villiers b Harris		94
I.R.Bell	c Boucher b Ntini	50	c Boucher b Ntini		20
P.D.Collingwood	c Smith b Kallis	4	c Boucher b Morkel		135
A.Flintoff	not out	36	c Amla b Harris		2
†T.R.Ambrose	b Kallis	22	b Morkel		19
R.J.Sidebottom	c Boucher b Ntini	2	c Amla b Morkel		22
J.M.Anderson	run out	1	b Kallis		1
M.S.Panesar	run out	1	not out		0
Extras	(B 1, LB 7, W 2, NB 5)	15	(B 8, LB 2, W 6, NB 3)		19
Total	**(77 overs; 334 min)**	**231**	**(98.2 overs; 432 min)**		**363**

SOUTH AFRICA

N.D.McKenzie	lbw b Flintoff	72	(2) lbw b Flintoff		22
*G.C.Smith	c Strauss b Flintoff	7	(1) not out		154
P.L.Harris	c Cook b Sidebottom	19			
H.M.Amla	c and b Anderson	9	(3) lbw b Panesar		6
J.H.Kallis	b Flintoff	64	(4) lbw b Flintoff		5
A.G.Prince	c Ambrose b Sidebottom	39	(5) c Ambrose b Anderson		2
A.B.de Villiers	c Sidebottom b Flintoff	5	(6) c Collingwood b Panesar		27
†M.V.Boucher	c Vaughan b Anderson	40	(7) not out		45
M.Morkel	lbw b Anderson	18			
A.Nel	b Sidebottom	0			
M.Ntini	not out	0			
Extras	(LB 35, NB 6)	41	(B 10, LB 8, W 2, NB 2)		22
Total	**(90.2 overs; 408 min)**	**314**	**(5 wkts; 80 overs; 341 min)**		**283**

SOUTH AFRICA	O	M	R	W	O	M	R	W	FALL OF WICKETS
Morkel	15	2	50	0	19.2	1	97	4	
Ntini	19	5	70	2	(3) 18	4	58	2	
Nel	17	7	47	3	(2) 20	3	79	1	
Kallis	15	5	31	3	20	5	59	1	
Harris	11	1	25	0	21	3	60	2	

									E	SA	E	SA
								Wkt	1st	1st	2nd	2nd
								1st	68	17	15	65
								2nd	68	94	39	78
								3rd	74	117	70	83

ENGLAND	O	M	R	W	O	M	R	W				
Sidebottom	25	9	81	3	10	1	26	0	4th	136	135	104	93
Anderson	26.2	6	72	3	13	0	60	1	5th	158	226	219	171
Flintoff	30	8	89	4	(4) 20	5	72	2	6th	173	238	221	–
Collingwood	2	0	12	0					7th	212	264	297	–
Panesar	7	0	25	0	(3) 33	3	91	2	8th	215	293	362	–
Pietersen					(5) 4	0	16	0	9th	230	298	363	–
									10th	231	314	363	–

Umpires: Alim Dar (*Pakistan*) (49) and S.J.Davis (*Australia*) (12).
Referee: R.S.Madugalle (*Sri Lanka*) (105).   **Test No. 1881/133 (E876/SA335)**

ENGLAND v SOUTH AFRICA (4th Test)

At Kennington Oval, London, 7, 8, 9, 10, 11 August 2008.
Toss: South Africa. Result: **ENGLAND** won by six wickets.
Debuts: None.

SOUTH AFRICA

*G.C.Smith	c Anderson b Harmison	46	lbw b Anderson		0
N.D.McKenzie	c Cook b Flintoff	17	b Broad		29
H.M.Amla	b Harmison	36	c Ambrose b Harmison		76
J.H.Kallis	lbw b Anderson	2	c Collingwood b Harmison		9
A.G.Prince	c Bell b Anderson	4	c Strauss b Flintoff		24
A.B.de Villiers	lbw b Panesar	39	b Panesar		97
†M.V.Boucher	c Ambrose b Anderson	3	c Collingwood b Anderson		12
M.Morkel	c Bell b Broad	17	c Bell b Panesar		10
P.L.Harris	not out	13	c Flintoff b Broad		34
A.Nel	c Ambrose b Broad	4	not out		3
M.Ntini	b Panesar	9	c Collingwood b Broad		2
Extras	(B 1, LB 1, NB 2)	4	(B 6, LB 8, W 5, NB 3)		22
Total	**(64.5 overs; 307 min)**	**194**	**(99.2 overs; 424 min)**		**318**

ENGLAND

A.J.Strauss	c Smith b Ntini	6	c Smith b Harris		58
A.N.Cook	c Boucher b Ntini	39	c Smith b Ntini		67
I.R.Bell	c Smith b Ntini	24	b Ntini		4
*K.P.Pietersen	c Kallis b Ntini	100	c McKenzie b Harris		13
P.D.Collingwood	c and b Kallis	61	not out		25
A.Flintoff	c Boucher b Kallis	9	not out		11
†T.R.Ambrose	c Smith b Kallis	4			
S.C.J.Broad	c McKenzie b Ntini	1			
S.J.Harmison	not out	49			
J.M.Anderson	lbw b Harris	13			
M.S.Panesar	run out	0			
Extras	(LB 4, W 1, NB 5)	10	(B 6, LB 7, W 1, NB 6)		20
Total	**(95.2 overs; 423 min)**	**316**	**(4 wkts; 52.5 overs; 221 min)**		**198**

ENGLAND	O	M	R	W		O	M	R	W
Harmison	18	6	49	2	(2)	25	9	84	2
Anderson	15	1	42	3	(1)	22	2	85	2
Flintoff	15	2	37	1		18	4	53	1
Broad	14	3	60	2	(5)	16.2	4	44	3
Panesar	2.5	0	4	2	(4)	17	5	37	2
Pietersen						1	0	1	0

SOUTH AFRICA	O	M	R	W		O	M	R	W
Morkel	22	3	78	0		13	2	43	0
Ntini	24	3	94	5		14	4	55	2
Nel	19.2	5	56	0	(4)	5	0	21	0
Kallis	15	2	51	3	(5)	1	0	10	0
Harris	15	4	33	1	(3)	19.5	5	56	2

FALL OF WICKETS

	SA	E	SA	E
Wkt	1st	1st	2nd	2nd
1st	56	7	0	123
2nd	103	51	82	147
3rd	103	111	119	147
4th	105	219	138	182
5th	118	233	161	–
6th	132	241	201	–
7th	158	248	218	–
8th	168	263	313	–
9th	172	316	313	–
10th	194	316	318	–

Umpires: Alim Dar (*Pakistan*) (50) and S.J.Davis (*Australia*) (13).
Referee: R.S.Madugalle (*Sri Lanka*) (106).   **Test No. 1882/134 (E877/SA336)**

SRI LANKA v INDIA (1st Test)

At Sinhalese Sports Club, Colombo, on 23, 24, 25, 26 July 2008.
Toss: Sri Lanka. Result: **SRI LANKA** won by an innings and 239 runs.
Debuts: Sri Lanka – B.A.W.Mendis.

SRI LANKA

M.G.Vandort	c Karthik b Sharma	3
B.S.M.Warnapura	c Dravid b Harbhajan	115
K.C.Sangakkara	c Dravid b Khan	12
*D.P.M.D.Jayawardena	c Karthik b Sharma	136
T.T.Samaraweera	c Laxman b Khan	127
T.M.Dilshan	not out	125
†H.A.P.W.Jayawardena	c Sharma b Harbhajan	30
W.P.U.C.J.Vaas	not out	22
M.D.N.Kulasekara		
B.A.W.Mendis		
M.Muralitharan		
Extras	(B 4, LB 5, W 3, NB 18)	30
Total	**(6 wkts dec; 162 overs; 705 min)**	**600**

INDIA

G.Gambhir	c Samaraweera b Muralitharan	39	st HAPW Jayawardena b Muralitharan	43
V.Sehwag	c Warnapura b Kulasekara	25	lbw b Muralitharan	13
R.Dravid	b Mendis	14	(5) c Warnapura b Mendis	10
S.R.Tendulkar	b Muralitharan	27	c Dilshan b Muralitharan	12
S.C.Ganguly	c Kulasekara b Muralitharan	23	(6) c Dilshan b Muralitharan	4
V.V.S.Laxman	b Mendis	56	(3) lbw b Mendis	21
†K.D.Karthik	c and b Muralitharan	9	c DPMD Jayawardena b Muralitharan	0
*A.Kumble	lbw b Mendis	1	b Muralitharan	12
Harbhajan Singh	c Warnapura b Muralitharan	9	b Mendis	15
Z.Khan	lbw b Mendis	5	b Mendis	3
I.Sharma	not out	13	not out	5
Extras	(LB 2)	2		
Total	**(72.5 overs; 298 min)**	**223**	**(45 overs; 187 min)**	**138**

INDIA	O	M	R	W	O	M	R	W		FALL OF WICKETS			
Khan	37	2	156	2							SL	I	I
Sharma	33	4	124	2						*Wkt*	*1st*	*1st*	*2nd*
Ganguly	8	1	24	0						1st	7	36	25
Harbhajan Singh	43	2	149	2						2nd	57	79	53
Kumble	37	4	121	0						3rd	212	79	82
Sehwag	4	0	17	0						4th	360	123	95
										5th	454	138	103
SRI LANKA										6th	545	147	103
Vaas	5	0	23	0	5	0	27	0		7th	–	170	103
Kulasekara	11	2	42	1	9	3	25	0		8th	–	181	120
Mendis	27.5	5	72	4	18	3	60	4		9th	–	188	133
Muralitharan	29	4	84	5	13	3	26	6		10th	–	223	138

Umpires: M.R.Benson (*England*) (24) and B.R.Doctrove (*West Indies*) (18).
Referee: A.G.Hurst (*Australia*) (18).　　　　**Test No. 1883/27 (SL178/I419)**

SRI LANKA v INDIA (2nd Test)

At Galle International Stadium on 31 July, 1, 2, 3 August 2008.
Toss: India. Result: **INDIA** won by 170 runs.
Debuts: None.

INDIA

G.Gambhir	lbw b Mendis	56	b Mendis		74
V.Sehwag	not out	201	c Dilshan b Vaas		50
R.Dravid	c Warnapura b Mendis	2	lbw b Muralitharan		44
S.R.Tendulkar	lbw b Vaas	5	c DPMD Jayawardena b Vaas		31
S.C.Ganguly	c Samaraweera b Mendis	0	st HAPW Jayawardena b Muralitharan		16
V.V.S.Laxman	c Samaraweera b Mendis	39	lbw b Mendis		13
†K.D.Karthik	lbw b Mendis	7	c Sangakkara b Muralitharan		20
*A.Kumble	st HAPW Jayawardena b Muralitharan	4	lbw b Mendis		2
Harbhajan Singh	b Mendis	1	c and b Mendis		11
Z.Khan	c HAPW Jayawardena b Muralitharan	2	(11) not out		1
I.Sharma	lbw b Mendis	0	(10) run out		0
Extras	(B 1, LB 4, W 7)	12	(LB 7)		7
Total	**(82 overs; 348 min)**	**329**	**(76.2 overs; 321 min)**		**269**

SRI LANKA

M.G.Vandort	c Dravid b Khan	4	lbw b Harbhajan		10
B.S.M.Warnapura	c Gambhir b Harbhajan	66	c Laxman b Sharma		0
K.C.Sangakkara	c and b Harbhajan	68	c Laxman b Khan		1
*D.P.M.D.Jayawardena	c Karthik b Kumble	86	c Dravid b Sharma		5
T.T.Samaraweera	lbw b Harbhajan	14	not out		67
T.M.Dilshan	c Gambhir b Harbhajan	0	c Karthik b Sharma		38
†H.A.P.W.Jayawardena	c Laxman b Harbhajan	24	c Ganguly b Harbhajan		4
W.P.U.C.J.Vaas	c Harbhajan b Kumble	1	lbw b Harbhajan		0
M.D.N.Kulasekara	not out	5	c Sharma b Kumble		1
B.A.W.Mendis	lbw b Kumble	0	c Kumble b Harbhajan		2
M.Muralitharan	c Ganguly b Harbhajan	0	c and b Kumble		0
Extras	(B 10, LB 12, NB 2)	24	(B 4, LB 2, NB 2)		8
Total	**(93.3 overs; 388 min)**	**292**	**(47.3 overs; 238 min)**		**136**

SRI LANKA	O	M	R	W	O	M	R	W
Vaas	19	2	74	2	13	4	32	2
Kulasekara	8	1	40	0	5	0	31	0
Mendis	28	1	117	6	(4) 27.2	4	92	4
Muralitharan	27	1	93	2	(3) 31	3	107	3
INDIA								
Khan	9	1	51	1	8	1	18	1
Sharma	8	1	36	0	15	8	20	3
Kumble	36	7	81	3	10.3	3	41	2
Harbhajan Singh	40.3	8	102	6	14	1	51	4

FALL OF WICKETS				
	I	SL	I	SL
Wkt	1st	1st	2nd	2nd
1st	167	4	90	4
2nd	173	137	144	5
3rd	178	144	200	10
4th	178	192	200	37
5th	278	192	221	113
6th	290	250	252	130
7th	317	255	255	131
8th	318	291	257	135
9th	323	291	257	135
10th	329	292	269	136

Umpires: B.R.Doctrove (*West Indies*) (19) and R.E.Koertzen (*South Africa*) (90);
M.R.Benson (*England*) (25) deputised for Koertzen (ill) after the first day.
Referee: A.G.Hurst (*Australia*) (19).   Test No. 1884/28 (SL179/I420)

SRI LANKA v INDIA (3rd Test)

At P.Saravanamuttu Stadium, Colombo, on 8, 9, 10, 11 August 2008.
Toss: India. Result: **SRI LANKA** won by eight wickets.
Debuts: Sri Lanka – K.T.G.D.Prasad

INDIA

G.Gambhir	lbw b Mendis	72	b Prasad		26
V.Sehwag	c HAPW Jayawardena b Prasad	21	c Samaraweera b Prasad		34
R.Dravid	lbw b Prasad	10	c DPMD Jayawardena b Mendis		68
S.R.Tendulkar	lbw b Prasad	6	(6) lbw b Mendis		14
S.C.Ganguly	c DPMD Jayawardena b Muralitharan	35	(4) lbw b Muralitharan		18
V.V.S.Laxman	st HAPW Jayawardena b Mendis	25	(7) not out		61
†P.A.Patel	lbw b Mendis	13	(5) lbw b Mendis		1
*A.Kumble	b Mendis	1	lbw b Muralitharan		9
Harbhajan Singh	c Vandort b Muralitharan	3	lbw b Vaas		26
I.Sharma	not out	17	(11) c Warnapura b Muralitharan		0
Z.Khan	st HAPW Jayawardena b Mendis	32	(10) run out		0
Extras	(B 1, LB 8, NB 5)	14	(B 5, LB 3, W 2, NB 1)		11
Total	**(80 overs; 325 min)**	**249**	**(87.5 overs; 345 min)**		**268**

SRI LANKA

M.G.Vandort	lbw b Khan	14	b Harbhajan		8
B.S.M.Warnapura	b Sharma	8	not out		54
W.P.U.C.J.Vaas	c Sehwag b Harbhajan	47			
K.C.Sangakkara	c Patel b Kumble	144	(3) c Gambhir b Khan		4
*D.P.M.D.Jayawardena	lbw b Harbhajan	2	(4) not out		50
T.T.Samaraweera	c Patel b Khan	35			
T.M.Dilshan	lbw b Kumble	23			
†H.A.P.W.Jayawardena	c Harbhajan b Khan	49			
K.T.G.D.Prasad	st Patel b Harbhajan	36			
B.A.W.Mendis	lbw b Kumble	17			
M.Muralitharan	not out	0			
Extras	(B 4, LB 14, W 2, NB 1)	21	(B 4, LB 3)		7
Total	**(134.2 overs; 585 min)**	**396**	**(2 wkts; 33.1 overs; 135 min)**		**123**

SRI LANKA	O	M	R	W	O	M	R	W
Vaas	12	1	44	0	5	0	20	1
Prasad	17	0	82	3	11	0	60	2
Mendis	28	4	56	5	(4) 34	7	81	3
Muralitharan	23	3	58	2	(3) 37.5	4	99	3

INDIA	O	M	R	W	O	M	R	W
Khan	32	5	105	3	6	1	22	1
Sharma	15.3	3	33	1				
Harbhajan Singh	40.3	8	104	3	(2) 14	2	44	1
Kumble	41.2	4	123	3	(3) 10	2	34	0
Sehwag	2	0	2	0	(4) 3	0	12	0
Ganguly	3	0	11	0	(5) 0.1	0	4	0

FALL OF WICKETS

	I	SL	I	SL
Wkt	1st	1st	2nd	2nd
1st	51	14	62	11
2nd	92	42	65	22
3rd	102	137	108	–
4th	151	141	109	–
5th	155	201	131	–
6th	190	244	216	–
7th	195	324	229	–
8th	198	367	266	–
9th	198	396	268	–
10th	249	396	268	–

Umpires: M.R.Benson (*England*) (26) and R.E.Koertzen (*South Africa*) (91).
Referee: A.G.Hurst (*Australia*) (20).

Test No. 1885/29 (SL180/I421)

INDIA v AUSTRALIA (1st Test)

At M.Chinnaswamy Stadium, Bangalore, on 9, 10, 11, 12, 13 October 2008
Toss: Australia. Result: **MATCH DRAWN**.
Debuts: Australia – C.L.White.

AUSTRALIA

Batsman	1st innings		2nd innings	
M.L.Hayden	c Dhoni b Khan	0	lbw b Khan	13
S.M.Katich	c Dhoni b Sharma	66	c Laxman b Harbhajan	34
*R.T.Ponting	lbw b Harbhajan	123	c Laxman b Sharma	17
M.E.K.Hussey	b Khan	146	b Harbhajan	31
M.J.Clarke	lbw b Khan	11	c Sehwag b Sharma	6
S.R.Watson	b Sharma	2	b Sharma	41
†B.J.Haddin	c Laxman b Sharma	33	not out	35
C.L.White	c Harbhajan b Sharma	6	not out	18
B.Lee	b Khan	27		
M.G.Johnson	b Khan	1		
S.R.Clark	not out	0		
Extras	(B 1, LB 10, W 1, NB 3)	15	(B 12, LB 11, W 6, NB 4)	33
Total	**(149.5 overs; 633 min)**	**430**	**(6 wkts dec; 73 overs; 326 min)**	**228**

INDIA

Batsman	1st innings		2nd innings	
G.Gambhir	lbw b Lee	21	b Johnson	29
V.Sehwag	c Hayden b Johnson	45	c Hayden b Clark	6
R.Dravid	lbw b Watson	51	c Ponting b Lee	5
S.R.Tendulkar	c White b Johnson	13	c Clarke b White	49
V.V.S.Laxman	c Haddin b Johnson	0	not out	42
S.C.Ganguly	lbw b Johnson	47	not out	26
†M.S.Dhoni	b Clarke	9		
Harbhajan Singh	c Haddin b Watson	54		
Z.Khan	not out	57		
*A.Kumble	lbw b Watson	5		
I.Sharma	b Clarke	6		
Extras	(B 24, LB 22, NB 6)	52	(B 16, LB 3, NB 1)	20
Total	**(119 overs; 551 min)**	**360**	**(4 wkts; 73 overs; 290 min)**	**177**

INDIA	O	M	R	W		O	M	R	W
Khan	29.5	4	91	5		17	4	46	1
Sharma	30	7	77	4		14	3	40	3
Harbhajan Singh	41	8	103	1		27	5	76	2
Kumble	43	6	129	0	(5)	8	0	31	0
Sehwag	6	0	19	0	(4)	7	1	12	0

AUSTRALIA	O	M	R	W		O	M	R	W
Lee	26	6	64	1		11	3	26	1
Clark	17	3	58	0		11	6	12	1
Johnson	27	4	70	4	(4)	8	3	23	1
Watson	19	4	45	3	(3)	5	2	8	0
White	13	2	39	0	(6)	18	4	49	1
Clarke	17	3	38	2	(5)	20	7	40	0

FALL OF WICKETS

	A	I	A	I
Wkt	1st	1st	2nd	2nd
1st	0	70	21	16
2nd	166	76	49	24
3rd	226	94	99	77
4th	254	106	115	138
5th	259	155	128	–
6th	350	195	203	–
7th	362	232	–	–
8th	421	312	–	–
9th	429	343	–	–
10th	430	360	–	–

Umpires: Asad Rauf (*Pakistan*) (20) and R.E.Koertzen (*South Africa*) (92).
Referee: B.C.Broad (*England*) (28). **Test No. 1886/73 (I422/A696)**

INDIA v AUSTRALIA (2nd Test)

At Punjab C.A. Stadium, Mohali, Chandigarh, on 17, 18, 19, 20, 21 October 2008
Toss: India. Result: **INDIA** won by 320 runs.
Debuts: India – A.Mishra; Australia – P.M.Siddle.

INDIA

G.Gambhir	c Haddin b Johnson	67	c Hussey b White		104
V.Sehwag	c Haddin b Johnson	35	c Haddin b Siddle		90
R.Dravid	b Lee	39			
S.R.Tendulkar	c Hayden b Siddle	88	(5) not out		10
V.V.S.Laxman	c Haddin b Johnson	12			
S.C.Ganguly	c Lee b White	102	(4) c Clarke b Lee		27
I.Sharma	c Katich b Siddle	9			
*†M.S.Dhoni	lbw b Siddle	92	(3) not out		68
Harbhajan Singh	b White	1			
Z.Khan	run out	2			
A.Mishra	not out	0			
Extras	(B 4, LB 10, W 5, NB 3)	22	(B 3, LB 4, W 5, NB 3)		15
Total	**(129 overs; 594 min)**	**469**	**(3 wkts dec; 65 overs; 291 min)**		**314**

AUSTRALIA

M.L.Hayden	b Khan	0	lbw b Harbhajan		29
S.M.Katich	b Mishra	33	c Tendulkar b Harbhajan		20
*R.T.Ponting	lbw b Sharma	5	b Sharma		2
M.E.K.Hussey	c Dhoni b Sharma	54	lbw b Harbhajan		1
M.J.Clarke	lbw b Mishra	23	c Sehwag b Mishra		69
S.R.Watson	lbw b Mishra	78	lbw b Sharma		2
†B.J.Haddin	b Harbhajan	9	b Khan		37
C.L.White	b Mishra	5	c Dhoni b Khan		1
B.Lee	c Dravid b Harbhajan	35	b Khan		0
M.G.Johnson	not out	9	c and b Mishra		26
P.M.Siddle	st Dhoni b Mishra	0	not out		0
Extras	(LB 13, NB 4)	17	(B 4, NB 4)		8
Total	**(101.4 overs; 454 min)**	**268**	**(64.4 overs; 287 min)**		**195**

AUSTRALIA	O	M	R	W	O	M	R	W
Lee	24	5	86	1	14	0	61	1
Siddle	28	5	114	3	15	1	62	1
Johnson	27	4	85	3	14	0	72	0
Watson	24	3	71	0	(5) 5	0	20	0
Clarke	7	0	28	0	(7) 1	0	6	0
White	19	0	71	2	(4) 8	0	48	1
Hussey					(6) 8	0	38	0
INDIA								
Khan	25	7	56	1	15	3	71	3
Sharma	21	4	68	2	13	4	42	2
Harbhajan Singh	29	9	60	2	20	3	36	3
Mishra	26.4	8	71	5	11.4	2	35	2
Sehwag					5	2	7	0

FALL OF WICKETS				
	I	A	I	A
Wkt	1st	1st	2nd	2nd
1st	70	0	182	49
2nd	146	17	224	50
3rd	146	62	290	52
4th	163	102	–	52
5th	305	130	–	58
6th	326	146	–	142
7th	435	167	–	144
8th	442	240	–	144
9th	469	262	–	194
10th	469	268	–	195

Umpires: Asad Rauf (*Pakistan*) (21) and R.E.Koertzen (*South Africa*) (93).
Referee: B.C.Broad (*England*) (29).   **Test No. 1887/74 (I423/A697)**

308

INDIA v AUSTRALIA (3rd Test)

At Feroz Shah Kotla, Delhi, on 29, 30, 31 October, 1, 2 November 2008
Toss: India. Result: **MATCH DRAWN**.
Debuts: None.

INDIA

G.Gambhir	b Watson	206	lbw b Johnson		36
V.Sehwag	lbw b Lee	1	b Lee		16
R.Dravid	c Hayden b Johnson	11	(4) b Lee		11
S.R.Tendulkar	c Haddin b Johnson	68	(5) c Hayden b White		47
V.V.S.Laxman	not out	200	(6) not out		59
S.C.Ganguly	c Ponting b Katich	5	(7) not out		32
†M.S.Dhoni	c Haddin b Watson	27			
*A.Kumble	lbw b Johnson	45			
Z.Khan	not out	28			
I.Sharma			(3) c Ponting b Clark		1
A.Mishra					
Extras	(B 6, LB 8, W 2, NB 6)	22	(LB 4, W 1, NB 1)		6
Total	(7 wkts dec; 161 overs; 703 min)	613	(5 wkts dec; 77.3 overs; 338 min)		208

AUSTRALIA

M.L.Hayden	lbw b Sehwag	83	not out	16
S.M.Katich	b Mishra	64	not out	14
*R.T.Ponting	b Sehwag	87		
M.E.K.Hussey	b Sehwag	53		
M.J.Clarke	c Khan b Mishra	112		
S.R.Watson	b Sehwag	36		
†B.J.Haddin	st Dhoni b Kumble	17		
C.L.White	b Sehwag	44		
B.Lee	lbw b Kumble	8		
M.G.Johnson	c and b Kumble	15		
S.R.Clark	not out	1		
Extras	(B 28, LB 17, W 2, NB 10)	57	(LB 1)	1
Total	(179.3 overs; 745 min)	577	(0 wkts; 8 overs; 27 min)	31

AUSTRALIA	O	M	R	W		O	M	R	W	FALL OF WICKETS				
Lee	30	2	119	1		17	3	48	2		I	A	I	A
Clark	33	9	69	0		12	6	22	1	Wkt	1st	1st	2nd	2nd
Johnson	32	4	142	3	(5)	12	0	23	1	1st	5	123	29	—
Watson	20	4	66	2	(7)	7	0	27	0	2nd	27	202	34	—
White	15	1	73	0	(6)	8	0	23	1	3rd	157	284	53	—
Clarke	14	0	59	0	(3)	20.3	7	56	0	4th	435	326	93	—
Katich	15	3	60	1	(4)	1	0	5	0	5th	444	399	145	—
Ponting	2	0	11	0						6th	481	426	—	—
INDIA										7th	579	532	—	—
Khan	23	5	86	0						8th	—	555	—	—
Sharma	25	5	84	0						9th	—	567	—	—
Kumble	43.3	9	112	3	(1)	4	0	14	0	10th	—	577	—	—
Mishra	47	12	144	2	(3)	2	0	2	0					
Sehwag	40	9	104	5	(2)	2	0	14	0					
Tendulkar	1	0	2	0										

Umpires: Alim Dar (*Pakistan*) (51) and B.F.Bowden (*New Zealand*) (49).
Referee: B.C.Broad (*England*) (30).   Test No. 1888/75 (I424/A698)

INDIA v AUSTRALIA (4th Test)

At Vidarbha C.A. Stadium, Jamtha, Nagpur, on 6, 7, 8, 9, 10 November 2008
Toss: India. Result: **INDIA** won by 172 runs.
Debuts: India – M.Vijay; Australia – J.J.Krejza.

INDIA

V.Sehwag	b Krejza	66	c Haddin b Lee		92
M.Vijay	c Haddin b Watson	33	lbw b Watson		41
R.Dravid	c Katich b Krejza	0	c Haddin b Watson		3
S.R.Tendulkar	lbw b Johnson	109	run out		12
V.V.S.Laxman	c Haddin b Krejza	64	b Krejza		4
S.C.Ganguly	c Clarke b Krejza	85	c and b Krejza		0
*†M.S.Dhoni	b Krejza	56	c Hussey b Krejza		55
Harbhajan Singh	not out	18	b Watson		52
Z.Khan	b Krejza	1	c Haddin b Krejza		6
A.Mishra	b Krejza	0	b Watson		7
I.Sharma	c Katich b Krejza	0	not out		1
Extras	(B 4, LB 2, W 1, NB 2)	9	(B 6, LB 3, W 6, NB 2, Pen 5)		22
Total	**(124.5 overs; 568 min)**	**441**	**(82.4 overs; 373 min)**		**295**

AUSTRALIA

M.L.Hayden	run out	16	lbw b Harbhajan		77
S.M.Katich	lbw b Khan	102	c Dhoni b Sharma		16
*R.T.Ponting	b Harbhajan	24	run out		8
M.E.K.Hussey	run out	90	(5) c Dravid b Mishra		19
M.J.Clarke	c Dhoni b Sharma	8	(4) c Dhoni b Sharma		22
S.R.Watson	b Harbhajan	2	c Dhoni b Harbhajan		9
†B.J.Haddin	c Dravid b Mishra	28	c Tendulkar b Mishra		4
C.L.White	c Sehwag b Harbhajan	46	not out		26
J.J.Krejza	lbw b Sharma	5	st Dhoni b Mishra		4
M.G.Johnson	c Khan b Mishra	5	(11) lbw b Harbhajan		11
B.Lee	not out	1	(10) c Vijay b Harbhajan		0
Extras	(B 12, LB 3, W 2, NB 6, Pen 5)	28	(B 6, LB 1, W 4, NB 2)		13
Total	**(134.4 overs; 570 min)**	**355**	**(50.2 overs; 247 min)**		**209**

AUSTRALIA	O	M	R	W		O	M	R	W	FALL OF WICKETS				
Lee	16	2	62	0	(2)	10	3	27	1			I	A	I	A
Johnson	32	11	84	1	(1)	14	4	22	0	*Wkt*	*1st*	*1st*	*2nd*	*2nd*
Watson	20	5	42	1	(4)	15.4	2	42	4	1st	98	32	116	29
Krejza	43.5	1	215	8	(3)	31	3	143	4	2nd	99	74	132	37
White	10	1	24	0		2	0	15	0	3rd	116	229	142	82
Katich	3	0	8	0						4th	262	255	163	150
Hussey					(6)	4	2	3	0	5th	303	265	163	154
Clarke					(7)	6	1	29	0	6th	422	266	166	161
										7th	423	318	274	178
INDIA										8th	437	333	286	190
Khan	28	8	68	1		8	0	57	0	9th	437	352	288	191
Harbhajan Singh	37	7	94	3	(3)	18.2	2	64	4	10th	441	355	295	209
Sharma	28	8	64	2	(2)	9	0	31	2					
Mishra	23.4	5	58	2	(5)	11	2	27	3					
Sehwag	18	2	38	0	(4)	4	0	23	0					
Tendulkar	2	0	13	0										

Umpires: Alim Dar (*Pakistan*) (52) and B.F.Bowden (*New Zealand*) (50).
Referee: B.C.Broad (*England*) (31).
Test No. 1889/76 (I425/A699)

BANGLADESH v NEW ZEALAND (1st Test)

At Chittagong Divisional Stadium on 17, 18, 19, 20, 21 October 2008.
Toss: Bangladesh. Result: **NEW ZEALAND** won by three wickets.
Debuts: Bangladesh – Naim Islam; New Zealand – J.D.Ryder.

BANGLADESH

Tamim Iqbal	c McCullum b Vettori	18		c and b Vettori	33
Junaid Siddique	lbw b O'Brien	0		c Redmond b Mills	6
Rajin Saleh	b O'Brien	20		lbw b Patel	6
*Mohammad Ashraful	lbw b Vettori	2		c Redmond b Vettori	0
Mehrab Hossain[2]	c Redmond b O'Brien	83		c Mills b Patel	6
†Mushfiqur Rahim	c How b Vettori	79		b O'Brien	32
Naim Islam	st McCullum b Patel	14	(8)	lbw b Vettori	19
Shakib Al Hasan	c Vettori b Patel	5	(7)	c Taylor b Vettori	71
Mashrafe Mortaza	c Ryder b Vettori	0		st McCullum b Redmond	44
Abdur Razzak	c McCullum b Vettori	11		c Taylor b O'Brien	18
Shahadat Hossain	not out	0		not out	0
Extras	(B 12, LB 1)	13		(B 4, LB 1, NB 2)	7
Total	(122.1 overs)	245		(107.3 overs)	242

NEW ZEALAND

A.J.Redmond	lbw b Shakib	19	(2)	c Siddique b Shakib	79
J.M.How	c Saleh b Shakib	16	(1)	b Razzak	36
J.D.Ryder	c Saleh b Shakib	1		run out	38
L.R.P.L.Taylor	lbw b Razzak	12	(5)	c sub (Mahbubul Alam) b Mortaza	9
†B.B.McCullum	c Razzak b Shakib	25	(6)	lbw b Razzak	2
D.R.Flynn	c Rahim b Islam	19	(7)	c Islam b Shakib	49
J.D.P.Oram	c Mortaza b Shakib	0	(8)	not out	8
*D.L.Vettori	not out	55	(4)	b Shakib	76
K.D.Mills	c Rahim b Shakib	4		not out	1
J.S.Patel	c Shakib b Ashraful	0			
I.E.O'Brien	b Shakib	5			
Extras	(B 8, LB 6, NB 1)	15		(B 13, LB 3, W 3)	19
Total	(64.5 overs)	171		(7 wkts; 137.5 overs)	317

NEW ZEALAND	O	M	R	W		O	M	R	W
Mills	19	7	46	0		18	2	55	1
O'Brien	23	11	36	3		17	7	28	2
Oram	20	11	14	0	(5)	8	2	19	0
Ryder	3	1	10	0					
Patel	21.1	7	67	2	(4)	20	7	53	2
Vettori	36	15	59	5	(3)	42	13	74	4
Redmond					(6)	2.3	1	8	1

BANGLADESH	O	M	R	W		O	M	R	W
Mashrafe Mortaza	7	4	13	0		14	4	37	1
Shahadat Hossain	11	0	35	0		11	1	46	0
Shakib Al Hasan	25.5	6	36	7	(4)	44.5	17	79	2
Abdur Razzak	16	1	51	0	(3)	50	15	93	3
Mehrab Hossain[2]	1	0	8	0		2	0	6	0
Naim Islam	3	0	11	1		12	2	16	0
Mohammad Ashraful	1	0	3	1		4	0	24	0

	FALL OF WICKETS			
	B	NZ	B	NZ
Wkt	1st	1st	2nd	2nd
1st	0	27	24	55
2nd	34	29	36	145
3rd	40	46	37	185
4th	44	52	49	209
5th	188	99	71	216
6th	229	99	127	298
7th	229	100	175	316
8th	229	126	180	–
9th	245	155	220	–
10th	245	171	242	–

Umpires: E.A.R.de Silva (*Sri Lanka*) (34) and D.J.Harper (*Australia*) (74).
Referee: J.Srinath (*India*) (10).
Mehrab Hossain[2] denotes a player born on 8 Jul 1987 (LHB/SLA). He is unrelated to Mehrab Hossain[1], who was born on 22 Sep 1978 (RHB/RM) and who played in nine Tests (2000-03).   **Test No. 1890/7 (B54/NZ343)**

BANGLADESH v NEW ZEALAND (2nd Test)

At Shere Bangla National Stadium, Mirpur, on 25‡, 26‡, 27‡, 28, 29 October 2008 (‡ no play).
Toss: Bangladesh. Result: **MATCH DRAWN**.
Debuts: Bangladesh – Mahbubul Alam.

NEW ZEALAND

A.J.Redmond	lbw b Mortaza	2	(2) not out		30
J.M.How	b Alam	8	(1) c Razzak b Mortaza		8
J.D.Ryder	c Mehrab b Razzak	91	not out		39
L.R.P.L.Taylor	b Shahadat	19			
†B.B.McCullum	c Ashraful b Shakib	66			
D.R.Flynn	not out	35			
*D.L.Vettori	b Ashraful	22			
G.P.Elliott	not out	8			
J.S.Patel					
I.E.O'Brien					
K.D.Mills					
Extras	(B 6, LB 3, NB 2)	11	(B 1, NB 1)		2
Total	**(6 wkts dec; 75 overs)**	**262**	**(1 wkt dec; 31 overs)**		**79**

BANGLADESH

Tamim Iqbal	c Taylor b Vettori	24
Junaid Siddique	st McCullum b Vettori	4
*Mohammad Ashraful	lbw b Vettori	0
Rajin Saleh	lbw b Vettori	0
Mehrab Hossain[2]	lbw b Patel	7
†Mushfiqur Rahim	c McCullum b O'Brien	7
Shakib Al Hasan	lbw b Vettori	49
Mashrafe Mortaza	c Flynn b O'Brien	48
Abdur Razzak	not out	16
Shahadat Hossain	c Vettori b O'Brien	4
Mahbubul Alam	not out	0
Extras	(LB 2, W 6, NB 2)	10
Total	**(9 wkts dec; 58.1 overs)**	**169**

BANGLADESH	O	M	R	W		O	M	R	W		FALL OF WICKETS			
												NZ	B	NZ
Mashrafe Mortaza	6	1	21	1		5	1	14	1		*Wkt*	*1st*	*1st*	*2nd*
Mahbubul Alam	8	0	37	1		3	1	12	0		1st	10	13	8
Abdur Razzak	25	2	72	1		7	1	12	0		2nd	10	13	–
Shahadat Hossain	8	0	39	1	(5)	6	0	20	0		3rd	49	13	–
Shakib Al Hasan	22	6	57	1	(4)	2	0	2	0		4th	186	26	–
Mehrab Hossain[2]	3	0	20	0	(8)	4	0	11	0		5th	201	44	–
Mohammad Ashraful	3	0	7	1	(7)	1	0	4	0		6th	233	44	–
Junaid Siddique					(6)	2	0	2	0		7th	–	122	–
Tamim Iqbal						1	0	1	0		8th	–	155	–
											9th	–	169	–
NEW ZEALAND											10th	–	–	–
Mills	9	4	22	0										
O'Brien	13.1	3	31	3										
Patel	15	6	45	1										
Vettori	19	6	66	5										
Redmond	2	0	3	0										

Umpires: E.A.R. de Silva (*Sri Lanka*) (35) and D.J.Harper (*Australia*) (75).
Referee: J.Srinath (*India*) (11).   **Test No. 1891/8 (B55/NZ344)**

SOUTH AFRICA v BANGLADESH (1st Test)

At OUTsurance Oval, Bloemfontein, on 19, 20, 21, 22 November 2008.
Toss: Bangladesh. Result: **SOUTH AFRICA** won by an innings and 129 runs.
Debuts: Bangladesh – Imrul Keyes.

SOUTH AFRICA

*G.C.Smith	b Alam	157
N.D.McKenzie	c Mehrab b Shahadat	42
H.M.Amla	b Mortaza	112
J.H.Kallis	c Ashraful b Shakib	16
A.G.Prince	not out	59
A.B.de Villiers	c Rahim b Shakib	3
†M.V.Boucher	b Shakib	15
M.Morkel	c Ashraful b Shakib	8
D.W.Steyn	c Iqbal b Shakib	1
M.Ntini	c Rahim b Alam	5
P.L.Harris	absent hurt	–
Extras	(B 2, LB 10, NB 11)	23
Total	**(122.5 overs; 553 min)**	**441**

BANGLADESH

Tamim Iqbal	b Steyn	7	c Boucher b Ntini		20
Imrul Keyes	c Amla b Harris	10	b Steyn		4
Junaid Siddique	c Prince b Morkel	8	c Boucher b Kallis		27
*Mohammad Ashraful	c McKenzie b Steyn	1	c McKenzie b Ntini		13
Mehrab Hossain II	c Boucher b Ntini	12	not out		43
Shakib Al Hasan	c De Villiers b Ntini	14	c Boucher b Steyn		0
†Mushfiqur Rahim	lbw b Kallis	48	run out		0
Naim Islam	c Harris b Ntini	8	c Boucher b Steyn		3
Mashrafe Mortaza	c and b Morkel	5	b Steyn		6
Shahadat Hossain	b Kallis	23	b Steyn		16
Mahbubul Alam	not out	–	c Prince b Kallis		0
Extras	(B 4, LB 2, W 4, NB 6)	16	(B 7, LB 17, NB 3)		27
Total	**(36.4 overs; 172 min)**	**153**	**(51.5 overs; 245 min)**		**159**

BANGLADESH	O	M	R	W		O	M	R	W
Mashrafe Mortaza	22	4	69	1					
Mahbubul Alam	24.5	8	62	2					
Shahadat Hossain	25	1	125	1					
Shakib Al Hasan	38	4	130	5					
Naim Islam	5	0	19	0					
Mehrab Hossain II	8	0	24	0					

SOUTH AFRICA	O	M	R	W		O	M	R	W
Steyn	9	2	36	2		18	4	63	5
Ntini	8	2	20	3		16	8	19	2
Morkel	8	0	55	2		13	6	36	0
Harris	7	1	26	1					
Kallis	4.4	1	10	2	(4)	4.5	0	17	2

FALL OF WICKETS

	SA	B	B
Wkt	1st	1st	2nd
1st	102	8	13
2nd	327	26	45
3rd	327	33	67
4th	352	33	80
5th	365	50	81
6th	404	59	81
7th	420	71	92
8th	427	88	108
9th	441	148	152
10th	–	153	159

Umpires: S.J.Davis (*Australia*) (14) and I.J.Gould (*England*) (1).
Referee: A.G.Hurst (*Australia*) (21).   Test No. 1892/7 (SA337/B56)

SOUTH AFRICA v BANGLADESH (2nd Test)

At Centurion Park (Verwoerdburg), Pretoria, on 26, 27, 28 November 2008.
Toss: Bangladesh. Result: **SOUTH AFRICA** won by an innings and 48 runs.
Debuts: Bangladesh – Raqibul Hasan.

BANGLADESH

Tamim Iqbal	c Boucher b Morkel	31	c McKenzie b Morkel		20
Imrul Keyes	c Smith b Ntini	6	c Smith b Ntini		5
Junaid Siddique	c McKenzie b Ntini	67	c Amla b Kallis		16
*Mohammad Ashraful	c and b Morkel	1	run out		21
Mehrab Hossain II	c Kallis b Ntini	3	run out		0
Raqibul Hasan	c Smith b Morkel	15	run out		28
Shakib Al Hasan	b Morkel	30	c Ntini b Morkel		2
†Mushfiqur Rahim	c De Villiers b Zondeki	65	b Ntini		4
Mashrafe Mortaza	c Kallis b Ntini	12	not out		23
Shahadat Hossain	c Boucher b Steyn	4	c De Villiers b Zondeki		0
Mahbubul Alam	not out	1	c Boucher b Zondeki		1
Extras	(LB 3, NB 12)	15	(B 5, LB 3, W 1, NB 2)		11
Total	(76.2 overs; 346 min)	250	(36.4 overs; 175 min)		131

SOUTH AFRICA

*G.C.Smith	lbw b Alam	27
N.D.McKenzie	c Raqibul b Mortaza	0
H.M.Amla	c Keyes b Shakib	71
J.H.Kallis	b Shakib	24
A.G.Prince	not out	162
A.B.de Villiers	st Rahim b Shakib	0
†M.V.Boucher	c Raqibul b Shakib	117
M.Morkel	b Shakib	0
M.Zondeki	c Rahim b Shakib	0
M.Ntini	c Ashraful b Shahadat	0
D.W.Steyn	b Shahadat	1
Extras	(LB 17, W 2, NB 8)	27
Total	(115.2 overs; 511 min)	429

SOUTH AFRICA	O	M	R	W		O	M	R	W
Steyn	17	4	80	1		8	2	23	0
Ntini	19.2	8	32	4		11	2	44	2
Kallis	12	2	30	0		6	1	24	1
Zondeki	10	2	32	1	(6)	4.4	2	10	2
Morkel	18	0	73	4	(4)	6	1	21	2
McKenzie					(5)	1	0	1	0

BANGLADESH	O	M	R	W
Mashrafe Mortaza	26	2	74	1
Mahbubul Alam	26	5	85	1
Shakib Al Hasan	28	3	99	6
Shahadat Hossain	22.2	2	89	2
Mehrab Hossain II	11	1	50	0
Mohammad Ashraful	2	0	15	0

FALL OF WICKETS

	B	SA	B
Wkt	1st	1st	2nd
1st	25	3	8
2nd	54	47	37
3rd	57	112	47
4th	71	134	57
5th	122	134	68
6th	159	405	77
7th	166	405	95
8th	186	405	126
9th	194	412	127
10th	250	429	131

Umpires: S.J.Davis (*Australia*) (15) and I.J.Gould (*England*) (2).
Referee: A.G.Hurst (*Australia*) (22).   **Test No. 1893/8 (SA338/B57)**

AUSTRALIA v NEW ZEALAND (1st Test)

At Woolloongabba, Brisbane, on 20, 21, 22, 23 November 2008.
Toss: New Zealand. Result: **AUSTRALIA** won by 149 runs.
Debuts: None.

AUSTRALIA

Batsman	1st innings		2nd innings	
M.L.Hayden	c Taylor b Southee	8	c McCullum b Martin	0
S.M.Katich	c McCullum b Southee	10	not out	131
*R.T.Ponting	c How b Southee	4	c Redmond b O'Brien	17
M.E.K.Hussey	lbw b Martin	35	c McCullum b O'Brien	0
M.J.Clarke	b Ryder	98	run out	9
A.Symonds	c McCullum b O'Brien	26	c McCullum b Martin	20
S.R.Watson	c McCullum b O'Brien	1	lbw b Martin	5
†B.J.Haddin	c How b Ryder	6	b Vettori	19
B.Lee	c McCullum b Southee	4	b Vettori	7
M.G.Johnson	c Taylor b Vettori	5	c Vettori b Elliott	31
S.R.Clark	not out	13	c Vettori b Southee	18
Extras	(LB 2, W 1, NB 1)	4	(LB 10, NB 1)	11
Total	**(77 overs; 328 min)**	**214**	**(81.2 overs; 346 min)**	**268**

NEW ZEALAND

Batsman	1st innings		2nd innings	
A.J.Redmond	c Ponting b Clark	3	c and b Clark	10
J.M.How	b Lee	14	c Ponting b Lee	0
J.D.Ryder	c Haddin b Watson	30	lbw b Johnson	24
L.R.P.L.Taylor	lbw b Lee	40	c Haddin b Johnson	75
†B.B.McCullum	c Ponting b Johnson	8	lbw b Clark	3
D.R.Flynn	not out	39	b Johnson	29
G.D.Elliott	b Watson	9	b Clark	4
*D.L.Vettori	c Symonds b Johnson	2	c Symonds b Johnson	10
T.G.Southee	c Symonds b Johnson	0	not out	12
I.E.O'Brien	c Clarke b Johnson	1	c Clarke b Clark	3
C.S.Martin	b Clark	1	b Johnson	1
Extras	(LB 3, NB 6)	9	(LB 5, W 2, NB 3)	10
Total	**(50 overs)**	**156**	**(54.3 overs)**	**177**

NEW ZEALAND	O	M	R	W	O	M	R	W
Martin	18	4	42	1	21	5	69	3
Southee	18	3	63	4	16.2	5	62	1
O'Brien	19	6	44	2	17	1	58	2
Elliott	10	4	29	0	6	1	15	1
Vettori	8	0	27	1	19	4	46	2
Ryder	4	1	7	2	2	0	8	0
AUSTRALIA								
Lee	16	5	38	2	9	0	53	1
Clark	15	2	46	2	17	5	43	4
Watson	10	2	35	2	(4) 5	1	19	0
Johnson	8	3	30	4	(3) 17.3	6	39	5
Symonds	1	0	4	0	4	0	12	0
Clarke					2	0	6	0

FALL OF WICKETS

Wkt	A 1st	NZ 1st	A 2nd	NZ 2nd
1st	13	7	0	1
2nd	22	44	40	30
3rd	23	64	40	40
4th	96	73	53	49
5th	132	108	109	133
6th	139	127	115	143
7th	152	143	156	160
8th	160	143	186	161
9th	183	149	239	164
10th	214	156	268	177

Umpires: B.R.Doctrove (*West Indies*) (20) and R.E.Koertzen (*South Africa*) (94).
Referee: B.C.Broad (*England*) (32).   **Test No. 1894/47 (A700/NZ345)**

AUSTRALIA v NEW ZEALAND (2nd Test)

At Adelaide Oval, on 28, 29, 30 November, 1 December 2008.
Toss: New Zealand. Result: **AUSTRALIA** won by an innings and 62 runs.
Debuts: None.

NEW ZEALAND

A.J.Redmond	c Symonds b Hauritz	83	c Clarke b Lee	19
J.M.How	c Haddin b Johnson	16	c Ponting b Lee	28
J.D.Ryder	c Clarke b Hauritz	13	c Symonds b Lee	3
L.R.P.L.Taylor	lbw b Clark	44	c and b Lee	1
P.G.Fulton	c Katich b Symonds	29	b Johnson	7
D.R.Flynn	b Lee	11	lbw b Johnson	9
†B.B.McCullum	c Haddin b Lee	30	not out	84
*D.L.Vettori	not out	18	c Hayden b Hauritz	13
T.G.Southee	c Katich b Johnson	2	c Ponting b Hauritz	11
I.E.O'Brien	c Haddin b Lee	0	lbw b Lee	0
C.S.Martin	b Lee	0	b Johnson	0
Extras	(B 4, LB 8, W 1, NB 11)	24	(B 7, LB 8, NB 13)	28
Total	**(98.3 overs; 400 mins)**	**270**	**(74.1 overs; 320 mins)**	**203**

AUSTRALIA

M.L.Hayden	run out	24
S.M.Katich	c Ryder b Vettori	23
*R.T.Ponting	c Fulton b O'Brien	79
M.E.K.Hussey	c Redmond b Martin	70
M.J.Clarke	c Ryder b O'Brien	110
A.Symonds	c McCullum b Martin	0
†B.J.Haddin	c Fulton b Redmond	169
B.Lee	c Taylor b O'Brien	19
M.G.Johnson	c McCullum b Redmond	23
N.M.Hauritz	b Vettori	1
S.R.Clark	not out	1
Extras	(B 2, LB 8, W 1, NB 5)	16
Total	**(157.4 overs; 640 mins)**	**535**

AUSTRALIA	O	M	R	W	O	M	R	W		FALL OF WICKETS			
Lee	25.3	8	66	4	25	5	105	5			NZ	A	NZ
Clark	20	6	56	1	10	5	22	0		Wkt	1st	1st	2nd
Johnson	25	5	56	2	15.1	7	29	3		1st	46	38	39
Hauritz	16	2	63	2	24	11	32	2		2nd	101	49	55
Symonds	12	2	17	1						3rd	130	155	58
										4th	194	244	63
NEW ZEALAND										5th	200	247	76
Martin	27	4	110	2						6th	228	428	84
Southee	27	1	100	0						7th	266	470	105
Vettori	59.4	20	124	2						8th	269	526	131
O'Brien	31	6	111	3						9th	270	532	181
Ryder	7	1	33	0						10th	270	535	203
Redmond	6	0	47	2									

Umpires: B.R.Doctrove (*West Indies*) (21) and R.E.Koertzen (*South Africa*) (95).
Referee: B.C.Broad (*England*) (33).   **Test No. 1895/48 (A701/NZ346)**

NEW ZEALAND v WEST INDIES (1st Test)

At University Oval, Dunedin, on 11, 12 (*no play*), 13, 14, 15 (*no play*) December 2008.
Toss: New Zealand. Result: **MATCH DRAWN**.
Debuts: New Zealand – T.G.McIntosh; West Indies – L.S.Baker, B.P.Nash.

NEW ZEALAND

T.G.McIntosh	c Baker b Gayle	34	not out		24
J.M.How	c Chanderpaul b Powell	10	b Powell		10
D.R.Flynn	lbw b Gayle	95	(4) not out		4
L.R.P.L.Taylor	c Marshall b Gayle	15			
J.D.Ryder	c Chanderpaul b Powell	89			
†B.B.McCullum	c Ramdin b Taylor	25			
J.E.C.Franklin	hit wkt b Edwards	7			
*D.L.Vettori	c Marshall b Powell	30			
K.D.Mills	lbw b Edwards	12	(3) b Powell		0
M R Gillespie	not out	16			
I.E.O'Brien	c and b Edwards	4			
Extras	(LB 16, W 9, NB 3)	28	(B 4, LB 1, NB 1)		6
Total	**(116 overs; 517 mins)**	**365**	**(2 wkts; 10 overs; 50 mins)**		**44**

WEST INDIES

*C.H.Gayle	c Franklin b O'Brien	74
S.Chattergoon	c O'Brien b Mills	13
R.R.Sarwan	c McCullum b Mills	8
X.M.Marshall	c Ryder b Vettori	20
S.Chanderpaul	b Vettori	76
B.P.Nash	c Ryder b Mills	23
†D.Ramdin	lbw b Vettori	5
J.E.Taylor	c McCullum b Vettori	106
D.B.L.Powell	lbw b Vettori	0
F.H.Edwards	c sub (S.W.Eathorne) b Vettori	0
L.S.Baker	not out	0
Extras	(B 1, LB 10, NB 4)	15
Total	**(100 overs)**	**340**

WEST INDIES	O	M	R	W		O	M	R	W	FALL OF WICKETS			
											NZ	WI	NZ
Taylor	23	7	61	1						*Wkt*	*1st*	*1st*	*2nd*
Powell	24	7	68	3		5	0	17	2	1st	10	66	33
Edwards	22	4	91	3	(1)	5	0	22	0	2nd	97	87	33
Baker	25	3	85	0						3rd	128	114	–
Gayle	21	2	42	3						4th	189	134	–
Nash	1	0	2	0						5th	278	162	–
										6th	289	173	–
NEW ZEALAND										7th	310	326	–
Gillespie	21	5	102	0						8th	327	326	–
Mills	24	6	64	3						9th	347	334	–
O'Brien	15	4	46	1						10th	365	340	–
Vettori	25	7	56	6									
Franklin	15	2	61	0									

Umpires: M.R.Benson (*England*) (27) and A.M.Saheba (*India*) (1).
Referee: J.Srinath (*India*) (12).   **Test No. 1896/36 NZ347/WI449**

NEW ZEALAND v WEST INDIES (2nd Test)

At McLean Park, Napier, on 19, 20, 21, 22, 23 December 2008.
Toss: West Indies. Result: **MATCH DRAWN**.
Debuts: None.

WEST INDIES

*C.H.Gayle	c McCullum b O'Brien	34	c McCullum b Patel	197	
S.Chattergoon	c How b Vettori	13	c Taylor b Patel	25	
R.R.Sarwan	c McCullum b Patel	11	lbw b Vettori	1	
X.M.Marshall	c Ryder b O'Brien	6	c Taylor b Patel	18	
S.Chanderpaul	not out	126	c and b Patel	0	
B.P.Nash	c Flynn b Franklin	74	c How b Franklin	65	
†D.Ramdin	b Vettori	6	c Flynn b Franklin	6	
J.E.Taylor	c McCullum b O'Brien	17	lbw b O'Brien	8	
S.J.Benn	c McCullum b O'Brien	0	(11) not out	4	
D.B.L.Powell	c McCullum b O'Brien	6	lbw b Vettori	22	
F.H.Edwards	c McCullum b O'Brien	0	(9) c Taylor b Patel	20	
Extras	(LB 6, W 1, NB 7)	14	(LB 2, W 1, NB 6)	9	
Total	**(107 overs)**	**307**	**(145 overs; 552 mins)**	**375**	

NEW ZEALAND

T.G.McIntosh	b Taylor	136	lbw b Taylor	3	
J.M.How	c Chattergoon b Edwards	12	c Gayle b Edwards	54	
D.R.Flynn	c and b Edwards	57	run out	33	
L.R.P.L.Taylor	c Ramdin b Edwards	4	lbw b Benn	46	
J.D.Ryder	c Ramdin b Edwards	57	not out	59	
†B.B.McCullum	c Ramdin b Taylor	31	c Ramdin b Taylor	19	
J.E.C.Franklin	c Gayle b Powell	0	not out	2	
*D.L.Vettori	c Ramdin b Edwards	29			
K.D.Mills	lbw b Edwards	18			
J.S.Patel	c Marshall b Edwards	2			
I.E.O'Brien	not out	0			
Extras	(LB 19, NB 6)	25	(W 2, NB 2)	4	
Total	**(126.4 overs; 551 mins)**	**371**	**(5 wkts; 51 overs; 233 mins)**	**220**	

NEW ZEALAND	O	M	R	W		O	M	R	W		FALL OF WICKETS				
Franklin	16	2	57	1	(5)	17	3	61	2			WI	NZ	WI	NZ
Mills	15	4	48	0		6	1	21	0		*Wkt*	*1st*	*1st*	*2nd*	*2nd*
Patel	25	12	41	1		46	16	110	5		1st	43	19	58	8
O'Brien	26	6	75	6	(1)	24	3	90	1		2nd	54	137	61	62
Vettori	22	4	71	2	(4)	52	21	91	2		3rd	63	145	106	96
Ryder	3	0	9	0							4th	74	245	106	170
											5th	237	316	230	203
WEST INDIES											6th	257	317	252	–
Taylor	23	6	76	2		13	2	67	2		7th	279	319	272	–
Powell	26	7	85	1		5	0	30	0		8th	279	367	342	–
Edwards	29.4	6	87	7		11	0	46	1		9th	299	368	363	–
Gayle	18	6	33	0	(5)	5	0	23	0		10th	307	371	375	–
Nash	6	2	22	0											
Benn	24	5	49	0	(4)	17	2	54	1						

Umpires: R.E.Koertzen (*South Africa*) (96) and A.M.Saheba (*India*) (2).
Referee: J.Srinath (*India*) (13).   Test No. 1897/37 NZ348/WI450

INDIA v ENGLAND (1st Test)

At M.A. Chidambaram Stadium, Chepauk, Chennai, on 11, 12, 13, 14, 15 December 2008.
Toss: England. Result: **INDIA** won by 6 wickets.
Debuts: England – G.P.Swann.

ENGLAND

A.J.Strauss	c and b Mishra	123	c Laxman b Harbhajan		108
A.N.Cook	c Khan b Harbhajan	52	c Dhoni b Sharma		9
I.R.Bell	lbw b Khan	17	c Gambhir b Mishra		7
*K.P.Pietersen	c and b Khan	4	lbw b Yuvraj		1
P.D.Collingwood	c Gambhir b Harbhajan	9	lbw b Khan		108
A.Flintoff	c Gambhir b Mishra	18	c Dhoni b Sharma		4
J.M.Anderson	c Yuvraj b Mishra	19	(10) not out		1
†M.J.Prior	not out	53	(7) c Sehwag b Sharma		33
G.P.Swann	c Dravid b Harbhajan	1	(8) b Khan		7
S.J.Harmison	c Dhoni b Yuvraj	6	(9) b Khan		1
M.S.Panesar	lbw b Sharma	6			
Extras	(LB 7, NB 1)	8	(B 10, LB 13, W 2, NB 7)		32
Total	**(128.4 overs: 539 mins)**	**316**	**(9 wkts dec; 105.5 overs; 502 mins)**		**311**

INDIA

G.Gambhir	lbw b Swann	19	c Collingwood b Anderson		66
V.Sehwag	b Anderson	9	lbw b Swann		83
R.Dravid	lbw b Swann	3	c Prior b Flintoff		4
S.R.Tendulkar	c and b Flintoff	37	not out		103
V.V.S.Laxman	c and b Panesar	24	c Bell b Swann		26
Yuvraj Singh	c Flintoff b Harmison	14	not out		85
*†M.S.Dhoni	c Pietersen b Panesar	53			
Harbhajan Singh	c Bell b Panesar	40			
Z.Khan	lbw b Flintoff	1			
A.Mishra	b Flintoff	12			
I.Sharma	not out	8			
Extras	(B 4, LB 11, NB 6)	21	(B 5, LB 11, NB 4)		20
Total	**(69.4 overs: 344 mins)**	**241**	**(4 wkts; 98.3 overs; 453 mins)**		**387**

INDIA	O	M	R	W		O	M	R	W	FALL OF WICKETS				
Khan	21	9	41	2		27	7	40	3		E	I	E	I
Sharma	19.4	4	32	1		22.5	1	57	3	*Wkt*	*1st*	*1st*	*2nd*	*2nd*
Harbhajan Singh	38	2	96	3	(5)	30	3	91	1	1st	118	16	28	117
Mishra	34	6	99	3	(3)	17	1	66	1	2nd	164	34	42	141
Yuvraj Singh	15	2	33	1	(4)	3	1	12	1	3rd	180	37	43	183
Sehwag	1	0	8	0		6	0	22	0	4th	195	98	257	224
										5th	221	102	262	–
ENGLAND										6th	229	137	277	–
Harmison	11	1	42	1		10	0	48	0	7th	271	212	297	–
Anderson	11	3	28	1		11	1	51	1	8th	277	217	301	–
Flintoff	18.4	2	49	3	(4)	22	1	64	1	9th	304	219	311	–
Swann	10	0	42	2	(5)	28.3	2	103	2	10th	316	241	–	–
Panesar	19	4	65	3	(3)	27	4	105	0					

Umpires: B.F.Bowden (*New Zealand*) (51) and D.J.Harper (*Australia*) (76).
Referee: J.J.Crowe (*New Zealand*) (27). **Test No. 1898/98 (I426/E878)**

INDIA v ENGLAND (2nd Test)

At Punjab C.A. Stadium, Mohali, Chandigarh, on 19, 20, 21, 22, 23 December 2008.
Toss: India. Result: **MATCH DRAWN**.
Debuts: None.

INDIA

G.Gambhir	c Cook b Swann	179	c Bell b Swann		97
V.Sehwag	c Prior b Broad	0	run out		17
R.Dravid	c Panesar b Swann	136	b Broad		0
S.R.Tendulkar	lbw b Swann	11	c Swann b Anderson		5
V.V.S.Laxman	lbw b Flintoff	0	run out		15
Yuvraj Singh	c Prior b Panesar	27	run out		86
*†M.S.Dhoni	c sub (O.A.Shah) b Anderson	29	c and b Panesar		0
Harbhajan Singh	c Swann b Panesar	24	not out		5
Z.Khan	b Flintoff	7			
A.Mishra	b Flintoff	23			
I.Sharma	not out	1			
Extras	(B 5, LB 5, NB 6)	16	(B 10, LB 8, W 5, NB 3)		26
Total	**(158.2 overs; 680 mins)**	**453**	(7 wkts dec; 73 overs; 330 mins)		**251**

ENGLAND

A.J.Strauss	lbw b Khan	0	not out		21
A.N.Cook	lbw b Khan	50	c Laxman b Sharma		10
I.R.Bell	b Sharma	1	not out		24
*K.P.Pietersen	lbw b Harbhajan	144			
P.D.Collingwood	c Dhoni b Mishra	11			
A.Flintoff	c Gambhir b Mishra	62			
J.M.Anderson	not out	8			
†M.J.Prior	c Dhoni b Harbhajan	2			
S.C.J.Broad	b Harbhajan	1			
G.P.Swann	b Khan	3			
M.S.Panesar	c Gambhir b Harbhajan	5			
Extras	(B 1, LB 7, W 1, NB 6)	15	(B 4, W 1, NB 4)		9
Total	**(83.5 overs; 368 mins)**	**302**	(1 wkt; 28 overs; 103 mins)		**64**

ENGLAND	O	M	R	W		O	M	R	W	FALL OF WICKETS				
											I	E	I	E
Anderson	32	5	84	1		19	8	51	1	Wkt	1st	1st	2nd	2nd
Broad	26	9	84	1		14	2	50	1	1st	6	0	30	18
Flintoff	30.2	10	54	3		13	1	39	0	2nd	320	1	36	–
Panesar	23	2	89	2	(5)	10	0	44	1	3rd	329	104	44	–
Swann	45	11	122	3	(4)	17	3	49	1	4th	337	131	80	–
Collingwood	2	0	10	0						5th	339	280	233	–
										6th	379	282	241	–
INDIA										7th	418	285	251	–
Khan	21	3	76	3		3	0	11	0	8th	418	290	–	–
Sharma	12	0	55	1		5	1	7	1	9th	446	293	–	–
Yuvraj Singh	6	1	20	0						10th	453	302	–	–
Harbhajan Singh	20.5	2	68	4	(3)	11	3	25	0					
Mishra	24	0	75	2	(4)	8	1	16	0					
Dhoni					(5)	1	0	1	0					

Umpires: Asad Rauf (*Pakistan*) (22) and D.J.Harper (*Australia*) (77).
Referee: J.J.Crowe (*New Zealand*) (28).   Test No. 1899/99 (I427/E879)

LEADING TEST AGGREGATES 2008

1000 RUNS IN 2008

	M	I	NO	HS	Runs	Avge	100	50
G.C.Smith (SA)	15	25	2	232	1656	72.00	6	6
V.Sehwag (I)	14	27	1	319	1462	56.23	3	6
R.T.Ponting (A)	14	25	–	158	1182	47.28	4	5
H.M.Amla (SA)	15	24	2	159	1161	52.77	3	6
G.Gambhir (I)	8	16	–	206	1134	70.87	3	6
V.V.S.Laxman (I)	15	27	4	200*	1086	47.21	2	7
N.D.McKenzie (SA)	14	23	3	226	1073	53.65	3	3
M.J.Clarke (A)	13	23	–	118	1063	50.61	4	5
S.R.Tendulkar (I)	13	25	3	154*	1063	48.31	4	3
A.B.de Villiers (SA)	15	22	4	217*	1061	58.94	4	2
S.M.Katich (A)	11	20	2	157	1021	56.72	4	4
K.P.Pietersen (E)	12	20	–	152	1015	50.75	5	1

RECORD CALENDAR YEAR RUNS AGGREGATE

	M	I	NO	HS	Runs	Avge	100	50
M.Yousuf Youhana (P) (2006)	11	19	1	202	1788	99.33	9	3

RECORD CALENDAR YEAR RUNS AVERAGE

	M	I	NO	HS	Runs	Avge	100	50
G.St A. Sobers (WI) (1958)	7	12	3	365*	1193	132.55	5	3

1000 RUNS IN DEBUT CALENDAR YEAR

	M	I	NO	HS	Runs	Avge	100	50
M.A.Taylor (A) (1989)	11	20	1	219	1219	64.15	4	5
A.N.Cook (E) (2006)	13	24	2	127	1013	46.04	4	3

50 WICKETS IN 2008

	M	O	R	W	Avge	Best	5wI	10wM
D.W.Steyn (SA)	13	442.1	1481	74	20.01	6-72	5	1
M.G.Johnson (A)	14	585	1828	63	29.01	8-61	2	1
Harbhajan Singh (I)	13	705	1987	63	31.54	6-102	2	1
B.Lee (A)	14	580.1	1884	57	33.05	5-59	3	–
D.L.Vettori (NZ)	14	590.3	1411	54	26.12	6-56	5	
M.Ntini (SA)	15	471.1	1537	54	28.46	5-94	1	–

RECORD CALENDAR YEAR WICKETS AGGREGATE

	M	O	R	W	Avge	Best	5wI	10wM
M.Muralitharan (SL) (2006)	11	588.4	1521	90	16.90	8-70	9	5
S.K.Warne (A) (2005)	14	691.4	2043	90	22.70	6-46	6	2

50 WICKET-KEEPING DISMISSALS IN 2008

	M	Dis	Ct	St
M.V.Boucher (SA)	15	58	56	2
B.B.McCullum (NZ)	14	53	50	3

RECORD CALENDAR YEAR DISMISSALS AGGREGATE

	M	Dis	Ct	St
I.A.Healy (A) (1993)	16	67	58	9
M.V.Boucher (SA) (1998)	13	67	65	2

20 CATCHES BY FIELDERS IN 2008

	M	Ct
G.C.Smith (SA)	15	30
J.H.Kallis (SA)	15	24
L.P.R.L.Taylor (NZ)	12	23
A.B.de Villiers (SA)	15	20
R.Dravid (I)	15	20

RECORD CALENDAR YEAR FIELDER'S AGGREGATE

	M	Ct
G.C.Smith (SA) (2008)	15	30

TEST MATCH CHAMPIONSHIP SCHEDULE

Months indicate the start of a series. Number of Tests in brackets.
All series involving Zimbabwe are subject to confirmation.

2009	May	**England hosts West Indies (2)**
	Jul	**England hosts Australia (5)**
		Sri Lanka hosts Pakistan (3)
		Bangladesh hosts West Indies (2)
	Aug	Sri Lanka hosts New Zealand (3)
		Zimbabwe hosts Bangladesh (2)
	Nov	**South Africa hosts England (4)**
		Australia hosts West Indies (3)
		India hosts Sri Lanka (3)
		Bangladesh hosts Zimbabwe (3)
	Dec	Australia hosts Pakistan (3)
		Pakistan hosts New Zealand (3)
2010	Jan	New Zealand hosts Bangladesh (2)
		Bangladesh hosts India (2)
	Feb	India hosts South Africa (3)
	Mar	**Pakistan hosts England (4)**
		New Zealand hosts Australia (3)
		West Indies hosts Zimbabwe (2)
	May	**England hosts Bangladesh (2)**
		West Indies hosts South Africa (4)
		Zimbabwe hosts India (2)
	Jul	**England hosts West Indies (4)**
	Aug	Pakistan hosts Bangladesh (2)
	Sep	South Africa hosts Zimbabwe (2)
	Oct	Bangladesh hosts New Zealand (2)
		Pakistan hosts South Africa (3)
	Nov	**Australia hosts England (5)**
		India hosts New Zealand (3)
		Sri Lanka hosts West Indies (3)
	Dec	South Africa hosts India (3)
		New Zealand hosts Pakistan (3)
		Bangladesh hosts Zimbabwe (2)
2011	Apr	Bangladesh hosts Australia (2)
		West Indies hosts India (4)
	May	**England hosts Sri Lanka (3)**
		West Indies hosts Pakistan (2)
	Jun	Australia hosts Zimbabwe (2)
	Jul	**England hosts India (4)**
		Zimbabwe hosts Bangladesh (2)
	Aug	Sri Lanka hosts Australia (3)
	Sep	South Africa hosts Australia (3)

		Zimbabwe hosts Pakistan (2)
	Oct	Pakistan hosts Sri Lanka (3)
		Bangladesh hosts West Indies (2)
	Nov	Australia hosts New Zealand (2)
		India hosts West Indies (3)
	Dec	Australia hosts India (4)
		New Zealand hosts Zimbabwe (2)
		Bangladesh hosts Pakistan (2)
		South Africa hosts Sri Lanka (3)
2012	Jan	**Bangladesh hosts England (2)**
	Feb	**Zimbabwe hosts England (2)**
		New Zealand hosts South Africa (3)
	Mar	West Indies hosts Australia (4)
		India hosts Pakistan (3)
	Apr	West Indies hosts New Zealand (3)

TEST MATCH CHAMPIONSHIP TABLE

(As at 22 March 2009)

		Tests	Points	Rating
1	Australia (1)	42	5361	128
2	South Africa (4)	45	5360	119
3	India (2)	43	5074	118
4	Sri Lanka (3)	34	3680	108
5	Pakistan (6)	22	2197	100
6	England (5)	47	4624	98
7	West Indies (8)	31	2752	89
8	New Zealand (7)	30	2426	81
9	Bangladesh (9)	23	0	0

*January 2008 positions in brackets.
Zimbabwe has a rating of 12 but has
played insufficient matches over the
current rating period (post-August 2004)
to qualify for inclusion in this table.*

MAJOR ICC EVENTS

Jun 2009	World Twenty20
Sep/Oct 2009	Champions Trophy
Apr/May 2010	World Twenty20
Feb/Mar 2011	World Cup

SECOND XI CHAMPIONSHIP FIXTURES 2009

3-DAY MATCHES (* 4-DAY)

APRIL

Tue 14	Northampton	Northants v Leics
Wed 15	Moseley	Warwicks v Glos
Wed 22	Kidderminster	Worcs v Yorks
Tue 28	*Smallwell	Durham v Lancs
	Ombersley	Worcs v Hants
	Abergavenny	Glam v Glos
Wed 29	Radlett CC	MCC YC v Notts
	Hove	Sussex v Surrey
	Kings Heath	Warwicks v Yorks

MAY

Tue 5	Longhirst	Durham v Scotland
	Todmorden	Yorks v Middx
Wed 6	Cardiff	Glam v Notts
	St Annes	Lancs v Derbys
	Taunton	Somerset v Northants
	Cheam	Surrey v Glos
Tue 12	Chelmsford	Essex v Surrey
	*Crosby	Lancs v Yorks
	Northampton	Northants v Glos
	Welbeck	Notts v Leics
Wed 13	Uxbridge	Middx v Sussex
	Kidderminster	Worcs v Derbys
Tue 19	Southampton	Hants v Kent
	Knowle & Dorridge	Warwicks v Middx
Wed 20	Leicester	Leics v Surrey
	Radlett CC	MCC YC v Glam
	Kidderminster	Worcs v Durham
Tue 26	Denby	Derbys v Leics
	*Cheltenham C	Glos v Worcs
	Southampton	Hants v Northants
Wed 27	Rugby S	Warwicks v Lancs

JUNE

Mon 1	Southampton	Hants v Middx
Tue 2	Darlington	Durham v Derbys
	Billericay	Essex v Glos
	tbc	Leics v Yorks
Wed 3	Usk	Glam v Worcs
Tue 9	Horsham	Sussex v Durham
	Uppingham S	Leics v Lancs
Wed 10	Denby	Derbys v Worcs
Tue 16	Charterhouse S	Surrey v Middx
	Coventry/N Warwick	Warwicks v Worcs
	Weetwood	Yorks v Scotland
Wed 17	Belper Meadows	Derbys v Glam
	Southampton	Hants v Sussex
	Taunton Vale CC	Somerset v Glos
Mon 22	Durham	Durham v Hants
Wed 24	Milton Keynes	Northants v Surrey
	Barnt Green	Warwicks v Leics
	Stamford Bridge	Yorks v MCC YC
Tue 30	Richmond	Middx v Kent

JULY

Wed 1	Todmorden	Lancs v Durham
	Leicester	Leics v Derbys
	Radlett CC	MCC YC v Worcs
	Taunton Vale CC	Somerset v Essex
	Hove	Sussex v Northants

	Leeds	Yorks v Notts
Tue 7	Derby	Derbys v MCC YC
	Bristol	Glos v Somerset
	Canterbury (King's S)	Kent v Northants
	Southend	MCC Universities v Essex
	*Purley	Surrey v Durham
Wed 8	Southport	Lancs v Worcs
	Welbeck	Notts v Warwicks
Mon 13	Southampton	MCC Universities v Hants
Tue 14	Glossop	Derbys v Scotland
	Coggeshall	Essex v Middx
	Millfield S	Somerset v Surrey
Wed 15	Chester-le-St	Durham v Warwicks
	Hatherley & R	Glos v Lancs
	Canterbury	Kent v Sussex
	Barnsley CC	Yorks v Glam
Tue 21	S Northumberland	Durham v Leics
	Wormsley	MCC Universities v Glos
Wed 22	Southend	Essex v Hants
	Cardiff	Glam v Warwicks
	Radlett CC	Middx v Somerset
	Worksop C	Notts v Worcs
Mon 27	Stirlands CC	Sussex v Hants
Tue 28	Cheltenham C	Glos v Kent
	Blackpool	Lancs v Scotland
	Milton Keynes	Northants v Essex
	*Worcester RGS	Worcs v Surrey
	York	Yorks v Derbys
Wed 29	Taunton Vale CC	Somerset v MCC Universities
	Ashby Hastings CC.	Leics v MCC YC

AUGUST

Mon 3	Beckenham	Kent v Somerset
Tue 4	Derby	Derbys v Lancs
	Bristol CC	Glos v Hants
	Worksop C	Notts v Durham
Wed 5	*tbc*	Leics v Glam
	Finedon CC	Northants v MCC Universities
	Kenilworth Wardens	Warwicks v MCC YC
Tue 11	Derby	Derbys v Notts
	Beckenham	Kent v Essex
	Radlett CC	Middx v MCC Universities
	Guildford	Surrey v Yorks
Wed 12	Seaton Carew	Durham v MCC YC
	Liverpool	Lancs v Glam
	Taunton Vale CC	Somerset v Sussex
	Worcester	Worcs v Leics
Tue 18	Southampton	Hants v MCC YC
	Manchester	Lancs v Notts
	Whitgift S	MCC Universities v Surrey
Wed 19	Cardiff CC	Glam v Durham
	Uxbridge	Middx v Northants
	Hove	Sussex v Essex
	Kidderminster	Worcs v Warwicks
Tue 25	Middlesbrough	Durham v Yorks
	Bristol	Glos v Middx
	Mkt Harborough	Leics v Scotland
	Rugby S	Northants v Notts
	Charterhouse S	Surrey v Kent

323

SECOND XI TROPHY FIXTURES 2009
1-DAY MATCHES

3-DAY COMBINED XI MATCHES (* 4-day)

APRIL

Mon 20	*Billericay	Essex/Kent v Durham
Wed 29	Beckenham	Kent/Essex v Middx

JUNE

Mon 8	*Beckenham	Kent/Northants v Yorks

MCCA FIXTURES 2009

KO   Knock-Out Trophy   MCCA   MCCA Championship

Date	Venue	Fixture
Sun 26 April		
KO	Netherfield	Cumberland v Cheshire (1)
KO	Ampthill	Bedfordshire v Oxfordshire (1)
KO	Audley	Staffs v Suffolk (2)
KO	S Northumberland	Northumberland v Herts (2)
KO	Exmouth	Devon v Cornwall (3)
KO	Devizes	Wiltshire v Herefordshire (3)
KO	Gerrards Cross	Bucks v Dorset (4)
KO	Pontardulais	Wales v Cambs (4)
Sun 3 May		
KO	Shrewsbury	Shropshire v Bedfordshire (1)
KO	Challow & Childrey	Oxfordshire v Cumberland (1)
KO	Manor Park	Norfolk v Northumberland (2)
KO	North Mymms	Herts v Staffs (2)
KO	Henley	Berkshire v Wiltshire (3)
KO	Colwall	Herefordshire v Devon (3)
KO	Woodhall Spa	Lincs v Wales (4)
KO	Clare College	Cambs v Bucks (4)
Sun 10 May		
KO	Workington	Cumberland v Shropshire (1)
KO	Christleton	Cheshire v Oxfordshire (1)
KO	Leek	Staffs v Norfolk (2)
KO	Woodbridge S	Suffolk v Herts (2)
KO	Instow	Devon v Berkshire (3)
KO	Truro	Cornwall v Herefordshire (3)
KO	Ascott Park	Bucks v Lincs (4)
KO	Bournemouth (Dean Pk)	Dorset v Cambs (4)
Sun 17 May		
KO	Wem	Shropshire v Cheshire (1)
KO	Bedford S	Bedfordshire v Cumberland (1)
KO	Manor Park	Norfolk v Suffolk (2)
KO	Longhirst Hall	Northumberland v Staffs (2)
KO	Falkland	Berkshire v Cornwall (3)
KO	Trowbridge	Wiltshire v Devon (3)
KO	Bracebridge Heath	Lincs v Dorset (4)
KO	Abergavenny	Wales v Bucks (4)
Sun 31 May		
KO	Challow & Childrey	Oxfordshire v Shropshire (1)
KO	Marple	Cheshire v Bedfordshire (1)
KO	Welwyn Garden City	Hertfordshire v Norfolk (2)
KO	Mildenhall	Suffolk v Northumberland (2)
KO	Eastnor	Herefordshire v Berkshire (3)
KO	St Austell	Cornwall v Wiltshire (3)
KO	March	Cambs v Lincs (4)

Date	Venue	Fixture
KO	Dean Park	Dorset v Wales (4)
Sun 7 – Tue 9 June		
MCCA	Falmouth	Cornwall v Cheshire
MCCA	Great & Little Tew	Oxfordshire v Dorset
MCCA	Usk	Wales v Wiltshire
MCCA	Falkland	Berkshire v Devon
MCCA	Eastnor	Herefordshire v Shropshire
MCCA	Longton	Staffs v Cambs
MCCA	Sleaford	Lincs v Norfolk
MCCA	Sedbergh S	Cumberland v Hertfordshire
MCCA	Benwell Hill	Northumberland v Bucks
MCCA	Ipswich (Ransomes)	Suffolk v Bedfordshire
Sun 14 June		
KO	Quarter-Finals	Match 1 – Winner 3 v RU 1
KO	Quarter-Finals	Match 2 – Winner 2 v RU 3
KO	Quarter-Finals	Match 3 – Winner 4 v RU 2
KO	Quarter-Finals	Match 4 – Winner 1 v RU 4
Sun 21 – Tue 23 June		
MCCA	Chester Boughton Hall	Cheshire v Berkshire
MCCA	Brockhampton	Herefordshire v Cornwall
MCCA	Bridgnorth	Shropshire v Wales
MCCA	Trowbridge	Wiltshire v Oxfordshire
MCCA	Torquay	Devon v Dorset
MCCA	March	Cambs v Cumberland
MCCA	Manor Park	Norfolk v Staffs
MCCA	Luton Town & I	Beds v Northumberland
MCCA	Tring	Bucks v Lincs
MCCA	Hertford	Hertfordshire v Suffolk
Sun 28 June (*Reserve* day 29th)		
KO	Semi-Final	Winner Match 3 v Winner 1
KO	Semi-Final	Winner Match 2 v Winner 4
Sun 5 – Tue 7 July		
MCCA	Banbury	Oxfordshire v Wales
MCCA	Dean Park	Dorset v Berkshire
MCCA	Shifnal	Shropshire v Devon
MCCA	Nantwich	Cheshire v Herefordshire
MCCA	Camborne	Cornwall v Wiltshire
MCCA	Barrow	Cumberland v Staffs
MCCA	Ipswich S	Suffolk v Norfolk
MCCA	March	Cambs v Bucks
MCCA	Cleethorpes	Lincs v Northumberland
MCCA	Bishop's Stortford	Hertfordshire v Bedfordshire
Sun 12- Tue 14 July		
MCCA	Bedford Modern S	Bedfordshire v Norfolk

Date	Venue	Fixture
Wed 15 July		
	Chester Boughton Hall	Cheshire v MCCA
Wed 22 July	*(Reserve day 23rd)*	
KO	Chester-le-Street	MCCA KO FINAL
Sun 26 – Tue 28 July		
MCCA	Corsham	Wiltshire v Herefordshire
MCCA	Alderley Edge	Cheshire v Dorset
MCCA	Exmouth	Devon v Wales
MCCA	Finchampstead	Berkshire v Shropshire
MCCA	Challow & Childrey	Oxfordshire v Cornwall
MCCA	Jesmond	Northumberland v Cumberland
MCCA	Grantham	Lincs v Cambs
MCCA	Gerrards Cross	Bucks v Beds
MCCA	Knypersley	Staffs v Suffolk
Sun 9 – Tue 11 August		
MCCA	Dean Park	Dorset v Shropshire
MCCA	Colwall	Herefordshire v Oxfordshire
MCCA	Salisbury South Wilts	Wiltshire v Berkshire
MCCA	Abergavenny	Wales v Cheshire
MCCA	Truro	Cornwall v Devon
MCCA	Jesmond	Northumberland v Staffs

Date	Venue	Fixture
MCCA	Wisbech	Cambs v Suffolk
MCCA	Slough	Bucks v Hertfordshire
MCCA	Carlisle	Cumberland v Lincs
Sun 16 – Tue 18 August		
MCCA	Norwich Manor Park	Norfolk v Hertfordshire
Thu 20 August		
	Lord's	MCC v MCCA
Sun 23 – Tue 25 August		
MCCA	Falkland	Berkshire v Oxfordshire
MCCA	Pontardulais	Wales v Cornwall
MCCA	Whitchurch	Shropshire v Cheshire
MCCA	Sidmouth	Devon v Herefordshire
MCCA	Dean Park	Dorset v Wiltshire
MCCA	Manor Park	Norfolk v Cambs
MCCA	Long Marston	Herts v Northumberland
MCCA	Bury St Edmunds	Suffolk v Lincs
MCCA	Stone	Staffs v Bucks
MCCA	Dunstable	Bedfordshire v Cumberland
Sun 6 – Wed 9 September		
MCCA	E Division winner	Championship FINAL

PRINCIPAL FIXTURES 2009

CC1	LV County Championship (1st Div)
CC2	LV County Championship (2nd Div)
F	Floodlit
FCF	First-Class Friendly
FPT	Friends Provident Trophy
LOI	Limited-Overs International

P40[1]	NatWest Pro40 League (1st Div)
P40[2]	NatWest Pro40 League (2nd Div)
T20	Twenty20 Cup
[T20]	Other Twenty20 Game
TM	npower Test Match
UCCE	Univ Centre of Cricketing Excellence

Thu 9 – Sun 12 April
FCF   Lord's   MCC v Durham

Fri 10 – Sun 12 April
   The Oval   Surrey v Leeds/Brad UCCE

Sat 11 – Mon 13 April
FCF   Cambridge   Cambridge UCCE v Yorkshire
FCF   Durham   Durham UCCE v Lancashire
FCF   Leicester   Leics v Loughborough UCCE
   Northampton   Northants v Cardiff UCCE
FCF   Oxford   Oxford UCCE v Worcs

Wed 15 – Sat 18 April
CC1   Southampton   Hampshire v Worcs
CC1   Taunton   Somerset v Warwicks
CC2   Chelmsford   Essex v Derbyshire
CC2   Leicester   Leics v Northants
CC2   The Oval   Surrey v Glos

Wed 15 – Fri 17 April
FCF   Cambridge   Cambridge UCCE v Sussex
FCF   Durham   Durham UCCE v Durham
FCF   Canterbury   Kent v Loughborough UCCE
FCF   Oxford   Oxford UCCE v Glamorgan

Sun 19 April
FPT   Chester-le-St   Durham v Yorkshire
FPT   Chelmsford   Essex v Northants
FPT   Bristol   Glos v Sussex
FPT   Southampton   Hampshire v Worcs
FPT   Manchester   Lancashire v Glamorgan
FPT   Nottingham   Notts v Leics
FPT   Birmingham   Warwicks v Somerset

Mon 20 – Wed 22 April
FCF   Leicester   Leics v West Indians

Tue 21 – Fri 24 April
CC1   Nottingham   Notts v Worcs
CC1   Hove   Sussex v Lancashire
CC2   Bristol   Glos v Essex
CC2   Canterbury   Kent v Northants

Wed 22 – Sat 25 April
CC1   Chester-le-St   Durham v Yorkshire
CC1   Birmingham   Warwicks v Hampshire
CC2   Derby   Derbyshire v Surrey
CC2   Lord's   Middlesex v Glamorgan

Wed 22 – Fri 24 April
   Taunton Vale   Somerset v Cardiff UCCE

Sat 25 – Mon 27 April
FCF   Chelmsford   Essex v West Indians

Sun 26 April
FPT   Derby   Derbyshire v Glamorgan
FPT   Bristol   Glos v Surrey
FPT   Belfast   Ireland v Worcs
FPT   Leicester   Leics v Hampshire
FPT   Lord's   Middlesex v Scotland
FPT   Northampton   Northants v Lancashire
FPT   Taunton   Somerset v Kent
FPT   Leeds   Yorkshire v Sussex

Tue 28 April – Fri 1 May
CC1   Taunton   Somerset v Durham
CC1   Leeds   Yorkshire v Worcs
CC2   Cardiff   Glamorgan v Derbyshire
CC2   Southgate   Middlesex v Leics
CC2   Northampton   Northants v Glos

Wed 29 April – Sat 2 May
CC1   Southampton   Hampshire v Sussex
CC1   Manchester   Lancashire v Notts
CC2   Chelmsford   Essex v Kent

Thu 30 April – Sun 3 May
FCF   Derby   England Lions v West Indians

Sun 3 May
FPT   Chester-le-St   Durham v Surrey
FPT   Chelmsford   Essex v Glamorgan
FPT   Southampton   Hampshire v Leics
FPT   Manchester   Lancashire v Derbyshire
FPT   Southgate   Middlesex v Kent
FPT   Nottingham   Notts v Ireland
FPT   Birmingham   Warwicks v Scotland
FPT   Leeds   Yorkshire v Glos

Mon 4 May
FPT   Derby   Derbyshire v Essex
FPT   Chester-le-St   Durham v Sussex
FPT   Canterbury   Kent v Scotland
FPT   Leicester   Leics v Ireland
FPT   Northampton   Northants v Glamorgan
FPT   Bath   Somerset v Middlesex
FPT   Worcester   Worcs v Notts
FPT   Leeds   Yorkshire v Surrey

Tue 5 May
FPT   Cardiff   Glamorgan v Notts
FPT   Taunton Vale CC   Somerset v Northants
FPT   Croydon   Surrey v Glos

Wed 6 – Sun 10 May
| TM1 | Lord's | **ENGLAND v WEST INDIES** |

Wed 6 – Sat 9 May
CC1	Nottingham	Notts v Somerset
CC1	Hove	Sussex v Durham
CC1	Birmingham	Warwicks v Yorkshire
CC1	Worcester	Worcs v Lancashire
CC2	Bristol	Glos v Leics
CC2	Canterbury	Kent v Glamorgan
CC2	Northampton	Northants v Essex
CC2	The Oval	Surrey v Middlesex

Wed 6 – Fri 8 May
| | Derby | Derbyshire v Leeds/Brad UCCE |
| FCF | Southampton | Hants v Loughboro' UCCE |

Sun 10 May
FPT	Chelmsford	Essex v Lancashire
FPT	Bristol	Glos v Durham
FPT	Eglinton	Ireland v Hampshire
FPT	Canterbury	Kent v Warwicks
FPT	Northampton	Northants v Derbyshire
FPT	Nottingham	Notts v Worcs
FPT	Hove	Sussex v Surrey

Mon 11 May
FPT	Bristol	Glos v Yorkshire
FPT	Canterbury	Kent v Middlesex
FPT	Taunton	Somerset v Scotland
FPT	Hove	Sussex v Durham

Tue 12 May
FPT	ᶠCardiff	Glamorgan v Essex
FPT	Southampton	Hampshire v Notts
FPT	Manchester	Lancashire v Northants
FPT	Birmingham	Warwicks v Middlesex
FPT	Worcester	Worcs v Leics

Wed 13 May
FPT	ᶠDerby	Derbyshire v Lancashire
FPT	The Oval	Surrey v Glos
FPT	Leeds	Yorkshire v Durham

Thu 14 – Mon 18 May
| TM2 | Chester-le-St | **ENGLAND v WEST INDIES** |

Thu 14 May
FPT	Dublin	Ireland v Leics
FPT	Edinburgh	Scotland v Middlesex
FPT	Taunton	Somerset v Warwicks
FPT	Worcester	Worcs v Hampshire

Fri 15 May
FPT	ᶠDerby	Derbyshire v Northants
FPT	ᶠCardiff	Glamorgan v Lancashire
FPT	The Oval	Surrey v Durham
FPT	ᶠHove	Sussex v Glos

Sat 16 May
FPT	Dublin	Ireland v Notts
FPT	Canterbury	Kent v Somerset
FPT	Leicester	Leics v Worcs
FPT	Edinburgh	Scotland v Warwicks

Sun 17 May
| FPT | Lord's | Middlesex v Somerset |
| FPT | Northampton | Northants v Essex |

Mon 18 May
FPT	Chelmsford	Essex v Derbyshire
FPT	Southampton	Hampshire v Ireland
FPT	Lord's	Middlesex v Warwicks
FPT	Edinburgh	Scotland v Kent
FPT	Hove	Sussex v Yorkshire

Tue 19 May
FPT	Swansea	Glamorgan v Northants
FPT	Leicester	Leics v Notts
FPT	The Oval	Surrey v Sussex

Wed 20 May
FPT	Chester-le-St	Durham v Glos
FPT	Cardiff	Glamorgan v Derbyshire
FPT	Manchester	Lancashire v Essex
FPT	Nottingham	Notts v Hampshire
FPT	Edinburgh	Scotland v Somerset
FPT	The Oval	Surrey v Yorkshire
FPT	Birmingham	Warwicks v Kent
FPT	Worcester	Worcs v Durham

Thu 21 May
| LOI | Leeds | **England v West Indies** |

Sat 23 May (*no reserve days*)
| FPT | Quarter-Finals | |

Sun 24 May
| LOI | Bristol | **England v West Indies** |

Mon 25 May
T20	Cardiff	Glamorgan v Somerset
T20	Southampton	Hampshire v Sussex
T20	Canterbury	Kent v Essex
T20	Lord's	Middlesex v Surrey
T20	Northampton	Northants v Warwicks
T20	Nottingham	Notts v Durham
T20	Worcester	Worcs v Glos
T20	Leeds	Yorkshire v Leics

Tue 26 May
LOI	Birmingham	**England v West Indies**
T20	Chester-le-St	Durham v Derbyshire
T20	Manchester	Lancashire v Yorkshire
T20	ᶠThe Oval	Surrey v Sussex

Wed 27 May
T20	ᶠCardiff	Glamorgan v Glos
T20	ᶠLord's	Middlesex v Kent
T20	Taunton	Somerset v Warwicks
T20	ᶠThe Oval	Surrey v Hampshire

Thu 28 May
T20	Manchester	Lancashire v Notts
T20	Leicester	Leics v Derbyshire
T20	ᶠHove	Sussex v Essex

Fri 29 May
| T20 | ᶠDerby | Derbyshire v Notts |
| T20 | Chester-le-St | Durham v Leics |

T20	FChelmsford	Essex v Surrey
T20	Canterbury	Kent v Middlesex
T20	Northampton	Northants v Glamorgan
T20	Taunton	Somerset v Glos
T20	FHove	Sussex v Hampshire
T20	Birmingham	Warwicks v Worcs
T20	Leeds	Yorkshire v Lancashire

Sat 30 May

T20	Cardiff	Glamorgan v Warwicks
T20	Worcester	Worcs v Northants

Sun 31 May

T20	Chesterfield	Derbyshire v Yorkshire
T20	Chester-le-St	Durham v Notts
T20	Southampton	Hampshire v Surrey
T20	Canterbury	Kent v Sussex
T20	Leicester	Leics v Lancashire

Mon 1 June

T20	Chelmsford	Essex v Kent
T20	Bristol	Glos v Worcs
T20	Taunton	Somerset v Glamorgan
T20	Hove	Sussex v Middlesex
T20	Birmingham	Warwicks v Northants

Tue 2 June

T20	Manchester	Lancashire v Derbyshire
T20	Uxbridge	Middlesex v Hampshire
T20	Leeds	Yorkshire v Durham

Wed 3 June

T20	FChelmsford	Essex v Sussex
T20	Bristol	Glos v Northants
T20	Leicester	Leics v Notts
T20	Worcester	Worcs v Somerset

Thu 4 June

T20	FDerby	Derbyshire v Leics
T20	Cardiff	Glamorgan v Worcs
T20	FSouthampton	Hampshire v Essex
T20	Manchester	Lancashire v Durham
T20	Northampton	Northants v Somerset
T20	FHove	Sussex v Kent
T20	Birmingham	Warwicks v Glos
T20	Leeds	Yorkshire v Notts

Sat 6 – Tue 9 June

CC1	Chester-le-St	Durham v Hampshire
CC1	Manchester	Lancashire v Somerset
CC1	Birmingham	Warwicks v Notts
CC1	Leeds	Yorkshire v Sussex
CC2	Chesterfield	Derbyshire v Glos
CC2	Chelmsford	Essex v Middlesex
CC2	Cardiff	Glamorgan v Surrey
CC2	Leicester	Leics v Kent

Thu 11 – Sun 14 June

CC1	Chester-le-St	Durham v Lancashire
CC1	Southampton	Hampshire v Notts
CC1	Worcester	Worcs v Sussx
CC1	Leeds	Yorkshire v Somerset

CC2	Derby	Derbyshire v Glamorgan
CC2	Northampton	Northants v Surrey

Thu 11 – Sat 13 June

FCF	Cambridge	Cambridge UCCE v Essex
FCF	Durham	Durham UCCE v Warwicks
	Weetwood	Leeds/Brad UCCE v Glos
	Richmond	Middlesex v Cardiff UCCE

Tues 16 – Fri 19 June

CC1	Hove	Sussex v Somerset
CC1	Birmingham	Warwicks v Durham
CC1	Worcester	Worcs v Yorkshire
CC2	Cardiff	Glamorgan v Northants
CC2	Tunbridge Wells	Kent v Essex
CC2	Leicester	Leics v Surrey

Wed 17 – Sat 20 June

CC1	Liverpool	Lancashire v Hampshire

Wed 17 – Fri 19 June

FCF	Oxford	Oxford UCCE v Notts

Thu 18 – Sun 21 June

CC2	Bristol	Glos v Middlesex

Mon 22 June

T20	FChelmsford	Essex v Middlesex
T20	Bristol	Glos v Warwicks
T20	Tunbridge Wells	Kent v Hampshire
T20	Liverpool	Lancashire v Leics
T20	Nottingham	Notts v Yorkshire
T20	FHove	Sussex v Surrey

Tue 23 June

T20	FDerby	Derbyshire v Durham
T20	FSouthampton	Hampshire v Middlesex
T20	Northampton	Northants v Glos
T20	Taunton	Somerset v Worcs
T20	Birmingham	Warwicks v Glamorgan

Wed 24 – Sat 27 June

FCF	Hove	Sussex v Australians

Wed 24 June

T20	Chester-le-St	Durham v Yorkshire
T20	Nottingham	Notts v Leics
T20	The Oval	Surrey v Kent
T20	Worcester	Worcs v Glamorgan

Thu 25 June

T20	FDerby	Derbyshire v Lancashire
T20	Taunton	Somerset v Northants
T20	The Oval	Surrey v Essex

Fri 26 June

T20	Chester-le-St	Durham v Lancashire
T20	FCardiff	Glamorgan v Northants
T20	Bristol	Glos v Somerset
T20	FSouthampton	Hampshire v Kent
T20	Leicester	Leics v Yorkshire
T20	Lord's	Middlesex v Essex
T20	Nottingham	Notts v Derbyshire
T20	Worcester	Worcs v Warwicks

Sat 27 June

T20	The Oval	Surrey v Middlesex

Sun 28 June

T20	Chelmsford	Essex v Hampshire
T20	Bristol	Glos v Glamorgan
T20	Beckenham	Kent v Surrey
T20	Leicester	Leics v Durham
T20	Lord's	Middlesex v Sussex
T20	Northampton	Northants v Worcs
T20	Nottingham	Notts v Lancashire
T20	Birmingham	Warwicks v Somerset
T20	Leeds	Yorkshire v Derbyshire

Tue 30 June – Fri 3 July

CC1	Chester-le-St	Durham v Worcs
CC1	Nottingham	Notts v Lancashire
CC1	Taunton	Somerset v Yorkshire
CC2	Derby	Derbyshire v Leics
CC2	Beckenham	Kent v Gloucester
CC2	Lord's	Middlesex v Surrey

Wed 1 – Sat 4 July

FCF	Worcester	England Lions v Australians

Wed 1 – Fri 3 July

FCF	Edgbaston	Warwicks v England XI

Sat 4 July

Lord's		Oxford U v Cambridge U

Sun 5 July

FPT	Semi-Finals	

Tue 7 – Fri 10 July

CC1	Birmingham	Warwicks v Sussex
CC2	Chelmsford	Essex v Glamorgan
CC2	Northampton	Northants v Derbyshire
FCF	Cambridge	Cambridge U v Oxford U

Wed 8 – Sun 12 July

TM1	Cardiff	ENGLAND v AUSTRALIA

Fri 10 – Mon 13 July

CC1	Manchester	Lancashire v Worcs
CC1	Taunton	Somerset v Hampshire
CC1	Leeds	Yorkshire v Durham
CC2	Leicester	Leics v Middlesex
CC2	The Oval	Surrey v Kent

Sun 12 – Wed 15 July

CC2	Cheltenham	Glos v Derbyshire

Mon 13 July

P40[1]	[F]Chelmsford	Essex v Sussex

Tue 14 July

P40[2]	[F]Birmingham	Warwicks v Middlesex

Wed 15 – Sat 18 July

CC1	Nottingham	Notts v Durham
CC1	Arundel	Sussex v Hampshire
CC1	Birmingham	Warwicks v Lancashire
CC2	Cardiff	Glamorgan v Kent
CC2	Guildford	Surrey v Essex

Wed 15 July

P40[1]	[F]Worcester	Worcs v Yorkshire

Thu 16 – Mon 20 July

TM2	Lord's	ENGLAND v AUSTRALIA

Fri 17 July

P40[1]	Cheltenham	Glos v Worcs
P40[2]	[F]Derby	Derbyshire v Northants

Sun 19 July

P40[1]	Cheltenham	Glos v Essex
P40[1]	Nottingham	Notts v Somerset
P40[1]	Arundel	Sussex v Hampshire
P40[1]	Scarborough	Yorkshire v Durham
P40[2]	Manchester	Lancashire v Derbyshire
P40[2]	Northampton	Northants v Leics
P40[2]	Guildford	Surrey v Middlesex
P40[2]	Birmingham	Warwicks v Glamorgan

Mon 20 – Thu 23 July

CC2	Cheltenham	Glos v Northants

Tue 21 – Fri 24 July

CC1	Southampton	Hampshire v Warwicks
CC1	Worcester	Worcs v Somerset
CC1	Scarborough	Yorkshire v Notts
CC2	Derby	Derbyshire v Middlesex
CC2	Leicester	Leics v Essex

Tue 21 July

P40[2]	[F]Cardiff	Glamorgan v Kent

Wed 22 July

P40[2]	[F]Manchester	Lancashire v Surrey

Fri 24 – Sun 26 July

FCF	Northampton	Northants v Australians

Fri 24 July

P40[1]	Cheltenham	Glos v Durham

Sat 25 July

FPT	Lord's	FINAL

Mon 27 July

T20		Quarter-Finals 1

Tue 28 July

T20		Quarter-Finals 2 & 3

Wed 29 July

T20		Quarter-Finals 4

Thu 30 July – Mon 3 August

TM3	Birmingham	ENGLAND v AUSTRALIA

Fri 31 July – Mon 3 August

CC1	Chester-le-St	Durham v Sussex
CC1	Manchester	Lancashire v Yorkshire
CC1	Taunton	Somerset v Nottinghamshire
CC1	Worcester	Worcs v Warwicks
CC2	Bristol	Glos v Glamorgan
CC2	Canterbury	Kent v Derbyshire
CC2	Lord's	Middlesex v Northants
CC2	The Oval	Surrey v Leics

Tue 4 August

P40[2]	[F]Northampton	Northants v Lancs

Wed 5 – Sat 8 August

CC1	Horsham	Sussex v Notts

CC1	Birmingham	Warwicks v Somerset
CC2	Southend	Essex v Glos
CC2	Colwyn Bay	Glamorgan v Leics
CC2	Canterbury	Kent v Middlesex

Wed 5 August
| P40¹ | ᶠSouthampton | Hampshire v Yorkshire |
| P40² | Croydon | Surrey v Derbyshire |

Thu 6 – Sun 9 August
| CC1 | Southampton | Hampshire v Lancashire |
| CC2 | Croydon | Surrey v Derbyshire |

Thu 6 August
| P40¹ | ᶠChester-le-St | Durham v Worcs |

Fri 7 – Tue 11 August
| TM4 | Leeds | ENGLAND v AUSTRALIA |

Sun 9 August
P40¹	Southend	Essex v Notts
P40¹	Taunton	Somerset v Yorkshire
P40¹	Horsham	Sussex v Glos
P40²	Colwyn Bay	Glamorgan v Northants
P40²	Canterbury	Kent v Middlesex
P40²	Birmingham	Warwicks v Leics

Tue 11 August
CC1	Basingstoke	Hampshire v Yorkshire
CC1	Manchester	Lancashire v Durham
CC1	Nottingham	Notts v Warwicks
CC1	Hove	Sussex v Worcs
CC2	Leicester	Leics v Derbyshire
CC2	Lord's	Middlesex v Essex
CC2	Northampton	Northants v Kent

Wed 12 August
| P40² | ᶠThe Oval | Surrey v Glamorgan |

Thu 13 August
| P40¹ | ᶠBristol | Glos v Somerset |

Sat 15 – Sun 16 August
| | Canterbury | Kent v Australians |

Sat 15 August
| T20 | Edgbaston | Semi-Finals and ᶠFINAL |

Sun 16 August
| P40¹ | Lord's | Middlesex v Leics |

Mon 17 August
| P40¹ | ᶠTaunton | Somerset v Sussex |

Tue 18 August
| P40² | ᶠLeicester | Leics v Kent |

Wed 19 – Sat 22 August
CC1	Chester-le-St	Durham v Warwicks
CC1	Nottingham	Notts v Hampshire
CC1	Taunton	Somerset v Sussex
CC1	Leeds	Yorkshire v Lancashire
CC2	Chesterfield	Derbys v Northants
CC2	Colchester	Essex v Surrey
CC2	Leicester	Leics v Glos

Wed 19 August
| P40² | ᶠCardiff | Glamorgan v Middlesex |

Thu 20 – Mon 24 August
| TM5 | The Oval | ENGLAND v AUSTRALIA |

Thu 20 – Sun 23 August
| CC2 | Swansea | Glamorgan v Middlesex |

Sun 23 August
P40¹	Chester-le-St	Durham v Hampshire
P40¹	Colchester	Essex v Worcs
P40²	Chesterfield	Derbyshire v Kent
P40²	Leicester	Leics v Lancashire

Tue 25 – Fri 28 August
| CC1 | Worcester | Worcs v Notts |

Tue 25 August
| P40¹ | ᶠSouthampton | Hampshire v Glos |

Wed 26 –Sat 29 August
CC1	Scarborough	Yorkshire v Warwicks
CC2	Chelmsford	Essex v Leics
CC2	Northampton	Northants v Glamorgan

Wed 26 August
| P40² | ᶠLord's | Middlesex v Lancashire |

Thu 27 – Sun 30 August
| CC1 | Southampton | Hampshire v Somerset |
| CC2 | Lord's | Middlesex v Glos |

Thu 27 August
| LOI | Belfast | England v Ireland |
| P40² | ᶠCanterbury | Kent v Surrey |

Fri 28 – Mon 31 August
| CC2 | Canterbury | Kent v Surrey |

Fri 28 August
| LOI | tbc | Scotland v Australia |
| P40¹ | ᶠHove | Sussex v Durham |

Sat 29 August
| P40¹ | Nottingham | Notts v Worcs |

Sun 30 August
| [T20] | Manchester | England v Australia |
| P40¹ | Scarborough | Yorkshire v Sussex |

Mon 31 August
| P40¹ | Worcester | Worcs v Hampshire |
| P40² | Northampton | Northants v Warwicks |

Tue 1 – Fri 4 September
| CC1 | Chester-le-St | Durham v Somerset |

Tue 1 September
| [T20] | ᶠOld Trafford | England v Australia |

Wed 2 – Sat 5 September
CC1	Manchester	Lancashire v Sussex
CC1	Birmingham	Warwicks v Worcs
CC2	Derby	Derbyshire v Kent
CC2	Bristol	Glos v Surrey
CC2	Leicester	Leics v Glamorgan
CC2	Northampton	Northants v Middlesex

Wed 2 September
| P40¹ | ᶠNottingham | Notts v Yorkshire |

Thu 3 – Sun 6 September
| CC1 | Nottingham | Notts v Yorkshire |

Thu 3 September
P40[1]   [F]Chelmsford   Essex v Hampshire

Fri 4 September
LOI   [F]The Oval   **England v Australia**

Sat 5 September
P40[1]   Chester-le-St   Durham v Essex

Sun 6 September
LOI   Lord's   **England v Australia**
P40[2]   Manchester   Lancashire v Kent
P40[2]   Leicester   Leics v Glamorgan
P40[2]   Birmingham   Warwicks v Derbyshire

Mon 7 September
P40[1]   [F]Hove   Sussex v Notts

Tue 8 September
P40[1]   [F]Taunton   Somerset v Essex

Wed 9 September
LOI   [F]Southampton   **England v Australia**

Wed 9 – Sat 12 September
CC1   Chester-le-St   Durham v Notts
CC1   Taunton   Somerset v Lancashire
CC1   Hove   Sussex v Warwicks
CC1   Worcester   Worcs v Hampshire
CC2   Uxbridge   Middlesex v Kent
CC2   The Oval   Surrey v Northants

Thu 10 – Sun 13 September
CC2   Cardiff   Glamorgan v Essex

Thu 10 September
P40[1]   [F]Leeds   Yorkshire v Glos

Fri 11 September
P40[2]   [F]Derby   Derbyshire v Leics

Sat 12 September
LOI   Lord's   **England v Australia**

Sun 13 September
P40[1]   Chester-le-St   Durham v Notts
P40[1]   Southampton   Hampshire v Somerset
P40[2]   Canterbury   Kent v Warwicks
P40[2]   Uxbridge   Middlesex v Derbyshire
P40[2]   Northampton   Northants v Surrey

Mon 14 September
P40[1]   [F]Worcester   Worcs v Somerset
P40[2]   [F]Cardiff   Glamorgan v Lancashire

Tue 15 September
LOI   [F]Nottingham   **England v Australia**

Tue 15 – Fri 18 September
CC1   Southampton   Hampshire v Durham
CC2   Chelmsford   Essex v Northants
CC2   Canterbury   Kent v Leics
CC2   Uxbridge   Middlesex v Derbyshire

Wed 16 – Sat 19 September
CC1   Taunton   Somerset v Worcs
CC1   Hove   Sussex v Yorkshire
CC2   Cardiff   Glamorgan v Glos

Wed 16 September
P40[2]   [F]The Oval   Surrey v Warwicks

Thu 17 September
LOI   [F]Nottingham   **England v Australia**

Sat 19 September
P40[1]   Southampton   Hampshire v Notts
P40[2]   Uxbridge   Middlesex v Northants

Sun 20 September
LOI   Chester-le-St   **England v Australia**

Wed 23 – Sat 26 September
CC1   Manchester   Lancashire v Warwicks
CC1   Nottingham   Notts v Sussex
CC1   Worcester   Worcs v Durham
CC1   Leeds   Yorkshire v Hampshire
CC2   Derby   Derbyshire v Essex
CC2   Bristol   Glos v Kent
CC2   Northampton   Northants v Leics
CC2   The Oval   Surrey v Glamorgan

Sun 27 September
P40[1]   Nottingham   Notts v Glos
P40[1]   Taunton   Somerset v Durham
P40[1]   Worcester   Worcs v Sussex
P40[1]   Leeds   Yorkshire v Essex
P40[2]   Derby   Derbyshire v Glamorgan
P40[2]   Canterbury   Kent v Northants
P40[2]   Manchester   Lancashire v Warwicks
P40[2]   Leicester   Leics v Surrey

ICC WORLD TWENTY20 2009

Group Stage

Group A	Group B	Group C	Group D
India (A1)	Pakistan (B1)	Australia (C1)	New Zealand (D1)
Bangladesh (A2)	England (B2)	Sri Lanka (C2)	South Africa (D2)
Ireland	Netherlands	West Indies	Scotland

Fri 5 June	Lord's	England v Netherlands	17.30
Sat 6 June	The Oval	New Zealand v Scotland	10.00
	The Oval	Australia v West Indies	13.30
	Nottingham	India v Bangladesh	17.30
Sun 7 June	The Oval	South Africa v Scotland	13.30
	The Oval	England v Pakistan	17.30
Mon 8 June	Nottingham	Ireland v Bangladesh	13.30
	Nottingham	Australia v Sri Lanka	17.30
Tue 9 June	Lord's	Pakistan v Netherlands	13.30
	Lord's	New Zealand v South Africa	17.30
Wed 10 June	Nottingham	Sri Lanka v West Indies	13.30
	Nottingham	India v Ireland	17.30

Super Eight Groups

Group E	Group F
A1	B1
B2	A2
C1	D1
D2	C2

(NB: If the two seeded teams from Groups A-D qualify, they will remain as A1 and A2, regardless of where they finish in the league. If one of the unseeded teams qualifies, it will replace the seeded team. So if Ireland qualified and India did not, Ireland would become A1.)

Thu 11 June	Nottingham	D1 v A2	13.30
	Nottingham	B2 v D2	17.30
Fri 12 June	Lord's	B1 v C2	13.30
	Lord's	A1 v C1	17.30
Sat 13 June	The Oval	C1 v D2	13.30
	The Oval	D1 v B1	17.30
Sun 14 June	Lord's	A2 v C2	13.30
	Lord's	A1 v B2	17.30
Mon 15 June	The Oval	B1 v A2	13.30
	The Oval	B2 v C1	17.30
Tue 16 June	Nottingham	D1 v C2	13.30
	Nottingham	D2 v A1	17.30
Thu 18 June	Nottingham	Semi-Final 1	17.30
Fri 19 June	The Oval	Semi-Final 2	17.30
Sun 21 June	Lord's	FINAL	15.00

INTERNATIONAL UNDER-19 CRICKET

England v Bangladesh

TM1	Scarborough	Mon 6 – Thurs 9 July		LOI	Northampton	Tue 21 July
TM2	Derby	Sun 12 – Wed 15 July		LOI	Hove	Thu 23 July
LOI	Leicester	Sat 18 July		LOI	FHove	Fri 24 July
LOI	Leicester	Sun 19 July		LOI	Sleaford	Tue 28 July
				LOI	Sleaford	Wed 29 July

WOMEN'S INTERNATIONAL FIXTURES

England v Australia

				LOI	Stratford-upon-Avon	Fri 3 July
T20	Derby	Thu 25 June		LOI	Wormsley	Sun 5 July
LOI	Chelmsford	Mon 29 June		LOI	Lord's	Tue 7 July
LOI	FChelmsford	Tue 30 June		TM	Worcester	Fri 10 – Mon 13 July

WOMEN'S ICC WORLD TWENTY20 2009

Group A	*Group B*
Australia	India
New Zealand	England
West Indies	Sri Lanka
South Africa	Pakistan

All Group fixtures to be played at Taunton

Thu 11 June	West Indies v South Africa		12.00
	India v England		16.00
Fri 12 June	Australia v New Zealand		12.00
	Pakistan v Sri Lanka		16.00
Sat 13 June	West Indies v New Zealand		12.00
	India v Pakistan		16.00
Sun 14 June	Australia v West Indies		12.00
	England v Sri Lanka		16.00
Mon 15 June	New Zealand v South Africa		12.00
	India v Sri Lanka		16.00
Tue 16 June	Australia v South Africa		12.00
	England v Pakistan		16.00
Thu 18 June	Nottingham	Semi-Final A1 v B2	13.30
Fri 19 June	The Oval	Semi-Final B1 v A2	13.30
Sun 21 June	Lord's	FINAL	10.30

MCC UCCE CHALLENGE

Tue 21, Wed 22 April

Weetwood	Leeds/Bradford v Cambridge
Oxford	Oxford v Durham

Tue 28, Wed 29 April

Loughborough	Loughborough v Cardiff

Fri 1, Sat 2 May

Weetwood	Leeds/Bradford v Oxford

Sat 2, Sun 3 May

Durham	Durham v Cardiff

Thu 7, Fri 8 May

Cambridge	Cambridge v Durham
Newport	Cardiff v Oxford

Fri 15, Sat 16 May

Weetwood	Leeds/Bradford v Loughboro'

Sun 24, Mon 25 May

Loughborough	Loughborough v Cambridge

Sun 14, Mon 15 June

Oxford	Oxford v Loughborough

Mon 15, Tue 16 June

Usk	Cardiff v Cambridge
Durham, MC	Durham v Leeds/Bradford

Sat 20, Sun 21 June

Cambridge	Cambridge v Oxford
Panteg	Cardiff v Leeds/Bradford
Durham	Durham v Loughborough

Mon 29 June

Lord's	FINAL

FIELDING CHART

(For a right-handed batsman)

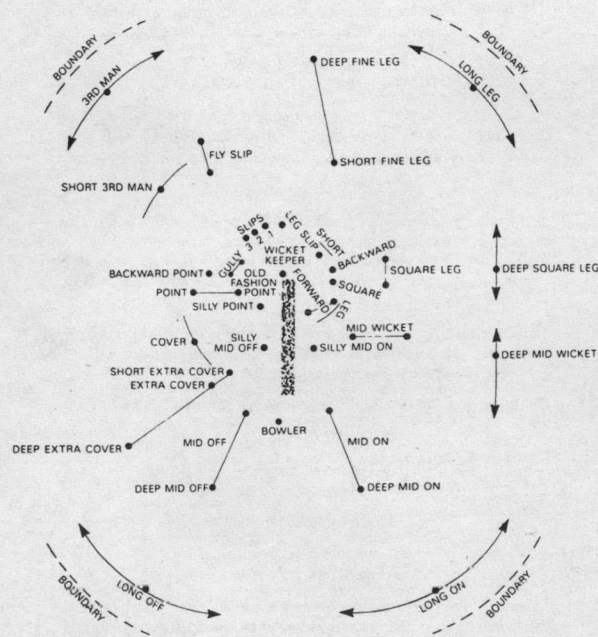

First published in 2009 by
HEADLINE PUBLISHING GROUP

Cover photographs:
(*Front and Spine*) Ricky Ponting © Prakash Singh/AFP/Getty Images
(*Back*) Kevin Pietersen © Adam/Davy/EMPICS Sport/PA Photos

1

Cataloguing in Publication Data is available from the British Library

ISBN 978 0 7553 1746 2

Typeset in Times by
Letterpart Limited, Reigate, Surrey

Preface by Jonathan Agnew

Printed and bound in Great Britain by
Clays Ltd, St Ives plc

HEADLINE PUBLISHING GROUP
An Hachette UK Company
338 Euston Road
London NW1 3BH
www.headline.co.uk
www.hachette.co.uk